St Michael BOOK OF THE GARDEN

St Michael® BOOK OF THE GARDEN

Editors: Robert Pearson and Susanne Mitchell

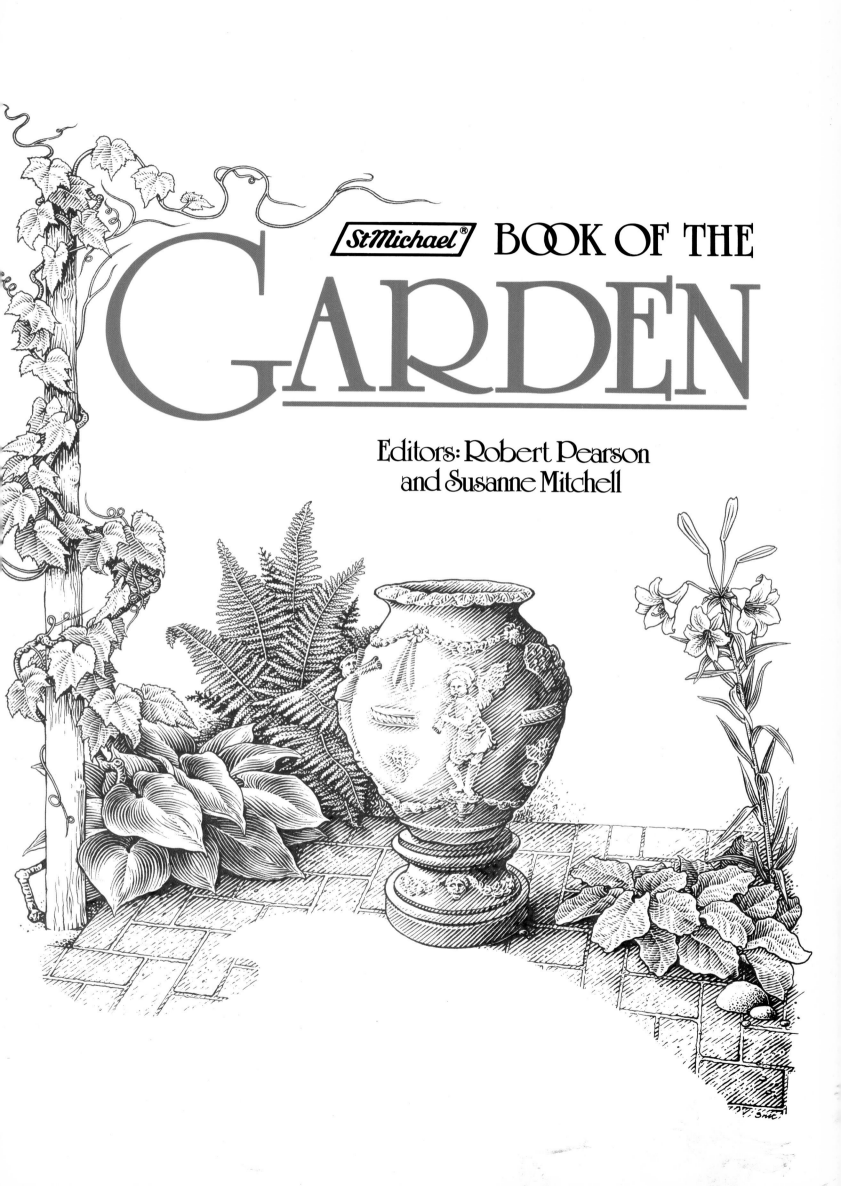

The Authors:

Edward Fawcett Mr Fawcett is Events Organiser for The National Trust and has a wide knowledge of British gardens generally and garden history in particular.

Michael Gibson Rose specialist and author of highly regarded books on this flower, Mr Gibson is Deputy President of The Royal National Rose Society.

Royton E. Heath F.L.S., F.R.I.H. (N.Z.). Mr Heath is an alpine plant specialist who has achieved outstanding success as a cultivator and exhibitor. His books include the acclaimed gardening classic – *The Collingridge Guide to Collectors' Alpines*.

Arthur Hellyer M.B.E., F.L.S., V.M.H. Doyen of horticultural journalists and a gardening writer whose many books have guided countless gardeners in the pursuit of their hobby, Mr Hellyer was for many years Editor of *Amateur Gardening* magazine. He is a Vice-President of The Royal Horticultural Society.

Bill Heritage Mr Heritage is one of Britain's leading authorities on every aspect of water gardening, a subject which has been his speciality for well over 30 years.

Patrick Johns N.D.H. One-time adviser with the Ministry of Agriculture, Fisheries and Food, then head (for eight years) of the Department of Horticulture at the Hampshire College of Agriculture, Mr Johns is now gardening adviser for an international chemical company.

Alan Titchmarsh Kew-trained Mr Titchmarsh, former Deputy Editor of *Amateur Gardening*, is a gardening journalist well-known for his magazine and book writings, and even more for his regular appearances on television and radio programmes.

Alan Toogood Since training as a student at Wisley in the early 1960s, Mr Toogood has been in horticultural journalism and education. He was with *The Gardener's Chronicle* and *Amateur Gardening* before moving to the Merrist Wood Agricultural College in Surrey as a lecturer in horticulture. He was afterwards Editor of *Greenhouse* magazine and is now a free-lance journalist.

Dennis Woodland A former Wisley student and outstanding plantsman, Mr Woodland has for many years been Horticultural Consultant to Hillers Nurseries of Ampfield, near Romsey, Hampshire giving garden owners both in this country and abroad advice on every aspect of gardening and plant care.

Tom Wright B.Sc. (Hort.). Mr Wright is Senior Lecturer in Landscape and Amenity Horticulture at Wye College, University of London, and has a deep knowledge of British gardens and garden history.

Kenneth Lemmon Mr Lemmon is the Editor of *The Northern Gardener*, the journal of the Northern Horticultural Society and a much-respected gardening historian, well-known for his writings on this and other gardening subjects.

Robert Pearson One-time Wisley student and subsequently Deputy Editor of *The Gardener's Chronicle*, Mr Pearson is Gardening Correspondent of *The Sunday Telegraph* and Publisher of Collingridge Books, with a long career in gardening journalism and publishing. He is a member of the Council of the Royal National Rose Society.

Eric Robson Mr Robson is Gardens Adviser to The National Trust for Scotland and immensely knowledgeable on the gardens and, indeed, every aspect of gardening in that country.

Mark Rumary Mr Rumary is a talented landscape designer who is a director of a landscaping company within the East Anglian-based Notcutt group of nurseries. He owns a beautiful garden in Suffolk, and knows the gardens of East Anglia intimately.

F. W. Shepherd N.D.H. (Hons.), F.I. Biol., V.M.H. At one time Director of the Rosewarne Experimental Horticulture Station at Camborne, Cornwall, Mr Shepherd was afterwards Senior Horticulture Adviser of the Government's National Agricultural Advisory Service. Now retired, he is a member of The Royal Horticultural Society's Examinations Board.

Anne Stevens Mrs Stevens is an amateur gardener with a beautiful garden in Dorset, and a detailed knowledge of the gardens of the West Country, on which she lectures. She is a contributor to *Amateur Gardening* magazine.

The Editors:

Robert Pearson (see above)
Susanne Mitchell, B.Sc. (Hort,), Editor, Collingridge Books.
Design Editor, Christopher Pow
Designer, Karel Feuerstein

The Artists:

A distinguished team of artists was specially commissioned to provide illustrations for this book, drawing upon their knowledge and experience of creating accurate artwork to accompany the botanical descriptions.

Preliminary pages and garden plan – Charles Stitt

Herbaceous perennial plants, trees, shrubs, conifers and climbing plants – Stephen Kirk (*The Hayward Art Group*)

Flowering bulbs, corms and tubers – Tim Hayward (*Linden Artists*)

Roses – Kristin Rosenberg H.R.M.S.

Alpine and rock plants – Cynthia Pow

Water and marginal plants – Pat Harby (*Linden Artists*)

House plants – Stuart Lafford (*Linden Artists*)

Additional line drawings throughout by Charles Stitt, Norman Barber, Ian Garrard, Hayward Art Group, Mei Lim.

The Photographers

All the photographs in this book are by Michael Warren and Edward Gabriel of Photos Horticultural, Ipswich with the exception of the following:
Boughton House and The Dower House by Valerie Finnis
Ashridge and Tresco Abbey by Robert Pearson
Hyde Hall by the Harry Smith Horticultural Photographic Collection
Achamore House, Brodick Castle, Crarae, Duncombe Park, Inverewe and Packwood House by Arthur Hellyer

The photographs of gardens taken by Michael Warren and Edward Gabriel were specially commissioned for this book and appear here for the first time.

Acknowledgements

The publishers would like to thank Hollingbourne Nusery of Hollingbourne, Kent, Hillier Nurseries (Winchester) Ltd., and The Royal Botanic Gardens, Kew for providing plant specimens for artists' references.
The garden shown in the photograph on 130 was designed by David Stevens.

First published in 1984 exclusively for
Marks and Spencer p.l.c., Baker Street, London
by Newnes Books
a division of The Hamlyn Publishing Group Limited
84–88 The Centre, Feltham, Middlesex, TW13 4BH

Copyright © Newnes Books 1984
ISBN: 0 600 35759 7
The A to Z of Botanical and Gardening Terms has been reproduced from *The Collingridge Illustrated Encyclopedia of Gardening*
Copyright © Arthur Hellyer and The Hamlyn Publishing Group Limited 1976, 1982

Printed and bound by Graficromo s.a., Cordoba, Spain

Contents

An Introduction to the Garden

A garden for some people is little more than a setting for their house; for others it is a place in which their children can play in safety. Many people will want to use it as an outdoor room in which they can take meals or relax in pleasant, tranquil surroundings; the more energetic may wish to grow the ingredients for those very meals. Another may feel its best use is to offer varying habitats for wild life, whilst for the owner whose pleasure is to grow plants, it must provide for them the best conditions.

Usually the garden needs to fulfil not one requirement but several, and above all is expected to look attractive. If this is to be achieved, the most made of the site, and boring work reduced to a minimum, careful planning is essential. Every garden is a combination of individual situation, quality of soil, share of sun and rain, plus the skill of its designer, and the application and knowledge of its keeper. As little or nothing can be done about the first three it is essential that the design and maintenance should be the best that can be achieved.

Because to most of us gardens mean flowers and plants, there is a tendency to devote too little time to the preparation of the overall plan and to start choosing, and even purchasing plants, before it is even known where they are to go. This is not to say that the type of plants liked may not fundamentally dictate the style of the garden. For instance, a desire to cultivate rhododendrons would indicate an informal, shady garden, whereas hybrid roses not only thrive but look better in an open, reasonably formal setting.

Whilst every garden is unique, the actual components out of which it is created are common to all. How many will be used, and what form they will take, will depend on the needs and tastes of the owner and the size of the plot, but what is paramount is that they are welded together to form an harmonious whole and not a series of unrelated features.

The Terrace or Patio

This should be the link between house and garden; in effect an outdoor room with a 'floor' composed of paving which, if possible, should be in keeping with the style and period of the house. One of the walls ideally should be the south wall of the house, whilst others could be composed of hedges or trellis, sited to provide privacy and to deflect cold winds. There might even be a 'ceiling' in the form of a pergola or timber arbour whose dappled shade will be welcome on the hottest days and which would give a certain measure of privacy if the garden was overlooked.

Because it needs to be in sun for much of the day, and should have the best views of the garden, the patio might need to be sited at the side of the house rather than at the back, or even completely away from the building and, since it would mainly be used for sitting and dining, the area should be as large as space and good proportions will allow. In fact with small courtyard gardens the whole plot would become a patio. It need not be a simple rectangle, it could be 'L' shaped, circular or curved in outline, but whatever its shape it must interlock with the remainder of the garden.

Lawns and Grass

In the gardens of northern Europe all areas not planted or paved will almost certainly be grassed, close mown on lawns and paths, but with longer rougher grass, needing to be cut only two or three times a year, in orchards and wild areas. The lawn may initially be for children's games but it has an important design function which is to form the largest open space, a contrast to smaller enclosures and mass planting. For this reason it should not be intersected by paths or broken up with fussy beds. Its shape should be a pleasing one, especially if the edges are clearly visible and the lawn does not disappear into the shade of trees and shrubs. Grass paths need to be wider than paved ones, if they are not to show wear, and they, as well as lawns, should be designed to make mowing easy. Short, weed-free sward will increase the apparent size of a lawn and produce a restful effect. Longer grass will provide a home for native wild

flowers as well as naturalized bulbs. It also provides a useful contrast of texture when seen next to close-mown grass, for instance where there are islands of longer grass within a lawn, or surrounding it, or where a mown path runs through an orchard.

Water and Water Plants

Any opportunity to use water in the garden should be seized for it can provide movement, sound and sparkle, or alternatively the stillness and reflections of a mirror. It also enables the cultivation of a whole new range of aquatics and semi-aquatic plants but if the point of incorporating water into the design is to reflect the sky and the surroundings, then most, if not all of the water surface, must be kept clear of water-lilies or other plants.

Whether water is used formally with an obviously man-made pool of geometric shape or whether it does its best to appear natural, as with a free form pond or a stream, will depend on the overall design of the garden. A rectangular pool with a fountain looks as out of place next to a rock garden as does a rock-strewn waterfall in a setting of formal flower beds.

Rock Gardens

A decision to include rock in the garden is not to be taken without careful consideration. Of all features it is the most difficult to incorporate successfully, and the most demanding in maintenance. Great skill in placing the stone is needed if the outcrops are to appear natural; in addition rock is very expensive over much of the country. Nevertheless, rock, and rock and water gardens, continue to exercise great fascination over many people and if one is to be constructed an essential requirement is a change in level, engineered by excavation and mounding if one does not occur naturally, so that rock can be set into a bank to look as if it has been exposed by nature. The boulders must be married together, with any strata running the same way but should not be scattered at regular intervals.

Whilst alpines may look most at home growing between rocks they can be successfully cultivated in a raised bed and in the joints of a dry retaining wall, both of which may fit more easily into the modern garden.

Greenhouse and Conservatory

The serious gardener will soon wish to have some method of growing plants under glass and it is unfortunate that modern metal greenhouses are unattractive in appearance. If the plot is large enough the greenhouse with a frame, tool shed, compost heap and bonfire area can be grouped into a neat work unit hidden behind hedges or shrub borders.

In the small garden it may be quite impossible to screen the greenhouse but it helps if there can be taller planting behind it in order to break up the outline. Care must be taken, however, to see that trees do not overhang or shade the greenhouse. The small octagonal and hexagonal timber houses are better looking and easier to incorporate, but have limited practical use.

A larger greenhouse can serve as a conservatory with flowering and exotic foliage plants in large pots. Ideally the conservatory should be attached to the house, with tender climbers such as mimosa and plumbago set against the house walls.

Garden Structures and Ornaments

Vertical structures such as arches, pergolas and trellises are among the most attractive garden features, particularly when covered by some well chosen climbers, and they are particularly useful in giving height to the new garden before the trees and shrubs have grown. Many can be made by the keen amateur carpenter, using either rustic or sawn timber, a choice which must depend on the style of the garden.

Pergolas should always 'roof' a path which leads from one part of the garden to another, or at least to a seat or some focal point. Archways should also straddle a patch and are most effective if they form the link between one part of the garden and another.

Ornamental Conifers
See pages 89 to 95

Flowering Bulbs, Corms and Tubers
See pages 38 to 51

Garden Hedges
See pages 103 to 105

Garden Trees
See pages 82 to 88

**Flowering, Foliage
and Fruiting Shrubs**
See pages 62 to 81

**Lawn Making
and Aftercare**
See pages 9 to 12

**Herbaceous
Perennial Plants**
See pages 16 to 37

**Alpine
and Rock Plants**
See pages 106 to 109

**Annuals
and Biennials**
See pages 13 to 15

**A Diversity
of Roses**
See pages 52 to 61

**Climbing and
Wall Plants**
See pages
96 to 102

**Garden
Pools and
Water
Plants**
See pages
122 to 129

**House
Plants for
Home and
Conservatory**
See pages 136
to 155

**The Patio
Garden**
See pages
130 to 135

An idealised garden plan which incorporates all the features discussed in this book and illustrates how a small space can be utilised to the maximum extent.

The needs and tastes of the owner, however, should dictate how many such features are actually used.

Ornaments can either be purely decorative, such as a statue or a sundial, or functional, as with seats, bird-baths and plant pots. Any of these can be used as a focal point, drawing the eye not only to themselves but in a particular direction, or they can be pleasing incidents along the way, in which case they are likely to be smaller, and grouped with plants. The important point in selecting ornaments is to keep in mind the style of the house and garden and not to overload the garden with them.

The Plants

Having completed the plan we can at last choose and arrange the plants which will give the garden life. The choice is vast, as will be seen from later chapters of this book, and in order to make a reasonable selection and in order to use them to the best advantage, it is essential to get to know a range of all types – from trees to rock plants – and to know them as thoroughly as possible; not only their needs regarding soil, climate and other conditions, but their eventual size and shape, the size, texture and colour of their leaves and flowers, and the flowering season. To do this we should not only seek out information from books such as this but visit gardens open to the public (see p. 158 to 232) to see therein which plants make an effective screen, provide scent, cloth a dry bank or a shady corner, which stand out like living sculpture and how they can be grouped together to form a restful or stimulating colour scheme.

Trees Trees are the largest growing items in the garden, although they may take many years to reach their ultimate size. Their roots will also have the widest spread, and those of poplars and willows especially can cause damage if they come too near services or foundations on heavy clay soils. It therefore pays to think ahead and to make a choice only after carefully researching the subject in books and nursery catalogues. Their role in the design may be to provide shelter or screening, in which case they need to be planted close together, their individual shape being sacrificed in order to form a solid mass of twigs and foliage; to provide shade for other plants as in a wood or spinney, or as a focal point on a lawn or isolated specimen within a shrub border. Trees with unusual coloured or variegated foliage, showy flowers, a weeping habit, or some other eye-catching attribute are best reserved for this last use.

Shrubs These are the prime components of the modern garden. Planted in borders or beds, on their own, or in combination with trees, they form the background against which everything else is viewed, and at the same time they create the enclosures of which the garden is composed. The most important are the evergreens for they sustain the design during the winter months, followed by the deciduous kinds which, because of their outstanding form, habit or foliage, are attractive when not in flower. These two should be used in bold groups to form the backbone against which shrubs like roses, hydrangeas and buddleias, grown for their flowers alone, can display their beauty in due season.

Climbers Climbers and wall shrubs provide an invaluable means of improving the appearance of our houses and gardens, for there are few buildings which will not be enhanced by some well chosen and carefully trained climbers, while there are a great many more houses which desperately cry out for a covering of foliage and flowers, to say nothing of miles of ugly fencing! In addition climbers can be used to give new life to old trees or dull shrubs and hedges.

In choosing a climber it is essential to decide if it is suitable for the aspect in question and for the area to be covered. The size and density of the foliage and the colour of the flowers or berries in relation to the colour of the wall should also be taken into account.

Hedges There are basically three sorts of hedges – the first marks a boundary and excludes intruders and may also be required to act as a barrier against wind and noise. The second is used within the garden to separate one part from another, whilst the third edges beds or paths or is used to create geometric or free-flowing designs as in the knots and parterres of earlier centuries. The first needs to be impenetrable, and if privacy is important it must be evergreen or capable of retaining its leaves over the winter. For this our native hedging plants such as quickthorn, beech, hornbeam and holly are difficult to beat.

With internal hedges it is necessary to decide if a close-textured wall-like appearance is required or if a lightly trimmed informal hedge is more suitable. The former provides the best background to other planting and should be composed of yew, box, thuja or other plants which can withstand close clipping. For a flowering hedge almost any shrub can be used as long as it naturally remains clothed to the ground and responds to pruning; many, however, cannot be kept narrow without loss of flowers or berries.

Roses From the designer's viewpoint roses can be loosely divided into three kinds; firstly the modern, quickly repeating, mainly cluster varieties which produce massed flowers and which can be employed like bedding plants where their bright hues are welcome and where their frankly unattractive appearance in winter does not matter. Secondly there are those modern and old large-flowered varieties which produce beautiful blooms but not massed colour, and these are best used in groups with other shrubs or in the mixed border. Finally there is a select band of species and their hybrids, like 'Canarybird', 'Rubrifolia', 'Nevada' and varieties of *Rosa rugosa*, whose solid growth and attractive leaf pattern enable them to be used as part of the garden structure rather than just decoration.

Herbaceous Plants Amongst hardy herbaceous plants there are species and varieties for every type of soil and every condition. Many produce beautiful flowers whilst others have magnificent foliage and some make good ground cover. There are, however, disadvantages; with a few notable exceptions the plants die down in winter, indeed in some cases almost before the end of summer. The most colourful often have undistinguished foliage or shape, whilst staking may be necessary. They need, therefore, to be chosen with care. Large herbaceous borders when well planned and managed provide a magnificent spectacle but a mixture of herbaceous plants, shrubs, roses and bulbs is frequently much more successful.

Bulbs, Corms and Tubers Bulbs are invaluable for providing flowers and interest in late winter and spring, and again in late autumn, and many never look better than when planted in generous drifts in grass, though the less vigorous are better used in the rock garden, in a raised bed, or between low-growing plants at the front of borders. Beds of regimented tulips and hyacinths are much used in our public parks but in the small garden they look better as casual groups in herbaceous or mixed borders where their decaying foliage will eventually be hidden by the foliage of plants and shrubs. Summer flowerers like gladioli, alliums, dahlias and lilies can be used in the same way.

Annuals and Biennials The energies of a short-lived plant are directed to producing masses of flowers in order to produce seed. This makes annuals excellent for positions where splashes of bright colour are required, for instance in tubs and window boxes, in the mixed border, or between shrubs, particularly in the early stages when the permanent plants are still small. Annuals include a few of the sweetest scented plants we possess, and space beside seats or under windows should be reserved for patches of night-scented stock, tobacco plants and mignonette.

KEY TO THE SYMBOLS used in the garden plant information included between pages 18 and 129.

⊘	Deciduous	◖	Requires shelter	◑	Partial sun	❈	Good drainage
▲	Semi-evergreen	✿	Flowering season	●	Suitable for shade	△	Alkaline soil
△	Evergreen	♻	Ornamental fruit and season if applicable	◼	Wet soil	▼	Acid soil
♠	Slightly tender	○	Sunny position	◼	Dry soil	△▼	Any soil

Lawn Making and Aftercare

An existing well established lawn is most likely to consist of a number of different grass species that vary according to various contributing factors. The soil itself is important in that an alkaline soil will no doubt support a high proportion of coarse grasses; an acid soil is more inclined to grow fine species. Mowing height also has a bearing on the type of grass to be found: close cutting tends to reduce the amount of rough grasses and encourage the finer grass.

Given a choice, the majority of people would prefer a lawn consisting of fine grasses for the ornamental area in a garden. Unfortunately fine grasses do not usually put up with rough treatment and wear and so, for an area where children play, it is better to grow coarse grass which is likely to withstand rougher wear and yet still look presentable.

Various grass mixtures are available already blended and ready for use, or a mixture can be made up at home.

Grasses for Different Purposes

Top quality turf like that in bowling greens is often made from sowing creeping red fescue (*Festuca rubra* ssp *rubra*) and browntop bent (*Agrostis tenuis*). The former has bristly leaves and does particularly well on light sandy soils due to its tolerance of dry conditions. It will also tolerate wet and cold and is hard wearing so far as fine grasses are concerned. Browntop bent forms tufts of short flat leaves and is tolerant of dry conditions, but does best on medium to heavy lawns. It will tolerate close

A well maintained lawn is an asset to any garden, whether used as a feature on its own or to complement the flowers. This one is at Tintinhull House,

mowing. A mixture of 70 per cent creeping red fescue plus 30 per cent browntop bent would produce turf of the highest quality. The mixture should be sown at the rate of 1oz per sq yd (34g per sq metre).

A slightly coarser turf but still of extremely high quality would result from sowing 70 per cent chewings fescue (*Festuca rubra* ssp *commutata*), a dark green sward tolerant of dry conditions, and 30 per cent browntop bent. Sow the seed at the rate of 1oz per sq yd (34g per sq metre).

A good high quality ornamental lawn may also contain smooth-stalked meadow grass (*Poa pratensis*). This grass is tolerant of dry conditions but does not flourish under wet heavy soil conditions, particularly if the soil is acid. It is, however, reasonably hard wearing and included at no more than 10 per cent of the total, mixed with the species mentioned above, would make a most admirable lawn.

For really hard-wearing lawns, it is usual to add perennial rye grass (*Lolium perenne*) to the mixture. There are a number of dwarf growing varieties which are suitable for all types of soil, and do reasonably well in shady situations. A suitable mixture would consist of 50 per cent perennial dwarf ryegrass, 40 per cent creeping red fescue and 10 per cent smooth stalked meadow grass sown at the rate of 1oz per sq yd (34g per sq metre).

Lawns from Seed

Autumn is usually a good time to sow grass seed; the soil is still warm so that seed germinates to establish before the cold weather sets in. Late spring is also a suitable time except that, should a long dry spell occur in the summer, the young grass plants would barely have time to send down their roots deep enough in the ground to find sufficient moisture to survive. Seed should not normally be sown in midsummer unless sufficient irrigation can be given to ensure proper germination. Even where irrigation can be given, the surface of the soil may pan and produce a hard crust which would inhibit germination of seed, or the seed may be washed together into puddled groups.

Preparing the Site Adequate soil preparation is essential before sowing grass seed. The site should be dug over at least one spit deep to remove deep rooted weeds and debris. Heavy soils are best dug in late summer or autumn so that winter frost will crumble the clods to enable a good fine tilth to be produced in spring time. Clay soil should not be dug when it is wet and the same can be said for any other type of soil which sticks to the footware, otherwise the soil will be almost impossible to rake fine.

The best lawns are those with a firm level surface and so the ground should be allowed to settle before seed is sown. When time is at a premium, the soil can be made firm by treading it with a shuffling motion. Time spent settling the ground will be well rewarded in future years so that dips and mounds are avoided. Next rake over the site to make it level and at the same time break down any clods of soil. Stones and other debris will be brought to the surface and these should be removed and the site raked again.

When the site is perfectly level, a general fertilizer may be applied. One which contains nitrogen, phosphate and potash is ideal and the rate to be applied will depend on the concentration of each of the nutrients in the mixture but will be in the region of 4oz per sq yd (136g per sq metre) depending on brand. The fertilizer should be lightly forked into the surface of the soil, which is then finally raked over.

Residual weed seeds are likely to be in the soil and it is often beneficial to wait for these to germinate before sowing the grass seed. Weed seedlings can easily be dealt with by the application of a weedkiller that becomes inactivated as soon as it touches the soil so that grass seed can, if necessary, be sown the following day. Subsequent weed seeds that germinate will not be of great importance because they will no doubt be controlled when grass cutting begins.

Sowing Seed Grass seed should be sown evenly and thinly. It is often tempting to sow very thickly just in case the seed does not germinate well. Unfortunately thickly sown seed is very susceptible to disease attack and large patches of young grass plants may die off. In case of doubt, it is often preferable to mark off the site with string in yard squares before sowing the seed. The correct amount of seed may then be scattered over the surface with ease.

After sowing, the seed may be very lightly raked into the surface of the soil which should be kept moist so that germination may take place without check. Most seed is treated with bird repellent and so loss is unlikely from that quarter. Birds and cats do have a liking for freshly raked soil and so it would be as well to take precautions in the form of nylon threads crisscrossed over the site.

Aftercare When the grass has grown to a height of approximately 2in (5cm) it should be topped by using very sharp hand shears; when a mower is used, great care should be taken to avoid ripping the young grass plants from the ground. A light rolling may be given provided the soil is not wet.

Generally, the domestic lawn does not require rolling at any time because it is likely to get sufficient firming from the weight of the mower and by general use. New lawns may require rolling in the early stages of establishment and especially after frost, although lawns should never be walked on when frost is present otherwise much damage will be done to the sward.

Once the grass is established, frequent mowing will keep the turf in a healthy condition although the grass should never be cut so short that it is scalped, otherwise vigour will be lost and weeds will become established; moss invasion invariably occurs when grass vigour has been lost.

Lawns from Turf

New lawns can also be established by laying turves. These may be purchased locally and it is always better to inspect the area from which the turves are being taken, so that the amount of weed growth, if any, and the quality of the turf can be ascertained. Turves vary in the grass species they contain but do provide the opportunity for an instant lawn. It is, of course, just as important to prepare the site properly for turves as it is for sowing seed.

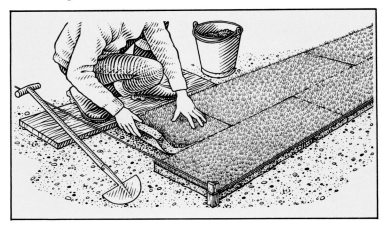

Stagger the turves so that the joins bond well. If necessary use a half turf at the end of each alternate row.

When the turves have been put into position, they should be tamped down with the back of a spade to ensure good contact with the soil below. The crack where each turf joins its neighbour should be filled in by brushing friable soil, or preferably a mixture of soil, peat and sand, over the area.

Routine Maintenance

Just as other parts of the garden respond to treatment, so will the lawn look that much better for the extra care given to it. The grass plants should be kept healthy by frequent mowing and feeding. Fertilizer containing a high level of nitrogen compared with the other ingredients of phosphate and potash will be required in the spring. During early autumn a further application of fertilizer may be given. This time the nitrogen and phosphate should be at a lower level than potash so that the grass plants will harden up to withstand the winter weather.

Irrigation is important to keep the roots moist during dry weather. It is far better to give the lawn a thorough soaking rather than a dribble, which would only bring the roots to the surface. Empty tins placed over the area will give a good indication of how much water has been applied.

A certain amount of undecomposed organic matter often builds up at the base of plants in a well established lawn. This 'thatch' impedes percolation of water and soon causes deterioration in the turf. Good cultural technique will avoid the build up of thatch. This includes regular mowing with a grass box attached to collect the clippings, fertilizer and water application as necessary, spiking the turf with a digging fork at 6in (15cm) intervals 4in (10cm) deep to allow air to penetrate and raking with a mechanical scarifier or lawn rake from time to time.

Weeds can be troublesome even in the best kept lawn. Fortunately they do not present too much of a problem when they are caught at an early stage. When only a few are present, they may be removed with a small fork but the method is rather tedious when there are many. In that case it would be more convenient to use one of the selective hormone type weedkillers made especially for turf. This type of herbicide will only kill broad-leaved plants and will not harm the lawn provided the lawn is well established and not suffering from drought.

Various pests and diseases are liable to infest the lawn from time to time. Worms often throw up casts, especially when the soil is alkaline or if clippings are not removed at the time of mowing. Casts are best brushed away regularly, otherwise weeds will become a problem and the surface of the lawn will be very uneven.

Leatherjacket grubs and wireworms tend to feed on the roots of grass plants, chafer grubs are also a pest in this way from time to time. Usually the first sign of these pests being present is when starlings and other birds are seen pecking at the turf, in some cases ripping the turf away to feed on the grubs below. These pests can be controlled by certain insecticides available from garden centres and stores.

Turf diseases can be seen in the form of yellow patches on the lawn. Close inspection often reveals small cotton-like threads attached to the end of the infected grass leaf. This disease, known as red thread, is usually caused by a low nitrogen content in the soil. Unfortunately it often occurs during autumn when

Left: Spiking a lawn with a garden fork. Right: Raking to remove thatch.

nitrogen is not required to any great extent by the plant. However, the disease is readily controlled by using a fungicide and a note should be made to feed the grass adequately the following year. Turf diseases are normally rectified by a general fungicide sold for the purpose, which again is available from garden centres and stores.

Moss does tend to be a severe problem in some lawns and no wonder when the reasons for its existence are considered. Moss is a problem where the sward lacks vigour for some reason. Shade cast by trees or the dwelling is often enough to reduce vigour; other factors such as lack of fertilizer or irrigation, keeping the grass too short, poor drainage so that the roots are unable to function properly, all contribute to a lack of vigour and the development of moss. Mosskillers may be purchased to deal with the existing growth but if it returns, than the cause of the problem should be found and rectified.

Choosing and Using Mowers

Choosing a mower is rather like choosing a car, there is no shortage of makes and designs although there are likely to be some limiting factors. But first it is worth considering why a mower is necessary at all. Clearly the grass in a lawn needs to be kept reasonably short otherwise the whole garden is likely to look an untidy mess; mowing helps to keep a good quality, dense, healthy sward.

Regular mowing also reduces weed growth by continually removing part of the leaf and resulting in a weakening of the plant. The same could be said for grass plants, unless the turf is mown regularly so that the grass is not allowed to grow too long and rank, when severe topping would have an adverse effect. The main difference between broad-leaved weeds and grass is that weeds often grow with a terminal point to the stem and this is continually being removed by mowing leaving the older, less active leaves to nourish the plant, which soon weakens. Grass, on the other hand, continually makes new growth from the crown and so the older part of the plant is removed by mowing. Unfortunately weed plants have a habit of modifying their growth to survive and so certain weeds like daisy are able to form a ground-hugging rosette to avoid the mower blades.

Proper use of the mower can help the grass during drought. A considerable quantity of water is taken out of the ground by grass plants in hot weather. One way to reduce the uptake is to raise the mowing height so that a leaf long enough to shade its neighbour is left on the plant after mowing. Most mowers can have the cutting height raised, or lowered, but it is worth checking before the final decision is made when buying a machine.

Cutting height has a bearing on root activity; grass kept very short is likely to have shallow roots unable to search for moisture and nutrients in the soil. This puts the plant under stress which in turn makes it prone to infection by diseases and invasion by weeds. Ideally no more than one-third of the growth should be removed at each mowing and during good growing weather that means mowing at least once each week. That in itself is a good reason for selecting the right mower that will do the job properly without continually breaking down or making hard work of the task.

The mower should not be too heavy to handle. Pushing a heavy mower or trying to control a powerful machine can be exhausting and some soil types compact easily under the weight and this, in turn, causes sickly grass growth. Try to avoid turning in the same place each time the lawn is cut, the best way to avoid excessive compaction and wear in those areas is to alternate mowing patterns, so that the mowing direction is changed each time. Some mowers leave stripes on the lawn so that mowing direction can be seen easily.

Whilst it is not always necessary to remove clippings from the lawn after cutting, there are certain times when it is essential: some weeds are easily spread over the lawn by allowing the clippings to fly, cast-forming worms are encouraged and an undecomposed layer of 'thatch' is inclined to build up around the base of the plants. During hot sunny weather when the grass is still growing there can be certain advantages in allowing the clippings to return to the ground: the main immediate advantage is that they act as a mulch to reduce water loss from the soil by evaporation. When clippings are allowed to fly, it is most important that the grass is cut regularly so that only a very thin layer is present at any one time, otherwise diseases would soon be encouraged. Unless lawn clippings are raked up after each mowing, it would be as well to choose a mower with a grass collecting box or bag which can be removed as the occasion arises. Since the container is likely to be removed several times during the course of mowing, it is important to choose one that is easy to remove and so it is worth trying it out at the time of purchase.

Cylinder Mowers So far as the actual cutting blades are concerned, there are basically two different types. Cylinder mowers have a number of cutting blades joined together to form a cylinder which cuts the grass leaf as it passes between the cylinder and fixed blade in a scissor action. Cylinder mowers have been used since gardeners first took pride in their lawns; they are considered by many professional groundsmen to give a better and closer finish to the lawn and they give an attractive striped effect to the area. These mowers are available in sizes suitable for a pocket handkerchief to a lawn the size of a meadow; they can have either a petrol or electric powered motor, or they can be purchased without a motor and be pushed by hand.

Rotary Mowers These have a blade which spins in a horizontal circular motion below a cover close to the ground. This type of mower is of particular benefit for steep slopes, especially when of the wheel-less hover type, and can be used when cutting long grass. Not all rotary mowers have the grass collecting facility and it is worth checking before a final decision to purchase is made. Electric and petrol driven machines are available and where the grass is likely to be tough, a petrol-driven engine will probably be of benefit. Although possibly less expensive to buy, rotary mowers use more fuel and tend to be more noisy than cylinder mowers.

Some rotary mowers are made with wheels so that they may be pushed over the surface of the ground, the very large ones are propelled by an engine which also drives the cutting blade. Other types do not have wheels but glide over the ground on a cushion of air, they are very light and easy to handle but do not always leave a bowling green finish if that is required. However, areas below shrubs and close to trees and other obstructions do not present a problem with these, as they can do with wheeled mowers.

Motor Mowers Motor mowers are inclined to be noisy and some are difficult to start. Other things being equal, 4-stroke engines are easier to start than 2-stroke where the oil is mixed with the petrol. Electric motors are quiet but a wandering cable can sometimes be something of a nuisance, in that case battery-operated models are available which must be recharged from time to time. Hand-propelled mowers are less expensive than motor-driven ones and, of course, they do not use fuel. Maintenance is also less of a problem and unless motor mowers are properly maintained, they can be very inconvenient and expensive. When large areas need to be cut, a ride-on mower is of considerable benefit and the lawn is rolled at the same time. It is doubtful whether any sort of motor mower is justified for a lawn measuring less than 15 paces by 10 paces.

Mower Maintenance A motor mower is likely to be one of the most expensive items used in the garden, but it is a worthwhile investment and one that will last for many years provided it is maintained properly. Good maintenance begins as soon as the machine is first used.

Moving parts of the machine will begin to wear as soon as the engine is started up; minute fragments of metal will find their way into the lubricating oil and since few motor mowers have filters in the system, these fragments must be removed before they cause damage to pistons, rings, cams and various other parts of the engine. Drain out the oil when the mower has been used a few times and then refill the sump with fresh. From then on the oil level should be checked before starting, on no account should the machine be run with the oil below the recommended level otherwise considerable damage could be done to the working parts.

Check and adjust the cutting blades from time to time. Cylinder mowers should be adjusted so that the edge of the blades is left bright after use. They are inclined to wear too quickly when set tightly against the fixed blade and that also puts undue strain on the engine. Rotary mower blades tend to wear quickly because they must of necessity be made of comparatively soft metal so that they do not shatter if they make contact with a hard obstruction. This is due to the very high speed the blades need to turn for them to cut the grass properly.

Cylinder mower blades may be sharpened by attaching a special device on to the mower, or alternatively they may be taken to a service engineer who has a grinding machine made especially for sharpening cylinder mower blades. Rotary mower blades require sharpening much more frequently and it is not unusual to sharpen them after each hour or so of use. It is important to keep the edge sharp otherwise the grass sward is bruised and an untidy appearance results. Rotary blades are easily sharpened by using a reaper file which can be purchased at any ironmongers and it is a job well worth doing.

Check nuts and bolts for tightness each time after the machine is used, it takes but a few seconds and can save much time and money by avoiding accidents. Drive chains should occasionally be checked for tightness; the degree of tension is important and instructions will be found in the service book for the particular model. Chains and cables will need lubricating.

Petrol engines are sometimes difficult to start. 2-stroke engines in particular suffer from starting problems and usually this can be traced to an incorrect mixture of petrol and oil. Special 2-stroke oil must be used, never ordinary engine oil. Each model has its own mixture ratio and so the maker's handbook should be consulted. Two star, low octane petrol is used for both 4-stroke and 2-stroke engines; high octane petrol is likely to damage the engine and so it should not be used. Petrol can deteriorate when stored and it is wise to start the new season with fresh fuel. Remember that fuel left in the engine for any length of time may cause starting problems and so it is wise to let the engine run until the carburetter is empty when the machine is likely to stand for any length of time.

Remember to clean the fuel filter at intervals recommended in the instruction book supplied with the machine. A dirty filter will choke the engine and use far more petrol than it should.

Grass finds its way into all sorts of places. Cylinder mowers pick up long grass which winds itself around spindles; cut sward clings to various parts of the casing and deflector plates. Rotary mowers fling grass to stick under the hood and all of this should be removed before the machine is put away after each period of use. The best tool to remove grass from these areas is a piece of thin wood; a stiff brush is useful to remove clippings from cables and other areas which may be damaged by using a solid object. Professional groundsmen often hose down their machines from time to time and that is no bad thing provided the equipment is allowed to dry off before storing away. A rub over the bright parts with an oily cloth after washing down will do much to keep the metal in good condition.

It is often recommended to store mowers away for the winter months. Whilst the mower should certainly be serviced and any necessary repairs carried out at the end of the main growing season, generally it is better to keep the mower handy so that it can be started up and run for a few minutes from time to time. A run up every three or four weeks through the dormant season should keep the points and other parts in good working order. The machine will then be ready to tackle any growth that has been made during a particularly mild winter. Not only that, but the mower really will be ready for that first cut in spring when so often the service engineer is swamped with machines that will not start.

Calendar of Events – A Guide

January
Remove snow from lawn as soon as possible to prevent disease and moss.
Avoid walking on frosted grass.

February
Watch for diseases and moss and treat as necessary.
Brush off debris including twigs from nearby trees.
Spike to aerate the surface.

March
Remove debris by sweeping.
Growth often starts in earnest this month but avoid taking too much away when mowing.
Use roller on turf if necessary where frost has lifted it.
Spring fertilizer dressing may be given in mild southern counties.
Tidy lawn edges with half-moon tool.

April
Apply spring fertilizer dressing if not already done.
Increase frequency of mowing to once a week.
Rake to remove thatch and debris provided moss is not present, otherwise kill moss first to prevent spread.
Reseed thin patches.

May
Apply selective hormone-type weedkiller if necessary.
Reduce height of cut gradually to ¾in (19mm).

June
Continue mowing regularly.
Water to prevent roots from drying out.
Spike surface with digging fork if water lays on surface after irrigating.

A wheeled fertilizer distributor ensures the even distribution of fertilizer.

July
If drought conditions prevail, raise height of cut and allow clippings to fly without being collected up.

August
Apply hormone weedkiller if necessary.
Switch lawn with long cane or besom broom to control crane flies if present.

September
Apply autumn fertilizer.
Spike lawn and apply topdressing of proprietary mixture, or mix soil, sand and peat. No more than ¼in (6mm) depth is necessary, brushed into the surface.
Sweep away worm casts.

October
Brush away dew before mowing.
Raise cutting height and continue to mow all the time grass is growing.
Repair worn patches by turfing or seeding.
Watch for leatherjacket damage and apply insecticide if necessary.
Sweep away worm casts.
Complete grass seed sowing.

November
Have mower serviced.
Sweep away fallen leaves.

December
Complete turfing before Christmas.

Annuals and Biennials

Annuals and biennials are amongst the most colourful and easiest to grow of all our flowers; in addition, they are the quickest to show results. A look first at which plants we are talking about.

Classification

Most outdoor flowering plants are classified as either HA (hardy annual), HHA (half-hardy annual), HB (hardy biennial) or HP (hardy perennial). This indicates what sort of a plant is being dealt with and, consequently, how it should be grown and when it will flower.

The real key to cultivation is whether a plant is hardy, half-hardy or tender. Hardy means that it will normally survive outdoors throughout its life; half-hardy, that it is only safe outside when there are no frosts and tender, that it is better suited to the greenhouse or indoors.

Within this grouping, plants are either annuals, biennials or perennials. Annuals grow and flower in the same year and then die. Biennials grow one year, flower the next and then die. Perennials grow in their first year and then flower at the same time every year more or less indefinitely.

There are, of course, 'in-between' plants that are botanically one kind but which gardeners treat as another. In fact, wallflowers and polyanthus are perennials but as they are only kept for one flowering season they are treated as biennials.

Making the Best Use of Annuals and Biennials

These plants are normally grown outdoors in borders, either on

Mixed plantings of annuals bring a blaze of colour to the garden. Included here are phlox, asters, French marigolds, lobelia and alyssum.

their own or in combination with other plants, such as bulbs. Simple though it sounds, this covers an immense range of possibilities. It means that they can be grown formally, as in the bedding schemes that can be seen in towns and cities all over the country, or informally, where complete beds are sown with different annuals to give a tidy but natural appearance.

Then again, they can be used to fill up the space between trees and shrubs and as edging plants around other borders. The rock garden is also an excellent place for suitably dwarf plants. To make the most of them, though, requires the use of a certain amount of imagination because there are a wealth of other places where they can enhance the beauty of a garden; window boxes and hanging baskets are just a couple. Nor should it be forgotten that a great many make first rate cut flowers for the house.

Propagation

Because annuals are some of the easiest plants to grow, it follows that they are also simple to propagate. The majority of hardy annuals are grown from seed sown outdoors where the plants are to flower and the best time to sow is in the early spring (March/April).

The ground is dug as far in advance of sowing as possible to allow it to consolidate properly. When preparing the actual seed bed, tread the soil down well and rake it to give a firm and fine surface. This is the secret of growing good annuals from direct sowing, it produces stocky plants that are full of flowers. Always sow the seeds sparingly to give the future seedlings room to develop. With biennials, it is normal to sow them in nursery rows on a spare piece of ground for later transplanting.

Half-hardies can be sown direct outdoors from about the middle of May onwards but the usual practice is to sow them in pots or seed trays under cover during late March or early April and plant them out when the frosts have gone. The obvious advantage of this is that they flower much sooner than if sown outdoors. If a lot of plants are needed, then a seed tray would be the best container for the seeds but a pot is quite ample for a small number. Fill the container with a good proprietary seed compost, sow the seeds thinly and cover them lightly with sifted compost. Press the surface down gently with something flat and, after standing the container in a saucer of water until moisture seeps through to the surface, cover it with some glass or polythene to keep the surface moist.

Keep the pot reasonably dark and look at it every day to check if the seeds have germinated. Once the seedlings are large enough to handle, they should be 'pricked out' singly into either small individual pots or, where there are a lot of plants, into seed-trays of potting compost so that the little plants are about an inch apart. They are grown on like this until the risk of frosts has passed when they can go outside.

Formal Bedding

The sort of display that this refers to are the massed bedding schemes seen in the local parks. As a rule, two plantings are carried out each year. One in about October, for flowering in the spring, and the other during May to provide the summer show. The spring-flowering scheme usually consists of suitable biennials (wallflowers, polyanthus, forget-me-nots), which were raised in the open. These are planted with bulbs such as tulips or hyacinths. Summer bedding plants are normally raised

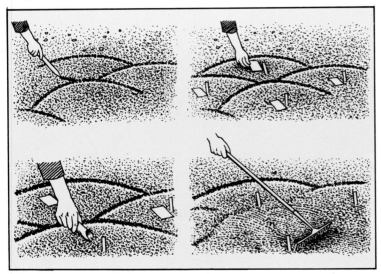

Preparing a mixed planting of annuals.

under cover. As the overall effect has to be formal and spectacular, direct sowing is not carried out and all plants should be set in strict rows and patterns. To add interest to what could otherwise be a rather flat display, a few larger and contrasting 'dot' plants are often grown as well. Preparation of the border takes place as soon as the previous display has been removed and should consist of thorough digging and the incorporation of plenty of well rotted garden compost or farmyard manure. Work in some general fertilizer with the final cultivation. When planting, always make sure that the plants are firm in the ground.

Informal Displays

These require a very different technique because, for the most part, they are composed of hardy annuals which are sown where they are to flower.

If a complete border is to be given over to them, it should first be planned so that it is known exactly where each packet

is to be sown. The best system is to break down the surface of the soil into a firm and fine seed bed and then to mark it out in drifts so that each different species is allocated its own area. After this, the actual seed rows can be marked out. Following sowing, cover the seeds lightly and firm them down with the flat of a rake before covering the whole bed with sticks or netting to keep the birds and cats away. If the soil is dry, give it a good watering.

Once the seedlings are an inch or two high, thin them out to the recommended distance apart and remember that any gaps can be filled with these thinnings.

Exactly the same routine is followed where the odd drift of annuals is wanted for filling up spaces in other borders but a little more thought has to go into the correct choice of plant so that the height and colour are in keeping with the surroundings.

Hanging Baskets and Window Boxes

Much the same plants that are used for formal bedding can be used in containers but they should be planted so that they look natural rather than regimented. Apart from using plenty of trailing plants around the edges, the choice is really one of personal preference but remember to put the plants in fairly close together to obtain an instant display.

Aftercare

The main tasks will be to keep the borders free of weeds and flowering for as long as possible. Most worthwhile annuals have a long flowering period and this can be ensured by regularly removing faded and dead flower heads.

With direct sown borders, you will also have to think about any support that may be needed. Although they tend to support each other, it is often a good idea, when the plants are still small, to push twiggy sticks into the ground amongst them. The plants cover these as they grow and seldom need anything more sophisticated.

The main need of plants growing in any kind of container will be for regular and sufficient watering and, though a hose or watering can will be the answer for tubs and troughs, hanging baskets are best taken down regularly and stood in a bucket of water for a few minutes. All will need feeding as well and, for this, a liquid tomato feed is better than most as it encourages more flowers to form. Feed the plants at least weekly once they start flowering.

A Selection of the Best Annuals and Biennials
Half-hardy Annuals

Ageratum – 6in (15cm) high. Bright blue rather feathery flowers. Good for edging. Formal.

Amaranthus (Love-lies-bleeding) – 12in (30cm). Curious rather than pretty, with red tail-like flowers that hang down. A good dot plant.

Antirrhinum (Snapdragon) – up to 24in (60cm). A perennial treated as HHA. A popular formal and informal bedding plant.

Coleus – 12in (30cm). Better known as a pot plant, the brilliantly coloured leaves make a startling display in a formal border.

Dahlia – 18in (45cm). Many good mixtures can be grown from seed. Superb for filling gaps in shrub borders.

Helichrysum – up to 24in (60cm). Grown solely for drying and winter use. One of the best everlastings.

Helipterum – 18in (45cm). A dainty everlasting with pink or white daisy-like flowers.

Impatiens (Busy Lizzie) – 12in (30cm). A popular pot plant and excellent for tubs and window boxes.

Ipomoea (Morning Glory) – A vigorous climber. Sky blue flowers like convolvulus. First rate in a greenhouse.

Kochia (Burning Bush) – 18in (45cm). Red or green feathery leaves. A good formal dot plant.

Lobelia – 6in (15cm). One of the best edging plants. Compact and trailing forms. Blue, white and near-red flowers.

Matthiola (Ten-week Stock) – 15in (38cm). Semi-formal. Heavily scented. Red, pink, white flowers.

Mesembryanthemum (Livingstone Daisy) – 6in (15cm). Bright multi-coloured daisy-like flowers. Rockery.

Nicotiana (Tobacco Plant) – Up to 24in (60cm). Good colour range of trumpet-shaped flowers. Sweetly scented. Informal.

Petunia – 9in (12cm). Large flowers. Good colour range.

Salvia – 15in (38cm). Brilliant red flower spikes. Very formal.
Senecio and *Cineraria* – 24in (60cm). Grown solely for grey foliage. Dot plants.
Tagetes (French and African Marigolds) – 6 to 24in (15 to 60 cm). Shades of orange or yellow. Mainly formal.
Tropaeolum (Nasturtium) – 12in (30cm). Compact or trailing. Large flowers; red, orange or yellow. Informal.
Verbena – 12in (30cm). Good colour range. Formal or informal.
Zinnia – 6 to 12in (15 to 30cm). Flowers like marigolds; many colours. Cut flowers, formal or informal.

The delightful white Lavatera trimestris 'Silver Cup'.

The Iceland poppy, Papaver nudicaule.

Hardy Annuals

Alyssum – 4in (10cm). Compact. Normally white flowers, Edging. Formal or rockery.
Calendula (English Marigold) – 15in (38cm). Orange or yellow. Informal.
Centaurea (Cornflower) – 15in (38cm). Pink, blue, white. Cut flower. Informal.
Clarkia – 12in (30cm). Multi-coloured. Informal.
Coreopsis – 18in (45cm). Large yellow/orange flowers. Informal.
Cosmos – 24in (60cm). Large and daisy-like. Pink or white. Informal. Cut flower.
Delphinium (Larkspur) – 18in (45cm). Pink, blue or white flower spikes. Cut flower. Informal.
Dianthus – 15in (38cm). Many colours. Mainly informal.
Eschscholzia (Californian Poppy) – 12in (30cm). Shades of pink, orange and yellow. Informal.
Godetia – up to 24in (60cm). Large flowers, many colours. Informal.
Gypsophila – 12in (30cm). Many small, pink or white flowers. Informal.
Lathyrus (Sweet Pea) – Climber. Many colours. Cut flower. Dwarf form exists. Sweetly scented.
Lavatera (Tree Mallow) – 24in (60cm). Large flowers. Pink or white. Informal.
Nigella (Love-in-a-mist) – 18in (45cm). Blue, pink or white. Feathery foliage. Informal. Seed heads can be dried.
Papaver (Poppy) – 24in (60cm). Many colours, mainly red, orange and yellow. Informal.
Scabiosa (Scabious) – 30in (75cm). Blue, lilac and white. Cut flower. Informal.
Statice (Sea Lavender) – 18in (45cm). Many colours. For drying. Informal.
Viola (Pansy) – 6in (15cm). Many and multi-coloured. Formal or informal.

Hardy Biennials

Bellis (Ornamental Daisy) – 6in (15cm). Large red, pink or white flowers. Good for edging.
Campanula (Canterbury Bells) – 36in (1m). Blue or white. Useful for cutting. Informal.
Cheiranthus (Wallflower) – 18in (45cm). Multi-coloured. Sweetly scented. Good for cutting. Formal and informal.
Dianthus (Sweet William) – 18in (45cm). Many and multi-coloured. Good for cutting. Informal.
Digitalis (Foxglove) – 36in (1m). Spikes of pinkish flowers. Informal.
Lunaria (Honesty) – 24in (60cm). Grown solely for drying. Informal.
Myosotis (Forget-me-not) – 12in (30cm). Tiny pale blue flowers. Formal or informal.
Polyanthus – 6in (15cm). HP treated as HB. Many colours. Formal. Informal and cut flower.

Brilliantly coloured Mesembryanthemum criniflorum.

Ipomoea 'Heavenly Blue'

Herbaceous Perennial Plants

Herbaceous plants are perennial plants, which means that they live for a long time, producing new growth and flowers annually. Most live for many years but can be kept indefinitely if regularly lifted and divided. Some, such as peony, naturally have an exceedingly long life and it is not unusual to come across clumps that are at least 50 years old. At the other extreme, some herbaceous plants are short-lived, like aquilegia, and these need replacing regularly.

The top growth of herbaceous plants – the stems and foliage – dies down each autumn, but in the spring new growth is produced and flowers following in spring, summer or autumn. The plants overwinter as dormant 'crowns' – roots, with a cluster of buds at soil level.

There are also evergreen perennials, which are not herbaceous in habit but retain their leaves all the year around. Examples of these are bergenias, many of the hellebores, iris like *I. foetidissima, Liriope muscari, Phormium tenax* and varieties and *Stachys olympica*.

Herbaceous plants have many uses in the garden and there are plants suited to all sorts of situations, from hot and dry to cool, moist and shady. In a well-planned garden they rank second in importance to shrubs and trees. No longer are herbaceous plants confined to borders on their own – as was the case in the past – these days they are mixed with all kinds of other plants.

The Mixed Border In most gardens these days beds and

Herbaceous plants are relatively trouble free and bring colour to the garden over a long season. This effective border can be seen at New College, Oxford.

borders are planted with a mixed collection of plants – chosen from those that look well together. The 'framework' of a mixed border consists of shrubs, both deciduous and evergreen. Between and around the shrubs are planted other subjects, including herbaceous plants, evergreen perennials, bulbs, and even hardy and half-hardy annuals.

When considering herbaceous plants to combine with shrubs, choose only those that look particularly good with their woody companions. The aim in such a border is to have something in flower or of interest all the year round.

Even in the winter there can be a great deal of colour, perhaps from a group of hamamelis, winter-flowering heathers and *Helleborus niger*. There is no problem in the summer, as this is when shrubs and perennials are at their most colourful, but for the autumn make sure you have some clumps of asters or Michaelmas daisies, perhaps planted around shrubs with good autumn leaf colour, completing the group with the various sedums.

In the spring, colour can be provided by *Doronicum* 'Miss Mason', some hellebores, and *Pulmonaria saccharata*, perhaps in association with spring-flowering shrubs like forsythia.

Other perennials which associate particularly well with

shrubs, giving a good contrast in foliage shape and texture, include *Acanthus mollis latifolius*, kniphofias, *Cynara cardunculus, Echinops ritro*, eryngiums, geraniums, hemerocallis, hostas, agapanthus, anemones and euphorbias.

Island Beds If you want to display herbaceous plants on their own then the modern way is to grow them in an irregular-shaped bed in a lawn, known as an island bed. It can be of any shape but should have gently curving edges for easy mowing.

The aim is to have something of interest all the year round and to grow only labour-saving plants – in other words, those which are self-supporting and need no artificial supports.

Ideally an island bed should be in an open sunny part of the garden. Generally the tallest plants are planted in the centre of the bed, intermediate kinds next and the shortest around the edges. However, do not stick too rigidly to this arrangement otherwise you will end up with an unnatural-looking graded effect. Instead, a few groups of short plants could be extended towards the centre, and one or two groups of taller kinds towards the edge of the bed.

Always try to plant in bold informal groups of each kind of plant – for example, groups of three or five plants. Single specimens dotted all over the bed result in an unattractive 'spotty' effect. This may mean restricting the number of varieties of plants you wish to grow. Suitable plants for spring display in an island bed include dicentra, doronicums, pulmonarias, brunnera, veronicas and violas.

There are many for summer colour, like achilleas, aquilegias, anaphalis, campanulas, coreopsis, dianthus, erigeron, gaillardias, *Gentiana asclepiadea*, geraniums, geums, hemerocallis, liatris, lysimachia, lythrum, monarda, oenothera, phlox, polygonums, potentillas, pyrethrums, rudbeckia, salvia, sidalcea, stokesia and tradescantia.

Autumn sees the Japanese anemones flowering, together with the asters or Michaelmas daisies, sedums, solidago and cerato-stigma. For winter do not forget the hellebores, including the Christmas rose, and make sure you have some evergreen foliage – bergenias, stachys and even some of the ornamental grasses.

Specimen Plants in a Lawn
Some herbaceous plants have such a distinctive shape that they make good isolated specimens in a lawn, or even in an area of gravel. Thus displayed, they are shown to best advantage. The kinds for this sort of situation include cynara, *Rodgersia pinnata*, *Macleaya cordata*, *Phormium tenax* and varieties, *Gunnera manicata* (needs plenty of moisture), *Aruncus dioicus* and the verbascums.

For Shade Many people think that it is difficult to grow plants in shade, but this is not so if suitable plants are chosen. There are two types of shade for practical purposes – shade with moist soil and, the more difficult of the two, shade with dry soil.

If you have a shady area with cool moist soil then you should choose from plants like meconopsis, hostas, *Polygonatum x hybridum, Cimicifuga racemosa, Astrantia major* and *Convallaria majalis*.

For shade with dry soil try some of the really tough plants like pulmonaria and the geraniums.

Hot and Dry Equally difficult for many people is trying to grow plants in an area with very dry soil and in full sun, so that in the summer it is like a little bit of the Mediterranean. However, many herbaceous plants relish these conditions, including acanthus, *Ballota pseudodictamnus, Centranthus ruber, Cheiranthus* 'Harpur Crewe', cynara, eryngiums, *Euphorbia myrsinites, Linaria purpurea* 'Canon Went', *Nepeta x faassenii*, potentillas and sedums. One can further create an impression of 'arid' conditions by covering the soil with gravel or shingle.

Ground Cover For covering the ground between and around shrubs and other larger plants, not only to create a pleasing effect but also to keep down weeds, there are several herbaceous plants to choose from, like bergenias, *Polygonum affine* 'Donald Lowndes', *Prunella webbiana* 'Loveliness', *Pulmonaria saccharata* and *Stachys olympica*.

Cultivation
Preparing the Soil Before planting herbaceous plants the soil must be prepared thoroughly, for they will remain where they are planted for several years. Ideally the bed or border should be double dug (this is to two depths of the spade) in the autumn and organic matter like well-rotted farmyard manure, garden compost, peat, leafmould, spent hops or pine bark added to each trench.

While digging remove all perennial weeds – roots as well – for these are virtually impossible to control once perennials have been planted.

Planting The best time to plant is a debatable point: some gardeners say autumn planting, others spring. Autumn planting is acceptable provided your soil is very well drained and does not lie wet over the winter. For instance, light sandy soils generally come in this category. One cannot go wrong, however, with spring planting – March or April. By this time the soil will be warming up and drying out, so the plants quickly become established.

A week or two before planting hoe into the soil surface a general-purpose fertilizer, such as Growmore. The previously dug ground should also be broken down fairly finely for easy planting, and moderately firmed by treading with your heels all over it.

Most gardeners will buy herbaceous plants in pots or other containers from a garden centre. Carefully remove them from the containers and try not to disturb the soil ball. Plant in a hole slightly larger than the rootball and firm the soil well around it. The crown of the plant should be at soil level.

If the plants are bare-root then take out a hole of sufficient depth that the roots are able to dangle straight down – on no account cram roots into a shallow hole.

General Care Weeds must be kept under control or they will compete with the plants for food and moisture. Weeds can be hoed off while they are in the seedling stage, choosing a warm dry day when the surface of the soil is dry. The odd perennial weed that may appear – such as dandelion – can either be dug out, root as well, or treated with a 'spot weedkiller'.

Perennials must be watered whenever the soil starts to dry out in spring and summer if optimum growth and flowering is to be achieved. This even applies to 'hot dry areas'. It is especially important to keep newly planted perennials well watered in dry periods to help them become established. To conserve soil moisture you might consider laying a mulch over the soil surface.

Like most plants herbaceous perennials are prone to attacks by pests and diseases. Slugs and snails will go for new shoots of many plants, particularly delphiniums, hostas and lupins. Put down slug pellets just as plants are coming into growth. Aphids or greenfly are another problem, but are easily controlled by spraying with a systemic insecticide. Michaelmas daisies are prone to mildew, a disease which appears as white patches over the foliage, and which can seriously affect growth and flowering. To prevent mildew, spray with benomyl fungicide.

Staking Some herbaceous plants will need artificial support to keep them upright. Plants with thin stems which are inclined to flop over, such as some of the Michaelmas daisies, can be supported with twiggy pea sticks inserted between and around the clumps when growth is only a few inches high. The stems will then grow up through them. Some plants have tall stems and heavy flower heads, like delphiniums, and these need more adequate supports. A stout bamboo cane should be provided for each stem which is tied in with soft garden string.

Removing Dead Growth Remove dead flower heads from all plants throughout the season, as in some cases this results in the plants producing more flowers. It also prevents seed setting, which uses up the plant's energy.

In the autumn the dead stems of herbaceous plants should be cut down as close to the dormant buds as possible. Also, regularly remove any dead leaves from evergreen perennials.

Lifting and Dividing Most herbaceous plants and evergreen perennials need lifting and dividing every three or four years to ensure they remain young, vigorous and free flowering. This can be done in the spring and while the bed or border is free of plants it should be dug thoroughly, and more organic matter added. While the plants are out of the ground keep the roots covered to prevent them from drying out. Full details of division will be found in the section on Plant Propagation, page 156.

Achillea filipendulina 'Gold Plate'

Achillea ptarmica 'The Pearl'

Acanthus mollis latifolius

Achillea millefolium 'Cerise Queen'

Acanthus mollis latifolius (syn A. mollis lusitanicus) Bear's Breeches, Europe. Acanthaceae

Vigorous plant with magnificent sinuate shiny leaves. The flower spike gives rise to an abundant densely clustered inflorescence. A versatile plant most impressive as a single specimen or set in a group where space permits. The rootstock may require some protection during severe winters. Excellent as a container plant for patio or indoor decoration. Propagate by division of the rootstock in autumn or early spring, or by seed. 3ft (1m)

⬭ ✿Summer ○ ◑ ▦ △▼

Achillea filipendulina 'Gold Plate', Yarrow. Compositae

Strong-growing plant with pungent, alternate, rough, hairy pinnately-lobed leaves. The large corymbs of bright yellow flowers produced over a long period on erect stems are good for cutting and drying provided the stems are gathered before flowers fade. The plants, spaced 2ft (60cm) apart, are best grown in groups. Propagation is by division in autumn or spring or by seed. 3ft (1m)

⬭ ✿Summer ○ ▦ △▼

Achillea millefolium 'Cerise Queen', Yarrow. Compositae

A most adaptable plant with spreading habit. The dark green, deeply segmented strap-shaped leaves are attractive and give the plant a healthy appearance. Bright red flowers most useful for cutting are borne on erect stems over a long period. New plants are easily raised by seed or by dividing the rootstock in autumn or spring and setting out the divisions 1ft (30cm) apart in the border. The type plant is often found growing as a weed in lawns and has been cultivated as a lawn plant where normal turf grasses will not flourish. The yarrow lawn is established by sowing seed in spring or during autumn when the soil is moist and still warm. 2¹/₂ft (75cm)

⬭ ✿Summer ○ ◑ ▦ △▼

Achillea ptarmica 'The Pearl', Sneezewort. Compositae

This valuable border plant spreads over its allotted space rapidly by way of creeping stems giving rise to narrow-lanceolate minutely toothed leaves. The terminal corymbs of double white flowers on erect stems useful for indoor decoration may be cut over a longer period by pinching out the stem apex occasionally. Propagate by seed sown in spring or autumn. 2¹/₂ft (75cm)

⬭ ✿Summer ○ ◑ ▦ △▼

Aconitum napellus, Monkshood, Europe. *Ranunculaceae*

Most attractive but poisonous plant with a dark-coloured fleshy tuberous rootstock which gives rise to branched stems clad in deeply cut, palmate leaves terminating in erect, tapering dense spikes of indigo-blue flowers. Best grown in small groups, the plants can be propagated by seed sown during spring or summer. 3ft (1m)

⬯☼Summer○◗●✕/▼

Agapanthus Headbourne Hybrids, S. Africa. *Liliaceae*

A thick fleshy creeping rootstock gives rise to handsome, linear, arching dark green leaves. The erect scape terminates in a large inflorescence of abundant exotic blue flowers to form an umbel. Although perfectly hardy, flowering is, in fact, enhanced by low temperature, the plant may be grown in a large container and makes an attractive feature for the conservatory when the leaves often persist green during winter. Seed germinates readily to produce plants that flower in 3 or 4 years and new plants are often raised by division of mature specimens. 3ft (1m)

⬯☼Summer○✕/▼

Alchemilla mollis, Lady's Mantle, Europe, Asia Minor. *Rosaceae*

The stout dark rootstock gives rise to grey-green lobed leaves with a toothed margin. Small yellowish-green flowers borne in panicles are used for flower arranging. An effective ground-cover plant for the front of a border. New plants can be raised from seed or by division. 1¹/₂ft (45cm)

⬯☼Summer○◗✕/▼

Anaphalis cinnamomea (syn *A. yedoensis*) India, Burma. *Compositae*

Attractive border plant with erect stems giving rise to alternate lanceolate silvery leaves, woolly on the lower surface, and abundant, small, white everlasting flowers much used for drying and flower arranging. Propagate by seed or division in spring. 2ft (60cm)

⬯☼Summer○✕/▼

Anemone × hybrida 'Honorine Jobert' (syn. *A. japonica*). *Ranunculaceae*

Fibrous-rooted bushy plant with most interesting toothed trilobed leaves. The abundant flower-buds presented on long pedicels are very attractive when the single white flowers are open. Much admired for its long flowering period the plant is propagated by division and then established in a container before setting out in the border. It can also be increased by root cuttings. 4ft (1.2m)

⬯☼Autumn○◗✕/▼

Anemone × hybrida 'Bressingham Glow', Japanese Anemone. *Ranunculaceae*

Flowering over a very long period during late summer and autumn with large semi-double rosy-red blooms, a group of plants will add much interest to the border. 3ft (1m)

⬯☂☼Summer○◗✕/▼

Aquilegia McKana Hybrids, Columbine. *Ranunculaceae*

Graceful plants producing attractive slightly glaucous fern-like foliage and large-spurred flowers of many shades and colours on wiry branching stems, and much used for border decoration and cutting. The plants are best set out in large groups and, although the fruits are attractive, they should be removed before ripe to avoid self seeding. New plants may be raised from selected seed or by division. 3ft (1m)

⬯☼Summer○◗✕/▼

Artemisia arborescens Europe. *Compositae*

A sub-shrub with silvery-white, erect woody shoots. The alternate much divided leaves are covered by attractive white down which is the main feature of the plant and makes an attractive setting for the terminal leafy panicles of small flowers. New plants are raised by cuttings taken with a heel during late summer. 2ft (60cm)

⬯🌢☼Summer○◗◧✕/▼

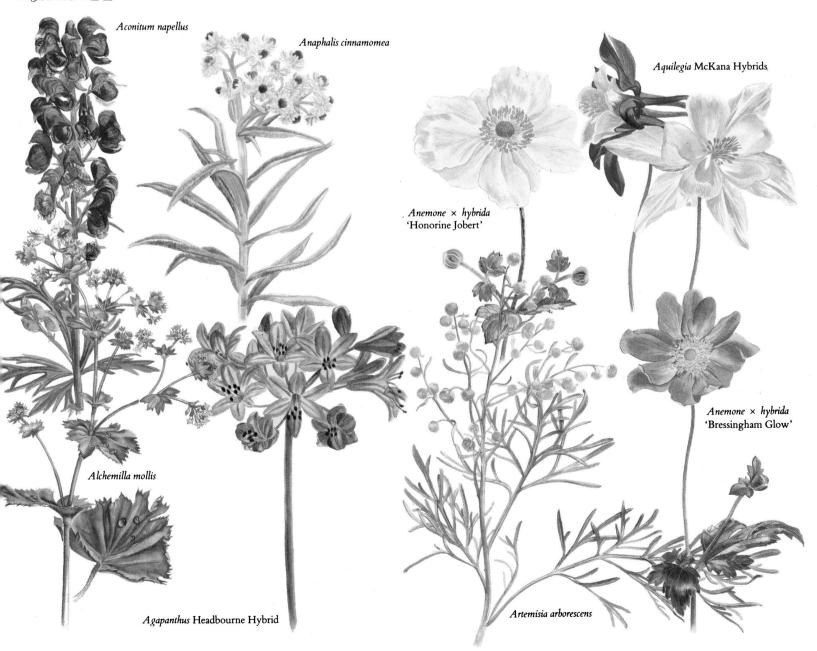

Aconitum napellus

Anaphalis cinnamomea

Aquilegia McKana Hybrids

Anemone × hybrida 'Honorine Jobert'

Anemone × hybrida 'Bressingham Glow'

Alchemilla mollis

Agapanthus Headbourne Hybrid

Artemisia arborescens

Aruncus dioicus (syn *A. sylvester*, *A. vulgaris*, *Spiraea aruncus*) Goat's Beard, Europe. **Rosaceae**

Bushy plant with tripinnate leaves composed of sharply serrated lanceolate-oblong leaflets. The abundant dioecious ivory white flowers occur on long compound plume-like panicles and make an interesting feature for a central bed in the lawn. New plants are propagated by division in spring or autumn and are slow to establish. 4¹/₂ft (1.4m)

⬯ ⛉Summer ◗ ▱ ✖ △▼

Aster amellus 'Brilliant', Italian Aster. **Compositae**

Most attractive plant flowering over a long period which has given rise to many hybrids. The long rough stem produces oblong-lanceolate leaves and large flower heads of abundant purple florets surrounding the rich yellow disk. Propagate by seed, cuttings or by division. 2ft (60cm)

⬯ ⛉Summer ○ ✖ △▼

Aster × frikartii. **Compositae**

A very elegant plant much grown for its long-flowering period from mid-summer to mid-autumn; the large flower heads are a pleasing blue and arise from branched stems. New plants are easily propagated by cuttings or by division. 2¹/₂ft (75cm)

⬯ ⛉Summer ○ ✖ △▼

Aster novae-angliae 'September Ruby', Michaelmas Daisy. **Compositae**

Vigorous plant with stem-clasping lanceolate leaves and abundant flowers composed of many bright ruby-red florets much liked by bees and butterflies. An attractive border plant usually free from the wilt disease but not the best for cutting, the flowers tending to close when taken indoors. Propagate by division or by cuttings. 4ft (1.2m)

⬯ ⛉Autumn ○ ✖ △▼

Aster novi-belgii 'Marie Ballard', Michaelmas Daisy. **Compositae**

The slightly hairy or glabrous much-branched stems give rise to lanceolate, slender-pointed stem-clasping leaves and abundant, double, violet-purple flowers in corymbose panicles. An excellent choice for border decoration and long lasting as a cut flower. Cuttings root readily or it can be propagated by division. 3ft (1m)

⬯ ⛉Autumn ○ ✖ △▼

Astilbe × arendsii 'Fanal'. **Saxifragaceae**

A showy plant which is most effective when grown in a group. The prolific panicles of dark crimson-red flowers are most attractive as are the ternate leaves which add interest to the border when the long flowering season is over. Propagate by division. 2ft (60cm)

⬯ ⛉Summer ○ ◗ ▱ ✖ △▼

Astilbe × arendsii 'Sprite'. **Saxifragaceae**

This dwarf-growing plant is one of the very wide range of hybrids available within the group. Attractive dark green fern-like foliage provides a good backdrop for the erect, spreading panicles of pale pink flowers. New plants can be propagated by division. 10in (25cm)

⬯ ⛉Summer ○ ◗ ▱ ✖ △▼

Astrantia major, Masterwort, Europe. **Umbelliferae**

The blackish-coloured roots give rise to an attractive vigorous plant with toothed, ovate-lanceolate lobed leaves. The umbels of star-like, pinkish-green flowers surrounded by bracts are most interesting. Propagate by division in spring. 2ft (60cm)

⬯ ⛉Summer ◗ ● ✖ △▼

Aster novi-belgii 'Marie Ballard'

Aruncus dioicus

Aster amellus 'Brilliant'

Aster × frikartii

Aster novae-angliae 'September Ruby'

Bergenia 'Silberlicht'

Brunnera macrophylla

Ballota pseudodictamnus

Astrantia major

Bergenia 'Ballawley'

Astrantia maxima

Astilbe × arendsii 'Sprite'

Astilbe × arendsii 'Fanal'

Astrantia maxima (syn *A. helleborifolia*, *A. heterophylla*) Masterwort, Caucasus. **Umbelliferae**

Graceful plant with trifoliate leaves, the ovate-lanceolate lobes being unequally toothed. Umbels of attractive light pink flowers are surrounded by bristly ovate-lanceolate bracts. Propagate in spring by seed or division. 2ft (60cm).

⟋ ☼ Summer ◕ ● ⊞ ◿

Ballota pseudodictamnus, Mediterranean. **Labiatae**

Attractive plant with grey, woolly foliage and stems somewhat woody at the base. The orbicular leaves are a feature of the plant, which is best set out in the border as a small group. Abundant, purple-spotted white flowers appear in whorls. Plants can be increased by division. 2ft (60cm)

△ ☼ Summer ○ ◧ ⊞ ◿

Bergenia 'Ballawley'. **Saxifragaceae**

One of the best of a wide range of available hybrids with characteristic large round, laurel green leaves, with some persisting during winter and so useful for ground cover. Red stems give rise to panicles of bright rose-red flowers. Propagate by division of rootstock. 1ft (30cm)

△ ▮ ☼ Spring ◕ ⊞ ◿

Bergenia 'Silberlicht' (syn 'Silverlight'). **Saxifragaceae**

An unusual cultivar of the group, this plant has white flowers and good foliage and is most useful for the border or for indoor decoration. New plants are raised by dividing the rootstock. 1ft (30cm)

△ ☼ Spring ◕ ⊞ ◿

Brunnera macrophylla (syn *Anchusa myosotidiflora*, *Myosotis macrophylla*) Caucasus. **Boraginaceae**

Interesting plant for the front of the border or light woodland area, the leaves are cordate and those on the stem smaller than the ones at the base. Abundant blue flowers with a yellow throat are borne in panicled racemes. Easily propagated by seed or division; the larger roots may be prepared as cuttings to make new plants. 1¹/₂ft (45cm)

⟋ ☼ Spring/Summer ◕ ⊞ ◿

21

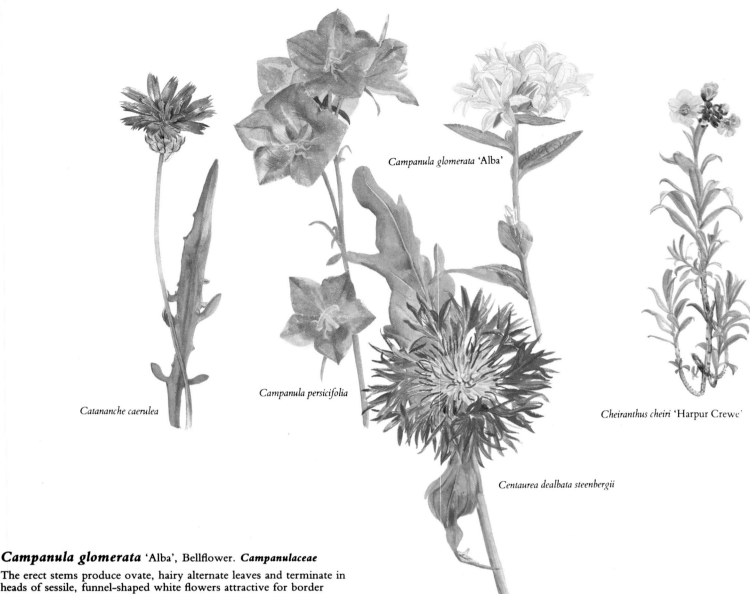

Campanula glomerata 'Alba'

Campanula persicifolia

Catananche caerulea

Cheiranthus cheiri 'Harpur Crewe'

Centaurea dealbata steenbergii

Campanula glomerata 'Alba', Bellflower. *Campanulaceae*

The erect stems produce ovate, hairy alternate leaves and terminate in heads of sessile, funnel-shaped white flowers attractive for border decoration and much used for cutting. Plants can be propagated by division of the rootstock. $1^1/_2$ft (45cm)

⊘☼Summer ◕ ✱ △▼

Campanula persicifolia (syn *C. crystalocalyx*) Bellflower, Europe, N. Africa, Asia. *Campanulaceae*

Handsome glabrous plant with a creeping branched rootstock which gives rise to a long smooth stem and alternate, leathery oblanceolate basal leaves with rounded teeth, the upper leaves being linear-lanceolate. Racemes of short-stalked blue flowers are excellent for cutting. Division of the rootstock is reliable, the new plants should be set out $1^1/_2$ft (45cm) apart to fill in. 3ft (1m)

⊘☼Summer ○ ◕ ✱ △▼

Catananche caerulea, Cupid's Dart, Europe. *Compositae*

A useful plant providing border decoration and semi-everlasting flowers for cutting. The abundant blue flowers are borne on long wiry stems arising from a rosette of narrow-lanceolate leaves. Raised by seed or by division, the new plants are set out $1^1/_2$ft (45cm) apart in the border. 3ft (1m)

⊘☼Summer ○ ◕ ✱ △▼

Centaurea dealbata *steenbergii*, Cornflower, Caucasus, *Compositae*

Good plant for cutting and border decoration, the heads of deep pink tubular florets are accompanied by deeply fringed involucral bracts and the finely divided foliage is grey-green. The stems may need support. Propagate by cuttings or division in spring. $2^1/_2$ft (75cm)

⊘☼Summer ○ ✱ △▼

Centranthus ruber, Red Valerian, Europe. *Valerianaceae*

Adaptable and showy border plant that combines particularly well with grey foliage. The panicles of abundant pale red flowers are offset by fleshy, glaucous, ovate leaves. New plants are raised by seed or cuttings or by rootstock division; they are best planted in a group for mass display. 3ft (1m)

⊘☼Summer ○ ✱ △ △▼

Ceratostigma plumbaginoides (syn *Plumbago larpentae*, *Valoradia plumbaginoides*) China. *Plumbaginaceae*

Beautiful, spreading mat-forming perennial with alternate, obovate leaves fringed with hairs arising from much-branched, reddish, slightly bristled angled stems. The brilliant purplish-blue flowers are carried in terminal and axillary heads. A fine plant for the border as it turns shades of red in autumn. New plants are easily raised by dividing the creeping underground rootstock or by cuttings but are often rather slow to establish in the open border. $1^1/_2$ft (45cm)

⊘☼Autumn ○ ◕ ✱ △

Cheiranthus cheiri 'Harpur Crewe', Perennial Wallflower. *Cruciferae*

An erect bushy plant with lanceolate leaves. The most attractive, yellow, fragrant double flowers are borne in racemes during late spring and summer. A good plant for the border or rock garden which can be increased by cuttings taken during late summer. $1^1/_2$ft (45cm)

⊘ ⬆☼Spring ○ ◕ ✱ △

Chrysanthemum maximum 'Mt Everest', Shasta Daisy. *Compositae*

This most popular vigorous border plant produces numerous stiff stems with toothed lanceolate leaves, the lower stalked. The solitary heads of flowers are excellent for border display and cutting and are borne on long peduncles. Propagate by division of the root stool and set out $2^1/_2$ft (75cm) apart in the border. 3ft (1m)

⊘☼Summer ○ ✱ △ △▼

Cimicifuga racemosa, Eastern N. America. *Ranunculaceae*

Very graceful racemes of small, white, short-stalked flowers, together with the divided, fresh green leaves, make this a desirable feature plant for the border. Best planted in a group, the seed should be sown when fresh under cold glass or the rootstock may be divided during spring. 3ft (1m)

⊘☼Summer ○ ◕ ✱ ▼ △▼

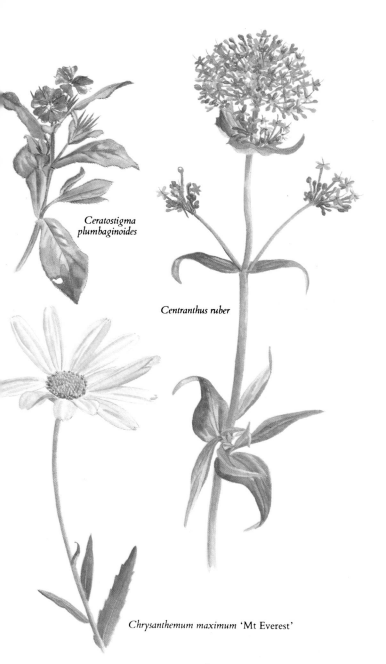

Ceratostigma plumbaginoides

Centranthus ruber

Chrysanthemum maximum 'Mt Everest'

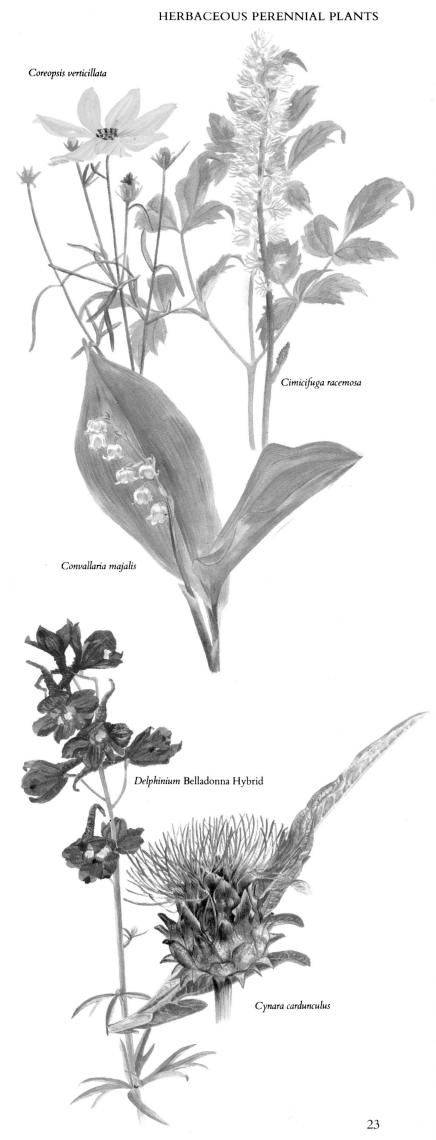

Coreopsis verticillata

Cimicifuga racemosa

Convallaria majalis

Delphinium Belladonna Hybrid

Cynara cardunculus

Convallaria majalis, Lily of the Valley, Europe, Asia, N. America.
Liliaceae

A rather invasive but most attractive plant with a slender creeping
rootstock giving rise to long-stalked, light green, elliptic-lanceolate
sheathed leaves. The six-lobed, white, bell-shaped fragrant flowers droop
most gracefully from the arched stems; they are much used for flower
arranging and bridal bouquets. Propagate by dividing the rootstock in
November and planting the rhizome close to the soil surface. 6in (15cm)

⬠☼Spring ○ ◑ ● ▩ △▼

Coreopsis verticillata (syn *C. tenuifolia*) E. United States.
Compositae

Beautiful shrubby plant with furrowed stem adorned by opposite leaves
much divided into narrow segments. The glorious and abundant bright
yellow flowers are supported by erect graceful stems. Most effective
when planted in a large group, the flowers are much used for cutting.
Propagate by division when lifting the rootstock, preferably every three
years, or raise from seed. 2ft (60cm)

⬠☼Summer ○ ▩ △▼

Cynara cardunculus, Cardoon, Europe. *Compositae*

Large thistle-like perennial herb with very large silvery-green pinnatifid
spiny leaves. The ovate involucral bracts protect purple flowers useful for
decoration at the rear of a border. Propagate by seed or by sucker offsets
arising from the rootstock. 5ft (1.5m)

⬠☼Summer☾Autumn ○ ◑ ● ▩ △ △▼

Delphinium Belladonna Hybrids. *Ranunculaceae*

Magnificent plants for the border and for cutting, the different cultivars
produce flowers in shades of blue, from pale to deep purple, pink and
white. The wiry stems with abundant flowers often need added support
to remain erect and tidy especially during prolonged rain or wind. Plants
raised from seed are often variable and a selected flower colour can be
perpetuated by rootstock division or by basal cuttings. 4ft (1.2m)

⬠🍃☼Summer ○ ▩ △▼

23

Dianthus 'Doris'

Dianthus 'Mrs Sinkins'

Dicentra spectabilis

Echinacea purpurea

Endymion non-scriptus

Dianthus 'Painted Beauty'

Doronicum 'Miss Mason'

Echinops ritro

Dianthus × allwoodii 'Doris', Modern Pink. *Caryophyllaceae*

One of the most well known of all Allwoodii varieties, 'Doris' produces abundant flowers over a long period and so is good for display in a group or in the mixed border, where the attractive grey-green foliage provides a good foil to the pink flowers. The flowers are also much used for cutting. Young plants produce good compact growth and can be propagated by layering during July or August or cuttings (pipings). The young plants are set out 9 to 12in (23 to 30cm) apart in the border. 10 to 15in (25 to 38cm)

🔺✿Summer ○ ✽ △ ◸▼

Dianthus 'Mrs Sinkins', Old-fashioned Pink. *Caryophyllaceae*

Very fragrant and delightful plant derived from *D. plumarius* which was introduced to Britain c1692 from E. Europe. The abundant double white large flowers make ideal decoration for the border particularly in association as underplants with roses. Propagate by layering or by cuttings (pipings). 10in (25cm)

🔺✿Summer ○ ✽ ◸▼

Dianthus 'Painted Beauty', Old-fashioned Pink, *Caryophyllaceae*

A favourite of cottage gardens, the old-fashioned pink is slower growing than others in this genus and is ideal for edging paths and beds. Many varieties are now unobtainable commercially but still occur in private gardens, and the one illustrated is typical of the single-flowered kinds. Increase by layering in summer or by 'pipings'. 10in (25cm)

🔺✿Summer ○ ✽ ◸▼

Dicentra spectabilis (syn *Dielytra spectabilis*) Bleeding Heart, Dutchman's Breeches, Siberia, Japan. *Fumariaceae*

This delightful plant produces glaucous, much-cut leaves on long stalks with obovate wedge-shaped segmets and rosy-red unusual flowers which droop from a graceful raceme. Care should be taken when planting to avoid damaging the fragile rootstock. Propagate by division to raise new plants which are at their best when planted amongst shrubs in the mixed border. 2ft (60cm)

◿ ◖ ✿Spring ◕ ✽ ◸▼

Doronicum 'Miss Mason', Leopard's Bane. *Compositae*

A bright plant forming neat clumps with abundant flowers early in the year composed of yellow ray florets surrounding the perfect disk florets. The alternate brilliant green leaves are heart shaped and most effective when the plants are set out in a large group. Although good for cutting the flowers tend to curl up unless the stems are immersed deeply in water for 24 hours. Propagate by division. 1½ft (45cm)

◿✿Spring ◕ ● ✽ ◸▼

Echinacea purpurea (syn *Rudbeckia purpurea*) Hedgehog Cone Flower, United States. *Compositae*

The stem is glabrous and roughish, with faintly toothed ovate-lanceolate basal leaves, the stem leaves being rather more narrow. The thick rigid peduncle terminates in a large solitary flower consisting of reddish-purple ray florets with greenish tips; the disk florets are orange and form a cone. Easily propagated by seed or the rootstock may be divided, although resulting plants are somewhat difficult to establish. Once set out in the border approximately 1½ft (45cm) apart, plants benefit from a permanent position. 3ft (1m)

◿✿Autumn ○ ✽ ◸▼

Echinops ritro (syn *E. ruthenicus*) Globe Thistle, E. Europe, W. Asia. *Compositae*

Handsome pinnatifid robust leaves with a cobweb covering on the upper surface and a downy underside, together with large, globose thistle-like flower heads attractive to bees, make this a valuable bushy plant for border decoration and cutting. Propagate by seed, division or root cuttings and set out the young plants in a group 3ft (1m) apart in the border. 3ft (1m)

⬡ ✿ Summer ○ � △▼

Endymion non-scriptus (syn *Scilla non-scripta, S. festalis, S. nutans, Hyacintha non-scripta*) Bluebell, Harebell, Wild Hyacinth, W. Europe. *Liliaceae*

The tunicated bulb gives rise to long, basal, sub-acute, concave strap-like leaves. Abundant blue, purple, white or pink fragrant flowers supported by curved pedicels on an erect raceme beyond the tall solitary scape are most effective in drifts during spring and much used for indoor decoration. Propagate by dividing the rootstock and set out where the plants may be allowed to naturalize. 1¹/₂ft (45cm)

⬡ ✿ Spring ○ ◑ ▬ ✖ △▼

Erigeron 'Dignity', Fleabane. *Compositae*

This is a popular plant for border decoration and cutting, the abundant semi-double flowers with numerous slim ray florets of a pleasing violet-blue colour are borne on a stout erect peduncle. Propagate by division in spring or by seed. 2ft (60cm)

⬡ ✿ Summer ○ ✖ △▼

Eryngium amethystinum, Sea Holly, Europe. *Umbelliferae*

This distinctive plant has erect, branching stems and pinnatisect basal leaves on winged stalks. The small blue flower heads are surrounded by dark blue bracts and are much used fresh or dried for flower arrangements. Propagate by seed, by root cuttings or by division. 2ft (60cm)

⬡ ✿ Summer ○ ✖ △▼

Eryngium variifolium

Eryngium amethystinum

Erigeron 'Dignity'

Euphorbia griffithii 'Fireglow'

Euphorbia characias

Euphorbia robbiae

Euphorbia myrsinites

Eryngium variifolium, Sea Holly, Morocco. *Umbelliferae*

Handsome plant with a rosette of small, toothed and spiny green leaves that are clearly marked with white veins. The small flower heads are grey-blue and have a spiny collar of bracts. It is propagated by seed or root cuttings. 1¹/₂ft (45cm)

△ ✿ Summer ○ ✖ △▼

Euphorbia characias, Spurge, Europe. *Euphorbiaceae*

The glaucous foliage of this attractive plant persists through the winter. The inflorescence is a cyathium and consists of yellow bracts surrounding several male flowers and a central female flower. The cyathia are borne in dense clusters in spring and remain decorative during summer. Propagate by seed which should be collected before the fruit dehisces, or by division. 4ft (1.2m)

△ ✿ Spring ○ ▬ ✖ △▼

Euphorbia griffithii 'Fireglow', Spurge. *Euphorbiaceae*

An imposing clump-forming plant with erect stems and good for ground cover; the heads of deep orange-red cyathia in early summer make a bright display for the border. New plants are produced by division of the rootstock. 3ft (1m)

⬡ ✿ Summer ○ ▬ ✖ △▼

Euphorbia myrsinites, Spurge, S. Europe. *Euphorbiaceae*

A low-growing plant with trailing stems giving rise to fleshy glaucous sessile leaves in spirals and yellowish green cyathia in wide heads during summer. An ideal plant for the front of the border or rock garden. Propagate by seed or by division. 6in (15cm)

⬡ ✿ Summer ○ ▬ ✖ △▼

Euphorbia robbiae, Spurge, Asia Minor. *Euphorbiaceae*

The branching, somewhat invasive, rhizomes give rise to evergreen stems with tough, glabrous, oblanceolate or broadly oblanceolate dark green leaves. Erect stems produce attractive panicles of cyathia with pale green bracts. Readily propagated by division. 2ft (60cm)

△ ✿ Summer ◑ ● ✖ △▼

Filipendula ulmaria 'Aurea'

Gaillardia × grandiflora

Gentiana asclepiadea

Geranium endressii 'Wargrave Pink'

Geranium wallichianum 'Buxton's Variety'

Filipendula ulmaria 'Aurea' (syn *Spiraea ulmaria aurea*) Meadow Sweet. *Rosaceae*

A decorative foliage plant with divided and veined leaves which at first are golden but become creamy-yellow during the summer. The flowers are insignificant and should be removed to prolong the attractions of the foliage. Propagate by division of the rootstock. 3ft (1m)

⟋ ✿ Summer ○ ◐ ▭ ▣ △▼

Gaillardia × grandiflora, Blanket Flower. *Compositae*

Useful for border display over a long period and for cutting; the erect wiry stems need support and carry large flowers with showy ray forets surrounding dark disk florets. Easily raised from seed and by stem cuttings taken during early autumn, or root cuttings can be taken in spring. Division of the rootstock in autumn is a simple and reliable method. 2¹/₂ft (75cm)

⟋ ✿ Summer ○ ◼ ▣ △▼

Gentiana asclepiadea, Willow Gentian, Europe. *Gentianaceae*

A beautiful plant rather variable in height from 6in (15cm) with leafy erect or arching stems clad in pale green ovate-lanceolate opposite leaves. The abundant, narrow bell-shaped, blue flowers are carried in the axils of the upper leaves. Propagate by fresh seed, cuttings in spring or by division. 2ft (60cm)

⟋ ✿ ✿ Summer ○ ▣ △▼

Geranium endressii 'Wargrave Pink', Crane's-bill. *Geraniaceae*

An attractive semi-evergreen spreading plant good for ground cover with long-stalked opposite leaves acutely lobed and toothed. The salmon-pink flowers veined red make a fine display from early summer to autumn followed by the interesting fruits. New plants are best raised by dividing the rootstock. 1¹/₂ft (45cm)

⟋ ✿ Summer ✿ Autumn ○ ◐ ▣ △▼

Geranium wallichianum 'Buxton's Variety', Crane's-bill. *Geraniaceae*

An outstanding long-flowering foliage plant much used for ground cover with deeply cut lobed leaves. Long penduncles give rise to blue flowers with a white centre. Propagate by division. 1ft (30cm)

⟋ ✿ Summer/Autumn ○ ◐ ▣ △▼

Geranium sanguineum lancastriense, Streaked Crane's-bill, Europe, W. Asia. *Geraniaceae*

Beautiful, low spreading plant which is good for ground cover. The branched stems give rise to graceful opposite leaves with lobes of linear segments. Abundant, large, flesh-coloured flowers with notched purplish-veined petals presented on long peduncles are most attractive over a long period. Propagate by seed or by division. 10in (25cm)

⟋ ✿ Summer ◔ ○ ◐ ▣ △▼

Geum 'Mrs Bradshaw'. *Rosaceae*

Deservedly one of the most popular herbaceous perennials, this attractive mound-forming plant has large cordate lobed leaves, the stem leaves being deeply cut. Erect wiry stems give rise to panicles of beautiful scarlet double flowers appearing over a long season. Plants do not breed true from seed and so should be increased by division. 2ft (60cm)

⟋ ✿ Summer ○ ◐ ▭ ▣ △▼

Gunnera manicata, S. Brazil. *Gunneraceae*

A very distinctive plant grown as a single specimen with gigantic, leathery, coarsely toothed lobed basal leaves on prickly stalks up to 8ft (2.4m) long. The minute greenish flowers are borne on long stout panicles which may be removed before maturity to enhance leaf growth. The rootstock may require some protection during winter by covering with leaves or bracken. New plants are raised by seed or division in spring. 12ft (3.6m)

⟋ ⬆ ◖ ✿ Summer ○ ▭ ▼

Helianthus 'Loddon Gold', Perennial Sunflower. *Compositae*

This bushy plant with broadly ovate leaves and strong stems giving rise to abundant double golden-yellow flowers can be rather invasive. The plant should be lifted every two years and replanted in fertile soil to maintain the attractive flower form. Plants are increased by division in spring or summer. 4¹/₂ft (1.4m)

⟋ ✿ Summer ○ ▣ △▼

Heliopsis scabra, N. America. *Compositae*

Much used for cutting, the plant is most attractive in the border with long-lasting, large flowers borne on long wiry stems and rough, lanceolate leaves. Propagate by division of the rootstock or by cuttings. 4ft (1.2m)

⟋ ✿ Summer ○ ◐ ▣ △▼

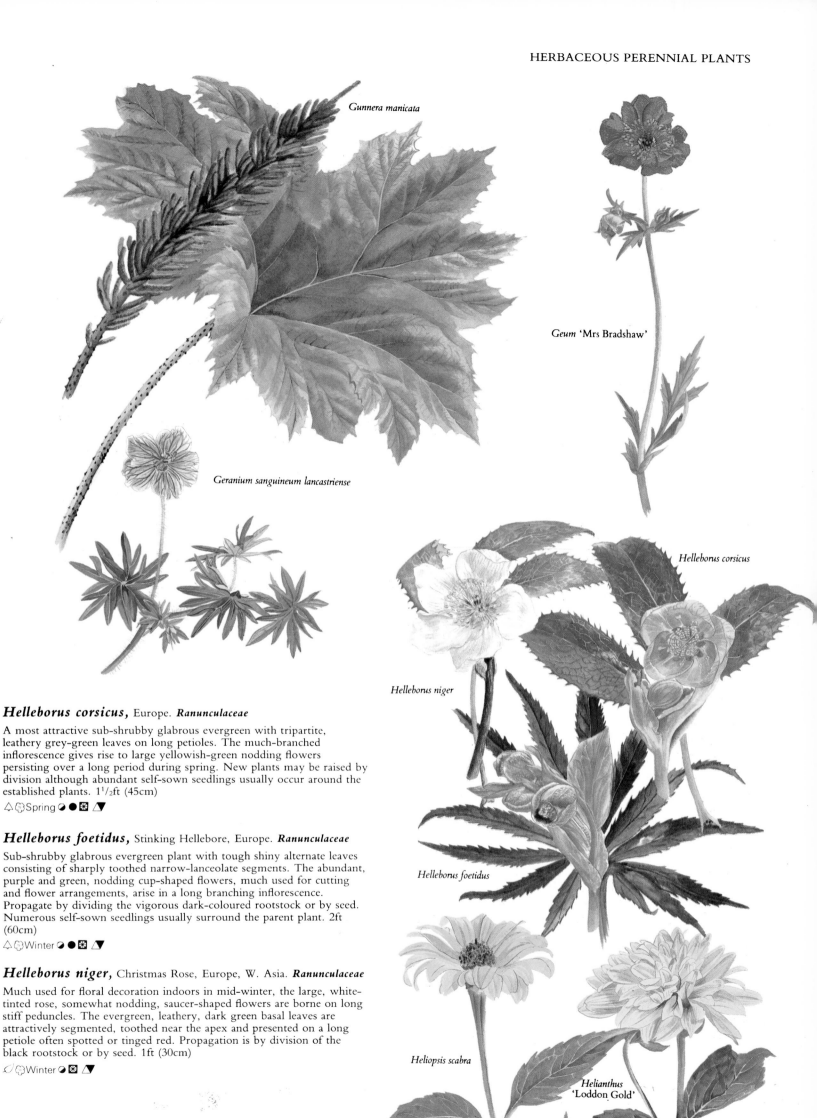

Gunnera manicata

Geum 'Mrs Bradshaw'

Geranium sanguineum lancastriense

Helleborus corsicus

Helleborus niger

Helleborus foetidus

Heliopsis scabra

Helianthus 'Loddon Gold'

Helleborus corsicus, Europe. *Ranunculaceae*

A most attractive sub-shrubby glabrous evergreen with tripartite, leathery grey-green leaves on long petioles. The much-branched inflorescence gives rise to large yellowish-green nodding flowers persisting over a long period during spring. New plants may be raised by division although abundant self-sown seedlings usually occur around the established plants. 1¹/₂ft (45cm)

△ ☼Spring ◐ ● ✸ △▼

Helleborus foetidus, Stinking Hellebore, Europe. *Ranunculaceae*

Sub-shrubby glabrous evergreen plant with tough shiny alternate leaves consisting of sharply toothed narrow-lanceolate segments. The abundant, purple and green, nodding cup-shaped flowers, much used for cutting and flower arrangements, arise in a long branching inflorescence. Propagate by dividing the vigorous dark-coloured rootstock or by seed. Numerous self-sown seedlings usually surround the parent plant. 2ft (60cm)

△ ☼Winter ◐ ● ✸ △▼

Helleborus niger, Christmas Rose, Europe, W. Asia. *Ranunculaceae*

Much used for floral decoration indoors in mid-winter, the large, white-tinted rose, somewhat nodding, saucer-shaped flowers are borne on long stiff peduncles. The evergreen, leathery, dark green basal leaves are attractively segmented, toothed near the apex and presented on a long petiole often spotted or tinged red. Propagation is by division of the black rootstock or by seed. 1ft (30cm)

◔ ☼Winter ◐ ✸ △▼

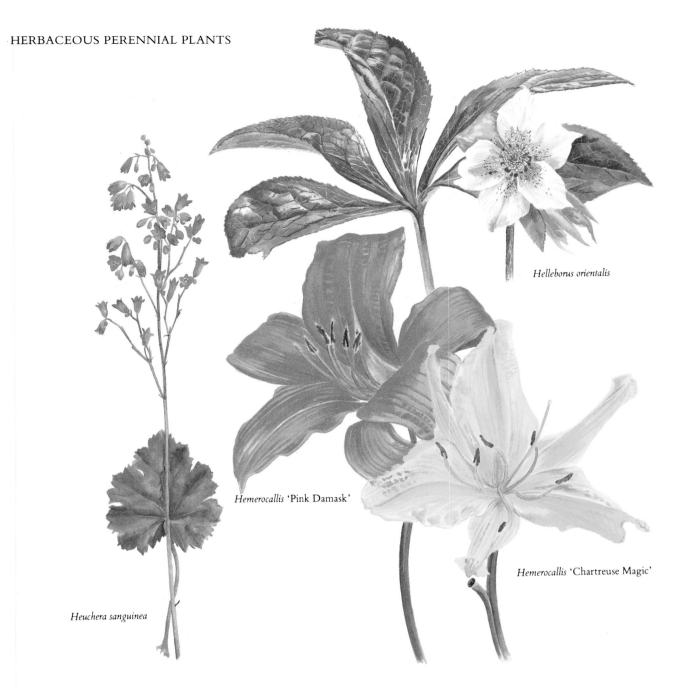

Helleborus orientalis

Hemerocallis 'Pink Damask'

Hemerocallis 'Chartreuse Magic'

Heuchera sanguinea

Helleborus orientalis, Lenten Rose, Greece, Asia Minor. *Ranunculaceae*

The branched rhizome gives rise to very large leathery basal leaves with 5 to 11 doubly serrated elliptic leaflets all on a long petiole. Large, basin-shaped white flowers change to dull yellow-green, although the many hybrids have shades of pink. Most valuable for the long flowering period from mid-winter to spring. Plants are increased by seed or division. 1¹/₂ft (45cm)

△ 🍂 🌣 Winter ◑ ⊞ △▼

Hemerocallis 'Pink Damask', Day Lily. *Liliaceae*

A delightful plant rather shorter growing than most of the group. The sessile strap-like leaves provide an opportunity to contrast the foliage with other plants in the border. A medium long scape gives rise to the beautiful flowers. Division of the rootstock is the method of propagation used and once set out the plants are best left undisturbed for a number of years. 1¹/₂ft (45cm)

⟳ 🌣 Summer ◑ ▬ ⊞ △▼

Hemerocallis 'Chartreuse Magic', Day Lily. *Liliaceae*

A taller growing variety of this very useful herbaceous perennial with yellow trumpet-shaped flowers that make a bright splash of colour for a long period in summer. Increase infrequently by division in autumn or spring and plant the roots 1½ft (45cm) apart. 3ft (1m)

⟳ 🌣 Summer ◑ ▬ ⊞ △▼

Heuchera sanguinea, Coral Bells. Mexico, Arizona. *Saxifragaceae*

Evergreen plant with most attractive cordate or roundish lobed leaves, the lobes toothed and hairy. A scape gives rise to an open panicle with the bright red bell-shaped flowers. An excellent subject and much used in the front of a border where the foliage maintains interest after flowers have faded. Propagate by division. 1¹/₂ft (45cm)

△ 🌣 Spring ◑ ⊞ △▼

Hosta fortunei 'Albopicta', Plantain Lily. *Liliaceae*

This most adaptable plant is one of the best available from the very large group. The attractive, cordate, yellow and green variegated leaves with long petioles are much used for flower arranging and the summer flowers are pale lavender. A desirable subject for a border to give ground cover or used as a group set in a lawn, alongside water or in container, the plant is happy in semi-shade or sun. Propagate by division. 2ft (60cm)

⟳ 🌣 Summer ○ ◑ ▬ ⊞ △▼

Hosta lancifolia (syn *H. japonica*), Plantain Lily, Japan. *Liliaceae*

A lovely plant for a mixed border or as a dense group to provide ground cover. The shining, deep green, long-pointed leaves arise on long petioles to complement the raceme of deep-lilac funnel-shaped flowers which appears in late summer. Plants can be increased by division in spring or autumn. 2ft (6cm)

⟳ 🌣 Summer ○ ◑ ▬ ⊞ △▼

Hosta sieboldiana elegans, Plantain Lily, Japan. *Liliaceae*

The most attractive glaucous ovate leaf tapers to a sheathing striated petiole providing interest from spring, when the leaves unfurl, until autumn frost. A simple raceme develops during summer, the nodding funnel-shaped flowers of white tinged purple giving added interest to the clump. New plants can be raised by division and set out 1¹/₂ft (45cm) apart in the border. 2ft (60cm)

⟳ 🌣 Summer ◑ ● ▬ ⊞ △▼

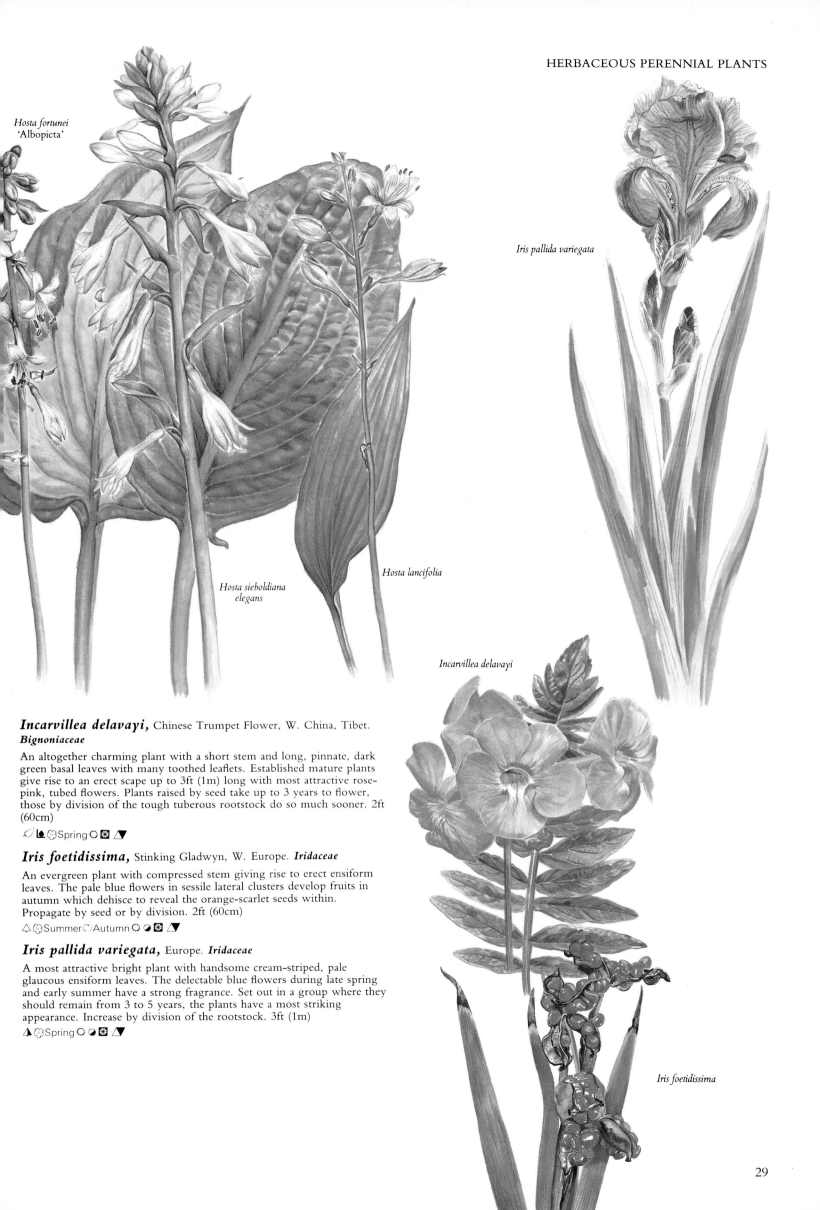

Hosta fortunei 'Albopicta'

Hosta sieboldiana elegans

Hosta lancifolia

Iris pallida variegata

Incarvillea delavayi

Iris foetidissima

Incarvillea delavayi, Chinese Trumpet Flower, W. China, Tibet. *Bignoniaceae*

An altogether charming plant with a short stem and long, pinnate, dark green basal leaves with many toothed leaflets. Established mature plants give rise to an erect scape up to 3ft (1m) long with most attractive rose-pink, tubed flowers. Plants raised by seed take up to 3 years to flower, those by division of the tough tuberous rootstock do so much sooner. 2ft (60cm)

⬧ ◖ ❀Spring ○ ◕ ✧ △▼

Iris foetidissima, Stinking Gladwyn, W. Europe. *Iridaceae*

An evergreen plant with compressed stem giving rise to erect ensiform leaves. The pale blue flowers in sessile lateral clusters develop fruits in autumn which dehisce to reveal the orange-scarlet seeds within. Propagate by seed or by division. 2ft (60cm)

△ ❀Summer ❀Autumn ○ ◕ ✧ △▼

Iris pallida variegata, Europe. *Iridaceae*

A most attractive bright plant with handsome cream-striped, pale glaucous ensiform leaves. The delectable blue flowers during late spring and early summer have a strong fragrance. Set out in a group where they should remain from 3 to 5 years, the plants have a most striking appearance. Increase by division of the rootstock. 3ft (1m)

△ ❀Spring ○ ◕ ✧ △▼

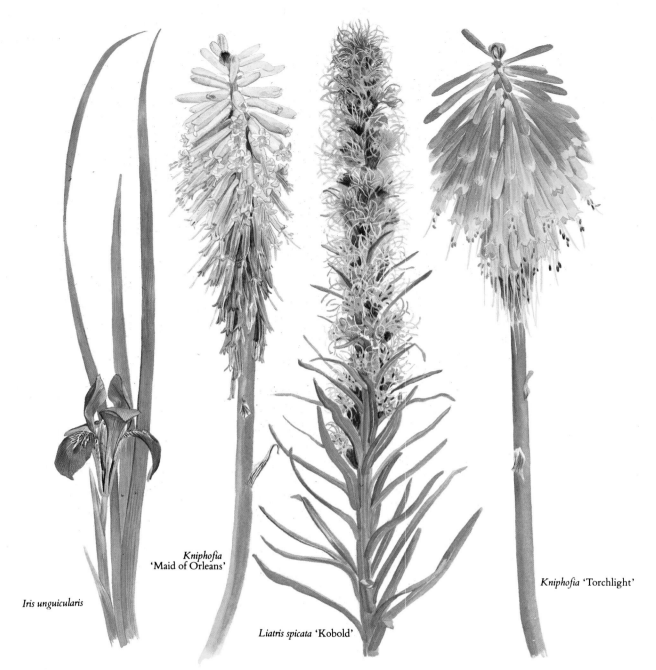

Iris unguicularis

Kniphofia
'Maid of Orleans'

Liatris spicata 'Kobold'

Kniphofia 'Torchlight'

Iris unguicularis (syn *I. stylosa*) Algeria. *Iridaceae*

A valuable plant flowering over a long period in mid-winter with
fragrant flowers of blue with an attractive yellow keel streaked with lilac
and much used for cutting. The narrow leaves forming an untidy tuft
should be cut back half way during mid- to late summer to initiate
flower bud development for the following winter. Much admired when
planted at the base of a south-facing wall. Propagate by seed or division.
2ft (60cm)
⛰ ✿Winter ○ ◐ ✣ ◿▼

Kniphofia 'Maid of Orleans'. *Liliaceae*

A tufted showy plant with grass-like leaves and a long scape which gives
rise to a dainty inflorescence of tubular, very creamy-yellow flowers
suspended by short peduncles. Most attractive when planted in a group
to form a bold clump. In colder districts, protect the crowns with a
heavy mulch in late autumn. Propagate by division in spring, taking care
to prevent the roots drying out during the process. 3ft (1m)
◿ ✿✿Summer ○ ✣ ◿▼

Kniphofia 'Torchlight', Red-hot Poker. *Liliaceae*

Handsome plant with greyish-green leaves that form a large clump. The
long erect scape gives rise to a bold spike of rich orange flowers. Much
used as a focal point in the garden, new plants are raised by division and
once planted should remain undisturbed. 3¹/₂ft (1m)
◿ ✿✿Summer ○ ✣ ◿▼

Liatris spicata 'Kobold', Blazing Star, Gay Feather, United States. *Compositae*

The linear-lanceolate fresh green leaves arise from the stem, which
develops into a dense and handsome inflorescence. The spikes of
abundant sessile flowers, bright mauve-pink with involucral scales, are
most attractive for border decoration and as a long-lasting cut flower,
fresh or dried. Propagate by seed or division in spring, setting out plants
1¹/₂ft (45cm) apart in the group. 2ft (60cm)
◿✿Summer ○ ✣ ◿▼

Libertia formosa, Chile. *Iridaceae*

Evergreen plant with long, ensiform, dark green leaves, and much
shorter sheathing leaves on the erect stem. Attractive white flowers borne
in dense clusters appear during spring. Propagate by seed or division of
the rootstock rhizomes which tend to be rather brittle. 1¹/₂ft (45cm)
⛰ ✿✿Spring ○ ◐ ✣ ◿▼

Ligularia dentata 'Desdemona' (syn. *L. clivorum* 'Desdemona'). *Compositae*

Striking plants with massive, rounded, purplish leaves. An erect stem
terminates in a head of daisy-like flowers. Good for weed suppression
and most spectacular when planted in a group. Propagate by division in
spring. 4ft (1.2m)
◿✿Summer ○ ◐ ▨ ◿▼

Linaria purpurea 'Canon Went', Toadflax. *Scrophulariaceae*

An attractive glabrous plant with erect glaucous stems giving rise to
linear-lanceolate leaves in whorls. The most interesting pink flowers with
an arching spur at the base of the corolla tube form a loose erect raceme.
Much used as a border group, the plant makes a delectable feature when
grown in a wall. Plants are increased by division or by basal cuttings in
spring. 3ft (1m)
◿✿Summer ○ ◐ ✣ ◿▼

Liriope muscari, E. Asia. *Liliaceae*

The stout compact rootstock gives rise to a dense clump-forming plant
with lanceolate leaves good for ground cover. The glabrous scape
terminates in a dense spike of abundant, small, bell-shaped purple flowers
so that the inflorescence resembles a poker. New plants are raised from
seed which should be sown fresh or by division of the rootstock. 1ft
(30cm)
⛰ ✿✿Autumn ○ ◐ ● ✣ ◿▼

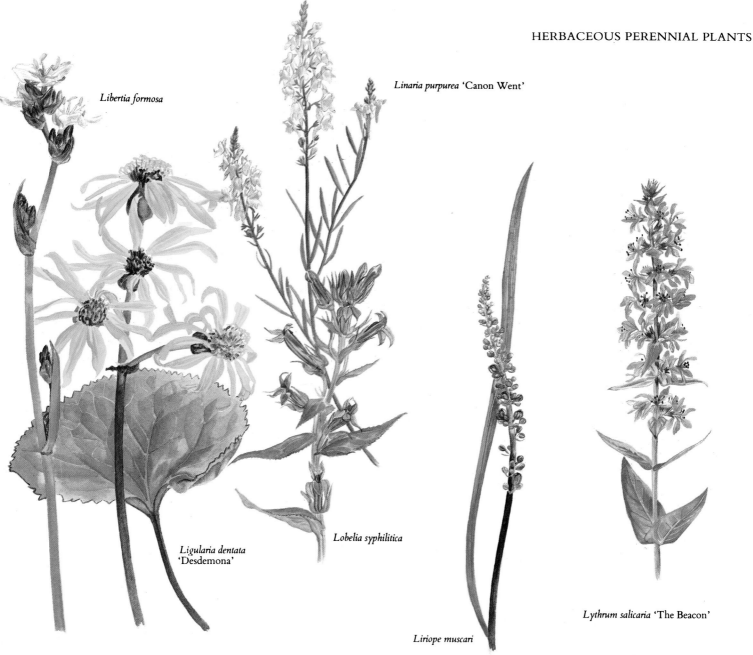

Libertia formosa

Linaria purpurea 'Canon Went'

Ligularia dentata 'Desdemona'

Lobelia syphilitica

Liriope muscari

Lythrum salicaria 'The Beacon'

Lobelia syphilitica, E. United States. *Campanulaceae*

This plant produces its leaves in a basal rosette and the erect stem gives rise to a raceme of blue flowers which last for many weeks. May be short lived and should be divided and moved every few years. Propagate by root division or stem cuttings during spring. 3ft (1m)

⟋ ✿ ✿ ☺Summer ○ ◑ ▩ ✳ △▽

Lychnis chalcedonica, Jerusalem Cross, Maltese Cross, E. Russia. *Caryophyllaceae*

Striking plant with a stiff erect branching stem glaucous and roughly haired. The cordate basal leaves are pointed with coarse hairs at veins and margin. Beautiful scarlet flowers arise in an abundantly dense corymb over a long period during summer. At its best when set amid blue-flowering plants in the border. Propagate by seed or division in spring. 3ft (1m)

⟋ ✿ ✿ ☺Summer ◑ ✳ △▽

Lysimachia clethroides, Loosestrife, China, Japan. *Primulaceae*

This border plant is good for cutting and produces an erect stem clad with opposite ovate leaves which turn bright red and orange in autumn. Abundant flowers are borne on a terminal bracteate arching spike. Propagate by division in autumn or spring. 3ft (1m)

⟋ ☺Summer ○ ◑ ▩ ✳ △▽

Lythrum salicaria 'The Beacon', Purple Loosestrife. *Lythraceae*

A bold plant for the border or water margin with an angled stem bearing opposite or whorled lanceolate leaves with a cordate base. The long spike terminates in abundant clusters of rosy-red flowers with narrow, oblong, wrinkled petals. Propagate by division. 3ft (1m)

⟋ ☺Summer ◑ ● ▩ ✳ △▽

Lychnis chalcedonica

Lysimachia clethroides

Macleaya cordata (syn *Bocconia cordata*, *B. yedoensis*) Plume Poppy, China, Japan. *Papaveraceae*

This handsome plant has a spreading root which gives rise to leafy stems. The large, cordate, glaucous, deeply veined and lobed leaves make an attractive sculptured feature ideal as a focal point set in a lawn or at the rear of a border. Large panicles of abundant creamy petal-less flowers tower above the leaves during summer. Readily propagated by division or by root cuttings, the plant can also be raised by seed. 8ft (2.4m)
⟋❀Summer○◐✿ △▼

Meconopsis betonicifolia (syn *M. baileyi*) Himalayan Blue Poppy, Tibet, China, Upper Burma. *Papaveraceae*

The most beautiful sky-blue large flowers with silky petals surrounding the showy yellow stamens are borne on axillary pedicels from a stem often clad with red hairs, as are the oblong-cordate leaves with long petioles, whereas the stem-clasping leaves are sessile. The plants are best set out where they may naturalize and give rise to self-sown seedlings. 5ft (1.5m)
⟋🌢❀Summer◐✿ △▼

Mentha × *rotundifolia* 'Variegata', Round-leaved Mint. *Labiatae*

Underground rhizomes give rise to stout erect stems bearing green variegated yellow, toothed, roundish-ovate, sessile opposite leaves somewhat wrinkled above and hairy below. Abundant purplish-white flowers are borne on attractive conical spikes. Plants are easily increased by cuttings or by lifting rooted rhizomes and setting them out 1ft (30cm) apart. Good for ground cover. 2ft (60cm)
⟋❀Summer○◐✿ △▼

Monarda didyma 'Prairie Dawn', Oswego Tea, Bee Balm, Bergamot. *Labiatae*

This robust plant has the square stem typical of the family giving rise to bright green and fragrant, opposite, ovate-lanceolate, toothed leaves with a hairy petiole. The flowers arise in twin or solitary bracteolate whorls throughout summer to early autumn. Best grown as a large group in moisture-retentive soil they revel in a light situation. Propagate by division in spring. 3ft (1m)
⟋❀Summer○◐▭✿ △▼

Nepeta × *faassenii*, Catmint. *Labiatae*

This semi-evergreen aromatic catmint is often labelled *N. mussinii* in gardens but is, in fact, a sterile hybrid much used as an edging plant and for ground cover. The stem divides at the base to give rise to many weak branches. Attractively silvered, grey, small, wrinkled, lanceolate opposite leaves are deeply indented at the margin. The abundant, spotted-blue flowers appear in whorls on a long erect inflorescence throughout late spring to early autumn. Plants are increased by division in spring or cuttings in mid-summer and set out in the border during the following spring. 1ft (30cm)
▲⬆❀Spring○✿ △▼

Paeonia officinalis 'Rosea Plena'

Macleaya cordata

Nepeta × *faassenii*

Monarda didyma 'Prairie Dawn'

Oenothera missouriensis

Mentha × *rotundifolia* 'Variegata'

Meconopsis betonicifolia

Oenothera missouriensis (syn *Megapterium missouriense*) S. United States. *Onagraceae*

A somewhat decumbent plant with pubescent stems up to 2ft (60cm) long clad in lanceolate to ovate or obovate bright green leaves. The abundant, large, attractive, saucer-shaped yellow flowers with a calyx frequently spotted red, open during the evening to give the appearance of a yellow carpet. An adaptable plant much used for ground cover and edging. Plants are propagated by cuttings or division in spring or by seed. 6in (15cm)

⟋ ✿Summer ○ ◐ ✣ ◺▼

Paeonia officinalis 'Rosea Plena'. *Paeoniaceae*

Most handsome deeply cut leaves and large rich pink double flowers with obovate spreading petals make this a magnificent plant for the border. Planted in well prepared soil and set shallow, the crown will develop into a plant which should remain undisturbed for a number of years. 2ft (60cm)

⟋ ✿Spring ○ ◐ ✣ ◺▼

Paeonia lactiflora 'Sarah Bernhardt'. *Paeoniaceae*

Considered by many enthusiasts to be one of the best plants of a very wide range available, the double pink flowers are most decorative for the border and excellent for cutting on the long rigid red-tinged stems. 2ft (60cm)

⟋ ✿Spring ○ ◐ ✣ ◺▼

Papaver orientale 'Mrs Perry', Oriental Poppy. *Papaveraceae*

A bright showy plant with an unbranched erect stem giving rise to pinnatifid leaves with lanceolate segments. The attractive flower has pink petals surrounding the abundant dark stamens which, in turn, surround the interesting globose capsule. Propagate by root cuttings taken from autumn to spring or by division in spring. 3ft (1m)

⟋ ✿Spring/Summer ◔Summer ○ ◐ ✣ ◺▼

Phlox paniculata 'Border Gem'. *Polemoniaceae*

This bright plant has dense corymbs of large, deep violet-blue flowers on strong erect stems with pointed, oblong entire leaves, the lower ones opposite. Plants are readily increased by basal cuttings preferably in spring; if stem eelworm infests the plants, root cuttings should be taken by cutting roots into short lengths. 3ft (1m)

⟋ ✿Summer ○ ◐ ✣ ◺▼

Phormium tenax 'Bronze Baby', New Zealand Flax. *Agavaceae*

An architectural plant which is smaller than most in the group with erect, tough, leathery, deep coppery-bronze ensiform leaves. Established plants give rise to a panicle of bronze-red flowers. Most attractive as a specimen plant or when grouped with the yellow-variegated form. The rootstock may be protected by covering with bracken or other material during severe winter weather. Propagate by division in early spring. 2ft (60cm)

△ ⬈ ✿Summer ○ ◐ ▭ ✣ ◺▼

Physostegia virginiana (syn *Dracocephalum variegatum*) Obedient Plant, N. America. *Labiatae*

A showy erect plant with square stem giving rise to opposite, lanceolate, sessile leaves with irregular sharp teeth. The inflorescence is a simple erect spike or, in fertile soil, a panicle of abundant, attractive, white-throated purple flowers which tend to stay in place when moved. Plants are increased by seed or by division. 4ft (1.2m)

⟋ ⬈ ✿Summer ○ ✣ ◺▼

Platycodon grandiflorus, Chinese Bell-flower, China, Japan. *Campanulaceae*

A most attractive fast-growing glabrous plant with fleshy tap roots supporting erect stems giving rise to ovate-lanceolate leaves with a toothed margin. The large blue or white bell-shaped flowers in a cyme develop from interesting inflated buds. A useful plant for the border and attractive when mass planted in a flower bed. Propagation is by seed, division or by basal cuttings. 1ft (30cm)

⟋ ✿Summer ◐ ✣ ◺▼

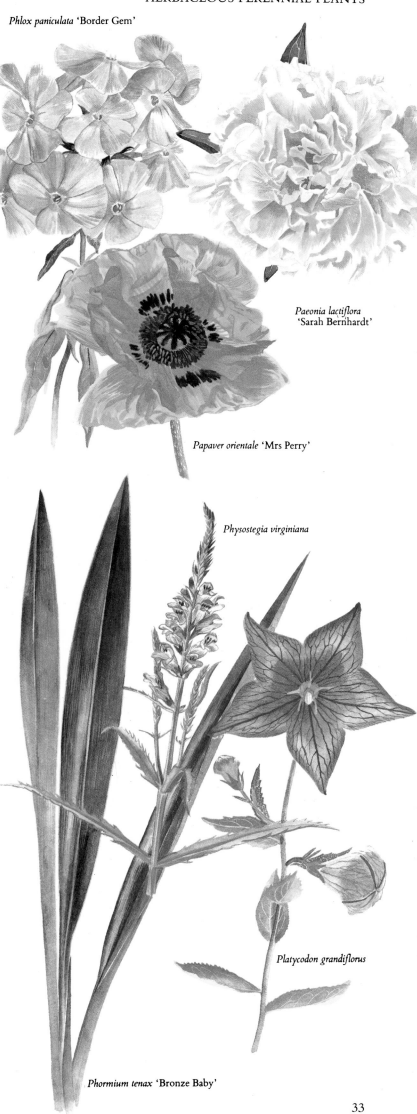

Phlox paniculata 'Border Gem'

Paeonia lactiflora 'Sarah Bernhardt'

Papaver orientale 'Mrs Perry'

Physostegia virginiana

Platycodon grandiflorus

Phormium tenax 'Bronze Baby'

Polemonium caeruleum

Polygonatum × *hybridum*

Polygonum bistorta 'Superbum'

Potentilla 'William Rollison'

Polemonium caeruleum, Charity, Greek Valerian, Jacob's Ladder, Europe. *Polemoniaceae*

The rootstock gives rise to an erect, hollow, angled stem bearing alternate leaves with many oblong-lanceolate leaflets; the lower leaves are borne on long petioles. The most attractive, open, bell-shaped flowers are usually blue or rarely white and carried in loose panicles. Readily propagated by seed. 2¹/₂ft (75cm)

⟋❀Summer ◕✠ ◿▼

Polygonatum × hybridum, Solomon's Seal. *Liliaceae*

An underground rhizome gives rise to long arching stems with alternate lanceolate leaves on short stem-clasping petioles. Attractive, pendulous, waxy flowers have a most pleasing appearance especially when planted amid shrubs or below trees. Plants are increased by rootstock division; if potted up and forced in a greenhouse or conservatory they make a fine display early in the year; after flowering plant outside in the border. 4ft (1.2m)

⟋❀Summer ◕●✠ ◿▼

Polygonum affine 'Donald Lowndes'. *Polygonaceae*

This charming compact mat-forming plant is good for ground cover with oblanceolate deep green leaves turning bright red then bronze in autumn and winter. The abundant flowers borne on erect dense spikes are much used for cutting and drying for arrangements. Easily propagated by division, the resulting plants set out 1ft (30cm) apart in the border. 1ft (30cm)

⟋❀Summer ◯ ◕✠ ◿▼

Polygonum bistorta 'Superbum', Bistort, Snakeweed. *Polygonaceae*

The spreading and erect stems give rise, mainly at the base, to long petioles terminating in oblong-ovate wavy leaves with a glaucous lower surface. A dense spike of flowers persists over a long period from early summer to early autumn. Effective when planted alongside a water feature and useful as ground cover in drier soils. Plants are increased by division. 3ft (1m)

⟋❀Summer ◯ ◕✠ ◿▼

Potentilla 'William Rollison', Cinquefoil. *Rosaceae*

A delectable hybrid plant with orange-red flowers and attractive palmately lobed leaves. This is a popular plant for its contrasting flower colour against the healthy green leaves and is good for ground cover. Propagate by division. 15in (38cm)

⟋❀Summer ◯ ◕✠ ◿▼

Prunella webbiana 'Loveliness'. *Labiatae*

The sub-erect square stems root where they touch the soil and are clad with ovate leaves somewhat blunted at the apex. The dense terminal spikes of lilac flowers appear in whorls and unless faded flowers are removed they produce abundant seed which germinates readily, the resulting seedlings sometimes becoming invasive, particularly in ornamental turf when this is adjacent to the parent plants. 1ft (30cm)

⟋❀Summer ◯ ◕▬✠ ◿▼

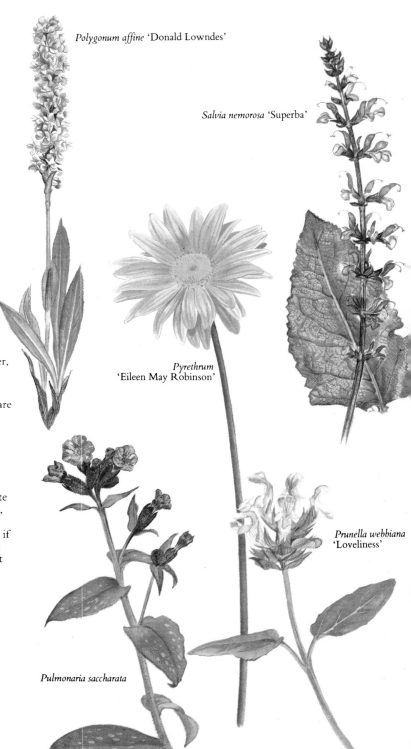

Polygonum affine 'Donald Lowndes'

Salvia nemorosa 'Superba'

Pyrethrum 'Eileen May Robinson'

Prunella webbiana 'Loveliness'

Pulmonaria saccharata

Pulmonaria saccharata (syn *P. picta*) Bethlehem Sage, Europe. *Boraginaceae*

This handsome plant has interesting bristly leaves elliptic or narrowly ovate with pronounced white blotches. The stem terminates in cymes of pinkish-red flowers which turn blue with maturity. Increase by dividing the rootstock. 1ft (30cm)

⬭🖤Spring◗●▰✺⬭▼

Pyrethrum 'Eileen May Robinson' (syn *Chrysanthemum coccineum*). *Compositae*

A popular plant for the border and much used for cutting. The rootstock gives rise to wiry stems with finely cut pinnate leaves. Most attractive, large, single salmon-pink flowers appear on long peduncles. Plants respond to lifting and dividing every three years and can be increased by division. 2ft (60cm)

⬭🖤Summer○◗✺⬭▼

Rodgersia pinnata, China. *Saxifragaceae*

The rhizome gives rise to a hollow stem with lateral shoots. The leaves are digitately pinnate and the central leaflet with its long stem is different from the sessile neighbours. Pale pink flowers appear in a large panicle. Propagate by division during late autumn to early spring. 6ft (1.8m)

⬭🍃🖤Summer◗▰✺⬭▼

Rudbeckia fulgida 'Goldsturm', Coneflower. *Compositae*

A beautiful plant with bright orange flowers with a dark central disk borne on stiff, wiry bristly stems over a long period. Most effective when set in a large group, the plants are self-spreading and can be increased by division in spring or autumn. 3ft (1m)

⬭🍃🖤Summer○◗✺⬭▼

Salvia nemorosa 'Superba'. *Labiatae*

This striking plant has much-branched stems bearing glaucous ovate-oblong fragrant leaves. The bright violet-blue flowers are accompanied by red bracts which persist long after the flowers have faded and make this a valuable plant for the border. Much used for cutting and drying for arrangements. Plants are raised by sowing seed or by division of the rootstock. 3ft (1m)

⬭🌢🖤Summer○◗✺⬭▼

Sedum 'Autumn Joy'. *Crassulaceae*

A most showy plant with large heads of bright salmon-pink flowers much liked by butterflies. The stout erect glaucous stems clad by toothed, fleshy leaves make this an interesting plant for the front of the border, particularly with the magnificent autumn flowers. Increase by division or cuttings. 1¹/₂ft (45cm)

⬭🖤Autumn○◗✺⬭▼

Sedum spectabile, China. *Crassulaceae*

This plant offers much interest throughout the year with its erect fleshy glaucous stems giving rise to almost sessile, fleshy obovate glaucous leaves usually in threes. The abundant pink flowers in corymbs up to 6in (15cm) wide contain stamens 1¹/₄ times as long as the petals. Attractive to butterflies, the plant is much used set in a group to the front of a border. Propagate by seed, division or cuttings taken during summer. 1¹/₂ft (45cm)

⬭🖤Autumn○◗✺⬭▼

Sedum telephium, Orpine, Live For Ever, Europe. *Crassulaceae*

The thick tap root gives rise to a stout shoot bearing alternate oblong-ovate leaves circulated about the stem. Striking red-purple flowers with narrow scales appear in sub-globose cymes during late summer and autumn. New plants can be raised by division or by cuttings taken during the summer. 1¹/₂ft (45cm)

⬭🖤Autumn○◗✺⬭▼

Sidalcea malviflora 'Crimson Beauty'. *Malvaceae*

A most attractive sturdy plant of pyramidal shape worthy of its name with an interesting range of assorted leaf shapes, the basal leaves being roundish with crenately cut lobes, the stem leaves palmate. The abundant flowers are borne on a wiry raceme. Propagate by division. 3ft (1m)

⬭🖤Summer○✺⬭▼

Solidago 'Goldenmosa', Golden Rod. *Compositae*

A colourful, comparatively low-growing plant with abundant golden flowers arranged on slender recurving branches. The alternate leaves are a most pleasing yellow and the plant is often set to contrast with Michaelmas daisies which flower at the same time. Readily propagated by division in spring or autumn. 2¹/₂ft (75cm)

⬭🖤Summer○◗✺⬭▼

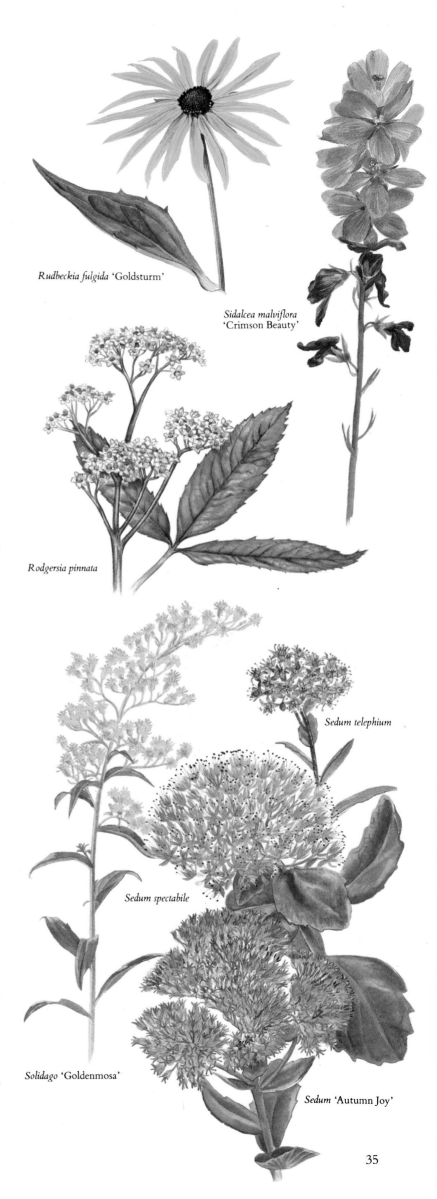

Rudbeckia fulgida 'Goldsturm'

Sidalcea malviflora 'Crimson Beauty'

Rodgersia pinnata

Sedum telephium

Sedum spectabile

Solidago 'Goldenmosa'

Sedum 'Autumn Joy'

Stachys macrantha 'Superba'

Stachys olympica

Tellima grandiflora

Stokesia laevis

Thalictrum delavayi 'Hewitt's Double', Meadow-rue. *Ranunculaceae*

A totally beautiful plant with attractive foliage consisting of decompound leaves with mostly trilobed leaflets. The panicles of abundant double mauve flowers arise on glabrous stems and are much used for cutting and persist when dried for arrangements. Plants are increased by division in spring and subsequent growth should be supported by concealed twigs to avoid wind damage. 3ft (1cm)

Tradescantia × andersoniana 'Osprey', Spiderwort, Flower of a Day, Trinity Flower. *Commelinaceae*

Showy plant with a long flowering period although individual flowers fade after one day. The branching stems give rise to linear-lanceolate leaves and white three-petalled flowers in umbels. An excellent plant for the front of the border which is increased by division of the rootstock. 1¹/₂ft (45cm)

Trillium grandiflorum, Wake Robin, Eastern N. America. *Trilliaceae*

Beautiful plant with short rhizome giving rise to the solitary stem with rhombic-ovate leaves almost sessile and pointed at the apex. The long peduncle terminates in an attractive flower with three petals first white then rose-pink. Plants can be raised from seed, the seedlings taking up to three years to produce the first flower, or propagation may be by division but resulting plants take a considerable time to establish. 1¹/₂ft (45cm)

Trillium grandiflorum

Thalictrum delavayi 'Hewitt's Double'

Verbascum phoeniceum

Tradescantia × andersoniana 'Osprey'

Stachys macrantha 'Superba'. *Labiatae*

This attractive plant with wrinkled, broadly ovate-cordate downy leaves borne on a stiff erect stem gives rise to whorls of abundant purplish-pink flowers over a long period during the summer months. Most useful when set in a group in the border. Increase by seed or by division of the rootstock. 2¹/₂ft (75cm)

Stachys olympica (syn *S. lanata*) Lamb's Tongue, Caucasus to Persia. *Labiatae*

The silvery appearance of this plant is due to the dense white woolly hairs persisting over all its parts. The fleshy and wrinkled, velvety, oblong-elliptic leaves make a fine setting for the abundant small purplish flowers arranged in whorls upon the spike. The plant is most spectacular when massed in a border especially with blue-flowering subjects. Propagation is by seed or division of the rootstock. 1¹/₂ft (45cm)

Stokesia laevis, Stokes' Aster, N. America. *Compositae*

A delectable plant whose blooms, in which the marginal florets are larger than the inner, are carried over a long period. A fine plant for the border which can be propagated by division. 1¹/₂ft (45cm)

Tellima grandiflora, N. America. *Saxifragaceae*

The stout stem gives rise to roundish, cordate-lobed, hairy leaves with a toothed margin. Abundant, greenish nodding flowers turning reddish with maturity appear in racemes. A good plant for ground cover which can be propagated by seed or division. 2ft (60cm)

Viola × williamsii 'Rebecca'

Veronica 'Heidi Kind'

Veronica spicata

Viola 'Maggie Mott

Verbascum phoeniceum, Purple Mullein, Europe, Asia.
Scrophulariaceae

This elegant plant has a tall erect inflorescence arising from ovate or
oblong leaves. The solitary flowers borne in a long slender raceme are
decorative over a long period. Set in a group, the plants are most
effective and may be increased from seed, by division or by root
cuttings. 5ft (1.5m)

⬭☺Summer ◑ ◐ ▦ △▽

Veronica spicata, Europe. *Scrophulariaceae*

Elegant plant with abundant bright blue flowers forming dense racemes
above the green, opposite, ovate or oblong leaves. Most effective planted
in a group towards the front of a border and easily propagated by
division in spring. 1¹/₂ (45cm)

⬭♣☺Summer ◑ ▦ △▽

Veronica 'Heidi Kind'. *Scrophulariaceae*

An easily grown plant which makes a good edging for the border.
Green, lanceolate, opposite leaves give rise to dense racemes of
raspberry-pink flowers that are borne for a long period in summer. Lift
and divide plants in spring. 10in (25cm)

⬭♣☺Summer ◑ ▦ △▽

Viola × williamsii, 'Rebecca' Viola, Tufted Pansy, Violetta.
Violaceae

An interesting group of hybrid plants derived from crossing *V. ×
wittrockiana* (garden pansy) with *V. cornuta*. The wide colour range of the
flowers gives a fine display for borders and is particularly effective when
massed in a bed. New plants are raised by sowing seed in summer and
planting the resulting seedlings in their final position during autumn. 1ft
(30cm)

⬭☺Summer ◑ ◐ ▦ △▽

Viola 'Maggie Mott', Garden Pansy. *Violaceae*

One of a large number of varieties which provide some of the most
appealing flowers for the garden. Ideal for use as an edging plant where
the fragrant flowers can be fully appreciated. Plants do not come true
from seed and are propagated by softwood cuttings of non-flowering
shoots taken in summer and rooted in a frame. 9in (23cm)

⬭☺Summer ◑ ◐ ▦ △▽

Flowering Bulbs, Corms and Tubers

A true bulb is rather like an oversize bud. It is composed of numerous fleshy overlapping scales which store food and moisture and it contains one or more growing points and possibly also the embryo of a flower or flowers. Its purpose is to allow the plant which produces it to survive periods of dryness or extreme temperatures that could be unfavourable for active growth, and to emerge at the end of it ready to grow fast, produce its flowers, set and ripen seed before the unfavourable conditions return. The onion is a typical bulb and anyone who has sliced through one will recognise the construction just described.

Corms, Tubers and Rhizomes

But bulbs are not the only storage organs produced by plants to help them through difficult periods. There are also corms, tubers and rhizomes and, because most of these share the ability of most bulbs to be kept out of the soil for a time and marketed dry, they often appear in the same catalogues as those that list true bulbs and are loosely referred to as bulbs. All differ from true bulbs in being solid flesh throughout, not a compact package of overlapping scales. A corm is a modified stem, usually surrounded by a papery membrane and often with several growth buds but no embryo flowers. The gladiolus and the crocus are two familiar examples of corm-producing plants. Rhizomes are similar for they, too, are modified stems, but they show their derivation more clearly as they have retained their stem shape, but thickened and usually lying more or less hori-

How welcome are the clear bright colours of the bulbs in spring. This brilliant display of tulips and daffodils is at Springfield Gardens.

zontally on or just below the surface of the soil. The common bearded or German iris is a familiar example of a rhizome-producing plant.

Tubers may be either swollen underground stems or roots. The dahlia is a typical root tuber, with growth buds clustered around the base of the old stems still attached to it, and the potato, though it seems to be root, is actually a stem tuber with the growth buds, or eyes, formed in it.

Planting Times

There are three main planting seasons for bulbs, corms and tubers. Those that flower in autumn or winter, such as the colchicums and autumn-flowering crocus species, are planted in late summer (July to August). Spring-flowering bulbs and corms such as daffodils, tulips, hyacinths and crocuses, are planted in autumn (September to November). This is also the best time to plant most lilies though, in practice, they are seldom available so early and often do not appear in the shops until late winter and then it is best to start them growing in pots and plant them out when conditions are more favourable in the spring. Most of the summer-flowering bulbs and corms, and tubers including gladioli, crocosmias and dahlias, are planted in spring (March to May), the precise time depending a good deal on situation and climate.

Survival Times of Unplanted Bulbs.

Although bulbs, corms and tubers all permit plants to be out of the ground for periods, the length of time they will survive without damage differs greatly. There is no general rule about this; no way in which, just by looking at one of them, it is possible to know just how long it will live out of the ground. Most lily bulbs look far larger and fatter than tulip bulbs but lilies suffer much more rapidly than tulips when they are removed from the soil. This is because, in nature, they are not accustomed to be completely dormant for long periods. Once they have completed one year's growth, produced their flowers, ripened and distributed their seeds and lost all or most of their leaves they are soon making roots again, even though it may be many months before any new shoots and leaves appear above ground. Some, such as the Madonna lily (*Lilium candidum*), are actually producing new leaves by August only a couple of months after they have flowered and so they have a very short shelf life in the shops and garden centres. Another limiting factor in the life of lily bulbs out of the soil, and this applies to all of them, not just the early flowering types, is that their scales are relatively loose and not contained within an outer skin to act as a protective bag. In consequence they lose water readily and need to be kept in damp moss or something of the kind even when in store.

Other bulbs, such as the snowdrops, though they look very normal and give little outward sign of being idiosyncratic, in fact dislike being disturbed even when quite dormant and transplant most successfully in February and March either in flower or immediately after flowering. But this means that they must be moved green like herbaceous plants, preferably with soil around their roots, and as a rule only specialist nurseries will undertake this. In the shops and garden centres snowdrops are sold dry in autumn like other spring-flowering bulbs, and as a result many die or take a year or so to recover fully.

Cultivation

Because bulbs, corms, rhizomes and tubers are produced by so many totally different plants, some hardy, some tender, some grown for ornament, some for food, it is impossible to generalise much about their treatment. Most are easy to grow, at any rate in their first year, because all or most of the essentials for growth are already there. Sturdy hyacinth bulbs are often grown in special glass jars with a swollen neck to hold the bulb with its base just touching the water which fills the rest of the jar. The bulbs, if well cared for, will produce flower spikes as fine as any that could be produced by similar bulbs growing in soil but they are doing this by drawing on the resources within themselves and, as these cannot be replenished by water alone, the bulbs are exhausted by late spring and will not be able to repeat the performance a second year.

Planting Depths

Most rhizomes like to grow almost on the surface of the soil and, when planted, are only covered with sufficient soil to keep them in place. As they become established they will probably push themselves up on to the surface and this is nothing to worry about as it is their natural habit.

No such blanket directions can be given for bulbs, not even for bulbs belonging to the same genus. The Madonna lily, already mentioned, likes to be on the surface like a rhizome yet most other lilies prefer to be covered with at least 4in (10cm) of soil, since many make roots above as well as below the bulbs.

Many bulbs like to be covered with about their own depth of soil e.g. a daffodil bulb measuring 2in (5cm) from bottom to top would need a hole 4in (10cm) deep, and this is suggested as a useful rule of thumb whenever more precise advice is not available. It is not likely to do much harm even if it is not ideal for the plant in question and bulbs do have a considerable ability to adjust themselves in the soil to the most favourable depth,

though they may take a year or so to accomplish this.

Tubers also vary greatly in the depth at which they grow best and though one might suggest a 2in (5cm) covering as a fair average this would not suit cyclamens at all well for they like to have their bun-shaped tubers almost on the surface. Neither do cyclamen tubers transplant well when dormant though they are often sold in this state. When such dry tubers are purchased, it is best to start them growing in shallow trays filled with damp peat into which the tubers can be pressed but not completely buried. Not until they have made some roots and leaves is it completely safe to transfer the hardy kinds to the open ground.

Lifting and Replanting

There is a widespread belief that bulbs need to be lifted and replanted every year. In fact this is more a matter of convenience than of necessity. When hyacinths and tulips are used for mass display in the spring it may be convenient to dig them up as soon as their flowers fade so that they can be replaced with something else that will flower during the summer. But then the lifted bulbs should be replanted immediately somewhere else, even though this may be no more than lining them out thickly in shallow trenches and throwing soil over their roots so that they may complete their growth. Later they can be lifted, cleaned, sorted and stored in a cool dry place for replanting in the autumn but they would almost certainly have done better if they had been left alone. It is only when such hardy bulbs become overcrowded that it is essential to lift and split up the bulb clusters and then replant.

There are other considerations with tender bulbs, corms and tubers. Outdoors they may be killed by frost, though it is surprising how much protection a covering of 3 to 4in (8 to 10cm) of soil can give. But with gladioli and dahlias it is customary to lift the plants in the autumn, remove most of the top growth and store the corms or tubers dry in a frost-proof place where they will remain until it is safe to replant them outdoors the following spring.

Bulbs increase in numbers by seed and also by forming offsets i.e. small bulbs beside the parent bulbs. After a few years the clumps of bulbs so produced become so large and crowded that they starve each other and it is then that lifting, dividing and replanting becomes essential. Some corms produce new corms on top of the old ones, which wither away, and they may also produce tiny corms, known as cormels, around the new corms. These cormels are not usually sufficiently large to produce flowers the following year but if 'sown' rather like large seeds, about an inch deep in a nursery bed they will grow to flowering size in a year or so. This may not be worth doing with common kinds but it can be very profitable with scarce varieties.

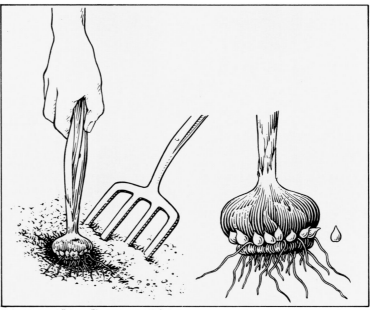

Gladiolus corms should be lifted in the autumn. The tiny cormels can be used for propagation.

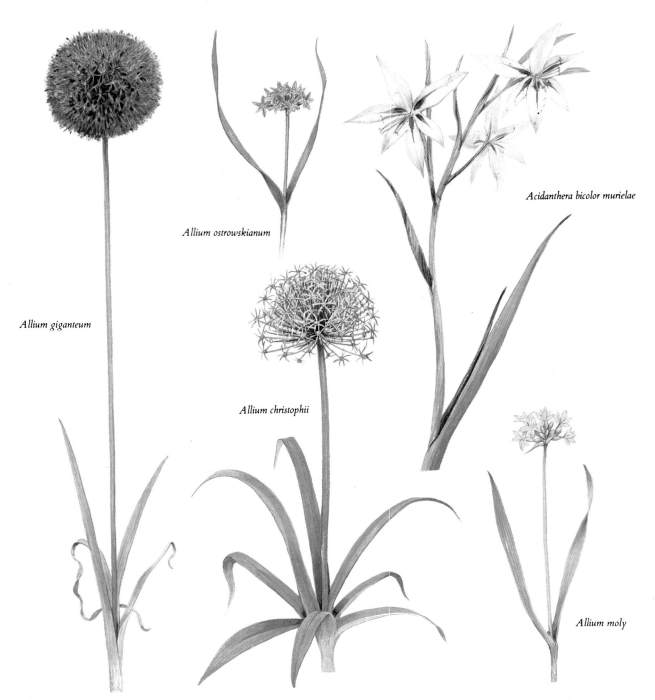

Allium ostrowskianum

Acidanthera bicolor murielae

Allium giganteum

Allium christophii

Allium moly

Acidanthera bicolor murielae (syn *Gladiolus callianthus*) Abyssinia. *Iridaceae*

The small globose tunicated corm gives rise to an unbranched stem with linear leaves. Most fragrant flowers containing a white, straight perianth tube with purple spot appear in a loose spike. An excellent plant for cutting and growing in large containers, or for permanent planting 5in (12.5cm) deep in the border. Frost protection is necessary, otherwise the corms should be lifted each autumn, cleaned and stored free from frost and replanted in spring. Propagate by seed which takes up to 3 years to reach flowering size plants, or by corms. 3ft (1m)

✎ ☂ ✿ Autumn ○ ▦ ◹◿

Allium christophii (syn *A. albopilosum*) Persia. *Liliaceae*

A delectable globose-bulbed plant from the many available in this large genus. The erect scape terminates in an umbel of flowers with a metallic sheen. Strap-shaped leaves glabrous above have white hairs on the underside. Propagate by seed or by division of bulbils. 2ft (60cm)

✎ ✿ Summer ○ ▦ ◹◿

Allium giganteum, Himalaya. *Liliaceae*

The bulb produces a long scape which rises above the wide blue-green leaves and terminates in a dense spherical umbel of abundant, lilac star-shaped flowers. A magnificent plant for the border. Propagate by seed or by division of the bulbs. 4ft (1.2m)

✎ ✿ Spring ○ ◕ ▦ ◹◿

Allium moly, Lily Leek, Mediterranean Region. *Liliaceae*

The grey ornate bulb gives rise to an erect scape terminating in an hemispherical umbel of green-striped flowers on long pedicels. The long glaucous foliage is pointed at the apex. A vigorous plant, good for cutting and naturalizing in the border or rock garden. Propagated by seed or division of the bulbils. 1ft (30cm)

✎ ✿ Spring/Summer ◕ ▦ ◹◿

Allium ostrowskianum (syn *A. oreophilum ostrowskianum*) Persia. *Liliaceae*

An attractive plant of the onion tribe with distinctive garlic aroma. The scape arises through few inconspicuous and flaccid linear leaves to produce a globose head of pretty, star-shaped red flowers. A showy plant for the border or rock garden and plants may be increased by seed or bulbs. 10in (25cm)

✎ ✿ Summer ○ ◕ ▦ ◹◿

Allium siculum, Europe. *Liliaceae*

A majestic plant producing a thick whitish bulb giving rise to a long scape surrounded by inconspicuous, linear-lanceolate leaves. The striking umbel of flowers has a green stripe on the reverse of the outer segments. Ideal for border decoration and much used for cut flowers. Increase by seed or by division. 3ft (1m)

✎ ☂ ✿ Spring ○ ◕ ▦ ◹◿

Alstroemeria ligtu, Chile. *Amaryllidaceae*

These tuberous-rooted hybrid plants have umbels of pink, red or whitish flowers with usually yellow upper segments. The stems give rise to narrow linear leaves becoming linear-lanceolate higher up. Tubers should be planted at least 6in (15cm) deep to avoid frost damage and remain undisturbed for best results. Increase by sowing ripe seed thinly and transplanting without undue root disturbance or by careful division of the roots in autumn or spring. A good plant for container growing. 2ft (60cm)

✎ ☂ ✿ Summer ○ ▦ ◹◿

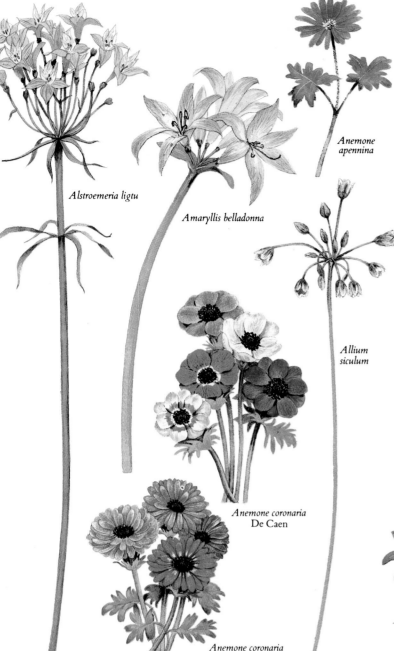

Alstroemeria ligtu

Amaryllis belladonna

Anemone apennina

Allium siculum

Anemone coronaria De Caen

Anemone coronaria St Brigid

Anemone nemorosa, Wood Anemone, Europe. *Ranunculaceae*

The slender horizontal-branched rhizome produces ternate leaves containing acute, lanceolate, deeply toothed segments, the involucral leaves with a petiole. Scapes terminate in a white flower tinged pink on the outside. A variable plant good for the rock garden or below trees. Propagate by seed or by division. 6in (15cm)

✐❀Spring❍◗✻/▼

Arum creticum, Crete. *Araceae*

A tuberous herbaceous plant with hastate-sagittate leaves on a long petiole. The swollen, pale green convolute spathe tube with a lanceolate-oblong cream blade arises on a long peduncle. The attractive foliage should be kept vigorous by copious watering during the growing season. Plants may be increased by division 1ft (30cm)

Bulbocodium vernum (syn *Colchicum vernum*) Europe. *Liliaceae*

An oblong, almost black, corm gives rise to concave then flat, broadly strap-shaped leaves which appear after the purple flowers with their white-spotted claws. The corms should be lifted every second autumn, divided and replanted to avoid congested etiolated growth. An attractive plant in grass or on the rock garden. 6in (15cm)

✐❀Spring❍◣✻/▼

Camassia cusickii, Quamash, Western N. America. *Liliaceae*

The large bulb produces long, glaucous, slightly wavy leaves and a very long scape terminating in an inflorescence of star-shaped pale blue flowers. Ripe seeds germinate readily and take up to 4 years to produce flowering size plants, or bulbs may be planted in autumn and left undisturbed to naturalize. 3ft (1m)

✐❀Spring❍◗◣✻/▼

Amaryllis belladonna (syn *Callicore rosea*) Belladonna Lily, S. Africa. *Amaryllidaceae*

The large brown-skinned bulb produces, strap-like, channelled leaves during winter and early spring, followed much later when the leaves have withered by fragrant flowers. Planted during mid-summer 6in (15cm) deep, the bulbs should remain undisturbed. Useful for container growing and, when propagation is required, divide during dormancy in summer. 3ft (1m)

✐❦❀Autumn❍✻/▼

Anemone apennina, Europe. *Ranunculaceae*

The short fleshy prostrate rhizome gives rise to binately pinnate leaves, the segments deeply toothed. Erect solitary flowers terminate long pedicels. A delectable plant especially good below trees and attractive on the rock garden. Readily increased by division or by seed. 6in (15cm)

✐❀Spring❍◗✻/▼

Anemone coronaria, Europe, Asia. *Ranunculaceae*

Small brown tubers give rise to segmented leaves. Large solitary flowers terminate long pedicels. Good for border display or cutting and readily propagated by seed which produces various flower colours. The named varieties should be increased by division to retain type. There are a number of strains, the best known being De Caen with single flowers in various shades from purple to scarlet, and St Brigid with double flowers in the same colour range. 9in (23cm)

✐❦❀Spring❍✻/▼

Anemone × fulgens, S. France. *Ranunculaceae*

A beautiful hybrid plant with abundant scarlet flowers containing obovate sepals arising on a long pedicel from a brown tuber. An attractive plant for border and cutting. Propagated by division. 10in (25cm)

✐❀Spring❍◗✻/▼

Anemone × fulgens

Anemone nemorosa

Bulbocodium vernum

Arum creticum

Camassia cusickii

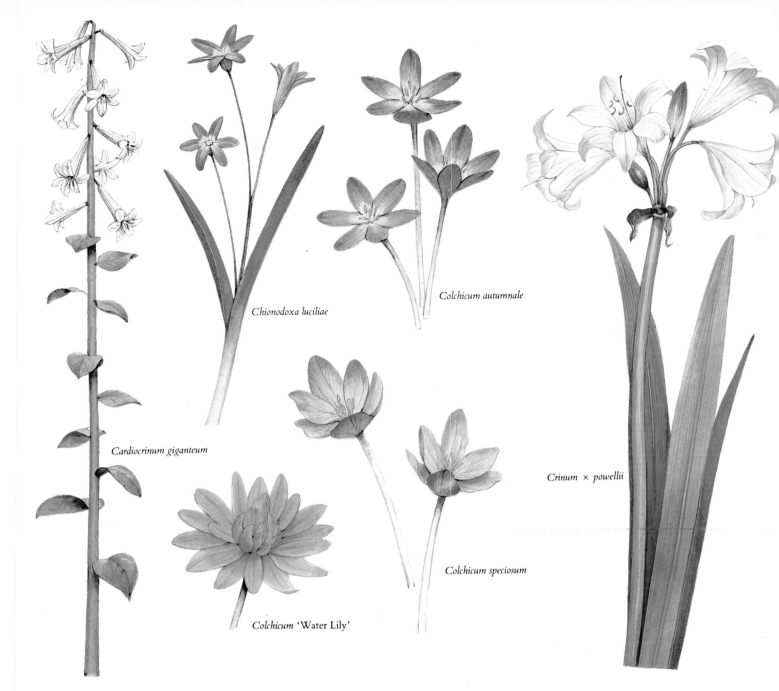

Chionodoxa luciliae

Colchicum autumnale

Cardiocrinum giganteum

Crinum × powellii

Colchicum speciosum

Colchicum 'Water Lily'

Cardiocrinum giganteum (syn *Lilium giganteum*) Himalaya. *Liliaceae*

The large bulb produces large ovate-cordate shiny leaves. A raceme of abundant funnel-shaped white flowers with purple throats terminates the stem. A magnificent plant especially when set amid trees or shrubs and readily propagated by seed or division. 10ft (3m)

⬯☸Summer ○ ◑ ✷ △▼

Chionodoxa luciliae (syn *C. forbesii*) Glory-of-the-Snow, Asia Minor, Crete. *Liliaceae*

A glorious little bulbous plant with star-shaped flowers. Bulbs planted in a group during autumn make a fine display the following spring. Most attractive when planted in pots for indoor decoration; the roots becoming well established before the pot is brought inside. Plants may be increased by offsets or by seed. 6in (15cm)

⬯☸Spring ○ ◑ ✷ △▼

Colchicum autumnale, Meadow Saffron, Europe. *Liliaceae*

A corm-producing plant with rather variable flowers. The lanceolate vernal leaves wither before flowers appear and it is important that they remain until shrivelled. Corms should be planted in July or early August and the plants are most effective when grown amid shrubs or in a drift to the front of a border. Readily increased by division in July or raised by seed which takes up to 5 years to produce mature plants. 6in (15cm)

⬯☸Autumn ○ ◑ ✷ △▼

Colchicum speciosum (syn *C. veratrifolium*) Caucasus to Asia Minor. *Liliaceae*

The large brown tunicated corm gives rise to wide, oblong vernal leaves which wither before the large pink, purple or white flowers appear in late summer to early autumn. Plant corms during July or early August and leave undisturbed to naturalize. New plants may be raised from seed or by division when the offsets should be replanted immediately. 1ft (30cm)

⬯☸Autumn ○ ◑ ✷ △▼

Colchicum 'Water Lily'. *Liliaceae*

A corm-producing hybrid plant with magnificent pink-coloured flowers, up to 6 appearing at the same time during autumn after the foliage has withered. Most prolific in making new corms, the plants should be divided after a few years when they become crowded so that flower quality is maintained. 1ft (30cm)

⬯☸Autumn ○ ◑ ✷ △▼

Crinum × powellii. *Amaryllidaceae*

A handsome bulbous plant producing abundant, spreading, ensiform, slender-pointed bright green leaves and a very long glaucous scape terminating in an umbel of large pink or white with a greenish tube. A good plant for container growing, which is recommended in a very cold climate so that winter protection may be given. Plants may be increased by offsets taken away carefully to avoid damaging the roots. 2ft (60cm)

⬯↟☸Summer ◑ ▬ ✷ △▼

Crocosmia masonorum (syn *Tritonia masonorum*) S. Africa. *Iridaceae*

The corm gives rise to a cylindrical stem with ensiform leaves and prolific bright orange-red ascending flowers. A most attractive plant when set out in a group and readily propagated by division. 3ft (1m)

⬯☸Summer ○ ◑ ✷ △▼

Crocus chrysanthus, Greece, Asia Minor. *Iridaceae*

A delectable plant with tunicated corm giving rise to a sheathed scape terminating in yellow or orange flowers with a glabrous throat surrounded by ensiform leaves with a ciliated keel. Much planted around the base of trees, the plants are attractive in grass where they should be allowed to naturalize. Propagate by division or by ripe, fresh, thinly sown seed. 10in (25cm)

⬯☸Spring ○ ◑ ✷ △▼

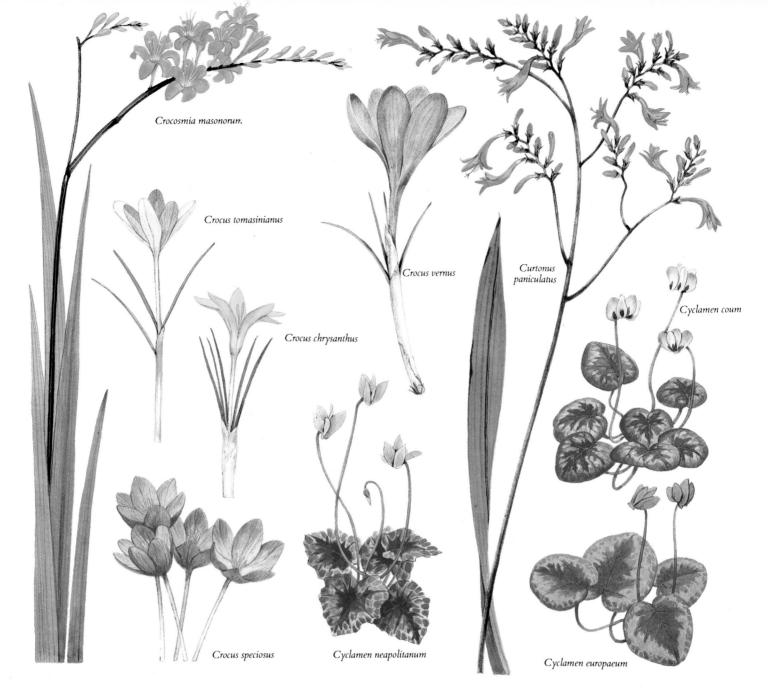

Crocosmia masonorum.

Crocus tomasinianus

Crocus vernus

Crocus chrysanthus

Curtonus paniculatus

Cyclamen coum

Crocus speciosus

Cyclamen neapolitanum

Cyclamen europaeum

Crocus speciosus, S. Russia, Asia Minor, Persia. *Iridaceae*

A corm-producing plant with variable and always attractive autumn flowers in shades of blue standing well above the ciliate leaves which may not appear until after flowering. Cormlets form around the base of the parent and may be removed for propagation. 15in (38cm)

⊘❁Spring ○ ◑ ▩ △▼

Crocus tomasinianus, Yugoslavia. *Iridaceae*

A nearly spherical corm gives rise to most attractive long narrow flowers with a white bearded throat and pale pinkish-blue segments. One of the earliest flowering within the group to brighten the winter garden. Plants may be increased by division or by seed. 10in (25cm)

⊘❁Spring ○ ◑ ▩ △▼

Crocus vernus, Europe. *Iridaceae*

The fleshy corm with sheathing fibrous tunic produces a sheathed scape terminating in flowers varying in colour from white to purple with a wide-throated tube. Slender ensiform leaves appearing with the flowers and persisting afterwards contain a striking white line. The plants may be increased by division or by seed. 1ft (30cm)

⊘❁Spring ○ ◑ ▩ △▼

Curtonus paniculatus, S. Africa. *Iridaceae*

A beautiful plant with sub-globose corm giving rise to a stem terminating in a panicle of zig-zag spikes of flowers. The ensiform or lanceolate leaves can be up to 3in (7.5cm) wide. Corms should be planted 8in (20cm) deep and given frost protection for the winter in very cold areas, or the plants may be grown in containers. Readily propagated by offsets or by ripe fresh seed. 4ft (1.2m)

⊘ ♠❁Autumn ○ ◑ ▩ △▼

Cyclamen coum, E. Europe, S.W. Asia. *Primulaceae*

Roots emerge from the middle of the underside of a small flattish corm which produces roundish reniform or obcordate, dark green often silvered leaves before the flowers. The carmine flowers contain ovate corolla lobes and ovate-lanceolate sepals. Planted in drifts and most effective below spring-flowering shrubs, the corms persist for many years. Propagate by seed. 3in (7.5cm)

⊘❁Winter ○ ◑ ▩ △▼

Cyclamen europaeum (syn C. *littorale*, C. *clusii*) Europe. *Primulaceae*

The globose or flattened corky corm persists for many years often growing to a very large size, rooting all over the surface and giving rise to abundant, solitary, carmine, fragrant flowers; the most attractive widely triangular sepals with the oblong or ovate corolla lobes and almost evergreen silver-zoned leaves make this a delightful plant. New plants may be raised from seed. 3in (7.5cm)

⊘❁Autumn or Spring ○ ◑ ▩ △▼

Cyclamen hederifolium (syn C. *neapolitanum*) Europe. *Primulaceae*

The flattish corky corm with a hemispherical base roots from the upper surface only and gives rise to pinkish-red or white flowers. The crenate or entire rather variable leaves, usually obcordate, have interesting markings and appear after the flowers. Good for naturalizing and persisting for many years to make a very large corm. Plants may be propagated by seed. 4in (10cm)

⊘❁Autumn ○ ◑ ▩ △▼

Cyclamen repandum, Europe. *Primulaceae*

Roots appear from the centre of the base of a globose or flattish hairy corm which gives rise to bright carmine, solitary, most fragrant flowers upon a graceful peduncle. The soft, cordate silvery leaves with reddish reverse have undulate lobes. A beautiful little plant for the garden and for growing in containers. Propagate by seed. 3in (7.5cm)

⟋❀Spring ○ ◐ ▦ △▼

Dahlia hybrids. *Compositae*

Most attractive tuberous-rooted plants in a wide range of forms with bright flowers terminating long erect stems, good for garden display and for cutting. Plants may be increased by dividing the tubers complete with the immature buds adjacent to the stem, by cuttings or by seed. 3ft (1m)

⟋ ♠❀Summer ○ ◐ ▬ ▦ △▼

Dierama pulcherrimum, Wand Flower, S. Africa. *Iridaceae*

The large corm gives rise to a slender stem with long, narrow leaves often persisting through the winter and terminating in a panicle of drooping branches of bright purple or dark red flowers with almost white bracts. A striking plant effective when planted near water. Propagate by seed or by division. 6ft (1.8m)

△❀Autumn ○ ▦ △▼

Eranthis hyemalis, Winter Aconite, Europe. *Ranunculaceae*

A dwarf herbaceous perennial with tuberous rootstock producing a short stem with stalked roundish basal leaves, those on the flowering stem sessile, broad linear and rounded at the tip and forming a rosette close to the cup-shaped flower. Most attractive when planted amid shrubs and trees to naturalize. The tubers should be set in summer or early autumn and plants may be increased by division or by sowing ripe fresh seed. 4in (10cm)

⟋❀Winter ○ ◐ ▦ △▼

Erythronium dens-canis, Dog's Tooth Violet, Europe, Asia. *Liliaceae*

A charming bulbous plant with broadly oval basal leaves blotched in purple-brown and white. The solitary drooping flowers terminate the scape. Attractive when planted in large groups and left to naturalize, the plants combine well with others on the rock garden. Propagate by offsets immediately leaves have withered after flowering, or raise new plants from seed. 6in (15cm)

⟋❀Spring ◐ ▦ △▼

Fritillaria imperialis, Crown Imperial, W. Himalaya. *Liliaceae*

The large bulb produces an erect stem with partly scattered leaves, the uppermost whorled. A magnificent umbel of bright yellow or bronze flowers terminates the stem. Increased by offsets or from seed which takes a considerable time to produce mature plants. 4ft (1.2m)

⟋ ♠❀Spring ○ ▦ △▼

Fritillaria meleagris, Snake's Head, Europe. *Liliaceae*

A fascinating and most attractive plant with usually solitary, pendulous bell-shaped flowers with purple and white netting or white with green veins and green linear nectary. The almost spherical bulbs should be planted during early autumn and left undisturbed. Most attractive grown in grass or on the rock garden. Propagate by offsets or by sowing seed. 1ft (30cm)

⟋ ♠❀Spring ○ ◐ ▦ △▼

Galanthus elwesii, Snowdrop, Asia Minor. *Amaryllidaceae*

This plant is variable in time of flowering, size and flower colour with wide, glaucous leaves and charming flowers whose inner segments are often marked with green. Plant in autumn in groups under trees, on the rock garden, on banks and elsewhere to naturalize. Propagate by division. 10in (25cm)

⟋❀Winter and Spring ◐ ▦ △▼

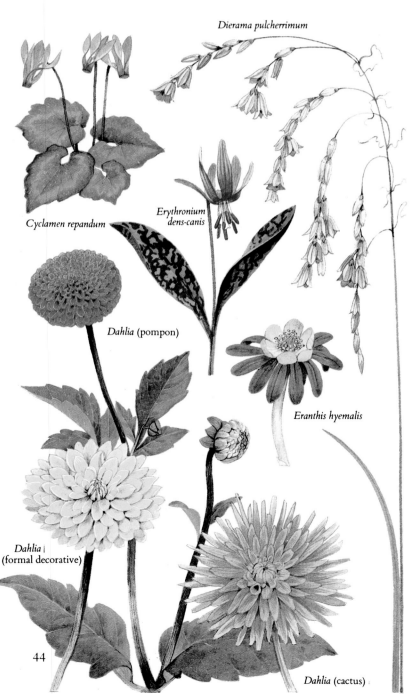

Dierama pulcherrimum

Cyclamen repandum

Erythronium dens-canis

Dahlia (pompon)

Eranthis hyemalis

Dahlia (formal decorative)

Dahlia (cactus)

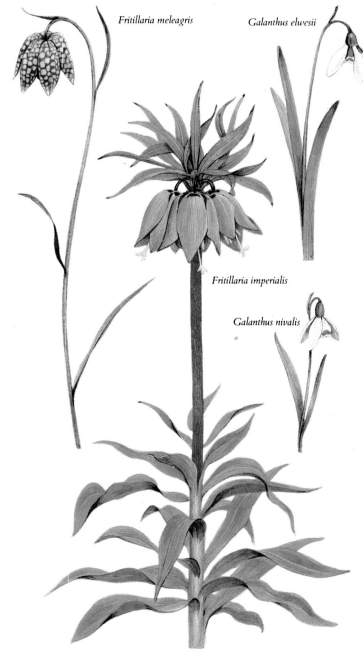

Fritillaria meleagris

Galanthus elwesii

Fritillaria imperialis

Galanthus nivalis

Galanthus nivalis, Common Snowdrop, Europe. *Amaryllidaceae*

The tunicated bulb produces a sheathed scape terminating in a pendant white flower with a green streak and apical spot. An excellent plant for growing in pans provided forcing is avoided; the bulbs should be planted in autumn to establish abundant root before taking them indoors to flower during winter. Planted outdoors, the bulbs should be allowed to naturalize. Propagate by division as soon as foliage has withered, or by fresh ripe seed. 8in (20cm)

⬭ ❀ Winter and Spring ◕ ▣ ◿

Galtonia candicans (syn *Hyacinthus candicans*) S. Africa. *Liliaceae*

The large round bulb gives rise to basal lanceolate leaves surrounding an erect majestic scape terminating in a raceme of fragrant, pendant flowers. A beautiful plant grouped for border decoration or for growing in a container. Increase by division. 4ft (1.2m)

⬭ ❀ Summer ◯ ▣ ◿

Gladiolus byzantinus, Mediterranean Region. *Iridaceae*

A showy cormous plant with long ensiform deep green leaves and a rigid stem terminating in spikes with bright red flowers. Most effective planted in a mixed flower border, the corms may also be used for conservatory decoration in a container. Propagate by seed which often produces flowering sized plants the following year or by division of the spawn surrounding the parent corm. 2ft (60cm)

⬭ ❀ Summer ◯ ◕ ▣ ◿

Ipheion uniflorum (syn *Brodiaea uniflora, Milla uniflora, Triteleia uniflora*) Spring Starflower, South America. *Amaryllidaceae*

This most attractive bulbous plant produces straggling linear-lanceolate leaves and abundant somewhat limp stems terminating in solitary, fragrant, pale blue, star-shaped flowers. Best planted in groups, the bulbs should be lifted, divided and replanted every two to three years. 6in (15cm)

⬭ ⬆ ❀ Spring ◯ ◕ ▣ ◿

Iris danfordiae, Asia Minor. *Iridaceae*

A delectable little plant with bright yellow solitary flowers terminating a short rigid scape surrounded by ensiform leaves arising from the bulb. Readily propagated by division, the plant is good for pan culture and for naturalizing out of doors. 4in (10cm)

⬭ ❀ Spring ◯ ▣ ◿

Iris histrioides, Asia Minor. *Iridaceae*

The bulb produces a very short stem terminating in an attractive blue flower with spreading falls and erect standards. The leaves often appear after the flowers and should be allowed to mature and then wither before lifting to divide bulbs when propagation is desired. May also be propagated by sowing seed. 10in (25cm)

⬭ ❀ Spring ◯ ◕ ▣ ◿

Iris reticulata, Caucasus. *Iridaceae*

The bulb gives rise to a tuft of slender angled leaves surrounding attractive, variable flowers often with deep purple falls containing a white-bordered orange ridge and erect, oblanceolate standards. Valued for its early flowers, the bulbs should be planted in a small group preferably within view of a window so that the flowers may be admired during the most inclement weather. Propagate by division. 1ft (30cm)

⬭ ❀ Spring ◯ ◕ ▣ ◿

Galtonia candicans   *Gladiolus byzantinus*

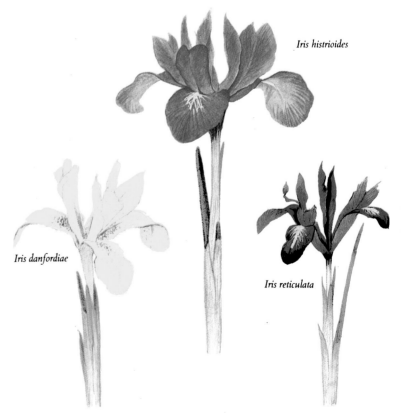

Iris histrioides

Iris danfordiae

Iris reticulata

Ipheion uniflorum

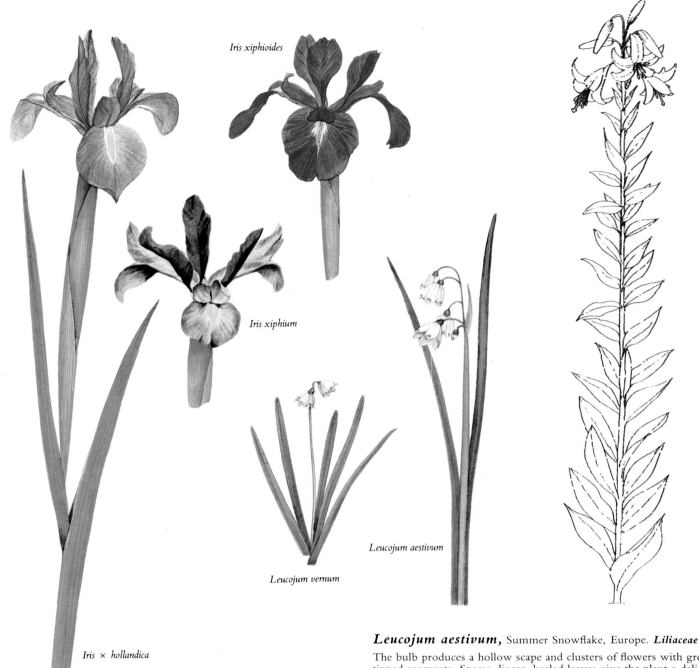

Iris xiphioides

Iris xiphium

Leucojum aestivum

Leucojum vernum

Iris × hollandica

Iris × hollandica hybrids, Dutch Iris. *Iridaceae*

A hybrid bulbous plant much used for general planting in beds and borders due to its ease of culture and the prolific production of daughter bulbs. An excellent plant for cutting for indoor decoration with its long stem and the wide range of bright-coloured flowers which may be obtained from a mixture of bulbs. Ideal for planting amid tulips and other spring-flowering plants. 28in (71cm)

🌣 ⚘ ❀ Spring ○ ◐ ▦ △▼

Iris xiphioides (syn *I. anglica, Xiphion latifolia*) English Iris, Pyrenees. *Iridaceae*

The bulb gives rise to a long erect stem clad with 3 or 4 leaves below the spathe and lower leaves 1ft (30cm) long and deeply channelled. Most attractive large flowers available in a wide range of colours from white to various shades of blue contain roundish falls and erect standards. Much used for cutting and good for prolonging spring border decoration into summer. Readily propagated by division. 2ft (60cm)

🌣 ⚘ ❀ Summer ○ ◐ ▦ △▼

Iris xiphium, Spanish Iris, Europe. *Iridaceae*

A bulbous plant with graceful appearance and erect stems clad with leaves. Large flowers containing orbicular reflexing falls in a variety of colours from white, yellow or blue clad with a yellow or orange patch make this a most attractive plant for border or indoor flower display. Propagate by division. 2ft (60cm)

🌣 ⚘ ❀ Summer ○ ◐ ▦ △▼

Leucojum aestivum, Summer Snowflake, Europe. *Liliaceae*

The bulb produces a hollow scape and clusters of flowers with green-tipped segments. Sparse, linear, keeled leaves give the plant a delicate appearance. An easy and most attractive plant to grow in a border and readily increased by division which is carried out every 3 years after flowering when the foliage has ripened. New plants may also be raised by seed. 1¹/₂ft (45cm)

🌣 ⚘ ❀ Summer ○ ◐ ▬ ▦ △▼

Leucojum vernum, Spring Snowflake, Europe. *Liliaceae*

A charming little bulbous plant with white, pendulous, fragrant bell-shaped flowers containing green-tipped segments. A most hardy plant well equipped to naturalize in a border or, preferably, in grass. New plants may be raised by sowing fresh ripe seed. 6in (15cm)

🌣 ❀ Spring ○ ◐ ▦ △▼

Lilium auratum, Golden-rayed Lily of Japan, Japan. *Liliaceae*

A magnificent and stately plant with a non-tunicated bulb containing overlapping fleshy scales and giving rise to a long, erect, rigid stem which roots at the base and is clad with alternate linear-lanceolate leaves. The stem terminates in a triangular raceme of abundant fragrant white flowers with a yellow band and deep purple spots. An excellent plant for the border or pot culture and readily propagated by seed or bulb scales. 8ft (2.4m)

🌣 ⚘ ❀ Summer ○ ◐ ▦ △▼

Lilium candidum, Madonna Lily, E. Mediterranean. *Liliaceae*

A much grown, beautiful, fleshy-scaled bulbous plant with pure white, most fragrant, trumpet-shaped flowers. The basal leaves form a tuft. Bulbs should be planted shallowly with the top 1in (2.5cm) below the soil surface and the best time for planting is August. Propagate by division of bulb scales. 5ft (1.5m)

🌣 ❀ Summer ○ ◐ ▦ △▼

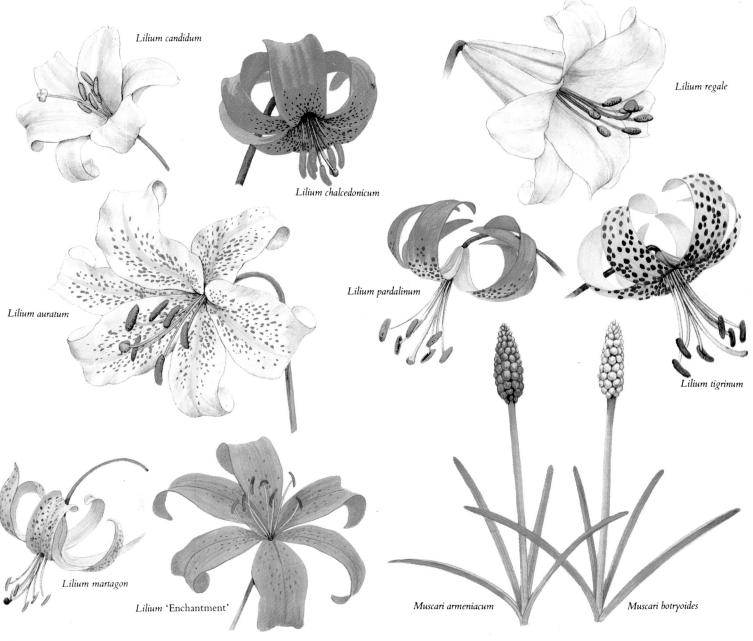

Lilium candidum

Lilium chalcedonicum

Lilium regale

Lilium auratum

Lilium pardalinum

Lilium tigrinum

Lilium martagon

Lilium 'Enchantment'

Muscari armeniacum

Muscari botryoides

Lilium chalcedonicum, Greece. *Liliaceae*

The bulb gives rise to a long erect stem clad with abundant, scattered, ovate-lanceolate silver-edged leaves. Bright scarlet, strongly recurved waxy flowers nod from long pedicels to make this a most striking plant. Propagate by bulb scales or by seed. 4ft (1.2m)

⊘ ۞ Summer ○ ◐ ✦ △▼

Lilium 'Enchantment'. *Liliaceae*

An Asiatic hybrid bulbous plant with erect stem and beautiful, large and abundant red flowers. Easy to grow and as rewarding in a container as it is planted in the border. New plants may be readily obtained by removing and growing on the axillary bulbils produced on the stem during late summer. 4ft (1.2m)

⊘ ۞ Summer ○ ◐ ✦ △▼

Lilium martagon, Turk's Cap Lily, Europe, Asia. *Liliaceae*

The ovoid, scaly bulb produces an erect, more or less hairy stem with mainly whorled ovate-lanceolate leaves, and terminating in a raceme of purple-dotted rose-purple nodding flowers, the segments strongly recurved. Many find the flower scent disagreeable. Most effective when planted in a group for naturalizing, the seed may well give rise to variable plants, otherwise propagation may be achieved by division. 3ft (1m)

⊘ ۞ Summer ◐ ✦ △▼

Lilium pardalinum, Leopard Lily, California. *Liliaceae*

A striking plant with a rhizomatous bulb producing an erect stem with narrow-lanceolate leaves in whorls and terminating in an inflorescence with red, fragrant, nodding reflexed flowers containing an orange centre and large purple spots. Plants should be lifted every three years and increased by division before replanting. 6ft (1.8m)

⊘ ۞ Summer ○ ✦ △▼

Lilium regale, China. *Liliaceae*

Most prolific in producing viable seed, which reaches maturity in 2 or 3 years, the rigid, purplish stem roots at the base and is clad with many scattered narrow leaves. The inflorescence contains attractive, fragrant, white funnel-shaped flowers tinted reddish-purple outside with a yellow throat, the segments recurved at the tip. 5ft (1.5m)

⊘ ۞ Summer ○ ◐ ✦ △▼

Lilium tigrinum (syn *L. lancifolium*) Tiger Lily, China, Korea, Japan. *Liliaceae*

A beautiful lily with an erect purplish-black pubescent stem rooting at the base and terminating in an inflorescence of purplish-black spotted, bright orange-red pendant flowers with strongly recurved segments. The flower colour is enhanced by the abundant glossy green linear leaves scattered along the stem. Readily propagated by removing the bulbils from the leaf axils. 4ft (1.2m)

⊘ ۞ Summer ◐ ✦ △▼

Muscari armeniacum, Grape Hyacinth, Asia Minor. *Liliaceae*

The tunicated bulb gives rise to glabrous, rather fleshy, linear basal leaves surrounding a simple scape terminating in a crowded raceme of blue flowers, the sterile terminal flowers are a bright blue. Plants may be increased by seed, or offsets can be removed from the parent and planted in groups to naturalize. 1ft (30cm)

⊘ ۞ Spring ○ ✦ △▼

Muscari botryoides, Grape Hyacinth, Europe. *Liliaceae*

A delectable little bulbous plant much planted in English cottage gardens and good for pot culture to give colour during winter and early spring. The pale blue or white flowers are borne on a short, dense, almost globose, raceme terminating the scape and surrounded by slightly glaucous, erect, stiff, linear foliage. Readily propagated by seed or by division. 8in (20cm)

⊘ ۞ Spring ○ ◐ ✦ △▼

47

Narcissus bulbocodium (syn *Corbularia bulbocodium*) Hoop Petticoat Daffodil, Europe, N. Africa. *Amaryllidaceae*

A most charming bulbous plant with slender scape terminating in a solitary yellow or white flower with obconic perianth tube and large funnel-shaped corona, the segments lanceolate and ascending with a green keel. An admirable plant for container growing and delightful when naturalized in grass. Seed produces variable plants and selections may be increased by division. 6in (15cm)

⟋ ⬆ ✿ Spring ○ ◐ ▦ △▼

Narcissus cyclamineus, Portugal. *Amaryllidaceae*

An elegant little plant with a long scape terminating in a solitary drooping flower containing a very short tube and strongly reflexed pale yellow segments, the attractive orange-yellow corona is delicately ribbed. Grass-like foliage complements the dainty plant which is excellent for pot culture or for naturalizing. Propagate by seed or by division. 6in (15cm)

⟋ ⬆ ✿ Spring ○ ◐ ▦ △▼

Narcissus triandrus albus, Angel's Tears, Europe. *Amaryllidaceae*

The bulb gives rise to a slender scape terminating in a head of from 1 to 6 flowers nodding from a pedicel. The lanceolate, reflexed, white perianth segments extend from the white tube, and the white cup-shaped corona is truncate at the throat. An elegant plant and most attractive when set in groups. Propagate by division or by seed. 10in (25cm)

⟋ ⬆ ✿ Spring ○ ◐ ▦ △▼

Narcissus 'Rockall'. *Amaryllidaceae*

This delightful bulbous plant produces a long scape terminating in a solitary flower of the Small-cupped division with a small corona. An excellent plant for cutting as well as for border decoration, especially when massed planted and allowed to naturalize. 1¹/₂ft (45cm)

⟋ ✿ Spring ○ ◐ ▦ △▼

Narcissus 'February Gold'. *Amaryllidaceae*

A bulbous plant of medium size belonging to the Cyclamineus hybrid division with slightly reflexing yellow perianth segments and pale orange-yellow trumpet-shaped corona. A very good plant for forcing once the bulb has produced established roots; also effective on the rock garden and for planting in drifts. 10in (25cm)

⟋ ✿ Winter/Spring ○ ◐ ▦ △▼

Narcissus 'Sempre Avanti'. *Amaryllidaceae*

The bulb gives rise to a long scape with solitary flower belonging to the Large-cupped division. A bright orange corona is set off by the background of yellow perianth segments to give a generous display when planted in a group to naturalize. Propagate by division. 1¹/₂ft (45cm)

⟋ ✿ Spring ○ ◐ ▦ △▼

Narcissus 'Silver Chimes'. *Amaryllidaceae*

This bulbous plant flowers later than the majority within the group and produces strong stems terminating in clusters of beautiful flowers of small to medium size. Belonging to the Triandrus division, the flower consists of smooth white perianth segments and pale yellow cup-shaped corona standing well above the healthy dark green foliage. Excellent for container growing the plants may be propagated by division. 10in (25cm)

⟋ ✿ Spring ○ ◐ ▦ △▼

Narcissus 'Texas'. *Amaryllidaceae*

A vigorous bulbous plant belonging to the Double division and giving rise to rigid stems terminating in a large, rounded double flower with dark yellow outer perianth segments, the inner segments orange and yellow. The flowers last well and the plant is particularly good for forcing in containers or for naturalizing out of doors. Plants may be increased by division. 15in (38cm)

⟋ ✿ Spring ○ ◐ ▦ △▼

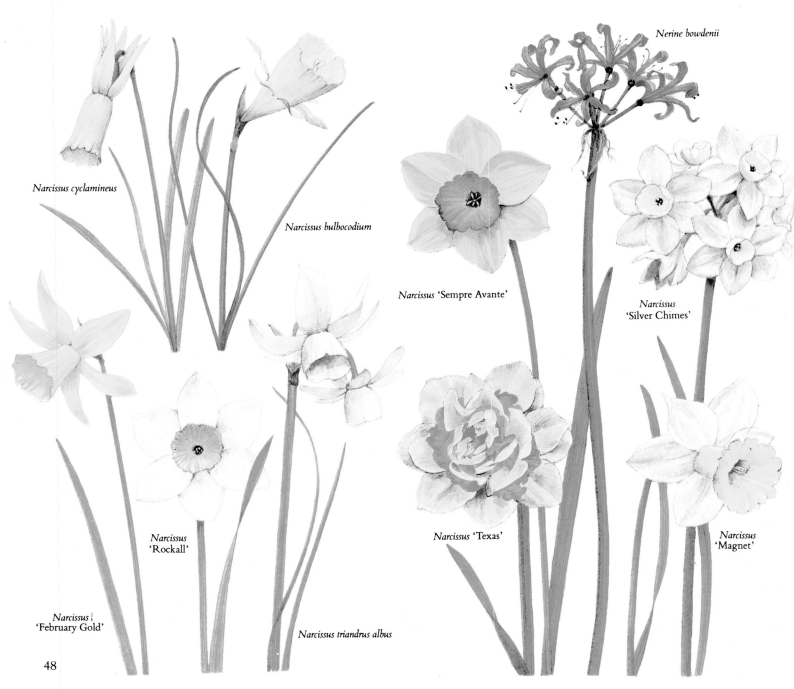

Narcissus cyclamineus

Narcissus bulbocodium

Narcissus 'Sempre Avante'

Nerine bowdenii

Narcissus 'Silver Chimes'

Narcissus 'Rockall'

Narcissus 'Texas'

Narcissus 'February Gold'

Narcissus triandrus albus

Narcissus 'Magnet'

Puschkinia scilloides

Ornithogalum nutans

Schizostylis coccinea 'Major'

Ranunculus asiaticus

Narcissus 'Magnet'. *Amaryllidaceae*

The bulb gives rise to a stout stem terminating in a large flower belonging to the Trumpet division with white perianth segments and large creamy-yellow trumpet-shaped cup which lasts well in the border or as a cut flower. Propagate by division by removing daughter bulbs from the parent. 1¹/₂ft (45cm)

⌀✿Spring ○ ◕ ▦ △▼

Nerine bowdenii, South Africa. *Amaryllidaceae*

A delectable plant producing a long-necked bulb which gives rise to a long scape terminating in an umbel of pink flowers with long segments recurved at the tip. The flower is followed by glossy green, long linear leaves which eventually begin to turn yellow. At that stage water should be withheld to induce the resting period and cool conditions should be given to pot-grown plants. Water plants in autumn when the flower spike or leaves appear and then continue as required until the resting stage. Propagate by offsets or by seed. 1¹/₂ft (45cm)

⌀ ✿Autumn ○ ◕ ▦ △▼

Ornithogalum nutans, Star of Bethlehem, Europe. *Liliaceae*

A beautiful bulbous plant with limp strap-shaped leaves and a scape terminating in a one-sided raceme of white and green nodding flowers. An excellent plant for naturalizing in the border or in grass below trees. The plants may be raised by sowing fresh ripe seed or by division of offsets which will flower after 1 or 2 years. 1ft (30cm)

⌀ ✿Spring ◕ ▦ △▼

Puschkinia scilloides, Striped Squill, Caucasus. *Liliaceae*

This charming bulbous plant produces sparse, lanceolate, dark green basal leaves and a scape terminating in a one-sided raceme of blue or whitish flowers on a slender pedicel. Plants may be increased by division every 2 or 3 years. An excellent subject to naturalize for the border or rock garden. 10in (25cm)

⌀✿Summer ○ ◕ ▦ △▼

Ranunculus asiaticus, Garden Ranunculus, Orient. *Ranunculaceae*

This plant is rather variable but always interesting. The small tuberous claw-like roots give rise to a simple or branched stem clad with segmented leaves and terminating in large white, yellow or red flowers with blunt ovate petals. After flowering and when the leaves turn yellow, the roots should be lifted and overwintered in dry airy conditions and replanted the following spring. Propagate by division. 15in (38cm)

⌀ ✿Summer ◕ ▦ △▼

Schizostylis coccinea 'Major', Crimson Flag, Kaffir Lily. *Iridaceae*

A most striking plant with clustered erect stems arising from the rhizome and clad with linear or narrow ensiform sheathing leaves. Abundant bright red scattered flowers appear in a distichous spike. An excellent plant for border decoration or for cutting, as the flowers are long lasting, and makes a good subject for container growing. Plants may be increased by division in spring. 2ft (60cm)

⌀ ✿Autumn ○ ▦ △▼

Scilla sibirica (syn *S. amoena siberica*) Russia. *Liliaceae*

A charming bulbous plant from within a genus offering many gems. The tunicated bulb gives rise to fleshy scapes with horizontal or slightly drooping deep blue flowers on short pedicels. Strap-shaped basal leaves appear with the flowers. A good plant for growing in containers in the cold greenhouse or frame, or planting out of doors. Propagate by offsets or seeds, but the latter may take up to 5 years to produce flowering-size plants. 6in (15cm)

✏ ❀ ✿ Spring ○ ◗ ❖ △▽

Sternbergia lutea (syn *Amaryllis lutea*) Yellow Star Flower, Lily of the Field, Winter Daffodil, Europe. *Amaryllidaceae*

An attractive plant which produces a solitary funnel-shaped flower with a yellow perianth upon a short scape. The blunt, keeled, strap-shaped leaves are dark green. Unusual for autumn and good for permanent planting. Plants may be increased by division during July. 4in (10cm)

✏ ◖ ✿ Autumn ○ ❖ △▽

Tulipa batalinii, Bukhara. *Liliaceae*

A genus which offers so many lovely species and some of the easiest of plants to grow. This select little dwarf with a tunicated bulb produces grass-like leaves in a rosette and a solitary yellow flower with a green blotch upon a short scape. An excellent plant for pan culture or for naturalizing. Propagate by offsets. 6in (15cm)

✏ ✿ Spring ○ ◗ ❖ △▽

Tulipa clusiana, Lady Tulip, Persia, Afghanistan, Kashmir. *Liliaceae*

The round bulb gives rise to slightly glaucous linear-lanceolate leaves and a slender scape terminating in a solitary, white, flat (and star-shaped when open) flower, the outer elliptic-lanceolate segments externally red. A charming plant for naturalizing. Plants may be increased by division. 10in (25cm)

✏ ✿ Spring ○ ❖ △▽

Tulipa fosteriana 'Red Emperor' (syn 'Mme Lefeber'). *Liliaceae*

A striking plant with globose bulb producing more or less glaucous leaves and a stem which terminates in a very large, solitary, bright red shiny flower opening flat with long, bluntly pointed segments. A magnificent plant which often responds favourably to lifting after the leaves have withered, then replanting during spring after dry winter storage. Propagate by offsets. 2ft (60cm)

✏ ❀ ✿ Spring ○ ❖ △▽

Tulipa greigii 'Red Riding Hood'. *Liliaceae*

A beautiful, bright, cup-shaped flower with large, reflexing segments with a recurving margin. The pubescent scape is surrounded by wide leaves with purple zones. A plant generous in flower colour and size ideal for naturalizing. Increase by division of offsets. 8in (20cm)

✏ ✿ Spring ○ ❖ △▽

Tulipa 'Holland's Glory'. *Liliaceae*

This magnificent Darwin hybrid has a long stem and very large, orange-scarlet globose flower with a black base to the segments. An outstanding plant for bedding schemes and for cutting for indoor decoration. Plants may be increased by offsets. 2½ft (75cm)

✏ ✿ Spring ○ ❖ △▽

Scilla sibirica

Sternbergia lutea

Tulipa batalinii

Tulipa clusiana

Tulipa fosteriana 'Red Emperor'

Tulipa 'Keizerskroon'

Tulipa 'Holland's Glory'

Tulipa kaufmanniana 'Stresa'

Tulipa greigii 'Red Riding Hood'

Tulipa kaufmanniana 'Stresa', Water-lily Tulip. *Liliaceae*

One of the earliest to flower, this charming plant has a solitary long-lasting flower opening to a star shape during bright weather, the narrow elliptic red segments showing a yellow interior. The pubescent scape is surrounded by long, broad, slightly glaucous leaves. Excellent for naturalizing and may be increased by offsets. 8in (20cm)

⌀ ❀Spring ○ ▧ △▼

Tulipa 'Keizerskroon'. *Liliaceae*

An outstanding single early, semi-dwarf tulip with large scarlet-red flowers with a broad yellow margin. This plant has stood the test of time as being very good for border decoration and for growing in containers. Propagate by offsets. 1ft (30cm)

⌀ ❀Spring ○ ▧ △▼

Tulipa 'Mariette'. *Liliaceae*

A plant of perfect form with deep pink, elegant single flowers with long, pointed, recurving segments and a member of the Lily-flowered class. Very good for bedding and cutting for indoor decoration. Plants may be increased by division of offsets. 1¹/₂ft (45cm)

⌀ ❀Spring ○ ▧ △▼

Tulipa 'Mrs John T. Schleepers'. *Liliaceae*

In keeping with others belonging to the Cottage class, the plant is a vigorous grower and has beautiful, very large, single, clear-yellow elongated flowers. Once planted, the bulbs may be left undisturbed to naturalize. Good for bedding and cutting the plants may be increased by division of offsets. 1¹/₂ft (45cm)

⌀ ❀Spring ○ ▧ △▼

Tulipa 'Peach Blossom'. *Liliaceae*

This plant, with its large pink flower, belongs to the Double Early class, often known as the Paeony-flowered group – an apt description of the beautiful-shaped blooms. The long-lasting flowers make a fine bedding display and may also be grown in containers. Propagate by division. 1ft (30cm)

⌀ ❀Spring ○ ▧ △▼

Tulipa praestans 'Fusilier'. *Liliaceae*

The ovoid bulb gives rise to a multi-flowered plant with bright scarlet-red bluntly pointed segments forming a cup shape. A most attractive plant with wide channelled leaves for the border or rock garden. Plants may be increased by division. 10in (25cm)

⌀ ❀Spring ○ ▧ △▼

Tulipa 'Queen of Bartigons'. *Liliaceae*

Beautiful and much grown, the Darwin class includes many fine plants, this being one of the better ones with large salmon-pink shiny flowers which have a white base to the segments. The long robust stem makes the plant ideal for cutting and bedding display. Propagate by division of the offsets. 2¹/₂ft (75cm)

⌀ ❀Spring ○ ▧ △▼

Tulipa tarda (syn *T. dasystemon*) Turkistan. *Liliaceae*

The ovoid bulb with a yellow tunic produces a short scape with 1 to 6 star-shaped flat flowers with yellow-based segments becoming white towards the apex with green and red marks. A most interesting and attractive little plant with glabrous leaves forming a rosette and almost prostrate. A good plant to naturalize and completely at home in the rock garden. May be increased by seed or by division. 6in (15cm)

⌀ ❀Spring ○ ▧ △▼

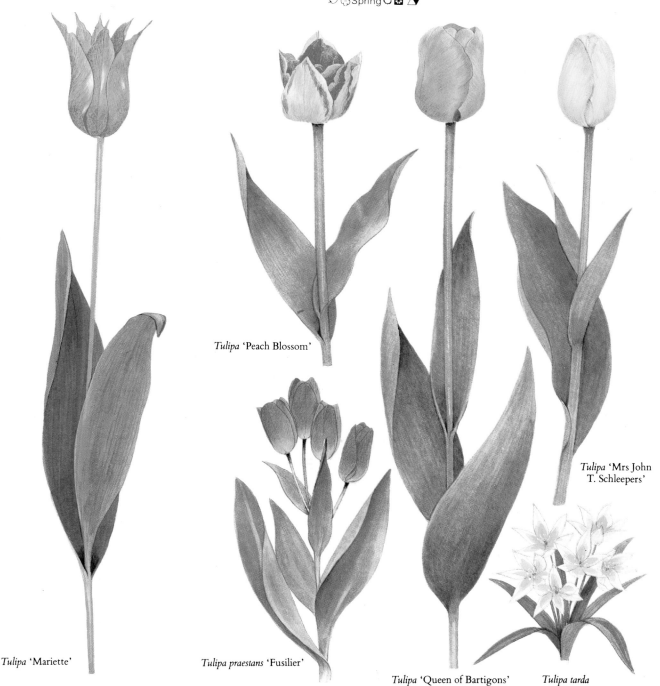

Tulipa 'Peach Blossom'

Tulipa 'Mrs John T. Schleepers'

Tulipa 'Mariette'

Tulipa praestans 'Fusilier'

Tulipa 'Queen of Bartigons'

Tulipa tarda

A Diversity of Roses

All of us want beautiful roses in our gardens. Provided that you have chosen the best varieties to start with, and a good rose nursery will advise you on this, here is the way to get them.

The Site
Roses will do best if they are given full sun for most of the day and grown in a good, medium loam, moisture-retentive but well drained. They like a soil that is slightly acid (about 6.5 on the pH scale). The addition of peat will increase acidity, and nitro-chalk, which is also a fertilizer, will increase alkalinity. But whatever the soil, about three months before you are to plant your roses, dig well-rotted farmyard manure or well-rotted compost, plus a liberal helping of bonemeal and hoof and horn meal into the top spit of earth. Double digging and the addition of coarse peat should only be necessary on the heaviest clay soils, primarily to improve drainage.

Do not plan to plant new roses in a bed from which you have taken old ones. The soil will have become what is known as rose-sick, and the plants will never do well, even if fertilizers are added. The soil must be replaced or another site picked.

Planting
November is the best month for planting as the rose roots can begin to establish themselves before the really cold weather sets in, but they can in fact be planted at any time up to the end of March, though not during a frosty spell or if the ground is waterlogged. Late planting means that they will be later getting

A spectacular array of roses can be seen in Queen Mary's Rose Garden, Regent's Park. Roses are unrivalled for their long flowering season.

away, but no harm will come to them.

If planting cannot be carried out at once when the roses arrive, they can be left, still in their packing, in a cool, frost-proof shed for a week or so. If the delay has to be for longer that this, they should be heeled in. This means putting them, after unpacking, in a shallow trench with at least 6in (15cm) of earth over the roots. They will be happy like this for quite a while, but do plant as soon as possible.

When you unpack the roses, either for planting or for heeling in, inspect them carefully. Cut back damaged or diseased shoots to a healthy bud and shorten thick, strong roots by about two-thirds. If you are planting in the spring, prune the main shoots as well. Cut them to 3 to 4in (8 to 10cm). If the plants look dry, put them in a bucket of water and leave them there for at least an hour. While this is going on prepare some planting mixture, which will help the roses to settle in and make new feeding roots quickly. This should consist of soil and granulated peat in equal parts (approximately one large shovelful to each rose), with about one handful per rose of bonemeal well mixed in.

How far apart you plant your roses depends on the vigour and habit of growth of the varieties you have chosen. A compact, upright grower needs less space then one which sprawls, but 18in to 2ft (45 to 60cm) between them can be taken as an average. Planting holes should be wide enough so that the roots can be well spread out, and deep enough so that the budding union is just below soil level. With the rose held in position in the hole, check the level and pack planting mixture round the roots, finally pulling in earth from the surrounding bed to fill the rest of the hole. Tread firmly but not too hard, and re-firm the soil once more if there should be hard frost during the ensuing winter. Keep well watered.

Should you find when you unpack them that the roots of your roses all point in one direction (a consequence of the mechanical planting of the rootstocks) so that they cannot be spread out evenly all round in the planting hole, position the rose to one side of it and arrange the roots fanwise over the rest of it. The same technique is used in planting climbers against a wall, where the soil is likely to be exceptionally dry. The planting hole should be at least 18in (45cm) away from the wall and the roots encouraged to grow outwards towards moister earth. When planting a standard rose, put the supporting stake in position first. Driven in later, it might cause root damage.

Training

Train the shoots of climbers on a wall or fence along horizontal wires which are strung between vine eyes and about 3 to 4in (8 to 10cm) from the wall's surface. If the shoots were allowed to grow straight up the flowers would all form at the top, but properly trained like this there will be flowering side shoots at all levels. The same result will be achieved with a pillar rose by spiralling the shoots round the support rather than, once again, letting them go straight up.

Pruning

Roses are pruned to encourage strong new shoots to form each year, to get rid of weak and spindly ones, and also those that are diseased or even dead. In addition pruning should open out the centre of the bush if this is needed to improve air circulation, and help the plant to grow into a nicely balanced, shapely specimen. Though pruning can be done at any time during the winter or spring when the bushes are dormant or nearly so (provided that there is no frost about), traditionally the pruning months are March in the south of the country and April in the colder north. If you follow this pattern you will not go far wrong. Prune with secateurs, which should be kept sharp and

When pruning, remove old and weak shoots and cut to an outward pointing bud, keeping the centre of the bush open.

clean at all times. The actual pruning cut should be made about ¼in (6mm) above a bud, sloping down away from it on the opposite side. Cut to a bud which is facing the way in which you wish the shoot which will grow from it to go.

When pruning large-flowered (Hybrid Tea) and cluster-flowered (Floribunda) roses, first get rid of all dead, diseased or spindly shoots, and if two shoots should be rubbing together, cut back one of them. The aim at this stage is to achieve a framework of strong, firm, green shoots, none of which is much less than pencil thickness. Finally, for large-flowered roses

cut these shoots back to 8 to 10in (20 to 25cm) and for cluster-flowered to 12 to 14in (30 to 35cm). In the latter case also reduce strong side shoots by about two-thirds.

Climbing roses need only their laterals or side shoots cut back by about two-thirds in autumn. If they have become bare at the base, a main shoot cut back hard should encourage new growth low down. Ramblers are pruned immediately after blooming, the shoots which have flowered being removed to ground level and the new ones, which will form each year, being tied in their place. If there are not enough new shoots, leave a few old ones, which will still produce some flowers.

For the taller varieties of miniature rose, follow the pruning pattern as for cluster-flowered kinds. The shorter ones can just be clipped over to keep them tidy and even, and any that form a thick tangle of shoots should have these thinned out. Shrub roses, though they vary enormously in size and habit, in general benefit from having their side shoots cut back by two-thirds, after flowering with the non-recurrent varieties, and in winter with those that are recurrent. Wild or species roses should not be pruned, other than for the removal of dead wood. Pruning would destroy their natural charm.

Routine Maintenance

At pruning time and again in July, sprinkle a small handful of a proprietary rose fertilizer round each bush and hoe it lightly into the soil. Do not use fertilizer after July as this would encourage soft autumn growth which the frosts of winter would kill off.

In late spring of each year, mulch the beds with well-rotted stable manure, compost, peat or pulverised forest bark. This will help to keep in moisture, will smother weed seedlings, will help to maintain an even soil temperature and, as it rots down, will improve its structure. The first two will provide plant foods as well.

Dead-heading should be carried out regularly throughout the flowering season. As the blooms fade and die, they should be removed to stop hips forming. If this is done the rose will produce further flowers to take their place in a more or less continuous display. However, do not just pull the spent blooms off. Cut to a bud about 4 to 5in (10 to 13cm) down the stem. A much stronger new shoot will be the result, bearing much better flowers.

Suckers are shoots coming from the rootstock (the rose's roots), rather than from the cultivated variety growing on it. They should be pulled away from the root as cutting them off would be the equivalent of pruning and would simply encourage new and stronger growth. Generally the leaves, thorns and stems of a sucker will look very different from those of the rest of the rose. But if in doubt, scrape some soil away until you find the point from which the suspected sucker is growing. If it comes from the roots below the budding union, it is a sucker.

Pests and Diseases

The most common pests are greenfly – small green and some-times brown insects that cluster on new rose shoots and flower stems. These and most other rose pests can be dealt with very effectively by spraying the plants with a systemic insecticide. An exception is the leaf-rolling sawfly, which curls up the rose leaves into little tapering cylinders. Preventative treatment must be given before this happens, using a spray containing fenitro-thion at the end of April and again early in May.

The most common and troublesome rose diseases are powdery mildew, the name of which describes its appearance well, and black spot, seen as fringed black spots on the leaves. The latter is the more serious of the two as the spots quickly grow in size and the leaves will eventually turn yellow and fall, thus weakening the plant. Both diseases can be controlled, mildew more effectively than black spot, by fungicides containing benomyl, thiophanate-methyl, bupirimate-triforine, fenarimol and a few others. Spray as soon as either disease appears as both spread quickly. Do not spray in hot sunshine. The evening is the best time.

'Fragrant Cloud'

'Ernest Morse'

'Double Delight'

'Alec's Red'

'Blessings'

Large-flowered (Hybrid Tea) Roses: 'Alec's Red'

The abundant, large, full, and most fragrant light crimson blooms of good form terminate vigorous erect stems clad with glossy green disease-resistant leaves. An excellent cultivar for border display, for cutting and exhibition, it has been awarded many distinctions including The Royal National Rose Society's President's International Trophy, Gold Medal and Henry Edland Memorial Medal, the Belfast Gold Medal and Fragrance Award. 3ft (1m)

'Blessings'

A prolific disease- and weather-resistant plant with abundant flowers extending from the early season through to the end and their persistence compensates for the moderate size. Much used for bedding, the cultivar has been awarded the Royal National Rose Society's Certificate of Merit and the Baden Baden Gold Medal. 3ft (1m)

'Double Delight'

This vigorous upright grower with disease-resistant foliage terminates in large, most fragrant flowers of somewhat unusual pigmentation. An All American Rose Selection, the cultivar has also been awarded the Rome Gold Medal and the Baden Baden Gold Medal. 3ft (1m)

'Ernest H. Morse'

Dependable and sweetly scented, the weatherproof flowers are well formed except for the centre ones which can be weak. An excellent plant for bedding and cutting, bearing semi-glossy leaves inclined to be susceptible to mildew. Often seen on the show bench, the cultivar has been awarded the Royal National Rose Society's Gold Medal, the Award of Merit by the Royal Horticultural Society and The Hague Fragrance Medal. 3ft (1m)

'Fragrant Cloud' (syn 'Duftwolke', 'Nuage Parfume')

Delectably fragrant bright red flowers tend to fade with maturity and the moderate size may be increased by reducing the number of flower buds. The bushy growth gives rise to dark green semi-glossy leaves which are better if sprayed with fungicide against mildew and black spot. Excellent for cutting, border display and much grown for exhibition, the cultivar has been awarded the Royal National Rose Society's President's International Trophy and Gold Medal and the Royal Horticultural Society's Award of Merit. 2½ft (75cm)

'Grandpa Dickson' (syn 'Irish Gold')

The vigorous stems clad with, glossy, disease-resistant leaves terminate in slightly fragrant, large, weather-resistant flowers. An excellent plant for bedding, cutting and exhibition; the cultivar has been awarded many distinctions including the Royal National Rose Society's President's International Trophy and Gold Medal, an Award of Merit by the Royal Horticultural Society and the Belfast and Hague Gold Medals. 3ft (1m)

'Just Joey'

A distinctive plant with large, slightly fragrant, weather-resistant flowers. The bushy habit with dark green disease-resistant foliage makes this an ideal plant for bedding and cutting. The cultivar has been awarded the Trial Ground Certificate of the Royal National Rose Society and the Hague Fragrance Medal. 2½ft (75cm)

'Mischief'

The vigorous stems clad with semi-glossy leaves give rise to most prolific weather-resistant flowers, those produced towards the end of its long season often being darker. An excellent plant for bedding although somewhat susceptible to rust disease. The cultivar has been awarded the President's International Trophy and Gold Medal of the Royal National Rose Society. 3ft (1m)

'Grandpa Dickson'

'Pascali'

'Just Joey'

'Peace'

'Mischief'

'National Trust'

'Pink Favorite'

'Piccadilly'

'Wendy Cussons'

'Silver Jubilee'

'Troika'

'Rose Gaujard'

'Pink Favorite'

The most handsome, slightly fragrant, deep pink weather-resistant flowers appear in abundance upon erect stems. Seldom attacked by disease, the leaves appear dark green and glossy to make an attractive plant for border and exhibition. An Award of Merit has been presented by the Royal Horticultural Society. 2½ft (75cm)

'Rose Gaujard'

A prolific plant with large, slightly fragrant, weather-resistant, split centre flowers. An adaptable plant easy to grow and tolerant of indifferent soil. Black spot disease is inclined to attack during prolonged wet weather. The cultivar has been awarded the Royal National Rose Society's Gold Medal and Trial Ground Certificate together with an Award of Merit by the Royal Horticultural Society. 3ft (1m)

'Troika' (syn 'Royal Dane')

An excellent exhibition cultivar good for cutting with large, fragrant, long-lasting flowers and glossy, disease-resistant leaves. The plant was awarded a Certificate of Merit by the Royal National Rose Society. 3ft (1m)

'Wendy Cussons'

Easy to grow and outstanding in every way with prolific, fragrant, weather-resistant flowers. The bushy habit is enhanced by dark green leaves resistant to disease. An excellent plant for bedding or for growing as a standard. The Royal National Rose Society has awarded it its President's International Trophy and Gold Medal, the Royal Horticultural Society an Award of Merit, the Golden Rose is presented by The Hague and the cultivar has also received the Rome Gold Medal. 3ft (1m)

'Silver Jubilee'

A most attractive tufted plant giving rise to abundant fragrant flowers. Excellent for bedding with its relatively short stems and glossy disease-free leaves, the cultivar has been awarded the President's International Trophy and Gold Medal by the Royal National Rose Society. 2½ft (75cm)

Cluster-flowered (Floribunda) Roses: 'Allgold'

An appropriate name for such pure-coloured flowers presented in a cluster upon short stems. This plant has stood the test of time and still remains a favourite with disease-resistant glossy leaves and persistent flowering. The Gold Medal was awarded by the Royal National Rose Society and an Award of Merit by the Royal Horticultural Society. 2ft (60cm)

'Anne Harkness' (syn 'Harkaramel')

The beautiful and unusual saffron-yellow colour makes this a most attractive recent introduction. Long shoots develop before the double flower cluster appears in a large mass to brighten the border at a time when many cultivars lack colour between flushes. 3½ft (1m))

'Arthur Bell'

Erect vigorous stems clad with healthy glossy green leaves give rise to clusters of most fragrant, yellow, weather-resistant flowers becoming white in maturity to give the plant a somewhat unusual appearance. Good for the border and rather taller than most, the cultivar has been awarded the Royal National Rose Society's Certificate of Merit. 3½ft (1m)

'City of Leeds'

A most prolific repeat-flowering plant with attractive, slightly fragrant, salmon-pink petals inclined to be susceptible to rain spotting during inclement weather. The plant is adaptable, easy to grow and justifies the Gold Medal awarded by the Royal National Rose Society. 3ft (1m)

'Dearest'

A vigorous erect grower with most fragrant, double, salmon-pink flowers rather susceptible to weather damage. Foliage, although dark and glossy, is now rather prone to rust and black spot disease; never-the-less still a good plant for border display, cutting and exhibition, the cultivar has been awarded the Royal National Rose Society's Gold Medal and an Award of Merit by the Royal Horticultural Society. 2½ft (75cm)

'Elizabeth of Glamis' (syn 'Irish Beauty')

An elegant habit with semi-glossy foliage and fragrant, beautiful flowers make this an attractive plant for loamy fertile soils. Rather susceptible to black spot and mildew. It has received the Royal National Rose Society's President's International Trophy and Gold Medal and an Award of Merit by the Royal Horticultural Society. 2½ft (75cm)

'National Trust' (syn 'Bad Nauheim')

A low-growing vigorous plant with healthy dark green leaves and bright red, tightly packed petals producing a bloom of good form. Prolific long-lasting flowers make this a good plant for border decoration and for cutting. The cultivar has been awarded the Royal National Rose Society's Trial Ground Certificate. 2½ft (75cm)

'Pascali'

Beautiful medium-sized flowers upon erect stems with glossy leaves make this a delectable plant for cutting with good keeping qualities. Fragrance is not strong and the growth tends to be somewhat weak and rather susceptible to mildew. An All-American Rose Selection, the cultivar has also also been selected for the Golden Rose award by The Hague, the Royal National Rose Society's Gold Medal and Trial Ground Certificate. 3ft (1m)

'Peace' (syn 'Gloria Dei', 'Mme A Meilland')

A much-loved rose with outstanding, very large blooms. The vigorous stems clad with dark green glossy leaves make this a great favourite. Blind shoots should be shortened at an early stage to encourage further shoot development. Awarded the Royal National Rose Society's Gold Medal and Trial Ground Certificate, the Royal Horticultural Society's Award of Merit, the cultivar is also an All-American Rose Selection. 4ft (1.2m)

'Piccadilly'

The slightly fragrant, weather-resistant flowers, together with dark green leaves which are at first coppery, provide a lively plant for bedding and cutting. Awards include the Royal National Rose Society's Certificate of Merit, The Royal Horticultural Society's Award of Merit and the Rome Gold Medal. 2½ft (75cm)

A DIVERSITY OF ROSES

'Escapade'

An interesting plant with clusters of unusual coloured flowers and light green foliage. Suitable for mixing with others in the shrub border; delectable for cutting with a generous musky fragrance and equally attractive for exhibition. The Royal National Rose Society awarded its Certificate of Merit and the cultivar also received the Baden Baden Gold Medal. 2½ft (75cm)

'Evelyn Fison' (syn 'Irish Wonder')

Deservedly popular for its bright red flowers which resist inclement weather and persist well through the season. An excellent plant for border decoration and awarded the Royal National Rose Society's Gold Medal and Royal Horticultural Society's Award of Merit. 2½ft (75cm)

'Eye Paint'

Planted as a hedge the cultivar establishes quickly and is most attractive with its abundant, small and brilliant red flowers. May also be planted in a mixed border where it blends well. The cultivar received the Royal National Rose Society's Trial Ground Certificate and the Baden Baden Gold Medal. 4ft (1.2m)

'Iceberg' (syn 'Schneewittchen')

A most shapely and vigorous plant producing upright shoots giving rise to abundant, slightly fragrant, weatherproof flowers. The glossy light green leaves tend to be rather susceptible to black spot which may be avoided by generous spacing of the plant with others and the use of preventive fungicides. An excellent specimen plant for the border which has been awarded the Royal National Rose Society's Gold Medal and Award of Merit by the Royal Horticultural Society. 4ft (1.2m)

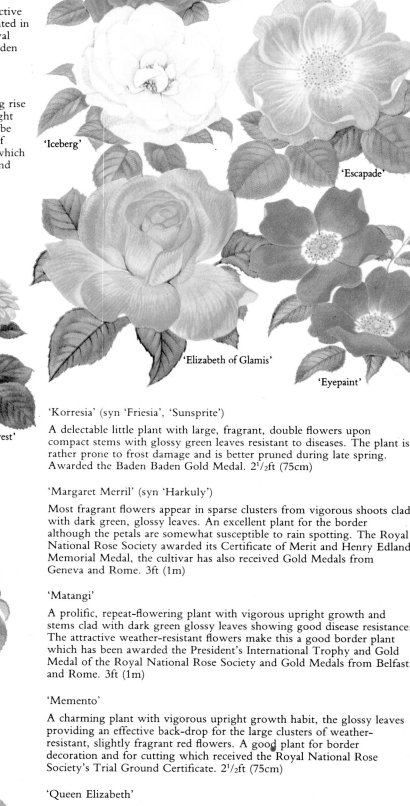

'Evelyn Fison'

'Korresia'

'Iceberg'

'Escapade'

'Elizabeth of Glamis'

'Eyepaint'

'Allgold'

'Dearest'

'City of Leeds'

'Arthur Bell'

'Anne Harkness'

'Korresia' (syn 'Friesia', 'Sunsprite')

A delectable little plant with large, fragrant, double flowers upon compact stems with glossy green leaves resistant to diseases. The plant is rather prone to frost damage and is better pruned during late spring. Awarded the Baden Baden Gold Medal. 2½ft (75cm)

'Margaret Merril' (syn 'Harkuly')

Most fragrant flowers appear in sparse clusters from vigorous shoots clad with dark green, glossy leaves. An excellent plant for the border although the petals are somewhat susceptible to rain spotting. The Royal National Rose Society awarded its Certificate of Merit and Henry Edland Memorial Medal, the cultivar has also received Gold Medals from Geneva and Rome. 3ft (1m)

'Matangi'

A prolific, repeat-flowering plant with vigorous upright growth and stems clad with dark green glossy leaves showing good disease resistance. The attractive weather-resistant flowers make this a good border plant which has been awarded the President's International Trophy and Gold Medal of the Royal National Rose Society and Gold Medals from Belfast and Rome. 3ft (1m)

'Memento'

A charming plant with vigorous upright growth habit, the glossy leaves providing an effective back-drop for the large clusters of weather-resistant, slightly fragrant red flowers. A good plant for border decoration and for cutting which received the Royal National Rose Society's Trial Ground Certificate. 2½ft (75cm)

'Queen Elizabeth'

An outstanding, elegant plant with vigorous erect stems clad with dark glossy green disease-resistant leaves. The beautiful flowers make excellent cut blooms. The cultivar is an All-American Rose Selection and has also been awarded the Royal National Rose Society's President's International Trophy and Gold Medal, the Gold Medal and Golden Rose of The Hague. 5ft (1.5m)

'Sunsilk'

'Southhampton'

'Matangi'

'Margaret Merril'

'Memento'

'Queen Elizabeth'

'Southampton'

A bright sunny plant with abundant, weather-resistant flowers upon vigorous stems clad with many dark green, disease-resistant leaves. An excellent plant for border decoration and cutting, and also desirable for hedging. Awarded the Royal National Rose Society's Trial Ground Certificate and the Belfast Gold Medal. 3ft (1m)

'Sunsilk'

This vigorous upright plant gives rise to stems clad with semi-glossy leaves somewhat prone to rust disease. The slightly fragrant double flowers stand well in water and the plant is good for border decoration. The Trial Ground Certificate has been awarded by the Royal National Rose Society and a Gold Medal by Belfast. 3ft (1m)

Shrub Roses: 'Ballerina'

In cultivation for many years, the compact bushy growth produces stems with abundant, minute, long-lasting, pale pink single flowers appearing repeatedly during summer and autumn. An excellent plant for hedging, it may also be grown in the mixed border or rose bed. 3¹/₂ft (1m)

'Chinatown'

This plant is very vigorous with a bushy habit giving rise to long shoots clad with abundant bright green, glossy, disease-resistant leaves. The fragrant, bright yellow double flowers with good form stand well and arise in clusters. An excellent plant for the border growing well in light soil. 5ft (1.5m)

'Frau Dagmar Hartopp'

A well established plant less vigorous than most within the group giving rise to wide-spreading stems clad with dark green healthy leaves turning golden-yellow in autumn. The attractive, fragrant, pink single flowers appear repeatedly and develop large red hips during autumn. A good plant for the border and hedge. 4¹/₂ft (1.4m)

'Fred Loads'

A most vigorous plant producing upright stems clad with abundant light green leaves and terminating in very large clusters of bright red, weather-resistant, fragrant flowers. An excellent repeat-flowering cultivar for the border. 6ft (1.8m)

'Frühlingsgold'

This very large spreading shrub with healthy light green foliage upon ascending stems has abundant, fragrant, pale yellow, large double flowers. An early-flowering shrub rose which should not be severely pruned by cutting back, otherwise flowering will be suppressed the following year; congested and spent growth should be removed by thinning. An excellent plant for the large border where it will spread 3¹/₂ft (1m) in each direction. 8ft (2.4m)

'Golden Wings'

Massive single flowers with a slight fragrance and a rich creamy-yellow colour which withstands inclement weather make this a delightful shrub. The bushy growth clad with light green disease-resistant leaves produces stems which flower repeatedly throughout the season provided faded blooms are removed. An excellent plant for the border. 6ft (1.8m)

'Nevada'

A most vigorous shrub with attractive ascending branches, the arching stems clad with abundant, small, light green leaves rather susceptible to black spot. The large, semi-double, slightly fragrant, pure white, then flushed pink flowers with pronounced yellow stamens appear in much abundance in early summer, less profusely in autumn. An excellent plant for the border where space permits. 7ft (2.1m)

'Penelope'

Vigorous wide-spreading shrub with shoots bearing abundant mid-green disease-resistant leaves and semi-double flowers composed of most fragrant shell-pink-shaded salmon petals. Tends to develop hips too readily at the expense of autumn flower unless the heads are removed as they fade. A good plant for the border or for hedge. 4ft (1.2m)

'Ballerina'   'Frühlingsgold'

'Chinatown'

'Frau Dagmar Hartopp'

'Fred Loads'

'Golden Wings'

'Nevada'

'Penelope'

'Roseraie de l'Hay'

'Empress Josephine'

'Charles de Mills'

'Chapeau de Napoleon'

'Roseraie de l'Haÿ'

This beautiful and most adaptable shrub has light green disease-resistant foliage which provides a contrasting back-drop to the most attractive and fragrant, bright purple, large double flowers. The plant will tolerate polluted air and is good for coastal districts; its vigour will overcome light soil not always favoured by roses. An excellent border plant which does equally well as a hedge. 6ft (1.8m)

Old Garden Roses: 'Chapeau de Napoleon' (syn 'Crested Moss')

The modified sepals enclosing the flower bud resemble Napoleon's hat. Nodding clusters of beautiful, double flowers with a delectable fragrance appear during summer upon spreading branches which form a bush of open relaxed habit. A charming rose for the border but rather susceptible to mildew. 5ft (1.5m)

'Charles de Mills'

A most attractive Gallica-type rose with large fragrant purplish-crimson flowers arising on vigorous shoots. A member of the type which has been grown in gardens of the West longer than any other and is still much appreciated. 4¹/₂ft (1.4m)

'Empress Josephine' (syn 'Francofurtana', 'Imperatrice Josephine', 'Souv. de l'Imperatrice Josephine')

A delectable plant with large, bright pink, rather loose flowers composed of petals with dark pink-coloured veins. A well furnished shrub for the border. 3ft (1m)

'Fantin Latour'

This beautiful old rose of the Centifolia group has dark green leaves upon vigorous stems giving rise to large, flat, most fragrant double flowers in an attractive blush-pink colour. 5ft (1.5m)

'Maiden's Blush' (syn 'Cuisse de Nymphe Emue')

The blush-pink at the margin which, together with the grey-green coloured foliage resistant to black spot, make this a charming member of the old-fashioned Alba group. A vigorous and easy plant to grow for the border. 6ft (1.8m)

'Reine Victoria'

A beautiful old rose of the Bourbon group with delicate silky petals forming a full flower. The growth is vigorous and now rather subject to black spot disease in some areas. 5ft (1.5m)

'Madame Hardy'

The most fragrant, pure white double flowers contain concentric rings of abundant petals which easily damage in inclement weather, as do the long ascending shoots typical of the Damask group. Given support, the plant deserves a place in the border provided preventive fungicide is applied to control mildew. 5ft (1.5m)

'Madame Isaac Pereire'

A most vigorous plant which makes a pillar or large bush. The very strong fragrance from the large, purplish-crimson double flowers is much appealing. A beautiful plant belonging to the Bourbon group and well worth border space provided support is given. 8ft (2.4m)

Climbing Roses: 'Climbing Cécile Brunner'

Delectable little buds of light pink arise in trusses on wood made the previous year and adorn the plant during mid-summer; the open double flowers exude a delicate fragrance and make charming table decorations. This vigorous climber with long, strong shoots is ideal for scrambling through an old tree, since little pruning is necessary other than the removal of dead stems and spent wood. 20ft (6m)

'Climbing Cécile Brunner'

'Reine Victoria'

'Madame Hardy'

'Maiden's Blush'

'Fantin Latour'

'Madame Isaac Pereire'

'Compassion' (syn 'Spectacular')

This plant of moderate vigour with abundant basal shoots, gives rise to stems bearing leathery, dark green, leaves and abundant, well formed, most fragrant pink blooms with salmon-orange shading. An ideal plant with which to furnish walls, fences or pillar, requiring little pruning other than the removal of dead and spent wood. 8ft (2.5m)

'Danse du Feu'

The slightly fragrant, most abundant, scarlet flowers mature to purplish-red and appear in clusters on laterals and young vigorous main shoots. Most attractive, disease-resistant, glossy bronze-tinted foliage blends well on a wall or the plant may be trained to a pillar. Prune by removing dead and spent wood. 8ft (2.5m)

'Dublin Bay'

At first bushy, the vigorous upright shoots produce glossy, dark green leaves and slightly fragrant, bright crimson, well-formed flowers in abundance. Little pruning is necessary other than the removal of dead and spent wood. 8ft (2.5m)

'Galway Bay'

Beautiful clusters of salmon-pink, slightly fragrant flowers of good form with healthy, medium green semi-glossy leaves, make this moderately vigorous plant ideal as a feature for a more confined space. Remove spent shoots and old overcrowded wood after flowering. 7ft (2.1m)

'Golden Showers'

A bushy climber with vigorous upright shoots giving rise to most attractive, glossy, deep green leaves rather susceptible to black spot disease. The slightly fragrant, weather-resistant and most abundant semi-double flowers appear in yellow clusters on long stems. Prune by removing dead and overcrowded shoots. 6ft (1.8m)

'Galway Bay'

'Golden Showers'

'Dublin Bay'

'Handel'

'Compassion'

'Danse du Feu'

'Pink Perpetue

'Swan Lake'

'Maigold'

'Parkdirector Riggers'

'Handel'   'Mermaid'

The most attractive fragrant creamy flowers flushed red at the petal margin appear during summer and autumn; the flowers are rain resistant and good for cutting. Rather susceptible to black spot disease, the glossy bronze-green foliage should be sprayed with preventive fungicide to keep it attractive. An excellent plant to train on pillar, fence or wall, and particularly attractive to brighten the wall of an outhouse. 10ft (3m)

'Maigold'

A most vigorous and handsome climber with thorny shoots clad with large healthy glossy leaves. The very fragrant, semi-double, bronzy-yellow flowers appear early in the season on lateral shoots arising from mature wood. A good plant for pillar or wall and may also be grown as a large shrub where space permits. 15ft (4.5m)

'Mermaid'

One of the most vigorous climbers with stiff, somewhat brittle shoots which should be carefully tied to supports to avoid damage. The plant often takes time to establish and is best planted facing a southerly aspect. Large, abundant fragrant flowers are produced on mature wood over a long period, single and at first pale yellow, they open to present their deep yellow stamens to view. Prune by removing dead wood and by tipping back young growth. 20ft (6m)

'Parkdirector Riggers'

A most vigorous climber with long shoots clad with abundant, glossy, dark green leaves and bright crimson, semi-double, slightly fragrant flowers often with a white centre. The weather-resistant flowers appear on lateral shoots arising from mature wood and so little pruning is necessary, other than cutting out dead wood and tipping back spent laterals. Removing the faded blooms will prolong flowering. 12ft (3.5m)

'Pink Perpetue'

This plant, although vigorous, may be confined to a restricted space by training. The stems give rise to attractive glossy leaves, somewhat prone to rust disease, and clusters of abundant, slightly fragrant, rose-pink, long-lasting, double weatherproof flowers. Since flowers are produced on laterals and old wood, little pruning is necessary other than the removal of dead tissue and the shortening of side shoots. A good semi-climber for fence or wall. 7ft (2.1m)

A DIVERSITY OF ROSES

'Swan Lake'

A vigorous climber with beautiful and abundant weather-resistant, large, slightly fragrant, white blooms containing a pinkish centre. The semi-glossy foliage is somewhat prone to attack by mildew and black spot disease and routine spraying with fungicide is necessary. 8ft (2.5m)

Ramblers: 'Albertine'

Vigorous fast-growing rambler with much semi-glossy foliage susceptible to mildew unless prevented by routine fungicide application. Abundant, very fragrant, pink, double flowers appear during summer in clusters on lateral shoots arising from mature wood. An excellent plant to ramble through a tree when little pruning is necessary other than the removal of dead wood and the shortening of lateral shoots to within 3in (7.5cm) of the main framework after flowering. 18ft (5.5m)

'Albéric Barbier'

This vigorous rambler produces abundant shoots giving rise to long pendulous laterals clad with small, glossy, disease-resistant leaves. The attractive, pale yellow fading to warm white, double and most abundant weather-resistant and slightly fragrant flowers arise on lateral shoots during early summer. An adaptable plant which is easy to grow, particularly good to train on a pergola and may be grown as a weeping standard. 25ft (7.5m)

'American Pillar'

A most vigorous rambler giving rise to abundant stems clad with large glossy leaves somewhat prone to mildew. The prolific, weather-resistant, single pink flowers with a white centre appear in clusters during summer, on lateral shoots from mature wood. A good plant for the pergola or other support where growth remains accessible so that flowering stems may be cut back to ground level in autumn. Stems arising from the ground during the current season are then tied in to flower the following year. 20ft (6m)

'Sander's White'

'Dorothy Perkins'

'American Pillar'

'Albertine'

'Alberic Barbier'

'Dorothy Perkins'

Rampant grower with glossy light green foliage susceptible to mildew attack. The double rose-pink flowers appear in abundant clusters during mid-summer. Much used to clamber over the pergola of well-established gardens, the plant may also be planted to form a screen but this must allow for fungicidal application. 15ft (4.5m)

'Sander's White'

Vigorous rambler giving rise to pendulous shoots clad with bright green glossy leaves somewhat prone to mildew. The semi-double, fragrant white flowers appear in large clusters on laterals from mature wood and open to present a yellow centre of abundant stamens. An ideal plant for ground cover or for growing over an archway. 10ft (3m)

Miniatures: 'Angela Rippon' (syn 'Ocaru')

This delectable little plant with its compact growth is ideal for the border or for container growing. The fragrant, pink double flowers are most prolific. Little pruning is necessary other than the removal of dead growth. 1ft (30cm)

'Baby Masquerade'

A vigorous little bushy plant easy to grow and giving rise to abundant clusters of slightly fragrant, semi-double, pale yellow flowers tipped rose-pink, the blooms maturing to light red. Faded blooms should be removed to extend the flowering period. 15in (38cm)

'Starina'

This delightful miniature has abundant, orange-scarlet double flowers with bright yellow on the reverse of the petals. Removal of the faded flowers extends the season until frost occurs during late autumn. An excellent bedding plant which may also be grown in a container. 1ft (30cm)

'Darling Flame' (syn 'Minuetto')

A bushy little plant giving rise to prolific, bright orange, slightly fragrant, double flowers with a golden yellow reverse. The healthy compact dark green and glossy foliage is an added attraction. 1ft (30cm)

'Pour Toi' (syn 'Para Ti', 'For You', 'Wendy')

Beautiful miniature with very dwarf bushy habit and small glossy leaves. The most prolific double flowers are white with a yellow tint at the base. 10in (25cm)

'Easter Morning'

This little plant produces large, weather-resistant, ivory-white double flowers and small glossy leaves. It is ideal for the front of a border or for growing in a container. 1ft (30cm)

Roses for Ground Cover: 'Fairyland'

A most vigorous plant with strong stems clad with glossy leaves. The prolific flowers are of delicate pink shade which fades to creamy white. An excellent plant for ground cover.

'Max Graf'

Vigorous trailing plant good for ground cover with prostrate stems rooting where they make contact with the soil. The fragrant clusters of single pink flowers with a white centre appear during summer.

'Swany'

This ground cover rose produces large, white, double flowers upon arching semi-prostrate growths. The shoots spread laterally to cover approximately 3$\frac{1}{2}$ft (1m).

'Rosy Cushion'

Delectable deep pink flowers arise on abundant arching stems clad with healthy green leaves to give good ground cover. The plant will extend to 3ft (1m) over the surface of the soil.

'Snow Carpet'

An excellent plant for ground cover with prostrate stems. The small white recurrent flowers arise in considerable profusion throughout the summer and autumn.

'Darling Flame'

'Baby Masquerade'

'Canary Bird'

Rosa moyesii

Rosa rubrifolia

oi'

'Angela Rippon'

rina'

'Easter Morning'

Rosa virginiana

'Snow Carpet'

'Complicata'

'Fairyland'

'Max Graf'

'Swany'

'Rosy Cushion'

Wild Roses: 'Canary Bird' (syn *Rosa zanthina spontanea*) N. China, Mongolia, Turkistan.

A vigorous shrub giving rise to abundant shoots clad with medium to light green leaves containing many segments. The canary-yellow, fragrant, single flowers appear most prolifically during early summer on lateral shoots arising from mature wood. The plant is somewhat prone to die-back. 5ft (1.5m)

'Complicata'

A most attractive shrub or semi-climber with large, well-shaped, fragrant, single pink flowers. The vigorous shoots are clad with large light green leaves. 6ft (1.8m)

Rosa rubrifolia (syn *R. glauca*, *R. ferruginea*) Europe.

This most attractive wild rose with interesting glaucous leaves upon almost thornless stems is much used for flower arrangements. The minute flowers give rise to bright red hips. An adaptable plant which will tolerate shade and grows well in light soil. 6ft (1.8m)

Rosa virginiana (syn *R. lucida*) E. North America.

A suckering shrub giving rise to bristly young shoots with sharply toothed leaflets. The bright pink flowers are most attractive and later produce red hips. Bright autumn tints add extra interest to the plant. An excellent plant when grown as a specimen or as a hedge. 5ft (1.5m)

Rosa moyesii, N.W. China.

Vigorous erect shrub with smooth arching shoots and decorative foliage. The bright red flowers produce most attractive, flask-shaped vermilion-red hips. An excellent plant when grown as a specimen. 9ft (2.7m)

Flowering, Foliage and Fruiting Shrubs

Shrubs are permanent plants in the garden and, once they have established themselves, it is unwise to cultivate at all deeply close to them. This is because most kinds make many of their roots close to the surface and if this is dug or forked it is inevitable that many of these roots will be broken and destroyed. Since these are the roots that gather most of the food the plant requires from the soil, the deeper roots being more concerned with anchorage and water supply, their loss will give a serious check to growth.

The Site

It is partly for this reason that cultivation before shrubs are planted should always be thorough. This soil needs to be dug or forked at least 18in (45cm), deep and be well broken up in the process. If animal manure of some kind is available, or even old mushroom bed compost, peat or anything else that will improve the texture of the soil and so help to make it more productive, it is best dug in a few weeks before planting. This will fortify the soil with humus which, though not itself a rich plant food, is a potent soil conditioner that will improve the food-retaining qualities of the soil. The chemicals that shrubs require can be added later as topdressings, which can be hoed or raked in. A balanced compound fertilizer can be used for this purpose, which means that it will have approximately equal quantities of nitrogen, phosphoric acid and potash, the three essential plant foods most likely to be in short supply in the soil. National Growmore is a fertilizer of this kind and it is

Shrubs have many attributes: form, foliage, fruit or flowers. The last is shown especially well by this planting of azaleas at Rosemoor Garden.

quite suitable for shrubs if scattered over the surface at 3 to 4oz per sq yd (100 to 136g per square metre). Spring is a good time to give the dressing and it can be repeated annually.

Most shrubs will grow in all reasonably fertile soils but a few dislike lime in any form. The most important of these are rhododendrons, azaleas and some heathers. If grown in soil containing lime the leaves of lime-hating plants will turn yellow, growth will cease and the plants will eventually die.

Buying and Planting

Shrubs bought at garden centres will mostly be in containers, most probably made of black polythene. This is fine for young plants but, as they get older and larger, they tend to starve in the containers unless they are well fed and watered. So if larger plants are required it may be better to get them from a nursery which grows them in the open ground. Sometimes this is the only way to obtain the less popular shrubs and it is a very satisfactory way provided a few precautions are observed.

First the plants must have been dug up with all, or at any rate most, of their roots intact. The roots must still be moist and pliable when they are replanted and this means that either they must be planted within a few hours of being lifted or that their roots must be protected in some way, maybe by a covering of moist peat or moss wrapped around with polythene or hessian. This is the way they are likely to arrive if obtained by mail order and if they cannot be planted very shortly after delivery the packs should be opened at the top to let the stems breathe but be kept closed around the roots to retain moisture. If there is any doubt about the dampness of the roots, then some water should be poured into the pack.

There is a difference in the method of planting shrubs from containers and those from the open ground. The roots of container plants will all be in a compact mass the shape and size of the containers, so the holes dug to receive them need be only a little bigger than the containers. With open ground plants the roots will look quite different, looser and more spread out, and so the holes made for them will also need to be wider. It is a good plan to put the plant momentarily on the ground where it is to go before actually digging the hole so that it can be seen just how far the roots do stretch.

Because the roots get so matted together inside containers and also because they are usually growing in almost pure peat, they are sometimes reluctant to grow out into the probably very different soil of the garden. It may help to loosen some of the outer roots with the fingers and lead them out into the new soil (though with really tight root balls this can be difficult) and it will certainly help if a mixture of equal parts garden soil and peat is prepared and a little of this is worked around the roots.

Holes for container plants need to be ½ to 1in (13mm to 2.5m) deeper than the container. For open ground plants they need to be deep enough and wide enough to contain all the roots naturally spread out and enable the uppermost to be covered with 2 to 3in (5 to 8 cm) of soil. Usually the nursery soil mark can be seen on the stems of the shrub and it should be planted with this mark ½ to 1in (13mm to 2.5cm) below the surface. Both shallow and deep planting should be avoided.

Soil should be made really firm around the roots, treading it down where necessary, but carefully so as not to bruise or break roots. Finish off with a scattering of loose soil over the surface or, better still, a scattering of peat or pulverised bark which will look tidy and will help to keep the soil moist.

As a rule newly planted shrubs do not need staking but there are exceptions. Some kinds, such as brooms, do not usually have a lot of roots when they come from the nursery and so are easily disturbed or blown out by wind. This can be fatal, so if there is any doubt stake for the first year or so.

Planting Time Bare root plants have a limited planting season, from late October to late March for deciduous (leaf losing) kinds and from late September to November and March until the end of April for evergreens, which are best left alone in mid-winter. Theoretically, container grown plants can be put in at any time since they suffer little or no root disturbance, but in practice spring and autumn are the easiest times and all extremes of heat or cold, wetness or dryness should be avoided.

Most gardeners plant shrubs too closely with the result that, after three or four years, they become overcrowded. If the ultimate width of the shrub is known leave sufficient space for this and do not let any other shrub encroach on it. If the width is not known but the height is (and most books and catalogues

give height though few give width) assume that the ultimate width will be the same as the height. It is not an accurate guide but it is better than none.

Aftercare Newly planted shrubs will take several months to get established and during this initial period they may require watering if the soil shows signs of getting dry.

Routine Maintenance

Established shrubs do not require a great deal of attention. They should be kept clear of weeds and grass, which will rob them of food and moisture and, for reasons already explained, this should be done without disturbing the soil deeply. The surface can be hoed or weeds can be pulled out. Occasional mulches of peat or pulverised bark spread ½ to 1in (13mm to 2.5cm) thick will tend to smother small weeds and make it much easier to hoe all weeds. Another possibility is to use a herbicide but it must be one that will not harm the shrubs. Paraquat, diquat and glyphosate are all suitable if properly applied, which means direct to the leaves of the weeds and not at all to the leaves of the shrubs or other garden plants.

Pruning

Many shrubs live out their lives without any pruning but some can be improved by pruning and it can be necessary if they threaten to grow too big. There are four basic kinds of pruning, cutting back, thinning, renewal pruning and summer pinching. Cutting back means just that and and is useful for some shrubs and climbers that flower late on stems made the same year and also for shrubs grown mainly for the colour of their bark. Four familiar examples are the purple buddleia (*Buddleia davidii* and varieties), *Hydrangea paniculata* and varieties, varieties of *Cornus sanguinea* and the summer-flowering *Clematis jackmanii*. All these can be cut back to within a foot or so of the ground every year, as early as February for the clematis, but left until March or even early April for the others. The result of this hard pruning will be fewer but sturdier young stems which will produce flowers or flower heads, or bark colour in the case of the cornus, of superior quality.

Such pruning applied to early-flowering varieties of clematis or any variety of *Hydrangea macrophylla* (the common ball headed or lace cap hydrangeas) would simply deprive them of all ability to flower, for they either bloom on or from stems made the previous year. So, if they need pruning, it must be a selective thinning out of stems that are overcrowded or are old and weakly. For the hydrangeas and many other shrubs, this can be done most safely and satisfactorily in February or March but for clematis it is best left until June but it is possible to thin at any time of the year and it is always best to get rid of damaged or diseased growth as quickly as possible. Renewal pruning has the same aim as thinning but is done in a more precisely regulated way. Examine a common forsythia in May or a mock orange (*Philadelphus*) in July and you will see, in addition to stems that are carrying the remains of faded flowers, that there are also new stems that have not yet borne any flowers. These young growths will almost certainly flower the following year, especially if they are given plenty of space and relieved of competition. So the old flowering stems can be cut out as far back as the new stems which are preserved at full length. The sooner this is done after flowering the better.

Summer pinching provides a useful method of restricting the growth of many shrubs and climbers. Look at a wisteria or a vine in July and you will see that they are making a great deal of new growth which, if left alone, may well find its way into house gutters or under tiles. This need not be, for every new shoot can be shortened to about five leaves in July and, if that is not enough, can be further cut back to 2in (5cm) in November. Pyracanthas trained against walls can have their young stems shortened in a similar way, taking care not to remove the clusters of green berries in the process. Japanese quinces (*Chaenomeles*) and evergreen ceanothus varieties can be pruned in the same way to keep them tidy. This is a very useful form of pruning with a wide field of application.

Acer palmatum 'Dissectum Atropurpureum'. *Aceraceae*

Typical of the group, the leaves are delicate and this shrub has the advantage of bright leaf colour throughout the summer. It is particularly striking when planted next to *A. palmatum* 'Dissectum'. A very slow-growing shrub suitable for container culture, especially when garden soil is unfavourable. Pruning is not necessary. 15ft (4.5m)

Acer palmatum 'Senkaki', Coral Bark Maple. *Aceraceae*

Slightly more erect than its close relatives, the bright coral stems are much appreciated during winter after the small palmate leaves have fallen. A very attractive feature when its golden autumn leaves carpet the ground below. Pruning is not necessary. 20ft (6m)

Aesculus parviflora (syn *A. macrostachya*) Dwarf Buckeye, S.E. United States. *Hippocastanaceae*

Suckering from below ground produces a neat and graceful broad dome-shaped shrub. The shoots give rise to many cylindrical panicles of white flowers at an unusual period in late summer. Fruit develops only during the warmer summer. The compound palmate leaves produce good autumn colour. Cut out dead wood in winter or early spring. 10ft (3m)

Arctostaphylos uva-ursi (syn *A. officinalis, Uva-ursi Uva-ursi*), Red Bearberry, N. Hemisphere. *Ericaceae*

A low, spreading shrub ideal for ground cover to suppress certain weeds; it makes a graceful drape over dwarf wall or rocks in a sloping bank. Thin out stems when congested. Easily propagated by seed from the ripe berries, or from tip cuttings; stems naturally rooted at the node may be severed and lifted. 1ft (30cm)

Arundinaria viridistriata, Bamboo, Japan. *Gramineae*

This woody grass is a very decorative bamboo, the elegant foliage being striped with yellow. Leaf curl indicates that more shade is necessary, the foliage transpiring moisture faster than can be taken up by the root. Easily propagated by division of the creeping rootstock in May or early autumn. Newly planted canes should be cut back half way the first year, the old canes being removed entirely as new shoots develop. (6ft (2m)

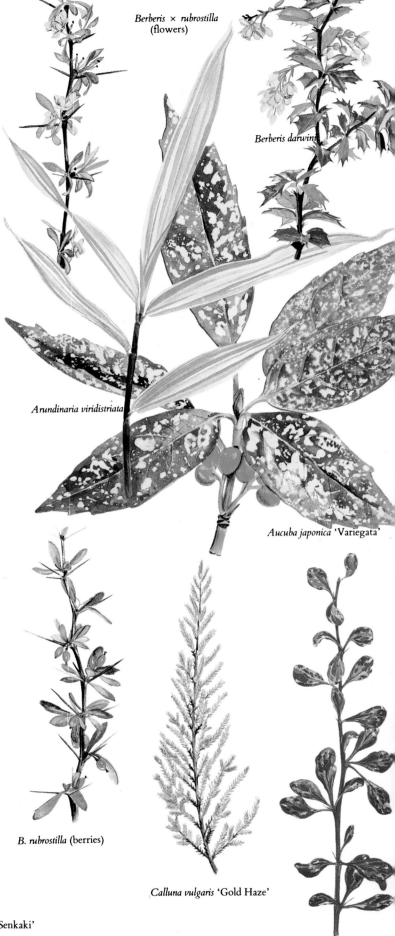

Berberis × rubrostilla (flowers)

Berberis darwinii

Arundinaria viridistriata

Aucuba japonica 'Variegata'

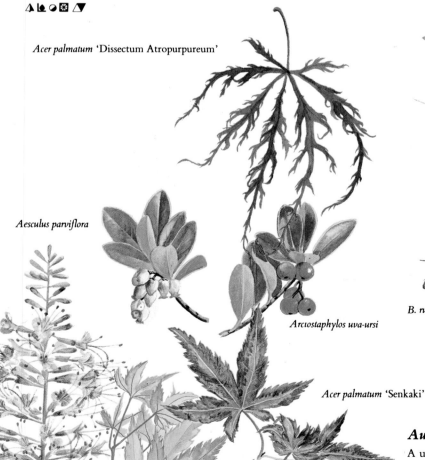

Acer palmatum 'Dissectum Atropurpureum'

Aesculus parviflora

Arctostaphylos uva-ursi

Acer palmatum 'Senkaki'

B. rubrostilla (berries)

Calluna vulgaris 'Gold Haze'

B. t. 'Rose Glow' (young shoot)

Aucuba japonica 'Variegata'. (syn *A.j.* 'Maculata') *Cornaceae*

A unisexual female bushy form producing a dense thicket of erect stems with thick gold-spotted leaves so good for indoor decoration. Competes well with roots of trees and thrives in the shade cast by their canopy, although better for good light. Tolerates air pollution. Easily propagated by stem cuttings which may be grown on in tubs and other containers. Growth can be kept within bounds by pruning in late spring. An adjacent male bush will provide pollen for berry development. 10ft (3m)

Berberis darwinii, Darwin's Barberry, Chile. *Berberidaceae*

One of the finest evergreen shrubs, densely branched with small oblong prickly leaves resembling miniature holly foliage. Dense pendulous clusters of flowers give rise to ornamental fruits attractive to visiting birds. Very easy to grow and can be contained by pruning out old wood in spring which reveals the yellow internal wood. 8ft (2.4m)
△⟐Spring◯Summer◯ ◑ ▣ △▼

Berberis × rubrostilla. *Berberidaceae*

The glaucous, oblanceolate, deciduous leaves are borne on arching, dark red, glabrous shoots with long spines. Much admired for its mass of ovoid, lustrous translucent red fruits suspended by short peduncles. A vigorous grower in fertile soils which may be thinned out and pruned after flowering or in winter after fruiting. 4ft (1.2m)
▲⟐Spring◯Summer◯ ◑ ▣ △▼

Berberis × stenophylla. *Berberidaceae*

Fast-growing shrub with many slender dense interweaving stems. Much admired graceful habit makes this a very popular evergreen subject. Thin out old wood in spring. 6ft (2m)
△⟐Spring◯Summer◯ ◑ ▣ △▼

Berberis thunbergii 'Atropurpurea'. *Berberidaceae*

Stiff, grooved branches with smooth reddish-brown bark form a shrub with a neat close habit eventually 6 to 7ft (2m) tall. The rhomboid-elliptic purple leaves, which colour exceptionally well in autumn, are borne in tufts along the branches and, together with the handsome red fruit, make this a most interesting subject. Ideal as a hedging plant. Prune after flowering unless fruit is required when old wood should be thinned the following spring. 7ft (2.1m)
▲⟐Spring◯Summer◯ ▣ △▼

Berberis thunbergii 'Rose Glow'. *Berberidaceae*

The young purple leaves are mottled silver-pink and bright rose-red, making this a striking plant. Prune after flowers fade. 4ft (1.2m)
▲⟐Spring◯Summer◯ ▣ △▼

Buddleia alternifolia, China. *Loganiaceae*

Distinguished from its relatives by producing lanceolate leaves which are alternately placed along the stem. A graceful pendulous habit similar to the weeping willow but with delicate lilac-coloured fragrant flowers. Much admired as a specimen set in the lawn or planted amongst others in a mixed border. Old spent shoots should be pruned away after flowering. 20ft (6m)
◔⟐Summer◯ ▣ △▼

Buddleia globosa, Chilean Orange Ball Tree, Chile, Peru. *Loganiaceae*

The fragrant, bright yellow flowers resemble small balls and differentiate this shrub from its relatives. Pruning, when necessary, should be carried out immediately after flowering and not in spring as is often the case with other members of the group. 10ft (3m)
◔⟐Summer◯ ▣ △▼

Calluna vulgaris 'Gold Haze' (syn *Erica vulgaris*) Heather, Ling. *Ericaceae*

Developed from wild plants rampant in N. Europe, Asia Minor and Eastern N. America and renowned for the special flavour it gives to honey produced by foraging bees. This plant sustains outstanding bright golden foliage all year round. The previous year's growth cut back by one-third every March does much to encourage the compact shape. Magnificent when planted in a group below a silver birch tree. 1ft (30cm)
△⟐Summer/Autumn◯ ◑ ▣ ▼

Camellia japonica 'Adolphe Audusson', Common Camellia. *Theaceae*

Often incorrectly considered to be tender, this exotic shrub with very attractive, lustrous, tough green leaves is one of the most satisfactory of hardy evergreens, but camellias should, nevertheless, be situated in a position that does not attract early morning sun to prevent the flowers from being damaged by frost. All camellias are inclined to suffer from bud drop caused by dry or waterlogged roots. Excellent when grown in a container provided the roots are kept moist during summer. If necessary, cut back shoots after flowering. 6 to 10ft (2 to 3m)
△⟐Spring ◑ ▣ ▼

Caryopteris × clandonensis 'Kew Blue', *Verbenaceae.*

An outstanding, dwarf rounded bush of compact habit with tubular rich blue flowers. The ovate-lanceolate to lanceolate grey-white leaves are aromatic. Propagated easily by half-ripe cuttings in summer. Prune to within 1 or 2 buds from old wood in spring. Following severe winter weather, new stems arise from below ground to flower the same year. 3ft (1m)
◔⟐Autumn◯ ▣ △▼

Berberis thunbergii 'Rose Glow'

Berberis × stenophylla

Berberis thunbergii 'Atropurpurea'

Buddleia alternifolia

Caryopteris clandonensis 'Kew Blue'

Camellia japonica 'Adolphe Audusson'

Buddleia globosa

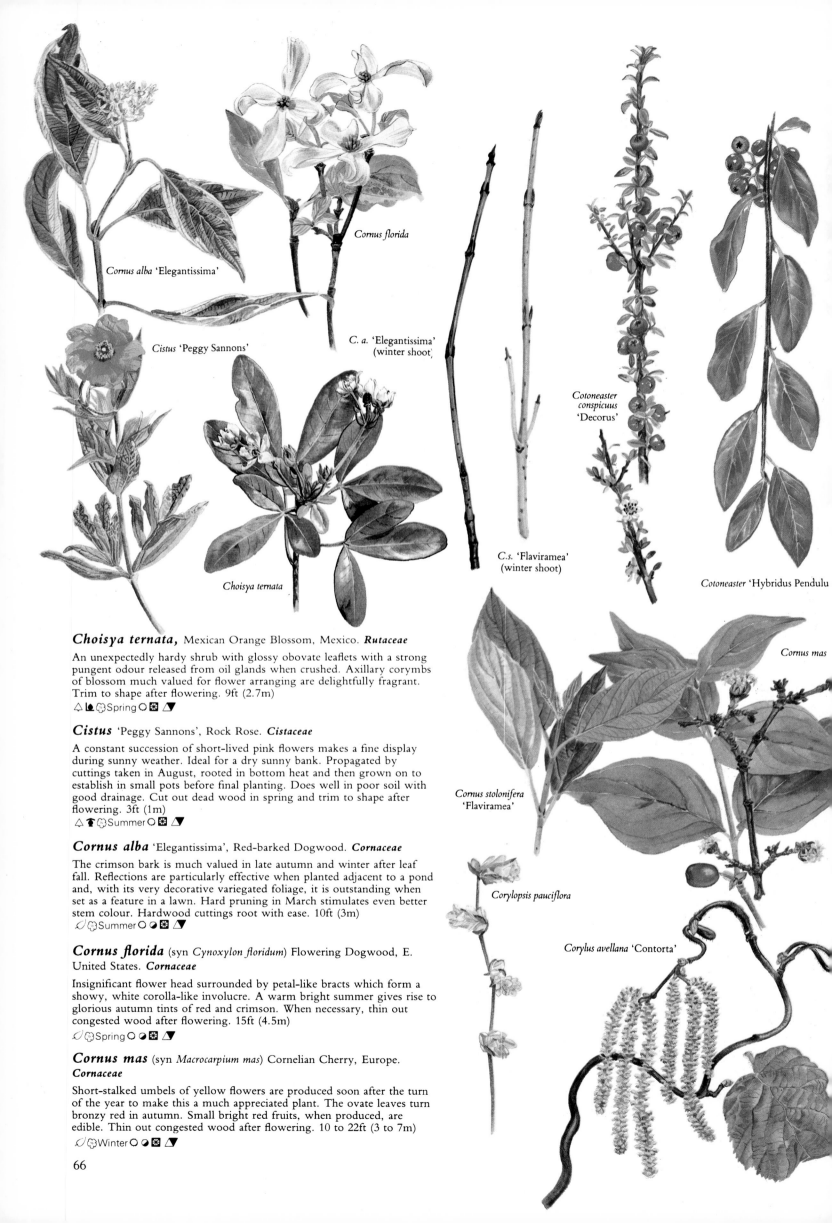

Cornus alba 'Elegantissima'

Cornus florida

Cistus 'Peggy Sannons'

C. a. 'Elegantissima' (winter shoot)

Cotoneaster conspicuus 'Decorus'

C.s. 'Flaviramea' (winter shoot)

Cotoneaster 'Hybridus Pendulu

Choisya ternata

Cornus mas

Cornus stolonifera 'Flaviramea'

Corylopsis pauciflora

Corylus avellana 'Contorta'

Choisya ternata, Mexican Orange Blossom, Mexico. *Rutaceae*

An unexpectedly hardy shrub with glossy obovate leaflets with a strong pungent odour released from oil glands when crushed. Axillary corymbs of blossom much valued for flower arranging are delightfully fragrant. Trim to shape after flowering. 9ft (2.7m)
△ ✿ ❀ Spring ○ ✽ △▼

Cistus 'Peggy Sannons', Rock Rose. *Cistaceae*

A constant succession of short-lived pink flowers makes a fine display during sunny weather. Ideal for a dry sunny bank. Propagated by cuttings taken in August, rooted in bottom heat and then grown on to establish in small pots before final planting. Does well in poor soil with good drainage. Cut out dead wood in spring and trim to shape after flowering. 3ft (1m)
△ ✿ ❀ Summer ○ ✽ △▼

Cornus alba 'Elegantissima', Red-barked Dogwood. *Cornaceae*

The crimson bark is much valued in late autumn and winter after leaf fall. Reflections are particularly effective when planted adjacent to a pond and, with its very decorative variegated foliage, it is outstanding when set as a feature in a lawn. Hard pruning in March stimulates even better stem colour. Hardwood cuttings root with ease. 10ft (3m)
◑ ❀ Summer ○ ◕ ✽ △▼

Cornus florida (syn *Cynoxylon floridum*) Flowering Dogwood, E. United States. *Cornaceae*

Insignificant flower head surrounded by petal-like bracts which form a showy, white corolla-like involucre. A warm bright summer gives rise to glorious autumn tints of red and crimson. When necessary, thin out congested wood after flowering. 15ft (4.5m)
◑ ❀ Spring ○ ◕ ✽ △▼

Cornus mas (syn *Macrocarpium mas*) Cornelian Cherry, Europe. *Cornaceae*

Short-stalked umbels of yellow flowers are produced soon after the turn of the year to make this a much appreciated plant. The ovate leaves turn bronzy red in autumn. Small bright red fruits, when produced, are edible. Thin out congested wood after flowering. 10 to 22ft (3 to 7m)
◑ ❀ Winter ○ ◕ ✽ △▼

Cotinus coggygria
'Royal Purple'

Cotoneaster
'Cornubia'

Cotoneaster horizontalis

Cornus stolonifera 'Flaviramea', Yellow-stemmed Dogwood. *Cornaceae*

Rampant underground stems send up many yellow suckers most attractive for winter display. Outstanding feature when planted alongside red-stemmed dogwood. Cut back hard during late spring. 7ft (2.1m)
⊘☼Spring○◐✲△▼

Corylopsis pauciflora, Japan. *Hamamelidaceae*

A charming little densely branched shrub with racemes of fragrant, primrose-yellow flowers much appreciated at a sparse time before the young pink-tinged broadly ovate, cordate leaves appear. Cut back after flowering to keep within bounds. Layering is the easiest method of propagation. 5ft (1.5m)
⊘🌢☼Spring○◐✲▼

Corylus avellana 'Contorta', Corkscrew Hazel. *Corylaceae*

Unusual curled and twisted growth forming a dense slow-growing thicket which is better for thinning every 4 years. The yellow catkins are prolific and most decorative in winter. 6ft (2m)
⊘☼Winter◐✲△▼

Cotinus coggygria 'Royal Purple', Smoke Tree. *Anacardiaceae*

Panicles of small flowers have a striking effect against the maroon-red backdrop of the glabrous orbicular or obovate leaves. The panicles turn smoky grey in autumn when the foliage is a spectacular blazing red. Prune to shape during the winter. 6 to 10ft (2 to 3m)
⊘☼Summer○✲△▼

Cotoneaster conspicuus 'Decorus'. *Rosaceae*

A ground-hugging shrub gracefully arched with prostrate branches forming a dense mat useful for weed suppression and attractive on a rock garden or growing amongst heather. Shining scarlet berries are complemented by the dark green leaves. Cut out upward-growing shoots. 2¹/₂ft (75cm)
△☼Summer☾Winter○✲△▼

Cotoneaster 'Cornubia'. *Rosaceae*

A very vigorous semi-evergreen leafy shrub supporting heavy pendulous masses of bright red fruit attractive to birds which make an interesting spectacle during autumn. Thin congested growth after flowering. 19ft (6m)
▲☼Summer☾Autumn○✲△▼

Cotoneaster horizontalis (syn *C. davidiana*) Fishbone Cotoneaster, China. *Rosaceae*

The interesting opposite branching and flat habit make this shrub ideal for growing without support against a wall, which may be north facing. The abundant oval leaves turn various shades of orange and red during autumn, younger leaves remaining green. The turn of the year brings leafless branches curiously similar to fish bones. Cut back straggly growth in winter. Easily propagated by cuttings. 10ft (3m) on wall; 2 to 3ft (60cm to 1m) free growing.
⊘☼Summer☾Autumn○✲△▼

Cotoneaster 'Hybridus Pendulus'. *Rosaceae*

A vigorous evergreen, glossy leaved ground-cover plant spreading at least 3ft (1m) each year to a maximum of 13ft (4m). Abundant fruit ripens brilliant red in autumn. Very adaptable and can be trained on a main stem to form a small weeping tree if required. Thin out congested growth in winter. 2ft (60cm)
△☼Summer☾Autumn○◐✲△▼

Cytisus battandieri, Moroccan Broom, N.W. Africa. *Leguminosae*

An outstanding vigorous shrub to clad a sunny wall. The large trifoliate silvery-green leaves are displayed on rather erect branches. Plump, cylindrical, vertical racemes of pineapple-scented flowers arise from lateral branchlets to make this one of the choicest of specimens. Pubescent pods contain seeds which germinate readily. Prune spent and spindly wood after flowering. 10ft (3m)
⊘☼Summer☾Autumn○✲△▼

Cytisus × praecox, Warminster Broom. *Leguminosae*

A bushy, deciduous shrub producing pendent shoots at first erect giving rise to most attractive long-lasting abundant axillary flowers with a somewhat unpleasant odour. Cut back to new growth after flowering but avoid cutting into bare old wood. Freely germinating seeds do not grow true to type although cuttings taken in August are reliable. 3 to 6ft (1 to 2m)
⊘☼Spring○✲△▼

Daboecia cantabrica 'Atropurpurea', St Dabeoc's Heath. *Ericaceae*

One of the best evergreen shrubs valued for its long period of rich red-purple flowers in terminal racemes. The underside of the dark glossy green, alternate, ovate oblong leaves is covered with white wool. Trim over plants in early spring removing old flower stalks and one-third of previous season's growth to promote compact habit and enhanced flowering. Propagation by cuttings easy. 2ft (60cm)
△☼Summer○◐✲▼

Daboecia cantabrica 'Atropurpurea'

Cytisus × praecox

Cytisus battandieri

67

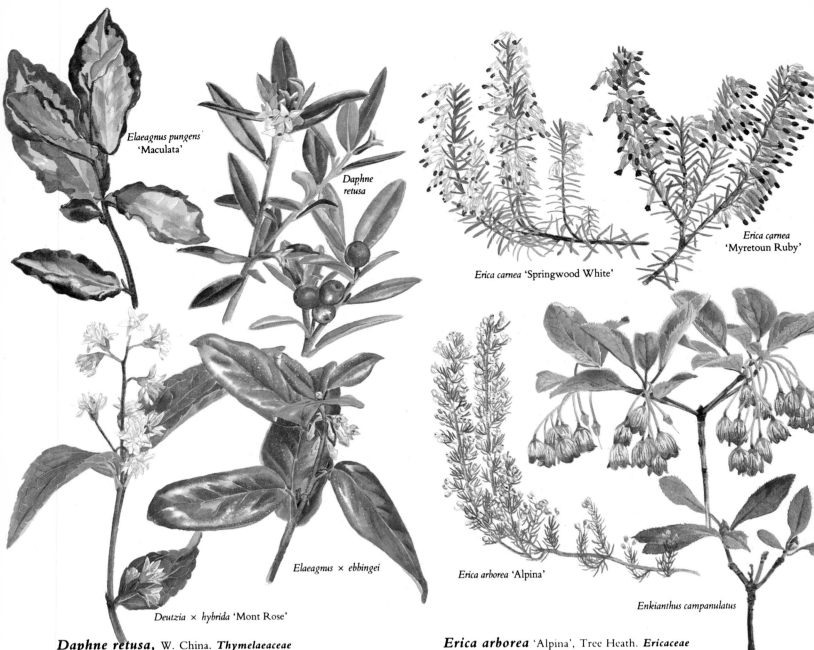

Elaeagnus pungens 'Maculata'

Daphne retusa

Erica carnea 'Springwood White'

Erica carnea 'Myretoun Ruby'

Deutzia × hybrida 'Mont Rose'

Elaeagnus × ebbingei

Erica arborea 'Alpina'

Enkianthus campanulatus

Daphne retusa, W. China. *Thymelaeaceae*

This slow-growing evergreen shrub produces stiff branches which give it
a rounded habit. The glabrous, obovate-oblong, dark green leaves
provide a foil to the terminal clusters of fragrant, pale rose-pink flowers
which are followed by red berries. No pruning required. 3ft (1m)
△ ✿Summer ✿Autumn ○ ◐ ✕ △▼

Deutzia × hybrida 'Mont Rose'. *Philadelphaceae*

A most beautiful shrub with many pink flowers on shoots made the
previous year. Pruning when required to thin out old spent wood should
be done as soon as flowers have faded by cutting exhausted stems at
ground level. 6ft (2m)
✿ ✿Summer ○ ◐ ✕ △▼

Elaeagnus × ebbingei. *Elaeagnaceae*

A broad, upright vigorous shrub with large leathery leaves producing
fragrant flowers on old wood. An excellent choice for screening as well
as for a specimen plant. Tolerates maritime situation. Thin out congested
wood and trim back in spring. 10ft (3m)
△ ✿Autumn ✿Winter ○ ◐ ✕ △▼

Elaeagnus pungens 'Maculata'. *Elaeagnaceae*

The oval or oblong evergreen leathery leaves are variegated with a broad
yellow patch covering the midrib and dotted with brownish scales, as are
the young stems. An outstanding shrub for year-round interest,
particularly in winter with its golden glow. Stems producing non-
variegated leaves should be removed. Thin congested growth and trim in
spring. 9ft (2.7m)
△ ○ ◐ ✕ △▼

Enkianthus campanulatus (syn *Andromeda campanulata*) Japan. *Ericaceae*

A deciduous free-flowering erect-branched shrub giving rise to reddish
young shoots. The leaves turn brilliant red and gold during autumn.
Long-lasting cup-shaped flowers are much appreciated for indoor
decoration. Thin congested growth after flowering. 6ft (2m)
✿ ✿Spring ○ ◐ ✕ ▼

Erica arborea 'Alpina', Tree Heath. *Ericaceae*

This vivid green shrub is sturdy with erect stems, the immature wood
has a mossy appearance due to many small, branched hairs. Fragrant
flowers make it a valuable plant for the heather garden. Trim over after
flowering to remove two-thirds of the previous year's growth. 4¹/₂ft
(1.4m)
△ ✿ ✿ ✿Spring ○ ◐ ✕ △▼

Erica carnea 'Myretoun Ruby', Heath. *Ericaceae*

One of the most attractive evergreen plants in this very large group
displaying clusters of bell-shaped carmine to ruby-red flowers during
winter and spring. Will tolerate alkaline soil and best grown in a group
for massed effect to give good ground cover and weed suppression.
Over-fertile soil will encourage lanky growth which can be made more
attractive by clipping over when the flowers have faded. 1ft (30cm)
△ ✿Winter ○ ◐ ✕ △▼

Erica carnea 'Springwood White', Heath. *Ericaceae*

Dwarf, semi-prostrate vigorous shrub with dense trailing habit;
undoubtedly the best white winter heath. Propagate by division, layering
or by cuttings taken in early August. Trim by removing two-thirds of
the previous year's growth after flowering. 1ft (30cm)
△ ✿Winter ○ ◐ ✕ △▼

Euonymus fortunei 'Silver Queen'. *Celastraceae*

A comparatively slow-growing shrub with cream-variegated leaves
producing rosy tints during winter. This adult form will slowly climb
and produces flowers and fruit on occasion. Thin out congested growth
in April. 6ft (2m)
△ ○ ◐ ✕ △▼

Euonymus japonicus 'Emerald n' Gold'. *Celastraceae*

Golden-variegated polished leaves make this dense shrub most attractive.
Useful for area subject to air pollution and tolerant of salt air. Shoots
giving rise to leaves without the golden variegation should be removed.
Thin congested growth in April. 4ft (1.2m)
△ ○ ◐ ✕ △▼

Exochorda racemosa (syn. *E. grandiflora*), China. *Rosaceae*

A spreading bush of great beauty with arching branches covered with many racemes of dazzling white flowers. Very attractive as a specimen or grouped with other plants. Thin congested growth after flowering. 10ft (3m)

⟋ ⬆☸Summer↻Autumn ○ ⊞ ◿

Fatsia japonica (syn *Aralia japonica, A. sieboldii*) Japan. *Araliaceae*

The thick stems form a handsome spreading bush with interesting, very large, palmate, glossy leaves eventually falling away to leave scars. Globose heads forming large panicles of white flowers give rise to black fruits. An attractive exotic-looking plant for a large container that will tolerate maritime air. Cut back straggly growth to the ground in April. 10ft (3m)

△☸Winter↻Summer ◖⊞ ◿

Forsythia 'Lynwood'. *Oleaceae*

A very adaptable shrub much in evidence during early spring in suburban gardens. One of the most spectacular of the group, the yellow flowers are borne on wood made during the previous year. Branches are erect and useful for cutting in tight bud for indoor decoration. Any thinning necessary should be carried out immediately after flowering by cutting back to old wood. 6ft (2m)

⟋☸Spring ○ ◖⊞ ◿

Forsythia suspensa 'Sieboldii', Golden Bell. *Oleaceae*

Slender pendent branches ideal for covering arbours, walls and steep banks form a mass of interlacing growth clad with flowers of great beauty. The shoots often root at the tip on contact with soil. Cut back spent shoots to 2 buds after flowering. 10ft (3m)

⟋☸Spring ○ ◖⊞ ◿

Fothergilla major (syn *F. alnifolia major*) Eastern N. America. *Hamamelidaceae*

The beautiful fragrant nude flowers composed of numerous long stamens give much pleasure before the leaves appear in spring. Young stems clothed in stellate hairs form branches making a charming, slow-growing, rounded deciduous bush with roundish-oval or broadly-ovate glossy-green leaves turning spectacular tints in autumn before leaf fall. Remove straggly shoots after flowering. Seed germination is slow often taking up to 2 years, plants can be increased by layering or by heeled cuttings in July with bottom heat. 8ft (2.4m)

⟋☸Spring ○ ● ⊞ ◿

Fremontodendron 'California Glory' (syn *Fremontia californica*). *Sterculiaceae*

An interesting large semi-evergreen shrub producing showy flowers which have no petals; the colourful calyx is at first cup shaped with down on the outside and hairy within the centre. Traditionally given the protection of a wall, the plant enjoys an open sheltered position, dislikes root disturbance and is best grown on in a container until planted in its final position. Remove dead wood in spring. 30ft (9m)

△☸Spring ○ ● ⊞ ◿

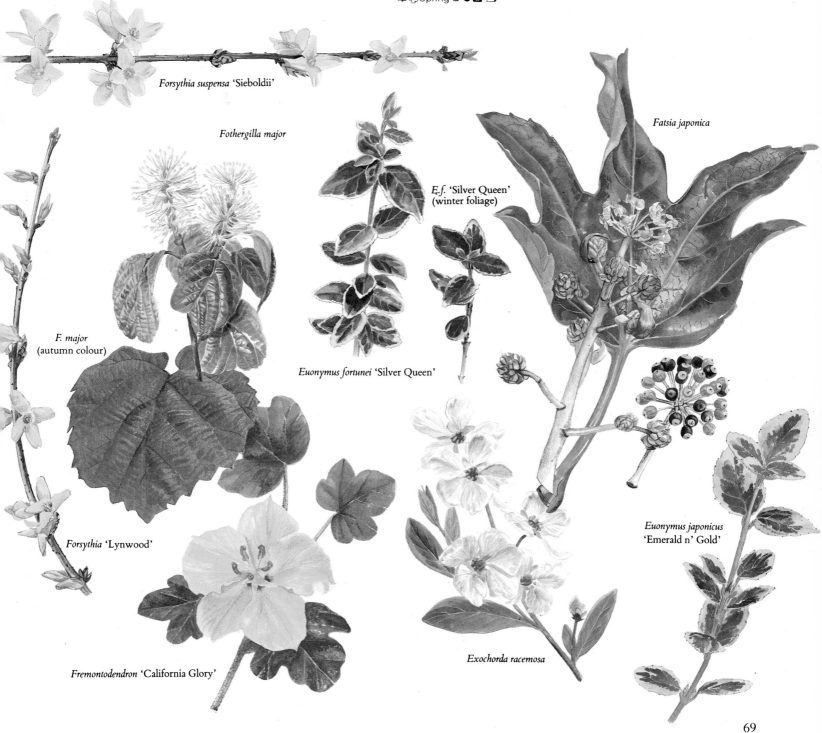

Forsythia suspensa 'Sieboldii'

Fothergilla major

E.f. 'Silver Queen' (winter foliage)

Fatsia japonica

F. major (autumn colour)

Euonymus fortunei 'Silver Queen'

Forsythia 'Lynwood'

Fremontodendron 'California Glory'

Exochorda racemosa

Euonymus japonicus 'Emerald n' Gold'

Fuchsia 'Mrs Popple'. *Onagraceae*

A favourite amongst so many hardy fuchsias displaying large flowers with carmine sepals and deep violet corolla over a very long period. The stems arising from soil level each spring form an arching bushy habit. Cut back old stems to ground level in spring. Propagation is by rootstock division or stem cuttings. 2¹/₂ft (75cm)
⊘❀Summer○⦿✵△▼

Fuchsia 'Riccartonii'. *Onagraceae*

The green ovate-lanceolate leaves have a purplish tinge and arise from vigorous straight stems which produce abundant flowers over a long period. Probably the hardiest of species in the genus. Makes a good hedge plant in addition to the more usual border specimen. Cut back damaged and dead growth in spring. 6ft (2m)
⊘❀Summer○⦿✵△▼

Gaultheria procumbens, Checkerberry, Creeping Wintergreen, Eastern N. America. *Ericaceae*

A vigorous shrub spreading by rooted offsets and useful for ground cover and to plant below sparsely branched subjects. The thick glossy obovate or oval leaves are aromatic and turn red during autumn. Pruning is not required. 2¹/₂ft (75cm)
△⬆⬆❀Summer◯Autumn⦿●✵▼

Genista aethnensis (syn *Spartium aethnense*) Mount Etna Broom, Sardinia, Sicily. *Leguminosae*

A beautiful shrub in summer with slender bright green drooping branches almost devoid of leaves and furnished with the golden-yellow flowers. Most suitable to plant at the rear of a border without overshadowing smaller plants. Cut back spent flower stems but not into old wood. 15ft (4.5m)
⊘❀Summer○✵▼

Fuchsia 'Mrs Popple'

Fuchsia 'Riccartonii'

Gaultheria procumbens |

Hamamelis × intermedia 'Jelena'

Genista aethnensis

Genista tinctoria 'Royal Gold'

Genista lydia

Genista tinctoria 'Royal Gold', Dyer's Greenwood. *Leguminosae*

Low-growing, spreading shrub suitable for the rock garden, front of a border or the top of a dry wall where its dark green linear-lanceolate leaves and dense racemes of rich yellow flowers will be displayed to their full effect. Cut back spent flower stems but not into old wood. 3ft (1m)
⊘❀Summer○⦿✵△▼

Genista lydia (syn *G. spathulata*) Europe, Syria. *Leguminosae*

The sub-terminal racemes of bright yellow flowers make a beautiful display and the interest is prolonged by wiry, grey-green arching stems. An ideal plant for the border and to add informality to a patio. Cut back spent flower stems but not into old wood. Cuttings taken in August will produce new plants. 2ft (60cm)
⊘❀Summer○✵▼

Hamamelis × intermedia 'Jelena', Witch Hazel. *Hamamelidaceae*

A beautiful, vigorous, spreading shrub with large, scented unusual flowers in dense clusters, the strap-like bi-coloured twisted petals appearing without damage during frost. Most striking autumn tints of orange-red and scarlet. Planted to the fore of a dark evergreen within view of a window, the plant can be admired during the most inclement weather. The sprigs may be cut in bud to open indoors. Remove damaged or badly placed branches in spring. 6ft (2m)
⊘❀Winter⦿✵▼

Hamamelis mollis 'Pallida', Chinese Witch Hazel. *Hamamelidaceae*

The stout zig-zag branches produce abundant clusters of pale yellow, very fragrant flowers before the roundish or broad-obovate leaves on wood made the previous year. Foliage turns a pleasing yellow in autumn. Certainly one of the best witch hazels in cultivation. Remove damaged or badly placed branches in spring. 10ft (3m)
⊘❀Winter⦿✵▼

Hebe armstrongii (syn *Veronica armstrongii*) New Zealand. ***Scrophulariaceae***

A small evergreen shrub giving rise to slender shoots adorned by small closely overlapping leaves producing a peculiar whipcord effect. The plant is easy to grow and propagation is by cuttings in late summer. Trim to shape in April. 3ft (1m)

△ ❀ Summer ○ ◑ ▦ ◿

Hebe 'Autumn Glory'. ***Scrophulariaceae***

The erect and rather sparse branches are clad with glossy, green-purple broadly elliptic leaves. The abundant, short, dense racemes of violet flowers continue over a long period. Planted in a group, the small shrubs give a most pleasing effect especially in autumn. Trim to shape in April. 1½ft (45cm)

△ ❀ Summer ○ ◑ ▦ ◿

Hebe pinguifolia 'Pagei'. ***Scrophulariaceae***

A very useful evergreen plant for ground cover or as a specimen in the rock garden. The stems are erect at first and then prostrate giving rise to obovate, glaucous blue-grey leaves. Trim to shape after flowering. 1ft (30cm)

△ ❀ Late Spring/Summer ○ ◑ ▦ ◿

Hebe salicifolia (syn *Veronica salicifolia*) New Zealand. ***Scrophulariaceae***

A vigorous, evergreen, freely branched dense shrub with roundish, smooth branchlets giving rise to pale green and smooth, lanceolate or oblong lanceolate leaves. The small flowers are tightly packed in slender cylindrical racemes up to 10in (25cm) long. Regrowth from the base and rootstock is usual after an abnormally severe winter when numerous variable seedlings develop after vernalization. Useful plant for maritime situation. Thin congested growth in spring. 10ft (3m)

△ ❀ Summer ○ ◑ ▦ ◿

Helichrysum serotinum (syn. *H. angustifolium*), Curry Plant, S. Europe. ***Compositae***

Small, dense shrub with narrow silver-grey foliage which has a rather pungent curry-like smell. The small yellow daisy-like flowers are carried in clusters in summer. No pruning required. Can be increased by summer cuttings rooted in a propagator. 1½ft (45cm)

△ ▙ ❀ Summer ○ ◑ ▦ ◿

Helianthemum nummularium 'Red Dragon', Sun Rose. ***Cistaceae***

A fast-growing, spreading, semi-shrubby evergreen plant good for ground cover, raised beds and dwarf walls. The green oblong leaves have a pleasing texture and flowers, although individually short lived, are showy and appear in succession to give a bright display. Straggly plants may be cut back after flowering. 1ft (30cm)

△ ❀ Summer ○ ▦ ◿

Helianthemum nummularium 'Wisley Primrose', Sun Rose, Rock Rose. Europe. ***Cistaceae***

A very attractive hybrid member of this wide range of plants. Easily propagated by stem cuttings devoid of flower buds in summer. Cut back straggly growth in spring. 1ft (30cm)

△ ❀ Summer ○ ▦ ◿

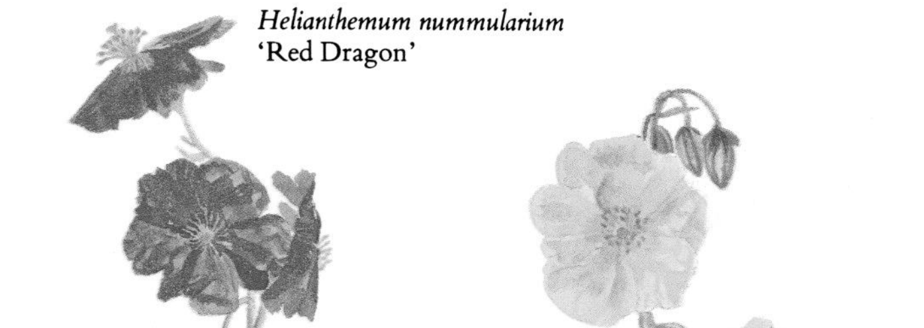
Helianthemum nummularium
'Red Dragon'

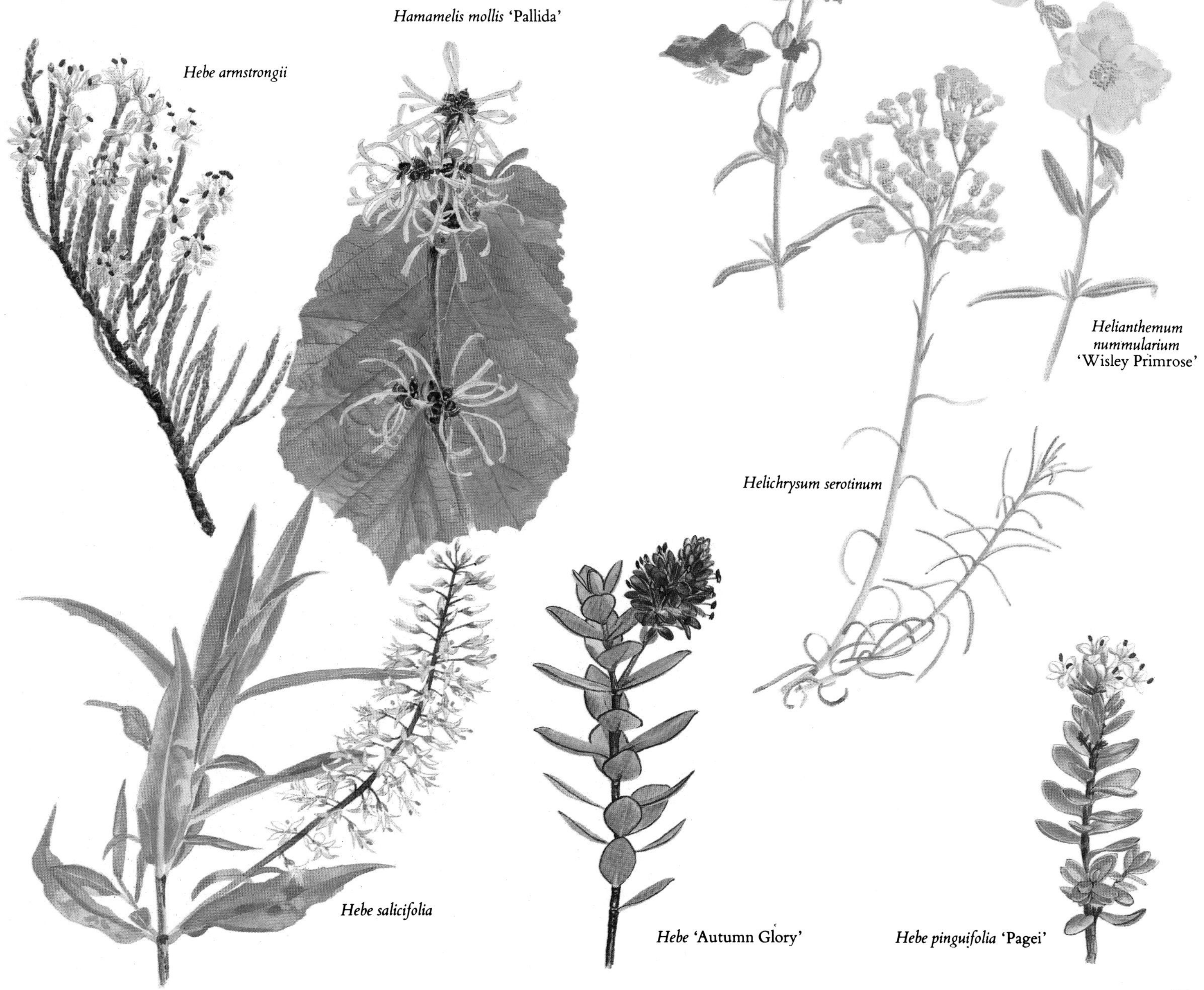
Hamamelis mollis 'Pallida'
Hebe armstrongii
Helianthemum nummularium
'Wisley Primrose'
Helichrysum serotinum
Hebe salicifolia
Hebe 'Autumn Glory'
Hebe pinguifolia 'Pagei'

Hibiscus syriacus 'Blue Bird'. *Malvaceae*

An erect deciduous shrub with bushy habit and smooth, fresh green, ovate leaves. A pleasing shrub with large solitary saucer-shaped flowers. Propagation is by cuttings or layering. Pruning is hardly necessary unless growth becomes straggly when it may be cut in spring. 6ft (2m)

🌣 ☝ 🌼 Summer ○ ❊ ◿

Hibiscus syriacus 'Woodbridge'. *Malvaceae*

The best red-flowered plant in this wide selection of much-liked plants. This one is well worth growing for the large single flowers. Cut back straggly growth in spring. 6ft (2m)

🌣 ☝ 🌼 Summer ○ ◑ ❊ ◿

Hippophae rhamnoides, Sea Buckthorn, Europe, Temperate Asia. *Elaeagnaceae*

A most striking deciduous shrub for winter effect with abundant bright orange-yellow berries produced by the female provided a male plant is grown alongside to give pollen. Birds are not attracted to the fruits which contain extremely acid yellow juice. Very good in maritime districts where it may be used as a hedge plant. Thin congested growth and trim in winter. Propagated by seed which produces both sexes or by layering. 13ft (4m)

🌣 🍂 Autumn ○ ❊ ◿

Hydrangea macrophylla 'Madame Emile Mouilliere', Hortensia Common Hydrangea. *Hydrangeaceae*

A rounded deciduous shrub with stout glabrous shoots giving rise to large, broadly ovate or oval, short-pointed, coarsely toothed leaves. The sterile flowers are displayed in a large mop-headed corymb most attractive when fresh and much used for flower arrangement when faded. Alkaline soil gives rise to chlorosis causing yellow leaves and can be corrected by the use of sequestered iron. Flower heads should persist through winter to protect buds below then be carefully removed in spring avoiding damage to the developing buds. Thin out growth in April if necessary. New plants are propagated by cuttings of non-flowering shoots in summer. 6ft (2m)

🌣 🌼 Summer ○ ◑ ❊ ▼

Hibiscus syriacus 'Woodbridge'

Hibiscus syriacus 'Blue Bird'

Hippophae rhamnoides

Hydrangea macrophylla 'Madame Emile Mouilliere'

Hydrangea paniculata 'Grandiflora'

Hydrangea macrophylla 'Bluewave'

Hypericum × *inodorum* 'Summergold'

Hydrangea macrophylla 'Bluewave', Lacecap Hydrangea. *Hydrangeaceae*

The large flat corymbs of blue fertile flowers are surrounded by sterile, coloured ray florets. Pink flowers are produced under certain soil conditions which can be amended by applications of aluminium sulphate to encourage blue flowers. Spent flowers can be carefully cut away in autumn. Thin out growth in April if necessary. 4$^{1}/_{2}$ft (1.4m)

🌣 🌼 Summer ○ ◑ ❊ ▼

Hydrangea paniculata 'Grandiflora'. *Hydrangeaceae*

A broad, deciduous shrub with semi-arching branches giving rise to oval or ovate leaves and mostly sterile flowers in large, closely packed pyramids of blossom first white then purplish-pink before fading to brown, when they are used for indoor decoration. Reduce length of shoots by pruning in late winter to encourage large flowers. 12ft (3.7m)

🌣 🌼 Summer ○ ◑ ❊ ▼

Hypericum 'Hidcote'. *Guttiferae*

A semi-evergreen, compact shrub with ovate-lanceolate leaves and saucer-shaped flowers larger than any other in the group and produced over a very long period. A most satisfying plant to grow as a specimen in the border. Thin out congested growth in April. 4$^{1}/_{2}$ft (1.4m)

▲ 🌼 Summer ○ ◑ ❊ ◿

Hypericum × *inodorum* 'Summergold'. *Guttiferae.*

Deciduous shrub with striking leaves which are acid-yellow in spring and early summer and then gradually turn green. Small yellow flowers produced in terminal cymes are followed by black fruits. Cut back to within a few buds from the old wood in early spring. 3ft (1m)

🌣 🌼 Summer 🍂 Autumn ○ ◑ ❊ ◿

Ilex × *altaclarensis* 'Golden King', Holly. *Aquifoliaceae*

Despite the name, this plant is female and will produce bright berried fruit provided a male plant is adjacent to release wind-borne pollen. One of the best of a very large group, the broad almost spineless leaves have a bright golden margin. Will tolerate polluted air and a maritime location. Trim to shape in April. 6ft (2m)

△ 🍃 🌼 Spring 🍂 Winter ○ ◑ ● ❊ ◿

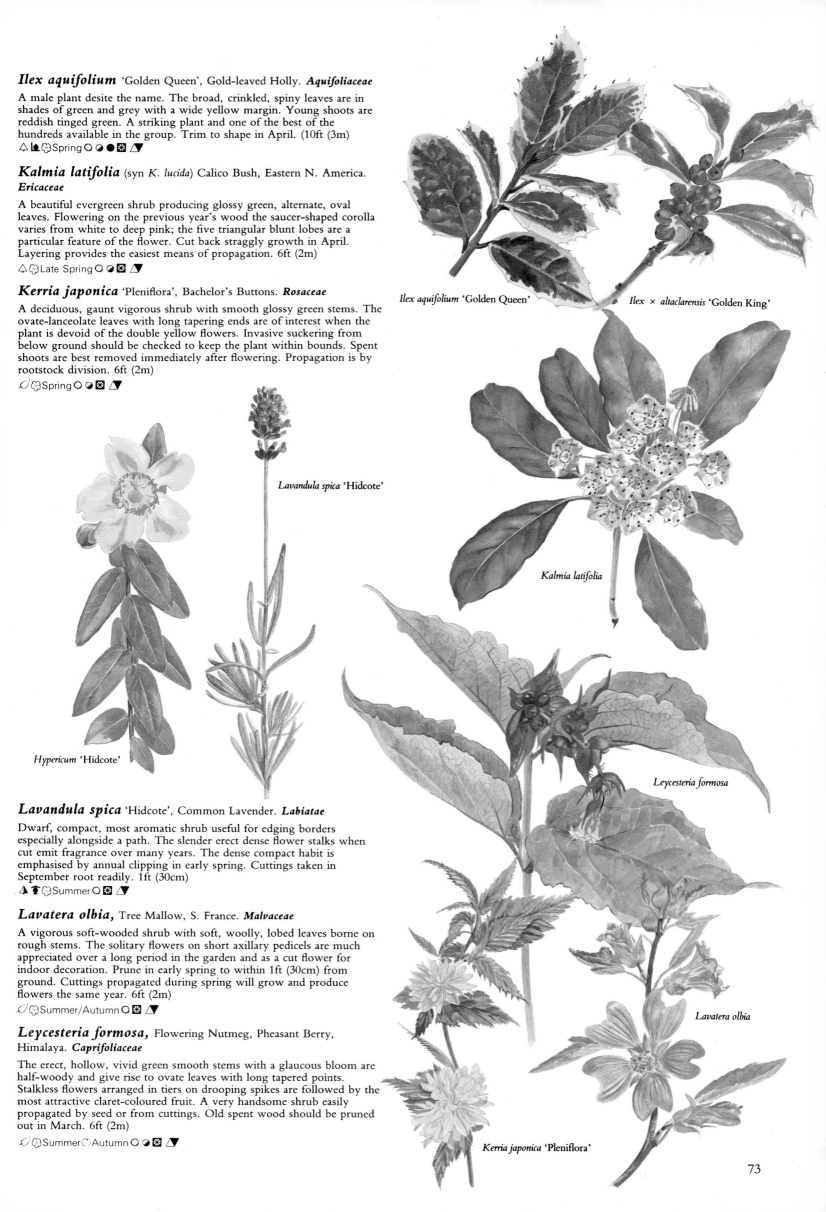

Ilex aquifolium 'Golden Queen', Gold-leaved Holly. *Aquifoliaceae*

A male plant desite the name. The broad, crinkled, spiny leaves are in shades of green and grey with a wide yellow margin. Young shoots are reddish tinged green. A striking plant and one of the best of the hundreds available in the group. Trim to shape in April. (10ft (3m)
△ ⚕ ✿Spring ○ ◐ ● ▨ △▼

Kalmia latifolia (syn *K. lucida*) Calico Bush, Eastern N. America. *Ericaceae*

A beautiful evergreen shrub producing glossy green, alternate, oval leaves. Flowering on the previous year's wood the saucer-shaped corolla varies from white to deep pink; the five triangular blunt lobes are a particular feature of the flower. Cut back straggly growth in April. Layering provides the easiest means of propagation. 6ft (2m)
△ ✿Late Spring ○ ◐ ▨ △▼

Kerria japonica 'Pleniflora', Bachelor's Buttons. *Rosaceae*

A deciduous, gaunt vigorous shrub with smooth glossy green stems. The ovate-lanceolate leaves with long tapering ends are of interest when the plant is devoid of the double yellow flowers. Invasive suckering from below ground should be checked to keep the plant within bounds. Spent shoots are best removed immediately after flowering. Propagation is by rootstock division. 6ft (2m)
⟋ ✿Spring ○ ◐ ▨ △▼

Lavandula spica 'Hidcote', Common Lavender. *Labiatae*

Dwarf, compact, most aromatic shrub useful for edging borders especially alongside a path. The slender erect dense flower stalks when cut emit fragrance over many years. The dense compact habit is emphasised by annual clipping in early spring. Cuttings taken in September root readily. 1ft (30cm)
▲ ⚑ ✿Summer ○ ▨ △▼

Lavatera olbia, Tree Mallow, S. France. *Malvaceae*

A vigorous soft-wooded shrub with soft, woolly, lobed leaves borne on rough stems. The solitary flowers on short axillary pedicels are much appreciated over a long period in the garden and as a cut flower for indoor decoration. Prune in early spring to within 1ft (30cm) from ground. Cuttings propagated during spring will grow and produce flowers the same year. 6ft (2m)
⟋ ✿Summer/Autumn ○ ▨ △▼

Leycesteria formosa, Flowering Nutmeg, Pheasant Berry, Himalaya. *Caprifoliaceae*

The erect, hollow, vivid green smooth stems with a glaucous bloom are half-woody and give rise to ovate leaves with long tapered points. Stalkless flowers arranged in tiers on drooping spikes are followed by the most attractive claret-coloured fruit. A very handsome shrub easily propagated by seed or from cuttings. Old spent wood should be pruned out in March. 6ft (2m)
⟋ ✿Summer/Autumn ○ ◐ ▨ △▼

Ilex aquifolium 'Golden Queen'

Ilex × altaclarensis 'Golden King'

Lavandula spica 'Hidcote'

Hypericum 'Hidcote'

Kalmia latifolia

Leycesteria formosa

Lavatera olbia

Kerria japonica 'Pleniflora'

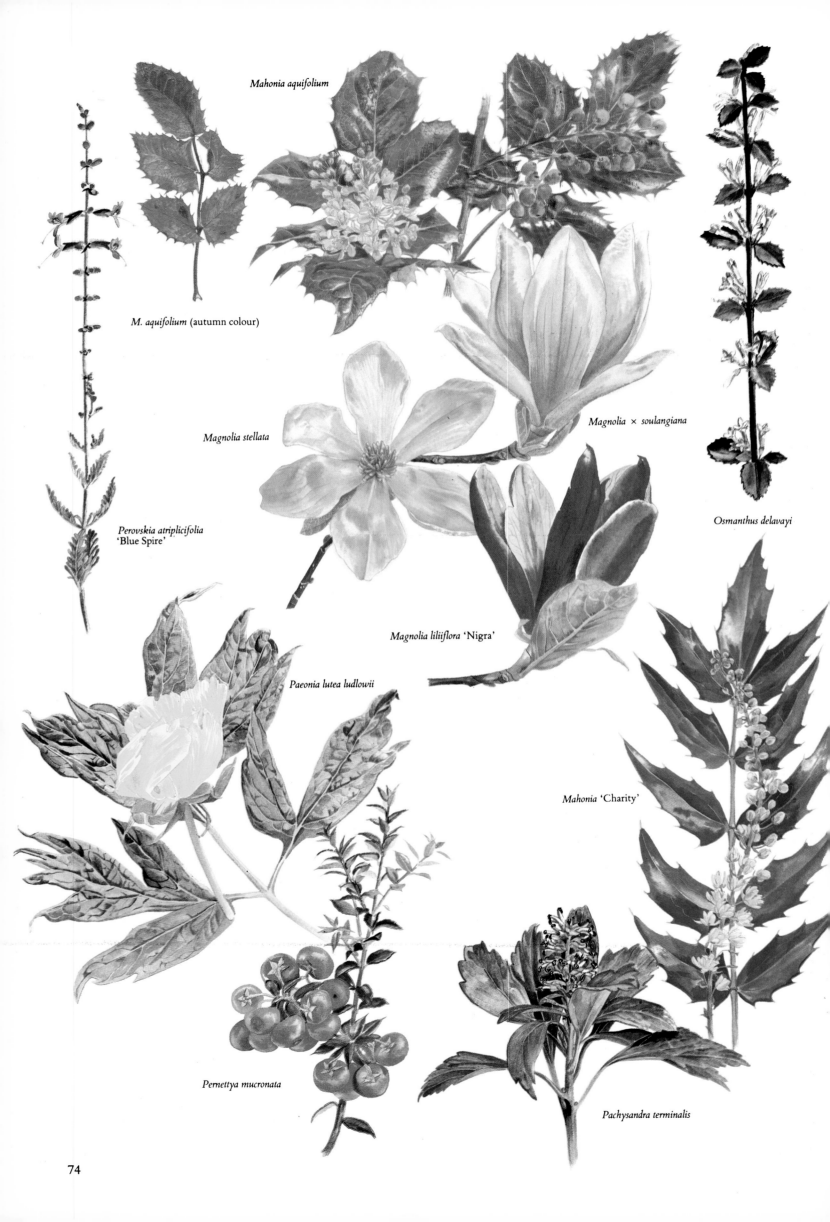

Mahonia aquifolium

M. aquifolium (autumn colour)

Magnolia stellata

Magnolia × soulangiana

Osmanthus delavayi

Perovskia atriplicifolia
'Blue Spire'

Magnolia liliiflora 'Nigra'

Paeonia lutea ludlowii

Mahonia 'Charity'

Pernettya mucronata

Pachysandra terminalis

Magnolia liliiflora 'Nigra'. *Magnoliaceae*

A deciduous bushy shrub with branches downy at the tips. The ovate to obovate healthy green leaves are attractive in spring and summer against the large, slender, bell-shaped flowers on very short pedicels. An interesting plant as a specimen for the lawn, flowering over a longer period than most in the group. Pruning not required. 10ft (3m)
⟋ ✿Spring○❊ ◢▼

Magnolia × soulangiana (syn *Conspicua soulangiana*) *Magnoliaceae*

A very popular plant with straggly relaxed branches giving rise to bell-shaped flowers before the leaves appear. Will tolerate polluted air. Good for the larger mixed border and especially as a specimen in a lawn. Pruning not required. 12ft (4m)
⟋ ✿Spring○❊ ◢▼

Magnolia stellata, Japan. *Magnoliaceae*

This deciduous, compact, rounded, slow-growing shrub produces many branches with aromatic silky immature bark. The fragrant star-shaped flowers with narrow oblong petals are borne on the branches before leaves appear. The very prolific flowers appear in succession replacing those which may be damaged by inclement weather. Suitable for smaller gardens; if underplanted with bulbs, it makes a most attractive feature in spring. Pruning not required. New plants can be raised by layering. 10ft (3m)
⟋ ✿Spring○❊ ◢▼

Mahonia aquifolium, Oregon Grape, Western N. America. *Berberidaceae*

The dark grey-brown stems sucker freely from below ground giving rise to an evergreen shrub with pinnate leaves consisting of up to nine spined leaflets. The leaves are glossy green in summer, some turning purplish in autumn. Abundant crowded flowers in erect racemes show colour at the turn of the year. They are followed by globose fruits good for preserves and most attractive to birds. A useful plant for ground cover or a difficult bank and effective below trees. Trim if necessary after flowering. Easily grown from seed, or suckers may be lifted. 6ft (2m)
△✿Winter◡Summer◐●❊ ◢▼

Mahonia 'Charity'. *Berberidaceae*

This erect evergreen shrub has most interesting long pinnate foliage and great spreading racemes of flowers treasured for their fragrance in mid-winter. The flowers are followed by abundant purple fruit much liked by birds. An excellent plant for the mixed border and when planted below the canopy of trees. Cut back if necessary after flowering. 6ft (2m)
△✿Winter◡Summer◐●❊ ◢▼

Osmanthus delavayi (syn *Siphonosmanthus delavayi*) China. *Oleaceae*

A charming, rounded, slow-growing, evergreen shrub with stiff downy young branches which spread as they mature. Glossy green ovate or oval leaves and clusters of abundant and extremely fragrant flowers are features of the plant. Trim to shape after flowering. Cuttings taken in July or August root faster with the aid of bottom heat. 9ft (2.7m)
△✿Spring○◐❊ ◢▼

Pachysandra terminalis, Japan. *Buxaceae*

A ground-hugging semi-woody plant with smooth stems. The obovate leaves persist for two to three years before making way for young stems arising from below ground as suckers. Much used as a ground-cover plant to suppress weeds, especially under trees. Pruning is not usually required unless stems become leafless then trim over in April. Division is easily undertaken by lifting rooted suckers. 6in (15cm)
△✿Spring◐●❊ ◢▼

Paeonia lutea ludlowii, S.E. Tibet. *Paeoniaceae*

Deciduous dwarf sub-shrub with a short glabrous woody stem and large green leaves. The magnificent, single flowers are saucer shaped. Old stems can be completely removed if they become leafless. 4¹/₂ft (1.4m)
⟋ ✿Summer◐❊△ ◢▼

Pernettya mucronata hybrids (syn *P. speciosa*, *Arbutus mucronata*) South America. *Ericaceae*

A range of dwarf evergreen shrubs spreading by underground suckers to form a thicket. The closely packed leaves on wiry stems give good ground cover and abundant white flowers produce persistent fruits varying in colour from white through pink, crimson, purple to almost black on the different plants. Useful for indoor decoration during winter. These shrubs are best planted in groups which include male forms. Thin out old wood in April. Propagate by division of the rootstock or by cuttings. 2¹/₂ft (75cm)
△🌢🍃✿Summer◡Autumn◐❊▼

Perovskia atriplicifolia 'Blue Spire'. *Labiatae*

Semi-woody deciduous shrub with stiff erect branches covered with down. The deeply cut grey-green leaves have a pleasant scent and the beautifully coloured flowers are produced in whorls. Old stems should be cut back in spring. Easily propagated by cuttings taken with a heel in July or August. 4ft (1.2m)
⟋ ✿Summer○❊ ◢▼

Phlomis fruticosa

Philadelphus 'Virginal'

Philadelphus 'Belle Etoile'

Philadelphus 'Belle Etoile', Mock orange. *Philadelphaceae*

A broad, deciduous shrub with long, semi-arching stems which give rise to the abundant, very fragrant single flowers. Spent stems should be pruned away close to mature wood immediately after flowering. Hardwood cuttings taken in October strike readily. 6ft (2m)
⟋ ✿Spring○◐❊ ◢▼

Philadelphus 'Virginal'. *Philadelphaceae*

A vigorous, erect, branched shrub producing abundant large double or semi-double fragrant flowers. Much admired for the shrub or mixed border. Cut back spent stems close to mature wood after flowering. 10ft (3m)
⟋ ✿Spring○◐❊ ◢▼

Phlomis fruticosa, Jerusalem Sage, S. Europe. *Labiatae*

Vigorous evergreen shrub with stout, grey-haired soft branchlets. The ovate-lanceolate, faintly aromatic, opposite leaves are wrinkled and grey-green in colour and the stalkless flowers are carried in dense clusters. A useful plant for the silver border. Thin out and cut back old flowering stems in late spring. Easily propagated by cuttings. 3ft (1m)
△✿Spring○❊ ◢▼

Potentilla fruticosa 'Elizabeth'

Potentilla fruticosa 'Tangerine'

Prunus glandulosa 'Albiplena'

Prunus laurocerasus 'Otto Luyken'

Pieris 'Forest Flame'

Poncirus trifoliata

Photinia × *fraseri* 'Red Robin'

Photinia × fraseri 'Red Robin'. *Rosaceae*

Spectacular evergreen shrub bearing brilliant red young foliage which matures to shiny green. It will liven up a shrub border and is very useful as a container plant for the patio. Cut back previous year's growth in late spring. 6ft (2m)

△ ○ ◑ ✶ ◿

Pieris 'Forest Flame'. *Ericaceae*

A handsome medium-sized evergreen shrub of bushy habit producing bright red new growth which turns pink then white to green. The abundant small pitcher-shaped flowers form large terminal drooping panicles. An excellent plant for the smaller garden. Trim if necessary after flowering. 6ft (2m)

△ ✿Spring ○ ◑ ✶ ▼

Poncirus trifoliata (syn *Aegle sepiaria*, *Limonia trifoliata*, *Citrus trifoliata*) Japanese Bitter Orange, N. China. *Rutaceae*

Slow-growing deciduous plant with dark green flattened branches armed with spines. The winged petiole terminates in a trifoliate glossy leaf with sessile leaflets. Very fragrant large white flowers are followed by globose fruits which ripen to yellow and contain many seeds. Trim shoots in summer if necessary. 15ft (4.5m)

◔ ✿Spring ✿Autumn ○ ✶ ◿

Potentilla fruticosa 'Elizabeth', Shrubby Cinquefoil. *Rosaceae*

Dense, rounded deciduous shrub with erect branches which is useful for weed suppression. Decorative pinnate leaves and especially valuable for its long period of flowering. Buds will not break from old wood and so hard pruning should be avoided. Propagate from cuttings taken in summer. 3ft (1m)

◔ ✿Summer ○ ◑ ✶ ◿

Potentilla fruticosa 'Tangerine', Shrubby Cinquefoil. *Rosaceae*

A dwarf shrub wider than it is tall and forming a dense mound. Very useful for ground cover when planted in a group. The pale copper-yellow flowers are more effective when grown in shade, otherwise they tend to fade. Cut back previous year's growth by half in March. 1½ft (45cm)

◔ ✿Summer ○ ◑ ✶ ◿

Prunus glandulosa 'Albiplena', Chinese Bush Cherry. *Rosaceae*

A rounded twiggy bush with ovate to lanceolate finely pointed leaves. The abundant double white flowers are most attractive. Cut back side shoots close to mature wood after flowering. 4ft (1.2m)

◔ ✿Spring ○ ✶ △ ◿

Prunus laurocerasus 'Otto Luyken', Common Laurel, Cherry Laurel. *Rosaceae*

This low-growing, compact, evergreen shrub with a wide-spreading habit is excellent for ground cover and to clothe difficult banks. The leaves are glossy dark green and complement the showy erect racemes of flowers followed by fruit. Trim, if necessary, after flowering. Useful for container growing. 4ft (1.2m)

△ ✿Spring ✿Autumn ◑ ● ✶ ◿

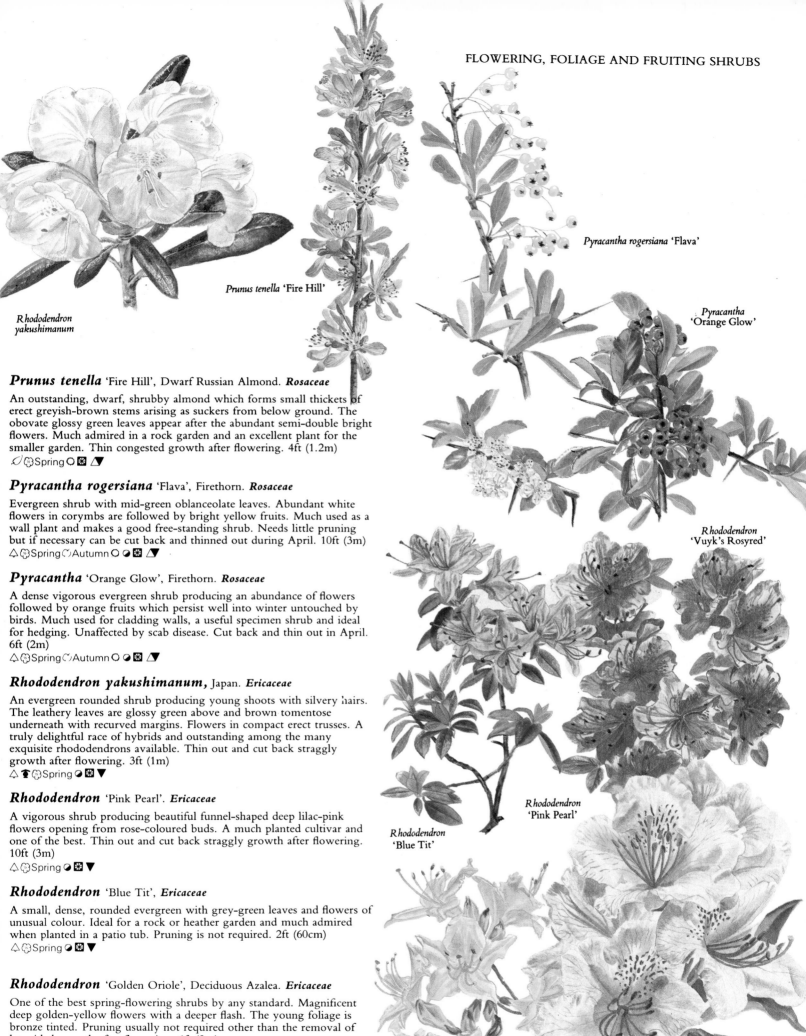

Pyracantha rogersiana 'Flava'

Pyracantha 'Orange Glow'

Rhododendron 'Vuyk's Rosyred'

Rhododendron yakushimanum

Prunus tenella 'Fire Hill'

Rhododendron 'Pink Pearl'

Rhododendron 'Blue Tit'

Rhododendron 'Golden Oriole'

Prunus tenella 'Fire Hill', Dwarf Russian Almond. *Rosaceae*

An outstanding, dwarf, shrubby almond which forms small thickets of erect greyish-brown stems arising as suckers from below ground. The obovate glossy green leaves appear after the abundant semi-double bright flowers. Much admired in a rock garden and an excellent plant for the smaller garden. Thin congested growth after flowering. 4ft (1.2m)
⊘ ☸ Spring ◐ ✖ △▽

Pyracantha rogersiana 'Flava', Firethorn. *Rosaceae*

Evergreen shrub with mid-green oblanceolate leaves. Abundant white flowers in corymbs are followed by bright yellow fruits. Much used as a wall plant and makes a good free-standing shrub. Needs little pruning but if necessary can be cut back and thinned out during April. 10ft (3m)
△ ☸ Spring ↻ Autumn ◯ ◐ ✖ △▽

Pyracantha 'Orange Glow', Firethorn. *Rosaceae*

A dense vigorous evergreen shrub producing an abundance of flowers followed by orange fruits which persist well into winter untouched by birds. Much used for cladding walls, a useful specimen shrub and ideal for hedging. Unaffected by scab disease. Cut back and thin out in April. 6ft (2m)
△ ☸ Spring ↻ Autumn ◯ ◐ ✖ △▽

Rhododendron yakushimanum, Japan. *Ericaceae*

An evergreen rounded shrub producing young shoots with silvery hairs. The leathery leaves are glossy green above and brown tomentose underneath with recurved margins. Flowers in compact erect trusses. A truly delightful race of hybrids and outstanding among the many exquisite rhododendrons available. Thin out and cut back straggly growth after flowering. 3ft (1m)
△ ✿ ☸ Spring ◐ ✖ ▼

Rhododendron 'Pink Pearl'. *Ericaceae*

A vigorous shrub producing beautiful funnel-shaped deep lilac-pink flowers opening from rose-coloured buds. A much planted cultivar and one of the best. Thin out and cut back straggly growth after flowering. 10ft (3m)
△ ☸ Spring ◐ ✖ ▼

Rhododendron 'Blue Tit', *Ericaceae*

A small, dense, rounded evergreen with grey-green leaves and flowers of unusual colour. Ideal for a rock or heather garden and much admired when planted in a patio tub. Pruning is not required. 2ft (60cm)
△ ☸ Spring ◐ ✖ ▼

Rhododendron 'Golden Oriole', Deciduous Azalea. *Ericaceae*

One of the best spring-flowering shrubs by any standard. Magnificent deep golden-yellow flowers with a deeper flash. The young foliage is bronze tinted. Pruning usually not required other than the removal of lop-sided growth after flowering. 6ft (2m)
△ ☸ Spring ◐ ✖ ▼

Rhododendron 'Vuyk's Rosyred', Vuyk Hybrid Azalea. *Ericaceae*

An interesting shrub producing many flowers with wavy deep rose petals. The large flower size is a feature of the plant. Pruning not required. 3ft (1m)
⊘ ☸ Spring ◯ ◐ ✖ ▼

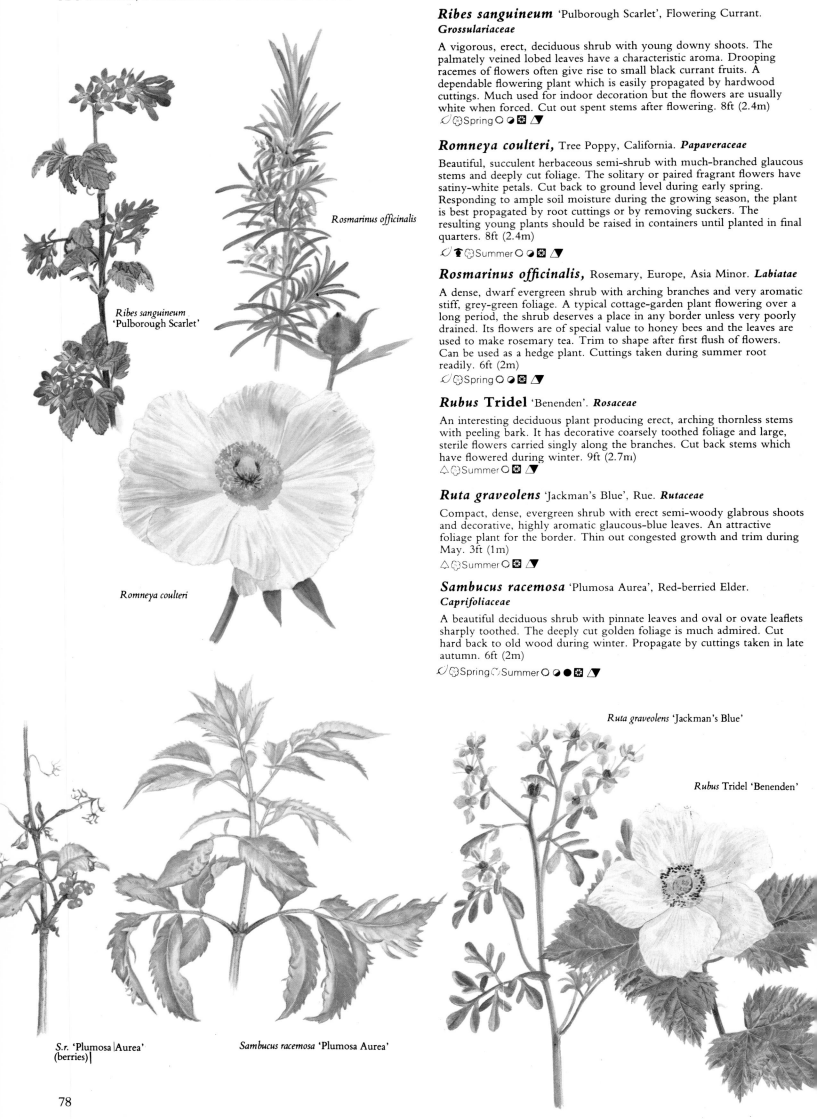

Ribes sanguineum 'Pulborough Scarlet', Flowering Currant. *Grossulariaceae*

A vigorous, erect, deciduous shrub with young downy shoots. The palmately veined lobed leaves have a characteristic aroma. Drooping racemes of flowers often give rise to small black currant fruits. A dependable flowering plant which is easily propagated by hardwood cuttings. Much used for indoor decoration but the flowers are usually white when forced. Cut out spent stems after flowering. 8ft (2.4m)
○❀Spring○◐▣△▼

Romneya coulteri, Tree Poppy, California. *Papaveraceae*

Beautiful, succulent herbaceous semi-shrub with much-branched glaucous stems and deeply cut foliage. The solitary or paired fragrant flowers have satiny-white petals. Cut back to ground level during early spring. Responding to ample soil moisture during the growing season, the plant is best propagated by root cuttings or by removing suckers. The resulting young plants should be raised in containers until planted in final quarters. 8ft (2.4m)
○♠❀Summer○◐▣△▼

Rosmarinus officinalis, Rosemary, Europe, Asia Minor. *Labiatae*

A dense, dwarf evergreen shrub with arching branches and very aromatic stiff, grey-green foliage. A typical cottage-garden plant flowering over a long period, the shrub deserves a place in any border unless very poorly drained. Its flowers are of special value to honey bees and the leaves are used to make rosemary tea. Trim to shape after first flush of flowers. Can be used as a hedge plant. Cuttings taken during summer root readily. 6ft (2m)
○❀Spring○◐▣△▼

Rubus Tridel 'Benenden'. *Rosaceae*

An interesting deciduous plant producing erect, arching thornless stems with peeling bark. It has decorative coarsely toothed foliage and large, sterile flowers carried singly along the branches. Cut back stems which have flowered during winter. 9ft (2.7m)
△❀Summer○▣△▼

Ruta graveolens 'Jackman's Blue', Rue. *Rutaceae*

Compact, dense, evergreen shrub with erect semi-woody glabrous shoots and decorative, highly aromatic glaucous-blue leaves. An attractive foliage plant for the border. Thin out congested growth and trim during May. 3ft (1m)
△❀Summer○▣△▼

Sambucus racemosa 'Plumosa Aurea', Red-berried Elder. *Caprifoliaceae*

A beautiful deciduous shrub with pinnate leaves and oval or ovate leaflets sharply toothed. The deeply cut golden foliage is much admired. Cut hard back to old wood during winter. Propagate by cuttings taken in late autumn. 6ft (2m)
○❀Spring○Summer○◐●▣△▼

Rosmarinus officinalis

Ribes sanguineum 'Pulborough Scarlet'

Romneya coulteri

Ruta graveolens 'Jackman's Blue'

Rubus Tridel 'Benenden'

S.r. 'Plumosa Aurea' (berries)

Sambucus racemosa 'Plumosa Aurea'

Senecio 'Sunshine'

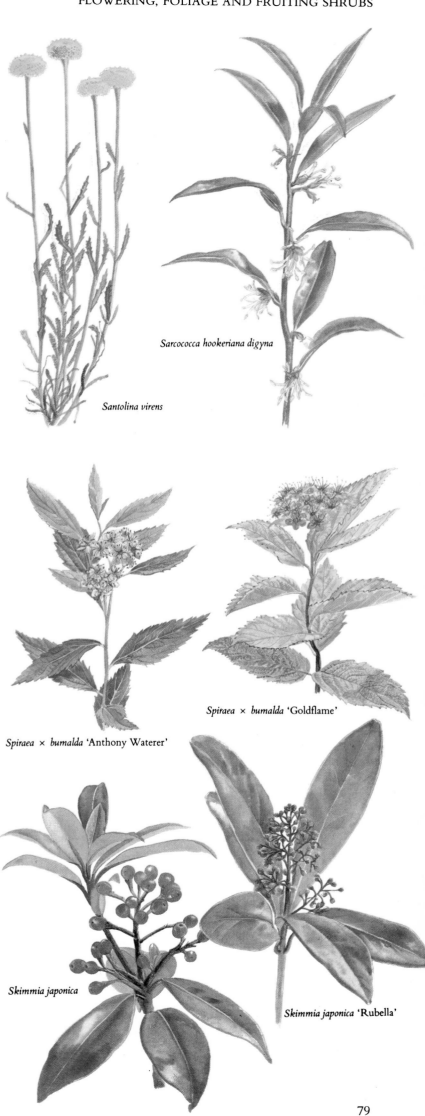

Sarcococca hookeriana digyna

Santolina virens

Spiraea × bumalda 'Goldflame'

Spiraea × bumalda 'Anthony Waterer'

Skimmia japonica

Skimmia japonica 'Rubella'

Santolina virens (syn S. viridis) Holly Flax, S. Europe. *Compositae*

A bushy shrub with smooth green stems giving rise to bright green aromatic thread-like leaves. The yellow flower heads appear at the apex of slender stalks. Remove spent flower stems and trim remainder after flowering. 2ft (60cm)
△ ⊕Summer ○ ⊞ △▼

Sarcococca hookeriana digyna (syn S. pruniformis hookeriana) Himalaya. *Buxaceae*

A charming, low-growing, erect evergreen shrub giving rise to new stems by suckering from below ground, with narrow lanceolate, alternate, shining leaves. The fragrant male flowers and petal-less female flowers occur in the same cluster and the plant is much appreciated when set to the front of the border. Trim back growth if necessary during spring. Propagated by cuttings taken during summer. 1¹/₂ft (45cm)
△ ⊕Autumn ● ⊞ △▼

Senecio 'Sunshine'. *Compositae*

A low, evergreen bushy shrub with straggly branches, the young stems covered with silver down as are the young oval or lanceolate leaves. Pyramidal panicles of abundant flowers are most attractive and, together with the silver-grey foliage, much used in flower arrangement. The stems may be shortened in early spring to retain a compact habit. 4ft (1.2m)
△ ⊕Summer ○ ⊞ △▼

Skimmia japonica, Japan. *Rutaceae*

A low, compact bush with foliage which is aromatic when bruised; the transparent glands arise on the lower surface of the leathery obovate leaves. On female plants the clusters of fragrant small flowers are followed by red berries if there is an adjacent male plant to provide pollen. Trim to shape if necessary in April. 4ft (1.2m)
△ ⊕Spring ⊘Autumn ○ ● ⊞ △▼

Skimmia japonica 'Rubella'. *Rutaceae*

This low, dense evergreen shrub with red winter buds gives rise in spring to fragrant male flowers. An ideal plant to set near the female form to encourage flower fertilization and subsequent berry production. Remove congested growth in April. 4 ft (1.2m)
△ ⊕Spring ○ ● ⊞ △▼

Spiraea × bumalda 'Anthony Waterer'. *Rosaceae*

The erect stems form a dwarf and elegant shrub with ovate lanceolate green leaves often variegated cream and pink. Flat compact corymbs of carmine flowers add interest to this very popular border plant. The stems may be pruned hard back in spring to retain a compact habit. Propagate by hardwood cuttings or cuttings taken in summer preferably from shoots showing abundant variegation. 2¹/₂ft (75cm)
⊘ ⊕Summer ○ ● ⊞ △▼

Spiraea × bumalda 'Goldflame'. *Rosaceae*

A striking dwarf deciduous shrub with bright gold leaves in spring. Much admired in the border and ideal to relax the lines of a formal patio. Prune stems hard in early spring to retain a neat habit. 2¹/₂ft (75cm)
⊘ ⊕Summer ○ ● ⊞ △▼

Viburnum × bodnantense 'Dawn'

Viburnum davidii

Symphoricarpos orbiculatus

Tamarix tetrandra

V. davidii (berries)

Symphoricarpos orbiculatus, Indian Currant, Coral Berry, E. United States. *Caprifoliaceae*

This shrub has a dense, bushy habit and clusters of small purplish-pink peristent berries following rather insignificant flowers. A good shrub for ground cover. Remove spindly growth during spring. 6ft (2m)

⟁ ✿Spring◐Autumn ◯ ◕ ● ▦ △▼

Tamarix tetrandra, Tamarisk, S.E. Europe, W. Asia. *Tamaricaceae*

A graceful deciduous shrub with smooth very dark branches eventually arching. The interesting, minute imbricated leaves are pointed and incurved at the apex. Abundant flowers are produced on wood made during the previous year. Pruning when necessary should be carried out immediately after flowers have faded. 10ft (3m)

⟁ ✿✿Spring ◯ ◕ ▦ △▼

Viburnum × bodnantense 'Dawn'. *Caprifoliaceae*

A deciduous much-branched shrub with lanceolate or ovate to oblanceolate leaves. The very fragrant flowers closely packed in clusters are carried through the winter. Much valued for indoor decoration. It is most important to keep the roots moist during July when flower buds are initiated. Pruning not usually required except to remove very old wood during May. 7¹/₂ft (2.3m)

⟁ ✿✿✿Winter ◯ ◕ ▦ △▼

Viburnum davidii, W. China. *Caprifoliaceae*

A distinct, evergreen, dense, compact shrub with warted branches giving rise to deeply veined leathery leaves. A plant good for ground cover and best planted in a group to offer cross pollination of the flowers. Pruning not usually required. 3ft (1m)

△ ✿✿Spring✿Summer ◯ ◕ ▦ △▼

Viburnum rhytidophyllum, China. *Caprifoliaceae*

Wide-spreading vigorous evergreen shrub with densely downy shoots giving rise to most interesting large, deeply wrinkled elliptic to oblong leaves. Two plants should be set adjacent to one another for adequate fruit development. Pruning not usually required. 20ft (6m)

△ ✿Spring◐Autumn ◯ ◕ ▦ △▼

Viburnum tinus, Laurustinus, S.E. Europe. *Caprifoliaceae*

This much-valued, dense, multi-branched evergreen shrub is decorative from late autumn to spring. The fragrant flowers arise in terminal cymes and open first on the south-facing side and subsequently around the bush. The luxuriant foliage is an additional feature making this a very useful plant for the border, as a specimen or for screening. Will tolerate maritime conditions. Pruning not usually required except to remove congested growth. 10ft (3m)

△ ✿Winter◐Summer ◯ ◕ ▦ △▼

Vinca major 'Variegata', Periwinkle. *Apocynaceae*

An evergreen semi-shrub with long trailing stems which is good for ground cover and particularly effective when flowing over a dwarf wall. The opposite variegated leaves are a feature of the plant providing a back cloth for the bright blue flowers arising on a slender stalk from the leaf axil. The barren stems should be cut away in spring. Easily propagated by lifting rooted stems. 1ft (30cm)

△ ✿✿Summer ◕ ● ▦ △▼

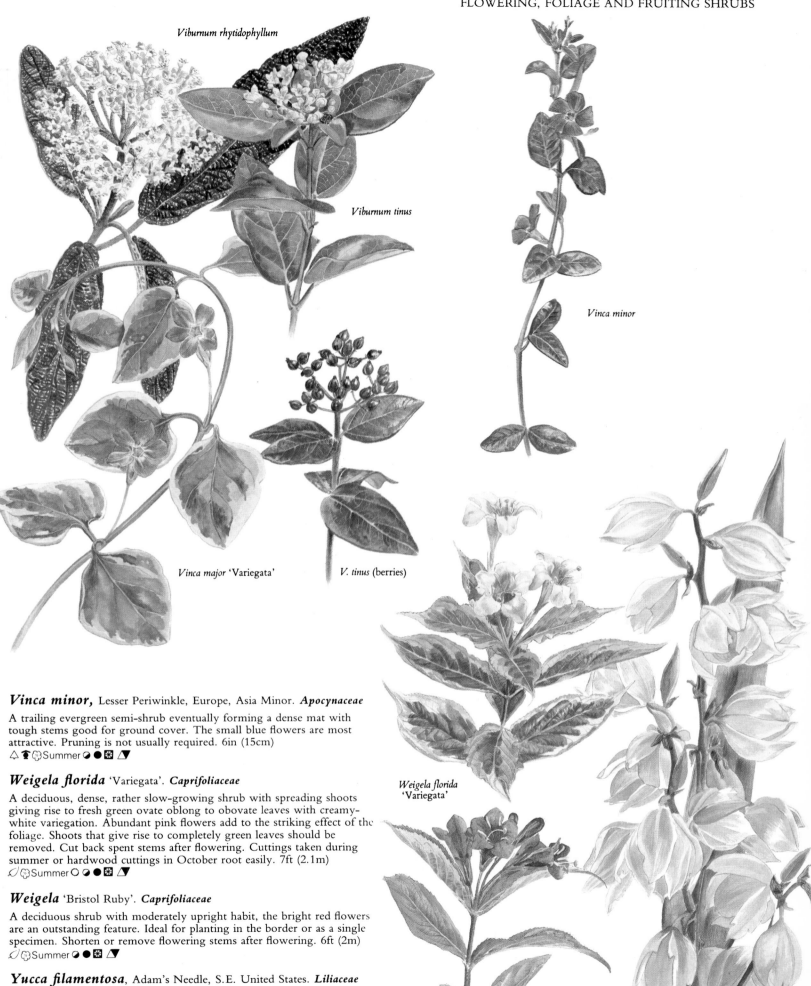

Viburnum rhytidophyllum

Viburnum tinus

Vinca minor

Vinca major 'Variegata'

V. tinus (berries)

Weigela florida
'Variegata'

Yucca filamentosa

Weigela 'Bristol Ruby'

Vinca minor, Lesser Periwinkle, Europe, Asia Minor. **Apocynaceae**

A trailing evergreen semi-shrub eventually forming a dense mat with tough stems good for ground cover. The small blue flowers are most attractive. Pruning is not usually required. 6in (15cm)

Weigela florida 'Variegata'. **Caprifoliaceae**

A deciduous, dense, rather slow-growing shrub with spreading shoots giving rise to fresh green ovate oblong to obovate leaves with creamy-white variegation. Abundant pink flowers add to the striking effect of the foliage. Shoots that give rise to completely green leaves should be removed. Cut back spent stems after flowering. Cuttings taken during summer or hardwood cuttings in October root easily. 7ft (2.1m)

Weigela 'Bristol Ruby'. **Caprifoliaceae**

A deciduous shrub with moderately upright habit, the bright red flowers are an outstanding feature. Ideal for planting in the border or as a single specimen. Shorten or remove flowering stems after flowering. 6ft (2m)

Yucca filamentosa, Adam's Needle, S.E. United States. **Liliaceae**

Low, tufted evergreen stemless shrub giving rise to side growths from the base of the plant with stiff, erect to spreading, lanceolate, slightly glaucous, spineless leaves. Curling thread-like filaments peel away from the leaf margin. The pendulous flowers arise from erect conical panicles. Pruning not required. Easily propagated by division. 3ft (1m)

81

Garden Trees

Choosing Trees for the Garden

There are available today many varieties of attractive garden trees in varying shapes and forms – both deciduous and evergreen and often effective at various times of year – which are suitable for even the smallest gardens.

For example, the very useful columnar or fastigiate trees which have a narrow upright growth habit. These range from small flowering trees, such as *Prunus* 'Amanogawa', *Malus* 'Van Eseltine', a crab apple with shell-pink, semi-double flowers followed by yellow fruits, or *Sorbus* 'Sheerwater Seedling', bearing, in autumn, clusters of orange-red berries, to the conifers such as the many forms of Lawson's cypress (*Chamaecyparis lawsoniana*), *Ginkgo biloba* 'Fastigiata' or *Taxus baccata* 'Fastigiata', Irish yew. Trees of this form are very useful for narrow confines, even in corners reasonably near to buildings if they are small growers such as *Prunus* 'Amanogawa'. Striking effects can be created by the use of several columnar conifers to make small avenues flanking paths or to provide 'horticultural exclamation marks' at focal points within the garden.

Another form, which might be described as conical or broadly pyramidal, is provided by such subjects as *Malus* 'Golden Hornet', *Acer pseudoplatanus* 'Brilliantissimum' and *Prunus* x *hillieri* 'Spire', the latter subject with soft pink flowers as well as autumn interest in the leaf colour. A number of Japanese cherries provide an upright spreading shape reminiscent of a 'Y' or wineglass, particularly *Prunus* 'Kanzan' and *P.* 'Tai-haku'. The very striking snake-bark maple, *Acer davidii*, and paper-

A delicate tracery of autumn colours provided by a group of acers at the Savill Gardens, Windsor Great Park.

bark maple, *Acer griseum*, also have this character and all will attain various heights up to 30ft (9m).

Round or ball-headed trees are equally available and the dense twiggy thorns, *Crataegus* species, and the Swedish whitebeam, *Sorbus intermedia*, are typical examples of these.

Mushroom-headed or semi-weeping is another interesting and attractive shape and the choice *Prunus* 'Shimidsu Sakura' with double flowers provides this requirement, while wider spreading trees often wider than high can be found in the fragrant, white-flowered *Prunus* 'Shirotae' and *Malus floribunda*.

Large weeping trees, such as the weeping willow, *Salix* x *chrysocoma*, are not suitable for small gardens, but small compact weeping trees may be found which are ideal as lawn specimens, providing focal points of interest for much of the year – *Pyrus salicifolia* 'Pendula', weeping silver-leaf pear, the neat and handsome crab apple *Malus* 'Red Jade' and *Salix purpurea* 'Pendula', weeping purple osier, are particularly good examples.

Given such a wide range of shape and form, it is easy to ring the changes and produce most satisfying effects in quite small areas. It is, however, vital to consider the ultimate size as well as the shape of the tree chosen, in order that it does not eventually shade windows, overhang or conflict in any other way with houses or other buildings or impede driveways.

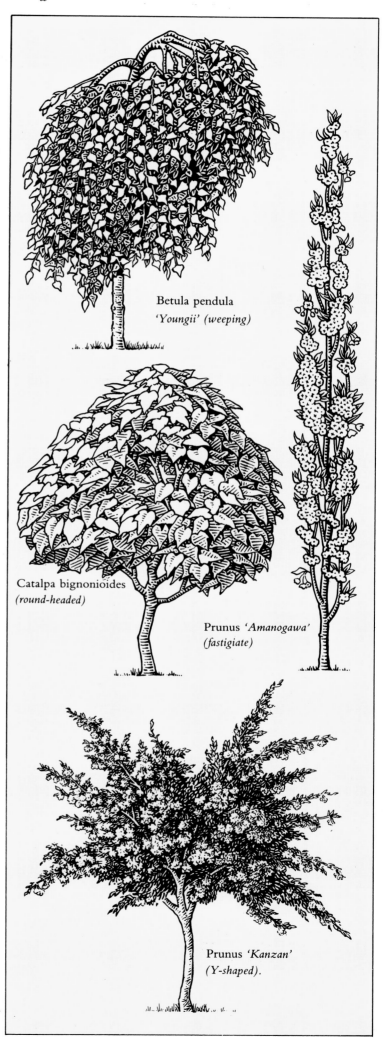

Betula pendula
'Youngii' (weeping)

Catalpa bignonioides
(round-headed)

Prunus 'Amanogawa'
(fastigiate)

Prunus 'Kanzan'
(Y-shaped).

To this end a careful planned siting of a selection of the trees mentioned above is rather more appropriate in small gardens than the use of forest trees, which are ultimately of large size and more suitable for parkland or more spacious circumstances where there is room for them to grow unrestricted to their full height and spread.

Siting Trees for Maximum Effect

If you have room for several trees in your garden, a variety of shapes can be used to give an aesthetically acceptable combination; some of the subjects should also be chosen for flower, others for foliage and some for both. Very often there is a need to screen nearby housing or undesirable objects – even distant pylons – and a tree of the right shape and ultimate size will usually achieve this; those that are of upright spreading, round or ball-headed, mushroom-headed or wide spreading shapes are particularly good for this task. *Crataegus* species, thorn, are notably useful for their dense, twiggy habit and are a reasonable substitute for evergreens for screening purposes. Most evergreens, other than conifers such as the cypresses, tend to start small and be of slow growth. If you are prepared to wait, the broad-leaved holly, *Ilex altaclarensis* and its cultivars, some of which are variegated, the holm oak, *Quercus ilex*, and the strawberry tree, *Arbutus unedo*, are all very useful as evergreen screeners and effective trees in their own rights.

Striking effects can be created by the use of trees with brightly coloured foliage, a feature often retained throughout the growing season. Foliage may be grey, purple, golden, or red and there are many examples of attractive variegation, both silver and yellow; such leaf colours effectively associate or contrast with one another and with the many shades of green of other trees and shrubs. For example, a satisfying association can be achieved by grouping as a focal point *Acer platanoides* 'Crimson King', a form of Norway maple with deep red foliage, with *Sorbus aria* 'Lutescens', a whitebeam with silver foliage, and placing in front *Gleditsia triacanthos* 'Sunburst', golden-leaved honey locust. *Acer negundo* 'Variegatum', variegated box maple, provides a striking silver-marginal variegation, while *A. negundo* 'Elegans' ('Elegantissimum') is similarly variegated with golden yellow.

Often, near the perimeter of the garden, screening can be achieved by using a variety of trees, perhaps of varying shapes and exhibiting a range of coloured foliage. These should not be sited less than 18 to 26ft (5.5 to 8m) apart in the majority of cases; some varieties need considerably more space otherwise they will foul one another and shape and form will be spoiled. However, it is becoming the custom increasingly today to treat the small garden as one might a room, refurnishing it after eight or ten years – a task often carried out anyway as the property changes hands – and planting trees more closely with this idea in mind. Pruning and shaping can usually be carried out as necessary and the trees thinned by removing every other one in four or five years time.

Tree Forms Available

Trees are usually available in various forms from nurserymen and garden centres; some may be container grown others will be bare rooted or balled.

Feathered Tree This is a young specimen of transplanted tree with a defined upright central leader and stem furnished with evenly spaced lateral shoots from near ground level upwards; the height is usually 5 to 8ft, but may be up to 10ft in certain species (1.5 to 2.5m and up to 3m). A standard or half-standard tree may be formed from a feathered specimen by correctly stopping the leading shoot and pruning or thinning the lateral branches to form a head; ultimately lateral twigs are removed nearly flush to the stem in order to form the standard or half-standard tree.

Standard and Half-Standard Trees These are usually supplied 7 to 10ft (2.1 to 3m) high, have formed heads and a stem about 5 to 6ft (1.5 to 1.8m) tall before branching starts, with a 3½ to 4½ft stem (about 1 to 1.2m) in the case of half-standards. Light standards with smaller heads may also be available.

In recent years, primarily to counter vandalism to trees planted in public places, heavy and extra heavy nursery trees have become available, which may be supplied initially from 10 to 18ft (3 to 5.5m) in height.

Preparation of the Planting Sites

Very often, if trees are sited around the perimeter of your garden, it will be advantageous to plant them in association with shrubs and perhaps herbaceous plants and ideally, in a cultivated area or border, perhaps 4 to 6ft or even 8ft wide (1.2 to 2.5m). Trees of upright spreading habit are the most useful in such a situation in order to allow for underplanting; reserving, perhaps, weeping or mushroom-headed specimens for use as accent points, at path junctions or as lawn specimens.

The perimeter border should, in the interests of all such planting, be cultivated to a depth of 18in (45cm) and well-rotted farmyard manure incorporated if the ground is poor, chalky or gravelly. Sometimes a rotavator is used for such an area, whereupon the depth of cultivation does not usually exceed 9in (23cm). If this is the case, individual sites for trees will need to be prepared at least 18in (45cm) deep and 3ft (1m) wide, in order that the tree roots can be properly spread and the tree has the best possible chance to succeed in its new site.

Isolated sites set in rough grass or lawn areas should be similarly prepared – the more generous the area cultivated and the less competition with rough grass or mown lawn, the quicker will the tree establish and grow away. In such circumstances cultivation areas of 3ft (1m) in diameter should be looked upon as the minimum size necessary.

Planting

If during the preparation of the site clay, chalk or poor sub-soil is encountered, this should be excavated to at least a depth of 18in (45cm) and fresh good top soil imported if necessary for use in planting the tree. On very poor soils, a bucketful of well-rotted farmyard manure dug into the bottom of the hole is a worthwhile addition. Ideally, this work should be done well in advance of planting, the holes being temporarily back-filled. Then at planting time, remove the loose soil to a depth of about 1ft (30cm) and thoroughly firm the remaining soil in the hole. Before attempting to plant, position the stake, which should be 2 to 3in (5 to 8cm) in diameter, driving the pointed end well into the firm soil at the bottom of the hole. Ideally, the bottom 2½ft (75cm) of the stake should be stripped of bark and the stake soaked in a suitable preservative which will not harm plant life. Thus treated the stake should then help to stabilise the tree until it is firmly anchored and growing well and should not break off at ground level which, without preservation, it may well do. From recent researches into tree staking it appears that feathered and light standard and standard trees, which are the kinds most usually planted in gardens, require shorter stakes than was formerly thought, say from 18in to about 3ft (45cm to 1m) above the ground, the object being to stabilise the root and lower part of stem, while encouraging the natural development of the specimen by the free movement of the head and upper part of stem.

Position the tree near the stake, spread the root system well out, and ensure that it is positioned so that the previous soil mark on the stem will be as near as possible to the finished soil level; a rod or cane laid over the hole should align with the soil mark on the stem as a guide. Fill back with a mixture of good top soil and moist peat or planting compost, shaking the tree gently to work the soil among the root fibres and leave no air spaces. A handful of compound fertilizer (Growmore or a slow-release fertilizer) can be incorporated at this stage. It is most important to firm the tree very thoroughly, using the full weight of the body behind the heel.

Finally secure the tree to the stake, using an adjustable purpose-made tree tie (one at the top of the stem should be all that is necessary); secure the tie to the stake with a nail if necessary in order to prevent it slipping down.

Larger trees (heavy, extra heavy or semi-mature) may require double staking or guying with galvanised wire hausers and

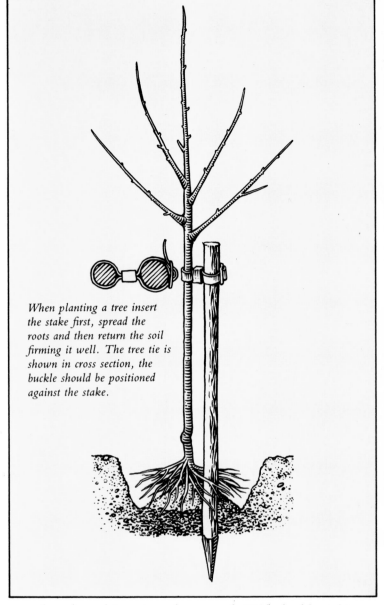

When planting a tree insert the stake first, spread the roots and then return the soil firming it well. The tree tie is shown in cross section, the buckle should be positioned against the stake.

wooden plugs driven into the ground. With double staking, a stake is used on either side of the trunk, the tree being secured between the two with a wooden cross-piece or rubber belting. Rubber reinforced hose could be used to prevent wire hausers damaging the bark of branches when these are to used to guy semi-mature trees.

Maintenance and Aftercare

Careful attention to watering and intelligent maintenance are very necessary and need not be arduous or time consuming. A newly transplanted tree has its greatest need for moisture in the spring and early summer of its first year following transplantation. During this period it is certainly worth giving at least two bucketfuls of water per tree each week, unless there is heavy rain. Trees set in grass are at greater risk, as they have to compete with the grass for all available food and moisture; the wider the cultivation area the better, but a minimum of 3ft (1m) is essential and this should be maintained free of grass or weed for the first three years following planting. A mulch of well-rotted leaves or pulverised bark fibre applied to this area will help to conserve essential moisture and maintain the cultivation area in a clean and weed-free condition.

Tree ties will require annual adjustment as the stem of the tree expands. This means loosening the buckle or re-fixing the rubber belting to allow the stem to grow without restriction, if neglected strangulation and considerable damage to the stem of the tree can result.

Once the tree is fully established, ground cover plants may be installed in the cultivated area. Shallow-rooted herbaceous or shrubby ground covers are ideal for this purpose such as lesser periwinkle, *Vinca minor*, in both green and variegated forms, varieties of hardy geranium or lady's mantle, *Alchemilla mollis*.

Acer platanoides 'Drummondii'

Aesculus × *carnea* 'Briotii'

Acer griseum

Acer pseudoplatanus 'Brilliantissimum'

Acer griseum, Paper-bark Maple, China. *Aceraceae*

This acer has handsome trifoliate leaves and highly decorative bark and is one of the finest of the ornamental maples. The leaves change to red and scarlet shades in autumn before leaf fall. The bark flakes away to reveal the orange-brown new bark underneath. Ideal for bark display, preferably with a conifer background to highlight the autumn colour. Flower and fruit of no decorative value. 30ft (9m)

Acer platanoides 'Drummondii', Norway Maple. *Aceraceae*

One of the most striking of variegated trees clothed with green leaves which have wide creamy white margins. The leaves provide interesting autumn colour in shades of yellow to brown and occasionally red. Small flowers appear in April before the leaves and subsequent seeds germinate easily to provide new plants. The handsome round-headed shape adds interest to the leafless tree during winter. Shoots giving rise to totally green leaves without the variegation should be removed as soon as they appear. 60ft (18m)

Acer pseudoplatanus 'Brilliantissimum', Sycamore. *Aceraceae*

A very handsome small tree useful for exposed sites but preferring light shade. The cordate leaves are coral pink when young, changing to pale bronze then greenish. This slow-growing tree is suitable for moderately-sized gardens although not one of the better maples for autumn leaf colour. 35ft (10.6m)

Aesculus × carnea 'Briotii', Red Horse Chestnut. *Hippocastanaceae*

A stately tree of rounded form with winter buds which are slightly sticky. The large, palmate, short-stalked dark green leaves with 5 or 7 leaflets, turn yellow in autumn. Very ornamental large flowers, deep pink and in panicles are followed by prickly rounded fruit containing large 'conkers'. It is considered that the type originated from cross pollination by an insect from *A. hippocastanum* and *A. pavia* and this cultivar was raised from seed from the type. Easy to grow and is best suited to large gardens. 45ft (14m)

Summer Autumn

Summer Autumn

GARDEN TREES

Amelanchier lamarckii, June Berry, Snowy Mespilus, Naturalised W. Europe. *Rosaceae*

The unfurling pink-tinged and copper-red ovate or oval leaves provide much pleasure before displaying rich orange and red autumn colour. Although relatively short lived, the racemes of flowers give the plant a spectacular appearance. It may also be grown as a small tree and is somewhat difficult to establish on thin chalky soils. 15ft (4.5m)

Spring Summer

Arbutus unedo, Strawberry Tree, Europe, Asia Minor. *Ericaceae*

A wide-topped evergreen with glandular pubescent immature shoots giving rise to oval or obovate dark green leaves toothed at the margin. The drooping panicles of white or pinkish bell-shaped flowers appear during autumn through to mid-winter followed by small globose orange-red edible fruits resembling strawberries, which persist until flowers appear next year. The brown shredding bark is a feature of the plant and most attractive. 20ft (6m)

Autumn/Winter Summer/Autumn

Betula pendula 'Youngii', Young's Weeping Birch. *Betulaceae*

This birch does not have a leading shoot as such and so should be trained to a 10-ft (3-m) stake to form a trunk to support the pendulous branches that will eventually weep to the ground. Undoubtedly the best weeping birch with its dome-shaped head and suitable for the smaller garden. Autumn leaf colour is good as is the bright bark. 15ft (4.5m)

Catalpa bignonioides (syn *C. syringaefolia*), Indian Bean Tree, E. United States. *Bignoniaceae*

A low, wide-spreading, bushy-headed tree which gives rise to shoots without a terminal bud. The tree is at its best as a specimen in a lawn. Young trees should be staked to form a trunk before allowing the head to develop. Mature trees produce ovate leaves up to 10in (25cm) long and almost as wide, although young plants often produce larger leaves. Delightful flowers, white with yellow markings and purple spots furnish the plant. Long seed pods up to 18in (45cm) are produced during favourable weather. 30ft (9m)

Summer Autumn

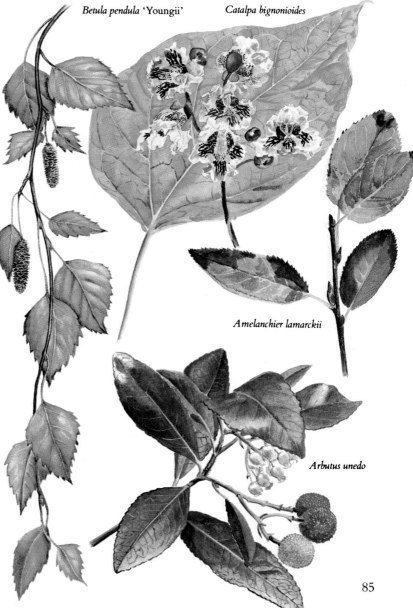

Betula pendula 'Youngii'

Catalpa bignonioides

Amelanchier lamarckii

Arbutus unedo

85

GARDEN TREES

Crataegus oxyacantha 'Paul's Scarlet', May. *Rosaceae*

The tree is armed with thorns up to 1in (2.5cm) long and this particular variety produces a fine display of double flowers. Often recommended as a specimen tree, it has now been in cultivation for well over 100 years. 15ft (4.5m)
⬭✿Spring◡Autumn○◐●✳ △▼

Eucalyptus gunnii (syn *E. whittingehamensis*) Cider Tree, Cedar Gum, Tasmania. *Myrtaceae*

This gum tree has opposite, orbicular and alternate juvenile leaves and sickle-shaped adult leaves. The juvenile leaf form can be retained by annual pruning to pollard the tree. The fast-growing tree has the typical eucalyptus aroma when the silver-grey leaves are crushed. Small, pot-grown plants are usually preferred for planting out, spring being the best time of year. 60ft (18m)
△☂○◐✳ △▼

Eucalyptus niphophila, Snow Gum, Australia. *Myrtaceae*

Year-round interest is provided by this gum: the bark takes on a dapple of silver-green, grey, fawn and cream as it matures. Leaves are large and strap shaped. The tree is less vigorous than might be expected and often grows at an interesting angle. 50ft (15m)
△☂○◐✳ △▼

Gleditsia triacanthos 'Sunburst', Honey Locust. *Leguminosae*

Unlike others in the group, this variety does not normally carry thorns. Very decorative pinnate leaves consist of many glossy green oblong-lanceolate leaflets. The attractive fern-like foliage emerges bright yellow through pale green and finishes with good autumn colour. A very tolerant tree where air pollution may still be a problem. 60ft (18m)
⬭☂○✳ △▼

Laburnum × watereri 'Vossii'. *Leguminosae*

All parts are poisonous, otherwise an ideal small tree for the garden, especially when space permits planting in a group of three. The long, slender, pendulous racemes of yellow flowers are most prolific and are followed by seed pods which should be removed if possible because they contain a harmful alkaloid substance. The tree benefits from the removal of these fruits by producing more flowers the following year. 25ft (8m)
⬭✿Spring◡Autumn○◐●✳ △▼

Liriodendron tulipifera, Tulip Tree, N. America. *Magnoliaceae*

This magnificent tree supports symmetrical branches from the columnar trunk. The leaves are a most interesting and unusual shape, resembling a saddle; fresh green during summer, they turn clear yellow in autumn before leaf fall. Tulip-shaped fragrant flowers produced by mature plants, add much to the splendour of the tree which is good as a specimen in a lawn. Air pollution is tolerated. 75ft (23m)
⬭✿Summer○◐✳ △▼

Malus 'Golden Hornet', Ornamental Crab. *Rosaceae*

A spreading tree with small, decorative white flowers producing much pollen, valuable to bees and for pollinating eating apples. The attractive yellow fruits persist on the tree until mid-winter and are then utilized for jelly or wine making. Set in a lawn and underplanted with crocus corms, this tree makes a fine spring feature and, later, a mature specimen provides shade for sitting out during summer. 30ft (9m)
⬭✿Spring◡Autumn○◐✳ △▼

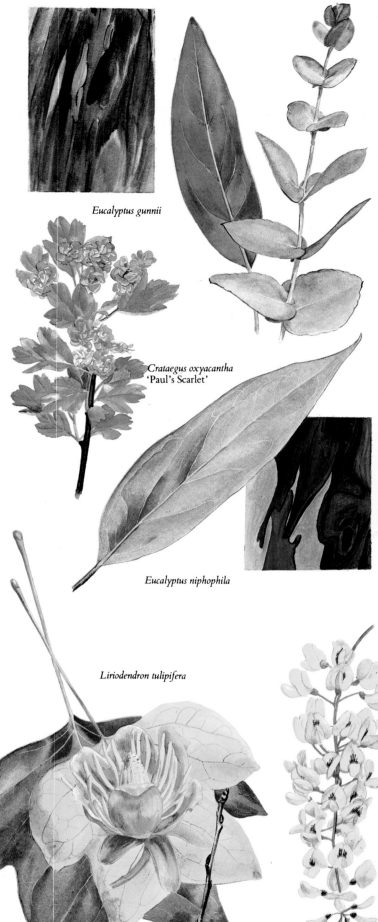

Eucalyptus gunnii

Crataegus oxyacantha 'Paul's Scarlet'

Eucalyptus niphophila

Liriodendron tulipifera

Laburnum × watereri 'Vossii'

Gleditsia triacanthos 'Sunburst'

Malus 'Golden Hornet'

Malus floribunda

Nyssa sylvatica

Parrotia persica

Prunus cerasifera 'Pissardii'

Prunus serrula (bark)

Prunus serrulata 'Amanogawa'

Prunus serrulata 'Kanzan'

Malus floribunda, Japanese Crab, Japan. *Rosaceae*

A very prolific-flowering round-headed tree, often shrubby in the immature state. The broad semi-pendulous branches are clothed in luxurious leaves and the crimson buds open to pinkish-white single flowers. Small globose, yellowish-red fruits are attractive in autumn. 30ft (9m)

⊘ ❀Spring ◯Autumn ◯ ◕ ✦ △▼

Nyssa sylvatica (syn *N. multiflora*, *N. villosa*) Tupelo, N. and E. America. *Nyssaceae*

A beautifully symmetrical slow-growing tree with variable leaves often obovate or oval in shape turning to brilliant red and yellow in autumn. The spectacular autumn tints progress from the base of the tree to give an interesting combination with the dark green apex. Dislikes root disturbance and is better for planting as a young specimen. The flowers are of no decorative value. 60ft (18m)

⊘ ◯ ◕ ✦ △▼

Parrotia persica, Iron Tree, N. Persia, Caucasus. *Hamamelidaceae*

The young hairy twigs mature into branches covered by grey bark which flakes from the trunk to reveal buff pink below. Magnificent tints of gold and crimson are produced by the ovate, oblong or obovate leaves. Lower branches should be removed during the early stages of establishment, otherwise the plant is inclined to remain stunted. The autumn colour and nude flowers in early spring make this a very desirable tree for any but the smallest of gardens, especially when planted amongst evergreens. 35ft (11m)

⊘ ❀Spring ◯ ✦ △▼

Prunus cerasifera 'Pissardii' (syn *P. c. atropurpurea*) Purple-leaved Plum. *Rosaceae*

Deservedly a popular tree for the foliage is a distinctive ruby red, changing to claret and then resembling the colour of the purple fruit which is rather spasmodically produced. The white blossom is well complemented by the leaves. Can also be grown as a decorative hedge. 25ft (8m)

⊘ ❀Spring ◯ ◕ ✦ △▼

Prunus serrula (syn *P.s. tibetica*) W. China. *Rosaceae*

The shining, brown, peeling bark resembles polished mahogany and the gleaming trunk is much appreciated during a bright winter day. Semi-erect branches become more relaxed to form a dome-shaped tree with arching limbs. 30ft (9m)

⊘ ❀Spring ◯ ◕ ✦ △▼

Prunus serrulata 'Amanogawa', Japanese Cherry. *Rosaceae*

A very slim, erect, tightly branched tree, suitable for a confined space and yet quite at home in a large garden. The clustered corymbs of semi-double, pink flowers are slightly scented. Immature leaves are pleasantly coloured bronze-green. 25ft (7.5m)

⊘ ❀Spring ◯ ◕ ✦ △▼

Prunus serrulata 'Kanzan', Japanese Cherry. *Rosaceae*

Large for an ornamental cherry, the tree produces vigorous upright branches, unless regulated by pruning during the summer months. The leaves appear bronze in spring-time, change to green and then turn bright red and orange during late autumn. The double pink flowers are very showy. 30ft (9m)

⊘ ❀Spring ◯ ◕ ✦ △▼

Prunus subhirtella 'Autumnalis', Autumn Cherry. *Rosaceae*

Large, fragrant white flowers are much appreciated during the bleak winter months and give the plant special value. The flowering shoots can be cut and used for indoor decoration. Autumn colour is particularly attractive when the foliage turns rich red and bronze. A good tree for the garden, regardless of size. 45ft (14m)

⊘ ❀Winter ◯ ◕ ✦ △▼

Prunus serrulata 'Tai Haku', Japanese Cherry. *Rosaceae*

This vigorous broad-headed tree produces very large pure white flowers, startling with their back drop of copper-red young foliage, which turns green as the leaves open. Autumn colours of yellow and orange provide an added bonus. One of the best white-flowered cherries available. 30ft (9m)

⊘ ❀Spring ◯ ◕ ✦ △▼

Prunus serrulata 'Ukon', Japanese Cherry. *Rosaceae*

Rather unusual, large, semi-double greenish-yellow flowers. The large green leaves turn deep purplish-red or brown rusty-red to give fine autumn colour. Nursery stock can be variable and the selection of a young tree with ample branches is desirable. The immature erect branches relax as the tree matures. 30ft (9m)

⌀ ✿Spring ○ ◑ ✺ ◺▼

Pyrus salicifolia 'Pendula', Willow-leaved Pear. *Rosaceae*

The young branchlets of this very elegant tree are covered with most attractive silky white down which vacates the upper surface to produce a glossy appearance. The small fruit, although ornamental, is of no culinary value. A weeping tree which is much more effective when staked to form a standard. 20ft (6m)

⌀ ✿Spring ↻Autumn ○ ✺ ◺▼

Rhus typhina (syn *R. hirta*, *R. viridiflora* [Male]) Stag's Horn Sumach, Eastern N. America. *Anacardiaceae*

A wide-spreading deciduous shrub with flat-topped habit and very pithy thick branchlets covered with small dense red hairs until mature. The very long pinnate leaves with oblong-lanceolate leaflets turn to shades of orange, red and purple in autumn. The stems may be cut back close to ground level every spring to produce superior foliage. Propagation by lifting rooted suckers. 10ft (3m)

⌀ ✿Summer ○ ◑ ✺ ◺▼

Prunus serrulata 'Ukon'

Pyrus salicifolia 'Pendula'

Prunus subhirtella 'Autumnalis'

Prunus serrulata 'Tai Haku'

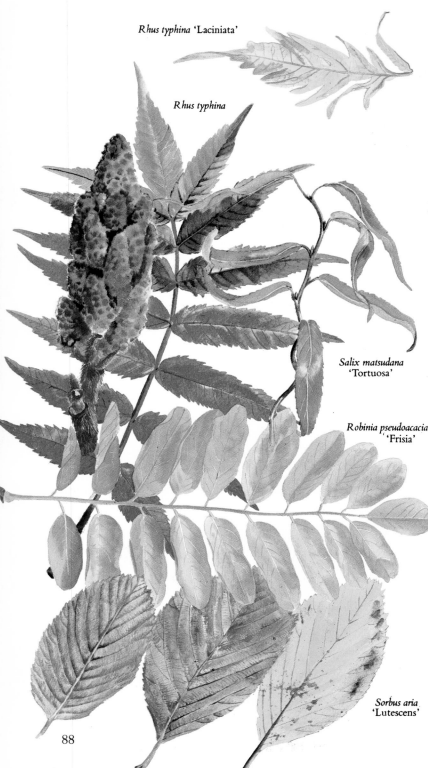

Rhus typhina 'Laciniata'

Rhus typhina

Salix matsudana 'Tortuosa'

Robinia pseudoacacia 'Frisia'

Sorbus aria 'Lutescens'

Rhus typhina 'Laciniata', Stag's Horn Sumach. *Anacardiaceae*

This female form has delightful finely cut leaves producing excellent autumn colour in shades of yellow to orange-red. An easy plant to grow in the garden. 20ft (6m)

⌀ ✿Summer ○ ✺ ◺▼

Robinia pseudoacacia 'Frisia', Locust, False Acacia. *Leguminosae*

Much appreciated for its deeply furrowed bark and graceful feathery pinnate leaves with delicate oval or ovate leaflets. The young branches tend to be rather brittle and prone to wind damage when grown in over-rich soil. The bright yellow foliage is emphasised if provided with a back drop of dark foliage and is complemented by purple-leaved plants. Suckers appearing from below ground should be removed. The young leaves and inner bark are poisonous. 30ft (9m)

⌀ ✿Summer ↻Autumn ○ ✺ ◺▼

Salix matsudana 'Tortuosa', Contorted or Corkscrew Willow. *Salicaceae*

Most unusual upright spiralling stems add much interest to the garden, especially during winter months after leaf fall. Will grow in any soil type. Good for flower arrangements. 40ft (12m)

⌀ ✿Spring ○ ◑ ● ▥ ◺▼

Sorbus aria 'Lutescens', Whitebeam. *Rosaceae*

An outstanding tree, especially in spring. The rounded head spreads from an immature pyramidal shape as it matures. The silvery oval or obovate leaves with yellow down, turn green above and grey below as the season progresses. Fruit cannot be guaranteed every year. 40ft (12m)

⌀ ✿Spring ○ ◑ ✺ ◺▼

Ornamental Conifers

Conifers are very ancient plants which, millions of years ago, developed a way of living that has enabled them to survive, often supremely well, in conditions no broad-leaved trees could endure. Some grow high up mountains and some inhabit sub-arctic regions. Conifers often make large trees in places where the soil is so poor that most of the other vegetation is dwarf.

Conifers include the tallest of all trees, since redwoods in Californian forests grow to a height of 300ft (91m), or even more. Some also live to a very great age and some of the bristle cone pines that are still alive in Californian mountains are believed to be several thousand years old.

There are only three truly native conifers in Britain, the Scots pine, yew and common juniper but this is not because our soil and climate are unsuitable for them. Long ago many more kinds grew here but they were destroyed when the ice came south in one of the ice ages and, when the ice receded again, our island character prevented us from being re-colonised from places in Europe where they had survived.

Characteristics of Conifers

Most conifers are evergreen and have leaves that are either very small or very narrow, which enables them to conserve moisture well. Many make conical trees which give a spiky effect quite different from that of broad-leaved trees, which are predominantly rounded in shape. This contrast in form can be used to great effect in the landscape either when conifers are grouped or when they are planted as isolated specimens.

Conifers bring all-year-round colour as well as varied shapes to the garden. This display is at The Wansdyke Nursery and Pygmy Pinetum.

Most conifers bear cones which contain their seeds and in some species these cones are very handsome. They vary greatly in size, shape and colour but they are only produced by mature trees. The word 'conifer' actually means cone bearing and is the popular form of 'coniferae', which was the original name used by botanists for the group of plants. But the group includes some non-cone bearing trees or shrubs such as the yews (*Taxus*) which have red berry-like fruits and the junipers (*Juniperus*) which also have berry-like fruits of various colours. Botanists now recognise eight distinct families where there was formerly but one and give them distinguishing names but gardeners usually continue the old convention of calling them all conifers. So in nursery catalogues under the general heading 'conifers' will be found such very different plants as pines, firs, spruces, cypresses, thuyas, cedars, junipers, yews, araucarias (monkey-puzzle trees) and ginkgos, the last with broad lobed leaves rather like single leaflets of the maidenhair fern greatly enlarged, for which reason it is popularly known as the maidenhair tree.

There is great variation in the colour of conifer leaves. Even in the wild they may be various shades of green or grey and in gardens other colours, which would not survive under natural conditions, have been preserved and are increased vegetatively

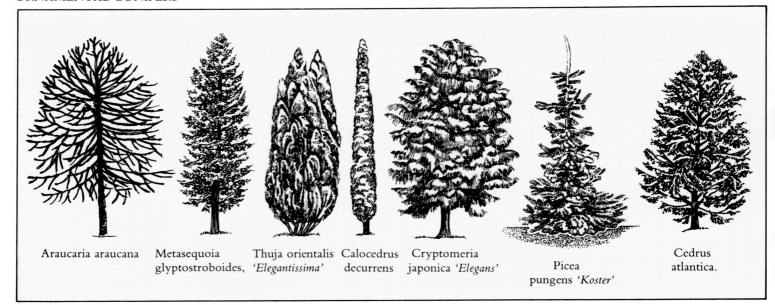

Araucaria araucana   Metasequoia glyptostroboides,   Thuja orientalis *'Elegantissima'*   Calocedrus decurrens   Cryptomeria japonica *'Elegans'*   Picea pungens *'Koster'*   Cedrus atlantica.

so that all the characteristics of the plant are maintained. Usually these garden forms are of some shade of yellow or they may be grey or silvery. This is another characteristic of conifers that can be put to good use when planning gardens or landscapes.

There is a popular belief that the leaves of conifers, and especially the needles of pines, are harmful to other plants because they contain resin. In fact pulverised bark of pines, which also contains resin, is now much used as a soil dressing, particularly as a loose surface mulch to retain moisture and smother weeds. The idea possibly arose because in dense conifer forests there is not much undergrowth but this is because of the lack of light not the fallen leaves.

For Providing Shelter

Because the evergreen conifers give just as much shelter in winter as in summer, they are extremely valuable as shelter trees both for protection from wind, which can be essential for many of the exotic plants grown in gardens, and for shade from the sun, which is necessary for many shade-loving plants including rhododendrons. However, when used for overhead shelter, conifers must not be planted closely, as they well may be when planted as windbreaks, or they may deprive the plants beneath them of too much light. Very often the best shade for other plants is given by a mixture of conifers and broad-leaved deciduous trees.

Some conifers grow very fast and these kinds can be useful to make a quick effect or to give rapid protection from wind. For many years one of the fastest growing kinds was the Monterey cypress (*Cupressus macrocarpa*) and this was much used as a windbreak. Unfortunately it is not completely hardy and, as it ages, it is liable to die or lose some of its branches. For these reasons, and also because it is even faster growing, this cypress has now been largely replaced for shelter by a fully hardy hybrid between it and the Lawson cypress (*Chamaecyparis lawsoniana*) which is named Leyland cypress (*Cupressocyparis leylandii*). This can add 4ft (1.2m) to its height every year.

Equally fast growing is the dawn redwood (*Metasequoia glyptostroboides*) which was only discovered in China in 1941 though it is very ancient. It looks much like the swamp cypress (*Taxodium distichum*) and, like it, is deciduous the leaves turning yellow and then brown before they fall in the autumn, but it grows at least twice as fast as the swamp cypress.

Planting

Some conifers transplant badly, especially after the first couple of years. Foresters overcome this difficulty by planting quite young seedlings which can be handled with little root damage and usually transplant well. Nurserymen frequently grow conifers in containers, which enables them to be planted with little or no root breakage. If larger plants are lifted from the open ground they are usually dug up with plenty of soil around the roots and this is wrapped in polythene or hessian, a process known as 'balling'. This protective material is best left in position until the plant is ready to go into its planting hole, when it should be removed carefully to retain as much as possible of the nursery soil around the roots.

Conifers, like other evergreens, transplant best in spring or autumn but, if grown in containers, they can be planted at any time. Because they are mainly evergreen and so present a fairly solid face to wind, newly planted conifers, unless very small, nearly always need to be staked but after a year or so they will be able to look after themselves.

The actual method of planting conifers is exactly the same as for broad-leaved trees and shrubs (see page 84). Most kinds will grow in all reasonably fertile soils but a few have special requirements and some dislike lime. The swamp cypress will grow in shallow water but will also succeed in ordinary drained soil.

Pruning

Conifers grown as individual specimens or in small ornamental groups seldom need much pruning. However, if branches get broken they must be removed and it is usually best to take the whole branch out even if only the end is damaged. It is all too easy to spoil the shape of conifers by cutting back branches part way and as conifers do not make new growth buds from bare stems as do many broad-leaved trees, truncated branches remain that are unsightly.

If branches get pulled down by the weight of snow collecting on them and do not go back into place of their own accord it may be possible to repair the damage by tying them in. Small-leaved conifers and narrowly erect varieties, such as some of the garden varieties of cypress and junipers, are particularly liable to suffer in this way but some varieties are much stiffer and shorter stemmed than others and so better able to support the weight of snow. It is desirable, if it is physically possible to do so, to shake snow off conifers before it has time to do this kind of damage.

All the really small-leaved conifers, such as the cypresses, thuyas and junipers, can be clipped any time from May to August and this is essential if they are grown as formal hedges. It can sometimes be useful even when they are planted as single specimens.

Dwarf Varieties

Some conifers are naturally dwarf and many conifers produce dwarf variants which will retain their character if propagated vegetatively. Dwarf conifers have become very fashionable for planting as miniature trees or shrubs in rock gardens or for growing in mini-pinetums i.e. collections of dwarf conifers usually on their own though some times they may be associated with other small plants. Some caution is necessary in choosing dwarf conifers since they vary greatly in their rate of growth and eventual size. Some will never get much above a foot in height, others will grow several feet high and there are conifers, misleadingly sold as dwarf, which grow slowly for a few years but then gradually accelerate until eventually they may become large shrubs or even trees. It is best to buy dwarf conifers from specialist nurseries or to make quite certain that the varieties offered are genuinely dwarf, see page 108.

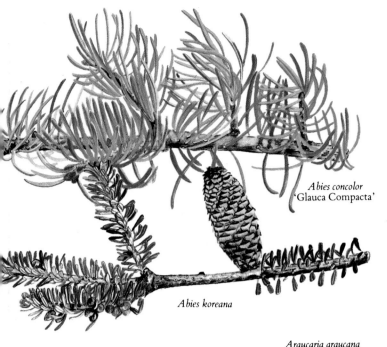

Abies concolor
'Glauca Compacta'

Abies koreana

Araucaria araucana

Calocedrus decurrens

Cedrus atlantica glauca, Atlas Cedar, Blue Cedar, N. Africa. *Pinaceae*

A handsome tree with very effective silvery-blue leaves. The older branches spread horizontally. An excellent specimen tree for a lawn provided sufficient space is available. Sometimes comes true from seed. 120ft (36.5m)

Chamaecyparis lawsoniana 'Ellwoodii'. *Cupressaceae*

This slow-growing, elegant, compact conical bush has short feathery sprays of dense grey-green juvenile foliage. Useful as a specimen for the rock garden or border and effective when grown in a container. 9ft (2.7m)

Chamaecyparis lawsoniana 'Pembury Blue'. *Cupressaceae*

This is a beautiful conical tree and one of the best of a large group. Most effective silver-blue foliage. 20ft (6m)

Chamaecyparis lawsoniana 'Stewartii'. *Cupressaceae*

An elegant tree of pyramidal habit with slightly erect branches giving rise to striking golden-yellow foliage. The colour tends to lose impact when over-shadowed. 25ft (7.6m)

Chamaecyparis lawsoniana 'Tamariscifolia'. *Cupressaceae*

A slow-growing multi-stemmed bush with relaxed habit when immature. The blue-green fronds resemble fans and create an altogether pleasing appearance. 15ft (4.5m)

Abies concolor 'Glauca Compacta'. *Pinaceae*

A compact slow-growing conifer of dense habit with egg-shaped resinous winter buds arising on yellowish glabrous shoots at first olive green. The immature cylindrical cones are green or purplish maturing to light brown. The silvery-blue leaves make this an outstanding plant for the rock garden or as a specimen set in a lawn. 2¹/₂ft (75cm)

Abies koreana, Korea. *Pinaceae*

This small slow-growing attractive conifer has slightly hairy, furrowed shoots giving rise to brownish winter buds covered with resin. Most attractive violet-purple cones are a feature of the neat conical plant which bears the cones on young specimens. 60ft (18m)

Araucaria araucana, Monkey Puzzle, Chile Pine, Chile, Argentine. *Araucariaceae*

An unusual, evergreen pyramidal or rounded tree with an erect cylindrical bole with resinous bark giving rise to regular tiers of whorled branches. The glossy green, spine-tipped, leathery leaves are spirally arranged and overlapping. Globose female cones develop over two years and shed conical seeds in early autumn. Easily raised from the edible seed, a resulting plant is best grown as an isolated specimen in a lawn. 65ft (20m)

Calocedrus decurrens (syn *Libocedrus decurrens*) Incense Cedar, S.W. United States. *Cupressaceae*

An elegant, slow-growing tree with a stiff columnar habit with vertical flattened branchlets and dark glossy green leaves. Much admired when planted as a single specimen or in a small group. 60ft (18m)

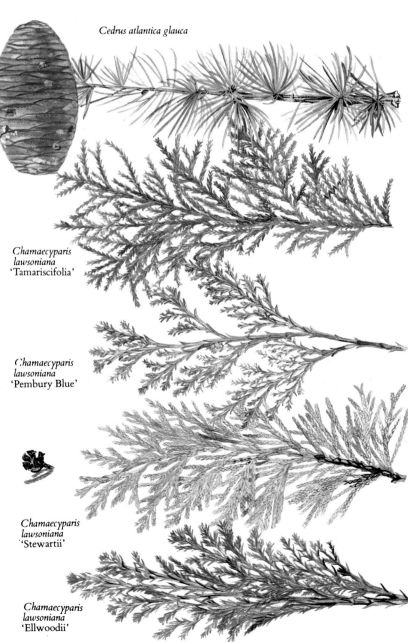

Cedrus atlantica glauca

Chamaecyparis
lawsoniana
'Tamariscifolia'

Chamaecyparis
lawsoniana
'Pembury Blue'

Chamaecyparis
lawsoniana
'Stewartii'

Chamaecyparis
lawsoniana
'Ellwoodii'

91

ORNAMENTAL CONIFERS

Chamaecyparis lawsoniana 'Wisselii'. *Cupressaceae*

Vigorous tree of columnar habit with upward twisting branches giving rise to blue-green leaves. The red male strobili are an unusual feature of the plant in spring. 30ft (9m)

△◔○◕▦ ◿

Chamaecyparis obtusa 'Nana'. *Cupressaceae*

Attractive slow-growing dwarf conifer forming a flat-topped dome with horizontal branches giving rise to flattened leaf-bearing branchlets. Blunt, fleshy, scale-like blue-green leaves are most appealing. An ideal plant for the rock garden or raised bed. 2ft (60cm)

△☁🌢○◕▦ ◿

Chamaecyparis pisifera 'Boulevard'. *Cupressaceae*

A dense, dwarf bush of conical habit with silvery blue-green, narrow, flat, pointed juvenile leaves soft to the touch. An excellent plant for the smaller garden. 6ft (2m)

△○◕▦ ◿

Cryptomeria japonica 'Elegans', Japanese Cedar. *Taxodiaceae*

An interesting plant in that the soft slender juvenile foliage is retained permanently. The supple trunks are covered by peeling, red-brown bark and this gives the tree a most striking effect especially in autumn when the shoots and leaves turn bronzy red, most unusual for an evergreen. Top-heavy trees may be lopped to prevent them falling. 22ft (7m)

△○◕▦ ◿

× Cupressocyparis leylandii (syn *Cupressus leylandii*) Leyland Cypress. *Cupressaceae*

Very vigorous pyramidal bi-generic hybrid which is much used for screening due to its rapid growth of approximately 3ft (1m) per year once established. The fresh green leaves arise from attractive drooping branches. Will tolerate maritime conditions and hard pruning. 65ft (20m)

△○◕▦ ◿

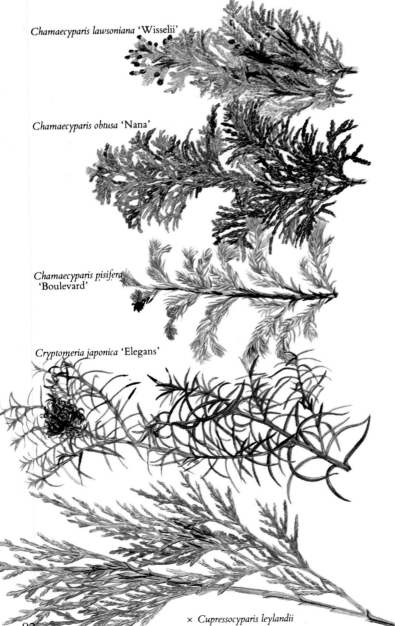

Chamaecyparis lawsoniana 'Wisselii'

Chamaecyparis obtusa 'Nana'

Chamaecyparis pisifera 'Boulevard'

Cryptomeria japonica 'Elegans'

× *Cupressocyparis leylandii*

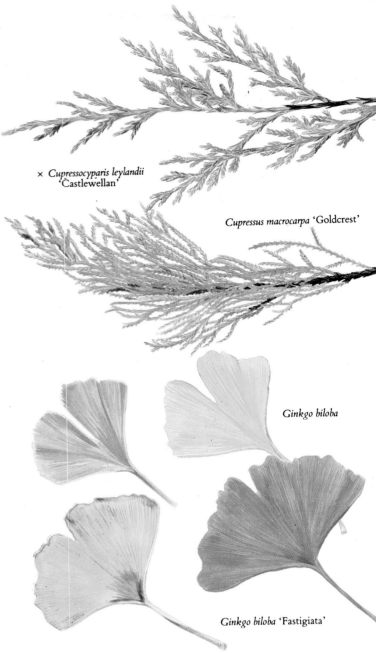

× *Cupressocyparis leylandii* 'Castlewellan'

Cupressus macrocarpa 'Goldcrest'

Ginkgo biloba

Ginkgo biloba 'Fastigiata'

× Cupressocyparis leylandii 'Castlewellan'. *Cupressaceae*

Striking golden form of the very popular screening plant. The form retains the vigorous growth habit and can be pruned to keep it within bounds as necessary. 65ft (20m)

△○◕▦ ◿

Cupressus macrocarpa 'Goldcrest', Monterey Cypress. *Cupressaceae*

An attractive conical tree of dense compact habit supporting bright golden-yellow juvenile foliage. Much used as a hedge plant for screening. Hard pruning into old wood should be avoided. 30ft (9m)

△○▦ ◿

Ginkgo biloba, Maidenhair Tree, China. *Ginkgoaceae*

This interesting, deciduous unisexual conifer is probably the most ancient of existing flowering plants. The erect whorled branches give rise to spreading secondary branches which are pendulous at the end. The fan-shaped, irregularly notched leaves with parallel veins, arise on long stalks and turn an attractive butter yellow in the autumn. Will tolerate polluted air. 70ft (21.3m)

∅🌢◔○▦ ◿

Ginkgo biloba 'Fastigiata', Maidenhair Tree. *Ginkgoaceae*

A most decorative columnar tree with upright branches. Especially good as a specimen tree for the smaller garden. 20ft (6m)

∅🌢◔○▦ ◿

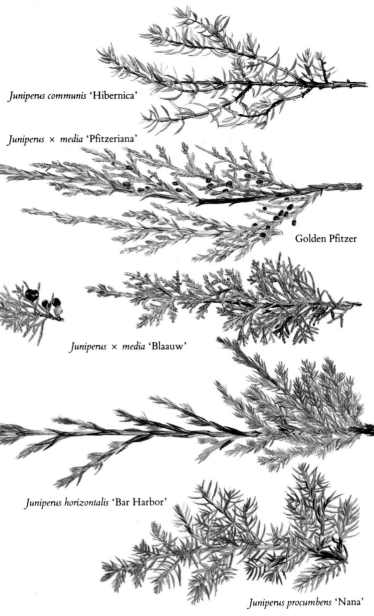

Juniperus communis 'Hibernica'

Juniperus × *media* 'Pfitzeriana'

Golden Pfitzer

Juniperus × *media* 'Blaauw'

Juniperus horizontalis 'Bar Harbor'

Juniperus procumbens 'Nana'

Juniperus communis 'Hibernica', Irish Juniper. *Cupressaceae*

An ideal plant for a formal setting as the dense stiff and fastigiate silvery column is very slow growing. The leaves are awl shaped and sharp pointed with one band of stomata along the centre of the concave upper surface. Attractive when set amongst heathers. 9ft (2.7m)
△◐○◑❈ ◿

Juniperus horizontalis 'Bar Harbor', Creeping Juniper. *Cupressaceae*

Low, spreading shrub rooting from the branches as it progresses over the soil; good for ground cover with dense stiff branchlets clad with sharply pointed awl-shaped leaves concave on the upper surface. The juvenile type and scale-like, sharply pointed adult leaves are carried in pairs. Will tolerate maritime conditions. 1¹/₂ft (45cm)
△○◑❈ ◿

Juniperus × *media* 'Blaauw'. *Cupressaceae*

Compact strong-growing shrub with feathery ascending branches and dense grey-green leaves. An attractive plant with many uses in the garden, especially good when flanking a drive or as a specimen set in a lawn or planted in a group for ground cover. 4¹/₂ft (1.4m)
△○◑❈ ◿

Juniperus × *media* 'Pfitzeriana', Pfitzer Juniper. *Cupressaceae*

A much appreciated wide-spreading conifer with stout ascending branches with mainly green, adult scale-like leaves; juvenile needle-like leaves arising occasionally. An excellent plant for ground cover and to camouflage unsightly manhole covers etc., or as a specimen set in a lawn. The Golden Pfitzer, displaying golden foliage in summer, is of equal importance and much used. 4¹/₂ft (1.4m)
△○◑❈ ◿

Juniperus procumbens 'Nana', Creeping Juniper. *Cupressaceae*

A low, compact spreading plant with abundant short branches clad with awl-shaped pointed leaves, very effective for ground cover to suppress weed growth. 1ft (30cm)
△○◑❈ ◿

Juniperus sabina tamariscifolia, Spanish Savin, S. Europe. *Cupressaceae*

Vigorous, evergreen flat-topped shrub with spreading branches which release a strong odour when touched. The opposite paired, or tripled, juvenile awl-shaped leaves have a sharp tip and concave upper surface. Adult scale-like and overlapping leaves arise on very slender branchlets. The intermediate stage leaf is larger and more pointed than the adult. 3ft (1m)
△○◑❈ ◿

Juniperus scopulorum 'Blue Heaven', Rocky Mountain Juniper. *Cupressaceae*

A vigorous, pyramidal evergreen with striking bright blue foliage. The juvenile leaves, awl-shaped in pairs and pointed, are present at the same time as ovate, adult, overlapping scale leaves. Mature trees with adult leaves only. A most useful plant for a heather garden or as a specimen set in a small lawn. 15ft (4.5m)
△○◑❈ ◿

Juniperus virginiana 'Skyrocket', Pencil Cedar. *Cupressaceae*

An aptly named vigorous plant with a very narrow slender columnar habit. The erect branches give rise to both juvenile and adult leaves, the former paired and awl shaped, pointed and concave inside. The adult ovate overlapping scale leaves are thickened and pointed. Much planted in smaller gardens as a lawn specimen and attractive as a dot plant amongst heathers. 15ft (4.5m)
△○◑❈ ◿

Metaseqoia glyptostroboides, Dawn Redwood, China. *Taxodiaceae*

Previously only known in fossil form and rediscovered in 1941, this vigorous deciduous conifer has feathery foliage consisting of linear, bright green leaves turning bronze then bright yellow in autumn. The dark brown, pendulous, cylindrical cones mature during their first year. An excellent tree for the larger garden. 100ft (30m)
◡◖◠○❈ ◿

Picea abies 'Nidiformis', Common Spruce, Norway Spruce. *Pinaceae*

This dwarf, dense, compact spreading bush is good for ground cover. The young shoots are smooth and hairy eventually giving rise to the most attractive reddish-brown winter buds. An interesting plant for a rock garden, difficult slope or border. 1¹/₂ft (45cm)
△○◑❈▼ ◿

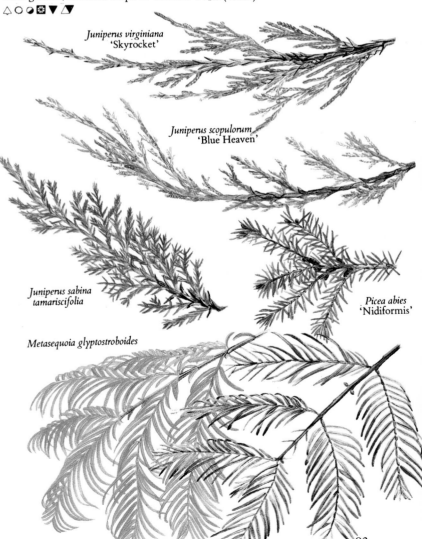

Juniperus virginiana 'Skyrocket'

Juniperus scopulorum 'Blue Heaven'

Juniperus sabina tamariscifolia

Picea abies 'Nidiformis'

Metasequoia glyptostroboides

93

Picea breweriana, Brewer's Weeping Spruce, California, Oregon. *Pinaceae*

A beautiful, slow-growing, stiff dense tree erect at first then becoming pendulous with long slender branchlets. The long, slender, flattened dark green leaves surround the shoot. Most interesting cones are first green becoming purple then brown. A first-class ornamental conifer for the larger garden. 100ft (30m)

△◌○◐▦▩▼◿

Picea omorika, Serbian Spruce, Yugoslavia. *Pinaceae*

Very narrow vigorous tree with a most slender reddish-brown trunk which gives rise to short drooping branches curving upwards at the tips and clothed with persistent down. Abundant adpressed leaves occur on the upper side of the branch with few below. The tapering blue-black cones maturing to dark brown have broad rounded scales with jagged margins. Will tolerate polluted atmosphere. 90ft (27m)

△◌○◐▩▼◿

Picea pungens 'Koster', Colorado Spruce. *Pinaceae*

Small, dense, pyramidal tree giving rise to short branches with sturdy young shoots and egg-shaped winter buds. The most attractive blue leaves are rigid and end in a sharp spine. A beautiful specimen tree. 30ft (9m)

△◌○◐▩◿

Pinus mugo pumilio (syn *P. montana pumilio*, *P. pumilio*) Mountain Pine, Europe. *Pinaceae*

A rather variable bush-like pine which gives rise to several greyish-brown curving stems often prostrate with smooth young green shoots. Most useful for ground cover over difficult slopes. An ideal plant amongst heathers or on the rock garden or scree. 6ft (2m)

△◖○▩◿

Pinus nigra maritima, Corsican Pine, S.E. Europe. *Pinaceae*

Stately tree with abundant foliage, light brown glabrous shoots and resinous cylindrical terminal buds with a slender point. The very minutely toothed, long, dark green leaves arise in pairs, as do the cones, or singly or in conical-shaped, bright brown clusters. A conifer for the larger garden which should be planted as young specimen to establish with certainty. 120ft (36m)

△◌○▩◿

Pinus nigra 'Pygmaea', Italy. *Pinaceae*

A very slow-growing form of Corsican pine with a dense globular shape giving rise to dull green needles which turn yellow in winter. Ideal for the rock garden or as a specimen for the smaller garden. 7ft (2.1m)

△◖○▩◿

Pinus sylvestris 'Aurea', Scots Pine, Scotch Fir. *Pinaceae*

This slow-growing small tree has smooth young green shoots and resinous winter buds. The paired leaves turn from green to yellow in the autumn and revert to green in the spring; it is interesting and unusual that these changes are made at least twice before the leaves fall. A most useful tree for any size of garden. 18ft (5.5m)

△◌○◐▩▼◿

Pinus sylvestris 'Watereri'. *Pinaceae*

A slow-growing bush or small tree with spherical habit and a most pleasing bluish-grey hue. An excellent plant for the smaller garden, particularly if set amongst heather, and with a useful life span in the rock garden before it eventually becomes too large. 22ft (7m)

△◌○◐▩▼◿

Taxodium distichum, Swamp Cypress, Deciduous Cypress, S. United States. *Taxodiaceae*

A beautiful deciduous pyramidal tree with more widespread branches at maturity and an erect, tapered, reddish-brown fibrous trunk, occasionally producing hollow roots which resemble knees growing into the air from below ground. The slender, annual, budless shoots fall in autumn together with the leaves. The soft, green feathery foliage turns rich brown in autumn providing a glorious display when reflected in water, a situation favoured by the plant which grows almost as well in drier soil. Pruning is often necessary during the formative years to establish a leading shoot. 75ft (23m)

◌○▦▼◿

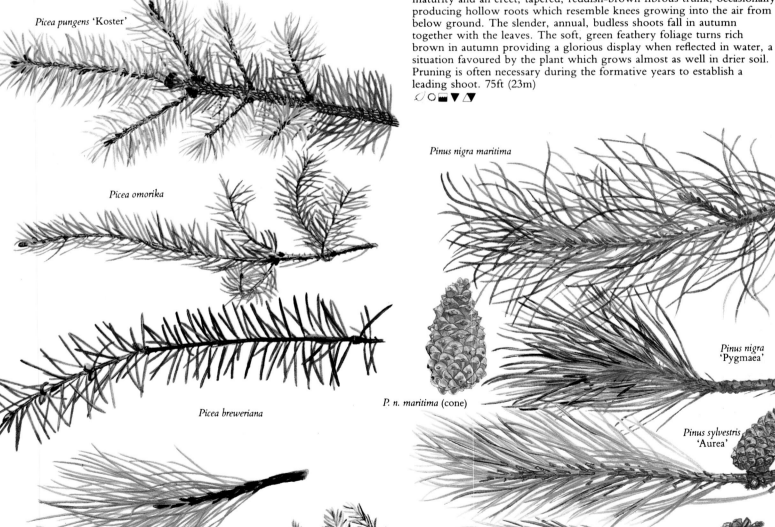

Picea pungens 'Koster'

Picea omorika

Picea breweriana

Pinus mugo pumilio

Taxodium distichum

Pinus nigra maritima

Pinus nigra 'Pygmaea'

P. n. maritima (cone)

Pinus sylvestris 'Aurea'

Pinus sylvestris 'Watereri'

Taxus baccata 'Fastigiata', Irish Yew. *Taxaceae*

An elegant, erect dense tree of columnar habit with stiff branches and branchlets giving rise to dark glossy leaves carried at right angles around the twigs. The unisexual flowers appear on separate trees, this being the female form. A most striking male form 'Fastigiata Aureomarginata' displays leaves with a yellow margin. Precautions are often necessary to protect the tree from snow loading by careful banding with wire which should be slackened periodically to avoid distorted growth. 15ft (4.5m)
△○◔●▧/▽

Taxus baccata 'Semperaurea'. *Taxaceae*

A wide-spreading dense shrub of semi-erect habit with bright yellow foliage which darkens with age. This slow-growing male form is most attractive and useful as a specimen plant set in a lawn. 6ft (2m)
△○◔●▧/▽

Thuja occidentalis 'Rheingold', American Arbor-vitae. *Cupressaceae*

Rather variable slow-growing shrub usually compact and eventually broadly pyramidal displaying gold colour in summer and copper during winter. The shrub becomes rather leggy when mature with slender branches giving rise to adult and juvenile leaves and pruning will prevent the inelegance. 10ft (3m)
△○◔▧/▽

Thuja occidentalis 'Smaragd'. *Cupressaceae*

A slow-growing emerald-green conifer with pyramidal habit. An excellent plant for hedges, as it tolerates pruning, or as a specimen. 30ft (9m)
△○◔▧/▽

Thuja orientalis 'Elegantissima' (syn *Biota orientalis elegantissima*), Chinese Arbor-vitae. *Cupressaceae*

Dense, columnar slow-growing bush giving rise to flattened branchlets at right angles to the branch. The very small, dense, yellow leaves, later turning golden bronze then green in winter, are triangular with minute stomata and only slightly aromatic when bruised. A distinct style and most attractive as a specimen for the border. 6ft (2m)
△○◔▧/▽

Thuja orientalis 'Rosedalis', Chinese Arbor-vitae. *Cupressaceae*

A dense, round-topped dwarf bush with soft juvenile foliage which is pale yellow in spring then green and turning purple in winter. Most attractive when used to flank steps or as a specimen in the rock garden. 2¹/₂ft (75cm)
△○◔▧/▽

Thuja plicata 'Fastigiata', Western Red Cedar. *Cupressaceae*

This erect, fast-growing conifer has dark, glossy green scale-like sharply pointed leaves which are aromatic when bruised. Ideal as a hedge plant, forming a tall dense screen, and will tolerate clipping. Its elegant appearance is much appreciated when it is grown as a specimen or in a small group. 100ft (30m)
△○◔▧/▽

Thuja plicata 'Stoneham Gold'. *Cupressaceae*

Small slow-growing conical bush with dense foliage which is bright yellow in summer and winter. An ideal plant for the rock garden. 3ft (1m)
△○◔▧/▽

Tsuga canadensis 'Pendula' (syn *Tsuga canadensis sargentiana*) Eastern Hemlock. *Pinaceae*

This large bush or small tree has dense weeping branches with young bright grey shoots giving rise to short-stalked linear leaves tapering to a blunt point. A most delightful specimen when set in a lawn or planted on a large rock garden. 6ft (2m)
△◔▧▼/▽

Taxus baccata 'Fastigiata Aureomarginata'

Taxus baccata 'Fastigiata'

Taxus baccata 'Semperaurea'

Thuja occidentalis 'Rheingold'

Thuja occidentalis 'Smaragd'

Thuja orientalis 'Elegantissima'

Thuja orientalis 'Rosedalis'

Thuja plicata 'Fastigiata'

Thuja plicata 'Stoneham Gold'

Tsuga canadensis 'Pendula'

Climbing and Wall Plants

Climbing plants have for long been considered important in garden design to give added height to planting schemes and their value in this respect is even more highly rated today when gardens are very much on the small side. In the modern pocket-handkerchief garden it is even more important to make use of as much vertical space as possible.

Climbers can be used on walls, fences, free-standing trellis screens, screen-block walls, pergolas, arches, and wooden posts erected specially for them. They can be grown over unsightly sheds and garages, grown up mature or semi-mature trees and even used to cover tree stumps.

Climbing plants are very versatile and can be used in a number of imaginative ways in the garden. This arch of large-flowered clematis is at Pusey House.

Opposite: Lonicera japonica halliana *climbing over trellis work to screen a domestic oil tank.*

Another use for some climbers is ground cover, particularly on steep banks as an alternative to grass, where they create not only colour and pleasing texture but a virtually maintenance-free area.

There are climbers suitable for all aspects, north-, south-, east- and west-facing walls and fences, so even the gloomiest wall can be clothed in greenery and brightened with flowers.

The term climber is used rather loosely in gardening to include plants that do not really climb in the true sense of the word. Many tall shrubs are used in a similar way to climbers, to clothe walls, fences and so on, but they are trained flat against their supports. These are perhaps more correctly called 'wall shrubs', but they are usually found listed with true climbers in catalogues. Examples are *Garrya elliptica*, chaenomeles, abutilon, ceanothus, chimonanthus and escallonia.

North- and East-facing Walls and Fencing
These aspects receive a limited amount of sun or none at all and therefore are considered shady and cold. Many people think nothing will grow in these situations but there are, in fact, many climbers and wall shrubs which may be used.

Chaenomeles, the ornamental quince, like the beautiful *C.* x *superba* 'Knap Hill Scarlet', will brighten such aspects early in the year. Equally valuable on account of its evergreen foliage and winter catkins is the shrub *Garrya elliptica*.

Ivies are a good choice and are grown for their ornamental evergreen foliage. Some have small leaves, like the popular green and gold variegated *Hedera helix* 'Goldheart', while others have large bold foliage, *H. colchica* 'Dentata Variegata' being a good example. All ivies are self-clinging, attaching themselves to any smooth surface by means of stem roots.

Also self-clinging is the climbing hydrangea, *H. petiolaris*, and the parthenocissus, which are grown mainly for their brilliant autumn leaf colour. The latter attach themselves to walls, fences and the like by means of little sucker pads.

Also giving good autumn colour, and fruits in a warm summer, is the vine *Vitis* 'Brandt'. *V. coignetiae* has massive leaves which also turn to fiery shades in autumn. These vines look particularly good when grown with the variegated large-leaved ivies.

The Russian vine, *Polygonum baldschuanicum,* is also suitable for shady walls, as are the ever-popular winter and summer jasmines – *Jasminum nudiflorum* and *J. officinale.* Try also the evergreen honeysuckle, *Lonicera japonica* 'Aureoreticulata' with gold-netted foliage.

South- and West-facing Walls and Fences
In these warm sunny situations it is possible to grow a very wide range of climbers and wall shrubs, including some which are on the tender side and need the protection that these walls provide, like abutilons, ceanothus, eccremocarpus, escallonias, passifloras and solanums.

Some climbers are grown for their attractive foliage, like the golden hop, *Humulus lupulus* 'Aureus', and the pink, white and green *Actinidia kolomikta*.

Winter flowers can be provided by *Chimonanthus praecox* 'Luteus', spring blooms by *Wisteria sinensis*, and summer colour from a wide range of choice plants like *Abutilon megapotamicum, Ceanothus* 'Topaz' and *C. thyrsiflorus*, clematis in variety (ideally for west walls or fences), *Eccremocarpus scaber, Escallonia* 'Iveyi', honeysuckles or loniceras, the passion flower or *Passiflora caerulea*, and *Solanum crispum* 'Glasnevin'.

For Growing up Large Trees
One of the most beautiful ways of displaying climbers is to grow them up reasonably large mature or semi-mature trees. You will need to start them off by guiding the stems up the trunks with bamboo canes, but once into the branches they will support themselves. A clematis growing through a deep green conifer, for example, is a beautiful sight and simple to achieve if you have large enough trees.

Other suitable climbers for arboreal supports are jasmines, honeysuckles, parthenocissus, Russian vine, vitis and wisteria.

Suitable for Ground Cover
To cover large areas of ground to make them labour saving, do consider some of the climbing plants. They are particularly suitable for clothing steep banks instead of grass. Clematis, the climbing hydrangea, the evergreen honeysuckle and ivies can all be used for this purpose. When buying ivies for ground cover, choose only those specially grown for the purpose – not plants trained to canes as these generally do not lie flat after planting.

Cultivation
Methods of Support Most climbers and wall shrubs are trained in such a way that a main or permanent framework of stems covers the support, whether it is a wall, fence, pergola, trellis screen, or whatever. With most climbers and wall shrubs this framework has to be tied in to a support system. If the plants are being grown against a flat surface, such as a wall or fence, then some provision will have to be made for tying in. This does not apply, of course, to self-clinging climbers, which are able to attach themselves to flat surfaces.

For non-clinging plants, the framework can be tied into a system of horizontal galvanised wires attached to the wall or fence and spaced about 12in (30cm) apart. These could be fixed to a wall by means of metal vine eyes or masonry nails, or to a wooden fence with metal hooks or eyes screwed into the timber. The wires should be held at least 1in (2.5cm) away from the wall or fence.

Alternatively, fix to the wall or fence proprietary trellis panels, which come in various shapes and sizes. Many of these are made of plastic-coated metal and may be green or white. Most good garden centres offer quite a good range of ornamental trellis panels. They can be fixed to the wall or fence in a similar way to wires.

Climbers growing up trees will eventually be able to support themselves once they start twining around the branches.

Planting Most climbers these days are supplied in containers or pots – very few being sold bare root or rootballed from open-ground nurseries. In theory this means they can be planted at any time of the year, provided the ground is not very wet or frozen. However, it has been found from experience that most climbers, especially those which may be on the tender side, establish very much better if they are planted in the spring as the soil is warming up and drying out. Evergreens, especially, should always be planted in spring, a good month being April.

Prepare the site well for each plant, by double digging an area of about 3ft (1m) square and incorporating organic matter in each trench, such as well-rotted farmyard manure, garden compost, peat, spent hops or mushroom compost. This is particularly important if the soil is inclined to dry out rapidly. Very often the soil immediately under a wall or fence is liable to remain on the dry side, so this organic matter will help to retain moisture.

Do not plant hard up against a wall or fence, or other support, but allow a gap of about 12in (30cm). The stems of the young plant can be initially guided to the wall by means of one or two bamboo canes. When planting, the plant can be tilted in slightly towards its support.

After planting water well whenever the soil starts to become dry, and continue this throughout the summer.

In the spring of each year apply a general-purpose fertilizer around each plant, and if available a mulch of organic matter such as manure (well rotted), compost, peat or pulverised bark.

Remember that clematis need a cool root run, so the root area should ideally be shaded by, say, some dwarf shrubs or other plants.

Pruning The only other attention needed by climbers and wall shrubs is pruning, and even this is minimal with some. Pruning details are given, where necessary, under the individual plant descriptions which follow.

Abutilon megapotamicum, Brazil. *Malvaceae*

This beautiful semi-evergreen shrub has slender shoots giving rise to cordate-based ovate leaves with coarsely toothed margins. The abundant lantern-shaped flowers are most charming and at their best on a south-facing wall. Prune in spring by thinning out old spent wood to make way for new. Can be propagated by seed or by cuttings taken during spring and summer. 6ft (2m)
⏶ ⏶ ✿ Spring ◐ ◉ ✕ △▼

Actinidia kolomikta, China, Japan, Manchuria. *Actinidiaceae*

A most attractive climber with large alternate ovate-oblong leaves which are purple when young but become variegated with age; the variegation is more pronounced when grown against a sunny wall. Cut back young stems in April to within 3 buds of the old wood. Can be raised from seed or by cuttings during late summer. 18ft (5.5m)
✐ ◐ ◉ ✕ △▼

Ceanothus 'Topaz'. *Rhamnaceae.*

A delightful deciduous shrub which makes a fine bush and produces panicles of indigo-blue flowers during the summer. Cut back to within 4 in (10cm) or so of previous year's growth in March. Propagate by soft cuttings taken during summer. The deciduous ceanothus are rather more hardy than the evergreen kinds. 5ft (1.5m)
✐ ✿ Summer ◐ ✕ △▼

Ceanothus thyrsiflorus, Californian Lilac, California. *Rhamnaceae*

An evergreen shrub with triple-veined, alternate, glossy green ovate leaves. The roundish clusters of abundant pale blue flowers arise on wood made the previous year. Pruning only required to thin out old wood and should be carried out immediately after flowering. Propagate by cuttings taken during summer. 20ft (6m)
△ ✿ Spring ◐ ✕ △▼

Abutilon megapotamicum

Actinidia kolomikta

Ceanothus thyrsiflorus   Ceanothus 'Topaz'

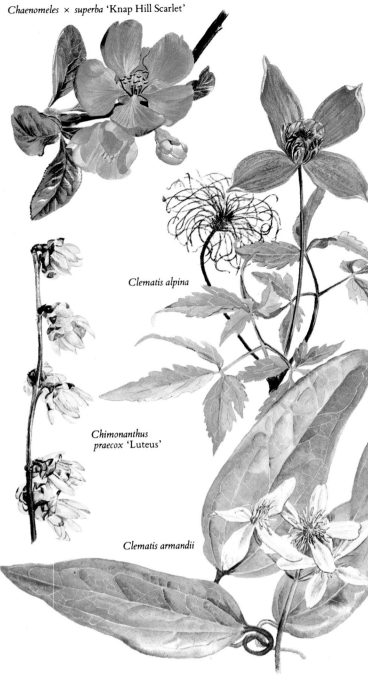

Chaenomeles × superba 'Knap Hill Scarlet'

Clematis alpina

Chimonanthus
praecox 'Luteus'

Clematis armandii

Chaenomeles × superba 'Knap Hill Scarlet'. *Rosaceae*

A most attractive hybrid with large orange-scarlet flowers. Summer pruning helps to establish flower bud initiation. Propagate by lifting rooted suckers or by layering. 6ft (2m)
✐ ✿ Spring ✿ Autumn ◐ ◉ ✕ △▼

Chimonanthus praecox 'Luteus', Winter Sweet. *Calycanthaceae*

Very desirable deciduous shrub with dark green ovate-lanceolate leaves. The most fragrant solitary or paired flowers are produced on wood made during the previous summer and are much used for indoor decoration. The plant takes several years to reach flowering size. Pruning should be carried out during the end of February or early March by removing weak and overcrowded growth, the remainder being shortened. 10ft (3m)
✐ ✿ Winter ◐ ◉ ✕ △▼

Clematis alpina, Europe, N. Asia. *Ranunculaceae*

Deciduous climbing plant giving rise to long doubly ternate leaves with ovate-lanceolate coarsely toothed leaflets. The nodding solitary flowers variously shaded blue produce tufted silky-styled achenes. An attractive plant for wall or pergola. Prune out any dead wood and cut back growth to within bounds immediately after flowering. 8ft (2.5m)
✐ ✿ Spring ✿ Summer ◐ ◉ ● ✕ △ △▼

Clematis armandii, China. *Ranunculaceae*

A beautiful evergreen climber, the young stems minutely downy giving rise to glossy green leaves with narrowly ovate-lanceolate leaflets. The abundant creamy-white to rose flowers appearing in dense axillary clusters. Growths should be tied to supports to avoid being blown down. Thin out and, if necessary, shorten stems after flowering. 20ft (6m)
△ ✿ Spring ◐ ◉ ✕ △▼

Clematis montana rubens

Clematis
'Ernest Markham'

Clematis × jackmannii

Clematis tangutica

Eccremocarpus scaber, Glory Flower, Chile. *Bignoniaceae*

A handsome semi-woody climber with herbaceous shoots giving rise to opposite doubly pinnate leaves with unequally lobed ovate leaflets. The plant is self-supporting by much-branched tendrils. The racemes of nodding flowers are a most attractive bright orange-red. Propagated by seed sown in heat during early spring, flowers appear during the first year. Pruning consists of cutting away dead branches in spring. 15ft (4.5m)
△ ✿☀Summer☀Autumn ○ ◕ ✳ △▼

Escallonia 'Iveyi'. *Escalloniaceae*

An attractive vigorous evergreen shrub with ovate, glossy, deep green leaves and large panicles of white flowers in July and August. The plant can be pruned immediately after flowering to keep it within bounds. Easily propagated by cuttings taken in late summer. 10ft (3m)
△ ◖☀Summer ○ ✳ △▼

Garrya elliptica, California, Oregon. *Garryaceae*

This vigorous evergreen shrub produces dark green oval leaves with wavy margins. The flowers are a feature of the plant being silvery-grey and densely packed on pendent catkins, the male up to 1ft (30cm) long. Thin out overcrowded growth in March. Propagate by semi-hardwood cuttings taken in July or August with bottom heat. The young plants should be grown on in containers to avoid root check at planting time. 15ft (4.5m)
△☀Winter ○ ◕ ✳ △▼

Hedera canariensis 'Gloire de Marengo', Variegated Ivy. *Araliaceae*

A self-clinging climber with large, glossy, lobeless or shallowly lobed leaves, green in the centre merging into silver-grey with cream margins set off by claret-coloured stems. Overwintering foliage damaged by severe frost is soon replaced by new leaves the following spring. An attractive plant to clad south-facing walls and fences. Pruning is not required other than to keep the plant within bounds. Easily propagated by cuttings or by lifting rooted stems. 25ft (7.5m)
△ ◖ ○ ✳ △▼

Garrya elliptica

Eccremocarpus scaber

Escallonia 'Iveyi'

Hedera canariensis
'Gloire de Marengo'

Clematis montana rubens, China. *Ranunculaceae*

A vigorous deciduous climber useful for covering pergolas and most attractive when the long bronze-purple shoots and leaves overhang a wall or fence. The abundant rose-pink flowers are a feature of the plant. Prune by cutting out old flowering shoots in June. Propagate by layering in spring or early summer. 30ft (9m)
⌀☀Spring ○ ◕ ✳ △▼

Clematis tangutica, China. *Ranunculaceae*

Most interesting deciduous climber with glaucous green leaves and ragged leaflets. The rich yellow solitary flowers, borne on downy pedicels, are much the best in the colour range and give rise to achenes with attractive, silvery feathered styles. Pruning should be carried out in March by cutting back to the base of the previous year's growth. An excellent plant for any situation where it can clamber. 15ft (4.5m)
⌀☀Summer☀Summer ○ ◕ ✳ △▼

Clematis × jackmannii. *Ranunculaceae*

A vigorous climber with large and abundant rich violet-purple flowers on the current year's growth. Pruning takes place in February or March by cutting all growth back to within 1ft (30cm) of the ground; plants otherwise become devoid of foliage at the base. Regrettably all large-flowered clematis are subject to an unidentifiable disorder known as 'clematis wilt'. Shoots that suddenly collapse for no apparent reason should be cut to the ground and replacement shoots may be healthy. 13ft (4m)
⌀✿☀Summer ○ ◕ ✳ △▼

Clematis 'Ernest Markham'. *Ranunculaceae*

Beautiful hybrid with very large, abundant, glowing red, velvety flowers produced on shoots made during the current year. The plant should be pruned hard to within 1ft (30cm) of the ground in February or March. 7ft (2.1m)
⌀☀Summer ○ ◕ ✳ △▼

Hedera colchica 'Dentata Variegata'

Hedera helix 'Little Diamond'

Humulus lupulus 'Aureus'

Hedera helix 'Goldheart'

Hydrangea petiolaris

Hydrangea petiolaris (syn *H. scandens, H. tileaefolia*) Climbing Hydrangea, Japan. *Hydrangeaceae*

This deciduous vigorous climbing plant is self clinging by aerial roots but often requires assistance to cling until established. the glossy green ovate leaves provide a most suitable back drop for the corymbs of blossom, small fertile florets in the centre surrounded by large white sterile flowers. A most attractive plant for a wall or other support. Remove dead wood and straggly shoots in early spring. Propagate by cuttings which root readily. 80ft (24m)

Jasminum nudiflorum, Winter Jasmine, China. *Oleaceae*

This rambling deciduous shrub is ideal for growing on a wall. The long slender green branches give rise to abundant yellow flowers in the axils of the previous season's leaves followed by lustrous trifoliate leaves. Attractive as a free-growing plant or scrambling amid the branches of an evergreen shrub to add interest during the dark months. Reduce shoots immediately after flowering to keep within bounds. Easily propagated by layering or by cuttings. 15ft (4.5m)

Jasminum officinale, Common Jasmine, China, N. India, Persia. *Oleaceae*

The beautifully fragrant clusters of flowers make this a good choice to clad a wall or clamber over a roof. A semi-evergreen, vigorous climbing shrub with pinnate leaves composed of up to nine leaflets. Little pruning is necessary other than thinning overcrowded growth. Increase plants by layering or by cuttings. 30ft (9m)

Lonicera japonica 'Aureoreticulata', Honeysuckle. *Caprifoliaceae*

A climbing plant with most attractive bright yellow veins in the leaf. The paired fragrant flowers are produced spasmodically over a long period during the summer months. Severe winter weather often kills the top growth which is refurbished the following summer. Cut back previous year's growth to healthy buds in spring. Propagate by layering or by cuttings. 20ft (6m)

Lonicera japonica halliana, Japanese Honeysuckle, Japan, China, Korea, Manchuria. *Caprifoliaceae*

Vigorous semi-evergreen or evergreen climbing plant with ovate, often lobed, leaves and very fragrant white flowers which change to yellow. A very good climber for concealing walls or other objects. Cut back the previous year's growth in spring. Increase by layering or by cuttings. 30ft (9m)

Hedera colchica 'Dentata Variegata', Persian Ivy. *Araliaceae*

The self-clinging rapidly climbing stems give rise to very large, most attractive ovate or heart-shaped green variegated yellow leaves often tinted with purple. Prune only to keep growth within bounds. The young shoots are enhanced by a covering of yellowish down. 25ft (7.5m)

Hedera helix 'Goldheart'. *Araliaceae*

A most attractive form of this popular ivy with small green leaves displaying a rich yellow central blotch. Rather slow to establish then rampant. Prune only to keep plant within bounds. 15ft (4.5m)

Hedera helix 'Little Diamond', Common Ivy. *Araliaceae*

An evergreen climber attaching itself to walls and other surfaces by root-like growths from the stem. The small, alternate, leathery green leaves are diamond shaped and variegated in grey-green and cream. Prune only to keep within bounds. Easily propagated by cuttings. 15ft (4.5m)

Humulus lupulus 'Aureus', Hop. *Cannabidaceae*

A hardy, vigorous herbaceous perennial twiner with soft yellow cordate leaves. Cut back stems close to ground after leaf fall. The plant is most effective trained over a pergola. Easily propagated by division. 15ft (4.5m)

A young plant of Hydrangea petiolaris *trained against a wall, lead-headed wall nails are used to support the plant until its aerial roots adhere to the structure.*

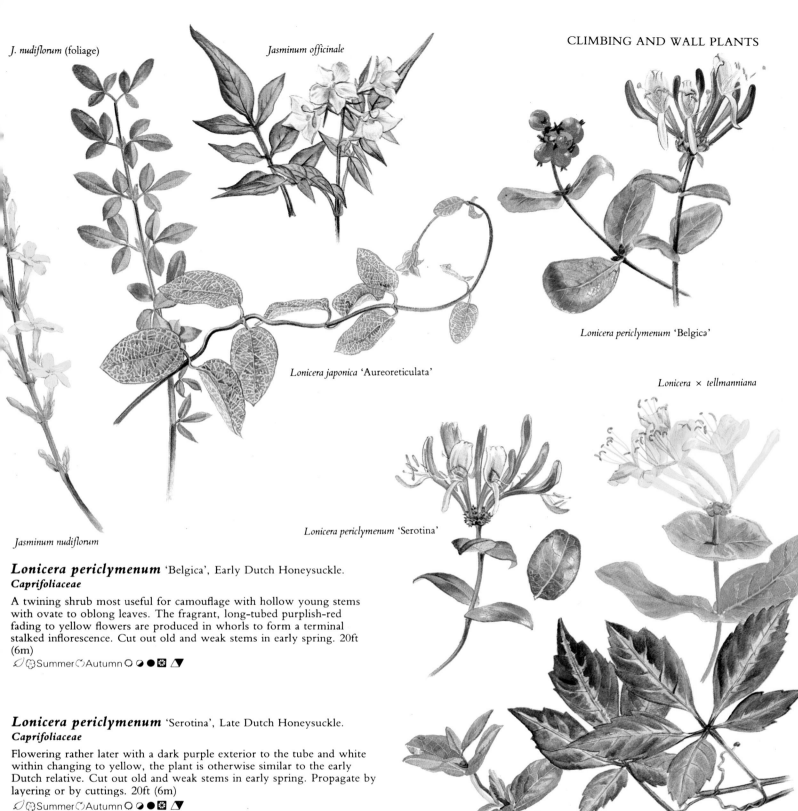

J. nudiflorum (foliage)

Jasminum officinale

Lonicera japonica 'Aureoreticulata'

Lonicera periclymenum 'Belgica'

Lonicera × *tellmanniana*

Lonicera periclymenum 'Serotina'

Jasminum nudiflorum

Parthenocissus henryana

Lonicera japonica halliana

Lonicera periclymenum 'Belgica', Early Dutch Honeysuckle.
Caprifoliaceae

A twining shrub most useful for camouflage with hollow young stems with ovate to oblong leaves. The fragrant, long-tubed purplish-red fading to yellow flowers are produced in whorls to form a terminal stalked inflorescence. Cut out old and weak stems in early spring. 20ft (6m)

✿ ❀Summer☾Autumn ○ ◐ ● ▦ ◿▼

Lonicera periclymenum 'Serotina', Late Dutch Honeysuckle.
Caprifoliaceae

Flowering rather later with a dark purple exterior to the tube and white within changing to yellow, the plant is otherwise similar to the early Dutch relative. Cut out old and weak stems in early spring. Propagate by layering or by cuttings. 20ft (6m)

✿ ❀Summer☾Autumn ○ ◐ ● ▦ ◿▼

Lonicera × tellmanniaña. Caprifoliaceae

One of the most attractive of the many honeysuckles available producing large elliptic to ovate leaves with the uppermost pair united. Large and abundant glowing flowers are presented in terminal clusters. Lack of fragrance has been inherited from the parents (*L. sempervirens* and *L. tragophylla*). Thin out growth if necessary after flowering. 20ft (6m)

✿ ❀Summer ○ ◐ ▦ ◿▼

Parthenocissus henryana (syn *Vitis henryana*) China. Vitaceae

A most decorative climbing vine self supporting by disc-tipped tendrils. The dark velvety digitate green leaves are variegated with silvery white and pink when grown on a north-facing or shaded wall. The leaves are outstanding in autumn when they turn brilliant red. Growth can be kept within bounds by pruning in late winter or early spring. Propagate by cuttings or layering. Seed sown in spring germinates better in heat. 40ft (12m)

✿ ☾Autumn ◐ ● ▦ ◿▼

101

Polygonum baldschuanicum

Passiflora caerulea

Parthenocissus quinquefolia

Parthenocissus tricuspidata

Solanum crispum 'Glasnevin', Chilean Potato Tree. *Solanaceae*

A beautiful fast-growing plant with ovate, ovate-lanceolate or cordate, minutely downy leaves. The delicate fragrant flowers are produced over a long period and give rise to globose fruit. An ideal plant for a wall or to grow over a structure; the growth can be kept within bounds by pruning in early spring. Cuttings taken during summer root easily. 20ft (6m)
🗡🌿❀Summer🌙Summer ◐ ◖ ▨ ◣▽

Vitis 'Brandt', Grape Vine. *Vitaceae*

A deciduous climber with multi-lobed leaves which give good autumn colour. The small fragrant flowers give rise to globose fruits which ripen during the best of summers. Prune by cutting back to within 2in (5cm) of the main rods in mid-winter. Easily propagated by hardwood cuttings. 30ft (9m)
🗡❀Summer🌙Autumn ◐ ◖ ▨ ◣▽

Vitis coignetiae (syn *V. kaempferi*) Japan. *Vitaceae*

A magnificent, very vigorous climber with tendrils in all except every third node. The massive green leaves turn to vivid crimson during autumn. Prune in winter to keep growth within bounds. Cuttings do not root readily and plants are usually raised by seed. Layering can be successful. 40ft (12m)
🗡🌙Autumn ◐ ◖ ▨ ◣▽

Wisteria sinensis, Chinese Wisteria, China. *Leguminosae*

A strong-growing deciduous climber at its best cladding a wall or clambering through a mature tree. The pinnate leaves with up to 11 green leaflets are most attractive. The beautiful fragrant racemes up to 1ft (30cm) long are produced on wood made the previous year and are followed by a second flush of flower during late summer. Summer pruning carried out immediately after the first flush of flower is essential to keep the plant within bounds and to secure blossom bud initiation for following year. Current season's shoots are cut back to 5 leaves which may again be shortened if necessary during winter. 40ft (12m)
🗡❀Summer ◐ ▨ ◣▽

Solanum crispum 'Glasnevin'

Vitis coignetiae

Wisteria sinensis

Vitis 'Brandt'

Parthenocissus quinquefolia (syn *Vitis quinquefolia, Ampelopsis quinquefolia*) Virginia Creeper, Eastern N. America. *Vitaceae*

One of the finest creepers with brilliant autumn colour and spectacular when cladding a wall or flowing over a structure; it will clamber through a tree to make an outstanding feature. The umbels of flowers form a multi-forked inflorescence and give rise to blue-black globose fruit. Keep growth within bounds by cutting back in early spring. Easily raised by hardwood cuttings taken in November. 40ft (12m)
🗡🌙Autumn ◐ ◖ ● ▨ ◣▽

Parthenocissus tricuspidata 'Veitchii' (syn *Ampelopsis veitchii, Vitis inconstans*) Boston Ivy. *Vitaceae*

Very vigorous climber with smooth young shoots self supporting by disc-tipped tendrils. The variable leaves are a feature of the plant and continue their dominance during autumn with spectacular crimson tints. Keep growth within bounds by cutting back in early spring. Plants are propagated by hardwood cuttings and should be potted into a container to form a good root system before final establishment. 60ft (18m)
🗡🌙Autumn ◐ ◖ ▨ ◣▽

Passiflora caerulea (Passion Flower) Brazil. *Passifloraceae*

A vigorous semi-evergreen with most unusual flowers and interestingly shaped palmate leaves. The fragrant flowers contain five sepals and five petals with a ring of thread-like growths known as the 'corona'. The thick-skinned, rather unpalatable fruit develops during a warm summer. The plant is inclined to die off above ground during severe weather usually growing up from the rootstock again. 15ft (4.5m)
▲ ❀Summer🌙Summer ◐ ▨ ◣▽

Polygonum baldschuanicum, Russian Vine, S.E. Russia. *Polygonaceae*

An extremely vigorous deciduous climber useful for growing over unsightly structures. The alternate leaves are pale green and ovate or heart shaped. Much showy blossom appears on lateral shoots to give a striking effect. Hard pruning is tolerated. Propagation is by hardwood cuttings or cuttings taken during summer with a heel. 40ft (12m)
🗡❀Summer ◐ ◖ ● ▨ ◣▽

Garden Hedges

There is no doubt that most people like privacy in their gardens and one way of achieving this is to plant hedges around the boundaries. Boundary hedges generally need to be dense and impenetrable, and often, because of lack of space, trained to a neat formal shape rather than being allowed to spread at will.

Hedges can also be used within the garden to divide it, so that the whole plot cannot be seen at a glance, and perhaps to screen utility parts such as the vegetable or fruit plot. Here ornamental shrubs can be used to good effect – perhaps to create an informal flowering hedge.

As well as ensuring privacy and screening parts of the garden, all hedges provide shelter from winds, the degree of shelter depending on the height. But a good thick hedge of about 6 to 8ft (1.8 to 2.5m) in height will certainly shelter the average-size garden well enough. Hedges do not stop the wind but filter it and slow it down, so, in windy weather, conditions are calmer on the lee side of the hedge.

Very low hedges are sometimes used in gardens, and these are purely for decorative effect, such as a lavender hedge lining each side of a path.

Basic Types of Hedges

Formal Formal hedges are trained to a definite shape and are clipped regularly to maintain a neat appearance – in other words, they are not allowed to grow at will in all directions. Because of this regular clipping they become very dense and, therefore, this type is ideal for boundary work.

A spectacular display of summer colour from a hedge of hebe, which makes a particularly good subject for a seaside garden.

A formal hedge is generally wedge-shaped – broad at the base and tapering to about half the width of the base at the top. In other words, the sides slope inwards. The top of the hedge may be squared off or rounded. This shape sheds snow easily, therefore preventing the hedge from splitting open under the weight. One with a rounded top is even better in this respect. On no account have a perfectly square hedge – one with straight sides and the same width at the top as at the bottom. Snow building up on the top will almost certainly split it open.

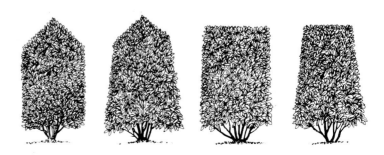

Well shaped hedges

103

There are many shrubs and trees which can be used to create a formal hedge. A favourite is *Fagus sylvatica* or beech, which is particularly suitable for chalky soils. Although the beech foliage dies in the autumn, the leaves are retained in the hedge throughout the winter, when they are a beautiful golden-brown shade. Plain green beech is normally used, but the purple-leaved variety is also suitable – try planting alternate blocks of green and purple. Plant 18in (45cm) apart.

Carpinus betulus or hornbeam is rather similar to beech, also liking chalky soils and planted at the same distance. The common holly, *Ilex aquifolium,* with its prickly, dark green, evergreen foliage, makes a really impenetrable hedge if planted 18in (45cm) apart. The quickthorn, *Crataegus monogyna,* is also very prickly and dense and a very appropriate subject for country gardens, as it is found growing wild in many parts of the country. Plant 12in (30cm) apart.

If you want to add to the already thousands of miles of privet hedge in this country, then choose the oval-leaf privet, *Ligustrum ovalifolium,* or its variety 'Aureum', the golden privet, with yellow foliage. Both are evergreen and planted 12in (30cm) apart. Another almost equally popular evergreen hedging plant is *Lonicera nitida,* with tiny leaves. Plant 12in (30cm) apart. It has the nasty habit, though, of suddenly dying out in patches. Also bear in mind that privet is very prone to the root disease known as honey fungus – which is very prevalent, especially in the south-east.

Laurel makes a good evergreen hedge, and is one of the largest-leaved hedging plants. Use the variety *Prunus laurocerasus* 'Rotundifolia' and plant 24in (60cm) apart.

Finally, a few evergreen conifers which are popular for hedging. x *Cupressocyparis leylandii,* the Leyland cypress, is possibly the fastest-growing hedging plant available, and consequently is very widely planted. Space plants 24in (60cm) apart. At the other extreme – much slower growing, but not as slow as many people imagine – is the yew, *Taxus baccata,* with dark green foliage. Plant 18in (45cm) apart. *Thuya plicata* 'Atrovirens' is a fast grower and has bright green foliage. Plant 24in (60cm) apart.

All of these subjects will make hedges in the region of 6 to 8ft (1.8 to 2.5m) in height. Most people prefer not to go above this height as trimming then becomes difficult.

Most of these hedges will need clipping several times in the

A low hedge of Berberis thunbergii *'Atropurpurea'.*

summer to keep them looking neat, and a start can be made in May or June. However, beech and hornbeam need clipping only once a year, the best time being August. Most can be clipped with shears or an electric trimmer, but large-leaved subjects, like laurel, are best trimmed with secateurs so that you do not cut through the leaves. Leaves cut in half will turn brown at the edges and result in an unslightly appearance.

Informal Informal hedges are allowed to grow naturally and need very little trimming, apart perhaps from shortening the odd shoots which grow very long and spoil the general outline. Such trimming can be done in the summer, or after flowering if applicable, using secateurs.

Flowering or berrying subjects often make very attractive hedges, like *Berberis darwinii,* with evergreen, tiny holly-like leaves and golden flowers in the spring. It will make a 6ft (1.8m) hedge and is planted 24in (60cm) apart. *B.* x *stenophylla* has an arching habit of growth, its evergreen shoots being wreathed with yellow flowers in the spring. Height and planting distance as above. Both make impenetrable hedges.

Escallonias will make 5 to 6ft (1.5 to 1.8m) hedges. They have evergreen foliage and flower in the summer, the blooms being red, pink or white. Plant 30in (75cm) apart.

Olearia x *haastii* is one of the daisy bushes, so called because white daisy flowers are produced in summer. The small evergreen leaves are white-felted below. Makes a good hedge in coastal areas. Plant 36in (1m) apart. Attains a height of 4 to 5ft (1.2 to 1.5m).

An impenetrable hedge is formed by the evergreen *Pyracantha rogersiana,* with red berries. It will make a hedge at least 6ft (1.8m) high; plant 18in (45cm) apart. Rose hedges are both colourful and impenetrable. Many kinds can be used, like the well-known pink 'Queen Elizabeth' which will make a 5ft (1.5m) hedge. Plant 36in (1m) apart. Varieties of *Rosa rugosa* can also be used, growing to 4 or 5 ft (1.2 to 1.5m). Plant 36in (1m) apart.

A rosemary hedge is suitable for milder parts of the country, using *Rosmarinus officinalis* or its variety 'Fastigiatus'. The aromatic foliage is evergreen and blue flowers are produced in spring and summer. A 4 to 6ft (1.2 to 1.8m) high hedge can be achieved and planting distance is 24in (60cm). Ideal for a seaside garden is the evergreen *Griselinia littoralis* with fresh green leaves. Inland it needs shelter. It will easily reach 6ft (1.8m) and should be planted 24in (60cm) apart.

Plants for dwarf hedges include *Berberis thunbergii* 'Atropurpurea Nana' with deciduous reddish-purple foliage. Can also be grown as a formal hedge. Height 2ft (60cm), planting distance 12in (30cm). For a lavender hedge, *Lavandula* 'Hidcote' is superb, with deep blue flowers and greyish evergreen foliage. Height about 2ft (60cm) and planting distance 12in (30cm). The cotton lavender, *Santolina chamaecyparissus* has silvery, woolly, evergreen foliage and heads of lemon-yellow flowers, which should be trimmed off when they are over. Height is about 18in (45cm) and planting distance 12in (30cm).

Cultivation

Planting a Hedge Prepare a strip of ground 3ft (1m) wide by double digging (to two depths of the spade) and incorporating well-rotted farmyard manure or garden compost in each trench. Allow to settle for a few months if possible. Eradicate all perennial weeds, either by digging them out or by using glyphosate weedkiller when they are in full growth.

Evergreen hedges are best planted in April or September. Deciduous kinds, if bare rooted, are planted between November and March. Containerised deciduous plants can be planted any time. Do not plant if the ground is very wet or frozen.

Most hedges are planted in a single row. However, if a very wide or particularly thick hedge is needed, then plant in double rows, but stagger the plants. Planting distances have been given, but if planting a double line the row spacing is the same as the planting distance in the row.

Obviously, to keep the row of plants perfectly straight, it will be necessary to put down a garden line and plant against this. Either take out individual holes for each plant, or a continuous trench. If plants are containerised do not disturb the rootball. If bare rooted, spread out the roots in the hole or trench and work fine soil between them. Plant to the same depth that the plants were originally growing. Firm the soil well with your heels around each plant.

When conifers are used to form a screen, allow them to grow to the required height before cutting the tops.

A method of using a garden line to achieve an accurate finish when trimming a low hedge.

Aftercare Do not allow hedges to grow too high too quickly or they may become thin at the base. In the first season or two trim back the tops of the plants to encourage them to bush out low down. Also lightly trim the sides evenly in the first season after planting, as this also encourages a bushy habit. As the hedge becomes bushy at the base allow it to increase in height.

To ensure maximum growth keep young hedges well watered in dry weather. It is especially important not to allow the plants to dry out in the first season after planting. Newly planted evergreens should be sprayed daily with water for about six weeks after planting (unless the weather is wet) to help them establish.

If available, mulch young hedges with a 2in (5cm) layer of organic matter in spring, such as well-rotted farmyard manure, garden compost, peat, spent hops or mushroom compost. This will help to conserve moisture and suppress weeds. A dense growth of weeds will retard the growth of a newly planted hedge: so keep weeds under control.

An annual application, in the spring, of a general purpose fertilizer will ensure the young hedge makes maximum growth in a season. Use a dry fertilizer and lightly hoe it into the soil surface. Water in if the soil is dry.

Planting a row of shrubs to form a hedge.

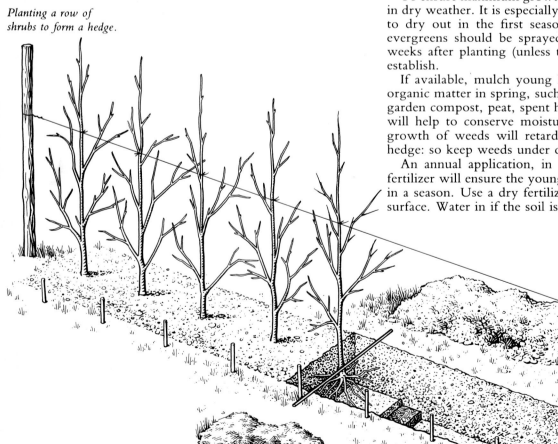

Alpine and Rock Plants

The Rock Garden

Interest in growing rock plants has greatly increased during the past decade or so. There are a number of reasons why this is so: the introduction of new species and hybrids from their native habitats and the opening up of parts of China, Japan, other Asiatic countries and the Andes to botanists and the general public. It is now possible to obtain a wide selection of rock plants from garden centres to form the nucleus of a collection. A large number of mail order nurseries also offer rock plants. Nurseries which specialise in the raising and selling of rock plants – both the easy species and varieties and the less easy but very desirable – are to be found in many parts of the British Isles. In their lists will also possibly be found a number of the new or recent introductions into cultivation which have been raised from imported seed.

Siting the Rock Garden

With the fast rising cost of land large gardens get fewer and fewer, for the tendency is to build the largest possible number of houses to the acre. Hence the attraction of rock plants, which, compared with most other plants, take up relatively little space. Even the smallest of gardens can be adapted to cultivate these small plants; the only drawback is where large, established trees are present. One often sees small mounds of soil planted with rock plants set among a few rocks placed almost up against tree trunks. No feature could be more doomed to failure, for in the matter of a year or so only the rocks will still be there – but it

A bed of alpine plants makes a most appealing feature for an open sunny site in the garden which has well drained soil.

is certain that the plants will have disappeared.

Where possible, choose a site which is open and sunny and away from surface-rooting trees. The drip from these will rapidly cause a large number of plant fatalities. If the garden is small or surface-rooting or surface-suckering trees are already established there – for example poplars, silver birch, elms or limes – it may be necessary to grow the plants in troughs and other containers, raised above the ground and sited as far as possible from the trees. If the garden is in half shade, (full shade is not suitable), it is still possible to grow the numerous dwarf ericaceous plants. There are many dwarf rhododendrons available from garden centres, also small shrubs which will tolerate half shade. The dwarf rhododendrons include *R. calostrotum*, 1ft (30cm) high with pink to purple flowers in May; *R.* 'Chikor', a good dwarf hybrid with terminal clusters of lemon-yellow flowers in May; *R. imperator* only a few inches high and about 1ft (30cm) wide with solitary, terminal, open-funnel-shaped, deep rose-purple flowers in May; the dwarf, spreading form of *R. pemakoense*, clear pinkish-purple flowers, and what is possibly the dwarfest of all the rhododendrons, *R. radicans*, less than an inch (2cm) in height with large (for the size of the plant) single flowers from light mauve to a deep purple. There is also a large range of small hybrids which are suitable for growing in this way, and a selection can be obtained from nurseries or local garden centres.

For all these ericaceous plants it is necessary for the garden soil to be lime-free, but here again such plants can be grown in troughs or other containers in a compost of four parts leafmould and one part of lime-free loam and sand, these proportions to be by bulk, not weight.

In a small garden not large enough to accommodate a rock garden, it should be possible to build up border edges, especially if there is a small lawn. On a sloping site a small dry wall could be constructed, thus providing a two-level plot, which will

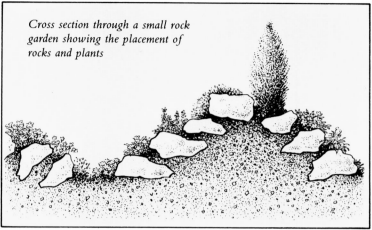

Cross section through a small rock garden showing the placement of rocks and plants

A peat garden on two levels constructed from peat blocks. The drainage should be good and the bed filled in with the compost described.

enable a selection of trailing plants to be grown; for example, arabis, alyssum in variety, the many colour forms of aubrieta, phlox, campanulas and helianthemums. These will give a display of colour starting in late March and continuing until the end of July. All these trailing varieties can be underplanted with suitable dwarf bulbs, extending the flowering season over six months.

Dividing the garden with a wall helps to give the appearance of greater length and depth if such a structure is combined with other features. Where necessary, too, it provides a natural division between different parts of the garden.

Soil

Unfortunately, it is seldom possible to choose the soil of one's garden, but much can be done to make existing soil suitable for rock plants. The best medium is a light open soil with faultless drainage. If possible, a lime-free medium is preferable, for lime can be added where this is required. Rock plants which approve of lime do not demand it, but lime-hating plants will only grow – and this is normally for a short period only – in specially prepared pockets of lime-free soil. So if you have an alkaline soil it is best to avoid growing all lime-hating plants. A rich

loamy soil can be made ideal for the vast majority of rock plants by adding really coarse sand or small gravel, and, for faultless drainage, the addition of a graded horticultural Perlite (an expanded volcanic rock that improves drainage, water availability and aerates the soil and composts). Perlite is inorganic, inert and stimulates root growth.

If the soil is of a heavy nature, clay for instance, it will be necessary to approach the problem in a different way. No attempt should be made to lighten it by adding drainage materials, a task which would perhaps be too difficult anyway. If you dig out pockets of soil, add drainage materials and then fill in again with a lighter mixture, you will find that you end up, after a heavy rainfall, with a series of pools, this in turn causing the rapid decline and almost certain death of plants growing in such hollows. If there is a natural slope it can be turned to good use by digging a pit at the base between 8 to 10in (20 to 25cm) deep and filling up with some coarse drainage material and then adding a layer of upturned turves or other roughage to prevent soil washing down and blocking the drainage. The rock garden is then built up about 8in (20cm) using a light, open compost. At least one quarter of the bulk of the compost around the drainage pit should consist of either leafmould or peat. This will provide an ideal spot for plants that prefer a greater quantity of moisture, such as Asiatic primulas and other kindred species.

Whatever soil is used over the clay it should have all perennial weeds removed; if this very important task is neglected, it will result in many hours being spent in attempting to remove these after planting has been completed, or, in bad cases, dismantling the rock garden with dire consequences to the plants. Nothing is more detrimental, for instance, than finding bindweed coming up in the centre of a rare alpine plant.

Constructing the Rock Garden

It is difficult to give exact instructions on building a rock garden. A great deal depends on the available area and the type of rock employed. The actual construction must be left to the gardener's choice, and provided a few simple principles are adhered to the result should appear natural and aesthetically pleasing. Natural stone suitable for the rock garden is available in three types – limestone, sandstone and tufa. It makes sense to choose a source and type of rock which is reasonably near to hand for rocks, expensive in themselves, are heavy and costly to transport.

First, the rock when positioned should have two exposed sides, one sunny, where plants can be placed which demand such a position to give of their best, the other in semi- or full shade for plants which require such conditions. Secondly, if the rock being used is limestone, which normally has distinctive strata, it should be placed almost horizontal to the surface, which gives it a natural look comparable to that of rocks in their natural surroundings. Lastly, it is only necessary to have one or two outcrops in a small rock garden, which should be kept simple with the planting carried out at the apex of the stone being used.

The next best rock to use (after limestone) is one of the local sandstones, which are found in many parts of the country; this is less costly and in many cases arrangements can be made to pick the stone up from the quarry, thus resulting in a considerable financial saving. Sandstone normally blends in better with the surroundings unless, of course, you live in a limestone area. If sandstone is used make sure that it is not composed of a large percentage of soft material, as this has a tendency to disintegrate after hard frosts.

Tufa is an ideal medium in which to grow less-easy alpine and extremely saxatile plants from high altitudes. It is light to handle, extremely porous and easy to drill. A small chisel can also be used to make holes in it to take plants without causing too much root disturbance to those already planted at the time of planting. Place in the base of the hole a small amount of flaked leafmould and detritus removed from the piece of tufa when making the hole. When planting in tufa obtain small specimen plants, seedlings, or even rooted cuttings. Remove the plant from its container, taking care not to fracture too many roots, gently remove any loose soil, and insert the plant in the hole sideways and gently work the planting mixture around the roots, firming gently. Topdress with small pieces of tufa around the neck of the plant. This method of planting has been used successfully over a number of years but there are a few problems. For one instance, tufa is costly, but this is offset to a certain degree by its weight as it is much lighter than other mediums and easier to handle. Unfortunately, it is only stocked by a few nurserymen, but if a source can be found locally it is possible to take a fair supply in the boot of a car.

If cost or other factors prevent the use of natural rock stone, a supply of broken paving stones from the local council yard can normally be purchased quite cheaply. Three or four layers should be placed one upon the other – each individual layer being inclined towards the mass of soil and made firm – with a light compost sandwiched between each layer and well firmed down. For the first year or so these slabs will look raw and artificial but, in due course, weathering will alter their appearance.

Bury as little of the stone as possible, consistent with firmness, making sure that there are no air spaces under the rocks so that the plants will have no difficulty in finding a cool root run. Dusting the base of each rock with HCH powder when settling them will prevent pests from taking a hold.

Scree Beds

Scree beds can be constructed as an edging to a lawn, flower border or path. With such features it is possible to grow a wide selection of plants without the use of a great deal of rockwork or even rocks at all. Wherever the beds are made they should be well clear of any adjacent trees, for the roots of the latter will quickly gain entry and exhaust the soil to the detriment of the rock plants. Scree borders should also be well away from the dense shade cast by buildings. Apart from these considerations, the actual aspect is not important, for there is a good number of rock plants that can be cultivated in sun or semi-shade.

A scree bed is made by placing paving stones so that they form a box. Such a scree bed can be of any length to suit the site. The width should be at least 16in (40cm). The material to use in building up the 'shell' can be natural York stone, but unless there is a supply locally this is very expensive. There are two alternatives, one broken paving stone obtainable from the local council yard, the other, made-up slabs of concrete, 14in by 5in and ¾in (36cm by 12cm and 2cm) deep, such as are sold by most garden centres. The paving stone should allow one to build a frame in which to grow a representative collection of rock plants. Once the size has been decided on, a base should be constructed to carry the walls. Depending on the width of the pieces of paving stone used, a fillet of cement 2¼in (6cm) deep should be laid under these to form the base for the stones. This concrete base should extend about a further 3in (8cm) beyond the stones and be made smooth, thus forming a narrow path between the scree bed and the lawn. This will allow a lawn mower to be used right up to the wall of the scree bed.

When laying the base, holes for drainage must be made at regular intervals. To prevent pests such as slugs, woodlice and so on gaining entry, small pieces of perforated zinc should be placed over these holes.

Whatever stone is used, this should be fixed on the base by the use of a cement mix and the walls built to a minimum height of 8 to 10in (20 to 24cm). A few weeks after completion of the building the scree borders are prepared, as follows. First, a good layer of broken crocks or roughage is added, followed by a well-firmed layer of peat or leaf roughage to prevent the compost filtering down and blocking up the drainage. The border is then filled to the top with either of the following mixtures: for sun lovers and bulbs equal parts of loam, leafmould and sharp sand, and for plants that require half shade the same mixture with an equal quantity of peat added. In each case a small handful of bone meal is spread over the surface of the compost, well watered in and left to settle. After a week or so the scree border will be ready for planting.

The chosen plants, which must not be pot-bound, should be carefully removed from their pots, the drainage material in the base removed and a few roots teased loose. Remove up to ¾in (2cm) of the old surface compost and plant in a prepared hole in the scree border and make firm. The surface should then be top dressed with ¾in (2cm) of stone chippings. Finally, a few decorative pieces of rock will put a finishing touch to the border.

Trough Gardens

Troughs are very popular today, but unfortunately the real thing is difficult to find and, if found, generally expensive. Most garden centres have artificial troughs for sale, and provided they are at least 5in (12cm) in depth these are suitable for growing a wide selection of rock plants. They can also be used to grow single specimens of plants or one variety of dwarf bulb.

The compost required is similar to that used in the scree border, and the same method is used in preparing the trough. Make sure that a lime-free loam is used if ericaceous plants are grown. Watering is very important, especially during the re-establishment of the plants for they must not be allowed to dry out.

The Peat Garden

A large number of plants requiring lime-free soil can be accommodated in this type of garden. The top 4in (10cm) of lime-free soil in a semi-shaded part of the garden should be dug over, all roots removed and plenty of well-rotted leafmould or peat mixed in. Peat blocks are used to construct the wall, and blocks measuring 10 by 5½in and 3in (24 by 12cm and 8cm) deep are ideal. Make sure that they are moist. They should be laid as when building a brick wall and two layers are necessary. A compost of four parts leafmould or peat, one part fibrous, neutral loam and one part coarse sand is used like a cement mix, working it into all the cracks as the wall is being built. Fill the rest of the bed with the same mixture. After planting, topdress the bed with 1¼in (3cm) of peat and water the plants in. This bed should be kept moist at all times to give of its best.

Dwarf Conifers

Irrespective of the size of the rock garden, large or small, or even if you are thinking in terms of troughs and sinks, space should be found to include a number of real dwarf conifers, suitably placed to enhance the whole. The variations in height these will provide will give a better balance to the planting overall and provide interest for the eye, especially during the drab winter months.

If space allows they can be planted in a bed of their own, suitable dwarf bulbous plants being planted underneath, but here care must be taken to use only the smallest of bulbs otherwise the balance of the planting will be badly affected. Crocus species and varieties are a good example of bulbs suitable for this purpose, and as these can consist of the autumn, winter and early spring flowering kinds it is possible to have colour throughout much of the winter.

A bed for conifers can be prepared by removing the turf from an irregular section of lawn or an area on one of its edges and then digging it over, adding peat or other humus-forming material as necessary, and planting the conifers to suit one's taste. Their diverse and sometimes fantastic forms and many types of different foliage colours and shapes make it possible to

This trough garden has been made from an old stone sink supported on brick pillars. The sink must be well drained. A piece of tufa provides additional height and a foothold for small plants.

create a garden feature which is attractive at all seasons.

Care should be exercised in choosing the plants, for a good number of supposedly dwarf or slow-growing conifers offered for sale rarely remain dwarf for long, and, if planted, will, in the course of a few years, become too large for the positions in which they are growing. This can, of course, cause real difficulties for they will have to be removed with the possibility of upsetting those plants with which they are associated. It may even be necessary to dismantle part of the rock garden. Plants should be obtained from a reputable source, there are a number of specialist nurserymen throughout the country who deal in these miniatures. A practice which the writer has carried out with success over a long period is to buy such conifers in late August when the annual growth is completed: a quick look at the new wood which has been made will give a general idea of ultimate size.

The following are ideal dwarf conifers. Unfortunately, space does not allow more than the mention of one species from each genus, but all of those described below may be planted with due confidence that they will not outgrow a small rock garden.

Abies balsamea var. *hudsonia*: A sterile form of the balsam fir with straight right-angled leaves, bright green above and with two sunken white-blue lines below. Annual growth ½ to ¾in (1 to 2 cm).

Chamaecyparis lawsoniana 'Pygmaea Argentea': A slow-growing, half-rounded bushlet with congested, slender semi-horizontal branches and narrow sprays of dark glaucous green, white-tipped narrow leaves. When young and grown under semi-shaded conditions it retains its white coloration. Annual growth ¼in (3cm)

Chamaecyparis obtusa 'Nana Caespitosa': There are three bun forms of *C. obtusa* 'Nana' which are ideal, namely 'Caespitosa', 'Juniperoides' and 'Minima'. They all make tight, rounded buns of congested foliage, 'Caespitosa' is deep green; 'Juniperoides' and 'Minima' are bright green. Annual growth not more than ¾ to 1¼ in (2 to 3cm). All are superb trough plants.

Juniperus communis 'Compressa': This is the Noah's Ark juniper making an upright symmetrical column of congested branches and needle-shaped leaves which are silver-grey if planted in an exposed, sunny position. Annual growth 1¼ to 2in (3 to 5cm).

Picea abies 'Gregoryana': There are many dwarf forms of the spruce and this is a tight hummock of small densely packed branches with congested pale green foliage having an annual increase of not more than ¾in (2cm).

Pinus sylvestris 'Beauvronensis': The Scots pine has produced a number of dwarf forms, but it is doubtful if there is any to beat this plant which will make a small tree and in 20 years is less than 16in (40cm) in height, rarely making more than ¾in

(2cm) annually. It is best obtained with a small trunk topped with a tight mass of shining green branches and needle-shaped grey-green leaves in pairs.

Dwarf Shrubs

Mention must be made of a few dwarf shrubs which add shape, height and colour to the rock garden, and if evergreen kinds are mixed with deciduous ones this will provide interest during the winter months.

Acantholimon venustum, about 5in (12cm) high, pink everlasting flowers, June; *Andromeda polifolia compacta*, no lime, 5in (12cm) high, pink, May; *Anthyllis montana rubra*, 2¼in (6cm) high, red, May; *Cassiope mertensiana*, 7in (18cm) high, white, May; *Ceanothus prostratus*, 1½in (4cm) high, blue, May; *Daphne collina*, 7in (18cm) high, lilac-pink, June; *Dryas octopetala minor*, 2in (5cm) high, white, May; *Gaultheria cuneata*, no lime, 7in (18cm) high, white, June, white fruits, October; *Genista delphinensis*, 5in (12cm) high, yellow, June; *Hebe pinguifolia pagei*, 7in (18cm) high, white, June; *Hypericum repens*, ¾in (2cm) high, yellow, June; *Linum elegans*, 3½in (9cm) high, yellow, June; *Penstemon rupicola*, 5in (12cm) high, crimson-pink, June; and *Salix apoda*, 1¼in (3cm) high, rose-pink catkins, April.

Propagation

There are two main methods of increasing rock plants, by seed or cuttings. First seed, John Innes seed compost is both a suitable and efficient germinating medium. A lime-free seed compost is also available. Seed of the normal types of rock plants is best sown in late February. This will provide the resulting plants with six months of growth during spring and summer so that they make sturdy specimens ready for planting out in September. Seed should be sown thinly and covered with a fine dressing of sharp sand, and be kept moist by immersing the seed pan in water, as necessary.

Cuttings provide a ready means of increase also, and in the great majority of cases green cuttings will root quite easily. They are best taken from small pieces of new growth, placed in a pot containing a mixture of equal parts sharp sand and fine peat. Generally, they should, where possible, be between ¾ to 1¼in (2 to 3cm) in length, the lower third of the stem being left clear of leaves (these leaves should be removed by giving each one a gentle upward pull). Insert the cuttings around the edge of the pot to a depth where the bottom leaves touch the rooting medium. Water the cuttings in well. Place a plastic bag over the whole pot and make firm with a rubber band. Rooting should take place in a few weeks, and signs of new growth will be evidence of this. The small plantlets are then grown on in John Innes No 1 potting compost until ready to plant in their permanent positions.

Acantholimon glumaceum (syn *Statice ararati*) Armenia. *Plumbaginaceae*

Slow-growing, dwarf, tufted, evergreen perennial with sharp-pointed, dark green, rigid, densely packed leaves. The abundant, bright red, star-shaped everlasting flowers appear on a scape. Plants are increased by division or layering in late summer; cuttings taken during early August will root by the following spring; seed germinates slowly. 6in (15cm)
△ ☝ ۞Summer ○ ◗ ⊠ △▼

Achillea clavenae, Europe. *Compositae*

Charming little perennial plant with alternate greyish coloured leaves. The white flowers arise in corymbs. Propagate by division. 6in (15cm)
◊ ۞Summer ○ ⊠ △▼

Adonis amurensis, Manchuria, Japan. *Ranunculaceae*

A most attractive perennial plant with linear, segmented, alternate leaves. The large solitary terminal flowers vary in colour from yellow and white to pink or striped red. Seed should be sown when fresh and is slow to germinate, the seedlings taking two years to flower; or plants may be increased by division in spring. 1ft (30cm)
◊ ۞Spring ○ ● ⊠ △▼

Aethionema 'Warley Rose'. *Cruciferae*

This sub-shrubby perennial has fleshy, glaucous, sessile leaves. The pinkish-red flowers arise in dense terminal roundish racemes. An easy plant to grow, given the protection of alpine house or frame. Propagate by seed or cuttings taken from the parent during summer. 6in (15cm)
◊ ۞Summer ○ ⊠ △

Ajuga reptans 'Burgundy Glow', Bugle. *Labiatae*

Perennial plant with thick, more or less hairy, erect stems. A four-sided pyramidal effect is achieved by the oval leaves which continue to the apex of the stem as leafy bracts between the flowers. The colour of these bracts forms the main attraction of this plant. Much used for ground cover, the plants are readily propagated by seed sown in spring or autumn or by division. 6in (15cm)
☝ ۞Summer ○ ⊠ △▼

Alyssum serpyllifolium, Spain. *Cruciferae*

A dainty perennial plant good for pan growing and producing a prostrate mat of very small hoary leaves. Abundant yellow flowers arise in terminal racemes to produce small orbicular pods with one or two seeds in each of the two cells. The seeds germinate readily or plants can be increased by cuttings taken during summer. 2in (5cm)
◊ ۞Summer ○ ⊠ △▼

Alyssum wulfenianum, Europe. *Cruciferae*

An evergreen shrub which is best suited to the rock garden. The small obovate to lanceolate leaves are hairy, more densely so on the underside. Short racemes of fragrant yellow flowers appear in late spring. Increase by heeled cuttings taken in summer. Plants can be kept dwarf and compact by restricting the roots. 1½in (4cm)
◊ ۞Summer ○ ⊠ △▼

Anacyclus depressus, Morocco. *Compositae*

An herbaceous perennial with alternate, leafy, lateral, prostrate branches giving rise to heads of white, reversed red, ray florets and regular disk florets. Rather susceptible to neck rot unless carefully watered and should be kept dry during winter. Propagate by seed sown in spring. 3in (8cm)
◊ ۞Summer ○ ⊠ △▼

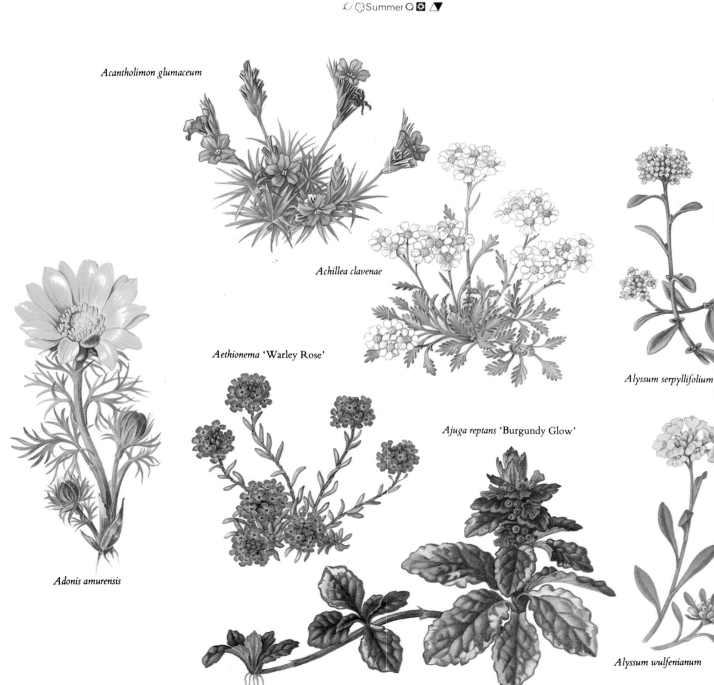

Acantholimon glumaceum

Achillea clavenae

Aethionema 'Warley Rose'

Alyssum serpyllifolium

Ajuga reptans 'Burgundy Glow'

Adonis amurensis

Alyssum wulfenianum

Anchusa caespitosa, Crete. *Boraginaceae*

The woody rootstock gives rise to a tufted growth habit. Abundant linear basal leaves with irregular dentate margins form prostrate rosettes containing the cymes of almost sessile, five-lobed, bright blue flowers. Wet root zone should be avoided during the winter. New plants can be raised by seed sown in spring. 12in (30cm)
⊘⊛Summer○�֎△▼

Andromeda polifolia 'Nana'. *Ericaceae*

This charming evergreen shrublet, with its leathery, almost linear leaves which are silvery grey on the underside, is suited to both rock garden and peat beds. Clusters of urn-shaped rose-pink flowers appear in May. This plant requires a soil with a high humus content and can be increased by softwood cuttings in summer. 2¹/₂in (5cm)
△⊛Spring○�֎▼

Androsace primuloides 'Chumbyi'. *Primulaceae*

This most delectable perennial tufted plant belongs to the Chamaejasme group within this large genus. The stolons give rise to rosettes of lanceolate to linear entire leaves covered with long hairs. Umbels of attractive pink flowers terminate axillary hairy scapes. Plants may be increased by runners. 4in (10cm)
⊘⊛Spring○◼✖△▼

Anemone obtusiloba, Himalaya. *Ranunculaceae*

An herbaceous perennial whose basal rosettes are composed of palmate, 3-lobed leaves on petioles, the leaf segments being wedge shaped and crenate. The cup-shaped flowers are blue, violet or cream. A good plant for the rock garden in soil with added humus. Increase by seed. 6 to 12in (15 to 30cm)
⊘⚘⊛Summer○✖▼△▼

Antennaria dioica 'Rosea'. *Compositae*

A charming herbaceous perennial plant with dioecious flower heads in crowded corymbs. The main attraction of the plant is in the mat of radical, spatulate, grey woolly leaves. Easily propagated by division in spring. 2 to 4in (5 to 10cm)
⊘⊛Summer○✖△▼

Anthyllis montana, S. Europe. *Leguminosae*

A charming miniature mat-forming deciduous shrub, the prostrate branches giving rise to alternate pinnate leaves with many silvery-haired linear-oblong leaflets. Attractive dark pink papilionaceous flowers borne in a hemispherical head arise on a long hairy peduncle. The plant is propagated by cuttings with a heel during August or by seed. 4in (10cm)
⊘⊛Spring○✖△▼

Aquilegia bertolonii (syn *A. reuteri*) Italy. *Ranunculaceae*

This delectable herbaceous perennial has long-stalked, dark green, fern-like, glaucous leaves. The nodding, blue, downy flowers with short-hooked spur appear with one to three others on the stem. Seed is unlikely to produce plants true to type when other plants of the species are grown and propagation is best restricted to division in early spring when it is desired to retain the type. 6in (15cm)
⊘⊛Summer○✖△▼

Aquilegia bertolonii

Anthyllis montana

Anacyclus depressus

Anemone obtusiloba

Anchusa caespitosa

Androsace primuloides 'Chumbyi'

Andromeda polifolia 'Nana'

Antennaria dioica 'Rosea'

111

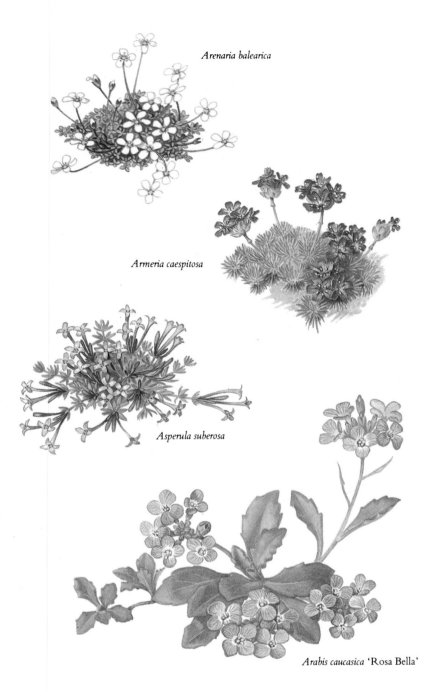

Arenaria balearica

Armeria caespitosa

Asperula suberosa

Arabis caucasica 'Rosa Bella'

Arabis caucasica 'Rosa Bella'. *Cruciferae*

An herbaceous perennial plant with tomentose, oblong, slightly toothed leaves. The attractive reddish-purple flowers are composed of oblong wedge-shaped petals. Readily propagated by division or by cuttings taken during the summer. 6in (15cm)

Arenaria balearica, Europe. *Caryophyllaceae*

This creeping herbaceous perennial has very small, fleshy, ovate, shining leaves. The solitary, white, small flowers appear on long peduncles over a long period throughout spring and summer. An excellent plant for the newly constructed rock garden but tends to smother adjacent plants unless checked. Easily propagated by seed sown in spring or by division during late summer immediately after flowering. 2in (5cm)

Armeria caespitosa, Spain. *Plumbaginaceae*

A charming, densely tufted perennial with short, linear, recurved, basal leaves. The most attractive pink flowers in a dense head terminate a leafless downy scape. Much used as a container specimen and for the scree, the plant is attractive when set in an old wall. Readily propagated by cuttings in summer or by division in autumn. 2in (5cm)

Asperula suberosa (syn *A. athoa*) Greece. *Rubiaceae*

Tufted, herbaceous, silvery-haired perennial plant with abundant stems clad in whorled leaves adorned by stipules. The attractive axillary and terminal, pink, tubular flowers arise on a spike. Specimens growing out of doors require protection during winter to prevent water collecting on the plant. Propagate by division in spring or early summer, subsequent growth being clipped back after flowering to retain the compact bun shape. 3in (8cm)

Aster alpinus 'Alba'. *Compositae*

A spreading herbaceous perennial plant with lanceolate-spatulate basal leaves and lanceolate stem leaves. The solitary flower heads of white ray florets surround hermaphrodite yellow tubular disk florets and develop from a bell-shaped involucre. Propagate by division in spring or autumn. 6in (15cm)

Astilbe simplicifolia, Japan. *Saxifragaceae*

This attractive herbaceous perennial tufted plant gives rise to deeply cut, ovate, glossy leaves. The inflorescence is arranged in slender panicles with short branches terminated by small white or pale pink flowers. Plants may be increased by division in spring and grown on in moist soil to prevent leaf curl; the compost kept rather dryer during dormancy. 6in (15cm)

Aubrieta 'Greencourt Purple'. *Cruciferae*

A graceful compact evergreen plant with lax terminal racemes which appear opposite the ovate leaves. The showy, purple, semi-double flowers make an attractive display and should be removed after they fade. Propagate by cuttings during spring or division in late summer. 4in (10cm)

Bellis perennis 'Dresden China'. *Compositae*

This showy, neat, almost stemless herbaceous perennial plant has semi-double solitary flower heads of deep pink quilled florets terminating a leafless peduncle. Young plants often flower better than old specimens and may be propagated by dividing the crowns after flowering. 4in (10cm)

Berberis × stenophylla 'Corallina Compacta'. *Berberidaceae*

A most interesting and charming small shrub suitable for pan culture, sink garden or rock garden. The attractive and abundant yellow flowers are followed by purple fruit covered by blue-white bloom. Propagation is by layering or by cuttings taken with a heel during summer. 6in (15cm)

Bruckenthalia spiculifolia, S.E. Europe, Asia Minor. *Ericaceae*

Closely related to the ericas, this tiny evergreen sub-shrub produces erect stems of grey-green heather-like foliage which is white on the underside. Bell-shaped pink flowers occur in terminal racemes. It grows best in a soil with added humus and requires a cool, moist root run. Increase by softwood cuttings taken in summer. 6in (15cm)

Campanula carpatica, Bellflower, E. Europe. *Campanulaceae*

The massed display of flowers produced by this spreading perennial is most attractive. The leaves on the lower part of the stem are cordate, roundish-ovate and toothed on a long petiole; those above are ovate with a short petiole. Abundant, bell-shaped flowers appear over a long period during summer. Readily propagated by cuttings in spring or by division. 12in (30cm)

Campanula cochlearifolia, Bellflower, Europe. *Campanulaceae*

This charming perennial spreads by underground runners and sends up slender branched stems carrying the bell-shaped, shallowly lobed flowers. The foliage is a fresh green, the basal leaves cordate and stalked, the stem leaves narrower and slightly notched. Plants can be increased by seed. 2in (5cm)

Cassiope 'Muirhead'. *Ericaceae*

An evergreen shrub with semi-erect stems covered in imbricate leaves. The ovoid-campanulate, solitary, white flower borne on a slender peduncle is most delectable. The plant dislikes a dry warm atmosphere and should be taken indoors only for flowering, then returned to a shady cool position preferably in cold frame. Propagate by cuttings taken in autumn. 6in (15cm)
△ ❀ ☺Spring ◗ ▩ ▼

Convolvulus cneorum, S. Europe. *Convolvulaceae*

An interesting sub-shrub for the alpine house with alternate, silky-haired, lanceolate leaves arising from the semi-prostrate branched stems. The heads of beautiful, funnel-shaped white or pinkish flowers appear on short peduncles throughout mid-summer. Plants may be increased by layering non-flowering shoots in June or by cuttings taken in July. 1¹/₂ft (45cm)
△ ◖ ☺Spring to Autumn ○ ▩ ◿

Cotoneaster dammeri radicans, China. *Rosaceae*

This is a charming, prostrate, evergreen shrub for the scree, sink garden or to clamber over rock. The self-rooting branches give rise to alternate, glossy green leaves, first woolly beneath but becoming glabrous. Attractive globose to obovoid fruit follows the purple-anthered, white, solitary flowers. Plants may be increased by lifting layered stems or by sowing seed. 6in (15cm)
△☺Summer ◖Autumn ○ ▩ ◿

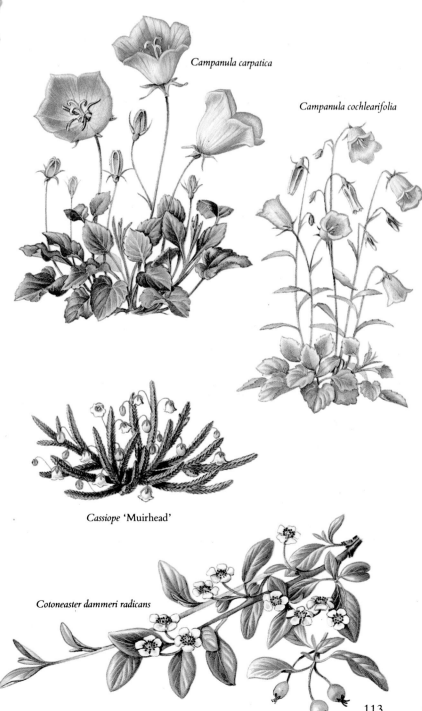

Aubrieta 'Greencourt Purple'

Astilbe simplicifolia

Bellis perennis 'Dresden China'

Berberis × stenophylla 'Corallina Compacta'

Convolvulus cneorum

Campanula carpatica

Campanula cochlearifolia

Cassiope 'Muirhead'

Aster alpinus 'Alba'

Bruckenthalia spiculifolia

Cotoneaster dammeri radicans

113

Crepis rosea (syn C. incana) Europe. *Compositae*

This compact, tufted, herbaceous perennial plant has attractive, clear pink, ligulate florets forming the composite flower heads which appear in succession over a period of weeks. Propagation is best achieved by division of the rootstock. 6in (15cm)
⟋❀Summer/Autumn ○ ◑ ▨ △▼

Cyclamen hederifolium (syn C. neapolitanum), Europe. *Primulaceae*

The deep green leaves with silvery markings persist well into the spring and appear after the dainty flowers. A lovely plant for naturalizing and usually long lived. New plants can be raised from seed. 4in (10cm)
⟋❀Autumn ○ ◑ ▨ △▼

Daphne cneorum, The Garland Flower, Europe. *Thymelaeaceae*

Tiny, trailing evergreen shrub with narrow oblong, deep green leaves, glabrous grey on the underside, spaced along the branches. The fragrant, rose-red, four-lobed tubular flowers are borne in dense terminal clusters. New plants can be raised by seed or cuttings of previous year's wood taken in summer. 6in (15cm)
△❀Spring ○ ◑ ▨ △▼

Dianthus alpinus, Europe. *Caryophyllaceae*

Mat-forming plant making loose cushions of bright green, narrow strap-shaped leaves. The large and attractive flowers vary in colour from white to deep pink with dark purple spots at the base of the petals. An attractive plant for the rock garden or trough increased by seed or by softwood cuttings taken during summer. 2in (5cm)
⟋❀Summer ○ ▨ △▼

Dianthus 'La Bourbrille'. *Caryophyllaceae*

A delectable little tufted perennial plant with narrow silvery leaves which, together with the most attractive bright pink flowers, make it a much admired plant for rock garden or container. Plants may be increased by cuttings taken during summer. 3in (8cm)
⟋❀Summer ○ ▨ △▼

Draba rigida (syn D. dicranoides) Armenia. *Cruciferae*

A neat tufted plant forming a dense cushion up to 3in (7.5cm) wide consisting of bristly, oblong-elliptic leaves. Clusters of flowers appear on smooth scapes. Rather susceptible to damping off disease should water collect on the plant and protection is needed against winter rain. Dying rosettes should be removed without delay to prevent rot spreading. Propagate by sowing seed during spring or by division. 1in (2.5cm)
⟋❀Spring ○ ▨ △▼

Dryas octopetala, Mountain Avens, N. Europe, N. America. *Rosaceae*

An evergreen mat-forming sub-shrub with alternate, elliptic-oblong, deeply crenate leaves arising from prostrate stems on petioles. The white solitary flowers terminate pubescent peduncles. Plants may be increased by lifting the rooted stems, by cuttings removed from the plant during summer or by seed, the resulting seedlings taking up to 3 years to flower. 6in (15cm)
△ ❧ ❀Summer ○ ▨ △

Edraianthus serpyllifolius (syn Wahlenbergia serpyllifolia) Balkans Peninsula. *Campanulaceae*

Dwarf, compact, mat-forming plant with oblanceolate basal leaves forming a rosette. Leafy stems of various length from 1 to 6in (2.5 to 15cm) give rise to terminal, solitary, bell-shaped flowers with bracts immediately beneath. An ideal specimen for the limestone scree and easily propagated by seed or by cuttings taken from non-flowering shoots during summer. 4in (10cm)
⟋❀Summer ○ ▨ △▼

Erigeron simplex, N.W. America. *Compositae*

This evergreen plant gives rise to clumps of hairy grey-green, basal leaves. The solitary daisy-like flowers are borne on scapes. A useful plant for the rock garden, scree bed or trough, it can be increased by seed. 2in (5cm)
△❀Spring/Summer ○ ▨ △▼

Cyclamen hederifolium

Crepis incana

Dianthus alpinus

Dianthus 'La Bourbrille'

Erinus alpinus, W. Europe. *Scrophulariaceae*

This delightful tufted plant forms cushions of deeply toothed and pubescent alternate spatulate leaves. The small pink flowers arise in a simple short raceme. Ideal for crevices and the wall of a raised bed. Plants may be propagated by seed sown during spring, self-sown seedlings appear to withstand hard winters better than those raised from stored seed. Plants may also be increased by division after flowering. 6in (15cm)
⟋❀Spring ○ ▨ △▼

Erodium chamaedryoides 'Roseum'. *Geraniaceae*

The deeply rooting stock gives rise to a densely tufted plant with small, stipulate, cordate leaves with a toothed margin. Attractive, solitary, deep pink flowers on a scape develop dehiscent fruit with spirally-twisted tailed carpels; the most interesting awn is hygroscopic and when contact is made with moist ground, it lengthens by untwisting and so pushes the fruit into the soil. In addition to seed, plants may be increased by stem or root cuttings. 3in (7.5cm)
⟋❀Summer ○ ▨ △ △▼

Erysimum alpinum 'Moonlight'. *Cruciferae*

This charming evergreen wallflower is a useful plant for the rock garden. The fragrant, pale yellow flowers are borne in late spring to early summer and the leaves are lanceolate. Plants may be increased by softwood cuttings in early summer. 2in (5cm)
△❀Spring/Summer ○ ▨ △▼

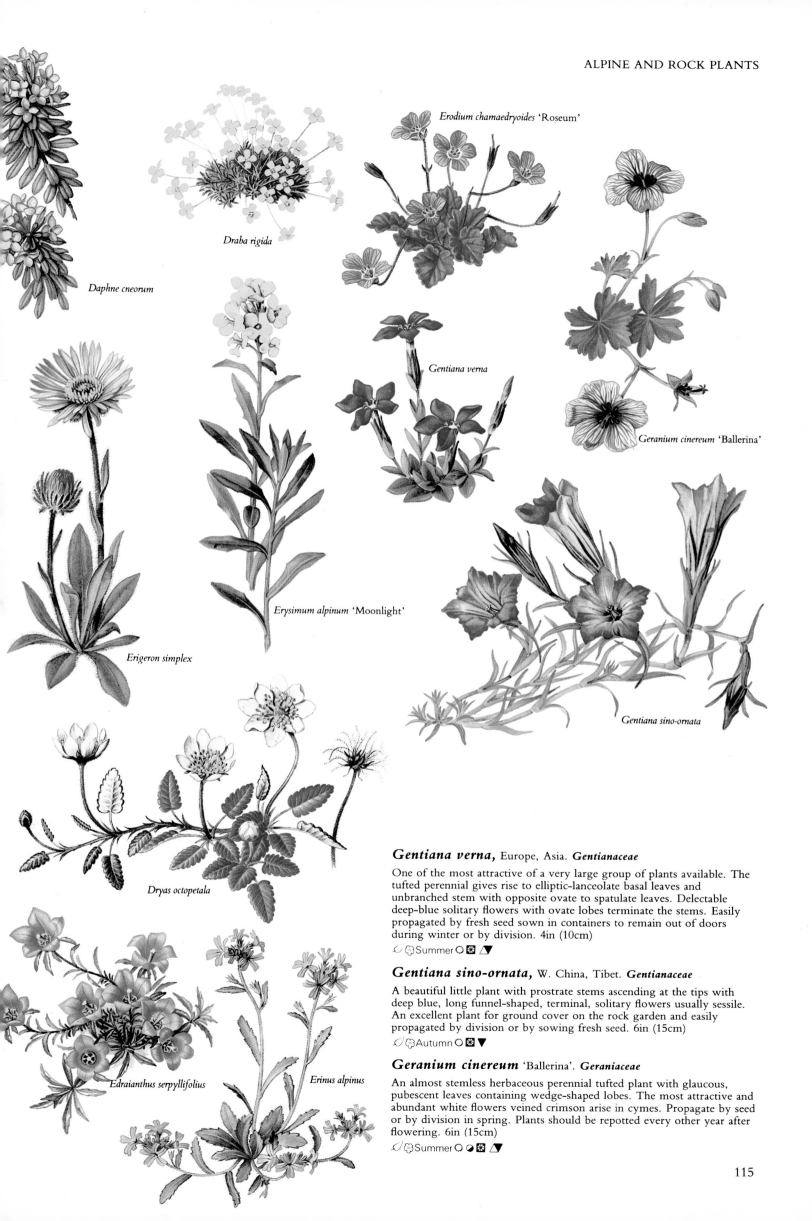

Daphne cneorum

Draba rigida

Erodium chamaedryoides 'Roseum'

Erigeron simplex

Erysimum alpinum 'Moonlight'

Gentiana verna

Geranium cinereum 'Ballerina'

Gentiana sino-ornata

Dryas octopetala

Edraianthus serpyllifolius

Erinus alpinus

Gentiana verna, Europe, Asia. *Gentianaceae*

One of the most attractive of a very large group of plants available. The tufted perennial gives rise to elliptic-lanceolate basal leaves and unbranched stem with opposite ovate to spatulate leaves. Delectable deep-blue solitary flowers with ovate lobes terminate the stems. Easily propagated by fresh seed sown in containers to remain out of doors during winter or by division. 4in (10cm)

○ ⊛ Summer ○ ⊞ △▼

Gentiana sino-ornata, W. China, Tibet. *Gentianaceae*

A beautiful little plant with prostrate stems ascending at the tips with deep blue, long funnel-shaped, terminal, solitary flowers usually sessile. An excellent plant for ground cover on the rock garden and easily propagated by division or by sowing fresh seed. 6in (15cm)

○ ⊛ Autumn ○ ⊞ ▼

Geranium cinereum 'Ballerina'. *Geraniaceae*

An almost stemless herbaceous perennial tufted plant with glaucous, pubescent leaves containing wedge-shaped lobes. The most attractive and abundant white flowers veined crimson arise in cymes. Propagate by seed or by division in spring. Plants should be repotted every other year after flowering. 6in (15cm)

○ ⊛ Summer ○ ◑ ⊞ △▼

115

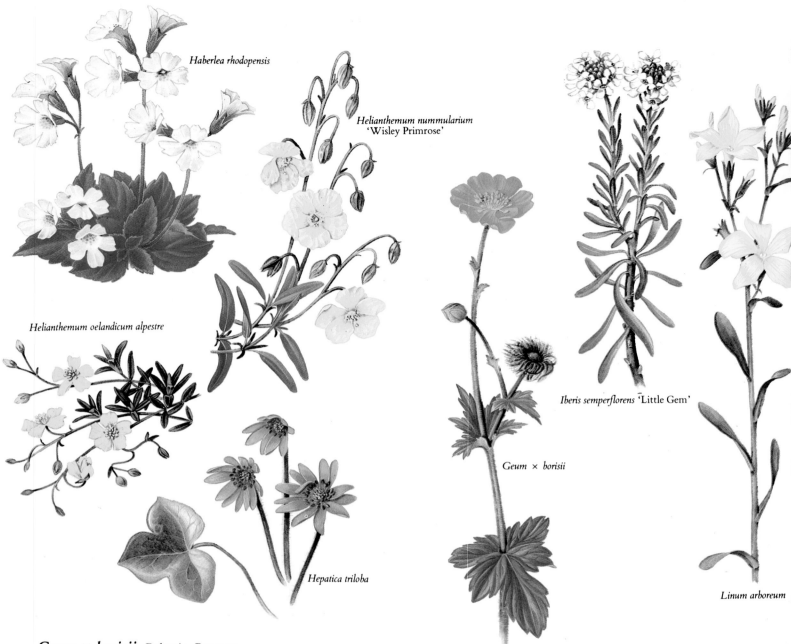

Haberlea rhodopensis

Helianthemum nummularium
'Wisley Primrose'

Helianthemum oelandicum alpestre

Iberis semperflorens 'Little Gem'

Geum × borisii

Hepatica triloba

Linum arboreum

Geum × borisii, Bulgaria. *Rosaceae*

This herbaceous perennial forms a basal rosette of attractive leaves giving rise to an inflorescence of solitary bright orange flowers in a panicle. The plant is best increased by division in spring or autumn and is most desirable for the rock garden or raised bed. 1ft (30cm)

⟁✿Summer ◐ ◕ ✺ ⬦▼

Haberlea rhodopensis, Bulgaria. *Gesneriaceae*

A tufted herbaceous perennial plant covered in soft hairs in which the ovate-oblong spreading leaves with a toothed margin form a basal rosette which gives rise to several long peduncles terminating in a drooping umbel of pale lilac flowers. An ideal plant for the alpine house or rock garden and easily propagated during spring by division or by leaf cuttings. 5in (12.5cm)

⟁✿Spring ◕ ✺ ⬦▼

Helianthemum nummularium 'Wisley Primrose', Rock Rose, Sun Rose. *Cistaceae*

A spreading semi-shrubby plant much used to flow over a dwarf wall and most attractive when planted at the edge of a raised bed. The attractive, oblong, opposite leaves are green on the upper surface and grey beneath covered with downy hairs. Abundant yellow flowers appear in terminal racemes to make this a most useful plant which should be trimmed back after flowering to avoid a straggly appearance. Propagate during summer by cuttings taken from non-flowering shoots. 1ft (30cm)

△✿Summer ○ ✺ ⬦▼

Helianthemum oelandicum alpestre, Rock Rose, Europe. *Cistaceae*

This little ground-hugging shrub with oval-lanceolate to obovate leaves, gives rise to pubescent shoots which form a tufted habit. The bright yellow flowers appear in terminal racemes during summer. An ideal plant for raised bed or rock garden and readily increased by taking cuttings from non-flowering shoots during summer. 3in (7.5cm)

△✿Summer ○ ✺ ⬦▼

Hepatica nobilis (syn *H. triloba*) Europe, Russia. *Ranunculaceae*

Most attractive pink or whitish flowers appear on a scape in spring before the new leaves. Mature leaves become glabrous and shiny beneath and usually persist throughout winter. The leaves are trilobed. Seed germinates readily or the plants may be increased by division. 9in (22.5cm)

⟁✿Spring ◐ ● ✺ ⬦▼

Iberis sempervirens 'Little Gem', Candytuft. *Cruciferae*

A bushy, glabrous, evergreen sub-shrub with alternate, narrow-obovate, somewhat fleshy, entire leaves. Most fragrant white flowers, which appear in closely packed racemes during winter, make this a delectable plant for the alpine house. Plants can be raised by sowing seed, by cuttings taken in June or the rootstock can be divided. 2ft (60cm)

△ ❀✿Winter ○ ✺ ⬦▼

Iris pumila 'Cyanea'. *Iridaceae*

The small rhizome gives rise to stout tufts of green, sword-like leaves. Miniature bearded-iris flowers are solitary and almost sessile. Propagate by division after flowers fade in June. 2in (5cm)

⟁✿Spring/Summer ○ ✺ ⬦▼

Lamium maculatum 'Salmonae', Dead Nettle. *Labiatae*

A trailing perennial plant with underground stolons giving rise to shoots with opposite, ovate leaves attractively variegated in silver. The two-lipped flowers appear in dense axillary clusters. Readily increased by division or by striking softwood cuttings during summer. 15in (38cm)

△✿Summer ○ ◐ ● ✺ ⬦▼

Lewisia cotyledon hybrid

Linaria alpina

Iris pumila 'Cyanea'

Lamium maculatum 'Salmonae'

Lithodora diffusum 'Heavenly Blue' (syn Lithospermum). *Boraginaceae*

Evergreen prostrate sub-shrub forming a mass of bristly stems which give rise to sessile, linear-oblong to lanceolate hairy leaves. The beautiful and abundant deep blue flowers are carried in terminal bracteate cymes which should be cut back when flowers fade to avoid a straggly appearance. Propagate by cuttings taken from previous year's growth. 8in (20cm)

△◌Summer ○ ✿ ▼

Lysimachia nummularia 'Aurea', Creeping Jenny. *Primulaceae*

A prostrate herbaceous perennial with glabrous yellow stems bearing short-petiolate, opposite, entire roundish leaves, also yellow. The bright yellow flowers arise on pedicels from the leaf axils. Planted in a container suspended from the roof of the alpine house it attractively utilises an often unused area; also good as ground cover in the rock garden and readily propagated by division in autumn or spring. 4in (10cm)

△◌Summer ○ ◑ ▭ ✿ ◬▼

Mazus reptans, Himalaya. *Scrophulariaceae*

This perennial plant has prostrate rooting stems giving rise to many tufted, lanceolate to elliptic, toothed leaves. The attractive large purplish-blue flowers with a blotched lip arise in axillary racemes. Plants may be increased by ripe seed or by division in spring. 2in (5cm)

◌◌Summer ○ ✿ ◬▼

Mimulus cupreus 'Whitecroft Scarlet'. *Scrophulariaceae*

This striking herbaceous perennial plant of tufted habit bears bright vermilion flowers over a long period of time and is well worth growing in a container which can be given frost protection during winter, when watering should be reduced from the very moist level enjoyed during summer. Propagate by division or by cuttings taken in spring. 6in (15cm)

◌ ♠◌Summer/Autumn ○ ◑ ✿ ◬▼

Lithodora diffusum 'Heavenly Blue'

Lysimachia nummularia 'Aurea'

Mazus reptans

Mimulus cupreus 'Whitecroft Scarlet'

Lewisia cotyledon hybrid. *Portulacaceae*

Herbaceous perennial plant with a thick fleshy rootstock and a dense rosette of obovate-spatulate, entire leaves. Most attractive panicles of pink-veined white to salmon flowers terminate numerous scapes. A good plant for pan culture in the alpine house or frame where protection from winter rain prevents over-wet compost. Plants may be increased by division or by seed. 6in (15cm)

◌ ♠◌Summer ○ ✿ ◬▼

Linaria alpina, European Alps. *Scrophulariaceae*

An attractive, prostrate, tufted herbaceous perennial with whorls of linear or linear-lanceolate glaucous leaves. The delightful, spurred, intense blue flowers with a deep yellow centre appear in racemes. A most adaptable plant suitable for growing in a dry wall or rock garden. Propagate by division in spring, by seed or by softwood cuttings during mid-summer. 6in (15cm)

◌◌Summer/Autumn ◑ ✿ ◬▼

Linum arboreum, Crete. *Linaceae*

Small, spreading, glabrous shrub with glaucous, sessile, spatulate, recurved leaves. Large golden-yellow flowers arise in close clusters of terminal panicles. An attractive plant for a container which should be given the protection of an alpine house or frame during winter. Propagate by softwood cuttings in summer. 1ft (30cm)

◌ ♠◌Summer ○ ✿ ◬▼

Myosotis alpestris, Europe. *Boraginaceae*

The perennial rootstock gives rise to petiolate basal leaves and erect stems with sessile, linear-oblong, cauline leaves to form a tufted pubescent plant. Most attractive, slightly fragrant blue flowers in a terminal cyme appear on short pedicels. Plants may be increased by taking cuttings or by sowing ripe seed in summer, or by division in spring. 6in (15cm)

⬭🌸○◐❖ △▼

Oenothera pumila (syn *O. perennis, Kneiffia perennis*) Eastern N. America. *Onagraceae*

An easily grown herbaceous perennial plant for the rock garden with slender stems clad with oblanceolate to spatulate or linear-lanceolate leaves. The abundant, small, showy, yellow diurnal flowers arise in a loose leafy spike. Propagation is by division in early spring or by cuttings taken late spring to early summer. 12in (30cm)

⬭🌱🌸Summer/Autumn○ ◐❖ △▼

Origanum rotundifolium, Marjoram, Europe. *Labiatae*

An aromatic plant with small entire leaves and wiry branches terminating in abundant purple flowers. Good for pan culture in frame or alpine house the plants may be increased by division in spring or by soft cuttings in summer. 1¹/₂ft (45cm)

⬭🍃🌸Summer○ ◐❖ △▼

Oxalis adenophylla, Chile. *Oxalidaceae*

A roundish bulb-like base gives rise to abundant leaves comprised of many obcordate, greyish or silvery-green, glabrous leaflets on long petioles which form a basal rosette. Large, solitary, pink, bell-shaped flowers terminate long peduncles. An interesting and adaptable plant for pan or scree where frost protection is given. Plants may be increased by offsets from the bulb-like base. 6in (15cm)

⬭🌸Summer○❖ △▼

Papaver alpinum, Alpine Poppy, European Alps. *Papaveraceae*

This charming tufted perennial plant has cauline lobed leaves with narrow, linear-lanceolate, glaucous, more or less glabrous, segments. The attractive white or yellow flowers terminate slender scapes. Good for pan culture, the plant may also be grown in the rock garden. Propagate by division in spring. 6in (15cm)

⬭🌸Summer○ ◐❖ △▼

Penstemon rupicola, W. United States. *Scrophulariaceae*

Prostrate, evergreen shrub which gives rise to hairy glandular stems clad with alternate, oval to orbicular, leathery, grey-green leaves. Most striking two-lipped crimson flowers arise on peduncles in a loose inflorescence. A good rock-garden plant. Propagate by cuttings taken in late summer. 4in (10cm)

△🌸Summer○❖ △▼

Phlox hoodii, Western N. America. *Polemoniaceae*

Grey-green perennial with tufted habit producing woolly branches and stiff, hairy, awl-shaped leaves. The solitary flowers are white with a soft, hairy calyx. A useful plant for the rock garden which can be increased from seed or by cuttings taken in summer. 2in (5cm)

△🌸Summer○ ◐❖ △▼

Phlox stolonifera (syn *P. reptans*) United States. *Polemoniaceae*

Low-growing, creeping perennial which roots at the nodes on the long sterile shoots. Obovate, obtuse leaves carried on sterile stems; oval, lanceolate ones on the erect flowering stems. Tubular, purple or violet flowers produced in a cyme. Increase by seed or cuttings in summer. 7in (18cm)

△🌸Summer○ ◐❖ △▼

Physoplexis comosa (syn *Phyteuma comosum*) Dalmatia, S. Tyrol. *Campanulaceae*

An admirable herbaceous perennial with long-stalked, sharply-toothed basal leaves and smaller, alternate, cauline leaves forming a tuft-shaped plant. The loose umbel-like clusters of short-stalked flask-shaped flowers make this a most useful plant for rock garden or alpine house. The plants should be protected from slugs which find them most attractive. Readily propagated by seed or division in spring. 4in (10cm)

⬭🌸Summer○❖ △▼

Primula juliae 'Wanda'. *Primulaceae*

A charming early-flowering plant with bright purple-red flowers on pedicels standing well away from the dense mat of coarsely dentate, reniform to orbicular leaves cordate at the base. Propagate by sowing fresh seed, the subsequent seedlings being potted firmly in well-drained compost which should be kept moist when growth is active. Remove dead leaves and allow the compost to become drier during the resting period. 4in (10cm)

⬭🌸Spring◐❖ △▼

Primula denticulata 'Ruby'. *Primulaceae*

A favourite primula whose oblong-obovate or spatulate, sharply denticulate, mealy-covered leaves grow to 1ft (30cm) long provided the soil is not too dry. A scape terminates in the globose head of flowers with yellow centres. Self-sown seedlings should be rogued to retain the choicest flowers and the best selections can be increased by division. 8in (20cm)

⬭🌸Spring◐❖ △▼

Primula marginata, Maritime and Cottian Alps. *Primulaceae*

The umbel of fragrant, lilac-blue, funnel-shaped flowers with farinose throats on farinose pedicels, terminates a long scape arising from the centre of obtuse, regularly dentate-serrate, oblong or obovate, evergreen leaves. The leaves are often completely farinose and the silver-white margin most attractive. Plants can be readily propagated by cuttings taken when flowers have faded. 4in (10cm)

⬭🌸Spring○ ◐❖ △▼

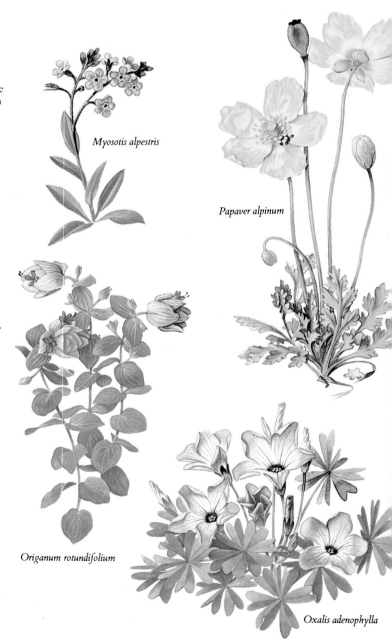

Myosotis alpestris

Papaver alpinum

Origanum rotundifolium

Oxalis adenophylla

Physoplexis comosa

Phlox hoodii

Primula juliae 'Wanda'

Phlox stolonifera

Penstemon rupicola

Oenothera pumila

Pulsatilla vulgaris

Pulsatilla vulgaris (syn *Anemone pulsatilla*) Pasque Flower, Europe. *Ranunculaceae*

The almost black-coloured fibrous rootstock gives rise to most attractive pinnate leaves with many partite segments. Beautiful violet flowers with yellow stamens terminate long hairy stems which support the feathery filaments that are a feature of the plant. Fresh seed germinates readily and plants can also be increased by root cuttings taken in July. 6in (15cm)

⌀ ✿ ❀ Spring ○ ◑ ✽ △▼

Ramonda myconi (syn *R. pyrenaica*) Pyrenees. *Gesneriaceae*

This stemless herbaceous perennial plant has hairy, ovate, cauline, deeply toothed leaves forming a rosette. The short leafless scape terminates in a showy flower head, each flower with 5 sepals and petals, the corolla lobes more or less obovate. An attractive plant for the rock garden or alpine house and easily propagated by seed or division in spring or by leaf cuttings in May. 3in (7.5cm)

⌀ ❀ Summer ○ ◑ ✽ △▼

Ranunculus alpestris, European Alps. *Ranunculaceae*

An interesting herbaceous perennial for the rock garden. It makes a small tufted plant with 3-lobed glossy green foliage and solitary white buttercup-like flowers. Plants may be increased from seed and should be kept fairly dry in winter. 4in (10cm)

⌀ ❀ Late Spring/Summer ○ ◑ ✽ △▼

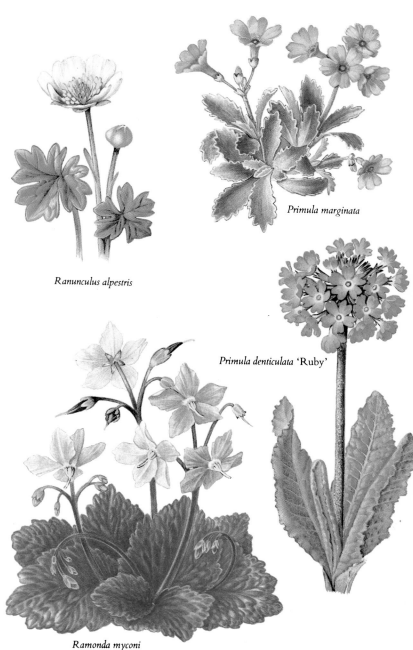

Ranunculus alpestris

Primula marginata

Primula denticulata 'Ruby'

Ramonda myconi

Saponaria 'Bressingham'. *Caryophyllaceae*

A herbaceous perennial for the rock garden or pan culture readily increased by cuttings with a heel in July. This choice little tufted plant is slow growing and produces abundant pink flowers. 2in (5cm)

⟋❀Summer○�✼△▽

Saxifraga burseriana, European Alps. *Saxifragaceae*

A much admired little cushion-forming spiny-leaved perennial plant. The dainty red-tinted stem arises through silver-grey leaves to produce reddish flower buds which open to display glistening petals. Readily propagated by division and grown on in a pan or planted in a raised bed or rock garden. 2in (5cm)

⟋❀Spring◑✼△▽

Saxifraga grisebachii 'Wisley Variety'. *Saxifragaceae*

An excellent form of this most attractive comparatively large cushion plant with basal rosettes of silvery-grey leaves up to 3in (7.5cm) in diameter. The flower stems are clad with red-haired leaves and terminate in deep red star-shaped flowers. Plants may be increased by division, seed often producing less favourable types. 9in (22.5cm)

⟋❀Spring◑✼△▽

Saxifraga longifolia 'Tumbling Waters'. *Saxifragaceae*

This magnificent evergreen herbaceous perennial with hybrid vigour produces spectacular panicles of white flowers. The basal, linear-ligulate, glabrous, greyish leaves grow up to 4in (10cm) long. Propagation is by seed taken from plants not cross pollinated by other silver saxifrages. 1¹/₂ft (75cm)

△❀Summer◑✼△ ▲▼

Saxifraga oppositifolia latina, Italy. *Saxifragaceae*

This delightful plant forms close mats of creeping stems densely covered with keeled, silvery-green leaves. Large pink flowers, borne on 1-in (2.5-cm) stems, add to its attractions. Increase plants by softwood cuttings in early summer. 2in (5cm)

△❀Spring◑✼△▽

Sedum palmeri, Mexico. *Crassulaceae*

Trailing mats of glaucous stems rooting where they touch the ground are clothed with glaucous leaves often grouped in loose rosettes. Abundant flowers arise in cymes which are rather drooping. Readily increased by lifting rooted stems or by stem cuttings. 8in (20cm)

△❀Summer○ ◑✼△▽

Sedum spathulifolium 'Capablanca'. *Crassulaceae*

Evergreen plant forming a dense cushion-like clump producing runners from the base. Spatulate leaves with pointed recurved tips arise on barren shoots to form a silver-white rosette, those on the erect flower stem are scattered, club shaped and spreading. Yellow flowers terminate the stem in cymes to provide a bonus to the attractive leaves. Propagate by division. 5in (12.5cm)

△❀Summer○ ◑✼△▽

Sempervivum arachnoideum, Houseleek, Europe. *Crassulaceae*

A thick fleshy herbaceous perennial forming rosettes. These are up to 2in (5cm) across and composed of densely packed, alternate, sessile, fleshy leaves with reddish or green tips all connected with cobweb-like hairs. Bright red flowers terminate an erect stem with scattered fleshy leaves. An easy plant to grow unless over-fed when the plant lacks colour, produces rank growth susceptible to stem rot. Plants should be increased by division to avoid seed variability. 2in (5cm)

△❀Summer○ ◑✼△▽

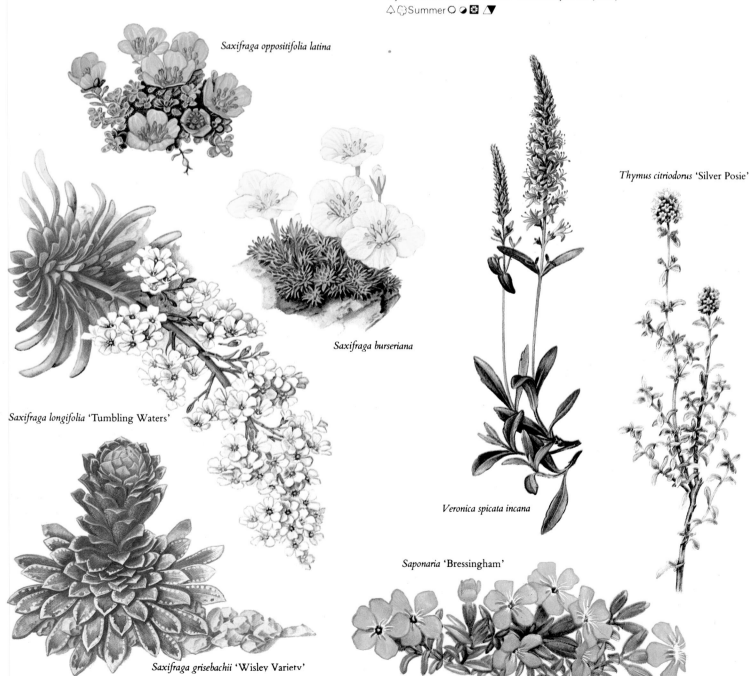

Saxifraga oppositifolia latina

Thymus citriodorus 'Silver Posie'

Saxifraga burseriana

Saxifraga longifolia 'Tumbling Waters'

Veronica spicata incana

Saponaria 'Bressingham'

Saxifraga grisebachii 'Wisley Variety'

Silene acaulis, Moss Campion, Cushion Pink, N. Hemisphere. *Caryophyllaceae*

Bright green perennial plant producing a densely tufted cushion with tightly packed, keeled, opposite and entire leaves. The spasmodically produced red, pink or white flowers terminate a short stem. Best grown on a moraine, the plants may be increased by division in spring, cuttings during mid-summer or by seed. 2in (5cm)

⟋ ✿ ❁ Summer ○ ▦ ⃤▽

Thymus citriodorus 'Silver Posie', Lemon Thyme. *Labiatae*

A rather variable lemon-scented hybrid bush with erect or ascending hairy shoots bearing short-petiolate, most aromatic, lanceolate, gland-dotted, glabrous leaves with revolute margin. The attractive pale lilac flowers appear on an oblong inflorescence. Propagate by cuttings during late summer. 1ft (30cm)

△ ❁ Summer ○ ▦ ⃤▽

Thymus caespititius, S.E. Europe. *Labiatae*

A mat-forming plant with slender, woody prostrate stems and erect, hairy flowering stems. The leaves are linear, gland dotted and glabrous but with hairy margins. Light lilac flowers are carried in a loose inflorescence arising from the leaf axils. Propagate by detaching rooted runners or by cuttings. 2in (5cm)

△ ✿ ❁ Summer ○ ▦ ⃤▽

Viola cornuta 'Alba'

Thymus caespititius

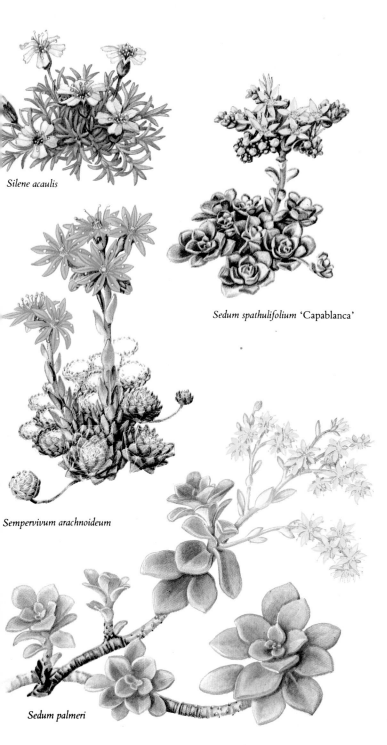

Silene acaulis

Sedum spathulifolium 'Capablanca'

Sempervivum arachnoideum

Sedum palmeri

Viola stojanowii

Verbascum 'Letitia'

Verbascum 'Letitia'. *Scrophulariaceae*

This charming little sub-shrub has woody stems clothed with rosettes of lanceolate, blue-grey woolly leaves. The open, saucer-shaped bright yellow flowers are carried in terminal racemes. A most attractive plant for the rock garden which can be increased by cuttings taken with a heel in late May. 6in (15cm)

⟋❁ Late Spring/Summer ○ ▦ ⃤▽

Veronica spicata incana, Europe. *Scrophulariaceae*

This herbaceous perennial is one of many useful plants within the genus. The opposite lanceolate leaves are toothed and the ascending flowering stems terminate in long dense racemes of blue flowers. Plants may be increased by cuttings in summer. 8in (20cm)

△❁ Summer ○ ▦ ⃤▽

Viola cornuta 'Alba'. *Violaceae*

The prostrate stems rooting at the nodes eventually ascend and give rise to large white flowers with a slender spur. Ovate or broadly ovate leaves on a long petiole arise from between attractive, deeply cut leafy stipules. A prolific flowering plant and easily propagated by division or by seed. 1ft (30cm)

⟋ ✿ ❁ Summer ○ ◗ ▦ ⃤▽

Viola stojanowii, Balkan Peninsula. *Violaceae*

Well suited to the rock garden, this small evergreen plant produces hairy, leafy stems from a slender erect rhizome. The leaves are entire, hairy and narrow lanceolate and the small flowers are yellow with a tiny spur. Increase by seeds sown as soon as ripe or by green cuttings in July. 4in (10cm)

△❁ Late Spring/Summer ○ ▦ ⃤▽

Garden Pools and Water Plants

A water feature adds another dimension to the garden and in some instances makes an ideal focal point. The pool shown here is at Stourton House.

Water-lilies, and the rest of the plants grouped together under the title of 'aquatics', are remarkably easy plants to grow. They are easy to establish, at the right season; they do not demand a lot of attention; they are not finicky about soil; immersed in water they need no watering, and they will survive a surprising amount of neglect. That does not mean, of course, that they will not do even better if some thought is given to their basic needs. Flowering will be improved all round; the splendid blooms of water-lilies will be larger, more numerous and even more magnificent, if care is taken over such elementary details as the position, the shape and the depths of the pool in which they will grow.

In the lakes and ponds where water-lilies occur naturally they are open to the sky, getting all the sunlight there is going. Lilies do not grow in the deeps: they prefer the shallower areas where the water warms up quickly in spring and where their leaves can easily reach the surface. At the lake's very edge, where the water is only inches deep, are ranked the reeds, rushes, irises and other marginal plants. These natural preferences signpost the way to the best position for the garden pool and to some extent decide its shape.

The Best Site

The idea that a pond would be just the thing to brighten up a dark corner must be dismissed: it would be the worst place. The best site is the one that gets most sunshine. A spot well clear of trees or overhanging bushes will not only gain light but will avoid pollution of the water by dead leaves and twigs. Another consideration is accessibility. A garden pool acts like a magnet; visitors will always make a beeline for it. If it can be sited close to an existing path so much the better. And if a fountain or waterfall is contemplated, or underwater lighting, it will ease the cable-laying problem if the pool is not too far from an undercover socket outlet.

Pool Design

The pool shape ought to match its surroundings. A rectangle or circle looks right on a patio or where lawns, paths and borders are straight-edged; an irregular shape will fit in with curved paths and borders. Whether geometrical or informal the best surface shape is a simple, open one. Complicated constricted shapes limit the spread of lily leaves, give no impression of a patch of water at a distance, and should not be considered.

The pool profile – the sectional shape – need not be complicated. The sides should slope steeply – 1in in for every 3in down (2.5cm in 8cm) – in order to achieve a good volume in relation to the surface area. Water plants vary somewhat in the depth of water they prefer but, given the flexibility conferred by container planting, the pool itself need provide only two levels.

One will be the main depth, from 18 to 24in (45 to 60cm), and it should extend over most of the bottom, not to be limited to one sump in an otherwise shallow pool. The second level is the shelf, 8 or 9 in (20 or 23cm) below the surface and 10 to 12in (25 to 30cm) wide, on which marginal plants will stand in their containers. No other complications are necessary and, except for fanciers of Koi carp, greater depths confer no advantage.

Materials

The most popular material for pool construction nowadays is a sheet of flexible plastic. Most garden centres offer two well-tried types.

Laminated PVC is two-coloured, usually black on one side and light brown on the other. Which way up it is used is a matter of personal choice; black makes an excellent background for plants and fish and (unexpectedly perhaps) looks very natural when installed. Laminated PVC will be found under such brand names as Aqualene, Wildwoods PVC, Pondalene, Duralay. Guarantees against defective material or workmanship vary from three to five years; the expectation of useful life is in the order of 10 to 15 years, or more, depending very much on how carefully it is installed. Damage is easily repaired with a PVC patch and Bostik clear adhesive.

Butyl Rubber is the longest-lasting and the most expensive type of pool liner; however, since its life expectation is more than four times that of PVC and its price less than double, in terms of cost-efficiency it can claim to be the most economical. Butyl liners are in fact a blend of butyl rubber and EPDM, in varying proportions, under names such as EP Butyl, Stapelite, and Lotylite. They claim a life expectation in excess of 50 years and are generally guaranteed for 15 years. Punctures or slits are repairable with special patches and tape.

Liner Installation Laminated PVC and butyl are both elastic and a similar installation technique is employed. The size of liner required for a given excavation is arrived at by adding twice the maximum pool depth to both the overall length and the overall width of the hole. It is not necessary to add on anything for overlap; that will be provided by the slope on the sides and the stretch in the material. An excavation 7ft (2.1m) long, 5ft (1.5m) wide and 2ft (60cm) maximum depth will need a liner 11ft by 9ft (3.3 by 2.7m).

The same calculation in reverse will show how large a pool can be made from a liner of a given size (garden centres usually offer half a dozen stock sizes off the shelf, though any required size can be made to order). Take, for example, a liner 16ft by 12ft (5 by 3.5m). If the pool is to be 2ft (60cm) deep at the most, then subtract twice the depth from the liner length and width: thus the pool surface shape can be anything within a rectangle 12ft by 8ft (3.5 by 2.5m). The simple open shape recommended is not only the most effective, but the least wasteful in trimmed-off material.

The excavation must offer an even bed for the liner, without sharp projections, and it can be lined with such materials as sawdust, sand, sifted soil, old carpet or underfelt, fertilizer bags, or even several thicknesses of newspaper. The liner is then placed over the hole, sagging so that it barely touches the bottom, and the edges weighted with bricks or paving. Water is run onto the sheet and by degrees its weight spreads the liner across the bottom, up the sides and over the shelves, moulded precisely to the contours of the excavation. Some of the weight may be taken off the edges to allow them to creep in but some tension should be kept on all the time to minimise wrinkling. Once the pool is filled surplus material is trimmed off with scissors (and some kept just in case a patch is ever needed) leaving a flap several inches wide on which paving stones will be bedded in a cement/sand mixture. Years can be added to the useful life of the liner (which is only degraded significantly by ultra-violet light *above* water level) if particular attention is paid to two points. One is to ensure, with a spirit level, that the pool rim is really level; the second is to project the paving stones 2in (5cm) over the water. One measure makes it possible to keep the water level high all round, the other casts shade; between

the two there is no reason why sunlight need fall on any part of the liner above water level.

Ready-made Pools Although pool liners offer freedom to make any desired shape, without limit on size, some gardeners prefer to choose from the range of ready-moulded shapes, of which there are several types. Glassfibre pools, when well made, are virtually indestructible and the more recently introduced moulded ABS pools seem likely to prove equally tough. They are both expensive compared with flexible liners. A tempting alternative, in terms of cost, is a pool made of moulded poly-propylene. Such pools are noticeably flimsy and, having a rela-tively short life, cannot be recommended except for temporary use, or as low-cost reserve pools for fry or live food or the children's frog-spawn and tadpoles.

Care is required in the selection of a moulded pool. Many are hopelessly small and shallow and will never make satisfactory features. Small may be beautiful in some spheres but not where pools are concerned. The greater the volume of water the fewer will be the problems. If ever a choice has to be made between two sizes, choose the larger. And remember that however large a pool may look propped against the garden centre fence, it will seem to shrink to half the size when sunk into the ground.

Installing a moulded pool requires the excavation of a hole several inches larger all round than the pool, but no deeper, so that its base can rest firmly on undisturbed soil. Once in position (and the level checked), backfilling can take place, particular care being taken to work soil in to give firm support under the shelves. The edge is again finished with paving stones. If the pool (whether moulded or made with a liner) is being sunk in a lawn it will not do to have the paving surround sitting on top of the grass. So take 2in (5cm) of turf off the whole area *including the surround* before excavating the pool profile. The top of the paving surround will then finish flush with the grass.

Green Water When the pool is filled (and tap water is per-fectly acceptable) it looks sparkling clear. In a very short time it will look as if it is filled with pea soup. Why? The answer is that nature allows no empty spaces and is busy colonising this new environment with microscopic life forms. The colour comes from single-celled algae, individually invisible plants in vast numbers. There is nothing wrong with this and it should cause no alarm but many gardeners panic at this point and change the water. To no avail: it simply does it again – and will do, again and again, as often as the water is changed. The way to make it go away is to ignore it – and plant the pond.

The green-water algae thrive on sunlight and on nutrients in the water. Cut off the sunlight with the spreading leaves of lilies, and floating plants, on the surface; starve them of nutrients by introducing competition in the shape of a flourishing bed of submerged oxygenators; be patient for a few weeks, and sud-denly, overnight even, the pool is clear. Chemicals may give temporary relief, but are no more a cure for green water than aspirin is a cure for toothache. Planting is the answer.

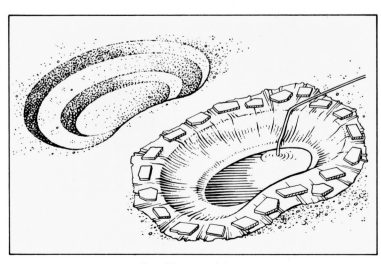

Installing a pool liner.

Water Plants

It will be seen that water plants serve two purposes, one ornamental, the other practical, and this has to be borne in mind when they are selected. They can be separated, very broadly, into four groups.

Submerged Plants These, generally referred to as oxygenators (and sometimes disparagingly as weeds) are important because they oxygenate the water. Even more vital is their function in absorbing dissolved mineral salts from the water and thus starving the algae. They are essentials.

Surfacing Plants These are plants which root in soil and produce flowers and leaves on the surface. Their great practical value is in intercepting at the surface the sunlight without which algae cannot flourish. Most are ornamental too. Water-lilies, supreme in both respects, are the most important plants in this group and, indeed, the most important in the pool.

Floating Plants This group embraces a mixed bag some of which float on the surface all the time, and some only spasmodically. They contribute to the light-excluding surface cover but, since some of them don't know where to stop, that job is best left to water-lilies, which have much greater ornamental value than any of the floaters.

Marginal Plants These are the ones that stand with their toes in water at the edge and lift their stems and flowers above it. They contribute nothing to pool balance so are not essential but they bring the beauty of attractive flowers or foliage.

A Selection of Hardy Water-lilies Water-lilies vary considerably in vigour and spread so choice is influenced by the dimensions of the pool. The most vigorous and easily propagated varieties are the most economical to produce. It may be assumed that a cheap water-lily is a vigorous one and, though the price and the size of the plant make it a tempting buy, it would not be a good choice for anything but a large pool. *Nymphaea laydekeri* 'Lilacea', though costing more, would prove in the long term a far better investment for a small glassfibre pool than a bulky inexpensive root of *Marliacea* 'Carnea'.

In the descriptions that follow, 'depth' refers to water depth over the crown and does not include the depth of the soil or container in which the plant is growing. Thus a lily in a container 8in (20cm) deep standing on the floor of a pool 20in (50cm) deep is at an effective planting depth of 12in (30cm).

RED LILIES

'Attraction'. A vigorous grower with very large flowers (often pinky white until established) and leaves. Spread 6ft (1.8m). Depth 15 to 36in (38cm to 1m).

'Escarboucle'. Superb crimson flowers, abundantly produced, make this the most popular of the medium-strong lilies. Spread 5ft (1.5m). Depth 12 to 30in (30 to 75cm).

'James Brydon'. Blooms are carmine-red bowls with golden centres, leaves bronzy-purple. Adapts well to limited space. Spread 3ft (1m). Depth 9 to 18in (23 to 45cm).

'Froebeli'. A free-flowering red even in cold areas: an ideal choice for small pools. Spread 2 to 3ft (60cm to 1m). Depth 7 to 15in (18 to 38cm).

PINK LILIES

'Mrs Richmond'. A vigorous lily with very beautiful 8 to 9in (20 to 23cm) blooms shading from pink to carmine. Spread 6ft (1.8m). Depth 15 to 36in (38cm to 1m).

Marliacea 'Rosea'. Strong, tough, prolific and beautiful, the colour deepening when the plant is established. Spread 5ft (1.5m). Depth 12 to 30in (30 to 75cm). *Marliacea* 'Carnea', of similar dimensions, and often sold as pink, is no more than lightly-blushed white.

'Mme Wilfron Gonnère'. Rich pink double flowers with the symmetry of a formal double camellia. Spread 4 to 5ft (1.2 to 1.5m). Depth 9 to 24in (23 to 60cm).

'Rose Arey'. Superb silvery pink blooms with elegantly pointed petals. Spread 4ft (1.2m). Depth 9 to 18in (23 to 45cm).

Laydekeri 'Lilacea'. An admirable choice for small pools: the flowers are lilac-pink. Spread 1½ to 2ft (45 to 60cm). Depth 5 to 12in (13 to 30cm).

WHITE LILIES

'Gladstoniana' (syn 'Gladstone'). Very robust, with massive leaves and flowers; it needs a lot of room. Spread 8ft (2.4m). Depth 18 to 36in (45cm to 1m).

Marliacea 'Albida'. As reliable and foolproof as any plant can be. Beautiful too, but big. Spread 6ft (1.8m). Depth 12 to 30in (30 to 75cm).

'Gonnère'. Marvellous globular flowers packed with dazzling white petals round a golden centre. Spread 4ft (1.2m). Depth 9 to 24in (23 to 60cm).

'Albatross'. A medium grower with apple-green foliage and pointed white petals. Spread 3 to 4ft (1 to 1.2m). Depth 9 to 18in (23 to 45cm).

'Candida'. An attractive small-pool or tub lily with 3in (8cm) white flowers. Spread 2ft (60cm). Depth 5 to 12in (13 to 30cm).

YELLOW AND 'SUNSET COLOURS'

Marliacea 'Chromatella'. A very popular and very vigorous lily with primrose-yellow flowers. Spread 6ft (1.8m). Depth 12 to 30in (30 to 75cm).

'Sunrise'. A very fine yellow whose flowers, held above the surface, respond to plenty of sunshine. Spread 4ft (1.2m). Depth 9 to 24in (25 to 60cm).

Odorata 'Sulphurea'. Many-petalled yellow flowers are held above marbled foliage. Spread 4ft (1.2m). Depth 9 to 24in (23 to 60cm).

'Graziella'. An unusual colour: orange-apricot with an underlying hint of pink. Spread 3ft (1m). Depth 7 to 15in (18 to 40cm).

'Paul Hariot'. This has quite large flowers for a small grower, a 'sunset' mixture from buff through pinky orange to red-centred deep pink. Spread 2ft (60cm). Depth 5 to 12in (13 to 30cm).

Pygmaea 'Helvola'. A true miniature with dainty 2in (5cm) pale yellow flowers and small leaves. For a bowl or a tub or the smallest pool. Spread 15in (38cm). Depth 3 to 9in (8 to 23cm).

The number of lilies a pool will hold depends on whether vigorous, moderate or small growers are chosen. The aim should be to cover half to two-thirds of the surface with foliage when the plants are established.

Other Surfacing Plants *Aponogeton distachyus*. Water hawthorn has unusual forked black-and-white flowers, vanilla scented. Blooms heavily spring and autumn, and lightly in between. Strongly recommended. Spread 2ft (60cm). Depth 4 to 18in (10 to 45cm).

Nymphoides peltata. Looks very much like a small water-lily, with round leaves and yellow flowers on the surface. Spread 2ft (60cm). Depth 5 to 12in (10 to 30cm).

Orontium aquaticum. Flower spikes like yellow waxy tapers on slender white stems have earned this plant the name golden club. Blue-green leaves float or stand erect depending on depth, anything from 2 to 18in (5 to 45cm).

Submerged Oxygenating Plants These 'maids of all work' provide oxygen, food and shelter, spawning beds and fry nurseries, all for the benefit of fish. And they play a vital part in keeping the water clear.

Ceratophyllum demersum, hornwort, does not need to be planted, and has slightly bristly foliage less palatable than most to fish, so is one of the most valuable. *Elodea crispa* (syn *Lagarosiphon muscoides* 'Major') and *Elodea canadensis* are particularly effective; other useful plants include *Myriophyllum spicatum*, *Potamogeton crispus*, *Fontinalis*, willow moss, and *Ranunculus aquatilis*. *Hottonia palustris* is the prettiest, and the most difficult to establish. Planting at the rate of one bunch for every 2 or 3sq ft (0.09 to 0.25sqm) of water surface area is recommended for initial stocking, using a mixture of several of the above species if possible.

Floating Plants *Azolla caroliniana*. Quickly spreads to form a mossy sheet across the surface, attractive in texture and variable green/grey/lilac/red colouring. Control difficult.

Lemna minor and *L. major*. A few specks of these duckweeds can soon become a smothering bright green blanket and they should never be introduced deliberately. *Lemna trisulca*, which stays submerged most of the time, is safe, and a useful fish food.

Hydrocharis morsus-ranae. Frogbit grows in June from a resting bud and develops a chain of rosettes of small round leaves with a few tiny white flowers. Much relished by snails.

Stratiotes aloides. The water soldier, a cluster of fleshy saw-toothed leaves, sits on the bottom most of the time, rising to the surface briefly to produce a white flower.

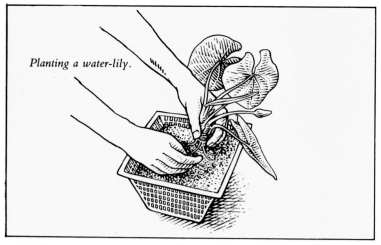

Planting a water-lily.

Eichhornia crassipes major. The tropical water hyacinth, with spikes of large violet-blue flowers borne on a raft of shiny dark green leaves, is the most beautiful of floating plants – grown under glass. Outdoors, in Britain, it is far from happy in summer and dead by winter.

Planting Aquatics

Water plants are different. Unlike roses and shrubs and fruit trees they are never moved when they are dormant. They should not be moved until growth is under way and the pond water warm enough to ensure that growth continues without check when they are transplanted. Some marginals and oxygenators will be fit to move in April, most by late May, and a few not until June. May and June are the peak months for pond planting but it can continue through the summer even into September. Plants that are already established in containers, as are increasingly being offered by specialist water garden centres, and which can be transferred from the garden centre to your pool *without root disturbance*, can of course be moved at any time.

Planting technique The most satisfactory planting technique is to use the plastic containers sold specifically for water plants. Soil goes only into containers and no soil (or gravel or pebbles) goes elsewhere on the pool floor. Compared with the older idea of spreading soil all over the floor and shelves, the container method economises on soil, controls rampant plant growth, gives fewer opportunities to fish for mud-stirring, and proves a boon when the pool needs cleaning out.

The most common fault lies in not using large enough containers. Nothing smaller than a 12in (30cm) square container will do for a water-lily – unless it is a miniature – and however odd a sprig of a marginal may seem when first planted in a 10-in (25-cm) container it will very soon prove it needs every bit of it.

Soil The ideal soil for pond plants is a heavy garden or pasture loam. Light sandy stuff has little value; putty-like clay should be used only as a last resort, and then only with a 50/50 mixture of peat. Except for this purpose peat has no use in the pond.

Fertilizer should be used sparingly, if at all. If it dissolves rapidly it will be as likely to promote the growth of algae as of the plants it is supposed to nourish. Leafmould and garden compost will foul the water and must never be used.

Planting Water-lilies `Any mature leaves on a lily at planting time may as well be removed since they will, in any case, die back very soon. The same applies to any white fleshy roots.

The lily rhizome will be one of two kinds: either a chunky lump or a banana-shaped tuber. The chunky sort is planted in the obvious way with the growing point kept above soil level and the rest firmly buried. The long type is planted almost horizontally, with no part of the rhizome completely buried, and a brick or stone to keep it firmly pressed into the soil until it is well rooted. The container should at first be positioned, propped on bricks if necessary, where there will be no more than 8 or 9 in (20 or 23 cm) of water above it. It does not matter if there are no leaves reaching the surface at this stage. After a few weeks the container can be lowered to whatever depth is appropriate for the variety growing in it. A layer of gravel or, better, pebbles placed on the soil will help if fish are to be introduced later.

Planting Oxygenators These are supplied as bunches of unrooted stems, usually held together by a twist of lead. There is a widely held belief that oxygenators are 'just dropped in'. If they are, some fragments will certainly root, but this is a very haphazard and wasteful way to set about establishing a flourishing bed of these vital plants. They should have their lower stems (the lead strip can remain) pushed firmly into soil. Or, if they won't stay put, the bunches can be laid flat with a stone to hold them down. They will root just as well that way. Since their roots are for anchorage (they absorb their nutrients through leaves and stems) they do not even need soil. Fine gravel or $\frac{1}{16}$in (1.5mm) aquarium grit makes an excellent rooting medium that does not muddy the water. Oxygenators can be planted in small pots; a plastic seed tray is perfect for half a dozen bunches. Oxygenators shrivel quickly out of water particularly in the sun. There must be no delay between unwrapping them and getting them into the pool.

Planting Marginals A planting container about 10in (25cm) square and 6in (15cm) deep contains enough soil to nourish a substantial clump of marginal growth; it also provides enough stability to prevent that clump from being blown over. Standing on a marginal shelf 8 to 9in (20 to 23in) deep it will provide the 2in (5cm) or so of water over the roots which suits the great majority of marginal plants. For those, like the calthas, which prefer to be barely covered, it is very easy to adjust the effective planting depth by slipping a tile or two under the container. A common mistake is to plant in the same container two or three different varieties which then struggle until only one survives. Whether it has one or two or three plants in it, the only safe rule is: one container, one variety.

Livestock

Fish add colour and movement to the pool. They also have a practical value in controlling the mosquitos and midges that would otherwise use it as a breeding ground. Goldfish, shubunkins, comets and other hardy goldfish varieties can safely be mixed with golden orfe (the insect-killers supreme), tench and rudd. Koi carp need special conditions (and are great destroyers of plants) and they cannot be recommended for the average garden pool.

No fish should be introduced (except perhaps a few small golden orfe) until the plants have been in for a month. This is for the sake of the oxygenators which, if nibbled and browsed

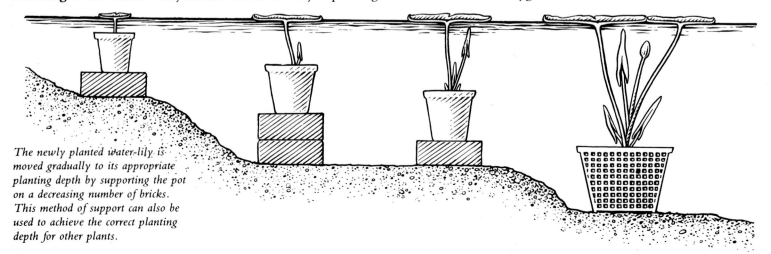

The newly planted water-lily is moved gradually to its appropriate planting depth by supporting the pot on a decreasing number of bricks. This method of support can also be used to achieve the correct planting depth for other plants.

on before they have time to get well-rooted, will disintegrate. And without oxygenators the water will never clear.

Both water snails and mussels are credited with the ability to clear water like magic. Mussels certainly do filter green algae out of the water but when they run out of food and die they pollute the water very badly. Add to that the fact that their larvae are parasitic on fish and it will be understood that they cannot be recommended. Snails have no effect on the colour of the water, and the commonest type, the big, pointed *Limnaea stagnalis*, has a destructive appetite for the choicest plants. The ramshorn snail, *Planorbis corneus*, is an acceptable, though by no means essential, member of the pool community.

Aftercare

Once established water plants do not demand constant attention. The few routine jobs necessary to keep them and the other pool occupants in good order are best reviewed on a seasonal basis.

February/March Frogs and/or toads may choose the pool as a nursery. Toad spawn is in strings, frog spawn in masses. The antics of courtship may upset plant containers but they don't last long. Before asking local conservation enthusiasts to remove frogs, toads and spawn to an alternative breeding site, consider that tadpoles are superbly efficient scavengers and spring cleaners of the pool.

April As the water warms fish become more active and feeding can be resumed. Changing from a third to half of the water will dilute the pollution of winter decay and greatly benefit the fish. Oxygenators can be planted now; if fish are already present the plants will have to be protected from them with a cage of small-mesh wire netting or they will have no chance to get established. Many marginals are ready to move now, including marsh marigolds (caltha) even though they are in flower.

May/June This is the optimum period for planting new stock and also for performing any operation which involves root disturbance, such as planting, replanting or splitting up. The great majority of aquatics are propagated by division. If you want to increase stock, or to tidy marginals that have outgrown their containers, now is the time to tip them out, split them up and replant young growth in new soil. Lilies that have been in a container for three years will probably need cutting up and replanting. If, after several years, the pool needs a total clearout, this is the time of year to do it, not the autumn.

Merely trimming off roots and shoots that have escaped from containers (without emptying the plant out) is a job that can be carried out at any time.

July/August Spells of close thundery weather can cause fish to gulp in distress at the surface; they may even die overnight. They are being affected by a surfeit of carbon dioxide which is not escaping through the surface as it would normally do. The problem is worst at night when plants as well as fish are exhaling carbon dioxide. Adding more oxygenators will not improve matters. The remedy is to churn up the water surface; do it with a hose, or even a stick, for a few minutes last thing at night and first thing in the morning. Better still, install a fountain or a waterfall and, as long as the thundery spell continues, keep it running all night.

September Oxygenators are an asset only during the summer. Decaying in the pool in the winter they become a hazard. It is wise to cut them back now (except for hottonia) to only a few inches.

October/November As long as the water is warm and fish have hearty appetites, feed them to build up reserves for the winter. When the temperature drops they will retire to the shelter of containers or (if you are thoughtful enough to provide them) drainpipes on the bottom where they will doze, living off their fat until the spring. To protect them from the dangers created by the surface being sealed over for a time with ice, consider installing a pool heater that will keep open a life-saving hole in the ice however long it freezes.

Apart from the invariably tender eichhornia and the sometimes vulnerable mimulus (as already mentioned) the pool plants described are hardy.

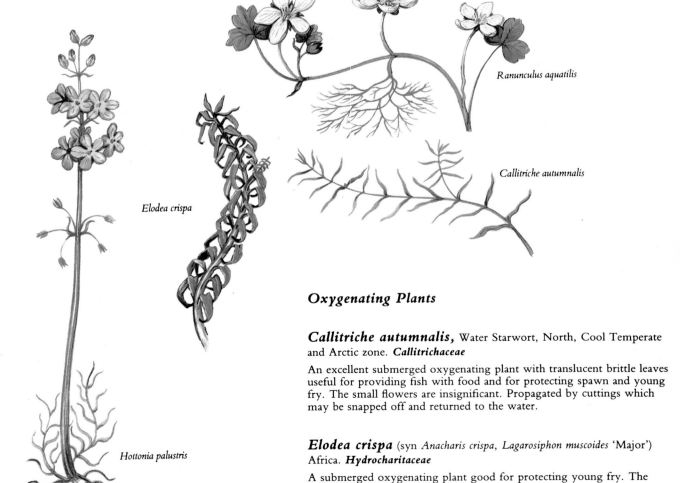

Ranunculus aquatilis

Callitriche autumnalis

Elodea crispa

Hottonia palustris

Oxygenating Plants

Callitriche autumnalis, Water Starwort, North, Cool Temperate and Arctic zone. **Callitrichaceae**

An excellent submerged oxygenating plant with translucent brittle leaves useful for providing fish with food and for protecting spawn and young fry. The small flowers are insignificant. Propagated by cuttings which may be snapped off and returned to the water.

Elodea crispa (syn *Anacharis crispa, Lagarosiphon muscoides* 'Major') Africa. **Hydrocharitaceae**

A submerged oxygenating plant good for protecting young fry. The ascending rope-like stem is clad with narrow reflexed leaves. Plants may be increased by cuttings and winter buds which sink to the bottom of the pool.

Hottonia palustris, Featherfoil, Water Violet, Europe, W. Siberia. ***Primulaceae***

A submerged oxygenating perennial plant with deeply pinnatifid, linear segmented, leaves. The spongy stem gives rise to abundant whorls of lilac flowers. Propagate by division or by sowing seeds in spring.
▲ ⚑ ✿Summer ○ ◑ ▧ △▼

Ranunculus aquatilis, Water Buttercup, Europe. ***Ranunculaceae***

Variable floating or submerged oxygenating plant with variously cut leaves, those submerged finely dissected, the floating leaves broadly lobed. The flowers arise above the water surface. Propagate by seed or division.
✿ ⚑ ✿Summer ● ▧ △▼

Surfacing Plants

Nymphaea 'James Brydon', Water-lily. ***Nymphaeaceae***

The hardy rootstock gives rise to purplish bronzy-green leaves and delectable paeony-shaped flowers in the form of a goblet and of a most luxurious rose-crimson colour. Good for the large or small pool and, with its relatively small leaves, equally at home in a tub. Propagate by division.
✿ ✿Summer ○ ▧ △▼

Nymphaea 'Sunrise', Water-lily. ***Nymphaeaceae***

This most popular plant has prolific large yellow star-shaped flowers. Propagate by division.
✿ ✿Summer ○ ▧ △▼

Nymphaea 'Rose Arey', Water-lily. ***Nymphaeaceae***

A delectable plant with elegant and fragrant star-shaped flowers that are rosy-red and may be up to 8in (20cm) across.
✿ ✿Summer ○ ▧ △▼

Nymphaea 'Escarboucle', Water-lily. ***Nymphaeaceae***

A beautiful hardy aquatic plant with fleshy rootstock and large floating leaves upon long petioles. The large, well-shaped, long-lasting, bright red flowers are produced freely and much more prolifically when the plant is located in bright light. Plants may be propagated by division of the rootstock in spring.
✿ ✿Summer ○ ▧ △▼

Nymphaea laydekeri 'Lilacea', Water-lily. ***Nymphaeaceae***

A most fragrant rosy-lilac to rosy-crimson, free-flowering medium-sized plant ideal for tubs and small pools. Propagate by division and plant to a depth of 9in (23cm) of water.
✿ ✿Summer ○ ▧ △▼

Nymphaea marliacea 'Rosea', Water-lily. ***Nymphaeaceae***

An interesting plant in that it often produces white flowers the first year after planting; from then on the large flowers appear deep pink. A large vigorous free-flowering plant suitable for the larger pool or lake. Plants may be increased by division.
✿ ✿Summer ○ ▧ △▼

Nymphaea laydekeri 'Purpurata', Water-lily. ***Nymphaeaceae***

A beautiful medium-sized compact plant ideal for the tub or smaller pond. The most prolific star-shaped rosy-crimson flower has white flecks and bright golden stamens. Plants may be increased by division.
✿ ✿Summer ○ ▧ △▼

Nymphaea 'Escarboucle'

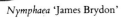

Nymphaea 'James Brydon'

Nymphaea laydekeri 'Lilacea'

Nymphaea marliacea 'Rosea'

Nymphaea 'Sunrise'

Nymphaea 'Rose Arey'

Nymphaea laydekeri 'Purpurata'

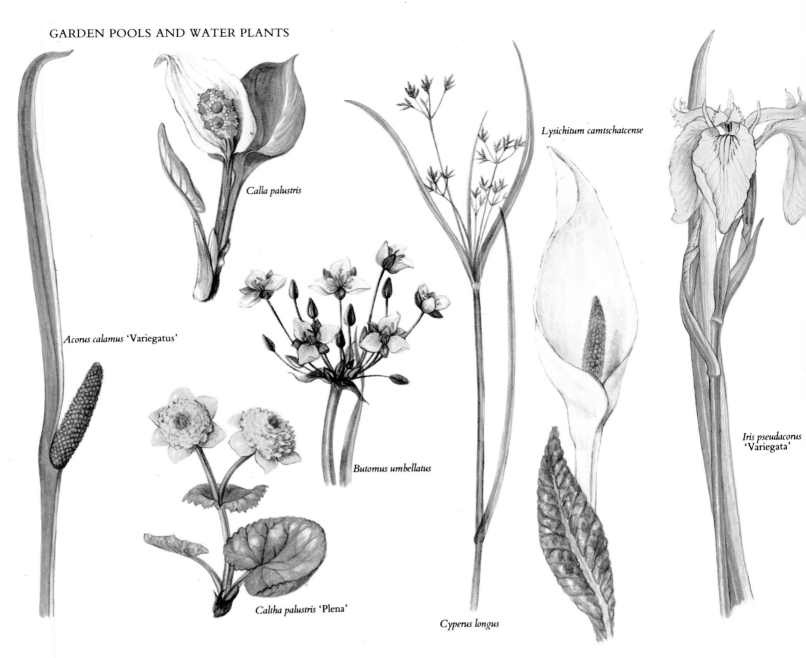

Calla palustris

Acorus calamus 'Variegatus'

Butomus umbellatus

Caltha palustris 'Plena'

Lysichitum camtschatcense

Cyperus longus

Iris pseudacorus 'Variegata'

Marginal plants

Acorus calamus 'Variegatus', Sweet Flag. *Araceae*

This attractive herbaceous perennial marginal plant has a creeping
rootstock which gives rise to erect, ensiform, cream and gold striped
leaves. The flat scape terminates in a spadix of insignificant greenish-
yellow flowers. An ideal plant for shallow water or moist loamy soil.
Plants may be increased by division in spring. 2½ft (75cm)

⟡ ☼ Summer ○ ◑ ▨ ◿

Butomus umbellatus, Flowering Rush, Asia, Europe. *Butomaceae*

A most handsome perennial marginal plant with a fleshy rootstock giving
rise to extremely sharp-edged ensiform leaves, bronze purple at first then
green. The erect naked scape rises above the leaves to terminate in an
umbellate bracteate inflorescence. An excellent plant for the water-side
and readily propagated by seed or by division of the rootstock in spring.
3ft (1m)

⟡ ☼ Summer ○ ▨ ◿

Calla palustris, Bog Arum, Europe, N. America, Siberia. *Araceae*

An excellent plant for camouflaging the edge of a pool; the rhizome gives
rise to creeping and floating stems with entire cordate, glossy leaves. The
leafy shoots produce an inflorescence during their second year of growth
with a spadix of small white flowers, the upper female and those below
hermaphrodite. Propagate by division. 9in (23cm)

△ ☼ Summer ○ ◑ ▨ ◿

Caltha palustris 'Plena', Marsh Marigold. *Ranunculaceae*

This attractive herbaceous perennial is suitable for the shallow water
margin and produces robust stems, usually branched, clad with shiny
green leaves, those arising during summer very large and sharply
toothed. The large flowers add much interest. Propagate by sowing ripe
seeds or by division in autumn. 1ft (30cm)

⟡ ☼ Spring ○ ◑ ▨ ◿

Cyperus longus, Galingale, Europe, N. America. *Cyperaceae*

A hardy perennial plant for the water's edge giving rise to an erect stiff
stem clad on the lower part with narrow, roughly edged, bright shiny
green leaves with reddish-brown sheaths at the base. The linear spikelets
appear in a loose panicle. A rather invasive plant and best grown in a
large pool. Propagate by seed or division. 4ft (1.2m)

⟁ ☼ Summer ○ ◑ ▨ ◿

Iris laevigata 'Variegata'. *Iridaceae*

This excellent marginal plant has attractive smooth ensiform leaves with
white variegation. The handsome clear blue flowers have broad falls and
erect oblanceolate standards. Propagate by division. 2ft (60cm)

⟁ ☼ Summer ○ ◑ ▨ ◿

Iris pseudacorus 'Variegata', Yellow Flag, Water Flag. *Iridaceae*

Stout forked stems, together with green and yellow variegated, ensiform,
glaucous leaves, provide much interest for the pool margin. The large
bright yellow flowers with roundish falls of orange-yellow with a dark
spot at the throat and radiating veins, together with the erect spatulate
oblanceolate standards make this a striking plant. Plants may be increased
by division. 2ft (60cm)

⟡ ☼ Summer ○ ◑ ▨ ◿

Lysichitum americanum (syn *Lysichiton americanum*) Yellow Skunk
Cabbage, Western N. America. *Araceae*

A robust and striking plant for the marshy edge of a pool, lake or stream
with a large, pale yellow boat-shaped spathe with a stalked green spadix
containing fertile flowers of somewhat unpleasant odour. The tufts of
long, erect, oblong-ovate dark-green leaves with a broad mid-rib succeed
the flowers. Propagate by division or by sowing fresh ripe seeds which
take some considerable time to become mature plants. 2½ft (75cm)

⟡ ☼ Spring ○ ◑ ▨ ◿

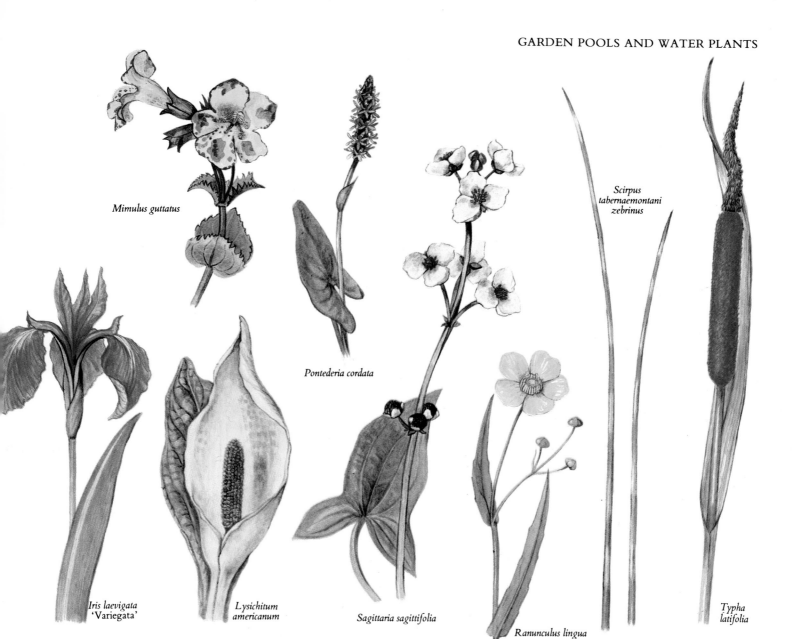

Mimulus guttatus

Pontederia cordata

Scirpus tabernaemontani zebrinus

Iris laevigata 'Variegata'

Lysichitum americanum

Sagittaria sagittifolia

Ranunculus lingua

Typha latifolia

Lysichitum camtschatcense (syn L. album, L. japonicum, Lysichiton camtschatcensis) Japan. *Araceae*

This attractive plant has a white spathe and flowers approximately one month later but otherwise resembles *L. americanum* except in height. Seeds do not germinate readily and the plant is better propagated by division. 2ft (60cm)

Summer

Mimulus guttatus (syn M. luteus guttatus, M. langsdorfii) Monkey Musk, California. *Scrophulariaceae*

An herbaceous perennial plant often without definite rootstock but with a stout, rooting, hollow stem ascending, clad with ovate or oblong, palmately veined, opposite leaves. The attractive, axillary, solitary yellow flowers have reddish purple-brown spots. A good plant for the margin of a pool or stream and readily propagated by seed or by cuttings. 1ft (30cm)

Summer

Pontederia cordata, Pickerel Weed, N. America. *Pontederiaceae*

Handsome herbaceous aquatic plant which has a creeping rhizome that gives rise to an erect stem and thick, bright glossy green, cordate leaves upon long petioles. The blue or white flowers with a greenish spot arise on a dense spike. An excellent plant set in water 6in (15cm) deep and readily propagated by division in spring. 2ft (60cm)

Summer

Ranunculus lingua, Greater Spearwort, Europe. *Ranunculaceae*

The densely fibrous root system gives rise to a long hollow stem clad with large, lanceolate, entire or toothed, partially stem-clasping sessile leaves. The large and attractive yellow flowers add much beauty to the plant which is ideal for the marshy pool margin and other damp areas which it soon colonises rampantly. Propagate by division or by seed. 3ft (1m)

Summer

Sagittaria sagittifolia, Common Arrow-head Water Archer, Europe. *Alismaceae*

An excellent plant for the smaller pool and equally at home in a slow-moving stream. The swollen stoloniferous rootstock gives rise to erect hastate leaves with long basal lobes. Long stout scapes support attractive whorls of white flowers with a purple centre. Propagate by fresh ripe seed or by division. 2ft (60cm)

Summer

Scirpus tabernaemontani zebrinus (syn S. zebrina) Porcupine Rush, Japan. *Cyperaceae*

A majestic perennial marginal plant with long green stems transversed with white bands. The sessile reddish-brown spikelets arise in a branched cyme terminating the stem. Readily propagated by suckers or by division of the rootstock. 4ft (1.2m)

Summer

Typha latifolia, Reed Mace, Cat's-tail, Britain. *Typhaceae*

A very large plant which should be restricted to lakes and large pools, the almost flat, obtuse, linear and somewhat glaucous leaves grow to 6ft (1.8m) in length. The dark brown flower spike is most decorative and much used for indoor arrangements. Plants may be increased by division or by seed and then planted in water 6in (15cm) deep. The colony tends to be invasive. 5ft (1.5m)

Summer

The Patio Garden

A clever use of brickwork and wood has achieved a variety of effects in this patio garden. Added interest comes from the small pool with its surrounding seat.

There can be no doubt about it, patio gardening as a concept has caught the imagination of the public, and its development over the past decade or so has been both rapid and sustained. One of its greatest attractions is that the patio garden, well designed and planted, is, in essence, a beautiful outdoor room which, changing with the seasons, is endlessly fascinating. It can be the whole garden area in an urban setting, or just a small part of a larger garden, and almost always in the latter case, as in the former, directly adjoining the house. It is an ideal place in which to relax, hopefully in complete privacy, have meals and generally enjoy the plants all around one whenever the weather allows. And really our climate is nothing like as bad as it is painted, for in a sheltered patio area open to plenty of sunshine – a patio garden should by definition be sheltered – it is often possible to sit out in complete comfort surprisingly early and late in the year.

It should not be overlooked either how much pleasure can be gained from a patio garden viewed from inside the house, especially if the house is modern with large window areas. Even in winter, if you have been wise enough to plant for year-round interest, there can be great joy from the harmonious blending of shapes, colours and textures. A smattering of suitable evergreen shrubs will provide both flowers and foliage – the winter-flowering *Viburnum tinus* 'Gwenllian' with pink buds, blush flowers and blue berries, for example, *Mahonia* 'Charity' and the much-loved heavily catkined *Garrya elliptica*, which is invariably grown as a wall shrub. But more of these later.

The Design of the Garden

The time has come now to say something of design in its broader aspects, as related to patio gardens. Including too many features in any garden is a great mistake; in a patio garden of small dimensions (we are usually thinking of an area of less than 60 by 60ft [18m by 18m] and sometimes far less) it can be disastrous. So exercise restraint, which is difficult if you are a mad-keen gardener. Also, take great care to vary the levels of interest by planting, if it is at all possible, at least one small tree (examples are suggested later); and using the house and other walls, fences or indeed any vertical surface that is available, as a support for climbing plants or background for shrubs which do especially well against such structures. Remember that in a garden where every inch of space is precious, shrubs and other plants grown in this way make a contribution out of all proportion to the area they occupy. Gardening upwards should be the order of the day, whenever possible.

Remember too, that a patio garden, snug and warm, is often the ideal home for so many plants of great beauty and interest but borderline hardiness. The lovely 20ft(6m) or so tall *Clematis armandii*, which bears its clusters of creamy-white flowers in March and April against a background of trifoliate, evergreen foliage, is a good example of what is meant; so is the very lovely 2ft (60cm) tall rhizomatous perennial from South Africa, *Schizostylis coccinea* 'Major', with rich red star-shaped flowers from late September to November. Warmth and all the sunshine that is going is what they and others like them need.

The popular conception of a patio garden is of a pleasing blend of paving, plants, features like raised beds, a small pool of formal outline and, of course, attractive garden furniture – and the popular conception is right. Grass has a very small part to play but it should not be ruled out altogether for even a narrow strip of verdant green can be enormously attractive combined with features such as those already mentioned.

Clearly, it is nice to have real stone paving but it is expensive, like hand-fired bricks, which are also, of course, highly suitable for this kind of purpose. Sometimes, however, local authorities have old paving slabs which are surplus to requirement and can be bought for quite modest sums. Usually, however, it will be a case of using precast concrete paving slabs and nowadays these can be very attractive. Gone are the days when concrete was looked on as an unsympathetic material. Advice on the construction of concrete paving slabs is given on page 134.

Cobbles and granite setts skilfully associated with paving can be extremely pleasing, and these associate just as well, of course, with patterned brickwork used, for instance, to delineate the planting area for a specimen tree or shrub. The quantity of bricks needed can be kept to a minimum.

Remember that, compared with a large garden, every feature, however small, assumes real importance; and balance (between the different features) is vitally important. For this same reason it is necessary to give much thought to the design of the containers you introduce into the garden – their shapes and the materials from which they are made. If you are going to have a wrought-iron table and chairs, for instance, then period-piece reproduction containers made of glass fibre could be just the right companion pieces to have in their vicinity. On the other hand, with wooden furniture, it might be best to opt for plant containers in the same material. With nylon-coated steel furniture it could well be that concrete containers are the best choice.

Provided they have merit, pieces of garden statuary and ornaments generally most certainly have their place in this kind of intimate garden atmosphere, especially if they are artistically associated with plants to contrast their shapes and textures with leaf and branch patterns. For obvious reasons, evergreen shrubs come into their own in this connection. Only in recent years, perhaps, have we come to realise fully how vitally important are leaves in the scheme of things. With evergreens, leaves are with us permanently, with deciduous plants for at least half the year and often considerably more, with (as an added bonus) the freshness of the new growth in spring and, quite often, fine autumnal tints as a 'grand gesture' before leaf-fall.

Concrete open-screen walling can provide a pleasing division where the patio is part of a larger garden, and this also is a feature which associates splendidly with shrub plantings to provide an interesting study in shapes, patterns and colours. You may, on the other hand, have to cope with surrounding brick walls, which, will possibly, with the passage of time, have become grimy and unprepossessing. Painting such walls with colour-wash in light colours (white best of all) will change the appearance of that part of the garden completely and act as a light reflector. The choice of fences is wide and a great deal depends on what you are prepared to pay, but if you are looking for such a screen to provide a support for plants close-board fencing is the best choice.

What is really being suggested is that you should think positively and imaginatively about the features to be included and try to get the right plants in the right places (clearly, of overriding importance is that the growing conditions should be as congenial as possible for the plant in question) but also to interrelate each to its neighbours and the 'grand design' overall. Nobody is suggesting that this is particularly easy. It isn't, which is why, if you do not have a special bent for garden design (some people do, without any formal training but most

do not) it is wise to seek professional help. Just getting a plan to which you can work is a major hurdle surmounted, if you are worried about doing the wrong thing. But get an estimate of the cost before you start from the landscape architect or designer you approach. Naturally, such a professional will oversee the complete construction and basic planting, if that is what is desired. If you decide to do everything yourself then hasten slowly, as the saying goes; think carefully before making major moves.

Plants in Paving

A very attractive, simple feature for a patio setting is to leave planting holes in paving, these spaces being of various sizes so that, for instance, dwarf or slow-growing conifers can be planted – the handsome, compact form of *Pinus mugo* named 'Humpy' with showy red buds, a rounded habit and eventual height of about 2ft (60cm) is one example, the foot-high (30cm) spreading *Juniperus communis* 'Hornibrookii' with grey-green foliage another – or perhaps small shrubs like the potentillas which flower virtually all summer. A very attractive choice of evergreen dwarf shrub which could be much valued in such a situation is *Euryops acraeus*, which has silver-coloured foliage and golden-yellow flowers in summer. It grows 1ft (30cm) tall, and, although it is of South African origin, it is fairly hardy.

There are many possibilities. Thymes and other typical paving plants such as erinuses, armerias and ajugas can also be planted in soil-filled gaps between paving stones with telling effect.

Pools

A pool, planted with water-lilies and other aquatics, can be a delightful feature, bringing to the garden a sense of peace and tranquillity and visual pleasure in many ways – from the water and the reflections in it just as much as the plants (see pages 122 to 125 for full details).

Bulbs

A patio garden would not be a patio garden either without its quota of spring and summer bulbs. From the snowdrops and crocuses very early in the new year, through the dwarf narcissi and irises, muscari, scillas, eranthuses, tulip species and hybrids and the rest to the lilies and smaller-growing gladioli of summer, and such autumnal delights as the crocus-like *Sternbergia lutea*, *Colchicum autumnale*, the so-called autumn crocus, and the autumn crocuses proper, varieties of *Crocus speciosus*. Perhaps loveliest of all, however, for a warm south-facing wall bed is the pretty *Nerine bowdenii*, preferably in its 'Fenwicks Variety', for in this form the highly distinctive pink flowers, comprised of narrow, reflexed segments, are especially fine. But with bulbs of all kinds you cannot go wrong. They give so much in return for so little work.

Rock Garden Plants

Alpine and rock garden plants are also 'naturals' for patio gardening, for so much of interest can be grown in such a relatively small space, whether one is thinking in terms of a raised bed (or beds) as the location, or perhaps immensely attractive trough and sink gardens. Alas, it is extremely difficult to get genuine stone troughs nowadays, and if they are available they are very expensive; but those made of modern, man-made materials are acceptable substitutes and some old fashioned glazed kitchen sinks can still occasionally be picked up, and these can be made presentable by facing them with hypertufa. Plastic containers are not suitable for alpine plants. They heat up too much in hot weather and, conversely, get too cold in arctic weather. All containers used for these plants must have a minimum internal depth of 6in (15cm) and preferably more, and plenty of drainage holes in the base.

Again, the choice of plants is extremely wide, but some of the loveliest, I feel, are spring gentians like *Gentiana verna* 'Angulosa', varieties of *Phlox douglasii*, the houseleek *Sempervivum arachnoideum*, and the thrift *Armeria caespitosa*. There are so many pretty small-growing dianthus, too, which are eminently

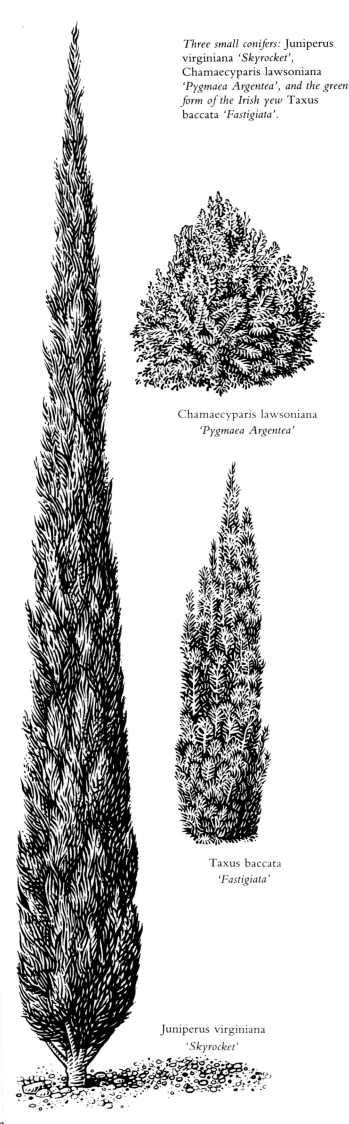

Three small conifers: Juniperus virginiana *'Skyrocket',* Chamaecyparis lawsoniana *'Pygmaea Argentea', and the green form of the Irish yew* Taxus baccata *'Fastigiata'.*

Chamaecyparis lawsoniana
'Pygmaea Argentea'

Taxus baccata
'Fastigiata'

Juniperus virginiana
'Skyrocket'

suitable for the purpose, likewise the smallest campanulas like *C. arvatica*, drabas, a huge number of saxifrages, small–growing geraniums, and, of course, small bulbous plants, the miniature roses mentioned below and many very attractive dwarf conifers, a selection of which is described on page 108.

Roses

Roses? Well who could make do without them, in terms of profusion of colour from early summer to autumn, in versatility and ease of cultivation. Like everything else, roses respond to good treatment and should be given such, but they are the most easy-going of decorative plants. The smaller growing cluster-flowered varieties (as the floribunda type are now called) are tailor-made for the patio garden – varieties like 'Anna Ford', orange-red, 'Topsi', of similar colouring, and 'Regensberg', pink and white. But, of course, tall newcomers like the new yellow 'Mountbatten' can also be used for special effects, as can large-flowered (hybrid tea) varieties with the quality of, say, the lovely 'Silver Jubilee' whose blooms are such a delightful blend of pink, cream, peach and apricot colouring. The same can be said, too, of fine modern shrub roses of modest stature like pink 'Ballerina' and its offspring 'Majorie Fair', with deep red flowers. The single flowers of both have white eyes, are very freely borne and very fetching. Both make bushes about 3ft to 4ft (1 to 1.2m) tall with a spreading habit.

Clearly, all the climbing roses from the ramblers to the repeat-flowering modern climbers and the sports of large-flowered and cluster-flowered varieties have their role to play in the patio garden. They give unrivalled returns for the space they occupy.

Don't overlook, either, the charm and usefulness of the miniature roses which are now so rapidly coming to the fore. These are extremely effective if grown in raised beds or even in containers. A height of 15in (38cm) or under is usual, although some do go to 18in (45cm). Their great appeal lies in their pleasing proportions, dainty flowers, dainty foliage – dainty overall effect.

Selected Trees and Conifers

One first–rate tree can transform a patio, but it must, of course, be one of suitable dimension for to plant anything which will completely out-grow its allotted space is plainly foolish – or worse – for it would eventually have to be mutilated or taken out completely. For small patios the choice should be confined to something like the very slim April to May flowering cherry *Prunus* 'Amanogawa', which will not grow more than 25ft (7.5m) tall nor have a width of much more than about 8ft (2.5m) – the flowers are shell-pink in colour – the little 15ft (4.5m) tall Fuji cherry, *P. incisa*, which bears white flowers (pink in the bud) in March; the well known Young's weeping birch, *Betula pendula* 'Youngii', again some 15ft (4.5m) tall and wide; and the exceedingly attractive mountain ash, *Sorbus vilmorinii*, marvellously effective with its fern-like foliage which colours up beautifully in autumn to shades of red and purple and bears fruits which pass from red to pink and then near-white. This is only a little larger than the others mentioned. Seek out trees of this calibre and of similar dimensions, if you would prefer something different. There is a wide choice.

Somewhat larger again (around 30ft [9m] tall) but a splendid patio tree in all but the most confined quarters is *Robinia pseudo-acacia* 'Frisia', which delights with its pinnate leaves of golden-yellow, a colour it holds with little diminution right through to autumn when the leaves turn an apricot shade before falling. The one fault of this splendid Dutch-raised garden tree (now very popular indeed) is that it has rather brittle branches which do tend to snap off if caught by very strong winds – so find a really sunny home, in a sheltered position, to bring out the colour fully. That it has a rather loose irregular outline is in its favour for it dissipates any suggestion of heaviness.

By far the most useful conifer for confined quarters where height is needed is *Juniperus virginiana* 'Skyrocket', which can make a column some 15 to 20ft (4.5 to 6m) tall eventually and still have a width of little over a foot. *Thuja occidentalis* 'Rheingold', which has a conical habit and eventually grows to some 10ft (3m) in height (it is slow growing), is another very effective performer being an old gold colour in summer turning to a more coppery-yellow in winter. Another golden conifer of real merit is the upright growing golden Irish yew, *Taxus baccata* 'Standishii', which is slow growing and decorative. Again, there are many more conifers of the right dimensions and appearance to seek out, and many can be found in garden centres these days.

Selected Climbers and Wall Shrubs

Do not overlook here the lovely *Garrya elliptica* which was mentioned early on in this chapter. It is a real joy when the catkins of greyish-green, usually 6 to 10in (15 to 25cm) long, are borne in great quantity against a background of dark green leaves in January and February. Against a wall it can reach a height of 15 to 20ft (4.5 to 6m).

Against walls which are warm and sunny you can also grow most effectively one or more of a range of 'japonicas', varieties of *Chaenomeles speciosa* and *C. superba* hybrids, or even one of the lovely ceanothuses – preferably a deciduous one like the 6ft (1.8m) tall and wide 'Gloire de Versailles' with palish blue flowers throughout summer – for these are hardier than the evergreen kinds. Then, of course, there are the very easy pyracanthas, and those marvellously effective climbers the ivies – you can grow any one of a number of *Hedera helix* varieties, including the golden foliaged 'Buttercup', or the striking large-leaved *H. colchica* 'Dentata Variegata', a form with very attractive leaf colouring of green, grey and creamy-white.

For wall beds with lime-free soils the camellias are fine plants, preferably with a west-facing aspect (south-facing walls get too hot and east-facing ones make the blooms liable in late spring to damage from sun scorch in the morning when they are covered in frost) or even a sheltered north-facing wall if needs be.

Cotoneaster horizontalis has no peer as a low cover under a downstairs window with its flattened growths (which have earned it the common name of herring-bone cotoneaster), being smothered in bright red berries in autumn and with bright red foliage too at that season.

The clematis in their wide diversity must be considered among the best of all true climbers for patios, both the large-flowered varieties and the species and their varieties like the splendid May-June flowering *Clematis montana* in its numerous forms; semi-doubled-flowered *C. macropetala* and glorious things like the earlier flowering *C. alpina*, which delights in April. For late summer and autumn colour one can turn to *C. orientalis* and *C. tangutica*, which have handsome seed heads in addition to their very attractive yellow flowers. Remember, too, the honeysuckles (loniceras) and the wisterias.

Other Shrubs

Brief mention of a few shrubs which integrate well with other plants in patio settings. First, two dwarf forms of popular barberries: *Berberis stenophylla* 'Coronilla Compacta' and *B. thunbergii* 'Atropurpurea Nana', the first evergreen and 1½ft (45cm) tall and the second deciduous and around 2ft (60cm) tall. The *thunbergii* form is not happy on very alkaline soils. 'Coronilla Compacta' is very showy in April when it bears a mass of bright yellow flowers which are red at the bud stage; 'Atropurpurea Nana' is also very attractive with its reddish-purple leaves and palish yellow flowers in spring, followed by brilliant red autumnal leaf colour.

Another berberis of real interest is the newly introduced *B. thunbergii* 'Helmond Pillar' with a height of up to 5ft (1.5m), a width of up to 1½ ft (45cm) and purple leaves. An ideal patio shrub.

If you have a lime-free soil, too, there are so many small rhododendrons which make a marvellous show in late spring and early summer, notably the hybrids from the exquisite *Rhododendron yakushimanum*, but also many more like the superb 'Elizabeth' with dark red flowers smothering a spreading bush no more than 4ft (1.2m) tall in April. Heathers can be put to good use also, but remember that with the exception of the winter-flowering *Erica carnea* varieties, the *E. darleyensis* and *E. erigena* (*E. mediterranea*) varieties and the Corsican heath, *E. terminalis*, all must be given a lime-free soil.

Of course, there are many more fine shrubs of modest size which can also be grown, like the daphnes *Daphne mezereum*

and *D. odora aureomarginata*; the small-growing lilac, *Syringa velutina* with rosy-lilac flowers in May, and, for later on (August and September) the splendid golden-yellow-flowered *Hypericum* 'Hidcote', a bush perhaps 4ft (1.2m) tall and 6ft (1.8m) wide. Investigate them all and choose wisely and well for the growing conditions you can offer.

Selected Perennials

With such a wealth of outstanding planting material of suitable size this brief note can give no more than pointers to the section of the book which deals fully with these plants (see page 16), but especially valuable in the patio garden are the hostas (primarily for their showy foliage but also for their lily-like flowers); the *Polygonum affine* varieties such as deep pink 'Donald Lowndes'; herbaceous geraniums in great variety, but especially the 2½ft (75cm) tall *Geranium psilostemon* with magenta-red, black-centered flowers in June and the charming, 4in (10cm) tall 'Ballerina' with lilac-pink flowers. The striking *Iris pallida variegata* is a splendid choice, not for its flowers but for its lovely grey foliage, striped with either yellow or white depending on the colour form. Find a place, too, for the much-loved *Alchemilla mollis* with its gossamer-light greenish-yellow flower sprays borne above pale green, roundish leaves with wavy edges from early June to late July. And consider, for good measure, the host of bergenias which bring such colour to the garden from late winter and early spring until May. For flowering the summer through with absolute abandon what better, too, than the cheery little *Coreopsis verticillata*, or the hybrid sedum 'Autumn Joy' for bringing the season to an end. A great favourite also is the lovely plate-headed, yellow-flowered *Achillea* 'Coronation Gold', which not infrequently continues in bloom after its recognized bowing out time of late September. The quest for just the right plants – like glorious *Salvia superba*, *Agapanthus* 'Headbourne Hybrids', winter-flowering *Iris unguicularis*, otherwise unmentioned in this chapter – can continue unendingly, which adds to the joy and the excitement of owning even a small patio garden.

Aucuba japonica *'Variegata', the spotted laurel, is a good tub plant that can cope with periods of dryness.*

Plants in Containers

An extremely wide range of plants has been grown in containers in gardens over the centuries but it is only now, at least in modern times, that they have had a significant role to play. This kind of gardening is so obviously in sympathy with what most of us want to achieve if we have a limited amount of space at our disposal, namely to make the maximum visual impact. The strange thing is that so many plants, from typical bedding plants raised from seed to shrubs and conifers, take on a quite different persona when so displayed. Perhaps it is because they are in a way more isolated from their immediate surroundings than when planted in beds. Perhaps the shape of the container used often has something to do with it, for some of these are extremely attractive. That is matter of opinion. But it certainly pays to take care in choosing such containers, and give attention to the position you have in mind for them. Will they, for instance, harmonise with the rest of the garden? Perhaps the best that can be said of most plastic containers is that they are inoffensive (some are, on the other hand, attractive); but most of us probably have an instinctive liking for wood, perhaps hardwood with a natural finish, although white-painted containers used, for instance, to display brilliantly coloured petunias or nasturtiums can be enormously attractive. White is a good, neutral colour but naturally the colour used can be anything you want, provided it is not obtrusive and so likely to kill the decorative qualities of plants in them. There are, too, the remarkably realistic and effective glass fibre reproductions of period vases and so on, usually expensive but very desirable. And, of course, concrete containers which can be much nicer than expected and, indeed, just right for some settings.

Before going in for container-style gardening in a big way, however, do take note of what you are letting yourself in for in long, dry spells in summer. Containers of all kinds are likely to dry out very quickly, and hanging baskets, of course, most of all. These last may need watering several times a day in exceptionally hot weather. Shrubs can suffer quickly from excessive dryness (hydrangeas and fuchsias – two of the finest kinds for growing in containers – in particular) and conifers even more so. They must be given proper attention.

For obvious reasons, the drainage of all containers must be impeccable, and with permanent plants like shrubs and conifers it is of course especially vital. So put plenty of stones, pieces of broken brick and the like in the base above the drainage holes and cover this with a good layer of roughage before adding the compost.

Grow permanent plants like those just mentioned above in compost of good quality. It is only in that way that the desired results will be obtained. For such permanent plants it is best to use John Innes No 3 potting compost. Plants with a reasonably limited life can go into John Innes No 2 and short-term plants like bedding plants and annuals generally into No 1 grade, or one of the numerous excellent proprietary soilless composts which are now on the market. Remember that with these last it is essential to feed the plants at regular intervals, for the fertilizer the composts contain does not last all that long. The John Innes composts are best for shrubs, conifers and so on for another reason, too: they provide a firmer base for the roots of the plants and so are more secure in periods of high wind (probably not a problem of much significance on usually well-sheltered patios). With all these composts, grow lime-hating plants only in versions which are lime-free. This is something which can get overlooked with unfortunate results.

Also, with all shrubs and conifers, remove with great care the top inch or so of compost in spring and topdress with some of the same type of compost as that originally used. This will give the plants a welcome boost just when they most need it.

Constructing Paved Surfaces

Once a patio garden is established, very little maintenance of the paved area is usually required for a considerable proportion of the surface consists of hard materials like stone and even the most pernicious weed finds that difficult to grow through. There are so many advantages to having an 'outdoor living room'. Even when darkness falls, garden lights may be switched

Bedding plants, pots and ornaments add colour and interest to this patio area. The house walls have been used for a variety of climbers.

on and such lighting is most effective, especially when set amid plants. One or two spotlights directed so that they fall on focal points add a great deal of interest. The patio can also accommodate a barbeque with charcoal grill and, perhaps, a giant chess games area where play can take place on a surface that can never become soggy and wet and is easily screened with plants or glass to prevent cold winds spoiling the pleasure.

Perhaps the most satisfaction of all is gained when the family collaborate in constructing the garden. They can all play their part in the building work, and when pebbles or small rocks are collected on family outings or holidays, then much more pleasure and fond memories are recalled as time goes by. Do-it-yourself jobs normally cost less but they must, of course, be done in a professional way, otherwise they are likely to be more costly in the long run.

A professional landscape gardener would start the job by first setting down the area with its dimensions on paper. Any gradients present should be taken into account so that some thought could be given to levelling the ground if necessary. Make a note of any underground services like gas, electricity, water and drains; they are usually well out of the way but it is as well to look out for them. A list can then be made of the main features to be included in the scheme: perhaps a raised bed, a barbeque, a pond, a sand pit for the children, a seat and so on. No doubt other features will come to mind as the early stages of work take shape but it is as well to have a rough plan drawn up before work proceeds too far otherwise much time and effort will be lost in altering the design.

Make sure the essential tools are to hand, it can be most frustrating to be short of a certain item when the shops are closed; a good deal of time could be lost when everything needs to be dropped to go out and acquire something before the next stage of work can proceed. Essential tools include a spade, bucket or water can, bricklaying trowel, rake, string and canes, spirit level, and a wheelbarrow when large quantities of materials need to be moved about. A flexible measuring tape will also be of use.

The amount of basic preparation rather depends on the site in question: uneven ground will need to be levelled and a sloping site will require attention. Ideally the ground should have a slight slope of no more than 1 in 80 to allow rainwater to run off away from the house. A slope of much steeper gradient will need to be levelled otherwise furniture will not stand evenly. If the site to be paved is at present a grass area, the turf could be used to lay a new lawn elsewhere, or the turves could be stacked to rot down and make excellent compost for a raised bed. If the soil is of good or even merely reasonable quality remove the top few inches and stack it away from the site for future use. The chances are that a certain amount of soil will have to be removed anyway for the level of the paved area should be at least 6in (15cm) below the damp proof course of the house.

The ground below the surface soil must be really firm to avoid subsidence and pit holes at a later date, for cracking of slabs and stone may also occur when the base is not sufficiently firm. Brick rubble is an excellent material to ram into the base. This can be done by using a heavy tamper or, when a large area is being prepared, it may be worth considering the hire of a small settling machine. Builders' merchants can supply large stones called rejects which will do the same job as brick rubble and these should be rammed into the base in the same way; a 3in (8cm) thickness of aggregate is usually satisfactory. Gaps left between the larger stones can be filled in with shingle and, when pre-set slabs are to be used for the patio, a layer of sand should then be spread over the area.

Check the level of the surface with a spirit level and if all is well, the patio slabs or other material can be set in place again, using the spirit level. Various materials are available including genuine sandstone or limestone. These natural stones can be very expensive to buy, especially when they have to be delivered from some distance away. Hand-fired bricks set in various designs make an attractive surface; pebbles set in concrete so that the rounded top protrudes like a cobbled pavement, or a combination of natural stone slabs and these is interesting. Setts, both straight and curved, are popular with designers and architects and a visit to the local shopping precinct may well throw up some ideas.

Concrete slabs and setts can easily be made at home and the

A variety of ways to use paving slabs, cobbles and bricks.

cost will be far less than for those purchased ready made. A simple mould can be made from lengths of timber, sufficient moulds being constructed to accommodate the quantity of concrete made up each time to avoid waste. Timber for the mould should be 2in (5cm) wide and ⅜in (10mm) thick, cut to the required length and then screwed together. A sheet of polythene is then laid on firm, level ground, the moulds are placed on top and all is now ready for the slab mixture.

Suitable ingredients for the slab mixture are clean builders' sand free from soil and other debris and Portland cement. Special dyes are available from builders' merchants if a colour other than the natural one is required. Measure out three parts of sand to one part of cement by volume, and then turn the mixture over very thoroughly three or four times before adding the water. Next make a depression in the top of the mound and add sufficient water to make a stiff mixture; on no account should the mixture be sloppy, otherwise the result will be inferior leading to subsequent frost damage and general weakening of the concrete. Having added the water, wait for a few minutes for this to soak in and then mix again until the moisture is uniform throughout the heap. Now shovel the mixture into each mould and tamp it down until all air bubbles have been released. After a few days the mould should be carefully removed when the cement is set – this will depend on the weather conditions prevailing at the time.

Instead of making individual slabs, lengths of timber can be set out on the prepared surface where the patio is to be made. This method avoids the almost inevitable cracking of the odd corner which may occur when slabs are taken from a mould. It is also a better method when the surface of the ground is not perfectly even, although more mortar is likely to be used on an uneven surface than one which has been made level. Use the same ingredients as those suggested for slabs and level the top off with a straight edge. When the concrete is perfectly hard the timber can be removed and it will appear as if patio slabs have been laid. Whichever of the two methods described is adopted, the next task is to fill in the gaps between the slabs. Although sand can be used, it does tend to attract weed seeds which later germinate and grow making the area look untidy. A better choice is mortar made by mixing together five parts of sand with one of cement. A dry mixture should be used to grout in between the slabs, otherwise the surface will be left with a permanent stain where the mixture flows over as filling proceeds.

When individual slabs are used for the patio, they are best set on blobs of dryish mortar, one blob at each corner and one in the middle. Slabs 1ft (30cm) or less square, should be set on a bed of dryish mortar or they are liable to become unstable after a period of use. Place ¼in (6mm) wooden pegs between each slab to keep them uniformly spaced. Slabs with the corner broken away can still be used: the missing area will be ideal to fill with soil and furnish with a ground–hugging plant.

Given time to harden off completely, all is now ready for the electrician to install lighting, if this is required, and the paved area can be enjoyed to the full.

House Plants for Home and Conservatory

Conservatories provide additional living space even if not on the scale of this one at Flintham Hall.

The house plant grower has now a greater range of plants from which to make a choice than ever before. Each year more new plants are introduced to add even greater variety to the ever-changing show on table and windowsill.

There are plants with handsome foliage that last for many years; some that flower without stopping, and others that have one brief but glorious display, after which they are discarded or planted out in the garden. Some are small and neat; others robust and handsome, and a few will climb up any support within their grasp. All of which means that you must know exactly what you are buying to be able to provide it with the conditions it appreciates and to enjoy the effect it provides.

Where and What to Buy
The best place to buy a house plant is undoubtedly the nursery where it was grown; from there you can transport it home confident that it will receive little shock to its system. The garden centre is the next best. Buy from chain stores only when the plants are fresh (they often have a week number or 'sell-by' date printed on the label). Never buy from a pavement display; the plants are sure to have been chilled to the sap.

Spring and summer are the best times of year to buy, for then the plants (many of which are native to tropical and sub-tropical parts of the world) are unlikely to be chilled in transit.

Make sure your plant is wrapped up for transportation, to prevent damage to its leaves and flowers and to keep it warm.

Before parting with your money, do give the plant a quick medical to make sure it's in good health. Refuse any plant that is spindly or drawn, showing signs of leaf scorch or pest and disease attack. Look for a shapely, bushy specimen (unless the variety is supposed to be tall and slender) that is turgid (not wilting).

Plants whose compost has shrunk from the sides of the pot should be avoided; they have been allowed to dry out at the roots and may later show signs of suffering.

If you're choosing a flowering plant, pick one which has a few blooms open and a few in bud. Tight-budded plants may refuse to open their flowers when given a change of environment.

When you're certain that the plant you are about to buy is healthy, consider whether you can provide the conditions it will enjoy. Does it prefer sun or shade; cool or warm rooms; dry air or reasonable humidity? If you are unable to fulfil its requirements, leave it where it is and choose a plant that will live happily with you.

The Plants at Home
Unwrap the plant as soon as you get home and stand it in the room where it is to grow. Don't place it in bright sunlight for

a few days (even if it is known to be a sun lover). Give it good but indirect light so that it can accustom itself to the temperature and atmosphere. Check that the compost is gently moist; water it only if it is dry. After a few days any plant that needs brilliant light can be moved to its permanent spot.

Think carefully about plant placement. Not only will the plant's requirements be of importance, but your own eye for design should be pleased, too. Plants always look good in groups and seem to enjoy each other's company, but stately specimens look well on their own, especially against a plain background. Pot-hiders of all descriptions can be used to mask ugly flowerpots and to contain water that flows from the drainage holes.

There are certain places in the home where no plant is happy to live. Avoid placing any plant near a radiator, in a draught or on top of the television (heat rising from the back and water spilling from the pot will make for mutual incompatability). On frosty nights don't leave your plants sandwiched between the curtains and the window or they may be chilled.

Temperatures You need not change your central heating system to suit your plants, provided you choose plants that will be happy in the same conditions as yourself. Each plant's requirements are covered in the illustrated section, so check there to see if you can keep it happy. The vast majority of house plants today will live happily in homes that are centrally heated, and they even enjoy the cooler temperatures that occur during the night (when the boiler is set to switch off) and the warmer days. Some plants, though, prefer rooms that are not heated (azaleas and cyclamen for instance), and will quickly burn to a crisp in hot, dry air. Others (like the poinsettia and dracaenas) flourish in the warmth. In summer all house plants must cope with the natural rise and fall in temperatures, which they seem to do with equanimity.

Light No plant will grow in total darkness, or where there is insufficient light to read by. Some plants insist on full and brilliant sunshine to do well (geraniums for instance), but most are quite happy in 'good, indirect light', such as that found 3 or 4ft (1m) from a window. One or two plants enjoy north light, where the sunlight is never direct, and some will tolerate shade. Check on the plant's light requirements before you buy it; you must be able to provide what it likes.

Humidity Dry air kills many house plants. Their leaves turn crisp and brown in a very short time if their foliage requires a humid atmosphere. Ferns are especially susceptible to this scorching but they, and almost any other house plant, will benefit from the extra humidity provided by a gravel tray. An old tin tray, or a large plate, filled with gravel which is kept constantly moist, will produce a mini-Turkish bath around any pot plant which is stood on it. Alternatively, spray the plant several times a day with a hand mister filled with water. Furniture will not enjoy the spray, though, so the gravel tray is a safer, and less laborious, alternative. Plant groups will thrive if plunged (still in their pots) into a large container of peat. Here the peat will not only improve humidity but it will also slow down the rate at which the plants dry out, so making visits with the watering can less frequent – a boon if you have to be away several days at a time.

Watering This is the most influential factor in plant life – and death. Most house plants that die are killed by overwatering. With just a handful of exceptions, house plants like to be watered when the compost in the pot begins to feel dry to the touch. Nearly all can be allowed to become dust dry on the surface, but only a few will tolerate being kept positively wet at the roots (the azalea and the cyperus). Ferns like a happy medium – gently moist at all times.

So, always feel the compost before you water, and if it is dry, give the plant a good soak. Do not water it again until the compost is dry once more. Peat-based composts shrink if they are allowed to dry out, so aim to keep these gently moist (but never soggy) at all times.

Watering is not something that can be carried out by the clock; it is influenced by weather conditions and the growth rate of the plant. In winter all plants need less water than they do in summer, and plants growing in full sun dry out faster than those growing in the shade.

Plants wilt when the compost is dry, but they will usually pull round when soaked. Plants also wilt when the compost is too wet, and then they will seldom recover.

There is no reason why a plant should not be watered from above, with a watering can or jug, unless it is impossible to penetrate its leaf canopy or rosette with the spout. When you do water from above, fill the pot to its rim (that's why there is a gap between the surface of the compost and the rim of the pot). One inch of water will travel downwards to a depth of 9in (23cm). Plants such as the African violet (saintpaulia) or the cyclamen, which make dense domes of leaves, can be watered from below. Fill a saucer or bowl with water and stand the plant in it. Leave it there for an hour or so and then tip out the excess. Within that time it will have taken up what it needs.

Where it is impossible to feel the surface of the compost (due to a thick covering of leaves) you will have to weigh the plant in your hand and get to know how light it is when dry.

If watering is something you cannot master, or absence from the house means that your plants always dry out, then automatic watering units will be a great help. Known as 'hydroculture' units, these devices consist of a basket of expanded clay granules in which the plant's roots grow, surrounded by a reservoir of water which is fitted with an indicator that shows the water level. All the gardener has to do is keep the water level topped up according to the indicator, and the plant's roots grow happily in the soilless medium. Hydroculture units are quite different to (and much more reliable than) self-watering pots which contain compost. These are tricky to keep in good order and the plants growing within them usually suffer as a result. Avoid them.

Feeding After a few weeks of active growth a plant will have extracted most of the nutrients from the compost within its pot and some additional food must be supplied. This can be most conveniently given in the form of a diluted liquid fertilizer sold especially for pot plants. Feeding is usually required once every fortnight, or once a month for slow-growing plants, during the growing season; that is, from spring to autumn. Only winter-flowering pot plants need be fed between autumn and spring. Always apply liquid food while the compost in the pot is moist, that way it can go straight into action without being too strong for the root hairs to cope with.

Display house plants in an intriguing way in a bottle garden. Drainage material and compost are poured in through a cardboard roll and the planting is done with simple home-made tools.

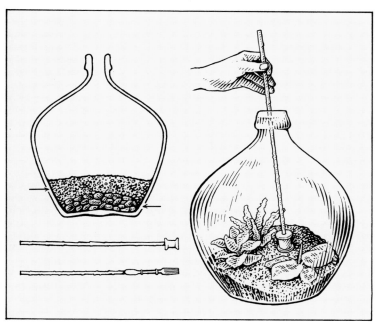

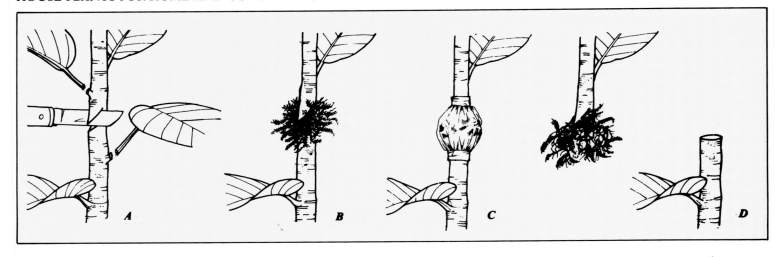

Flowering pot plants will enjoy diluted feeds of tomato ferti-lizer, which will often encourage the production of blooms on plants that are shy of flowering. It works especially well on African violets (saintpaulias).

If you can never remember to feed your plants, try using granular house plant foods which can be sprinkled on the surface of the compost and carried to the roots gradually by watering. Such applications will continue to feed the plant for several months.

Potting Most house plants will appreciate a larger pot and some fresh compost each year. Spring is the best time to pot them on, and you can use either a loam-based compost such as John Innes No 2 potting compost, or a peat-based alternative. Choose a pot that is 2in (5cm) larger in diameter than the previous container. Plastic pots are light and easy to clean, and

Air layering is an effective way of reducing the height of leggy plants. A: Make a slanting cut into the stem. B: Dust the cut with hormone powder and insert some moss. C: Enclose the area with more moss and wrap with polythene. D: Sever new plant when roots form.

they have plenty of drainage holes in the base to allow excess water to escape. Clay pots are heavier (and so more useful for anchoring top-heavy plants), but they should be provided with a layer of gravel or broken flower pots in the base so that their single drainage hole does not become bunged up with compost.

Water the plant before repotting it. Put some compost in the base of the new pot, sit the plant on top and fill around it with more compost. When potting is completed the root ball should sit just below the surface of the new compost which, in turn, should be between ½in and 2in (13mm and 5cm) below the rim of the pot (the larger the pot, the greater the distance). This allows for subsequent waterings, the first of which should be given immediately after the potting operation.

Staking Single-stemmed plants that grow quite tall can best be supported by a single cane, to which they are lightly tied with soft twine. Climbers will romp over wooden or plastic trellis, and plants that tend to fall open can be held together either with bare twigs pushed among their shoots and into the compost, or with three or four split green canes that are inserted around the edge of the pot and linked with soft twine.

Bushiness Unless a plant is meant to grow on a single stem it should be pinched out regularly to keep it shapely. Simply nip off the shoot tips of elongating stems whenever you notice that legginess is likely. Sideshoots lower down the stem will then grow out to furnish the plant more fully.

Really overgrown plants will often respond well to hard cutting back in spring and early summer. Always cut back to just above a bud or leaf.

Leaf Cleaning Remember to keep plant foliage clean. Flicking over it with a duster will not remove ingrained grime, so glossy-leaved plants are best washed from time to time with tissues dipped in rainwater or a mixture of equal parts milk and water. Hairy-leaved plants should be brushed free of dust with a dry paintbrush.

Pests and Diseases Scale insects and mealy bugs, whitefly and red spider mites are the four most common pests of house plants. All can be controlled by spraying with systemic insecti-cides offered in great variety by nurseries and garden centres. Check that any product you buy is suitable for both the plant and the pest and safe for use indoors. Diseases are not so common, but can usually be controlled by cultural methods – the removal of dead or fading leaves and flowers, adequate ventilation and careful watering. Plants severely attacked should be discarded and in no circumstances grown alongside healthy ones.

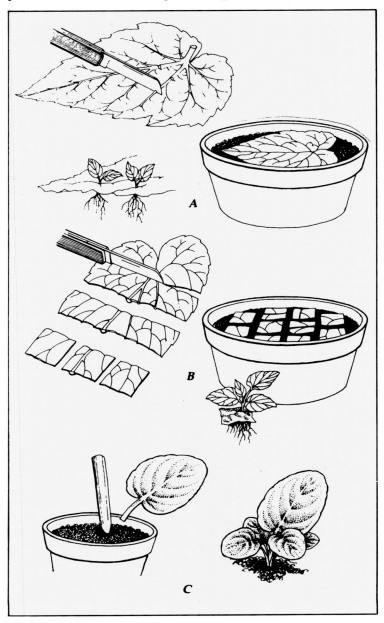

Various ways of propagating house plants from leaf cuttings. A and B: Begonia rex, C: Saintpaulia.

Vibrant colour from coleus, the most brilliant of all foliage plants for the house and conservatory.

Propagation As with most other plants, many house plants can be propagated by seed, cuttings and division of clumps. Some can also be increased by leaf cuttings – the individual leaf and its stalk (in the case of the saintpaulia) or portions of the leaf (in the case of streptocarpus and *Begonia rex*) being rooted in moist compost in a humid atmosphere.

The Conservatory

As an extension to the house a conservatory provides an environment in which humans find it easy to relax and plants find it easy to grow. Today there is no shortage of choice when it comes to design, for the conservatory, so beloved of the Victorians, is making a comeback.

All conservatories will admit plenty of light, but they should also be equipped with enough ventilators to allow a good circulation of air in summer when temperatures can rise dramatically. Roller blinds will also be needed to reduce the glare and consequent rise in temperature generated by brilliant sunshine.

Make the conservatory as large as possible; it must allow for free movement among the plants and if it is to act as an additional room there must be space for a table and chairs.

The floor may be quarry tiled and the plants grown on benches around the perimeter, or soil borders can be utilised by large, tender shrubs and climbers. Whichever is the case it should always be possible to damp down the floor with water, or to dampen a strip of gravel so that humidity can be provided. A bone-dry atmosphere will crisp plant foliage and delight red spider mites.

In winter the conservatory must be heated if tender plants are to survive. The alternative is to grow only those permanent residents which are happy to be given just a roof over their heads in winter; the summer show being provided by annuals that can be discarded after their season of spectacle.

For a dark corner of a room consider making an attractive and mobile display of house plants on a trolley which is fitted with overhead lighting tubes. Plants chosen for such a display should include a range of small foliage kinds, some of which are allowed to trail. Most flowering plants prefer natural light but African violets can cope with artificial lighting.

If heat is to be provided, some form of double-glazing and a thermostatically controlled heat source must be utilised to save money. The great advantage of a lean-to design (and most conservatories are attached to house walls) is the benefit derived from the central heating system within the home. The warmth given off by the wall will help to exclude frost, and if more heat is required, it is a simple job to run the domestic heating system through the wall of the conservatory to an additional radiator.

Begonia rex

Begonia pendula

Begonia 'Rieger Hybrid'

Begonia

There are many types of begonia grown as house plants – some for their leaf colour, others for their flowers – but all have the same basic requirements. Make sure they are kept warm (but not excessively hot) all the year round, and position them where the winter temperature is unlikely to fall below 13°C (55°F). All appreciate good but indirect light. Bright sunshine will scorch the leaves and flowers. The really tall varieties can be pinched out to encourage bushiness, but older specimens will need the support of a cane or two to prevent them from toppling over. All begonias carry separate male and female flowers. Water the plants freely when they are dry in summer, but allow them to go a little longer without water in winter.

Feed all begonias fortnightly in summer. Repot in spring when necessary using a standard soil-based or peat-based compost. Browning of the leaves and flowers may be caused by sun scorch, draughts, lack of water, or too dry an atmosphere.

Begonia pendula

(Strictly a name of no specific value, but one which is almost always used to describe these pendulous begonias which are really forms of tuberous begonia). Height 6 to 9in (15 to 23cm) spread 1ft (30cm). The flowers (single or double) may be pink, white, red, yellow or orange. The arching, pendent habit of these begonias makes them ideal subjects for hanging baskets. Like all plants grown in baskets, pendulous begonias will suffer from drought if the compost is not watered frequently in the summer months.

Begonia rex (syn *B. rex-cultorum*) (Assam) Fan Begonia, Painted Leaf Begonia, Rex Begonia.

Height up to 18in (45cm) spread up to 3ft (90cm). The most beautiful of the begonias grown for foliage. The plants have a tendency to grow rather one sided, but this can be avoided if the pots are turned from time to time. Be prepared for plants to deteriorate after two or three years, for they really grow best under warm conservatory conditions.

Begonia 'Rieger Hybrids'

Height and spread 1ft (30cm). This new race of begonias is very popular. They can be bought in flower at any time of year and will last for at least 3 months in the home. Kept in reasonable warmth and good, but indirect, light, the plant should perform well.

Saintpaulia (African Violet).

The saintpaulia's ease of culture has made it a widely popular house plant. It likes no place better than a bright windowsill – in shade it will not do well but in constant burning sunshine it may scorch – so stand it on a windowsill which faces north, east or west. Bring the plant inside the curtains at night. It is tolerant of fairly low temperatures in emergencies, but should be assured of at least 16°C (60°F) for preference. It hates draughts. Remove any faded flowers and leaves as soon as they are noticed. Damaged leaves should be snapped or cut off as close to the main stem of the rosette as possible.

The tightly packed leaves usually make watering from above rather difficult, so get used to weighing the plant in your hand and predicting by its lightness or heaviness if it needs watering. When it does it should be stood in a bowl of water for half an hour. Standing it on a saucer of moist gravel will increase the humidity around it. Let the compost dry out a little between waterings. Feed fortnightly in spring and summer with diluted tomato fertilizer to encourage flowering. Use at the dilution recommended for tomatoes to force older plants into bloom, but make up a half strength solution for younger ones. Repot every other spring using a peat-based compost. Propagate from leaf cuttings with stalks, inserting these in a warm propagator, pot or jam jar of water kept in a warm place.

Saintpaulia ionantha cultivars (Originally from the Tanzanian coast)

Height up to 4in (10cm) spread to around 1ft (30cm). The flowers are produced mainly in the lighter months of the year but can open even in winter if the plant is stood under fluorescent lights. The blooms may be single or double and cultivars are available with white, pink, mauve, purple, magenta and violet blooms. Some of the cultivars have crimped-edged flowers, while on others the flowers may be star shaped, crested in the centre or bicoloured. The leaves vary too. Some are plain (in which case they are referred to as 'boys'), others have a pale mark ('girls'), some are variegated with creamy white and others have turned up leaf edges and are known as 'spoons'. The variegated types tend to be rather more difficult to grow than the plain-leaved kinds.

Saintpaulia ionantha cultivar

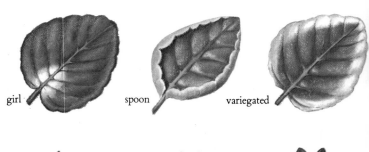

girl   spoon   variegated

star   crested   bicolour

Sinningia (Gloxinia)

Place in a bright draught-free spot out of direct sunlight with a minimum temperature of 16°C (60°F). Let the compost dry out on the surface between watering, then give it a good soak. Stand the plant on a tray of moist gravel or peat and feed fortnightly while it is in bud or flower. After the flowers have faded allow the compost to dry out between waterings. When the leaves turn yellow, stop watering. Once the foliage has died down remove the tuber and store it in dry peat or sand. In spring bed it, right side up (look for the dormant buds and a slightly concave surface), in a 5-in (13-cm) pot of moist peat-based compost. Water carefully at first, keeping the plant warm, and it will soon come into growth.

Sinningia speciosa cultivars (syn *Gloxinia speciosa*) (Originally from Brazil)
Height and spread up to 1ft (30cm). Large leaves and huge flared trumpet-like flowers of bright red, purple, pink, lavender or white, the deeper shades often margined with white.

Smithiantha (Gesneria)

Grow as for *Achimenes*. Start the rhizomes into growth at a temperature of 18°C (65°F). Do not pinch out the shoot tips.

Smithiantha zebrina (syn *Naegelia zebrina*)
Height and spread up to 1½ft (45cm). They need warmth and humidity.

Streptocarpus (Cape Primrose)

Place in good light but not direct sunshine. It likes warmth but will tolerate a minimum temperature of 13°C (55°F). Stand the pot on a tray of moist gravel. Water well as soon as the compost feels dry, then allow it to dry out a little before watering again. Feed fortnightly in summer and repot in a half pot filled with peat-based compost each spring. Dust the brittle leaves carefully with a dry brush when they are dirty. Propagate from leaf cuttings early in summer. Older plants can be divided in spring and seeds sown in heat at the same time. All originate from Africa and Malagasy.

Streptocarpus x **hybridus** 'Constant Nymph' (*S.* x *hybridus* 'Merton Blue' x *S. johannis*).
Height 1ft (30cm) spread up to 1½ft (45cm). The leaves are rather brittle. Flowers will be produced at any time from spring to autumn.

Streptocarpus x hybridus cultivar

Streptocarpus x hybridus
'Constant Nymph'

Sinningia speciosa
cultivar

Smithiantha zebrina

Achimenes cultivar

Columnea microphylla

Columnea x banksii

Streptocarpus x hybridus cultivars.

Height and spread 1ft (30cm). The larger-flowered hybrids are of mixed parentage.

Achimenes (Hot Water Plant)

These plants need a minimum temperature of around 13°C (55°F). They enjoy good light but should not be placed in brilliant sunshine all day. Achimenes are grown from small rhizomes which are potted on their sides, ½-in (13-mm) deep, in peat-based compost in late winter and spring (5 to a 4-in, 10-cm, pot). Start them into growth by keeping the compost slightly moist and a temperature of at least 16°C (60°F). Pinch out the tips of any shoots when they reach 3 in. (8 cm.) to encourage bushiness and flower production. Feed fortnightly as soon as flower buds are visible, stop feeding when flowers fade. Support taller varieties. After flowering, stop watering. When the compost is quite dry pull off the shrivelled growths. Take out the rhizomes, store them in dry sand or peat in a temperature of 13°C (55°F) until spring.

Achimenes cultivars (syn. *A.* x *hybridus*) (Originally Mexico)
Height 9 to 12in (23 to 30cm) spread 6 to 9in (15 to 23cm). The trumpet flowers are in shades of pink, magenta, mauve, purple, yellow and white and may be produced in large numbers right through summer into autumn.

Columnea (Goldfish Plant)

Fine for hanging basket plants in centrally-heated rooms, the columneas like a position in good but indirect light where temperatures are unlikely to fall below 13°C (55°F). Water well in summer whenever the surface of the compost shows signs of drying out, but keep it only just damp in winter when growth is slower. Feed fortnightly in summer and replant during spring only when the plant is showing signs of starvation (probably every other year). Use a peat-based compost for lightness. Smaller plants can be grown in suspended pots. Spray the plants daily if possible to maintain a humid atmosphere. Shorten any straggling stems after flowering. Propagate by taking stem cuttings in spring and summer and rooting these in a heated propagator.

Columnea x banksii (*C. oerstediana* x *C. schiediana*).
Trailing to 2ft (60cm) or more. The easiest columnea to grow.

Columnea microphylla (Costa Rica)
Trailing to 2ft (60cm) or slightly more. The flowers are produced in spring.

Fuchsia cultivars

Punica granatum var. nana

Pelargonium

These need full sunlight. Their leaves yellow and their stalks beome spindly in the slightest shade. They like an airy room and will tolerate temperatures only slightly above freezing point provided they are not too wet around the roots. Water, throughout the year, when the compost in the pot is quite dry to the touch. Stand plants outdoors in summer and pinch out the shoot tips to encourage bushiness. Remove all dead leaves and flower stalks. Feed monthly in spring and summer and repot in spring using a standard soil-based compost or a mixture of this and a peat-based compost. Propagate by taking 4-in (10-cm) long stem cuttings in spring and summer and rooting these around the edges of pots of sandy compost in a well-lit spot. The new F₁, hybrids can be propagated from seeds sown in a temperature of 21°C (70°F) in late winter, but these will not flower until late summer.

Old plants can be cut down in autumn and overwintered by keeping them cool and very dry at the roots. They are best discarded after one or two years and replaced with plants grown afresh fromcuttings. Rust disease may attack mature plants (yellow blotches appear on the upper surface of the leaf beneath which are circles of brown spores). Destroy any affected plants. Any plants distorted and mottled with virus diseases should also be destroyed.

Regal pelargoniums
These are larger than the zonals but only flower in summer. The fresh green leaves are whiskered at the edges, the flowers are large and beautifully marked. Sometimes listed as varieties of *P. x domesticum*.

Zonal pelargoniums
These are the aromatic-leaved plants grown in greenhouses and for summer bedding in Britain. They are frequently referred to as 'geraniums' and are often described as cultivars or varieties of *P. x hortorum* or *P. zonale*. They are called zonal pelargoniums because of the distinct horseshoe marking, often coloured, on the leaves of many varieties. They are available with double or single flowers in shades of red, orange, magenta, pink, white and mauve.

Regal pelargonium

Punica (Pomegranate)

This will survive in a winter temperature of 4°C (40°F) provided the light is good and the compost kept rather dry. In summer water more freely whenever the compost shows signs of drying out. Lightly pinch back any spindly shoots to encourage bushiness. Feed the plants fortnightly from spring until autumn. Repot in spring if the plant has outgrown its existing container using a standard soil-based compost. Propagate in spring by taking stem cuttings or sowing seeds.

Punica granatum var. **nana** (South-east Europe to Himalaya) Pomegranate.
Height 3ft (90cm) spread 2ft (60cm). A woody shrub with small oval leaves. The flowers are produced from late summer onwards and may give rise to small fruits. The leaves may fall in winter, but appear again the following spring. Large plants may be planted out in a sheltered sunny spot at the foot of a wall where they may survive mild winters.

Fuchsia

These need plenty of light to stop the shoots from becoming spindly, and a minimum winter temperature of 7°C (45°F). Avoid high temperatures in summer. Pinch out the tips of stems to encourage bushiness. Young plants should be pinched back while they are still quite small. Feed them weekly from spring to autumn. Water freely in the growing season, but keep the compost drier in winter when the leaves will probably fall (unless the plant is kept warm). Cut the stems down to within 2in (5cm) of the compost in spring and repot into a standard soil-based compost to encourage new growth. Avoid moving plants once they are in flower or the blooms may drop. Stem cuttings can be rooted in spring and summer. Grow pendulous varieties in hanging baskets or pots. Whitefly and red spider mite are common pests.

Fuchsia cultivars.
These vary greatly in height. Their flowers may be single coloured or combinations of white, pink, scarlet or purple. Those fuchsias offered as house or greenhouse plants are not reliably hardy outdoors in Britain.

Zonal pelargonium

Cyclamen persicum cultivar

Primula x *kewensis*

Primula malacoides

Cyclamen

Grow cyclamen in a room with a maximum temperature of 16°C (60°F) in good light, such as on a north-facing windowsill. Water only when the compost feels dry or as soon as the leaves become a little limp. Feed fortnightly while the plant is growing and flowering. Cyclamen may be discarded after flowering but they can be kept growing by watering carefully all the year round. Alternatively let the compost slowly dry out after flowering, to dry off the corms, and then repot them in fresh standard soil-based compost. The top of the corm should protrude above the surface of the compost. Water carefully at first, then more freely as growth begins. Propagation is by seeds sown in late summer.

Cyclamen persicum cultivars
(Originally Eastern Mediterranean including Greek Islands). Height and spread 1ft (30cm). The rounded leaves are often patterned with dark green and grey. The blooms may be white, pink, salmon, mauve, crimson or magenta and are sometimes frilled at the edges. Easily killed by excessive heat and water.

Primula

Give these good indirect light and a temperature of 10 to 16°C (50 to 60°F). Water thoroughly when the surface of the compost feels dry, and feed fortnightly when the plants are in flower. Discard the plants after flowering and raise new plants from seed.

Primula x kewensis (*P. floribunda* x *P. verticillata*).
Height 9 to 12in (23 to 30cm), spread 6in (15cm). The flowers are carried in winter and spring. The leaves are fresh green, often dusted with white farina.

Primula malacoides (Western China)
Fairy Primrose. Height 1 to 1½ ft (30 to 45cm) spread 9in (23cm). This plant has many stalks smothered in tiers of magenta, lilac, pink or white flowers which are sometimes exquisitely scented.

Hoya (Wax Plant)

Prevent temperatures falling below 13°C (55°F) in winter and position the plants where they will receive direct sunshine for at least part of the day; an east- or west-facing windowsill suits them well. Water the compost whenever the surface feels dry, but keep it drier in winter. The climbing species should be trained around wire hoops, over tripods of canes or up trelliswork. Old and overcrowding stems can be cut in spring. Spray daily with tepid water, except when the flowers are open. Feed fortnightly from spring to late summer, and in spring repot into a standard soil-based compost only when the plant is potbound. Cuttings of one-year-old shoots can be rooted in a heated propagator in spring, or younger shoots can be layered into pots of cutting compost during summer. Mealy bug and scale insects are common pests of hoyas.

Hoya carnosa (Australia)
Height and spread unpredictable as the plant is a vigorous climber in the right situation. It grows best when planted in conservatory borders but often flowers better in pots. The clusters of waxy flowers may be produced at any time between spring and autumn. Do not cut off old flower stalks – they will produce more blooms. The variety *H. c.* 'Variegata' is slower growing and more reluctant to flower than the true species but is a handsome foliage plant.

Stephanotis (Madagascar Jasmine)

Aim for a minimum temperature of 13°C (55°F) and keep the plant in good indirect light where the temperature is unlikely to fluctuate wildly. Water as soon as the compost feels dry, and spray with tepid water every few days. Keep the compost on the dry side in winter. Do not move the plant when it is in flower or the blooms may drop. Feed fortnightly from spring to late summer. Repot in spring every other year using a standard soil- or peat-based compost. Train the stems of the plant around a wire hoop or over trellis and cut out one or two old stems after flowering. Cuttings of firm shoot tips will root in a heated propagator in summer. Mealy bug and scale insects are frequently a problem.

Stephanotis floribunda (Malagasy)
Height and spread variable but to around 10ft (3m) The waxy flowers are powerfully scented and may be produced at any time from late spring to autumn.

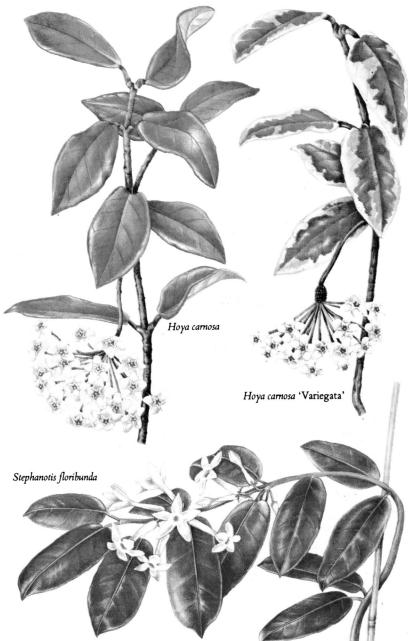

Hoya carnosa

Hoya carnosa 'Variegata'

Stephanotis floribunda

Hippeastrum (Amaryllis)

Hippeastrums are purchased as dry bulbs in autumn. Pot up each bulb singly in a 6-in (15-cm) pot of soil-based compost. Use moist compost and leave the upper half of the bulb exposed to view. If the compost is moist at potting time there will be no need to water it until the flower spike is well in evidence; it emerges before the leaves. Stand the pot in a well-lit spot out of direct sunlight and maintain a temperature of around 18°C (65°F) with a minimum of 13°C (55°F). During its flowering period the bulb will produce very few roots and if the compost is kept too wet the base of the bulb may rot, so water with care. Cut off the stalk once the blooms have gone, and water whenever the compost feels dry. Feed at fortnightly intervals as the leaves grow. In late summer allow the compost to dry off completely and remove the leaves when they are quite crisp. Bulbs that are kept growing all the year round seldom flower as well as those that are rested. Do not repot every year. Instead scrape away the top 2in (5cm) of compost in autumn and replace it with fresh, watering gently to encourage growth. This topdressing will give the bulb a boost without causing root disturbance. Offsets can be removed from large bulbs at repotting time. Mealy bugs may infest the growing point.

Hippeastrum cultivars
(Raised as a result of crossing *H. aulicum, H. elegans, H. reginae, H. reticulatum* and *H. striatum.*) (Originally natives of Central and South America). Height up to 2ft (60cm) spread 1½ft. (45cm). Two to four spectacular flowers emerge on a fat pale green stalk sometimes flushed with red. The massive blooms have 6 tepals (petal-like sepals) which may be crimson, scarlet, orange, pink or white, often suffused with a darker or lighter colour. The blooms usually open in spring but 'treated' bulbs bought from a specialist merchant can be flowered in winter.

Euphorbia pulcherrima

Euphorbia milii var. *splendens*

Euphorbia fulgens

Hippeastrum cultivars

Euphorbia (Poinsettia, Crown of Thorns)

Euphorbia fulgens (syn. ***E. jacquinaeflora***) (Mexico) Scarlet Plume Height 2 to 3ft (60 to 90cm) spread 2ft (60cm) Try to avoid winter temperatures below 16°C (60°F). In summer the plant can tolerate higher temperatures provided that the atmosphere is kept humid. Place in good light, even full sun. Cut back as required after flowering, keeping the milky sap away from your mouth and eyes. Water freely in summer, but keep it slightly drier and cooler in winter and spring immediately after flowering. Feed monthly in summer and repot when necessary in spring using a standard soil-based compost.

Euphorbia milii var. ***splendens*** (syn *E. splendens*) (Malagasy) Height 1ft (30cm) spread 3ft (90cm) There are relatively few leaves, but the plant is seldom out of flower. An easy plant to cultivate, it needs a minimum winter temperature of 7°C (45°F) and plenty of light. Water the compost thoroughly when it dries out in summer but keep it drier in winter. In spring cut out any unwanted stems (keep the sap away from your eyes and mouth) and repot when necessary in a standard soil-based compost mixed with a little sharp sand. Feed monthly in summer.

Euphorbia pulcherrima (syn. *Poinsettia pulcherrima*) (Mexico) Height 1 to 4ft (30cm to 1.2m) when treated with growth retardant but considerably larger in the wild. The coloured leaves (bracts) that surround the true flowers may be scarlet, pink or creamy white.

Maintain a minimum temperature of around 13°C (55°F). Keep the plant in good light and out of draughts. Water thoroughly when the compost feels dry and then let it dry out on the surface before watering again. Spray the plant occasionally with tepid water. When the bracts fade in spring the plant can be cut back to within 4in (10cm) of the compost. Then repot in a standard soil- or peat-based compost. Feed fortnightly in summer. The bracts will not colour up unless they have long dark nights, unbroken by electric light. To achieve this, place the plant in a completely dark cupboard at 6 p.m. each evening, and remove it the following morning at 8 a.m. Do this *every night* for 8 weeks, starting in early autumn. The plant should be in full colour after about 12 weeks. It will also be noticeable that the poinsettia will grow taller as the effect of the growth retardant wears off.

Rhododendron simsii

Rhipsalidopsis gaertneri (syn *Schlumbergera gaertneri, Epiphyllopsis gaertneri*) (Brazil)
Height 6ins (15cm) spread 1ft (30cm). The cool, winter resting period is important if flowers are to be produced regularly.

Schlumbergera (Christmas Cactus)

Another plant for good but indirect light and temperatures which do not fall below 10°C (50°F) in winter. Water when the compost shows signs of drying out between late spring and late summer; keep cool and dry in autumn and then water normally again in winter to encourage flower production. Feed monthly in summer and stand the plants outdoors, spraying them daily with tepid water. Repot after flowering every other year using the compost recommended for *Rhipsalidopsis*. Schlumbergeras are excellent in hanging baskets, where their stems can hang gracefully over the edge of the container. Propagation is as for *Rhipsalidopsis*. Flower drop is a common problem if the plants are moved when in bud, or if temperatures or moisture content of the compost are allowed to fluctuate too greatly at that time.

Schlumbergera x buckleyi (*S. russelliana* x *S. truncata*)
Height 9in (23cm) spread 1ft (30cm).

Schlumbergera truncata (syn *Zygocactus truncatus*) (Eastern Brazil) Crab Cactus, Thanksgiving Cactus.
Height 12in (30cm) spread 18in (45cm) Blooms are produced from late autumn to early winter. Recently many new cultivars have been offered for sale with flowers in shades of red, orange, paler pinks and white; all are spectacular when in flower.

Rhipsalidopsis gaertneri

Schlumbergera x buckleyi

Schlumbergera truncata

Rhododendron (Indian Azalea)

The secret of success with the pot-grown azalea is to give it the two things it most needs: cool temperatures and plenty of water. Stand it in good light but not direct sunshine – this is a good plant for a north-facing window – and choose for it a room which is not very warm. In temperatures over 16°C (60°F) it will rapidly fade. Every day the plant should be plunged in a bucket of rainwater for half an hour so that the pot is immersed. Remove and drain it afterwards and then return it to its spot in the room. Let the compost get even slightly dry or the air around the plant become too warm and the flower buds will turn brown and drop before they have a chance to open. When you buy a rhododendron in a pot, always choose one which has a few blooms open, but still plenty of buds unfurled. In this state the plant will stand the best chance of succeeding. Make sure that the compost is moist at the time of purchase. An occasional spray with tepid rainwater will keep the plant in good condition. Take off the blooms as they fade.

In spring, when there is no longer any danger of frost, plunge the plant to its pot rim in the garden and keep the compost moist through the summer - spraying the foliage with rainwater whenever you remember. Feed fortnightly and never allow it to dry out and it may produce buds the following autumn. Then bring the plant indoors to decorate your rooms. It is not fully hardy and if left in the garden through the winter it will probably perish. When the plant has outgrown its pot, repot it in spring into a lime-free peat-based compost before plunging it in the garden.

Rhododendron simsii (syn *Azalea indica*) (China, Thailand, Burma, Taiwan)
Height 1½ft (45cm) or so, spread up to 3ft (90cm). The blooms may be red, mauve, pink, orange or white and the coloured shades are sometimes contrastingly edged with white. They open in winter.

Rhipsalidopsis (Easter Cactus)

Place in good indirect light and maintain a minimum temperature of 10 to 13°C (50 to 55°F). Water freely in spring and summer whenever the compost looks dry; keep them cool and drier in winter giving just enough water to prevent shrivelling. Stand the plants outdoors in summer and spray them daily with tepid water. Bring them inside again before frosts threaten. Feed monthly in summer, and repot them each year as the flowers fade, using a basic soil-based compost plus an equal amount of ground bark or peat. Propagation is easy. Snap off stem tips, which consist of 3 or 4 flattened sections, and root these in a propagator or individual 3-in. pots of peat and sand covered by a polythene bag.

Nephrolepis exaltata 'Bostoniensis'

Adiantum capillus-veneris

Adiantum (Maidenhair Fern)

One of the most difficult plants to keep alive in the home unless you know the secrets of success. First, give the plant good but indirect light. Bright sunlight will scorch the fronds, as will draughts and heat sources such as radiators. Maintain a minimum temperature of 10°C (50°F) and keep the compost in the pot moist at all times – even in winter. The leaves are so thin that they can quickly desiccate and turn brown in a living room, so stand the plant on a tray or bowl filled with gravel which is kept constantly wet. Feed the plant monthly in summer and repot it into a basic soil-based compost with a little peat added when it outgrows its existing container. Spring is the best time to repot, and mature plants can be divided at the same time – use a sharp knife to cut the clump into several pieces and pot up the offspring in the recommended compost. Keep them warm and shaded for a few weeks to hasten establishment. Cut off any fronds that do turn brown to prevent them from rotting and damaging other parts of the plant. Avoid spraying the plants with insecticides or leaf-cleaning compounds which may burn the fronds.

Adiantum capillus-veneris (Cosmopolitan, including Britain) Common Maidenhair, Southern Maidenhair
Height 9in (23cm) spread 12in (30cm)

Nephrolepis (Ladder Fern)

Place in good but indirect light or gentle shade. Humidity is essential if the fronds are not to turn brown. Spray the plant each day with tepid rainwater and stand it on a tray of wet gravel. Temperatures as low as 10°C (50°F) will be tolerated, but warmer conditions will produce more luxuriant growth. If plants do become brown and ragged they can be cut down to pot level. Never let the compost in the pot dry out, but conversely do not keep it waterlogged. In conservatories the plants look good when grown in hanging baskets, but in the home this kind of culture is likely to lead to excessive drying out of compost and foliage. Repot the plants in a peat-based compost when they have filled their existing containers with roots. Spring is the best time to do this, and the plants can be divided into smaller clumps at the same time. Monthly feeds will keep the plants in good condition.

Nephrolepis exaltata 'Bostoniensis', Boston Fern
Height and spread 2 to 2½ft (60 to 75cm). A much more arching plant which is more common and has more grace than the true species. This is the form which is sometimes grown in hanging baskets.

Asparagus (Asparagus Fern)

Excellent foliage plants for cool rooms where their thin 'leaves' (really leaf-like stems known as cladodes) will not be dried out by excessive heat. They will tolerate temperatures as low as 7°C (45°F) and prefer a position in indirect light or light shade (sun will scorch them). Cut off completely any stems whose leaves have turned yellow, and trim away untidy growth in spring. Water thoroughly when the surface of the compost feels dry, but keep it barely moist in winter. An occasional spray over with tepid water will perk up the foliage, and a fortnightly feed in summer will keep the plants in peak condition. Repot every spring in a standard soil- or peat-based compost. Propagate by division at repotting time, or by seeds sown in gentle heat in spring.

Asparagus densiflorus (syn *A. sprengeri*)
Height 1ft (30cm) spread to 3ft (90cm). A graceful arching plant with soft fuzzy foliage that makes a perfect background for more dazzling plants. Nevertheless *A. densiflorus* is still worth growing on its own as a hanging-basket specimen or in suspended or wall-mounted pots. If grown as a climber it can be trained up a support system for 6ft (1.8m) or so. Easy to manage and tolerant of a fair amount of neglect. Clusters of small white flowers may be produced. Watch out for the tiny thorns.

Asparagus densiflorus 'Myersii' (syn *A. meyeri, A. myersii*).
Height 2ft (60cm) spread 3ft (90cm). Surely the most handsome of the asparagus ferns. Long lasting and well suited to cool conservatories and sunrooms.

Asparagus setaceus (syn *A. plumosus*)
Height 4 to 6ft (1.2 to 1.8m) spread to 4ft (1.2m). This is the wedding buttonhole asparagus fern and whilst the true species scrambles to 6ft (1.8m) or so, there is a much more compact form *A.s.* 'Nanus' (syn *A.p.* 'Nanus'). The feathery triangular fronds must be kept cool and away from heat sources if they are not to be shed. Flowers are seldom produced.

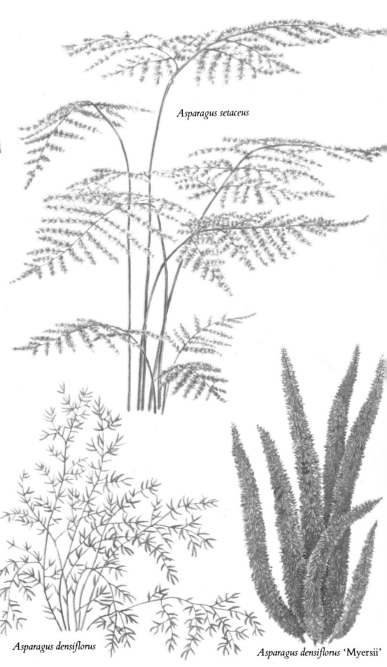

Asparagus setaceus

Asparagus densiflorus

Asparagus densiflorus 'Myersii'

Maranta (Prayer Plant)

These foliage plants are difficult to grow unless you can provide them with ideal conditions. A minimum temperature of 18°C (65°F) is necessary for them to produce new leaves and they need a spot in light shade where their humidity-loving leaves will not be scorched by sunlight. Spray them daily with tepid water or stand them on a tray of moist gravel or peat. The smaller species do well in bottle gardens and terrariums where their foliage can luxuriate in the humid atmosphere. Cut off any leaves as soon as they fade or other parts of the plant may rot off with them. Try to keep the compost evenly moist at all times and just damp in winter. Feed monthly in summer and repot in spring when necessary, usually every 2 years or so, using a peat-based compost. Propagate by dividing the clumps in spring. Pests are seldom a problem. Dry air and low temperatures will cause leaf browning. Over-watering causes stem rot. Generally known as Prayer Plants because of their habit of folding their leaves upwards at night.

Maranta leuconeura* var. *erythroneura (syn *M. l. erythrophylla, M. tricolor*) (Brazil) Herringbone Plant
Height 4 to 6in (10 to 15cm) spread 1ft (30cm) or more.

***Maranta leuconeura* 'Kerchoviana'** (syn *M. kerchoviana*) Rabbit's Foot.
Height 4in (10cm) spread 1ft (30cm). Probably the most popular maranta. Superb in group arrangements and terrariums if you can prevent the compost from getting too soggy.

Maranta leuconeura* var. *leuconeura (syn *M. l. massangeana*) (Brazil)
Height 4 to 6in (10 to 15cm) spread 1ft (30cm) or more. This plant contrasts well with the other two marantas.

Stromanthe

Grow exactly as for *Maranta*.

Stromanthe amabilis (Tropical America)
Height and spread 1ft (30cm). The vivid green leaves are marked with a darker tone in a clear herringbone pattern. The undersides are greyish green and the stems tinged with red. Well-grown plants always look fresh and healthy.

Peperomia

Most of the peperomias prefer warm rooms, though they will tolerate a winter temperature of 10°C (50°F) if they are kept rather dry at the roots. Indeed, the plants do better if allowed to dry out considerably between waterings even in summer – soggy compost leads to rotting of the main stem. Good but indirect light is preferred to bright sunshine or heavy shade. In summer spray the foliage daily with tepid water, or stand the plants on trays of moist peat or gravel. Feed monthly in summer, and repot only when absolutely necessary using a basic soil-based compost. Propagate by leaf, leaf bud or stem cuttings in spring and summer. Nearly all peperomias are good subjects for planting in bottle gardens and terrariums and in mixed arrangements in bowls. The trailing kinds are well suited to hanging baskets.

Peperomia caperata (Brazil)
Height 9in (23cm) spread 6in (15cm). A neat plant with corrugated leaves carried on rosy-red stalks. Mouse tail-like flower spikes of yellowish white may appear at any time during the growing season. There is a pretty variegated variety: *P.c.* 'Variegata' whose leaves are edged with creamy white. It is rather more difficult to grow than the true species.

***Peperomia magnoliifolia* 'Variegata'**
Of a similar height and spread to the true species, this variety is rather more commonly grown. Its leaves are most attractively marbled with creamy yellow, making the plant highly ornamental. The variegation is most pronounced in good light rather than shade.

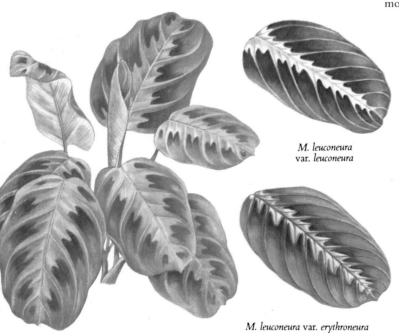

M. leuconeura var. leuconeura

M. leuconeura var. erythroneura

Maranta leuconeura 'Kerchoviana'

Peperomia magnoliifolia 'Variegata'

Stromanthe amabilis

Peperomia caperata

147

Pilea cadierei 'Minima'

Pilea (Aluminium Plant)

Try to maintain a minimum temperature of 10°C (50°F) for these plants, though they can tolerate lower temperatures in an emergency. The best pileas will be produced in good but indirect light. The plants will also cope with shade though the stems may become a little drawn as a result. The taller-growing types will benefit from being pinched back when the shoots are 4in (10cm) long; this will encourage branching and a bushier plant will be produced. Water well as soon as the compost feels dry to the touch in spring and summer. Allow it to remain dry for rather longer in autumn and winter. An occasional spray over with tepid water will keep the plants in good condition as all of them appreciate a little extra humidity. Repot every spring in a basic soil-based compost, though the plants are best renewed from cuttings or by division every two years or so. Feed fortnightly in summer. Stem cuttings, 3in (8cm) long, can be easily rooted in a warm propagator (or a polythene-covered pot) in spring and summer. Red spider mite can be a problem in a dry atmosphere.

Pilea cadierei 'Minima' (syn. *P.c.* 'Nana') (Vietnam)
Height and spread 8in (20cm). A most attractive modest-sized pot plant with oval pointed, glossy leaves that are rich green marked with silver grey. The markings are caused by air pockets under the upper surface of the leaf. The young, emerging leaves are pale bronze.

Pilea 'Moon Valley' (Often incorrectly described as *P. mollis*).
Height 9in (23cm) spread 12in (30cm). Bright green, roughly indented leaves with acute points are veined with deep brown. The colouring is more pronounced at the lower end of each leaf, giving a toned effect and making this an exceptionally handsome plant.

Pilea 'Moon Valley'

Dieffenbachia amoena

Dieffenbachia picta 'Exotica'   *D. picta* 'Superba'   *D. picta* 'Rudolph Roehrs'

Dieffenbachia (Dumbcane)

Increasingly popular plants which need just a little extra care to keep them in really good condition. Good but indirect light is what they most enjoy, though a little light shade will do them no harm. They need a fairly steady temperature regime, a minimum of 16°C (60°F) is necessary and the plants must be kept out of draughts. In centrally-heated rooms they will do well provided that the air around them is kept humid. Remove the lower leaves as they fade, peeling them away from the stem. In time a cluster of leaves will sit at the top of a tall stem and at this stage the plant can be cut back to within a few inches of compost level; the top section can be shortened and used as a cutting and the stump will produce new shoots if kept warm and the compost slightly moist. Do not overwater. If the compost around its roots is kept soggy its leaves will droop and shed tears. Wait until the surface of the compost is dry before watering well; let it remain slightly drier in winter. Feed monthly in summer, and repot in spring every year if necessary using a peat-based compost. Propagate by removing a section of stem and cutting it into 2-in (5-cm) long sections, each with a bud. Bed these into the surface of the rooting medium in a heated propagator and pot up the young plants that arise. Suckers can be removed from older plants in spring and potted up on their own. The sap of all these plants is poisonous and can cause inflammation of the tongue.

Dieffenbachia amoena (Tropical America) Giant Dumbcane
Height 5ft (1.5m) spread 2ft (60cm). Not the most spectacular species but one of the most shade tolerant. The arum lily-like flowers of this and the other species mentioned are rarely noticed due to their insignificant appearance.

Dieffenbachia picta 'Exotica' (Originally Brazil) Leopard Lily
Height 2 to 3ft (60 to 90cm) spread 1½ft (45cm). Due to its ease of culture this is the most widely grown of the group.

Dieffenbachia picta 'Rudolph Roehrs' (syn *D. p.* 'Roehrsii')
Height 2 to 3ft (60 to 90cm). The most brightly marked of the four. Here the leaves are a fresh green only around the edges and along the midrib. The rest of the surface is butter yellow. Like all heavily variegated plants it is rather more tricky than its plainer relations.

Dieffenbachia picta 'Superba'
Height 2 to 3ft (60 to 90cm) spread 1½ft (45cm). Smart and stately as a single specimen.

S. trifasciata 'Laurentii'

S. trifasciata 'Hahnii Variegata'

S. trifasciata 'Hahnii'

Sansevieria trifasciata

Sansevieria (Mother-in-law's-Tongue)

Ranking with the aspidistra for ease of culture, these plants are best pleased if you stand them on a sunny windowsill, though they will also tolerate some shade. Maintain a minimum temperature of 10°C (50°F) and the plants will come to no harm. Water only when the surface of the compost feels quite dry, the only way you can possibly kill this plant (short of setting fire to it or freezing it) is by overwatering. In winter be even more careful and keep the compost very much on the dry side, watering simply to prevent shrivelling. Feed monthly in summer, and sponge the leaves with tepid water at the same time. Repot only when the plant starts to grow out of its existing container, or when it cracks the sides. Repot in spring using a standard soil-based compost and a clay pot for added stability. Propagate by division at repotting time, or by rooting 2-in (5-cm) sections of leaf in a propagator in spring and summer.

Sansevieria trifasciata (South Africa)
Height and spread up to 3ft (90cm) or more. The tall, spiky leaves of this plant are thick and fibrous and twist gently as they ascend. The leaves are carried on thick rhizomes and these can be severed for propagation purposes. Whitish-green flowers may be produced on mature plants.

Sansevieria trifasciata 'Hahnii' (syn S. hahnii).
Height 6 to 9in (15 to 23cm) spread up to 1ft (30cm). This dwarf cultivar has much shorter, broader leaves and makes more of a rosette. The same attractive markings are present.

Sansevieria trifasciata 'Hahnii Variegata' (syn S. t. 'Golden Hahnii', S. hahnii 'Variegata')
As S. t. 'Hahnii, in stature; but here the leaves are longitudinally banded with broad butter-yellow stripes.

Sansevieria trifasciata 'Laurentii'
Similar in stature to the true species, but much more spectacular for the leaves are margined with broad butter-yellow stripes. Propagate by division, for the striping is lost when plants are raised from leaf cuttings.

Caladium (Angel's Wings)

As you would expect from the delicate appearance of the foliage, these plants need high temperatures and humidity, but only during the summer for they die down in autumn and remain dormant through the winter. Tubers or, more correctly, rhizomes (the root-like stems) are offered for sale in spring and can be planted just below the surface of peat-based potting compost in plastic pots. Keep the pots in a temperature of 24°C (75°F) at this stage and keep the compost moist, not soggy. As soon as growth is noticed, stand the pots in good but indirect light and maintain a temperature of 18 to 21°C (65 to 70°F). As the plants grow they should be kept out of direct sunlight and the temperature should never fall below 16°C (60°F). As more leaves are produced the compost can be watered more freely and as soon as three leaves have fully expanded a liquid feed can be applied fortnightly. Spray the foliage daily with tepid water and stand the plants on a tray of moist peat or gravel. When the foliage starts to look tired in late summer and early autumn, let the compost slowly dry out until the leaves are crisp and dry. Knock the compost from the pot and salvage the rhizomes, storing them in damp peat in a temperature of 13°C (55°F). Keep the plants out of draughts and do not place them where their fragile leaves may be knocked. The plants are collectively and individually known as Angel's Wings and were originally native to tropical South America.

Caladium x hortulanum cultivars
Height 1 to 1½ft (30 to 45cm) spread 1½ft (45cm). All the cultivars have generously proportioned arrow-shaped leaves which have a rubbery feel but are really quite thin; their translucency is part of their charm, for when viewed into the light the contrasting venation can be fully appreciated.

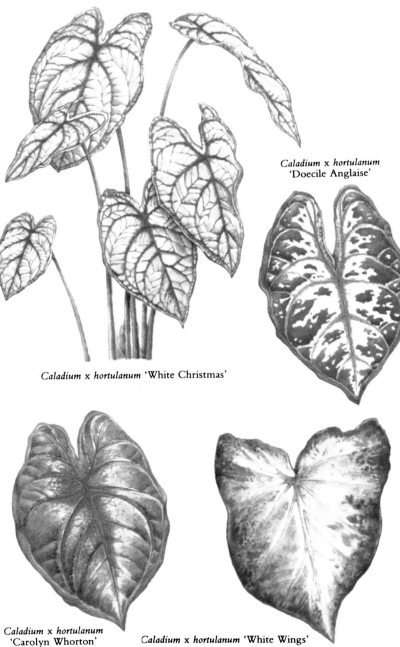

Caladium x hortulanum cultivars

Caladium x hortulanum 'Doecile Anglaise'

Caladium x hortulanum 'White Christmas'

Caladium x hortulanum 'Carolyn Whorton'

Caladium x hortulanum 'White Wings'

149

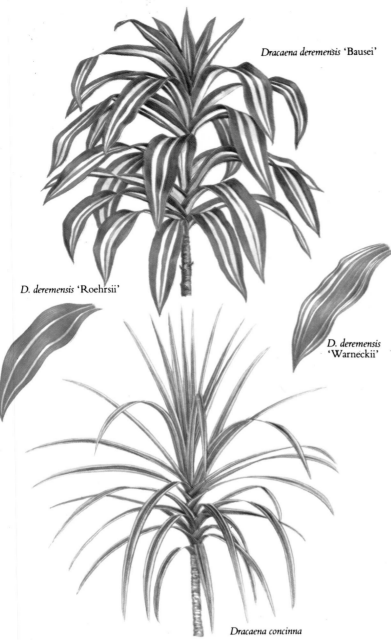

Dracaena deremensis 'Bausei'

D. deremensis 'Roehrsii'

D. deremensis 'Warneckii'

Dracaena concinna

Dracaena (Dragon Lilies)

These need a minimum temperature of 13°C (55°F) in winter and between 18 and 21°C (65 and 70°F) in summer. They thrive in indirect light. Peel off dead leaves as soon as they wither; this should only happen to the bottom ones, if the upper ones turn brown the plant is either in a draught, too near a heat source or a sunny window, too cold or too wet or dry at the roots. Water freely in summer as soon as the compost feels dry on the surface, but in winter keep it barely moist but never bone dry. Spray the foliage daily with tepid rainwater, or stand the plant in a tray or bowl of moist peat or gravel to increase humidity. Repot in spring when necessary, usually every other year, using a standard soil-based compost. Feed fortnightly in summer. Remove the insignificant flower heads as soon as they are seen. Older plants which outgrow available space can be decapitated and the top 6in (15cm) of stem rooted in a propagator. The stump left behind may sprout new shoots. Sometimes mature plants produce suckers and these can be removed and potted up at repotting time.

Dracaena concinna (syn D. marginata 'Tricolor', D. m. var concinna) (Malagasy, Mauritius) Rainbow Plant
Height 3ft (90cm) or more, spread 1 to 1½ft (30 to 45cm). The thin leaves open from the stem in the usual fountain pattern. Difficult to grow, it needs humidity to prevent the leaf tips from turning brown. Do not keep the plant too shaded or the colouring will become lacklustre. It is more susceptible than most species to overwatering. Spray regularly with tepid rainwater or the opening leaves may stick together and force the growing point to snap off. The plant offered as D. marginata has narrow, glossy dark green leaves edged with rosy red, but it lacks the yellow stripes.

Dracaena deremensis 'Bausei' (Originally Tropical Africa).
Height 3 to 10ft (90cm to 3m) in the home, spread around 2ft (60cm).

Dracaena deremensis 'Roehrsii' (syn. D.d. var. rhoersii)
Similar to 'Bausei'.

Dracaena deremensis 'Warneckii'
Almost a combination of the previous two cultivars, with many narrow white stripes running down the leaf.

Ficus (Ornamental Fig)

The ornamental figs are a varied group of plants with equally varied requirements. Generally speaking, all the taller and more shrubby plants like a position in good but indirect light; the creeping types prefer light shade. Keep all the figs reasonably warm in winter, a minimum temperature of 13°C (55°F) is ideal, though 7°C (45°F) can be tolerated for short periods of time. Water freely in summer, but only when the surface of the compost has dried out, for overwatering is a common cause of death. The compost can remain dry even longer in winter and the plant will not mind at all. Keep the creeping species moist (but not soggy) at all times. Taller species may need the support of a stout cane when their stems become top-heavy. Occasional misting with tepid rainwater will suit all species, as will a monthly feed in summer. Repot in spring when necessary – the large and shrubby species into a standard or rich soil-based compost and the smaller species into basic soil or peat-based compost. Propagate by sowing seeds in spring in a heated propagator, or by taking stem or leaf bud cuttings in spring and summer and rooting these with bottom heat. Tall, single-stemmed plants can be propagated and reduced in height by air layering. Scale insects and red spider mites are the only serious pests.

Ficus benghalensis (India, Tropical Africa) Banyan, Bengal Fig.
Height 10ft (3m) and more, spread 4ft (1.2m). A handsome species with a single or a branched stem. A vigorous but often neglected plant.

Ficus benjamina (Tropical Asia) Weeping Fig.
Height 6ft (1.8m) spread 4ft (1.2m) or more if given room to grow. Easily the most elegant ornamental fig. This plant often takes a while to settle in to a new home and some of its leaves will turn yellow and fall every time it is relocated. It soon recovers provided that it is given a spot in good light and away from draughts and heat sources. Its growth is rather slow but it makes an excellent specimen plant.

Ficus deltoidea (syn. F. diversifolia) (India, Malaysia) Mistletoe Fig.
Height 3 to 4ft (1 to 1.2m) spread 2ft (60cm). A quaint species with round, yellow-green berries carried all the year round. A slower grower.

Ficus benghalensis

Ficus benjamina

Ficus deltoidea

Codiaeum variegatum cultivars

x *Fatshedera lizei*
'Variegata'

x *Fatshedera lizei*

Fatsia japonica 'Variegata'

Fatsia japonica

Codiaeum (Croton)

This is one of the most popular house plants but one which often proves difficult. Give the plant what it needs and it will thrive. Maintain a minimum temperature of 16°C (60°F) and try to prevent too much fluctuation. Position the plant in good but indirect light, not in shade. The compost should be kept just moist at all times, never keep it soggy but similarly never let it dry out completely, even in winter. Codiaeum needs a humid atmosphere if its lower leaves are to be prevented from falling off, so stand it on a tray of moist gravel or peat which is kept constantly damp. Warmth, humidity and good light are the basic needs, but take care too that the plant is not positioned in a draught or the leaves will fall. Feed codiaeum fortnightly from spring to autumn (starvation is yet another cause of failure) and repot in spring every other year in a standard soil- or peat-based compost. Stem cuttings can be rooted in a heated propagator in spring and summer. The plants get rather tall with age but pinching out the growing point will encourage sideshoots to form, so making a bushier specimen. Tall plants can be reduced in size by air layering in spring.

Codiaeum variegatum cultivars (syn *C. variegatum pictum*) (Originally Pacific Islands and Malaysia) Croton, Joseph's Coat
Height 3ft (90cm) or more, spread 12 to 18in (30 to 45cm). A beautiful house plant when it is in peak condition, the croton is available in many forms. The leaves may be narrow or broadly oval and are often indented like the body of a violin. Whatever their shape they are almost always spectacularly veined, blotched or margined with red, orange or yellow on top of their basic shiny green. The flowers are insignificant.

x *Fatshedera* (Ivy Tree)

A cool and reasonably well lit room is really all that fatshedera needs. It cn even be grown outdoors in most parts of Britain. However, the plant might suffer if the air becomes too hot, so try to keep it in a well-ventilated room where temperatures are unlikely to rise above 24°C (75°F). Although the plant prefers to grow in good light (though not brilliant sunshine) it will put up with light shade, but growth will be slower and rather more spindly. Train the stems upwards around a central bamboo cane or a moss-covered stick, or let them hang over the edge of the pot from a shelf or window-ledge. Pinch out the tips of the stems if you want to encourage them to branch from lower down. Water the plant whenever the compost feels dry, but allow rather longer between waterings in winter – fatshedera does not like a waterlogged compost. Repot each spring in a standard soil- or peat-based compost, and feed monthly in summer. Propagation is by cuttings.

x *Fatshedera lizei*
Height and spread up to 10ft (3m) though usually considerably smaller when grown as a house plant. Repeated pinching out of the growing points on young plants will produce bushy specimens that can more easily hold themselves upright.

x *Fatshedera lizei* 'Variegata'
The variegated form has leaves irregularly margined with creamy white. It is slightly more difficult than the species and certainly needs quite bright light if its variegation is to be maintained.

Fatsia (False Castor Oil Palm)

This is grown exactly as *Fatshedera* except that the plant does not need staking. Cool conditions and good light are its prime requirements, but a little shade will be tolerated. It can be propagated from seed and cuttings in a warm propagator.

Fatsia japonica (syn *Aralia japonica, A. sieboldii*) (Korea, Taiwan, Japan)
Height and spread 3 to 5ft (90cm to 1.5m) in the home. The plant is very shapely, forming a rounded bush, and it is very easy to care for provided that the leaves are not scorched by sun and that the compost is not kept too soggy or too dry. Mist the leaves with water occasionally in summer.

Fatsia japonica 'Variegata'
The leaves are marbled with creamy white and relatively bright conditions will produce the best variegations.

151

Microcoelum weddellianum

Howea forsteriana   Howea belmoreana

Microcoelum weddellianum (syn *Cocos weddelliana, Syagrus weddelliana*) (Brazil)
Height and spread up to 3ft (90cm) in the home. A good potted palm but not so graceful as the larger types. Do not expect any coconuts!

Epipremnum (Scindapsus)

These must be kept warm; ensure a minimum temperature of 13 to 16°C (55 to 60°F) and keep in good, indirect light. Water freely in summer as soon as the surface of the compost feels dry, but let it remain barely moist in winter. Peel off any leaves that fade. Feed monthly in summer and provide the plant with some support (a moss-covered stick is best). It may dehydrate if grown as a trailing plant as it needs humid atmosphere, so spray frequently with tepid water. Repot in spring in a peat-based compost only when potbound. Propagate by taking cuttings comprising a leaf and a small portion of stem. Pinch out the shoot tips in the early stages to promote branching.

Epipremnum aureum (syn *Scindapsus aureus, Pothos aureus*) (Solomon Islands) Devil's Ivy, Golden Pothos.
Height and spread 6ft (1.8m) or more, depending on the size of the support system. Aerial roots should be trained into a mossed stick.

Monstera (Swiss Cheese Plant)

Make sure that the temperature never falls below 10°C (50°F) and keep around 18°C (65°F) during the day. Give it good light or slight shade. Push the tips of the aerial roots into a moss stick or the surface of the compost, never cut them off. Pull off any faded leaves. Feed weekly in summer and water the compost thoroughly whenever it feels dry on the surface. Keep it just damp in winter. Spray daily with tepid water and clean the leaves with rainwater once a month. Repot annually in equal amounts of a standard soil- and peat-based compost. Keep the plant warm, out of draughts, away from radiators, and do not overwater. Brown leaves (unless they are just old) indicate dry air or starvation; yellow leaves indicate starvation or overwatering (the latter also causes water to drip from the leaf edges). If the leaves are not perforated then the plant may be too young (they usually split after 3 or 4 years), underfed, in too small a pot or in poor light.

Monstera deliciosa (syn *Philodendron pertusum*) (Central America and Mexico)
Height and spread around 6ft (1.8m) when grown as a house plant. The creamy-white, pineapple-scented arum flowers rarely appear.

Monstera deliciosa

Epipremnum aureum

Howea (Kentia Palm)

Contrary to popular belief, palms grown as house plants do not enjoy blazing sunshine as it scorches their leaf tips and generally dries them up. Position them instead in light shade (they will even tolerate quite dark corners). Maintain a minimum winter temperature of around 10°C (50°F), although the palms may occasionally tolerate less than this. They need a relatively humid atmosphere which will stop the frond tips from drying out so stand them in a large jardinière or on a shallow tray filled with moist gravel. An occasional spray with tepid rainwater will also be beneficial.

Cut off cleanly any leaves that turn brown (the lower ones will do so quite quickly from time to time). If the tips of healthy leaves turn brown check that the plant is not too cold, positioned in a draught, near a radiator, or that it is not too dry at the roots. Palms detest soggy compost but they will soon suffer from drought. Aim to keep the compost moist from spring to autumn and slightly drier in winter so it is just damp. Clean the leaves once a month with a moistened sponge. A monthly feed in summer will keep the plants healthy, and they can usually do with repotting every other spring into a mixture of equal parts standard soil- and peat-based potting compost. Red spider mite is the only pest likely to be troublesome. Most problems are caused by faulty growing conditions. Gentle warmth and constant humidity, plus damp (rather than dry or soggy) compost are the secrets of success.

Howea belmoreana (syn *Kentia belmoreana*) (Lord Howe Island).
Height to around 6ft (1.8m) or more in the home, spread 3ft (90cm) or more. One of the finest specimen house plants and surprisingly tolerant of room conditions.

Howea forsteriana (syn *Kentia forsteriana*) (Lord Howe Island)
Height and spread similar to *H. belmoreana*. In this species the fronds arch less spectacularly, but it is the more popular of the two being, if anything, a little easier to grow.

Microcoelum (Coconut Palm)

Grow exactly as for *Howea*, but it prefers good indirect light and a minimum temperature of around 16°C (60°F).

Philodendron scandens var. *oxycardium*

Scindapsus pictus 'Argyraeus'

Philodendron selloum

Cissus antarctica

Cissus discolor

Rhoicissus rhomboidea 'Ellen Danica'

Rhoicissus rhomboidea

Philodendron

Varied plants in many shapes and sizes but with similar requirements when it comes to growing conditions. All prefer indirect light to bright sunshine which scorches the fleshy leaves, and one in particular, *Philodendron scandens*, will tolerate heavy shade. The latter can also put up with lower temperatures than most – around 10°C (50°F) – the others preferring a minimum of 13 to 16°C (55 to 60°F). Train the stems of the climbing kinds around a supporting framework or, better still, up a moss stick where they can sink their aerial roots into the moist material. Peel off any faded leaves as soon as they are noticed. Spray the plants daily with tepid water, or stand them on a tray of moist peat or gravel to improve atmospheric humidity. Clean the leaves once a month with a damp sponge. Water thoroughly in summer whenever the compost feels dry, but keep it only slightly damp in winter to prevent stem rot. Feed monthly in summer and repot every other spring into a peat-based compost. Propagation is by means of stem cuttings taken in spring and summer and rooted in a heated propagator or by air layering older plants at the same time of year.

Philodendron scandens var. **oxycardium** (syn *P. oxycardium*) (Tropical America) Sweetheart Plant, Parlour Ivy.
Height and spread dependent upon support system. The true *P. scandens* has leaves tinged with pink on their undersides, but it is this variety which is most commonly offered. Climbing stems display the leaves well. The plant also does well in suspended pots and is remarkably tolerant of poor growing conditions and neglect. Pinch out the shoot tips occasionally to keep it in trim. A reliable plant for any novice.

Philodendron selloum (Brazil) Lacy Tree Philodendron
Height 5ft (1.5m) or more, spread 6ft (1.8m). The long leaf lobes are wavy edged and so have a lacy appearance.

Scindapsus

Grow exactly as for *Epipremnum* to which it is closely related (the two were at one time grouped in the same genus).

Scindapsus pictus 'Argyraeus' (Indonesia, Malaysia) Ivy Arum, Silver Vine.
Height and spread dependent upon support system. This cultivar is said to be a juvenile form of the true species which has blotching of a more greeny colour. Not the easiest climbing house plant to grow as it needs plenty of heat and humidity to do well.

Cissus (Kangaroo Vine)

The two species described here need rather different growing conditions. *Cissus antarctica* is relatively easy to grow in good but indirect light in a cool room. Maintain a minimum temperature of 7°C (45°F) and train the stems around a support. Cut back the stems severely in spring if the plant becomes overgrown. In summer water well as soon as the surface of the compost feels dry, but in winter let it remain dry for longer. Feed fortnightly in spring and summer. Repot in spring when necessary using a standard soil- or peat-based compost. Spray occasionally with tepid water. Propagate from stem cuttings in spring or summer or sow seeds in spring. *Cissus discolor* is rather more difficult and prefers to grow in light shade with a minimum temperature of around 16°C (60°F). Stand the plant on a tray of moist gravel or peat to increase humidity, and otherwise train and cultivate as *C. antarctica*.

Cissus antarctica (syn *Vitis antarctica*) (Australia) Kangaroo Vine.
Height 3ft (90cm) or more, spread 2ft (60cm) or more. A good choice for a cool room which is well lit.

Cissus discolor (Java, Kampuchea) Begonia Vine
Height 6ft (1.8m) spread to 3ft (90cm) or so. Difficult to grow unless conditions are ideal.

Rhoicissus (Grape Ivy)

Cultivation is the same as for *Cissus antarctica*, but rhoicissus is more tolerant of shade and seems to survive (if not flourish) in dark corners. It is one of the most vigorous house plants available and can be trained on a light framework over walls and around arches.

Rhoicissus rhomboidea (South Africa)
Height and spread considerable. The rampant stems are rather wiry and coated in bronzy hairs. The young leaves as they unfurl are rich bronze and decorated with silky hairs.

Rhoicissus rhomboidea 'Ellen Danica' (syn *R. ellendanica*)
Similar in most respects to the species, but the leaves are quite deeply cut.

H. helix
'Little Diamond'

H. helix 'Luzii'

H. helix 'Gold Child'

Hedera canariensis 'Gloire de Marengo'

Hedera (Ivy)

Ivies are easy to grow if they are kept cool, but in stuffy centrally-heated rooms they often suffer. Position them in good light (especially important for the variegated varieties) but out of direct sun and where temperatures do not rise above 18°C (65°F); unheated rooms are ideal. Ivies can be trained over a framework of canes or some trellis. The aerial roots may cling to the surface of walls, but this makes decorating rather difficult. Smaller-leaved ivies are often grown as trailing plants in suspended pots or on shelves. Trim off unwanted shoots at any time, and pinch out shoot tips in spring to encourage bushiness. Feed monthly in summer and repot in spring when necessary using a standard soil-based compost; ivies prefer their roots to be rather restricted. Water freely in summer when the compost feels dry. In winter water less, but never let it dry out completely or the leaves will shrivel and fall. Spray daily with water. Propagate from stem cuttings. The aerial roots make ivy cuttings easy to strike. In hot, dry rooms, red spider mite can be a serious pest, and greenfly may colonize the shoot tips.

Hedera canariensis 'Gloire de Marengo' (syn *H.c.* 'Variegata', *H.c.* 'Souvenir de Marengo' (Originally Africa, Canaries, Madeira, Azores) Algerian Ivy, Canary Island Ivy.
Height and spread unpredictable. The youngest leaves bear the most striking variegations, and the young stems are a burgundy colour, as are the leaf stalks. Grow up a cane tripod.

Hedera helix (Europe, including Britain) Common or English Ivy.
Height and spread unpredictable. There are many different foliage variations and variegations in the common ivy. These are some popular varieties for indoor pot, trough and hanging basket culture:
'Gold Child' – The five-lobed leaves are slightly dished, greyish-green in the centre, margined with yellow. The stems and stalks are purplish. Difficult to grow well.
'Little Diamond' – Leaves three lobed, arranged in a diamond shape with a dull green centre and a whitish margin; stems and leaf stalks green.
'Luzii' – Leaves with five lobes, fresh green, mottled and marbled with yellow green; leaf stalks and stems purplish brown.

Tradescantia

Almost all the tradescantias need bright light. A windowsill suits their pendulous habit and they will tolerate a minimum temperature of 7°C (45°F). Central heating does not worry them, but if positioned in a hot, dry spot many of the leaves may turn brown; cut all the stems back to compost level and fresh shoots will grow. Cut out any very straggly or tatty shoots at any time of year, and pinch the shoot tips out of young plants. Water freely in summer whenever the compost looks like drying out, but keep it just slightly moist in winter. Feed monthly in summer. Repot each spring in peat-based compost, or, better still, discard old plants and insert three 4-in (10-cm) long shoot tips around the edge of a 4-in pot filled with moist compost. Kept moist and lightly shaded at first the shoots will soon root and grow away. Cuttings can also be rooted in jars of water. Greenfly are likely to be the only problem as far as pests are concerned, though red spider mite occasionally rears its ugly head if the atmosphere is too dry. All the species grow well in hanging baskets and suspended pots.

Tradescantia blossfeldiana (Argentina) Flowering Inch Plant, Wandering Sailor.
Trailing to 2ft (60cm) or more.

Tradescantia blossfeldiana 'Variegata'
Here the leaves are broadly but irregularly striped white and delicately flushed with pink.

Tradescantia fluminensis 'Quicksilver' (Originally South America) Wandering Jew
Trailing to 1½ft (45cm). A strong grower, but not so lengthy in the stem as the true species. The leaves are striped and are iridescent.

Tradescantia fluminensis 'Tricolor' Wandering Jew
Rather like *T.f.* 'Quicksilver' except that the leaves are slightly narrower and flushed with pink at the margins.

Tradescantia sillamontana (syn *T. pexata*, *T. velutina* of gardens, *Cyanotis sillámontana*, *C. veldthoutiana* of gardens) (Mexico) White Gossamer, White Velvet
Height 9in (23cm) spread 1ft (30cm) or more. More erect than the other species. The firm leaves are coated in white silky wool. Deep pink flowers are produced in summer and autumn. The most difficult to cultivate of the species described here. Keep the compost very much on the dry side in winter and keep the plant cool at the same time.

T. blossfeldiana
'Variegata'

Tradescantia
blossfeldiana

T. fluminensis
'Quicksilver'

T. sillamontana

T. fluminensis
'Tricolor'

Coleus blumei

Glechoma hederacea 'Variegata'

Aechmea (Urn Plant)

Although aechmea is native to tropical areas and enjoys reasonable warmth, it will tolerate a temperature as low as 10°C (50°F). Position it in good but indirect light. Keep the 'vase' in the centre of the rosette topped up with water at all times, but the compost should be just moist, not soggy. Keep the air around the plant as humid as possible. Feeding is not really necessary but some gardeners give a dilute foliar feed once a month in summer. If small specimens are acquired and repotting is necessary use a peat-based compost and a pot barely large enough to hold the roots. After flowering the large central rosette will die and one or more offsets should emerge to take over. Repot these individually in spring, cutting off and discarding the old rosette.

Aechmea fasciata (syn *A. rhodocyanea, Billbergia rhodocyanea*) (Brazil) Height and spread 1½ft (45cm) The massive rosette of green leaves is covered in a white farina that rubs off easily on the fingers. The 'urn' or 'vase' is quite pronounced, and from it a spiky head of pink bracts and lavender-blue flowers will emerge in summer if the plant is grown in a sufficiently high temperature around 24°C (75°F). The flower head will last for several months but can be cut off once it has turned brown, then the rosette will fade too.

Cryptanthus (Earth Star)

Cryptanthus do well in warm rooms where a winter minimum of 13°C (55°F) can be assured, and like a position in brilliant or indirect light. Only in the middle of summer might bright sunshine necessitate their being moved to a spot in more indirect light. Keep the compost around the roots only just moist, never soggy or the roots may rot; spray the foliage daily with tepid water and subsequent watering may not be necessary. Feeding is seldom necessary if the plants are grown in a good peat-based compost. Repot them in a peat-based compost only when absolutely necessary for they make very little root. Spring is the best time to move them. Propagation is by the removal and potting up of offsets in spring and summer.

Cryptanthus bromelioides 'Tricolor'
Height 6in (15cm) or more, spread 1ft (30cm) or more. One of the most spectacular.

Coleus (Flame Nettle)

They need the brightest light possible to keep their leaf colour brilliant and their habit shapely. Temperatures as low as 10°C (50°F) will be tolerated, but those a little higher are preferred. Pinch out the shoot tips regularly to encourage bushiness. Remove any flowers that form to encourage leaf production. If the plant looks a mess in winter, discard it, although it can be cut back within 3in (8cm) of the compost in spring. Water the compost thoroughly whenever it feels dry on the surface in summer, but keep it drier in winter (watch for the plant to wilt a little before watering). Feed the plant fortnightly from spring to autumn, and repot older plants in a standard soil- or peat-based compost when they have been cut back in spring. Stem cuttings root easily in compost or water. Sow seed in spring.

Coleus blumei (Java) Flame Nettle, Painted Nettle, The Foliage Plant. Height and spread 1 to 2ft (30 to 60cm). The brightest of foliage plants, the oval pointed leaves are toothed and may be mottled, margined and veined in bright green, acid yellow, fiery orange, fluorescent pink, crimson, caramel and plum purple. The blue flower spikes should be removed to encourage leaf production. Named cultivars are available in mixed colours and varying leaf shapes.

Glechoma (Variegated Ground Ivy)

This hardy ground-cover plant is useful for planting in hanging baskets indoors so long as it is kept cool and given plenty of light. Alternatively it will thrive for a year or so in a suspended pot until it runs out of root space and nourishment. Water the compost well in summer whenever it shows signs of drying out, but keep it rather drier in winter. Repot in spring when necessary using a peat-based compost for lightness, and feed monthly from spring to autumn. Cut out any old straggly growth. Cut back hard in spring to encourage the production of new stems. Propagate by stem cuttings and division of old plants in spring.

Glechoma hederacea 'Variegata' (syn *Nepeta hederacea* 'Variegata', *N. glechoma* 'Variegata') (Europe, Asia) Variegated Ground Ivy.
A trailing plant which can cascade for 3ft (90cm) or more from a suspended container. An easy fast-growing plant for a cool bright place such as a sunroom or conservatory.

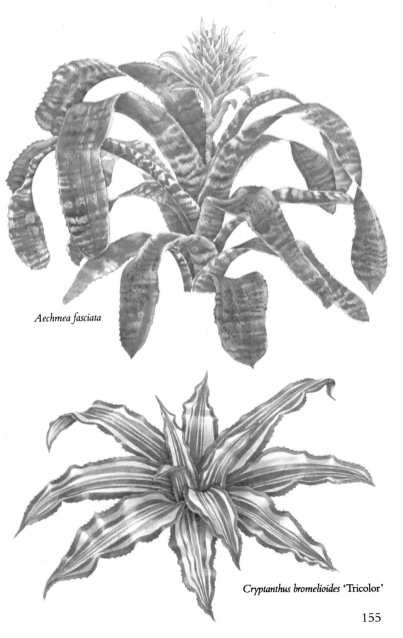

Aechmea fasciata

Cryptanthus bromelioides 'Tricolor'

Easy Methods of Plant Propagation

The cost of plants, like most other things, is constantly rising and for the keen gardener can be an inhibiting factor in acquiring some longed-for specimen. Many plants, however, are surprisingly easy to propagate and it is great source of satisfaction to produce one's own supply. Gardeners are very generous people and will, usually, provide cuttings and divisions from their plants very willingly.

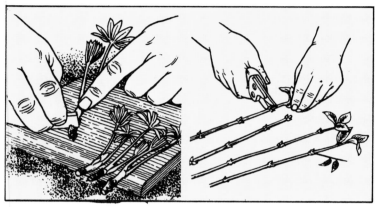

Left: Softwood cuttings. Right: Hardwood cuttings.

Stem Cuttings

The propagation of plants from stem cuttings is a very popular method used by amateur gardeners and simply involves encouraging a shoot to form roots of its own under suitable conditions. Shrubs, perennial plants, alpines, conifers and some fruits may be raised from cuttings, and there are three types that can be taken: softwood cuttings, semi-ripe and hardwood cuttings.

Softwood Cuttings These are prepared from very soft current year's side shoots before they turn hard and woody, and therefore are taken early in the year – between April and June as a rough guide.

Many shrubs can be propagated from softwood cuttings like weigelas, philadelphus, spiraeas, deutzias and hypericums; a wide range of alpines can also be increased at this time, together with hardy perennials such as lupins and delphiniums.

Healthy young shoots of shrubs should be used as cuttings. Collect them into a polythene bag to prevent wilting, then take them to a cool shady place to prepare and insert them.

The average length of shrub cuttings is 3in (8cm) and they are prepared by cutting immediately below a node or leaf joint at the base. The tips are left intact. Remove the leaves from the lower half of each cutting. Always use a very sharp knife or razor blade for preparation as clean cuts are important. Dip the base of each cutting (the lower ¼in (6mm) only) in a hormone rooting powder to speed up rooting.

The cuttings are then inserted up to the lower leaves in a cutting compost, consisting of equal parts peat and coarse sand. Use pots or seed trays, depending on quantity. Water the cuttings well in.

Softwood cuttings are rooted in warm humid conditions, ideally in a propagating case with a temperature of about 18 to 21°C (65 to 70°F). Alternatively root them on a windowsill indoors, enclosing the container in a clear polythene bag held up with a few short canes. Ventilate for an hour or so several times a week to prevent excess condensation forming.

When they have rooted – indicated by growth at the tips – pot off into small pots of John Innes potting compost No 1, and harden off in a cold frame before placing them outside.

Cuttings of alpines are treated similarly. With perennial plants like lupins and delphiniums, take cuttings when shoots are about 2in (5cm) high, removing them as close to the crown of the plant as possible, and provide the same conditions for rooting.

Semi-ripe Cuttings These are taken later in the year – July to October as a rough guide – when the current year's shoots are hardening or becoming woody. They are prepared in the same way as softwoods, except the base of the cuttings will be hard and woody, while the top will still be soft and green.

Many shrubs, climbers and conifers can be propagated from semi-ripe cuttings, including heaths and heathers. Cuttings of the last two will be small – about 2in (5cm) in length. All should be prepared and inserted as for softwoods, but these cuttings can be rooted in cooler conditions, such as a cold frame or unheated greenhouse.

Many evergreen shrubs, such as berberis, escallonia, lavender, laurel, rosemary, santolina and senecio, root particularly well under low polythene tunnel cloches. They can be taken in October, inserted in a well-prepared bed (mix in plenty of sand and peat), covered with a tunnel and by the following late spring they should have rooted. The tunnel is then taken off and the rooted cuttings lifted in the autumn.

Hardwood Cuttings Some fruits and various ornamental shrubs are easy to propagate from hardwood cuttings, which are taken when the plants are dormant in November or December, after the leaves have fallen.

Once again the current year's shoots are used, but by this time they will be well ripened – in other words, hard and woody. Cuttings are prepared with secateurs and, depending on the subject, are 6 to 9in (15 to 23cm) in length. The top cut is made just above a growth bud, and the bottom cut immediately below a bud.

Dip the lower ¼in (6mm) of the cuttings in hormone rooting powder, and then insert them to half to two-thirds of their length. Some, like privet and willows, can be rooted in a sheltered, well-drained spot out of doors. Take out a V-shaped trench, line the bottom with sharp sand, stand the cuttings in it, return the soil and firm well with your heels. Leave until the autumn of the following year, when they should be well rooted.

Some hardwood cuttings are best rooted in a cold frame, including the shrubs forsythia, *Cornus alba* or shrubby dogwoods, weigela, deutzia, philadelphus, buddleia, spiraea and ribes. Root them in a sandy/peaty soil, and lift the following autumn.

Division

About the easiest method of propagating many plants – particularly hardy perennials and alpines – is by division, which involves lifting a well-established clump and splitting it into a number of smaller portions, each with some roots and top growth or buds.

Many perennials are best lifted and divided every three or four years to keep them young and vigorous. The best time is between March and mid-April for most, but very early

Left: Dividing a clump with two forks. Right: Tease out small pieces from the outer part of the clump for replanting.

flowering perennials could be divided immediately after flowering. The German or bearded irises are divided after flowering in June.

Lift clumps with a fork and gently tease away most of the soil from the roots. You may be able to pull them apart with your hands (as for instance with Michaelmas daisies), but other clumps will be tough. The best way to deal with these is to insert two forks back to back through the centre of the clump and then lever the handles apart. These two portions can then be further split in the same way.

The centre part of each clump should be discarded as this is old and declining in vigour. Retain only the outer portions. Pieces which fit comfortably into the palm of your hand are the ideal size for replanting.

Iris divisions are somewhat different – each should consist of a portion of rhizome (swollen stem) with a fan of leaves attached.

Replant divisions as quickly as possible to prevent the roots from drying out. The rhizomes of irises are only lightly covered with soil.

Some perennials are best not lifted and divided unless it is absolutely necessary as they resent disturbance, and these include paeonia, helleborus and Japanese anemones.

Alpines which form mats, carpets, cushions and rosettes of growth are the ones to divide. Lift and divide in early spring, simply pulling them apart with your hands.

Simple Layering

This is an easy method of propagation for the amateur gardener and even allows one successfully to increase plants that may be difficult from cuttings;, like magnolias, rhododendrons, azaleas, camellias, witch hazels and so on. Indeed, a wide range of shrubs, trees and climbers can be propagated by layering.

Left: Pegging the wounded portion of the stem to the ground. Right: Cover the wounded area with soil and support the layer with a small cane.

Basically the technique involves rooting a shoot while it is still attached to the parent plant, provided it is possible to bend the shoot down to soil level. The shoots of most shrubs take about 12 months to form a good root system.

Layering is best done in the growing season – spring and summer. Use only young shoots or stems for layering – those formed in the current or previous season. Older stems may not root.

About 12in (30cm) from the top of the shoot remove a few leaves. This part of the shoot has to be wounded to encourage it to root. This can be accomplished in two ways. The easiest method is to hold the stem firmly with both hands and to give it a sharp twist to break some of the tissues. Alternatively, using sharp knife, make a 2in (5cm) long cut half way through the stem to form a 'tongue'. Keep this cut open by wedging it with a small stone or piece of wood.

The next stage is to make a 6in (15cm) deep depression in the soil, and to peg down the wounded area of the stem. A piece of thick galvanised wire bent into the shape of a hairpin makes a good peg. The wounded area must be in close contact with the soil. The remaining end of the stem should be carefully brought into an upright position and secured with a short bamboo cane and soft string. The part of the stem in contact with the soil should then be covered with 6in (15cm) of soil.

The soil around the layered stem must be kept moist, for if it is allowed to dry out rooting may not occur. In 12 months time carefully lift the stem, cut it away from the parent plant just beyond the roots, and replant elsewhere immediately to prevent the roots from drying out. If the stem has not rooted, then re-insert and leave for another 12 months.

With some climbers, such as clematis, jasmine, passion flower, honeysuckle, vines and wisteria, it is possible, as they have long stems, to peg down a stem in a number of places along its length so that it eventually produces several new plants. Preparation is the same as for simple layering.

Seeds

Raising plants from seeds can be a very economical way of obtaining new plants. Seeds of hardy perennials or herbaceous plants, alpines and trees and shrubs are available from the major seedsmen.

It is also possible to save seeds from your own plants, but a word of caution here: save seeds only from species of plants rather than from hybrids and varieties. The resultant plants from hybrids and varieties may not resemble the parent plants; they may have different characteristics, such as flower colour. Seeds from species, however, will result in plants which are exactly the same in every detail as their parents.

Seeds of herbaceous plants can be sown in the open ground in May or June, choosing a well-drained piece of ground in a sunny position. Prepare a good seed bed, firstly by digging, and then by firming and raking the soil down to a fine level surface. Rake in a general-purpose fertilizer.

Take out shallow drills about 12in (30cm) apart and sow the seeds thinly in these. Cover them with a depth of soil equal to twice their diameter. Keep the seed bed moist.

When the seedlings are large enough to handle they should be transplanted to a nursery bed to grow on. Prepare the site as for the seed bed. Lift the seedlings with a fork and replant them in rows 12in (30cm) apart, spacing the seedlings 6in (15cm) apart. Keep well watered in dry weather, and by the autumn the young plants will be large enough to transplant to their flowering positions.

Perennials with very small seeds are better sown in seed trays of John Innes seed compost and germinated in a cold frame. Subjects that are generally raised in frames include violas and pansies, primulas, delphiniums and lupins. The last two have large seeds but seem to germinate better in a frame. The seedlings are planted out as described above.

Seeds of many trees and shrubs can be sown in outdoor seed beds as described above, but making the sowings in March or April. Again very fine seeds are best sown in trays in a cold frame.

The resultant tree and shrub seedlings in outdoor beds can be left where they are until autumn, when they can be lifted and either replanted in a spare piece of ground to grow on, or in their final positions. Seedlings raised in trays are best potted individually into 3 ½in (9cm) pots, and planted out when large enough.

Most alpines are best sown in January or February. Sow in 3½in (9cm) pots of John Innes seed compost, and cover with a layer of coarse grit. Stand the pots in a cold, north-facing position and keep the compost moist. Most will germinate in the spring, but others may take much longer, so keep all pots of seeds at least until the second spring.

Seedlings of alpines are pricked out individually into 3in (8cm) pots of John Innes potting compost No 1. Get them established in a cold frame, and plant in the autumn or following spring. Overwinter potted alpines in a well-ventilated cold frame.

GARDENS TO VISIT

The descriptions and illustrations that follow are of a selection of the outstanding gardens of mainland Britain. The gardens included represent a comprehensive range of all the various types of garden, some notable for their historical associations, others for their plant collections or associated features. They are representative of the very much larger number of gardens that are open to the public at various times throughout the year.

What to See and Where

There can be no other country in the world which can show its centuries of garden history and evolution on the ground in such detail or display in its gardens such an immense variety of alien plants brought from every continent.

The Climate As is so often said we enjoy not so much a particular climate as 'weather', and it is our place in the Northern Temperate Zone which makes British gardens the congenial home of some 12,000 species of hardy plants, indeed it can be said, if we omit the Tropical Zone, that plants from every other floral region of the world can be and are grown in the open somewhere in Great Britain. If we take into account the many great palm houses and conservatories of our botanic gardens then we can well add to our plant-growing capacities the tropical zone as well so that visiting British gardens is almost a botanical tour of the world. It is these now 'naturalized' foreigners that have so lighted and coloured the drabness and dreariness of our native winters with early-flowering shrubs, with berrying trees and shrubs, the many evergreens from overseas and the textures and tints of the barks of exotic trees. They have illuminated our springs, mid-summers and autumns so vividly with the brightest and subtlest of colours and the delights of differing forms.

That said, we have to add to our British weather the benign influence of that so useful of phenomena to our western-shore gardens, the Gulf Stream, which gives Devon and Cornwall and the Western Coast of Scotland those climatic conditions where rhododendrons of the high Himalayas and the towering peaks of Tibet and China, the camellias of Japan, the magnolias of both China and Japan, and those rather incredulous Australian inhabitants, the tree ferns and bottle brushes and other related subjects, can flower as if in their native haunts. Such gardens are to be found in Scotland at Inverewe, Brodick Castle, Logan, the Edinburgh Botanic Garden, and in England, among many other gardens at Heaselands, Exbury, the Isabella and Waterhouse Plantations in Richmond and Bushy Parks, the Savill and Windsor Great Park Gardens, Cragside, Leonardslee and Wakehurst Place. In Cornwall and Devon one calls to mind particularly Lanhydrock. Trelissick, Trengwainton, Penjerric, and Knightshayes Court and Bodnant and Plas Newydd in Wales.

Roses These, so long the best-loved flower in British gardens, have, in larger gardens, their special place as a feature, and, in some botanical gardens, are planted to show the long history and evolution of the flower. We have these visual lessons at Oxford, at Ness in the Wirral and at The Gardens of The Rose, the Royal National Rose Society's gardens and trial grounds. Other larger scale gardens set out to display all that is best in our long tradition of rose growing, often give the old-fashioned and shrub roses pride of place, with these having a nomenclature redolent of a more leisurely and aristocratic past, both in this country and on the Continent. At the St Albans' garden the whole family can be seen, both old and new; at Mottisfont Abbey in Hampshire the National Trust has brought together in its collection all the old-fashioned and shrub roses still in cultivation in this country. At Castle Howard a charming Old World walled garden is the setting for old-fashioned and shrub roses and this collection is still being added to. There are rose gardens at Sissinghurst, Nymans, Hardwick Hall, Tintinhull, Queen Mary's Rose Garden in Regent's Park, at Wisley and at Kew. Large rose nurseries such as Mattocks at Nuneham Courtenay near Oxford and Harkness's at Hitchin, Hertfordshire are also open to view.

Tree Collections In the name of progress most of our wild native woodland and forests have gone from Britain, and on any trip into the heart of the country the tree lover is only likely to find a Forestry Commission clothing of hill and dale with exotic conifers rather than natural cover. But, fortunately for the tree lover, Great Britain can boast of some of the finest collections of both native and colourful exotic trees. Arboreta and pinetums are quite thick on the ground, and for our enjoy-

ment there are the Bedgebury National Pinetum; Bicton Park; Bressingham, and many other arboreta which include conifers in their extensive collections. These are to be found at Sheffield Park, Killerton, Batsford Park, Winkworth, Westonbirt Aboretum, the Edinburgh Botanic Garden, Hergest Croft, Wakehurst Place and Kew.

Rock Gardens A Victorian innovation which has grown rapidly since about the 1860s is the love of rock gardens and alpine plants. Most of our alpines were so named because they originally hailed from the European Alps, to be added to later by finds in Asiatic and North American highlands. Now, a great wealth of plants torn from snowy and scree-covered mountainsides are quite at home here, and some of the best displays are at Killerton, Ness and Wisley (where refurbishing is being carried out), and there are equally large and representative alpine rock gardens at the Edinburgh Botanic Garden and Kew. At both Bicton and at Harlow Car in Yorkshire there are sandstone and limestone rock gardens. Alpine plants and rock gardens are also to be seen at the Cambridge Botanic Garden, at Aberdeen University, Luton Hoo, at Threave in Scotalnd, at Alton Towers in Staffordshire where the plants clothe an almost precipitous high rock face, at Wakehurst and at Ascott.

Topiary For many years in our garden history topiary – the clipping of yews, privet, box and rosemary into all manner of pleasing and geometric shapes, taken from the Romans – was almost an essential feature of British gardens so fitting the style and feeling of the strictly formal gardens of Tudor, Elizabethan and Jacobean eras, and matching also the patterning on British soil of Dutch, Italian and French gardening. And there are still many fine specimens of the topiarist's art to be seen, the most historic and established being that at Levens Hall in Cumbria laid down in 1686 with much of the original planting still there. There is at Ascott a topiary sundial and examples both in hedging and figurines at Hidcote, Arley Hall, Antony House and Tyninghame, to name only a few. Packwood has its Sermon on the Mount and Dartington Hall its twelve apostles. Great Dixter, Crathes, Blickling Hall and Newburgh Priory as well as Penshurst Place have massive, handsomely shaped hedges and individual shapings.

Maze Probably because it is costly in time and labour and needs a fair amount of garden space that concomitant of the early formal garden, the maze or labyrinth is not all that numerous in British gardens. There are, however, still several well kept specimens of these 'greenery entertainments' so far from their mythical and penitential origins, the best known being Queen Anne's at Hampton Court, and a unique one at Glendurgan in Cornwall fashioned in laurel. One now covers the ground once looked over by Paxton's Great Stove at Chatsworth and, so much a part of their history, there are mazes at Hever Castle and Hatfield House.

Japanese Garden Although in design completely alien to the traditions of British landscape gardening, Japanese gardens were laid out here in the early years of this century, some of which still contrive to engender the philosophical ideals which are so much a part of the originals in their native setting. One of the best is at Tatton Park, there are others at Compton Acres, Cliveden, and Newstead Abbey.

Formal Gardens Japanese gardens are, as has been seen, a comparatively recent introduction but fortunately we do have, either carefully preserved and conserved or painstakingly reconstructed from old plans and drawings, period gardens ranging back to medieval times and evolving through Tudor, Elizabethan, Jacobean, Stuart and Georgian to Victorian fussiness. Formality, the ruler and set-square gardens, were the mode for many centuries and of these the cloister-surrounded ancient greenswards of our Oxford and Cambridge colleges are typical,

159

along with the reconstructed Monk's Garden at Ashridge, also at Newstead Abbey where a medieval fish pond accompanies a large green formal parterre with raised walk. Tudor and Elizabethan gardens with their under and over knots, small raised enclosed plots, sunken gardens with central pool or fountain and mounds are still with us, having been maintained or restored to show their original design. Hampton Court with its knots and the Pond Garden gives a useful picture of Tudor Gardening. The garden at Kirkby Hall is an accurate 17th-century reconstruction, and at Erddig a Badeslade drawing has been used to restore a garden of 1767/1789. There are knots at Moseley Old Hall, and a lovely old example is at Edzell Castle in Scotland as well as at Pitmedden, near Aberdeen, where the pattern of the compartments was taken from an original design of the period. There are knotted parterres at Holker Hall and at Dunham Massey.

There are mounds at New College and Wadham in Oxford and a terraced one at Northbourne near Deal, at Cranbourne Manor and at the Queen's Garden at Kew which is a replica of a 17th-century lay-out with gazebo, raised walks and pleached arbours. Melbourne Hall is one of the few remaining original 17th-century London and Wise designs with its long yew tunnel, long alleys, statuary in lead by Van Nost, a grotto enclosing a mineral spring, a lake and a truly beautiful wrought iron arbour. An idea of the Dutch garden, once so popular and influenced by William and Mary, can be seen in the white garden at Hidcote with its trees on 'stilts' and formal hedging.

Ornamental Buildings When the landscape revolution of the 18th century swept away, more or less, the formal geometric garden of compartmented parterres and their quincunx of trees and plantations, there first arose on the great estates of the landed gentry, before the 'natural' style of Brown and Repton came upon the land, the use of ornamental buildings to close a vista, provide a landmark, to evoke a mood, both classical and Gothic. As the Romantic and Picturesque mode became fashionable, the more outré ventures were added such as grottoes, hermitages, root houses and follies – those blossomings of aristocratic idiosyncracies. Very often in keeping with the classical Palladian mansions most aesthetically satisfying orangeries were built.

One of the earliest classically ornamented gardens can be seen at Rousham near Oxford where Kent shaped a series of idyllic scenes with classically based buildings, and at Stowe where he worked to ornament and enhance the ground with a wealth of temples, both Gothic and classical, with pavilions, a Corinthian arch, a pebble alcove, bridges and columnar monuments. Stourhead, in Wiltshire, is probably one of the most beautiful of 18th-century landscape conceptions, its lake, the Pantheon, a classic temple, the Gothic cottage making an idyllic garden picture. It has, too, one of the finest grottoes with statuary and running water. Two unusual 'tunnel' grottoes are at Studley Royal where an uphill, long black cavernous walk leads to a Gothic tea house on an upper terrace walk and at Bowood where, still in stygian gloom, rough steps lead steeply downhill to the foot of a cascade behind which are grotto rooms and tunnels. There are other grottoes at Chatsworth, Claremont, and at Melbourne, the last enclosing a mineral spring. In Scotland there is an example at Culzean Castle.

An approach to an Elysian landscape in the early 1700s was at Castle Howard in Yorkshire where Vanbrugh's Temple of the Four Winds closing a terrace walk, once the village high street, is still one of the most gracious of garden ornaments and is part of a landscape marked by a Roman Bridge, a great rotunda of a mausoleum, an obelisk, seemingly interminable avenue and romantic fortressed boundary walls and gateways. While at West Wycombe Park there is a mixture of classical and romantic ornamentation of a landscape with its temple of music, an 18th-century cascade, the Hell Fire Caves, Tower of the Winds, the church steeple meeting room and a much sculptured mausoleum. At Wrest Park there is an outdoor bathhouse. Kew

Gardens still retains some of its once many ornamental buildings, the Ruined Arch, the Pagoda, King William's Temple and at Shugborough there are ruins, a Chinese House, Tower of the Winds, the Lanthorn of Demosthenes and a triumphal arch. Wroxton Abbey displays well both the picturesque and the 'Gothic revival' in its dovecot, Drayton arch, Doric temple, obelisk, Chinese bridge and mount.

Follies dot the British landscape. At Spetchley there is a summer-house of knapped flints. Mottisfont has a barn like a castle.

Herb Garden So much a part of our gardening tradition and linking the present with a dim and distant past, herb gardens are currently making quite a come-back both for their culinary uses and as a garden feature both in period and modern designs, where they have been made into charming old world attractions. At Hardwick Hall, Hatfield House and at Scotney Castle the gardens are in strict keeping with the period as they are also at Moseley Old Hall and at the Queen's Garden at Kew.

Terrace Gardens Two unique 17th-century terrace gardens in England are at Duncombe Park and Rievaulx, near Helmsley, in North Yorkshire. The Rievaulx Terraces prompted Arthur Young to write of them 'Perhaps the most spectacularly beautiful among English landscape conceptions of the 18th century'. At Duncombe the terrace, created between 1711 and 1725, stretches for almost half-a-mile (0.8km) on top of a steep wooded escarpment with peeps below of the River Rye and its purling cascades. One end is terminated by an open rotunda above one of the earliest of ha-has from which the red pantiled roofs of Helmsley are viewed, the other by a Tuscan Temple. At Rievaulx, only a mile (1.6km) or so away (it was said the intention was to join it to Duncombe) the terrace was built in 1754, a landmark in the history of the picturesque movement. Again there is almost a half-mile (0.8km) of a sweeping curve leading from an Ionic Temple banqueting house to a Tuscan temple and on the way, through thick woodland on a most precipitous slope, there are 13 differing views of Rievaulx Abbey nestling in the valley beneath. 'Too elegantly beautiful to admit of description' said Arthur Young. Terracing, because of the elevated position of the house, is well illustrated at Powis Castle.

Water Features Fortunate are those who can command or have 'engineered' the charm of running water or the benison of limpid pools in their gardens. And of water gardens a notable one is that at Burnby Hall where two large pools and connecting streams were created to hold one of the largest collections of water-lilies (some 5,000) to be found in Europe. Blenheim Palace with its water parterre and Brown's lake makes a memorable picture, but it is the long canals, so much a feature of the once-fashionable Dutch gardening, which started the tradition for using water in gardens of a formal nature. Some of the best examples can be seen at Westbury Court, Wrest Park and Lochinch Castle. Other good water gardens are those at Sheffield Park with its four lakes, the bog and water garden at Savill Gardens and Windsor Great Park, and Wakehurst Place, where improvements are being carried out to the old water features. The streamside garden at Harlow Car with its thousands of primula and spiraea in bloom is an unforgettable sight. Hodnet Hall has its water feature and the Waterhouse and Isabella plantations are built round water courses. Newburgh Priory has its wild water garden where several spring-fed streams run downhill through mixed plantings. The Chatsworth cascade of 1694, the Emperor Fountain and canal, its aqueduct, waterfall on Robber's Stone and cascade on Wellington Rock as well as plant-lined streams and the Willow Tree Fountain and an artificial Stride are almost all Paxton's contributions to water gardening on a grand scale. The Studley Royal canals, pools and filmy cascades make for a tranquil scene in a steeply wooded valley.

Landscape Gardens Any reference to Brown is a reminder of the landscape revolution which swept formality from the face of our gardens starting with Switzer, Bridgeman and Kent in the late 17th century, continuing unabated during the whole of the 18th and fading out with the over emphasis on bedding-out by the Victorians. Once again we are fortunate in this country to have so many 'living' illustrations of this revolution. In landscapes either preserved or reconstructed from old drawings and plans as already noted at Erddig. There is Bridgeman's and Kent's work to be seen at Stowe, at Claremont where Bridgeman's great amphitheatre has been restored, and Rousham almost unchanged since Kent worked there. Brown's monumental clearances, his lakes, his 'belting and clumping' of park woodland are very much in evidence at Harewood House, Chatsworth, Bowood and Blenheim. Landscapes by Repton, who worked in a freer style than Brown, can be seen at Sheringham, Antony House, Tatton, and Plas Newydd.

To come to Victorian and Edwardian times W. A. Nesfield's parterre work, often in collaboration with Sir Charles Barry of House of Commons fame, is best seen at Broughton Hall, Trentham, the terrace at Harewood House, the Syon Vista and Broad Walk at Kew.

To come right up-to-date, the landscaping of the campus of York University by the late Frank Clark is modern landscaping at its best, or maybe one should call it 'waterscaping'. There are Venetian bridges, stepping stones, harbour walls, slipways and bollards with college buildings either projecting over or seemingly built in the water. Much of the present lay-out at Wisley is the work of the late Lanning Roper and Geoffrey Jellicoe. Russel Page's work can be seen at Tyninghame and Percy Cane's at Dartington.

Into this highly coloured, highly ornate style of garden planting came William Robinson (1839–1935) with a fierce antipathy towards Italianate gardens stocked with exotic plants. He was in favour of using native plants in mixed herbaceous borders and the wild garden and had the help of Miss Gertrude Jekyll to preach well-ordered, colour-scheme borders as against the kidney- or heart-shaped mosaics of eye-stabbing colours.

From the beginning of the 20th century until the start of the First World War there was a fashion for Japanese gardens in this country and among those still to be seen is Tatton Park in Cheshire. The First World War, purely on the matter of economy, did away with the elaborate schemes of bedding out and greenhouse growing, for neither labour nor money could be spared and British gardens on the big estates were almost back to Brownian grass but now punctuated with the wide range of shrubs and specimen trees which had offered the planters such an eclectic and bewildering choice.

As to the future, economics are going to rule as much as taste and smaller gardens are, as has been demonstrated so well at the Chelsea Flower Show these past few years, going to be a tasteful utilitarian blend of architectural layouts with patio, summerhouse, some water, modern statuary and shrubs and flowers chosen very carefully indeed to integrate with the overall plan. Many with the means to command the many landscape architects and gardeners who ply their trade will get this 'garden room' while the rest of us will imitate as well as we can. More and more of us will go for the labour-saving grace of the hundreds of flowering shrubs available, ground cover, miniature fruit trees and small specimen trees (many chosen for autumn colour) to make our home gardens less labour intensive but colourful, convenient and pleasing to look at and in which we can take our ease.

KEY TO GARDENS

P	Car park		Picnic areas
WC	Toilets		Plant sales
	Public transport		Guide book or leaflet
	Coach parties welcome		Shop
	Dogs allowed – usually on a lead		House or historic building open to the public
	Refreshments		Nature trails

10 miles sw of Hereford off B4347 — Location

SO 3831 — National Grid reference number

Mar to end Oct: daily 1030–1830 — Opening times

Peak months: June to Sept — Peak time, if any, otherwise garden is consistently interesting throughout the opening period

Reference should be made to the following publications for further information: Historic Houses, Castles & Gardens, The National Trust's booklet on properties, The National Trust for Scotland's Year Book, Gardens Open to the Public under the National Gardens Scheme and Scotland's Gardens, a guide to gardens open under Scotland's Gardens Scheme.

Abbey Dore Court HEREFORD and WORCESTER

Mrs C. L. Ward, nr Hereford.

10 miles SW of Hereford off B4347

SO 3831

Mar to end Oct: daily 1030–1830

Peak months: June to Sept

Here one can recognise one's own problems, for Mrs Ward has, since 1968, been reclaiming a fine garden – not too large to be beyond one's dreams – that had fallen into neglect. The reclaimed woodland garden beside the River Dore is a complete success with an underplanting of bluebells, poet's narcissus, sun spurge, Iceland poppy and forget-me-not, and many other shade- and moisture-loving plants. A natural and peaceful composition, combining happily with the sound and reflections of the river. Lovers of rock gardens will be interested in the one beyond the river that Mrs Ward has recently constructed. It contains a wide variety of well-labelled plants. The new herbaceous border set outside and against one of the red-brick walls of the erstwhile kitchen garden is interesting in the same way, for its varied profusion of plants, but the enquiring mind seeks for a reason why this plant should be here, not there, as no overall scheme of planting is apparent. The satisfaction of the new plantings at Abbey Dore is the possibility of identifying unusual attractive plants, for there is an excellent nursery and shop attached from which these delights may be purchased. **E.F.**

Abbotsbury Sub-Tropical Gardens DORSET

The Strangways Estates, Abbotsbury, Weymouth.
tel. Abbotsbury (030 587) 387

9 miles W of Weymouth, off B3157 Weymouth—Bridport road

SY 5685

Mid-Mar to mid-Oct: daily 1000–1800

Peak months: Mar to May, Aug and Sept

Set in a secluded position near Chesil Beach and protected from the cold north-east winds by the lovely Dorset hills behind, the gardens were created by the 1st Countess of Ilchester for her summer residence, Abbotsbury Castle. They were enlarged by the 4th Earl of Ilchester, who planted many unusual trees and tender shrubs in the damp shady woodlands surrounding the original walled garden. The gardens, which were greatly changed under the guidance of Lady Teresa Agnew, a descendant of the first owner, and John Hussey, former head gardener, now cover nearly 17 acres (7ha) of largely informal plantings where peacocks wander freely. Spring comes early to Abbotsbury with its almost sub-tropical climate, beginning with a wonderful display of camellias, azaleas, rhododendrons and magnolias, planted under such magnificent trees as *Pterocarya fraxinifolia*, Caucasian wing nut. A small stream feeds the ponds, where sloping banks provide ideal situations for moisture-loving primulas, gunnera and lysichitum. In the walled garden, large Chusan palms over 100 years old mix happily with *Cornus nuttallii* and *Robinia* 'Frisia'. Lacecap hydrangeas and shrub roses provide summer colour with trees grown for their coloured and textured bark, like the large collection of eucalyptus and the spectacular cinnamon-bark myrtle. **A.S.**

Abbotsford BORDERS

Mrs P. Maxwell-Scott, Melrose, (Roxburghshire).
tel. Galashiels (0896) 2043

On B6360, off A6091 between Galashiels and Melrose

NT 5034

Late Mar to end Oct: Mon to Sat 1000–1700, Sun 1400–1700. Reduced rates for parties

Peak months: May to June and Aug to Sept

It would be quite intolerable to believe that a property which was at one time the home of Sir Walter Scott could have an indifferent, or characterless garden. Sir Walter's love of trees is widely appreciated, and his devotion to his garden is no less apparent. The house was built between 1817–21 on a terrace above the right bank of the River Tweed. To the south of the house a formal garden has been developed as a combination of precisely trimmed yew hedge and historic sculpture, such as the five medallions which came from the old Mercat Cross in Edinburgh and which are inset in the hedge. The bowl of the centrally positioned fountain in the garden was also a part of the same Mercat Cross, and the formality is maintained with four yews planted one at each corner of the fountain lawn. At the other side of the house the garden drifts into the beautiful countryside associated with this stretch of the River Tweed, with the river itself, so beloved by Scott, passing close to the house. Beyond the river are pleasant groups of trees, many of which are reputed to have been planted by Scott himself. On either side of the south entrance one encounters plants of viburnum, old shrub roses, azalea and rhododendron. There is also an early 19th-century fernhouse with begonias, orchids and pelargoniums as well as ferns. **E.R.**

Achamore House Garden STRATHCLYDE

D. W. N. Landale, Esq., Isle of Gigha.
tel. Gigha (058 35) 253

Lying off the Mull of Kintyre in West Scotland, there are several small islands, including Colonsay, Jura and the smallest of all, the Isle of Gigha (pronounced Gia). Barely 3 miles (5km) long by no more than one mile (1.6km) at its widest point, it is nevertheless one of the most fertile of the Hebridean isles. Wild flowers in May are a marvellous sight. This small, windswept, island was purchased in 1944 by the late Lt Colonel Sir James Horlick, Bt., who made Achamore House his home, and the land that surrounds it into a splendid and most remarkable 60 acres (24ha) of woodland garden. Sir James brought from his former Berkshire home laundry basketfuls of rhododendrons, including many of his own hybrids, as the basis for his new garden. To these he added many more during the 29 years he continued to live on Gigha. It surprises many early visitors to find avenues lined with *Rhododendron ciliatum*, or carpets of candelabra primulas, the outstandingly vivid colours of the azalea garden, as much as the glades of wild hyacinths in more open woodland, amazingly sheltered from westerly winds. A walled garden serves both for vegetable growing and to house many outstanding treasures, such as *Rhododendron sinonuttallii*, *Metrosideros*, *Azara dentata* and a handsome and very uncommon *Abies delavayi* var. *delavayi*. **E.R.**

3 miles off Mull of Kintyre: take ferry from Tayinloan, 17 miles s of Tarbert on A83. Garden 1 mile s of ferry terminal: transport arranged through Gigha Village Stores or Gigha Hotel

Daily: 1000–dusk

Peak months: Apr to June

limited opening

Alton Towers STAFFORDSHIRE

J. L. Broome, Esq., Alton.
tel. 0538 702449

Alton Towers is no longer a Stately Home. It is a business', says Ron Sidwell. Evidence of this is clear at the entrance gates, where the charge reflects the range of attractions available, not always of a kind desired by garden lovers. But without the charges this 'oddest and most spectacular collection of ornamental garden architecture in the world', would have disappeared. It was called into being by Charles Talbot, 15th Earl of Shrewsbury, starting in 1812 and continuing under the 16th Earl, until 1835. J. C. Loudon, then arbiter of garden fashion, thought the whole project was 'in excessively bad taste'. His advice had been neglected. However time has been kind to Alton for woods and trees now clothe the hillsides, modify the starkness of the buildings, and blend them into a highly impressive landscape. Robert Abraham's domed Conservatory, and his striking Pagoda Fountain, are famous; both they, the Chinese Temple and the Screw Fountain, must be seen, as must the 'two storied Stonehenge'. Seen from a distance Alton Towers, the house ruinous but partly restored, is impressive and highly romantic; it is a rich man's folly on a scale that can never be repeated and an important, eccentric fragment of our garden history. **E.F.**

5 miles N of Uttoxeter, off B5032 Mayfield—Cheadle road

SK 0742

Late Mar to end Oct: daily 0930–dusk

No peak season

Anglesey Abbey CAMBRIDGESHIRE

The National Trust, Lode, Cambridge.
tel. Cambridge (0223) 811200

Anglesey Abbey was purchased by the first Lord Fairhaven in 1926 and during the next forty years, on flat, windswept farmland, he created a major work of art. The chosen style was a combination of 17th-century formal and 18th-century landscaping, thus the garden is divided by magnificent avenues of chestnut, lime and hornbeam whilst the land between is planted informally with a mixture of interesting trees. The scale for a garden made in this century is immense. The Great Avenue is over half a mile (0.8km) long and has four rows of trees on each side, whilst a broad grass walk between Norway spruce and a beech hedge, and decorated with busts of Roman emperors, stretches for a quarter of a mile (0.4km). The main components of the design are trees, grass, sculpture and water. Flowers there are, but in the 18th-century manner they are hidden from the main views. There are hedged enclosures for hyacinths, dahlias and classic herbaceous borders designed by Vernon Daniel. These are at their best in mid-summer. The wealth of antique garden ornaments and statuary is unrivalled and it has been placed with the same care and grasp of scale which characterises the whole of this magnificent garden. **M.R.**

6 miles NE of Cambridge on B1102

TL 5463

Apr to late May and 1st half of Oct: Wed to Sun (exc Good Fri) and Bank Holiday Mon. Late May to Sept: daily. 1400–1800. Reduced rates for parties of 15 and over by prior arrangement

No peak season

limited opening

limited opening

limited opening

5 miles w of Plymouth via Torpoint car ferry; turn north off A374 at Maryfield

SX 4256

Apr to end Oct: Tue to Thur and Bank Holiday Mon 1400–1800

Peak months: Mar to Apr

P
limited
by appointment only

Antony House CORNWALL

The National Trust, Torpoint, Plymouth.
tel. Plymouth (0752) 812191

From the avenues and tree-dotted park the south front of this early 18th-century house is viewed and entered through a central gate and square grass forecourt. The walls on either side of the gate are clothed with climbing roses and have a rose border in front and the brick arcades have some plants against them. A door on the west of the house leads to the now simplified grounds belonging to the National Trust. They include extensive lawns, some of which replace former Victorian flower beds, a great yew hedge and several free-standing *Magnolia grandiflora* and other individual trees. A clipped yew cone was designed as a garden pavilion and there are many ornaments associated with former generations of the Carew family. Borders in and outside the garden have been planted with many hemerocallis that once formed part of one of the largest collections of this genus in the country. This was the most easterly of the five estates in Cornwall visited by Humphry Repton but like the other four little from his 'Red Books' survives today. A bold group of flowering cherries was planted long after his visit and clumps of evergreen oak planted in 1760 were growing well before his time. A developing woodland garden around the perimeter of the estate with the usual camellias, magnolias and rhododendrons is open separately in the spring. **F.S.**

Between Northwich, Knutsford and Warrington, off B5391 (M6 Exit 19) and off B5356 (M6 Exit 20, M56 Exits 9 and 10)

SJ 6781

Easter to early Oct: daily exc Mon but inc bank holidays 1400–1830. Reduced rates for parties by prior arrangement

Peak months: mid May to Sept

Arley Hall and Gardens CHESHIRE

The Hon. M. L. W. Flower, Northwich.
tel. Arley (056 585) 203/284

The main framework of this unusual garden of 8 acres (3ha) was laid down by Rowland and Mary Egerton-Warburton between 1830 and 1860. Their outstanding contribution was the long, double herbaceous border of 1846 housing buttressing yews, one of the earliest in English gardens. Other features are a unique ilex avenue (*c.*1840) clipped to the shape of giant cylinders, an avenue of pleached limes and the furlong walk (220yd, 201m) bounding the garden. During the last 20 years the owners have made a series of gardens, a scented one of 1977, and a walled herb garden of 1969. The 18th-century walled kitchen garden now has a pond, a copy of one in the Vatican, Dawyck beeches, heraldic beasts, and borders planted with shrubs and herbaceous plants of foliage interest. The fish garden is cleverly planted with spiring cupressus, two *Prunus* 'Yukon' and holly hedges with stone-engraved epitaphs to Rowland Warburton's favourite horses. A 1900 vintage flag garden planted with floribunda roses and dwarf lavender is surrounded by walls clothed with honeysuckle, akebia and *Hydrangea petiolaris*. A former root tree garden, designed as a rock garden, is now planted with azaleas, rhododendrons and other flowering shrubs, ferns and salix. The rose garden was laid out in 1961 in the place of a former formal topiary garden. A romantic tea cottage has verses on the walls written by Rowland Egerton-Warburton to his wife and neighbours. **K.L.**

2 miles SW of Leighton Buzzard on A418 Leighton Buzzard—Aylesbury road

SP 8923

Apr to end Sept: Wed, Thur, and last Sun in each month, also Sat in Aug and Sept and late Aug Bank Holiday Mon 1400–1800. Parties must book in advance

No peak season

limited opening

Ascott BUCKINGHAMSHIRE

The National Trust, Wing, nr Leighton Buzzard.
tel. Wing (029 668) 242

Ascott was once a 17th-century farmhouse until purchased in 1873 by Baron Mayer de Rothschild, whose seat was the neighbouring mansion of Mentmore, for use as a hunting box. It was then purchased by Leopold de Rothschild who used the architect George Devey to build a rambling Tudor-style gabled house in which he housed his famous collection of fabulous works of art. He was also a talented gardener and with the help of Sir Harry Veitch of the Chelsea nurseries' fame, he laid out a remarkable garden of some 30 acres (12ha) whose essential features still survive today. They were completed by 1900. In 1949 the Rothschilds gave Ascott, its contents and grounds to the National Trust. On a pronounced south-facing slope, the gardens offer remarkable contrasts of formality and informality, remarkable and unusual in that the more formal gardens tend to be on the perimeters with essentially spacious lawns and parkland and orchards nearer the house. There is a splendid long terrace walk backed by a wall superbly planted in themes of blue, purple and white. A circular pool with Venus in a shell chariot provides an exotic incident along this terrace, which then ends in a loggia. An evergreen sundial is another unique feature. Further west is another surprise formal flower garden at right angles to the long terrace, superbly bedded out in the summer around a marble tiered fountain. A rock garden (rather wild), a fernery, and informal shrub areas are to be found and fine specimen trees nearer the house. **T.W.**

Ashridge HERTFORDSHIRE

Governors of Ashridge Management College, Berkhamsted.
tel. Little Gaddesden (044 284) 3491

The garden at Ashridge, covering some 90 acres (36ha), can fairly be described as one in which every prospect pleases, from the long vistas over coiffured lawns to the fine specimen trees on every hand and the grandeur of the mansion, which is the personification of early 19th century elegance in the Gothic style. Running the length of the mansion on the south elevation is a terrace bordered throughout its length by plant beds enclosed by cube-shaped, clipped yews. It is from this terrace vantage point that the most impressive vista unfolds: a magnificent avenue of wellingtonias (*Sequoiadendron giganteum*), some 120 years old, which are seen in the middle to far distance across sweeping tree- and shrub-framed lawns. One of the features of Ashridge is its series of individual gardens such as a circular, yew-enclosed rose garden ('The Rosarie') and another sunken rose garden; the Monk's Garden with its Holy Well and parterres of clipped box. Also a heather and conifer garden in a Westmorland limestone rock setting. There is a conservatory; great banks of rhododendrons and a fine arboretum featuring a ring of incense cedars (*Calocedrus decurrens*). For its first 250 years Ashridge was a monastery and then a Royal residence before passing into private ownership in the year 1605. The grandeur of the gardens owes much to Humphry Repton, who was commissioned in the early 19th century to lay out the gardens for the then new mansion. **R.P.**

4 miles N of Berkhamsted off A41

SP 9911

Apr to Oct: Sat and Sun 1400–1800

Peak months: May and June

P
by arrangement only
limited opening

Barnsley House GLOUCESTERSHIRE

Mr and Mrs David Verey, nr Cirencester.
tel. Bibury (028 574) 281

Although not large this garden is worth a lengthy visit, for it contains as many ideas and plants as any comparable space in England. It is tempting to compare David and Rosemary Verey with Harold Nicolson and Vita Sackville-West, the husbands contributing a strong sense of architectural design and the wives the controlled but profuse planting. Mrs Verey's second great contribution is her knowledge of garden history, which is shown not only in the arrangement of plants, but in such features as the tunnel of *Laburnum* 'Vossii', the knot garden and her intricate 'potager' with pyramids of roses and clematis, and cunningly contrived arbours. In the borders round the house, particularly those facing south, is a fascinating collection of plants chosen for shape, colour, scent and year-round interest. The pattern of the garden is set by a wide path of Cotswold stone pointed by pairs of Irish yews which leads to the garden gate and crosses at right angles the laburnum tunnel and its parallel box-lined path, terminating in the Rain Fountain. To the left of the path lies a Doric Temple, its columns and the echoing junipers reflected in a lily and goldfish pool. The main lawn to the west of the house has as its chief ornament an 18th-century summerhouse and terminates in a collection of sorbus and other interesting trees, including a paulownia. In a garden of this kind the house is of great importance, and Barnsley House is worthy of its gardens. Come to admire, to linger and to carry away treasures from the excellent nursery. **E.F.**

4 miles NE of Cirencester on A433 Cirencester—Burford road

SP 0705

Throughout year Wed 1000–1800 (dusk if earlier); also 1st Sun in May, June and July. Parties at other times by appointment

Peak months: Apr to Oct

P

Barrington Court SOMERSET

The National Trust, nr Ilminster.
tel. Ilminster (046 05) 2242

Though Barrington Court was built in 1514, the gardens were not designed until 1920 when Col A. A. Lyle leased the house and sent his plans for the garden to Gertrude Jekyll who made suggestions for the planting. Entering the gardens through the orchard, so beautiful in spring with many daffodils in bloom, a path leads towards the moat and the old 16th-century beef stalls where the old brick pillars and walls make an ideal background for climbing roses and honeysuckle. Nearby is the iris garden, looking at its best in early summer, with small beds filled with bearded irises. Large-flowered (hybrid tea) and clustered-flowered (floribunda) roses scent the summer air in the rose garden and next door is the lily garden where many water-lilies grace the pool and the mixed borders around contain crown imperials, crinums, azaleas and perennials. Very good use is made of every available area of wall space in these gardens, clematis and roses being the favourite climbing plants used. A well laid out kitchen garden is filled with many varieties of vegetables, the walls attractively covered with trained peach, apple and pear trees. The view from the lawn near the south border looks out to the tranquil park beyond the ha-ha, an arboretum stands to the right of this lawn with a lime walk nearby. **A.S.**

3½ miles NE of Ilminster; turn E off B3168 to Barrington, at eastern end of village

ST 3917

Early Apr to late Sept: Sun to Wed 1400–1730, also few days under National Gardens Scheme and Gardeners' Benevolent Society. Reduced rates for parties visiting garden

Peak months: May to Sept

P
by appointment only
limited opening

Batsford Park Arboretum GLOUCESTERSHIRE

Batsford Estates Company, Moreton-in-Marsh.
tel. Moreton-in-Marsh (0608) 50722 or Blockley (0386) 700409

1½ miles north of
Moreton-in-Marsh off
A44 Evesham—
Chipping Norton road

SP 1833

Apr to Oct: daily
1000–1700

Peak months: May,
June and Oct

☐ by appointment
only

The foundations of this garden arboretum were laid by Lord Redesdale, who created a garden in the oriental style with carefully considered groupings of water and rocks, garden buildings and ornaments, set among a collection of trees and shrubs. During the war, and until the present Lord Dulverton succeeded in 1966, little change was made to the garden. He then decided to reclaim it and expand its contents into an arboretum. The collection is now outstanding. A guidebook describes the arboretum in detail, but among the evergreens there are fine groups of cedars, Californian redwoods, Western hemlocks, and of that often bare-legged tree *Chamaecyparis lawsoniana* 'Erecta Viridis'. Batsford is naturally at its best either in spring, when the magnolias and cherries are in flower, or in autumn when the reds, yellows and golds from Japanese maples, red oaks, beeches, chestnuts, and cherries flame against the background of evergreens. There is an enormous variety of trees at Batsford, a mecca for students, but its well contrived effects make it a place that everyone will enjoy. **E.F.**

Beares SUFFOLK

S. A. Notcutt Esq., Saxtead, Woodbridge.
tel. Framlingham (0728) 723232

1 mile NE of Saxtead
Green on A1120

TM 2566

Open infrequently in
summer, frequently in
autumn, ring for
details

Peak months: June to
July, Sept to Oct

'Beares' is a delightful plantsman's garden created by the present owners over a period of twenty years. It covers 2½–3 acres (1ha) on a southern slope around an old farmhouse and its ponds. The soil is alkaline clay improved with pulverized bark, sharp sand and compost. The design grew around the existing paths, hedges and mature trees; only the raised terrace with its mixture of paving, lawn and beds was planned on paper. The rural nature of the site has been preserved by the informality, the retention of ditches, even when these cut across the garden, and in the cottage garden style of planting. The one element providing strong contrast is a wide, straight grass path, flanked by deep borders, running the full depth of the garden. Over 1000 varieties of trees, shrubs and plants are grown and all are labelled. A varied selection of evergreens forms a background for lilacs and hibiscus and for the autumn colours of rhus, photinia, acers and sorbus. Unusual trees include *Aesculus neglecta* 'Erythroblastos' with brilliant pink young leaves, and paulownia which regularly sets buds but flowers only in a good spring. Plants and alpines have been chosen for their ability to provide ground cover. The house is clothed with fremontodendron, carpenteria and *Abutilon* 'Kentish Belle.' **M.R.**

Bedgebury National Pinetum KENT

The Forestry Commission, Goudhurst, Cranbrook.
tel. Goudhurst (0580) 211392

10 miles SW of
Tunbridge Wells off
A21 on B2079

TQ 7234

Daily: 1000–dusk

Peak months: May to
July

limited opening

Scarcely a garden in the accepted sense, this unique place has been included in this book because it has probably the largest single collection of conifers in Europe and was designed from the outset to be a place of great landscape attraction. It has been developed over the past 50 years or so by the Royal Botanic Gardens, Kew and more recently the Forestry Commission, using part of the former grounds of nearby Bedgbury Park (now a girl's school). A well-wooded setting of valleys, streams and a lake proved an ideal place to establish the Pinetum although the soils are exceptionally acid, and frosts actually occur here every month of the year! In the original design by W. Dallimore of Kew, conifers are mostly grouped in genera, but interspersed with deciduous trees, many being fine old oaks once part of the ancient Wealden Forest. He also laid out rides and vistas now reaching fine maturity. Particular features are the unusual Brewers' weeping spruces in the Spruce Valley, the Lawson cypress collection of over 30 different cultivars, gold, silver, blue, weeping, dwarf and tall – a remarkable sight. The wellingtonia grove is still growing rapidly after 50 years and may reach impressive heights in the next century or so. In contrast, a comparatively new addition is the dwarf conifer collection near the information centre, nicely labelled and laid out. **T.W.**

Beningbrough Hall NORTH YORKSHIRE

The National Trust, Shipton-by-Beningbrough, York.
tel. York (0904) 470715

In a print of 1720 geometrically patterned parterres are shown on the south front of Beningbrough, to be replaced later in the century by large lawns and a ha-ha to give watermeadow views to the winding River Ouse. The wilderness and two small, restored privy gardens east and west of the hall entrance remain from the old style. That on the west has a simple geometric pattern of dwarf hedges with borders of red, yellow and orange plants while that on the east, paved and pebbled, holds more subtle colourings round a pool with central fountain. Predominant on the south lawn is a 14ft (4m) high vast Portugal laurel hedge. An attractive specimen of the variegated oak is at the east end of the terrace and the long border beyond, of fairly recent planting, leads to well-filled double herbaceous borders hemmed in by walls and a noble yew hedge. The kitchen garden is now grassed over but the central walk is arched over and avenued by espaliered and trained pears. A path by the far kitchen garden wall shelters a fig and the rare *Jasminum beesianum*. Further on is the American garden developed in the 19th century where rhododendrons, kalmia, sassafras and magnolia, a walnut and oaks keep up the name. On the west side of the house is a Victorian conservatory while the wilderness includes walnuts, bamboos, snowberries and hollies. **K.L.**

8 miles NW of York, turn W off A19 York—Thirsk road at Shipton (signposted)

SE 5258

Apr to end Oct: Tue to Thur, Sat, Sun, and Bank Holiday Mon 1100–1800

No peak season

P
⊘1-mile walk

Benington Lordship HERTFORDSHIRE

Mr and Mrs C. H. A. Bott, Benington, Stevenage.
tel. Benington (043 885) 668

Some gardens are exceptionally fortunate in their owners, witness the garden at Benington Lordship which has during the past decade been restored to a degree which gives it exceptional charm and interest. But this garden, with delightful vistas over rural Hertfordshire is unusual and intriguing in many ways. Mr Bott's grandfather bought the property early this century, adding a wing to the house and creating the garden in its present form. A Norman castle formerly occupied a site adjacent to the present house, where, in 1832, a folly incorporating an entrance gateway was erected. Behind this is a courtyard winter garden. The real delights of this intensely 'English' garden, however, lie on the west side of the house where below a lawn-framed formal rose garden, grass banks fall away to two Norman fish ponds, which have also been restored. At the end of one of these pools is a rock and water garden leading to turn to the superb double-sided herbaceous border which, for the summer-time visitor, is an unfailing attraction. There is also a small, intimate dell garden with lawns sloping down to a statue of Shylock. This is a garden in which all can delight. **R.P.**

4 miles E of Stevenage, midway between B1037 and A602

TL 2923

Easter Mon and May to July: Wed, Sun and May Bank Holiday Mon 1400–1700. At other times by appointment

Peak months: May to July

P
⊘not Sun
by arrangement only

Benthall Hall SHROPSHIRE

The National Trust, Broseley.
tel. Telford (0952) 882254

Benthall Hall came into horticultural history in 1886 when George Maw, its tenant and a local tile manufacturer, wrote his classic work there, 'The Genus Crocus'. His crocuses were grown in pits covered with frames. Their descendants, both spring and autumn flowering, so heavily hybridised as to make identification impossible, now occupy a large area of the garden. The Benthalls returned to their family home in 1934, and the present occupiers, Sir Paul and Lady Benthall, have kept the garden largely as they found it. The raised and terraced garden to the west of the house contains many unusual and interesting plants, including one of the few specimens in England of *Dipteronia sinensis*, a member of the maple family, the Japanese sacred cherry, which Sir Paul got from Collingwood Ingram; a white tree peony, *Paeonia suffruticosa alba*, and the Californian fuchsia, *Zauschneria californica*. *Rosa alba* 'Celeste' springs up unexpectedly here and there, a charming companion for 'Grüs an Aachen'. The beautiful Elizabethan house, the church (with its medieval tiles, Laudian altar rails and picture by Edward Burra), the garden and surrounding landscape fit happily together and make a satisfying visit. Come particularly in early spring, June or September. **E.F.**

4 miles NE of Much Wenlock; turn N off B4375 between Posenhall and Benthall

SO 6503

Easter Sat to end Sept: Tue, Wed, Sat and Bank Holiday Mon 1400–1800

Peak months: June and Sept

P

4 miles N of
Leominster on A49
Leominster—Ludlow
road

SO 5165

Apr and Oct: Sat,
Sun and Bank
Holiday Mon
1400–1700. May to
Sept: Wed to Sun
and Bank Holiday
Mon 1400–1800

No peak season

🅿️◼️⊕
🚻 by appointment
only
🕳️👜✠🏠

Berrington Hall HEREFORD and WORCESTER

The National Trust, nr Leominster.
tel. Leominster (0568) 5721

The house was begun in 1776 for the Hon Thomas Harley, the MP for Herefordshire, by Lancelot ('Capability') Brown and his son-in-law, Henry Holland. The park remains much as Brown left it, including the 14-acre (5.7-ha) lake in the south-east corner. The present Lord Cawley has been responsible for planting the collection of interesting, and sometimes rare shrubs and plants. The drive leading to the south front is flanked by the Chinese winter-sweet (*Chimonanthus fragrans*), magnolias, mountain ashes and the Syrian hibiscus. A woodland garden runs along much of the west boundary and is planted with many agreeable shrubs including the May bush (*Kolkwitzia amabilis*), mock orange, and deutzias. The lawns in front are, in early autumn, bright with the spires of ladies' tresses orchids, and followed by a carpet of *Cyclamen neapolitanum* in pink and white. The rare shrubs are planted on the sunny walls of the walled garden. The rarest is that perennial relation of the vegetable marrow *Thalidiantha oliveri*, a climber with rich yellow flowers. A striking combination is the large-flowered *Clematis* 'William Kennett', lavender blue, and the orange flowers of *Eccremocarpus scaber* from Chile. The mild climate also allows *Buddleia colvilei*, varieties of crinodendron, and *Carpenteria californica* to flourish. As a combination of Brown park and unusual plants Berrington has much to offer. **E.F.**

6 miles S of Tavistock
off A386 Plymouth—
Tavistock road

SX 4965

Apr to May: Sun,
May bank holidays
and infrequently in
summer under
National Gardens
Scheme. Other times
by appointment

Peak months: Apr and
May

🅿️◼️
⊖1-mile walk
🚻👜🍽️

Bickham House DEVON

The Lord Roborough, Roborough, Plymouth.
tel. Yelverton (0822) 852478

This series of gardens is entered along a curving drive through well-farmed parkland. The gardens open out from the level lawns and beds around the house to a long path through grass and shrubs to the more recently developed gardens below Bickham Barton. There the former farmyard has been cleared and now contains a pond with developing water plants. The former kitchen garden has been divided by rows of conifers and one half contains a good collection of wall shrubs with rose beds and borders giving a good summer display. Outside the walls, south-facing greenhouses and the sites of others allow tender plants, including a large fig, to be grown. Below them again a paddock is being planted with shrubs. At the bottom of this slope a curving path is flanked by an imaginative row of alternate white prunus and the lovely blue *Rhododendron augustinii* that flower together with striking results. At one end this path opens into an old wood with a few large trees, deciduous and coniferous, surviving but interplanted in recent years with more trees and many shrubs. Mown paths traverse this developing arboretum. Near the walled rose garden an enclosed lawn has seats and statuary with surrounding rhododendrons, including some ancient *R. arboreum* and younger plants of the scented Loder hybrids. Daffodils and other bulbs are plentiful in the spring and autumn cyclamen give a little late colour while extensive views from several vantage points add to the attractions. **F.S.**

1 mile N of East
Budleigh, W of A376
Budleigh Salterton—
Newton Poppleford
road

SY 0786

Daily, exc Christmas
and New Year weeks:
Apr to Oct
1000–1800; Nov to
Mar 1000–dusk

No peak season

🅿️◼️⊖🚻🕳️
👜🍽️✠✽🏠🌺

Bicton Park DEVON

Otter Leisure Enterprises Limited, East Budleigh.
tel. Budleigh Salterton (0395) 68475

Much of the gardener's craft of bygone days is preserved among the tourist attractions in this extensive garden. Separate greenhouses contain cacti, temperate and tropical plants, and birds. An important early greenhouse (*c.*1820), built tall for palms, is now filled with many tender plants. Spring and summer bedding provides splashes of colour when viewed from the curved range of greenhouses over the Italian-style terraces. The view takes in a rectangular pool, fountains and sculptures, to a distant obelisk through a landscaped gap in hill and woodland. The many and varied old deciduous and coniferous trees have received much skilled surgery and young replacements are starting on their long life. The original mansion now, with the surrounding farmland, the Devon College of Agriculture, overlooks a large lake and the trees. A comprehensive dwarf conifer collection is relieved by drifts of heather and provides useful examples for those who would add a few of these solid reliable plants to their own gardens. In the same way a new pergola beside a canal will provide interest when covered by the newly planted collection of climbing plants. There are rock gardens, wall and other shrubs, herbaceous and water plants, all bearing witness of continuing skilled attention – even if not within the gardeners' rules of 1842 still displayed on a large board on one of the walls. Visitors may walk or travel by miniature railway or ancient cars through these gardens, park and pinetum. **F.S.**

Blenheim Park and Gardens OXFORDSHIRE

His Grace the Duke of Marlborough, Woodstock.
tel. Woodstock (0993) 811325

Blenheim can justly claim to be one of the grandest and most spectacular gardens in Britain. The 1st Duke of Marlborough employed Sir John Vanbrugh as the architect and Queen Anne's gardener, Henry Wise, to build the magnificent palace and formal gardens. A great 77-acre (31-ha) formal parterre was laid out to the south of the palace and half a mile (0.8km) away a huge high-walled kitchen garden was made in the wooded park. Vanbrugh constructed the monumental grand bridge over what was then the very meagre River Glyme. In 1764 Lancelot ('Capability') Brown arrived to transform the garden and parkland, sweeping away the great parterre (his 'grass to the very door' approach), planting many belts and clumps of trees in the 2,000-acre (809-ha) park and most brilliant of all damming the River Glyme at its south end to create two great winding lakes, flowing through Vanbrugh's bridge, ending with a dramatic cascade in a rocky, picturesque landscape. A double avenue of elms was planted to the north representing the battle formation at Blenheim (still to be seen today). Some restoration of the formal style came in the 1920s when the 9th Duke engaged the French designer Achille Duchene to make an Italian garden and new terraces with fountains and hedged scroll pattern. All these features can be enjoyed today with many added family attractions to bring the vital revenue needed to maintain such a vast enterprise. **T.W.**

8 miles NW of Oxford on A34 Oxford—Stratford road

SP 4516

Mid-Mar to end Oct: daily 1100–1800. Reduced rates for parties

Peak seasons: spring and autumn

Blickling Hall NORFOLK

The National Trust, Blickling.
tel. Aylsham (0263) 733084

The enormous 400-year-old yew hedges flanking the forecourt give an indication of the delights to be enjoyed in the superbly maintained gardens of this romantic Jacobean house. They include a large parterre with clipped topiary and a central fountain, designed in the 19th century by Nesfield and Digby Wyatt, but simplified in the 1930s by Nancy Lindsey who reduced the number of beds and planted them with perennials and polyantha roses. It is unusual to employ herbaceous plants in such a setting but they are entirely successful, due to the subtle colour schemes and carefully graduated heights. Beyond the parterre a wide path bisects a 17th-century formal woodland garden and leads through azaleas and rhododendrons to a Doric temple. The woodland is intersected by radiating rides and surrounded by a raised terrace walk from which can be reached an orangery, probably designed by Repton or his son. The remainder of the garden consists of an early landscaped park, later improved by Repton, with a beautiful man-made lake over a mile (1.6km) in length. There is much of horticultural interest, including tender climbers, unusual shrubs, naturalised cyclamen, and a famous oriental plane which, by means of layering, has grown to a tremendous size. **M.R.**

10 miles S of Cromer on B1354 Saxthorpe—Aylsham road

TG 1828

Apr to late May and Oct: Tue, Wed, Fri to Sun (closed Good Fri) and Bank Holiday Mon 1400–1800. Late May to Sept: Tue, Wed, Fri, Sat and Bank Holiday Mon 1100–1800; Mon, Thur and Sun 1400–1800.

Peak months: May to Aug

limited opening
limited opening
limited opening

Bodnant Garden GWYNEDD

The National Trust, Tal-y-Cafn, Colwyn Bay.

Bodnant must be rated as one of the great gardens of the world. Developed since 1874 by three generations of Aberconways with three generations of Puddles as the head-gardeners, it is distinguished firstly for its amazing range of plants, next for its superb views to the mountains of Snowdonia, and then for the variety and scope of its design. The garden falls into three main sections, the Italianate terraces descending in front of the house constructed by the late Lord Aberconway between 1905 and 1915, the shrub borders above the River Hiraethlyn and flanked by the park, and the Dell, deep below full of great conifers, rhododendrons, and primulas. The soil is a stiff boulder clay, overlying a friable shaly rock. Pride of place goes to the rhododendrons, magnolias and camellias, all spring flowering, the summer display is concentrated on the terraces, roses, water-lilies and clematis, but throughout the garden there is leaf colour in the autumn. The basic structure of the garden is achieved by backgrounds of large native trees, mostly planted about 1792, by abundant running water, and by the dramatic fall of the land. Horticulturists will be overwhelmed by the endless variety of the species grown, and every visitor will be impressed by the views, the dramatic changes from sunny terrace to shady depths and by the knowledge and devoted skill that has made Bodnant into one of the wonder gardens. **E.F.**

8 miles S of Colwyn Bay on A470 Llanrwst road; entrance ½ mile down road to Eglwysbach

SH 8073

Mid-March to end Oct: daily 1000–1700. Reduced rates for parties of 20 and over by prior arrangement

Peak months: May to Sept

not Oct

TQ 3226

Mar and Oct: Sat and Sun. Apr to Sept: Wed, Thur, Sat, Sun and Bank Holiday Mon 1000–1800 (dusk in Oct). Reduced rates for parties of 20 or over

No peak season

🅿 ♿ 🚻 ☕ 🚻 ♥ 🌷 ❦ ✿

Borde Hill Garden WEST SUSSEX

Borde Hill Garden Ltd., Haywards Heath.
tel. Haywards Heath (0444) 450326

One of the largest Sussex gardens covering 400 acres (162ha) of ornamental gardens, woodland and parkland. The original house dates from the early 1600s but it was considerably enlarged in the last century in the neo-Elizabethan style by the Stephenson Clarke family. Robert Stephenson Clarke began the planting in the 1890s by creating a pinetum and arboretum on the grand scale, including many rare and unusual trees and shrubs and also developing ornamental gardens around the house. Two successive generations have continued his work and the family are members of the Borde Hill Trust which administers the gardens today. The more intensively designed gardens around the house are fascinating and full of interest. Rhododendrons, azaleas, magnolias, and camellias are brilliant, huge, and abundant in May and early June. The collection of rhododendrons alone is enormous. The more intimate herbaceous borders close to the house are lovely in June, edged with effective alchemilla. Several new and attractive features include the Bride's Pool, the replanted west bank terrace, using more half-hardy summer shrubs and colourful perennials, and the very clever conversion of the roofless old potting sheds to tiny garden rooms. Further afield are woodland trails and walks and then excellent restaurant and tea rooms to regale the wanderer on his return. **T.W.**

3 miles N of Kettering off A43 Kettering—Stamford road, on Geddington—Grafton Underwood road

SP 9081

Open frequently between spring and autumn. Ring for details

Peak months: Apr and June

🅿 ♿ 🚻 🚻 ♥
♥ when house open or by arrangement for parties
🚻 🌷 ❦ 🎪 🏠 ✿

Boughton House NORTHAMPTONSHIRE

His Grace the Duke of Buccleuch and Queensberry K.T., Geddington, Kettering.
tel. Kettering (0536) 82248

The magnificent, quintessentially English sweep of parkland in which is set the mansion of Boughton House – itself, on its north elevation, reminiscent of a palace in the style of Versailles – cannot but make one ponder Britain's past history and reflect that the English Channel, while a barrier in the physical sense, has never been an impediment to cultural influence. Originally the property of the Abbey of Bury St Edmunds, Boughton House passed into the ownership of the Montagu family in the early 16th century to be metamorphosised into the impressive mansion it remains to this day. The 1st and 2nd Dukes of Montagu created, in the late 17th and early 18th centuries, a huge parterre with fountains to the west of the mansion as well as other parterres and other water features, including large pools. One of these pools beyond the 'wilderness' garden of trees, shrubs and statuary, incorporated a cascade. Avenues, almost all of elm, were also planted at this time on a monumental scale. Because of Dutch elm disease none of these avenues remain, except some of small lime trees by the house, a magnificent lime tree avenue to the south of the house and an avenue to the west of the house, originally of elm but replanted with poplar. Virtually all the other garden features referred to were to fade away in the two centuries which followed. Some, however, have been re-created by the present owner, the Duke of Buccleuch and Queensberry, whose ancestors acquire the property in the mid-18th century, when the 3rd Duke of Buccleuch married the heiress and daughter of the last Duke of Montagu. So, today, it is possible to enjoy once more at Boughton the view of the Broad Water over sweeping lawns; the well-stocked lily pond and the star pond fed by the cascade. Also, a delightful, circular rose garden, a long south-facing herbaceous border, a symphony of soft colours in summer, and an abundance of magnificent trees in equally magnificent surroundings. Superb vistas abound. **R.P.**

3 miles N of Kettering off A43 Kettering—Stamford road, on Geddington—Grafton Underwood road

SP 9081

Open few times each year under National Gardens Scheme and occasionally by appointment

No peak season

🅿 ♿ 🚻 🌷

Dower House Garden NORTHAMPTONSHIRE

Sir David and Lady Scott, Boughton House, Kettering.

The Dower House, the home of Sir David and Lady Scott, needs no introduction to plantsmen for its garden, alas only opened to the public a few times a year, is a Mecca for those who appreciate fine plants. It comprises an intimate, enclosed garden adjoining the house which includes a superb collection of choice plants, from climbers and wall shrubs to roses, hardy plants in beds and alpines, and other dwarf plants in 23 stone sinks and a large stone trough. On a higher level, across a driveway, is a fruit and vegetable garden and some 200yd (183m) of raised beds which provide an ideal environment for another collection of outstanding small plants. Beyond that is some 2 acres (0.8ha) of garden devoted to trees, shrubs, bulbous plants and woodland plants grown for the most part in island beds set in mown grass. This is an exceptional garden of especial interest to the horticulturally well-informed. **R.P.**

Bowood House WILTSHIRE

The Earl of Shelburne, Calne.
tel. Calne (0249) 812102

The summer spectacle of hundreds of roses blooming in neat beds on the formal terraces in front of the magnificent orangery, contrasts well with broad columnar clipped yews standing in areas of lawn and divided by gravel paths, stone steps, walls and balustrades. *Magnolia grandiflora* and climbing roses are trained against the walls with lavender used as an edging plant in some places, stone urns placed at intervals along the walls are filled in summer with pelargoniums. From the East Terrace a breath-taking view of the Pleasure Grounds and long 40-acre (16-ha) lake can be seen, the latter designed by Lancelot ('Capability') Brown. A broad path leads towards the Cascade and Doric Temple at the north end of the lake, passing hollies, acres and hydrangeas planted in the shelter of the kitchen garden wall. Under the many superb trees, narcissi grow in great drifts, mingling with the carpets of bluebells. The pinetum that lies to the left of the path, was designed in 1848 and contains many notable conifers including redwoods, Sitka spruce, Monterey pine and monkey puzzle trees. During May and June, the rhododendron walks in the separate woodland gardens are open, where beech and oak shelter the numerous varieties of rhododendron that create such a blaze of colour. **A.S.**

2 miles w of Calne off A4 Chippenham— Calne road

ST 9769

Good Fri to end Sept: daily exc Mon but inc bank holidays. Suns in Oct 1100–1800. Reduced rates for parties by prior arrangement

Peak months: Apr to Sept

Branklyn Garden TAYSIDE

National Trust for Scotland, Dundee Road, Perth.
tel. Perth (0738) 25535

It was in 1922 that John and Dorothy Renton built their home, Branklyn. In subsequent years their interest in ericaceous and alpine plants increased as their knowledge extended, and so their garden grew until it reached the present size of just under 2 acres (0.8ha). Dorothy Renton was undoubtedly a cultivator of great ability. Fortunately for them they lived at a period especially rich in the results of plant collecting expeditions: their friends included, among others, George Sherriff. Specialities of the garden are numerous. Primulas and meconopsis are the backbone of an extensive collection, which includes rhododendrons, trees and shrubs, and an outstanding representation of alpine plants. To house all this there are two sections of rock garden, one recently rebuilt and extended, and a series of peat walls in various parts of the garden. At the far east end there are several large rhododendron, of which *R. fictolacteum* and *R. baurevie* are especially good. Most of the well-known meconopsis are represented, plus one or two rarer species, like *M. sherriffii*. The alpine for which the garden is particularly well-known is the fortunately now not so rare, *Paraquilegia anemoides*. It is indeed an outstanding plant with clear blue flowers and grey foliage. John Renton bequeathed Branklyn to The National Trust for Scotland in 1967. Today it reflects the interests of the Rentons and remains as a lasting memorial to two enthusiastic gardeners. **E.R.**

1½ miles E of Perth on A85 Dundee road

NO 1322

Mar to end Oct: daily 1000–dusk

Peak months: April to June

Bressingham Hall NORFOLK

Alan Bloom, Esq., Diss.
tel. Diss (0379) 88243

Bressingham Gardens are a place of pilgrimage for all who enjoy beautiful and original gardens, but especially for those who love hardy herbaceous plants, for here Alan Bloom has built up a collection of around 5,000 species and varieties. This collection is certainly the largest of its kind in Britain and it includes many plants which are the result of hybridisation or selection on his adjoining nursery. The garden covers 6 acres (2.4ha) and the planting incorporates many alpines, ornamental grasses, bog plants and aquatics, for which pools were constructed at the lowest point. A more recent addition has been a smaller area devoted to heathers and conifers. The garden is completely informal in style, with the plants growing in large island beds of curving outline on a gently undulating site, the contours being cleverly exploited by the placing of the beds and the retaining of banks by low walls of Norfolk flint. The design is particularly successful where the beds occupy most of the space and the grass is reduced to broad curving paths. The views are enormously enhanced by the presence of magnificent native trees to which have been added many introduced species, especially conifers. **M.R.**

2½ miles w of Diss on A1066 Diss—Thetford road

TM0880

Sun: May to Sept; Thur: June to 2nd in Sept; Wed: Aug; Easter Sun and bank holidays. 1330–1800

Peak months: June to Aug

171

1½ miles north of
Brodick off A841

NS 0139

Daily: 1000–1700.
Reduced rates for
parties

No peak season

P ■ ○ 市
■ limited opening
⚑ limited opening
♣

Brodick Castle Gardens and Country Park
STRATHCLYDE

National Trust for Scotland, Brodick Castle, Brodick, Isle of Arran.
tel. Brodick (0770) 2202

Brodick Castle had been the home of the Dukes of Hamilton since 1503, and remained as such until the death of Mary, Duchess of Montrose caused the estate to be accepted in lieu of Estate Duty, at which time it was placed in the care of The National Trust for Scotland. The garden now has an almost international reputation for the remarkable collection of rhododendrons to be found there. Rather surprisingly, it is not old, having been begun by the late Duchess around the 1920s with a large initial stock from Muncaster, Westmorland, and Tresco, Isle of Scilly. Contributions from plant-collecting expeditions proved very rewarding and undoubtedly many of these provided the basis of the outstanding quality of the plants which now exist. The other notable part of the garden is the formal walled garden to the east of the Castle, which has the date 1710 inscribed in the lintel of the north door. Formerly a kitchen garden, it was developed as a rose garden by the Duchess and has recently been restored to the Victorian style in which it was first conceived by her. There are many fine trees, which include exotic Chilean plants like the lantern tree, (*Crinodendron*), and the magnificent *Populus lasiocarpa* and several *Nothofagus*. The woodland garden is a wonderful fragrant place to be in spring, while the restored Victorian garden supplies ample colour during the summer. **E.R.**

6 miles w of Banbury
turn off A422
Stratford—Banbury
towards Alkerton and
take turning opposite
war memorial

SP 3743

Apr to end Oct: daily
by appointment and
several weekends
under National
Gardens Scheme

No peak season

P ■ ⚿
○ limited
☐ 市
■ limited opening and
for parties by
arrangement
⊞
♈ occasional
⊞ limited opening

Brook Cottage OXFORDSHIRE

Mr and Mrs David Hodges, Alkerton, nr Banbury.
tel. Edge Hill (029 587) 303

A lovely garden, outstanding in its clever and attractive designs, and modern in that it was begun less than 20 years ago and has been developing ever since. The original cottage, now sensitively enlarged, stands on quite a steep north-west facing slope. When Mr and Mrs David Hodges came here in 1964 they quickly realised the potentialities of the site, and in designing the garden they concentrated on four features in particular – terracing and levels, enclosure, the clever and varied use of water, and above all, a wonderful variety of plant associations carefully selected for colour and contrast of effects. The main terrace beyond the house leads from a tiny paved courtyard contained by the L-shaped house with cool green hostas and climbers. A new stone wall and yew hedges partially enclose the terrace and a border along one side is of mainly a blue, pink and grey theme. Columnar cypresses in sunken 'pedestals' of old millstones give a sense of formality here. Water suddenly appears as tiny rills running down each side of broad steps leading to the next level, the main lawn. A bed here of the rose 'Apricot Nectar' fronted by *Iris pallida variegata* is very striking. Mystery and surprise are also characteristic of so many other features of Brook Cottage; copper beech hedges around a secret garden, a beautifully planted pool, a broad expanse of the valley lawn with its new lake and tree planting, a wilder tree and shrub area with spring bulbs and, high above the garden, a prospect from the top terrace, where a fine stone wall shows off marvellous plant associations. **T.W.**

3½ miles west of
Skipton on A59
Skipton—Clitheroe
road

SD 9452

Open once a year
under National
Gardens Scheme.
Other days for parties
by appointment

Peak season: summer

P ■ ○
⚑ parties of 15–30 by
appointment only

Broughton Hall NORTH YORKSHIRE

H. R. Tempest, Esq., Skipton.
tel. Skipton (0756) 2267

One of the best surviving examples of William Andrew Nesfield's work is to be seen at Broughton Hall, the home of the Tempest family since Elizabethan times. Nesfield worked at Broughton for Sir Charles Tempest from 1855 to 1857 on what he said was his most difficult assignment. He had to excavate at the rear of the house not only to make way for an already designed conservatory and for a courtyard with balustraded retaining walls and a Dolphin fountain but also to give scale and effect to views from the house windows and open up the view. A rising lawn behind was created by him with a central path. The sloping lawn at the north front had already been given a retaining wall, balustrading and a terminating Italianate pavilion or open gazebo and this is where he laid down his magnificent scroll and feather parterre of his tapis verte, meticulously edged in box, the interstices filled with coloured spas and stone. Nesfield placed the existing statues in flower beds no longer there. A short distance from the parterre is the fairy walk along the top of the ha-ha covered with daffodils in spring and leading to the grove woodland. Broughton Beck, canalised and cascaded in 1792, runs through sloping parkland where mature trees grace the turf. The old kitchen garden's 18th-century walls are flued and there is a curiously ornamented stone building at the side of the rear lawn. **K.L.**

Brympton d'Evercy SOMERSET

Charles Clive-Ponsonby-Fane, Esq., nr Yeovil.
tel. West Coker (093 586) 2528

How imposing Brympton House looks, standing serenely in a wall-enclosed setting, the green of the well-kept lawns contrasting beautifully with the mellow stone, and borders in front of the house walls planted with shrubs, perennials and bulbs such as the lovely white-flowered *Allium triquetrum*. Roses climb the walls of the Priest House, now a country life museum, that lies to the right of the house and nearby St Andrew's Church completes this tranquil picture. Abutilon, euonymus and roses are trained up the south front and herbs grow along the terrace that runs below. From here the view is across gently sloping lawns to the very large pond, where ducks dabble among the water-lilies. There are herbaceous borders on either side of stone steps leading from the terrace. Around the pond are beds of newly planted shrubs, one devoted to golden-foliage specimens, while another is filled with grey- and red-leaved varieties to show how well plants of those two colours complement each other. Behind the Clock Tower the vineyard is situated with its neatly trained rows of vines stretched out most attractively across the terrace. A large bed of shrubs separates the vineyard from the old stables. **A.S.**

4 miles w of Yeovil off A3088 Yeovil—Taunton (Montacute) road

ST 5215

Easter weekend (Fri to Mon) and May to late Sept: daily (exc Thur and Fri) 1400–1800. Reduced rates for parties by prior arrangement

Peak months: May to July

Burford House Gardens HEREFORD and WORCESTER

John Treasure, Esq., Tenbury Wells.
tel. Tenbury Wells (0584) 810777

Control is the essence of this garden; nothing has been done without consideration; the self discipline of its maker is matched by his creative flair, and informed by an architectural training. John Treasure and his brother bought this fine 18th-century house with a derelict garden in 1954, their ambition being to create a modern garden, in keeping with the formality of the building, and to found a nursery to sell the plants grown. The starting point was 4 acres (1.6ha) of ground, bounded on one side by the River Teme, containing a London plane, a copper beech, a Scots pine, and a few boundary trees. It is not easy to invent a style that is suitable for the growing of a wide variety of plants, which creates points of view, vistas, open areas of parade and sequestered, secret gardens harmoniously blended, still providing the essential element of surprise, but this John Treasure has achieved. For those less interested in design, the wealth of plants is its own reward. Clematis were Mr Treasure's first love and some 130 examples are to be found, not all pinned against walls, but mounting trees, tangling with shrubs, or pegged along the ground. There are alpine gems below the heather slope, old-fashioned roses back several of the borders, and the stream gardens are rich with moisture-loving plants – all are healthy, have been placed with artistry and care, not a weed to be seen, a model for us all. **E.F.**

7 miles sw of Ludlow on A456, ½ mile west of Tenbury Wells

SO 5868

Good Fri to early Oct: daily 1400–1700. Reduced rates for parties of 30 and over by arrangement.

No peak season

Burnby Hall Gardens HUMBERSIDE

Stewart's Burnby Hall Gardens and Museum Trust, Pocklington.
tel. Pocklington (07592) 2068/2113

In 1904 after extensive world travels, Major P. M. Stewart made out of two ploughed fields at his home in Pocklington a pool, the Upper Water, for private fishing and swimming some 205yd (187m) long and 66yd (60m) wide and, in 1910, built a second pool, the Lower Water, with running water and cascades joining the two. In 1920 the Upper Water was extended to cover 1½ acres (0.6ha) and more trout were given a home. But in 1935 the whole project was changed and the Major started to build up a water-lily collection in his two pools, so that by 1950 some 5,000 plants in 58 species and varieties filled the Burnby Hall water with summer glory. Many other species and varieties were tried out but would not stand the northern climate so that now Burnby Hall has 5,000 blooms to show every day in July, though there are lilies to see from May to mid-September. The lakeside and walk by the stream, with pleasing glimpses of the Wolds in the distance, have been planted with hundreds of differing marginals and bog plants while rock gardens by the wayside display alpines and rock plants. There are decorative trees and shrubs too and 'tame' ornamental fish which almost eat out of the hand. In the grounds is a museum housing the Major's big game successes and ethnological exhibits from many countries, all given to Pocklington along with the gardens after Major Stewart's death in 1962. **K.L.**

13 miles E of York on B1247 in southern outskirts of Pocklington off A1079 York—Hull road

SE 8048

Easter to Sept: daily. Reduced rates for parties

Peak months: late June to mid-Sept

TL 4456

Mon to Sat (exc 25 and 26 Dec): 0800–1930 or dusk (summer), 0800–dusk (winter); also Sun (May to Sept) 1430–1830

No peak season

Cambridge University Botanic Garden

CAMBRIDGESHIRE

Cambridge

Cambridge University moved its Botanic Garden to the present 40-acre (16ha) site in 1831. From the first it was developed not only to provide facilities for botanical and horticultural education but also as a delightful park. It goes without saying that anyone with a knowledge of botany or ecology will find much of interest, but so can the ordinary flower lover and garden maker. There is an excellent range of glasshouses and a winter garden devoted to plants which provide interest from flowers, bark, berries or evergreen leaves in the darkest months, and which will be a revelation to those who think that a garden must of necessity lack colour between November and March. An outstanding feature is the rock garden. This rises dramatically from the edge of a small lake and has one section built of limestone and a second of sandstone. This allows a wide range of plants to flourish. Garden historians will enjoy the chronological bed in which familiar plants are placed in their order of introduction to this country and in the arrangement of roses to illustrate the descent of present-day hybrids from their wild ancestors, whilst conservationists will wish to see the collection of wild flowers of eastern England. **M.R.**

In town centre

TL 4456

Opening times vary for each college: apply Tourist Information Centre, Wheeler Street. Parties of 10 or more should register at the Information Centre

Cambridge University Colleges

CAMBRIDGESHIRE

Because there is such a wealth of fine architecture and historical assocations, few writers about Cambridge pay sufficient attention to the college gardens, which is unfortunate for without exception they are well planted, expertly maintained and contribute enormously to the beauty and atmosphere of the place, whilst several are major creations in their own right. The two features which do receive recognition are the velvety lawns and the 'Backs' which have been called the most perfect man-made view in England and which are at their loveliest when the meadows by the River Cam are filled with crocus and daffodils and the weeping willows are bursting into leaf. Amongst the best college gardens are those of *Emmanuel* which has attractive ponds, superb copper beeches and a dramatic herb garden; *Christ's* with an ancient mulberry and modern roof garden; *Pembroke* in which one court is treated quite informally; and *John's* which has a Georgian 'wilderness'. Best of all is The Fellows' Garden of *Clare*. This covers 2 acres (0.8ha) and has been skilfully sub-divided into a number of smaller enclosures and planted with artistry. Created in 1947 by Walter Barlow, then head gardener, it incorporates a sunken and a scented garden, and separate borders of blue, yellow and red flowers. **M.R.**

2 miles N of Enfield, just W of A10 Hertford road on A105

TQ 3499

Mid Apr to end Oct: Tue, Wed, Thur and Fri 1000–1630 (exc public and council holidays)

No peak season

🅿️⬛️◑
🅰️*limited parking*
🛆*limited opening*
🌱
🍂*occasional*

Capel Manor Institute of Horticulture and Field Studies

HERTFORDSHIRE

London Borough of Enfield Education Committe, Bullsmoor Lane, Waltham Cross.
tel. Lea Valley (9) 763849

For anybody living in north London or its adjoining counties (and especially those with easy access to the M25 and A10, which are adjacent to this establishment) regular visits to Capel Manor would be deeply rewarding. Administered by the London Borough of Enfield Education Committee it comprises a series of delightful formal gardens grouped around a late 18th-century house. These gardens with their botanical-type plant collections provide interest at all seasons. There is a 17th-century knot garden, a herb garden and collection of old roses. Also ornamental display glasshouses and a demonstration garden where fruit, vegetables, ornamental plants, formal bedding and so on can be seen at their best. The grounds also include a copper beech, reported to be the largest and oldest in the country, and a superb *Zelkova carpinifolia* and *Liriodendron tulipifera* (tulip tree). Courses for amateur gardeners leading to a City and Guild of London Institute Certificate cover a wide range of subjects. There are also special-interest courses on many aspects of gardening, as well as flower painting and botanical illustration. Details of courses are available from the address above. Overall, the Institute occupies 100 acres (40ha) of land on the Capel and Theobald's Park Estates. **R.P.**

Castle Howard NORTH YORKSHIRE

Lord Howard of Henderskelfe, York.
tel. Coneysthorpe (065 384) 333

The castle and its setting were Sir John Vanbrugh's first architectural and landscaping work, though the Earl of Carlisle was the presiding genius behind this elysium. The approach to its 45 acres (18ha) of formal gardens is through a 5-mile (8-km) avenue, mainly of limes, planted in 1709 with some of the original planting still standing near the house, and Vanbrugh's martial outerworks of fortified walls and towers. To the front of the house is the north lake while the garden front looks over what was once Nesfield's great parterre, now trim lawns, and the Atlas Fountain brought by Nesfield from the 1851 exhibition. Ray Wood, to the left of the house, now being underplanted with rhododendrons, flowering shrubs and exotic trees, is historic in that George London's plans for a great star of interconnecting rides which would have destroyed the ancient woodland, were dismissed for Switzer's waterworks of basins, cascades and fountains under the old tree cover – said to be a turning point in English landscape history. Down what was once Henderskelfe village street is the terrace walk to Vanbrugh's beautiful Temple of the Four Winds, the Roman Bridge and Vanbrugh's and Hawksmoor's great mausoleum. The south castle-reflecting lake overflows down a many-stepped cascade to the Roman Bridge, and in the 11-acre (4.5-ha) walled garden, with its Satyr Gate by Vanbrugh, is being built up a most important collection of old-fashioned and shrub roses. **K.L.**

5 miles W of Malton, between B1257 and A64

SE 7270

Late Mar to end Oct: daily 1030–1700. Reduced rates for parties by prior arrangement

No peak season

Charlecote Park WARWICKSHIRE

The National Trust, Wellesbourne.
tel. Stratford-upon-Avon (0789) 840277

Would that Charlecote still had the beguiling water garden to be seen in the painting of 1696 now hung in the drawing room. Alas this delight was swept away when Lancelot ('Capability') Brown was commissioned 'to alter the slopes and give the whole a natural easy corresponding level with the house on every side'. Gone are the fishing canal, the long sanded walks, the enclosed formal gardens but the lime avenue he was forbidden to touch. Much of the house and of the garden that we see today is Victorian, the result of alterations instituted by that lively and effective lady, Mary Elizabeth Lucy. In her day 20,000 bedding plants were produced annually, mostly for beds in the forecourt. Now there are good shrubs in the borders, and after the removal of brambles and overrun plants a border in the north garden contains a selection of flowers mentioned in Shakespeare's plays, primroses and heartsease, violets, columbine and cuckoo flowers. From the rose-planted terrace above the banks of the River Hele, the sound of the cascade is clearly audible and the herds of fallow deer, presumably descendents of those in Shakespeare's time, flicker up to its walls. For tranquillity Charlecote ranks high in the list of magic places. **E.F.**

4 miles E of Stratford, off B4086 Stratford—Kineton road

SP 2655

Apr and Oct: Sat, Sun, Bank Holiday Mon and Tue 1100–1700 (sunset if earlier). May to Sept: daily exc Mon and Thur but inc Bank Holiday Mon 1100–1800

No peak season

by appointment only
not Oct

Chatsworth DERBYSHIRE

Chatsworth House Trust Limited, Bakewell.
tel. Baslow (024 688) 2204

Successive generations have left their mark on Chatsworth gardens but what one sees now is mainly the work of the 6th Duke of Devonshire and Joseph Paxton. Of 17th-century provenance are the brick-built orangery, Floras's Temple, the Seahorse Fountain and the Great Cascade of 1694 with its water spouting temple by Archer of 1703. In 1761 Brown altered the line of the river and planted up the park as it is today. Paxton's work is most evident in his clothing of what were bare hillsides in woodland and pinetum, in his canal and Emperor Fountain – where lime trees date back to 1784 – his water works, the Wellington Rock, the Robber Stone Cascade, the ruined aqueduct, the Willow Tree Fountain and the site of his Great Stove, now a maze. His conservative wall greenhouse still houses camellias. A new greenhouse, however, houses the Amazonian lily which Paxton was the first in this country to bring to bloom. There is a grotto of the late 18th century, an azalea dell and a water and bog garden following the streams down the steep hillsides. A rose garden enhances the orangery lawns and a long, double herbaceous border leads from the house orangery. The round pond, with its Kentian Chiswick statuary, is surrounded by thick beech hedges and a serpentining beech walk of 1953 planting leads away from it. There can be few gardens which offer so much both historically and in beauty. **K.L.**

3 miles NE of Bakewell on B6012 off A6 Matlock—Bakewell road

SK 2670

Apr to end Oct: daily 1130–1700

Peak month: May

Limited

Northern outskirts of Chester on A41 outer ring road (signposted)

SJ 4170

Daily exc 25 Dec: 1000–1800 (summer); 1000–1 hr before dusk (winter)

No peak season

Chester Zoo Gardens CHESHIRE

North of England Zoological Society, Chester.
tel. Chester (0244) 380280

To see Victorian bedding-out at its most highly colurful go to Chester Zoo Gardens, where the mosaic carpets of flowers, changed three times a year and using 80,000 plants, are a floral experience. The colours are quite staggering and the beds set amidst extensive lawns centred by fountains of bronze statuary make for a delightful picture. To add to the colour are 15,000 roses in beds throughout the garden. In this 110 acres (44.5ha) of Zoo and gardens, developed by Mrs Mottershead, wife of the Zoo founder, even the animal enclosures are planted with trees, climbers and shrubs to make as natural a habitat as possible. Such is the high, arching Tropical House where exotic birds fly free and animals peer through naturally growing philodendrons, datura, bougainvillea, anthurium and orchids and a cascade 20ft (6m) high among towering shrubs gives a jungle effect. A rock garden with running water created in 1968 in memory of Mrs Mottershead is clothed in interesting rock plants and bounded by spiring conifers including the fossil tree (*Metasequoia glytostroboides*) now 30ft (9m) high. On this side of the garden is a new South American garden where tender subjects from that tree and shrub treasure land are being tried out, and the Jubilee garden which, until 1977, was a hole in the ground, but is now a green amphitheatre centred by a most distinctive fountain of bronze, Noah and the Four Winds. **K.L.**

8 miles N of Redruth on A30, 1 mile W of Zelah

SW 8050

Open frequently between Mar and end May by arrangement and some Sun for charity. Ring for details

Peak months: Mar to May

Chyverton CORNWALL

Mr and Mrs Nigel Holman, Zelah, Truro.
tel. Zelah (087 254) 324

The 250-year-old granite-faced house sits among native and exotic trees looking over a wide lawn that merges into grazed parkland. A small stream was dammed in the 18th century to provide a stretch of ornamental water that is now backed by large rhododendrons and other trees and shrubs. Part of the stream is filled with one of the largest stands of lysichitum in the country. The oldest trees and shrubs in the 15 acres (6 ha) of garden are more than 100 years old. The present owner's father bought the property nearly 60 years ago and started a regular planting programme. The present owner continued this policy when he inherited in 1959 while steadily eliminating all labour-intensive forms of gardening. Wind plays an important part in Cornish gardening but wind-damaged trees are being replaced and the garden is being extended by pushing out into extensive native woodlands by cutting tracks to additional glades kept under grass by regular machine cutting. The result is a very large collection of tree and shrub species with good forms and many cultivars. Most of them are suitably grouped and readily visible in these woodland clearings. To name the fifty genera that the owner claims to have added since he took over would far exceed the allotted space. The whole provides pleasant strolling for the non-gardener, the plantsman will find numerous woody plants to identify and admire, while the owner will tell much of his plants and their behaviour in Cornwall. **F.S.**

2½ miles S of Crewkerne off B3165 Lyme Regis road

ST 4106

Daily exc Sat but inc Easter Sat and Sats in May: 1000–1700; Sun 1400–1700. Reduced rates for parties by prior arrangement

No peak season

by appointment only

limited opening

Clapton Court Gardens SOMERSET

Capt. S. J. Loder, Crewkerne.
tel. Crewkerne (0460) 73220/72200

One of the most beautiful and best kept gardens in the West Country, Clapton Court has only been open to the public since 1979. The fascinating 10-acre (4-ha) gardens are filled with many interesting plants and provide good all-the-year-round colour. The biggest ash tree in Britain is just one of the many fine specimen trees to be seen in the woodland gardens. Entering the garden through a gateway from the plant centre, the terraces come into view. Grey and silver-leaved plants dominate the first terrace, while *Pyrus salicifolia* 'Pendula', the willow-leaved pear, is eye-catching planted as a central feature on the second terrace. A 'golden border' on the left of the highest terrace leads to the wild garden where old oaks and pine provide overhead protection for camellias, hydrangeas and the hundreds of small bulbs which carpet the ground in spring. The formal rose garden, enclosed by yew and hornbeam hedges, is fragrant on a hot summer's day with the blooming of many roses. Tiny streams meander through the delightful upper woodland which is filled with unusual and rare plants under a canopy of mature beech and ash. Many varieties of rhododendron and azaleas fill the leafy glades with glorious displays of colour in spring and ferns, hostas and primulas all act as ground-cover plants. **A.S.**

Claremont Landscape Garden SURREY

The National Trust, Esher.

This is included as a remarkable example of a recently restored early 18th-century landscape garden. The grand concept at Claremont was commissioned by the Duke of Newcastle in the 18th century when Vanbrugh built a strategically placed Belvedere on the hilly terrain that is such a feature of this part of Surrey, from which the Duke could survey several counties as well as the ponds and wooded grounds of his park. Then followed Charles Bridgeman's great 3-acre (1.2-ha) amphitheatre. William Kent in the 1730s enlarged the lake and made an island and pavilion and then in the 1770s Capability Brown was employed by the new owner Lord Clive of India to build a new mansion and extensively plant the estate. He altered the line of the main London/Portsmouth road to better improve the viewpoints! In 1975 work started to restore the gardens to the 1750 period. The most spectacular success was the uncovering of Bridgeman's unique amphitheatre, the terraces remarkably well preserved beneath a jungle of rhododendrons, laurels and also several massive cedars. The lake was dredged, the pavilion on the island restored, and the grotto rebuilt. Merrist Wood College provided valuable help to the National Trust in this programme. Do not expect flowers and sophisticated gardening at Claremont. Rather enjoy the sort of informal, yet designed pictorial landscape for which the 18th century in England became world famous. **T.W.**

On southern outskirts of Esher on A307

TQ 1363

Daily exc 25 Dec and 1 Jan: Apr to Oct 0900–1900 (sunset if earlier); Nov to Mar 0900–1600

No peak season

limited opening

Clevedon Court AVON

The National Trust, Clevedon.

The south-facing terraces, which may follow the line of earlier defence fosses, are probably of 18th-century construction. The top, or Esmond Terrace, so named as Thackeray's 'Henry Esmond' was begun there, is delightfully informal, and upon it grows a strawberry tree, *Arbutus unedo*, which seeds itself, the dwarf palm, *Chamaerops humilis*, and a Judas tree, *Cercis siliquastrum*. From it there are views of the house, lower garden and the Octagon. The main or Pretty Terrace, castigated by Gertrude Jekyll for its over-formality, is now more as she would have liked it, and its sunny length houses a fine variety of tender plants, *Buddleia colvilei*, with crimson dropping trusses, the semi-double, yellow spring jasmine, *Jasminum primulinum*, and various ceanothuses. At one end stands an 18th-century octagonal garden house, overlooked by Chusan palms, and at the other a Gothic garden shelter. In the lower garden is a fine collection of magnolias, while posts support a huge specimen of the Himalayan musk rose, *Rosa brunonii*. The whole garden exhibits a long history of loving care which makes it a delight to visit. **E.F.**

1½ miles E of Clevedon on B3130 Bristol road

ST 4272

Apr to end Sept: Wed, Thur, Sun and Bank Holiday Mon 1430–1730. Parties of 20 and over by arrangement

No peak season

Clive Memorial Garden STAFFORDSHIRE

Willoughbridge Garden Trust, Elds Wood, Willoughbridge, Market Drayton.
Tel. Pipegate (063 081) 411

There are two main planting dates for this garden; the first 1937 when Col. Harry Clive decided to make a woodland garden in a gravel pit, the second 1961 when the newly created Trust started to develop the sloping field between the road and the original garden. From the car park the visitor already sees interesting plants. The willow-leaved, weeping cotoneaster droops over the bank, and there are good specimens of that fine shrub rose, *Rosa californica* 'Plena'. On the left above the car park, there is a pool planted with water-lilies, and the usual range of waterside plants. The willow-leaved pear stands high above its neighbours. The scree garden above the pool is in complete contrast, closely planted with low, creeping plants and shrubs. Pinks, harebells, thymes and rock roses are plentiful. Pines and birches are an effective, contrasting background. The 1937 garden was planted under a canopy of oaks and birches. Large specimens of *Magnolia kobus* are now flowering freely. Much of the initial planting consisted of rhododendrons, but many others, which will be of interest from spring to autumn, are now growing well, catalpa, cedars, cherries, ginkgo, liquidambar and many varieties of conifer. Willoughbridge is already of interest, it will become increasingly beautiful. **E.F.**

9 miles SW of Newcastle-under-Lyme on A51 Stone—Pipegate road

SJ 4641

March to end Nov: daily 1100–1930 (or dusk if earlier)

Peak months: May to June and autumn

3½ miles NE of
Aberfeldy on Weem—
Strathtay road running
N of River Tay

NN 8751

Mar to end Oct: daily
1400–1800

Peak months: Apr to
June and Oct

Cluny House TAYSIDE

R. S. Masterton, Esq., Aberfeldy, (Perthshire).
tel. Aberfeldy (0887) 20795

It was in 1950 that the Mastertons bought the house and then 6 acres (2.4ha) – now 9 acres (3.6ha) – of land around Cluny in Perthshire, and set about the awesome task of creating a garden from the overgrown woodland and a bankside which descends steeply to the banks of the River Tay. Today, what is considered to be one of the best collections of primula is grown there with the Petiolaris group especially outstanding. Such primulas as *P. whitei*, *P. sonchifolia* and *P. gracilipes*, considered by many to require the protection of a glasshouse, grow happily out-of-doors and unprotected at Cluny. Meconopsis is another group of plants which do particularly well here. From a relatively open area in front of the house, paths wind through a woodland emerging occasionally into more open spaces where specimen trees such as *Prunus maackii* or *Magnolia sinensis* are planted to create interest. Here also one can find the 6- or 7-ft (2-m) stems of *Cardiocrinum giganteum* on the verge of the woodland, while in partial shade of the trees grow groups of trillium, fritillaria or erythronium. Spring and early summer are especially interesting times of the year, and so too is autumn when fruits and foliage of viburnum, cotoneaster, a good cercidiphyllum and several species of acer are equally rewarding. In 1982 Bobby Masterton was awarded the Scottish Horticultural Medal for outstanding service to gardening. This honour is ably reflected in the fascinating garden he has made with the remarkable collection of plants to be seen there. **E.R.**

Turn off A26
Tunbridge Wells—
Uckfield road onto
B2100; turn right at
2nd crossroads into
Tollwood Road

TQ 5231

Open several Sun
each year under
National Gardens
Scheme

Peak months: May to
Aug

Cobblers EAST SUSSEX

Mr and Mrs Martin Furniss, Crowborough.

Perfection in planting and design has always been the aim of Martin Furniss since he began making this remarkable garden over 25 years ago. When Mr and Mrs Furniss bought Cobblers in 1965 there were 2 acres (0.8ha) of land given over to pigsties, an old orchard and much jungle, with a small garden near the house. The design chosen for the garden is what Repton would have described as 'an irregular modern flower garden', a garden that flows in an orderly manner, so that the visitor is led onwards by vistas, tempting features and partially concealed views, offering the prospect of something new and exciting around each bend. Martin Furniss is an architect and the firm but flowing lines of the garden with ribbon-like brick paths, terraces, steps and retaining walls were all built by himself to a very high quality. The plant associations are carefully chosen to provide a succession of colour and interest with the emphasis on May to August. There are many different borders and habitats with over 2,000 species and varieties of plants. These range from the dry sun-loving rock and alpine types on the terraces round the house, a multitude of mixed borders with shrubs, perennials, roses, bulbs and foliage plants to the moisture-loving bog plants around the upper circular pond, and a superb range of aquatics and marginal plants in the serpentine main pool – one of the most cleverly designed and planted pools seen in any garden. In the coolest, lowest part of the garden is a rhododendron grove. **T.W.**

3 miles W of
Bournemouth, off A35
Bournemouth—Poole
road on B3065

SZ 0589

Apr to end Oct: daily
1030–1830. Reduced
rates for parties of 35
and over

No peak season

Compton Acres DORSET

J. and L. A. Brady, Canford Cliffs Road, Canford Cliffs, Poole.
tel. Canford Cliffs (0202) 708036

These famous gardens were first planned in 1914 by Thomas William Simpson, whose idea was to design a series of completely different gardens enclosed by hedges, walls and trees, thus making only one garden visible at a time. Beginning at the tiny Roman garden, encircled by mellow brick walls, a path leads through the herbaceous borders, seen at their best in summer, to the Italian gardens where formal beds surround the lovely cross-shaped lake filled with water-lilies. Behind these beds hundreds of roses grow in the long borders together with clematis climbing gracefully round pillars of Bath stone. A temple at one end of the lake and bronze statues of the 'Wrestlers of Herculaneum' at the other add to the character of this garden. A sub-tropical air is created by the eucalyptus, mimosa, palms and bamboos in the rock and water garden. There is a superb Japanese garden, complete with a pagoda, an Imperial tea-house over which wisteria elegantly climbs, and many oriental statues that look down on a sunken lake which may be crossed by stepping-stones. Every available space is massed with azaleas, flowering cherries and lilies for blooming in early summer and mingling with maples which provide a spectacular display of autumn colour. **A.S.**

Cotehele CORNWALL

The National Trust, St Dominick, nr Saltash.
Tel. St Dominick (0579) 50434

This sloping garden may be entered from the car park at Cotehele Quay on the River Tamar or from one of the others near the 600-year-old house. Leaving the quay a path above the riverside meadows, past the little 400-year-old chapel, leads to thick native woodland at the bottom of an east-facing valley. Paths on the north and south lead upwards through wicket gates and occasional cultivated plants are seen on either side. Gradually among fewer trees the native flora grows less and more garden plants are to be found. Rondlets and damp areas beside the stream support moisture-loving plants. The small, 15 by 10yd (14 by 9m) ancient fish pond has water-lilies and other water plants. Still higher there are more shrubs and other plants until one passes through or under the medieval garden wall, to arrive at the foot of four-er terraces below the east front of the house. Here are rose beds and, against the house, borders and wall shrubs as there are on other walls of the house and on the extensive garden boundaries. Paths lead round to the north, past shrubs in rough grass, to a formal pond with central island and surrounding lawns and flower borders. There is a garden for cut flowers and interesting old trees, all at about 250ft (76m) above the river. Beyond a back courtyard there is the south front and main entrance. The less energetic will enter here and enjoy the garden and the view from the terrace or below the roses. **F.S.**

8 miles sw of
Tavistock; between
A390 Tavistock—
Liskeard road and
A388 Saltash—
Launceston road

SX 4268

Daily: Apr to Oct
1100–1800; Nov to
Mar daylight

No peak season

🅿 ♿
🛏 by appointment
only
🍴 Apr to Oct: daily;
Nov to Christmas:
limited opening
🌿
🏛 limited opening
🎁 Apr to Oct
♣

Coton Manor Gardens NORTHAMPTONSHIRE

Commander and Mrs H. Pasley-Tyler, Coton.
Tel. Northampton (0604) 740219

Rarely can the past and the present have been so successfully related as at Coton Manor, where some 10 acres (4ha) of modern gardens have as their focal point a house with a long and eventful history. The original manor house, mentioned in the Domesday Book, was destroyed in the Civil War to be replaced by a small farmhouse in 1662, and much added to to become the present manor house in 1926, when the gardens had their origins. These gardens might have been created specifically for gardening enthusiasts to visit, such is their interest in terms of fine plants – trees, shrubs, herbaceous perennials, roses and so on – most beautifully displayed in what is, in effect, a series of interrelated gardens on different levels. Water features figure prominently, including a stream trilling through a natural garden with moisture-loving plants on its margins which flows into a large pool in the lowermost part of the property. These gardens, created by the parents of Mrs Pasley-Tyler, are a splendid achievement, restored (after unavoidable one-time neglect) and developed with the utmost dedication since 1950 by Commander and Mrs Pasley-Tyler. One unusual feature of the gardens is the extensive collection of water-fowl and other birds which have a home there. **R.P.**

10 miles N of
Northampton between
A50 and A428

SP 6771

Apr to Sept: Thur,
Sun and Bank
Holiday Mon, also
Wed in July and
Aug. Oct: Sun
1400–1800. Parties at
other times by
appointment

No peak season

🅿 ♿
🚶 1-mile walk
🛏 🚹 🍴 🏛 🌿 🎁

Cragside NORTHUMBERLAND

The National Trust, Rothbury, Morpeth.

Cragside, the romantic, almost fairy-tale castle built for Lord Armstrong by Norman Shaw on a high bluff, is surrounded by craggy moorland, a natural garden for thousands of rhododendrons and placid lakes in a deep ravine of Debdon Beck. From the house platform, high above soaring conifers, whether one looks up or down, in the right season the hillsides are painted with colours, the result of smothering the rocky outcrops with a varied selection of rhododendrons and azaleas, though in the 940 acres (380ha) encircled by a hilly drive, everywhere one looks it is *Rhododendron ponticum* and sweet-smelling *R. luteum* colouring the landscape. In the dell below the house the way is through woodland over which a graceful suspension bridge sways. Woodland walks may be taken by the stream, now placid then in a deep gorge and by waterfalls, to view on the way the North American conifers which have reached record heights, many over 140ft (43m). To be seen are the Western hemlocks, Douglas firs, and other spiring giants – the noble, red and great firs, Colorado spruce, the ornamental tiger tail spruce, the Swiss arolla pine and *Abies concolor* and *A. magnifica*. Banks of heather offer light relief under large stands of beech and birch. As has been said of Cragside 'It is not so much a garden as a rhododendron and azalea drive' or, a long 30-mile (48-km) hike. **K.L.**

11 miles sw of
Alnwick on B6341
Alnwick—Rothbury
road

NU 0702

Apr to Oct: daily
1000–1900. Nov to
Mar: Sat and Sun
1000–1600. Reduced
rates for parties of 20
and over

No peak season

🅿 ♿
🚶 1-mile walk
🛏 by appointment
only
🚹 🍴 🏛 🌿 🎁
🎁 limited opening
♣

9 miles N of
Wimborne Minster on
B3078

SU 0513

Apr to Oct: 1st Sat
and Sun of month
0900–1700 (Sat)
1400–1700 (Sun)

Peak months: May to
July and Oct

P WC ♿
🎁 by appointment
only
🌱 🏷

Cranborne Manor Gardens DORSET

The Marquess of Salisbury, Cranborne, Wimborne.
tel. Cranborne (072 54) 248

These very beautiful gardens were laid out in the early 17th century by
Mounten Jennings and John Tradescant (who supplied some of the original
plants) and contain many interesting features. Entering the gardens by the
pergola walk, then wandering through church walk where trained fruit trees
grow, one strolls down towards the river garden, a mass of daffodils under
flowering cherries in spring. Many unusual kinds of bulbs are mixed with
hellebores in borders either side of a little secluded path by the River Crane
sheltered from cold winds by a beech hedge. In June the air is filled with the
scent of old shrub and species roses flowering in the north court where they
mingle with herbaceous perennials. The Jacobean mount garden looks down
on the west lawn and a small knot garden that is planted with 16th- and 17th-
century flowers including crown imperials, *Fritillaria imperialis*. The chalk
wall garden contains a mixed shrub and perennial border, underplanted with
bulbs and spring- and autumn-flowering hardy cyclamen on one side, and a
yew hedge, clipped in places to form windows, on the other. A herb garden
crammed with many varieties of herbs set in small beds provides a final
aromatic treat before leaving. **A.S.**

13½ miles S of
Inveraray on A83
Lochgilphead road

NR 9897

Mar to end Oct: daily
0900–1800

Peak seasons: spring
and autumn

P WC 🚻 🐕
🚗 with permission
🌱

Crarae Woodland Garden STRATHCLYDE

Sir Ilay Campbell Bart. (Trustee), Crarae Garden Charitable Trust,
Inveraray, (Argyll).
tel. Inverary (054 66) 633

Crarae is one of the delights of Scottish gardens. It was made in a glen down
which the Crarae burn flows, having been started by Lady Campbell of
Succoth in 1912, and expanded by the late Sir George Campbell who, by the
time of his death in 1967, had created a garden which had become
internationally known and respected. To wander through the 40-acre (16-ha)
garden in spring is a pleasure one has to experience to fully appreciate. The
path offers a dramatic view over the lower stretch of the Crarae burn to Crarae
Lodge surrounded by acer and eucryphia, backed by a low hill clothed with
azalea and the Lodge itself furnished with interesting plants such as *Hydrangea
integerrima*. The path follows the course of the burn as it rises to over 100ft
(30m) above the waters of the loch, past the impressive shape and size of the
large-leaved rhododendrons, *R. macabeanum* and *R. hodgsonii* and strategically
placed plants of *Clethra delavayi* and *Disanthus cercidifolius* to the western limit
of the garden. It is around this area that further expansion has been made to the
garden in recent years to include more species of eucalyptus, several of the
fragrant *maddenii* series of rhododendrons, set in a magnificent backcloth of
pines and larch. The return path is on the other side of the burn. It is rarely that
one has an opportunity, even in Scotland, to enjoy an outstanding collection
of plants in a beautiful and natural setting such as Crarae. It is undoubtedly one
of Scotland's great gardens. **E.R.**

15 miles SW of
Aberdeen on A93
Banchory road

NO 7396

Daily: 0930–dusk

No peak season

P WC ♿
🍽 limited opening
🚗 🌱
🏷 limited opening
🏛 limited opening
♣

Crathes Castle Gardens GRAMPIAN

National Trust for Scotland, Crathes Castle, by Banchory (Kincardineshire)
tel. Crathes (033 044) 525

That the garden has been in existence for a great many years, is clearly evident
from the massive old yew hedges bordering the four small gardens on the
upper level, but the present splendid display is the direct result of two people,
the late Sir James and Lady Burnett of Leys. Fortunately, their skills and
interests were complementary in that Sir James had a great knowledge of and
love for trees and shrubs, and Lady Burnett, with a remarkable flair for colour
combination, produced the outstanding herbaceous borders. There are eight
small gardens in all, each with a specialised interest. The skills of both the
former owners have enabled collections of several genera to be represented
and a great many of the more uncommon or rare herbaceous perennials.
Happily, most of these are dispersed throughout the garden forming an
important role in colour or foliage combinations rather than being grouped
together as so often is the case. Sir James spent many years creating an
arboretum in the policies, or parkland, but the majority of trees were
destroyed in a severe gale of 1958, fortunately several species of importance
somehow managed to weather the storm. Crathes is one of the most
interesting and colourful gardens on Royal Deeside, a Mecca for the
plantsman, but a place of enjoyment no matter how little the extent of one's
plant knowledge may be. **E.R.**

Cruickshank Botanic Garden
GRAMPIAN

The Cruickshank Trust and the University of Aberdeen, St Machar
Drive, Aberdeen.
tel. Aberdeen (0224) 40241 ext. 348

The Botanic Garden was founded in 1898, to serve both as the University
Botanic Garden and as a place of leisure for the public. But apart from some
trees, the design of the garden dates from later. As a botanic garden, emphasis
is naturally on collections of plants for research and teaching, but the garden
also serves to present ideas in garden design and planting to the public. The
chief features are the sunken garden (conifers, rhododendrons, heathers), the
rock and water garden built in 1970 (alpines, bulbs, aquatic and marsh plants),
the woodland border (rhododendrons, meconopsis, hellebores, trillium,
gentians), the patio garden (wall, trough and paving plants) and the long
herbaceous border, with a rather 'botanical' emphasis. There is a small range of
glasshouses, open on application to the Head Gardener, with a large collection
of succulent plants. The Garden, including a small young arboretum, covers
approximately 11 acres (4.5ha), with lawns, specimen trees and varied shrub
collections forming a frame to the special features mentioned above.

*In Old Aberdeen, 1½
miles north of city
centre*

NO 9507

*Jan to Dec: Mon to
Fri 0830–1630, also
Sat and Sun in May
to Sept 1400–1700*

*Peak seasons: spring
and summer*

Culzean Castle Garden and Country Park
STRATHCLYDE

National Trust for Scotland, Culzean Castle, (Ayrshire).

The south-west side of Culzean Castle is occupied by a formally designed
Fountain Court Garden, immediately in front of an attractive terrace built by
Robert Adam, who was also responsible for the present design of the Castle, as
well as the home farm, now the Country Park Centre. Throughout the
woodland, areas have been selected for specialised treatment so that a pleasant
country walk will unexpectedly give way to a colourful glade, such as that
found around the camellia house, a Victorian Gothic-style building where
magnolias, camellias and rhododendrons provide a variable interest in spring
and early summer. Summer and early autumn is catered for in the extensive
herbaceous borders and rose garden found in the walled garden. General plant
interest is not lacking as one may see from long established trees of libocedrus
or *Pinus montezumae* and several eucalyptus or pittosporum. For generations
the property was in the possession of the Earls of Cassillis, later the Marquis of
Ailsa, until 1945 when it was presented to The National Trust for Scotland.
Since becoming a Country Park in 1969, financed by four Local Authorities,
both the garden and countryside activities have given pleasure and relaxation
to many thousands of visitors who find the Castle, excluded from the Country
Park, combines well with the several interests in the grounds to make an
enjoyable day for the family. **E.R.**

*4 miles W of Maybole
off A719*

NS 2310

*Daily: 1000–dusk.
Reduced rates for
parties exc July and
Aug*

*Peak months: Apr to
Oct*

limited opening

limited opening
limited opening

Dartington Hall DEVON

Dartington Hall Trust, nr Totnes.
tel. Totnes (0803) 862367

Several youngish trees outside the imposing entrance prepare one for the
extensive gardens within. Inside the gates a giant swamp cypress stands
sufficiently aside to allow ample views of the ancient buildings which are
lightly clothed with restrained plantings of wall plants and flanked by a few
trees and shrubs around the central lawn. Thence by way of the south-east,
south and west, a series of gardens bear evidence of the work of the Elmhirsts,
transformers from 1925 of this ancient and then derelict site, and of the
succession of garden architects and advisers from both sides of the Atlantic
who planned and suggested the planting and use of these varied and
undulating grounds. Extensive lawns and rougher grass give space for long
views and walks. Formal hedges shut off the private garden but well planned
additional groups break the severe straight lines and add to the protection of
the inner garden. Despite the decision only to plant to suit the design and
situation and not merely to achieve a collection of plants there is a goodly
range of interesting subjects among some stately trees of the past. Modern
buildings blend with the old and their lines are broken or hidden by careful
plantings. The main activities of the estate – music, speech, drama and the
visual arts – are in evidence much of the time and blend suitably with the
artistic development of the gardens with Henry Moore's and Willi Soukop's
figures standing amongst the shrubs. **F.S.**

*2 miles N of Totnes,
off Totnes—
Buckfastleigh road*

SY 7962

Daily: dawn–dusk

*Peak months: Apr to
May, Oct/Nov*

*by arrangement
only*

Deene Park NORTHAMPTONSHIRE

Edmund Brudenell, Esq., nr Corby.

½ mile W of A43 midway between Kettering and Stamford

SP 9592

June to Aug: Sun, also Easter, Spring and Summer bank holiday Sun and Mon 1400–1700

Peak months: May to July

🅿🚻🍴🍴🏕
⚲ *occasional*
🏪🏮

Imposing is the word best used to describe Deene Park, which has been the home of the Brudenell family since 1514. The mansion had its origins in medieval times and was extensively developed in the 16th and 17th centuries with further additions being made in the 19th century. The vista from the south face of the house impresses, with the climber-clad walls, the borders abutting these walls well furnished with shrubs and herbaceous perennials and the grass sward sweeping from the terrace to the banks of the river which, at the eastern end of the garden, is crossed by a stone, balustraded bridge, and, far distant, at the other end of the gardens, by a smaller bridge. It is this panorama and the fine specimen trees which frame the view which give Deene Park especial appeal. Not to be missed also is the delightful 'white' garden with its plantings including roses, cistus, lilacs, lilies and irises. But throughout the garden the visitor will find trees, shrubs and herbaceous perennials to admire, species, varieties and forms which indicate discernment of choice and flair in their association to provide maximum enjoyment. **R.P.**

Denmans WEST SUSSEX

Mrs J. H. Robinson, Fontwell, nr Arundel.
tel. Eastergate (024 368) 2808

5 miles SE of Chichester and just S of A27 Chichester— Arundel road in Denmans Lane adjacent to Fontwell racecourse

SU 9407

Late Feb to end Oct: Sat and Sun 1400–1800. Other times by appointment

No peak season

🅿
limited
by appointment only
🍴*by arrangement only*
⚲

The gardens at Denmans have been created over the past 35 years by their energetic and single-minded owner, Mrs J. H. Robinson, who with the help of one gardener transformed a one-time market garden and small holding into a home for many exciting plants. The setting is the old 19th-century bothy, stable block and service buildings of the adjacent Westergate House (since sold) and its walled garden. The exotic and secluded character of Denmans derives largely from the clever planting design using bold specimens and informal groupings, the emphasis being on the shape, colour and texture of the whole growing picture rather than the individual plants. The entrance drive is planted with mainly spring- and autumn-colouring trees and shrubs. A warm sunny terrace on the south of the cottage is luxuriant with massed cistus, brooms, grey-foliaged shrubs, dwarf conifers, groups of California tree poppies and many others. The main informal garden has winding paths through drifts and islands of specimen trees and shrubs, the surface material being mostly gravel. All manner of plants seed into this with most effective results. A more recent feature is a dry stream in pebbles and stones winding down through an arboretum, with willows, grasses and stony plantings. Ingenious plant associations are everywhere at Denmans including a glasshouse full of luxuriant conservatory plants. **T.W.**

Duncombe Park NORTH YORKSHIRE

Trustees of Duncombe Park, Helmsley

13 miles W of Pickering on A170 Thirsk—Pickering road

SE 6183

May to end Aug: Wed 1000–1600

No peak season

🚶*1-mile walk*

Duncombe Terrace is the attraction here in a landscape with Bridgeman/Switzer overtones where, created for Thomas Duncombe *c*.1715, it sweeps for half a mile (0.8km) of lawn in a great concave curve above the valley of the River Rye. At one end is a Vanbrugh-designed Ionic domed rotunda of 1718 above a serpentining wall, one of the earliest of ha-has. Terminating the far end of the terrace is a closed circular Doric temple of a slightly later date. Through woodland planted on the river valley side are views down to the meandering river and its cascades. From the open rotunda the peep is over the pantiled roofs of Helmsley. Formality came from the straight-sided yew hedges, etoiles and avenues on the far side of the terrace. The walk to the terrace from the Vanbrugh-inspired, but Wakefield-built house, now a school, is by way of a square lawn, said to be by Barry, to a life-size Van Nost lead Father Time sundial. Walks on the far side of the terrace give on to a secret garden and an old ruined orangery. To the west of the terrace, from the Tuscan temple along another escarpment, a walk turns off into the Terrace Bank Wood wherein is the tallest lime (154ft, 47m) and the tallest ash (148ft, 45m), in this country. **K.L.**

Dunham Massey CHESHIRE

The National Trust, nr Altrincham.
tel. 061-941 1025

A medieval mount which may even have been a motte of a Norman Castle still remains at Dunham Massey, along with part of the moat which now runs into an ornamental pond. In Kip's view of 1697 the mount is of elaborate design with circling hedges and topped by an ornamental building, the moat encircles the house round which are small formal gardens from which long radiating avenues stem. Today the National Trust is refurbishing this long established garden of which several fine paintings of 1696 and 1751 remain to show its impressive grandeur. Fortunately there are still obelisks from the old days, one to be seen in Langham Grove, of 1714 date, an orangery on the north-east corner of the house, a well house of the early 19th century by a rustic arbour and an Elizabethan mill of 1616 which has been put in working order. There are deer in the park and a 1740 deer house. A wooden rustic bridge and a bog garden have been created recently to give some colour and interest to the moat stream and in the woodland of the park and house surrounds many rhododendrons have been planted along with other flowering shrubs and herbaceous borders on the house lawns. While many of the early statuary gracing the grounds have gone, there are still two life-sized lions guarding the entrance forecourt and a sundial supported by a kneeling blackamoor. **K.L.**

3 miles SW of Altrincham, W of A56 on B5160

SJ 7487

Apr to end Oct: daily exc Fri 1100–1800

No peak season

1400–1800; parties by appointment only

Dyffryn Botanic Garden
SOUTH GLAMORGAN

Mr D. V. Goddard (Director), St Nicholas, Cardiff.

Situated in the Vale of Glamorgan, this 50-acre (20-ha) garden was landscaped in the 20th century by Thomas Manson for the owner John Cory, who was a prominent figure in the commercial, religious and philanthropic life of South Wales. The garden was further developed by his son, Reginald Cory, an eminent horticulturist, who increased the plant collections and established Dyffryn as one of the finest botanic centres in Wales. As a botanic garden, priority is given to the collection of plants, but the garden is also open to the public to encourage ideas in planting and design and as a venue for leisure events. Its chief features are individually designed gardens, (e.g. paved, sunken, pool, heart, Roman gardens each enclosed by magnificent yew hedges), an extensive arboretum, herbaceous borders, a newly established heather and rock garden, a rose garden, lawns and attractive water features. Of the plant houses, the 50-ft (15-m) high palm house is the most dramatic architecturally and contains many exotic plants and a large collection of citrus fruits. Other houses contain interesting collections of orchids, cacti and succulents. Amongst the trees are large specimens of paper bark maple, Brewer's weeping spruce, wing nut and roble beech. The Japanese maples and magnolia species are particularly outstanding.

6 miles W of centre of Cardiff, off A48 in the village of St Nicholas

ST 0975

Apr to Sept: daily

Peak months: May, July to Sept

Dyrham Park AVON

The National Trust, nr Chippenham.
tel. Abson (027 582) 2051

The curving drive, laid out by C. Harcourt-Masters, the Bath surveyor, around 1780, provides superb views of the house below. This part of the park was originally an immense, formal, Baroque water garden, with cascades, fountains and pools, of unrivalled quality made by George London for William Blathwayt in the latter half of the 17th century. By 1780 it was neglected and was 'reconciled to the modern taste'; this landscape park, containing a famous herd of fallow deer, has in turn required replanting. The orangery on the east was built about 1701, and now, in addition to lemons and oranges, is curtained with the pale-blue of plumbago, and scented by *Jasminum polyanthum*. The original stream still plunges underground to reappear on the garden side of the house, to feed two pools connected by a cascade. This garden is overlooked by a stone-paved terrace, level with the house and church, and Humphry Repton is thought to have planted the leaning holm oaks. The south-facing retaining walls provide warmth and shelter for *Magnolia delavayi*, *Solanum crispum*, and the climbing roses 'Mermaid' and 'Gloire de Dijon'. In the southern end of the garden recent plantings have reintroduced trees used in the time of William Blathwayt, including the Virginia pine and the tulip tree. The dramatic position of this park and the views over the Vale of Severn towards Bristol are unforgettable. **E.F.**

12 miles E of Bath: W of A46 Bath—Stroud road, 2 miles south of exit 18 on M4

ST 7575

Apr, May and Oct: daily exc Thur and Fri; June to Sept: daily exc Fri 1400–1800. Other times with written permission

No peak season

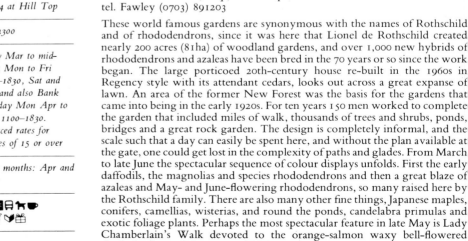

Edzell Castle TAYSIDE

7 miles N of Brechin off B966

NO 5969

Apr to Sept: Mon, Wed, Fri and Sat 0930–1900, Thur and Sun 1400–1900; Oct to Mar: Mon, Wed, Fri and Sat 0930–1600, Thur and Sun 1400–1600. Closed 25 and 26 Dec and 1 Jan

Peak months: June to Sept

Secretary of State for Scotland, Edzell, (Angus).
tel. Edzell (035 64) 631

Edzell Castle may well have remained just another ancient monument, had not the late Dr James Richardson, formerly Chief Inspector of Ancient Monuments, sought to restore the former glory of the pleasance originally created by Sir David Lindsay, Laird of Edzell. It was in 1604 that Sir David returned to Edzell, having travelled widely, and set about the creation of a beautiful early 17th-century garden. No expense was spared in securing highly skilled stonemasons to embellish the walls with the seven planetary deities, the seven liberal arts and the seven cardinal virtues. Overlooking the square garden stood the Castle at one corner, with a well house at the south-west corner and a charming corner summerhouse in the south-east. In his restoration Dr Richardson has used a centrally positioned circular yew on a mound as a centre-piece, with four ball-shaped yews as guardians. A square boxwood surround encloses four major parterre patterns, each with a subsidiary triangular parterre set inside the boxwood corners. To fill the designs, modern red and yellow cluster-flowered (floribunda) roses have been used, which is certainly effective, whereas the white and blue Lindsay colours recreated with alyssum and lobelia may cause an eyebrow to raise. Nevertheless, this is one of very few period garden restorations to have taken place in Scotland, and as such we should applaud the achievement, as much as admire the very high standard of maintenance of the garden. **E.R.**

Erddig CLWYD

On southern outskirts of Wrexham, off A483 Wrexham–Ruabon road

SJ 3348

Apr to Sept: daily exc Fri but inc Good Fri 1200–1730. Oct: daily exc Fri 1400–1630. Reduced rates for parties of 20 or over by prior arrangement

No peak season

by appointment only

The National Trust, nr Wrexham.
tel. Wrexham (0978) 355314

The remains of formal gardening in Britain are few. Launcelot Brown saw to that. Badeslade's engraving of 1738 shows a layout of a central gravel walk leading to a long, straight canal and through the White Gates there is a view of the country beyond. This is the arrangement of the original garden made by John Meller in 1718. The intention has been to return the garden as far as possible to the condition of the Badeslade engraving. The orchards have been replanted, and fruit trees, of ancient varieties especially propagated, have been placed against the walls. The middle section of the broad walk has been planted with double rows of limes, *Tilia euchlora*, which are pleached to make a low formal connection between the lawns and the canal. The gates at the end of the canal made by Robert Davies, the Wrexham smith, replaced the earlier White Gates in 1905. The south-facing side of the garden terminates in a fishpond, but the remainder was devoted to fruit, and has been replanted with ranks of apples, trained into pyramids. There will also be pears, peaches, apricots and plums from the walls. South of the canal walk the central section is devoted to a Victorian flower garden, which includes the rambler rose 'Dorothy Perkins' and *Clematis jackmanii*. This garden lies between yew hedges and a moss walk. **E.F.**

Exbury Gardens HAMPSHIRE

9 miles s of Southampton, turn off B3054 at Hill Top

ST 4300

Early Mar to mid-June: Mon to Fri 1300–1830, Sat and Sun and also Bank Holiday Mon Apr to June 1100–1830. Reduced rates for parties of 15 or over

Peak months: Apr and May

E. D. de Rothschild, Esq., Southampton.
tel. Fawley (0703) 891203

These world famous gardens are synonymous with the names of Rothschild and of rhododendrons, since it was here that Lionel de Rothschild created nearly 200 acres (81ha) of woodland gardens, and over 1,000 new hybrids of rhododendrons and azaleas have been bred in the 70 years or so since the work began. The large porticoed 20th-century house re-built in the 1960s in Regency style with its attendant cedars, looks out across a great expanse of lawn. An area of the former New Forest was the basis for the gardens that came into being in the early 1920s. For ten years 150 men worked to complete the garden that included miles of walk, thousands of trees and shrubs, ponds, bridges and a great rock garden. The design is completely informal, and the scale such that a day can easily be spent here, and without the plan available at the gate, one could get lost in the complexity of paths and glades. From March to late June the spectacular sequence of colour displays unfolds. First the early daffodils, the magnolias and species rhododendrons and then a great blaze of azaleas and May- and June-flowering rhododendrons, so many raised here by the Rothschild family. There are also many other fine things, Japanese maples, conifers, camellias, wisterias, and round the ponds, candelabra primulas and exotic foliage plants. Perhaps the most spectacular feature in late May is Lady Chamberlain's Walk devoted to the orange-salmon waxy bell-flowered rhododendron of that name. **T.W.**

Eyhorne Manor KENT

Mr and Mrs Derek Simmons, Hollingbourne.
tel. Hollingbourne (062 780) 514

A delightful and quite unique cottage garden wonderfully reflecting the character and charm of an old manor house, and equally the personality and instinctive tastes of the owners. Eyhorne Manor is a small historic hall or yeoman's house, oak timbered and tiled roof, which has been completely and carefully restored. It now combines a comfortable family house with a unique museum of country life, a wealth of things to see. The garden was, like the house, in a sad state when the Simmons family came here in 1952, disused chicken runs, vegetable patches, rubbish tips, 'privvies' and an old apple tree. Old hedges were tidied up and retained and gradually the garden took shape. The design is apparently informal, but within little more than an acre (0.4ha), quite different intimate spaces have been created, with narrow pathed walks, tiny lawns and everywhere massed associations of old-fashioned plants. From spring to midsummer this garden is an aromatic and nostalgic dream. Violets, purple honesty, pheasant-eye narcissus, lilacs, sweet rocket, old double crimson peonies, herbs of every description are followed in early summer by masses of old scented roses, of which there are over 100 different kinds in the garden. There are different levels too, to add interest, with sunken paths between rock walls richly planted with a host of small and attractive plant associations. **T.W.**

5 miles E of Maidstone just N of A20 Maidstone—Ashford road on B2163

TQ 8355

Good Fri to end Sept: Sat and Sun, also bank holidays and in Aug Tue to Thur 1400–1800. Parties at other times by appointment

Peak months: May to July

Falkland Palace Garden FIFE

National Trust for Scotland, Falkland Palace, Falkland.
tel. Falkland (033 75) 397

Although Falkland Palace and its garden are in the care of The National Trust for Scotland, it is a Royal Residence and therefore a property of Her Majesty The Queen. During the Second World War the garden became a forest nursery and then in 1945 was again newly contrived by the then Captain, Constable and Keeper of Falkland, the late Major Michael Crichton Stuart, who commissioned Percy Cane to design a garden appropriate to the historical significance of the Palace of Falkland. Cane based his design upon a print of a former garden, modified to make the most of the relatively small 7-acre (3-ha) garden by creating seemingly long vistas over immaculately kept grass, with beds and borders around the perimeter to support the illusion of space. No attempt was made to select plants of a particular period, consequently the garden reflects the skilful ingenuity of Percy Cane seen in herbaceous borders, a wide selection of shrubs and trees, with a potentially large cut-leaved beech and a purple sycamore dominating the central grass walk. At the north end of the garden beyond a charming Victorian glasshouse, a later addition, the pool garden, is a complete contrast which is almost too severe, relying, as it does, upon foliage for effect. All the same, the Palace of Falkland makes a unique background for a most charming garden. **E.R.**

11 miles N of Kirkcaldy on A192

NO 2507

Apr to Oct: Mon to Sat 1000–1800, Sun 1400–1800. Reduced rates for parties

Peak months: June to Sept

Flintham Hall NOTTINGHAMSHIRE

M. T. Hildyard, Esq., nr Newark-on-Trent.

The ornate Victorian mansion at Flintham is set in a 19th-century park with a lake and woodland with walks aglow in spring with snowdrops and other early flowers. Roses, particularly shrub roses, are one of the glories of Flintham along with a flowering shrub garden and herbaceous borders. A 19th-century pheasantry is one of the features of the extensive grounds as well as a garden house, an aviary and walled gardens. Flintham, however, is probably best known for its c. 1850 conservatory, the best surviving example of these large-scale palatial adjuncts to gracious living. Its high curved glass roof and its balcony make it most distinctive as one looks down upon the ivy and jasmine embowered masonwork of the great arched windows. Still remaining are the Lily Gaslights – glass-petalled arum lilies above exquisitely modelled small statuettes holding gas jets. The conservatory is reached from the house by the library from where the two-tiered tinkling fountain can be seen and just heard. An umbrella of a mimosa soars up to the arched roof and other luxurious plantings enrich the aesthetically satisfying lines of the architecture. **K.L.**

17 miles NE of Nottingham on A46 Leicester—Newark-on-Trent road

SK 7445

Open under National Gardens Scheme

No peak season

Forde Abbey DORSET

M. Roper, Esq., nr Chard.

1 mile s of B3167 Axminster— Crewkerne road

ST 3505

Mar, Apr and Oct: Sun 1400–1630, plus Easter Sun and Mon 1400–1800; May to Sept: Sun, Wed and Bank Holiday Mon 1400–1800. Reduced rates for parties

Peak months: Apr to Sept

🅿 🚻 🍴 🐕 🛍 🌹 🌿 🎁 🏠 *limited opening*

Originally designed in the 18th century by the Gwyn Family, who laid out the lawns and altered the existing stew ponds, and further landscaped and planted with many conifers by the Evans family, these largely informal gardens today extend over 25 acres (10ha). Borders in front of the long pond are massed with perennials for a superb display of colour throughout the summer months. Hundreds of narcissi in spring carpet either side of the drive leading to the great pond, the first of a line of four ponds joined by a series of cascades. The great pond covers 4 acres (1.5ha) and along one edge an interesting bog garden is planted with royal ferns, iris, lysichitum, primulas and enormous gunneras. The beech house stands overlooking the cascade flowing down to the canal pond and on to mermaid pond with a lovely statue of 'Leda and the Swan' situated in the centre of the water. Acers, pieris, kalmia and eucryphia, colourful in both spring and autumn, are among a great variety of trees and shrubs surrounding this area. Hellebores bloom in early spring in the park garden, beyond which stands the arboretum planted in 1947 by G. D. Roper with a marvellous collection of rare trees and shrubs. **A.S.**

Glasgow Botanic Gardens
STRATHCLYDE

City of Glasgow Parks Department, Great Western Road, Glasgow. tel. Glasgow (041) 334 2422

On the Great Western Road, junction of Byres Road and Queen Margaret Drive

NS 5865

Daily: 0700–dusk

No peak season

🚻 ♿ 🏠 *by appointment only*

🐕 🍴 🌹 🌿 🎁

The Gardens offer an extensive range of interest for visitors and act as a widely used resource centre. Links with the University of Glasgow date from their foundation in 1817 and they have been owned by the City since 1891. The Kibble Palace, just a few yards from the main gate, makes a good starting point for a visit. This large curvilinear iron glasshouse, named after John Kibble who had it erected here in 1873, is of special architectural merit. It contains a world famous collection of tree ferns and plants from warm temperate regions arranged geographically. The entrance area has two wings, one with an exhibit on 'The Plant Kingdom' and the other a visitor centre (open every afternoon throughout the summer). The main range of glasshouses consists of eleven sections, each devoted to special groups of plants. Among those of major interest are the orchids (here there is an internationally recognized collection of orchid species); the begonias (the gardens have the National Collection of Begonias – non-tuberous); economic plants – those used in commerce, industry and medicine. Within the 40 acres (16ha) of grounds the areas of interest include a systematic garden, a herb garden, a chronological border and an arboretum.

Glendurgan House CORNWALL

The National Trust, Helford, Mawnan Smith, nr Falmouth.

4 miles sw of Falmouth and ½ mile sw of Mawnan Smith on road to Helford Passage

SW 7728

Mar to end Oct: Mon, Wed and Fri (closed Good Fri) 1030–1630

Peak months: Apr to June

🅿 🚻 ♿ *limited* 🍴 🌿

Two realistic, life-size, stone foxes stand watch over the not easily seen entrance to this valley garden. They remind us that this was one of several estates developed locally by the Fox family of Falmouth in the 19th century and since. Once inside, a drive curves through short grass under tall established and more recently planted trees and shrubs, down to the house which stands some 200ft (61m) above and 700yd (640m) from Durgan, a tiny former fishing village on Helford river. Winding paths, some steeply sloping, take one to all parts of this 28-acre (11-ha) woodland garden and, finally, to the water's edge. Those that would avoid the climb back may do so by turning off the main path but still enjoy lovely views and many plants. The plan shows sixteen viewpoints, most of them in the upper half of the garden and giving a glimpse of the sea over and through a canopy of exotic trees and shrubs. There is colour of flowers from early spring through much of the summer but always variety of form provided by many long-established conifers with deciduous and evergreen trees. There has been steady recent planting giving greater interest and many stretches of grass contain bulbs in their season as well as naturalized primulas and columbines. Gunnera and bamboos add more variety to the pattern of leaf and plants. A laurel maze is a great rarity in Cornwall and near the top a wall garden has slightly more formality than the rest. **F.S.**

Great Comp KENT

Great Comp Charitable Trust, Borough Green, Sevenoaks.
tel. Borough Green (0732) 882669

A remarkable garden developed over the past 30 years by two people, Mr and Mrs Cameron, who until quite recently were entirely responsible for its development and maintenance. When they bought the property in 1957 they found a sturdy 17th-century house, mature lime trees, and an Edwardian-style garden and some woodland and a paddock and to this they added two more acres (0.8ha) of market garden land, transforming the whole 7 acres (3ha) into the present mature and interesting garden. Thoughtful advance tree planting of fast-growing pines, birches and evergreens soon gave shelter and the woodland glade effect they wanted. A natural, and informal style was favoured, with vistas and glades using unusual trees and shrubs of great variety and association, underplanted with carefully selected ground cover using heathers, conifers, brooms and other maquis-forming shrubs. In the more shaded woodland areas are hostas, hardy geraniums, ferns and naturalized bulbs. An excellent printed guide lists in detail the 3,000 or more plants to be found in this garden. More formal terraces and enclosures around the house are sensitively planted, lavenders, roses and many other plants providing fragrance and summer colour for the visitors enjoying the delicious home-made teas, or attending performances in the delightful barn theatre the Camerons skillfully converted. Music festivals are an added appropriate attraction to the pleasures to be found at Great Comp. **T.W.**

Between Maidstone and Sevenoaks, turn s off A25 onto B2016 at Wrotham Heath and ½ mile w at 1st crossroads

TO 6357

Apr to end Oct: daily 1100–1800

No peak season

🅿 wc ♿
🚌 *by appointment only*
limited opening and for parties by arrangement

Great Dixter EAST SUSSEX

Quentin Lloyd, Esq. (Director), Northiam.
tel. Northiam (079 74) 3160

No garden existed in 1910 when Mr Nathaniel Lloyd bought the neglected old farmhouse and asked Edwin Lutyens to help him restore it and to lay out the gardens. Another local timbered house was grafted on to the original house and Lutyens designed the gardens, incorporating the great oast houses, old barns and buildings into the clever design that largely characterises the gardens today. He skillfully linked the different levels by means of walls, terraces, steps and paths, using as always local material. Nathaniel was responsible for the many yew hedges and topiary. This architectural framework thus became furnished with a rich array of carefully selected plants, originally the genius of Mrs N. Lloyd but in recent years chosen by the plantsman and author, Christopher Lloyd, one of her sons. This is a garden of contrasts and everchanging seasonal effects. In spring and early summer the old orchards and the meadow garden in front of the house are flowering meads of wild flowers and naturalized bulbs, and from June to October in particular, the famous mixed border is a magnificent blend of shrubs, perennials and annuals. The sunken pool garden, the old rose garden with its many highly scented varieties, and the many walls clad with clematis, roses and many unusual climbers are only a few of the fascinating features to be explored at Dixter. **T.W.**

8 miles NW of Rye and ½ mile w of A28 Tenterden—Hastings road (signposted in Northiam village)

TQ 8225

Apr to mid-Oct: Tue to Sun and Bank Holiday Mon 1400–1700. Open 1100 Sun in July and Aug and late May and Aug Bank Holiday Mon. Reduced rates for parties by prior arrangement

No peak season

🅿 wc ♿
🚌 *by appointment only*

Great Thurlow Hall SUFFOLK

Ronald A. Vestey, Esq., Haverhill.

This handsome Georgian house is set in a fine, immaculately maintained 16-acre (6.5ha) garden. When purchased by the present owners hardly anything existed except the old walled kitchen garden. Development began in 1947 to the designs of Vernon Daniel. In the best tradition of English mid-20th century gardens it has wide lawns, terraces, yew-hedged enclosures, interesting shrubs and trees, a profusion of flowers, with formality around the house melting gradually into natural lines. On the west side of the house flows the River Stour and the land between has been stepped down to it. The top terrace is occupied by a rose garden whilst the lower levels contain excellent herbaceous borders. A timber bridge along which is trained wisteria and honeysuckle provides access to a stone-columned pavilion. There is a gold-fish pond with fountain statue in an enclosure to the south of the house and beyond a big open lawn ending at a ha-ha with views of unspoilt countryside. Between the two main axis, grass paths lead to the upper reaches of the river and a newly made trout lake. This part of the garden is delightful in April, being planted with great drifts of modern varieties of daffodil. **M.R.**

4 miles N of Haverhill, turn E off B1061 Newmarket road at Great Thurlow crossroads

TL 6750

Open frequently between spring and autumn

No peak season

🐕 ♿

7 miles w of Skegness
on A158 Skegness—
Horncastle road

TF 4766

Apr to end Sept:
Thur 1400–1800;
Tue, Wed and Fri by
written appointment
only

Peak Months: June
and July

Gunby Hall LINCOLNSHIRE

The National Trust, Gunby, nr Spilsby
tel. Scremby (075 485) 212

Known for its veteran roses, Gunby Hall gardens were first laid out when the
house was built for Sir William Massingberd in 1700. The existing garden on
the main front is of 1900 vintage, a yew-bounded enclosure with a central
sundial and formal flower beds, a paved central path and clipped golden
privet. Enclosures beyond, formed by yew hedges, make bowling alleys. On
the east are mellowed brick-walled gardens originally containing vegetables
and orchards. There are still apples, along with clematis and trained fruit on
the walls, and in beds are roses, many of which are rarely seen today such as
'Reine Marie Henriette', raised 100 years ago and exclusive to Gunby until
propagated by the National Trust, 'Mrs Oakley Fisher' (1921), which has
come to be known as the Gunby Rose, 'Mrs Wemyss Quin' (1914), 'Cardinal
de Richelieu' (1840), and 'Easlea's Golden Rambler' (1932). Among them are
modern shrub roses, and many climbing Bourbons and the old walls make a
fitting backcloth for herbaceous borders and a herb garden. Within these
walled gardens several old buildings survive, a pigeon house or dovecot
possibly older than the house itself and a stone summerhouse. Along the
southern wall of the gardens a long pool is known as the Ghost Walk Pond for
obvious reasons. A cedar of 1812 planting on the east has other young ones
round to follow on, a characteristic of the house wherein is contained the
Gunby Tree Book – a record of planting from round about 1670. **K.L.**

2 miles SE of Castle
Cary on A371

ST 6531

Tue, Wed and Thur
1000–1700; Sun (Apr
to Oct) 1400–1700.
Other times by
appointment

Peak seasons: spring
and summer

Hadspen House SOMERSET

Paul Hobhouse, Esq., Castle Cary.
tel. Castle Cary (0963) 50200/50427

Hadspen House was surrounded by fields until 1880, although the walled
gardens were already established then, situated a little way from the house.
Slowly the gardens began to take shape so that by 1900 many trees and shrubs
had been planted and a water garden created. Penelope Hobhouse took over
the supervision of the garden in 1966 and was responsible for introducing
many of the unusual plants still to be seen here today. Walking across the lawns
of this 8-acre (3-ha) south-facing sheltered garden that looks over fields
beyond the ha-ha, one follows a path which leads past a charming little cottage
upon which *Hydrangea petiolaris* climbs. The nearby beds are crammed with a
varied collection of ground-cover plants consisting of white-flowered
comfrey, pulmonaria, cowslips, bergenias and hellebores. The path to the
walled garden is backed on one side by a wall covered with roses and clematis,
and on the other by a herbaceous border which looks down on the lily pond.
From the top of the old walled kitchen garden looking down the central path
bordered by beech hedges, many unusual and rare plants can be seen with a
marvellous collection of hostas and rheums mixed with roses and tender
shrubs. Coming back towards the house a flowering cherry hangs gracefully
over a sunken garden with pool and fountain. **A.S.**

On A308 Kingston to
Staines road

TQ 1667

Open daily throughout
the year except for 24
to 26 Dec, Jan 1 and
Good Fri

No peak season

Hampton Court Palace Gardens
GREATER LONDON

Dept. of the Environment, East Molesey, Surrey.

The gardens which surround the Tudor palace at Hampton Court have a
grandeur and historical importance which immediately impresses itself on the
visitor, and most of all when surveying the scene from the Broad Walk, over
the Great Fountain to the tree-lined Long Water which forms the central axis
of the goose-foot pattern of lime trees. The clipped yews in the foreground of
this view lead the eye onwards to one of the most noble garden prospects in
Britain. Gardening enthusiasts, moreover, find delights at every turn, from
the grand herbaceous border and the superb bedding to the proliferation of
fine climbing and wall plants which beguile the eye and, of course, the features
for which Hampton Court is famous: the Privy Garden with its colourful
parterre, the pond gardens and the knot garden, the rose garden, the famous
maze and the vinery with its equally famous Black Hamburgh grape vine.
This was planted in 1769, has a branch spread of well over 100ft (30m) and
regularly produces over 500 bunches of grapes each year. Roughly triangular
in shape and embraced on two sides by a loop in the River Thames, the many
features of Hampton Court Gardens are interlinked by paths and driveways of
which the most impressive is, of course, the Broad Walk referred to earlier.
R.P.

Hardwick Hall DERBYSHIRE

The National Trust, Doe Lea, nr Chesterfield.
tel. Chesterfield (0246) 850430

Bess of Hardwick's house of 1597 still retains its original surrounding garden walls, heavily crenellated, the gatehouse and the 18th-century parkland in which is ancient timber, one of them, the Hardwick Oak, of 15ft 5in (4.7m) girth and probably growing in Bess's time. One of the original walled enclosures, the one on the south, is the garden proper. A long border is a feature in the entrance courtyard and from here the visitor reaches the south garden laid out by Lady Egerton from about 1870. It is divided into four by yew and hornbeam hedges and walks, and in arbours cut in the hedge are 18th-century lead statues. The north side is marked by a mixed border of herbaceous plants and shrubs with a silvery sheen while on the east is a wild border in which plants such as the 10-ft high (3m) giant hogweed are to be seen. A lawn here with magnolias contrasts with the two eastern sections planted as an ornamental orchard. Borders here are of shrub roses and lavender, while on the south side is a row of mulberry trees. During recent years part of the old vegetable garden has been turned over to an Elizabethan herb garden and here can be seen the white-margined foliage of the Hardwick lily-of-the-valley. An 18th-century gate leads to the east garden with pond, yew hedges, lots more shrub roses and a double row of limes planted in the shape of an inverted wine glass in the 1930s to be seen over the park. **K.L.**

8 miles SE of Chesterfield off A617 Chesterfield— Mansfield road (signposted)

SK 4564

Apr to end Oct: daily exc Good Fri 1200–1730

Peak months: June and July

🅿 WC
🚌 *by appointment only*
🐕
🍽 *limited opening*
♿ 🍴 ♨ 🌱
🎁 *limited opening*
🏠 *limited opening*
🌿

Harewood House WEST YORKSHIRE

The Earl of Harewood, Harewood, Leeds.
tel. Harewood (0532) 886225

'One of the most delectable of landscapes' wrote Dorothy Stroud of Brown's work at Harewood carried out for the 1st Earl in 1772. Here he enlarged the lake, moulded the rough farmland into an undulating park to match scenic Wharfedale, planted trees and banished the pleasure grounds to beyond the lake. A change of character came in 1843–48 with the Barry terrace on the south front of the house from where the view is still of Brown at his best. This balustraded terrace with its statuary and fountains is now being restored to its Victorian parterred splendour. The side lawns and walk under the terrace are planted with specimen trees, climbers, rhododendrons and flowering shrubs. A path passing the Carr stable block and bird garden goes downhill through thick woodland to the cascade bridge at the far end of the lake which overlooks a sunken garden – a bowl of rhododendron and azalea colour with a Japanese look stemming from the gunnera, primula and astilbe lined rocky stream and its oriental-style summerhouse. The path then leads through mature woodland underplanted with rhododendrons, many bred at Harewood, to the pleasure and rose gardens. The roses, mainly large and cluster flowered, are in two terraces. On the lawn overlooking the lake is a period summerhouse built into the wall by ancient mulberry trees and more rose beds. **K.L.**

8 miles N of Leeds at junction of A659 and A61 Leeds—Harrogate roads

SE 3144

Apr to end Oct: daily 1000–dusk Feb, Mar, Nov: Sun, Tue, Wed and Thur. Reduced rates for parties

Peak months: late May to Oct

🅿 WC
🐾 *1-mile walk*
🚌 🐕
🍽 *parties by appointment*
♿ 🍴 ♨ 🌱 🎁 🏠

Harlow Car Gardens NORTH YORKSHIRE

Northern Horticultural Society, Crag Lane, Harrogate.
tel. Harrogate (0423) 65413

Harlow Car Gardens, of some 60 acres (24ha), set out to be the 'Wisley of the North' when started upon by the Northern Horticultural Society in 1948, when only the roughest of pasture and overgrown woodland and an old hydropathic mineral spring establishment were there. Today it ranks as one of the finest of post-war garden creations. Apart from its native woodland, underplanted with rhododendrons, and its arboretum with its nature trail, wild life pond and hide, the garden acts as a touchstone for northern gardeners for almost every department of gardening. There are trials of heathers, delphiniums, annuals, perennials, roses and vegetables. The gardens accommodate the national collection of hypericums, a replica one of pyracanthas, one of the four 'vegetable sanctuaries' for endangered kinds. There are both vegetable and fruit plots and display collections of cane fruits, strawberries, and the national collection of rhubarb. Its model suburban gardens and collections of hostas, bergenias, hellebores, its peat garden and both limestone and sandstone rock gardens are object lessons in growing, as are the hedging and ground cover trials and the bog garden by the streamside. A most colourful display house gives shelter for a rare collection of alpines with an eclectic collection of greenhouse plants. **K.L.**

On SW outskirts of Harrogate just north of B6162 Beckwithshaw road

SE 2855

Daily: 0900–dusk

Peak months: May to Sept

🅿 WC 🍴 🚌 🍽
♿ 🍴 ♨ 🌱 🎁

5 miles E of Horncastle off A158 Lincoln—Skegness road, signposted at end of Hagworthingham village

TF 3773

Apr to end Sept: Wed and Thur 1200–2000, and several Sun for charity, inc National Gardens Scheme 1400–1800. Other times by appointment

Peak months: May to Aug

Sun only

limited opening

Harrington Hall LINCOLNSHIRE

Lady Maitland, nr Spilsby.

All the evidence seems to point to the Harrington Hall Garden as being the one Tennyson invited Maud to enter. It is still unspoiled by the passage of time and matches its 17th century with an early Elizabethan origin. Old brick walls surround one garden where gate piers are dated 1722 by steps leading to a raised terrace from which it would have been possible to see the once elaborate Jacobean parterres laid out in knots. Today its supporting walls are clothed in roses and its herringbone brick pathways are spilled over by herbs and herbaceous planting while a large holly, *Ilex aquifolium* 'Ferox Argentea', stands sentinel. *Rosa banksiae* 'Lutea' climbs the house walls while the entrance drive is through rhododendrons and azaleas to a large lawn bounded by a mellow brick wall on which sprawls lonicera and climbing roses. Under it luxuriates a herbaceous border of reds, mauves, pinks and white. The kitchen garden, approached by way of a high hedge of yew, has a flower border and a mulberry of 17th-century planting. A summerhouse built into the wall of the second terrace lawn leads to a south-facing walk where the wall supports shrub roses, *Pittosporum tenuifolium*, magnolias and viburnums. Some very old roses are planted in a box-edged square to be viewed from the drawing room window – Charles de Mills (1836), Mme Pierre Oger (1878) Alister Stella Gray (1894) and La Reine Victoria (1872). **K.L.**

Opposite Hatfield BR station

TL 2308

Late Mar to early Oct: Mon 1400–1700; Tue to Sat 1200–1700; Sun 1400–1730. Reduced rates for parties over 20 by prior arrangement

No peak season

not Mon

Hatfield House HERTFORDSHIRE

The Marquess of Salisbury, Hatfield.
tel. Hatfield (30) 62823

Hatfield House is a place of pilgrimage. Architecturally distinguished and full of treasures, it has a fitting counterpart in the beautiful gardens which surround it – gardens which have changed greatly since the house was built by Robert Cecil, 1st Earl of Salisbury in the early 17th century. This was due to changing fashions and the vicissitudes of the Cecil family. Indeed, the original gardens disappeared in the 18th century to allow landscaped parkland to sweep right up to the walls of the mansion. In the mid-19th century, however, both house and gardens were restored to the original Jacobean style. To the west of the mansion is an extremely attractive parterre garden enclosed by yew hedges in which patterned beds planted with roses, shrubs and herbaceous perennial plants have as their centrepiece a formal pool and fountain. Beyond this, on a lower level, is the scented garden, opened in 1979, a place of enchantment with its wealth of aromatic herbs, its scented trees, shrubs and other flowering plants in beautiful associations. Another addition is the knot garden, completed in 1981, in the courtyard of the remaining wing of the 15th-century Palace of Hatfield. Here plants grown in the 15th, 16th and 17th centuries are displayed. Another parterre garden of great charm and the famous maze lie to the east of the mansion, while to the south is the Wilderness Garden. **R.P.**

2 miles NW of Stowmarket, off A45 Stowmarket—Bury St Edmunds road (signposted)

TM 0263

May to Sept: Tue 1500–1800

Peak month: May

by appointment only

Haughley Park SUFFOLK

A. J. Williams, Esq., nr Stowmarket.
tel. Elmswell (0359) 40205

The 'bones' of the garden which surround this red brick Jacobean house are mainly Victorian but over the last 20 years they have been re-clothed with a well-chosen selection of ornamental shrubs, with the assistance of Frederick Barcock of Drinkstone. The old laurels and hollies have been utilised to form a background to log-edged borders of rhododendrons, viburnums and hydrangeas, including *Hydrangea villosa*. A dell in the shade of chestnuts is planted with mahonias, bamboos, Solomons seal and other shade lovers, whilst a large lily pond has been created. The heart of the garden adjoins the north face of the house and here there is a big lawn with, as a centre-piece, a wide spreading *Magnolia soulangiana*. In the borders are azaleas, rhododendrons, *Cornus alternifolia* 'Variegata' and *Davidia involucrata*; to the west a small paved courtyard with pool and fountain. The house is set within an old park with good trees, and there is a large oak, birch and pine wood planted with *Rhododendron ponticum* and *R. luteum* (*Azalea pontica*), at their best in early June. Connecting the wood to the house is a wide grassy path bordered by mainly native shrubs such as sea-buckthorn, Guelder rose and spindles. **M.R.**

Heaselands WEST SUSSEX

Mrs E. G. Kleinwort, Haywards Heath.
tel. Haywards Heath (0444) 458084

A remarkable garden extending to over 20 acres (8ha), in a particularly beautiful part of the Sussex Weald where there has been a full and discerning exploitation of all the natural features of the site in making the garden. An old farmhouse and buildings were enlarged and renovated by the Kleinworts in 1932 and they began making the garden creating the enclosed areas around the house, and planting the main tree groups until the onset of the 1939–45 war, and then developing the valley ponds, woodland and water gardens over the past thirty years. The house stands on a terrace, below which most of the garden unfolds on a descending slope, so that there are superb prospects of the valley ponds and woodland gardens, brilliant with massed rhododendrons and azaleas and a vivid blue under-carpet of bluebells in May. A formal sunken lily pool lies near the house. The enclosed gardens each have a special personality and planting themes. The walled garden with its raised beds massed with dwarf rhododendrons and fine flowering dogwoods; a new paved garden of roses enclosed by yew hedges; and the secluded warm garden from which can be seen tempting views into the wooded glades below. The valley ponds and streams are richly planted and there are pleasant walks in the woods around. To the north of the house is a mature rock garden. An aviary of wildfowl is also a traditional attraction. **T.W.**

1 mile S of Haywards Heath Hospital on A273 to Burgess Hill

TQ 3124

Open few times each year under National Gardens Scheme. Parties at other times by appointment

Peak months: May, July and Oct

🅿 ♿ ⊘
🚽 *by appointment only*
♨ 🚍 ❦

Helmingham Hall SUFFOLK

The Lord Tollemache, Stowmarket.
tel. Helmingham (047 339) 363

A sense of calm and peacefulness pervades the gardens of this Tudor mansion set within an ancient deer park and sheltered by huge cedars. It is as though time has stood still since the turn of the century. Like the house, the gardens are surrounded by a moat, starred with water-lilies. The main flower garden is walled on three sides but open to the house on the fourth. It consists of a lawn with an urn in the centre, surrounded by box-edged beds planted with traditional bedding plants. Against the walls are wide borders devoted to an interesting collection of 'old' and shrub roses, edged with lavender. Two charming little timber arbours provide alternately a shady and a sunny retreat. Fine wrought-iron gates lead into a big walled kitchen garden of the old style, divided into four by grass paths, and devoted to expertly grown vegetables, soft fruit, and picking flowers. Beautifully trained peach, plum, pear and fig trees line the 18th-century red brick walls. Through the centre and against the outsides of the walls are colourful borders filled with an unsophisticated mixture of shrubs, hardy plants and annuals. **M.R.**

11 miles N of Ipswich on B1077 Ipswich— Diss road

TM 1857

Easter Sun to Sept: Sun 1400–1800; parties by appointment Wed p.m.

Peak months: June to Sept

🅿 ♿ 🚽 🐕 ♨
🚍 🍴 ❦ 🎁

Hergest Croft Gardens
HEREFORD and WORCESTER

W. L. and R. A. Banks, Kington.
tel. Kington (0544) 230218

There are herbaceous borders as good, rock and water gardens of equal interest, but nowhere that rhododendrons can be seen in a more spectacular manner than in Park Wood at Hergest Croft. In 1910 W. H. Banks purchased Park Wood and planted it with masses of rhododendrons, mostly the standard garden hybrids of the time, although he later became interested in species and first crosses. After the First World War some 200 species were obtained. A pool has been created in the cleft of Park Wood by damming a stream, and from the bridge the full effect of 'Flower Fall', a cascade of rhododendrons, can best be seen. The Loderi hybrids are particularly splendid. The edges of the pool at Park Wood are planted with bamboos and with such bog plants as lysichitums, osmundas and rodgersias. The garden proper begins with small rock and water gardens. In spring this part is brilliant with snowdrops, and daffodils. *Scilla bifolia* has naturalised, as has *Crocus vernus* and *Anemone apennina*. The walled garden is an interesting mixture of vegetables and herbaceous borders; iris and anemones stand out. The other great feature of Hergest Croft is its range of trees, planted over most of the 50 acres (20ha). Acers are particularly well represented. There are large specimens of *A. griseum* and *A. palmatum* 'Senkaki'. There is also an extensive collection of deciduous azaleas. **E.F.**

20 miles NW of Hereford and ½ mile S of A44 on western outskirts of Kington

May to mid-Sept: daily; Oct: Sun 1330–1830. Reduced rates for parties of 20 and over by prior arrangement

Peak months: May, June and Oct

🅿 ♿ 🚽 🐕
♨ *limited opening*
🚍 🍴 ❦ 🎁

4 miles NE of
Chipping Campden;
turn east off A46
Broadway—Stratford
road at Mickleton

SP 1644

Apr to end Oct: daily
exc Tue and Fri
1100–2000. Parties of
15 and over by
appointment only

No peak season

P WC
limited opening

Hidcote Manor Garden   GLOUCESTERSHIRE

The National Trust, Hidcote Bartrim, Chipping Campden.
tel. Mickleton (038 677) 333

Hidcote, created by the American, Major Lawrence Johnson, is one of the seminal gardens of the 20th century. The Hidcote style has been, and still, in most cases, is the accepted manner in which to lay out gardens today. Johnston started work before the First World War and continued until his death in 1958. He was working at a time when the plants of the world were available to him, and when the history of gardening had become a subject of interest. Hidcote is thus a synthesis of much that has gone before. Its emphasis on structure, the avenues, the cross vistas, the thrust of the central spine starting in the old garden, through the circle, up the red borders, mounting the steps by the garden pavilions, along the stilt garden to a magnificent view of the open country, is derived essentially from the classical period of French gardening, but its planting is English, the planting of cottage gardens, but with an immeasurably enriched palette. Colour control is Miss Jekyll's principal contribution to gardening, and Lawrence Johnston learned her art; his red borders, the greens and yellows of the garden he named after his mother, Mrs Winthrop, the whites, silvers, pinks and mauves of the old garden testify to this. After a period of decline, in Johnston's later years, the garden is now meticulously and sympathetically maintained by the National Trust. **E.F.**

8 miles N of
Bournemouth, off
B3072 Bournemouth—
Verwood road

SU 0802

Easter Sun to 1st Sun
in Sept: Sun and
Bank Holiday Mon
1400–1800. Parties at
other times by
appointment

No peak season

WC ⊙ 🍵
🅿 ⚥ 🌿

Highbury   DORSET

Mr and Mrs Stanley Cherry, West Moors.
tel. Ferndown (0202) 874372

This fascinating half-acre (0.2ha) garden, filled with hundreds of unusual and rare plants in a setting of mature trees, was bought in 1966 by Mr and Mrs Stanley Cherry in a state of neglect. Since then it has been restored to the original design of 1909. There is much here to interest keen gardeners, plant collectors and botanists and all the plants are clearly labelled. Variegated and silvery leaved shrubs and ground-cover plants grow in beds near the front of the house with a collection of slow-growing ones nearby. Overlooking these are two very beautiful *Amelanchier lamarckii* trees which provide blossom in spring and also good autumn colour. Crinodendron and embothrium mingling with other interesting shrubs help to enclose the small paved garden which is filled with a good collection of herbs. In a narrow bed between this and the north walk 16th- and 17th-century plants grow. The lower garden is full of exciting plants, *Cunninghamia lanceolata* and the variegated lily-of-the-valley, *Convallaria majalis* 'Variegata', blend with collections of dwarf conifers, grasses, herbaceous perennials and bulbs. Next to the orchard, which is underplanted with snowdrops, daffodils and bluebells and divided by a hedge, a mixed border runs down to the greenhouse and small weather station. **A.S.**

On A272
Winchester—
Petersfield road 1 mile
W of Bramdean

SU 5928

Open few times each
year under National
Gardens Scheme

No peak season

Hinton Ampner House   HAMPSHIRE

The Rt Hon. The Lord Sherborne, nr Alresford.

It is perhaps surprising that these magnificent gardens are not better known, but their creator, Ralph Dutton (Lord Sherborne) has not sought publicity or large numbers of visitors. The fine Georgian-style house was re-built after a fire in 1960 and the gardens were created over the past 40 years. The house is sited on a south-facing ridge so that the terraced gardens can be viewed in part from its main windows with the unfolding countryside beyond. A bold, flagstone terrace runs the entire length of the house, a warm place for massed associations of sun-loving plants. The next level below is a dramatic wide grass terrace of even greater length and a procession of Irish yews terminate each end with a fine statue. Massed borders of shrubs and old roses run along the terrace, while below a ha-ha looks over a pastoral landscape, a real touch of the 18th century here. To the east a fine sunken garden leads to a more informal wilderness area. Moving downwards towards a shaded dell, towering 'cliffs' of box, scented philadelphus, yews, hollies, and cascades of Russian vine and the Kiftsgate rose give a breathtaking effect. This is a garden above all intended for meditation and sauntering, and before returning slowly to the house there is the old orchard, more shrubberies and a perfect kitchen garden to explore. This is an Englishman's garden conceived with style and bravura on classical lines; a visit is unforgettable. **T.W.**

Hodnet Hall Gardens SHROPSHIRE

Mr and the Hon. Mrs A. Heber Percy, Hodnet, Market Drayton.
tel. Market Drayton (0630) 84202

The gardens of Hodnet Hall have enormous natural advantages. The house stands high and below it a series of terraces descends to the main pool, the last of a string of lakes. At the level of the house, beyond the private garden, stretches a wide grassy meadow overlooked by hanging bluebell woods, while to the south is the run of fascinatingly shaped lakes. A walk along the mown paths beneath the yellows and greens of the springtime oaks, looking across grass thick with bluebells and ragged Robin, to their reflections in the water is pure pleasure. It is only as we approach the more heavily planted areas that questions arise. It is unfortunate that some of the most frequently planted azaleas and rhododendrons come in violently clashing colours, chrome yellow, cerise, magenta and scarlet. They flower together and the result is visual cacophony. The magnolia walk, alongside a path leading from an entrance gate to the tea room is excellent. The white theme continues with a snowdrop tree, *Halesia monticola vestita*, and on the lower level a bed of white camassias, with white Persian lilac nearby. Spring and autumn are the peak periods for this large, handsome garden. The smell of the azaleas is overwhelmingly seductive, and the space is large enough to take their blaze. **E.F.**

12 miles NE of Shrewsbury at junction of A53 Shrewsbury—Market Drayton road and A442 Whitchurch—Wellington road

SJ 6128

Apr 1 or Easter to late Sept: Mon to Sat 1400–1700; Sun and bank holidays 1200–1800. Reduced rates for parties of 25 or over

Peak months: May to June

🅿 wc 🚽 ♿ ✝
❥limited opening: parties by appointment
✝ ❦ 🌿 🎁

Holker Hall CUMBRIA

Mr and Mrs Hugh Cavendish, Cark-in-Cartmel, Grange-over-Sands.
tel. Newby Bridge (0448) 53328

Set between Morecambe Bay and the Lakeland hills, both of which can be seen from this 22 acres (9ha) of formal Victorian garden and woodland, the present design is largely by Paxton, for this is a Cavendish home. Paxton is also said to have suggested the formal Italianate steps descending between ilex hedges to a central pool and fountain. The gardens have been altered over the years several times from the early Dutch design to the present day when the new flower garden and lawn were completed in 1875. A long walk meanders through herbaceous borders and a wide ranging selection of shrubs and trees including azaleas and rhododendrons, magnolias and one of the first four monkey puzzle trees to be planted in England by Paxton for the 6th Duke of Devonshire. Also relishing the mild climate here are specimens of *Catalpa* (Indian bean tree), the tulip trees, *Gingko biloba*, *Hoheria lyallii*, a cut-leaf beech, a tree-sized *Magnolia acuminata*, *Drimys winteri*, *Embothrium*, *Paulownia*, *Staphylea holocarpa*, *Osmanthus yunnanensis* and *Myrtus luma*. In the spring daffodils and cherries brighten the scene and a double Banksian rose climbs the house wall. A paved sunken garden with a shelter and pergola designed by Thomas Mawson in 1912 is home for many species and old-fashioned roses including gallicas, cabbage, damask and noisette. Heather beds by the west wing are of 1769 planting. **K.L.**

5 miles W of Grange-over-Sands on B5278

SD 3577

Easter to end Sept: daily exc Sat 1030–1630. Reduced rates for parties

Peak seasons: spring and early summer

🅿 wc 🅿 ♿ 🚽 ✝
❥ ✝ 🌿 🎁 🏛

Horsted Place EAST SUSSEX

Lady Rupert Nevill, Uckfield.
tel. Isfield (082 575) 315

An ornate Victorian Gothic mansion built by G. Myers in 1851 (Pugin influence) provides the dominating feature of the attractive and cleverly designed gardens at Horsted Place. Approached down a long, wooded drive, a huge turkey oak stands near the garden entrance with picnic seats thoughtfully provided in its grassy shade. There are many attractive and surprising contrasts, the result of the combined mastery of an overall design by the landscape architect, Sir Geoffrey Jellicoe, with Lady Rupert Nevill's philosophy of creating scent, rhythm and blended harmony, for 'planting to feel unrestricted except where there is a specially made framework to contain it'. The more formal garden near the house has a distinct early-Victorian style with a boundary of pleached limes, rose-covered arches and arbours, and the delightful painted iron rose baskets 'floating' across the lawns inspired by Humphry Repton's designs for the Brighton Pavilion. Beyond is an inviting laburnum tunnel leading to a serpentine shrubbery where massed shrubs chosen for colour, scent and foliage contrasts are well sited against a backdrop of mature sheltering trees. A cool, hidden round garden is encircled with azaleas, hydrangeas, hostas and day lilies. Fragrant flowers and herbs are given especial emphasis. The gardens look lovely from May onwards. **T.W.**

2 miles S of Uckfield on A26 Uckfield—Lewes road

TQ 4718

End Apr to end Sept: Wed, Thur, Sun and bank holidays 1400–1800

No peak season

🅿 ♿ 🚽

6½ miles E of Forfar, just S of A932 Forfar—Arbroath road

NO 5649

Open frequently in spring and summer, ring for details

Peak months: May and July

P ⊞ ⊟ ♱
🍴by arrangement only
🍷occasional
⊓ 🌱 🎁

House of Pitmuies TAYSIDE

Mrs Farquhar Ogilvie, by Forfar, (Angus).
tel. Friockheim (024 12) 245

The new House of Pitmuies is reputed to have been built in 1730 and at that time it was the possession of David Ogilvie. In 1919 the property was sold to a Major Crombie who was instrumental in recreating the garden, which by this time was in a neglected state. The Crombies were the first to plant delphiniums at Pitmuies, for which the property was later to be well known. In 1945 the property was purchased by Major and Mrs Ogilvie, and later came into the possession of Mr and Mrs Farquhar Ogilvie. Sadly Mr Farquhar Ogilvie died early in 1983. The fact that Mrs Farquhar Ogilvie, the present owner, is the daughter of Mr Gerald Annesley of Castlewellan may account for much of the excellence of the present garden at Pitmuies. At the height of the season, in June and July, one has the feeling of stepping into a garden overflowing with flowers. The main attractions are herbaceous perennials, largely contained in two borders, and roses including hybrid teas (large-flowered), polyantha as well as a delightful selection of shrub roses. To extend the season in the early part of the year there are shrubs, early-flowering perennials, meconopsis and foliage plants. All this and an avenue of lime trees as well as outstanding beeches and a Spanish chestnut, all planted prior to 1877, lend Pitmuies a long established, and rather reverent character, which, all things being considered, is a right and proper one for such a charming and very delightful garden. **E. R.**

7 miles SE of Chelmsford take East Hanningfield turning off A130 at Rettendon Bell public house and then 2nd right

TL 7700

Open few times each year under National Gardens Scheme. Parties at other times by appointment

Peak months: Apr to Aug

P ⊞ ⊟ ♱
🍴open days and by arrangement
🍷open days only
⊓ 🌱
🎁open days only

Hyde Hall ESSEX

Hyde Hall Garden Trust, Rettendon, Chelmsford.
tel. Chelmsford (0245) 400256

This major garden has been created around an old Essex farmhouse during the past 25 years, but the owners had no intention of doing this when they purchased it. Had they done so they might not have chosen a wind-swept hilltop, heavy clay overlying in places impermeable gravel, and the lowest rainfall in England! There were, however, compensations; plenty of sunshine, little frost, neutral soil and several old ponds. There is no hint now of early struggles – even apparent drawbacks have been used to advantage. Trees and hedges planted for shelter have provided shade for rhododendrons and camellias whilst the dry, sunny climate has encouraged ceanothus, watsonias, hebes and other tender plants to thrive. The garden covers 8 acres (3.2ha), with a further 12 acres (5ha) devoted to specimen trees. The range and quality of the plants is impressive as is the meticulous maintenance. Roses form a major element, from climbers to miniatures which are grown in raised beds. There is a mainly herbaceous border with a graduated colour scheme, an iris border and a corner devoted to golden foliage. The garden possesses the national collections of viburnums and malus. A high greenhouse accommodates treasures such as mimosa, daturas and lapageria. **M.R.**

6 miles NE of Gairloch on A832, by Poolewe

NG 8582

Daily: 0900–2100, or ½ hour before dusk if earlier. Reduced rates for parties

Peak months: May to July

P ⊞ ♱
🍴limited opening
⊓ 🌱 🎁 🍁

Inverewe Garden HIGHLAND

National Trust for Scotland, Inverewe House, Poolewe, (Ross and Cromarty).
tel. Poolewe (044 586) 200

In 1862, Osgood Mackenzie began to make Inverewe garden which, in the course of the next 100 years, established an international reputation for its plant content as well as the tremendous attraction it has for gardeners everywhere. High as the reputation of Inverewe may be, the gardens more than fulfil expectations. Originally there was only one tree, 3ft (1m) in height, growing in the heather-covered peninsular of Am Ploc Ard, as Inverewe was at one time known. Mackenzie planted the whole area with pines, and waited patiently for them to grow before clearing areas within the shelter they provided to grow many of the plants which now rank amongst the more valuable in the garden. On Mackenzie's death in 1922, his daughter, Mairi Sawyer, continued his work for a further 30 years before handing over the garden into the care of The National Trust for Scotland. Like Brodick, Inverewe owes much to a craze known as 'Rhododendron-mania' which commonly seized the country at the turn of the century. Species rhododendrons are now a feature of the garden. However, other collections are well established with primula, meconopsis, olearia and celmisia strongly in the forefront. Two extensive herbaceous borders offer a wealth of summer colour, together with a host of unusual bulbs, rare shrubs and trees, all contributing to that particular magic inside the garden, with unparalleled views of the Torridonian mountains adding to one's enjoyment. **E. R.**

Isabella and Waterhouse Plantations
GREATER LONDON

Dept. of the Environment, Richmond Park and Bushy Park.
tel. (01) 948 3209

For lovers of beautiful woodland gardens nothing could be more satisfying than a visit to the Isabella and Waterhouse Plantations at the height of their beauty in May and June, a perfectly feasible proposition on the same day, if so desired, for they are only a few miles apart – the Isabella Plantation in Richmond Park, the Waterhouse Plantations (for there are two) in Bushy Park, adjoining Hampton Court. Both rely for their effectiveness on mass planting of such colourful shrubs as rhododendrons, azaleas and camellias which delight in the dappled shade that high-branched trees provide. In the Isabella Plantation a meandering stream provides the ideal conditions for moisture-loving plants like primulas and hostas, while the presence in the Waterhouse Plantations of the man-made Longford River provides the opportunity to use water as a feature in its own right in a dramatic way. But if these gardens have a late spring peak, nobody should be discouraged from visiting them at other times, for they are always rewarding. **R.P.**

*Isabella Plantation:
Off A307, A205,
A306 and A3*

TO 1971

Daily: 0700–dusk

*Peak months: May to
June*

*Bushy Park: Off
A308 Kingston to
Staines road*

TQ 1668

Daily: dawn–dusk

*Peak months: Apr to
June*

🅿 wc ♿
🪑 *by permit only*
🐕 🐑 *in park*
🚗 *in park*

Jenkyn Place HAMPSHIRE

Mr and Mrs Gerald Coke, Bentley.
tel. Bentley (0420) 23118

One of the finest private gardens in the country could well be described as an outstanding plantsman's formal garden, developed continually over the past 30 years or so on the Hidcote/Sissinghurst principle of a number of enclosed gardens each with its own very specialised character and planting theme. The late 17th-century house overlooks the garden which falls away steadily to the south east, towards the River Wey, the fertile upper greensand soils and warm slope playing an important part in the range and the rarity of the plants to be found here. Connected by beautifully detailed and designed gates, arches, steps, and paths, there are many exciting gardens to explore. Near the house a charming intimate Dutch garden concentrates on scented plants around a delightful fountain. A sundial garden leads to an elegant rose garden with elongated pool, rose beds and many fine and rare plants on the walls. Dominating a terrace on the next level are two superb herbaceous borders, deliberately designed to provide maximum colour and effect in high season. An Italian garden, a herb garden, a sunken garden are also to be discovered here and new gardens are still in the making. Rare plants abound, beautifully grown and maintained and the setting of the house and many old mature trees add to the sense of combined maturity and development of Jenkyn Place, the creation of a husband and wife team with their gardeners since the Second World War. **T.W.**

*4 miles SW of
Farnham just N of
A31 Farnham—Alton
road at Bentley
crossroads*

SU 7844

*May to end Aug:
Suns, plus other times
by appointment for
parties*

No peak season

🅿 wc ♿🪑
🍴 *occasional*
🐕

Kailzie Gardens BORDERS

Mrs Angela Richards, The Garden House, Kailzie, Peebles, (Peeblesshire).
tel. Peebles (0721) 20007

Whether you intend to garden in Peeblesshire, or simply look at the several fine gardens to be found in that country, it is important to remember that nowhere is the land less than 500ft (152m) above sea level. Consequently winters are cold and areas can be very exposed even if, like Kailzie, shelter would appear to be adequate. Before it was demolished, Kailzie House, a large 19th-century building, stood on a dominant site, just south of the walled garden. A modern house was built in the south-east corner of a large walled garden, which has been largely recreated by the present owner during the past 15 years. About half of it is devoted to beds containing a selection of interesting shrubs and trees, while the remainder is more formal with herbaceous borders with several old-fashioned and unusual subjects, a rose garden and a splendid conservatory, built in Regency style with a quite fascinating selection of pelargoniums, orchids and camellias. The surrounding woodland is particularly attractive in the early part of the year, enhanced by a stream winding through the garden on its way to the Tweed, planted along its length with primula, astilbe and other moisture-loving plants. A very pleasant area, known as the 'Major's Walk', is devoted to meconopsis, several ericaceous shrubs and foliage plants. The attractions of the property extend beyond gardening, and include an aviary, art exhibits, garden centre as well as a tea room. **E.R.**

*2 miles E of Peebles
on B7062*

NT 2939

*Daily: Mid Mar to
mid Oct 1030–1730*

*Peak months: Mar to
July*

🅿 wc 🪑🐕 🐑
🚗 🍴 🐕 🎁

195

3 miles NW of
Pittenweem on B9171

NO 5204

Daily: 1000–dusk.
Reduced rates for
parties of 20 and over

Peak months: late
June to July

🅿️🚾🚹🐕🚼
♈occasional
🎁
🏛️limited opening

Kellie Castle FIFE

National Trust for Scotland, Kellie Castle, Pittenweem.
tel. Arncroach (033 38) 271

Robert Lorimer spent his boyhood at Kellie, which his father, Professor James Lorimer, had restored from a ruinous state. Here it was that Robert first developed his taste for garden design, and began by establishing the basis of creating a 'garden within a garden' seen in many gardens he subsequently made. In later years when he came to live at Kellie, his greater and more mature experience enabled him to further develop the garden and in 1904 received the accolade of an admirable account by Gertrude Jekyll following her visit to the garden. When the Trust acquired the property in.1970 it was a relatively simple matter to restore the garden with the help of Hew Lorimer, Sir Robert's son. Compared to gardens such as Brodick and Inverewe, Kellie is tiny, being just over 1 acre (0.4ha) in size, enclosed by a stone wall and situated on the north side of the Castle, thus denying a quarter of this small area of land any direct sunlight. The object was to create a 'cottage garden'. The patterns for the new borders were gleaned from an article which appeared in the July 1906 edition of 'Country Life'. Today the garden is all but complete, and seen in August is full of the colour and freshness of roses, herbaceous plants and many annuals, seemingly in gay disorder, with only the neat, regular rows of the vegetable plots and the primly cut box edging to remind one that it appears so by careful design and intention. One can almost look through the eyes of Gertrude Jekyll and experience the delight she obviously had for Kellie by seeing, once again, the plants she so admired. **E. R.**

6 miles NE of Exeter
city centre on B3185,
between B3181
Exeter—Cullompton
and A396 Exeter—
Tiverton roads

SS 9701

Daily: dawn–dusk

No peak season

🅿️🚾♿
🍴by appointment
only
🐕🍼🎁
🏛️Apr to Oct

Killerton House DEVON

The National Trust, Broadclyst, nr Exeter.
tel. Exeter (0392) 881345

The garden on this estate of more than 6,000 acres (2,428ha) is entered by a small door beside the house just beyond the front door. The first impression is of limited gardening on a flat site. There are several shrubs and climbers in narrow borders below the house and above the dwarf wall opposite that divides the garden from the lower farmland. Then, at the end of the short south front of the house, the 15 acres (6ha) of garden open up with extensive finely trimmed lawns rising to groups and banks of trees and shrubs. First there is a 'terrace' garden and borders beside the low wall with many herbaceous plants and a few shrubs. Beyond, the lawns and paths continue west and up past a rock garden in an old quarry. Alpine gardeners will find few of their plants among the shrubs and even trees that spring from the rocks. Up again beyond the long level beech walk the garden boundary is reached some 150ft (46m) above the bottom lawn and one can turn east through many trees and shrubs back to the house. John Veitch, the young Scot who founded the famous nursery, advised on planting here in the 1770s. Successive generations of that family have added many new trees and shrubs including, it is said, the first seedlings of the giant redwood that now stand tall among numerous neighbours. Now, in National Trust hands for 40 years, the policy continues of felling old trees and replanting similar species and thus providing an interesting and well-kept garden. **F.S.**

2 miles N of Tiverton;
turn E off A396
Tiverton—Bampton
road at Bolham

SS 9515

Apr to end Oct: daily
1100–1800. Reduced
rates for parties by
prior arrangement

Peak months: Apr to
Oct

🅿️♿
♿1-mile walk
🍴by appointment
only
🐕🚼♈🍼🎁
🏛️1330–1800

Knightshayes Court DEVON

The National Trust, Bolham, Tiverton.
tel. Tiverton (0884) 254665

This Victorian house stands high above the site of once prim Victorian gardens now completely transformed by the former owners and, since 1973, the National Trust. The top terrace now has rare and unusual permanent plants in the borders and on the walls above. South of the terrace semi-formal beds of roses and herbaceous plants thrive among fine lawns. Lower still the south garden has bulbs and rhododendrons. East from the house, up steps past modern junipers, there are separate and distinct small gardens; first a paved garden with statuary and mainly grey foliage and pink-flowered plants, fronted by a bank of alpines. Then a former bowling green now with a pool in the middle and surrounded by statues and yew hedges. Opposite, mown grass emphasizes the 60-year-old fox and hounds topiary. Still to the east the 'garden in the wood', the 'glade' and other areas provide contrasting settings for a wide range of plants. The beds and borders with shade-bearing plants are different from the wild and woodland shrub gardens elsewhere. Behind the house to the north-west a 20-year-old willow garden is growing rapidly around a pond and among earlier plantings of azaleas and rhododendrons. At 450ft (137m) above the sea there are extensive views of the 200 acres (81ha) of park and woodland and the Devon countryside but the gardens of more than 40 acres (16ha) can hold the attention with their great variety of form, colour and species. **F.S.**

Lanhydrock CORNWALL

The National Trust, Bodmin.
tel. Bodmin (0208) 3320

The majority of visitors are attracted to the turreted gate house and impressive castellated house, with its long gallery and preserved living rooms. Outside there is much to see for those who would walk and sit. Three main gardens can be distinguished within the 28 acres (11ha) or so. First, the formal, levelled, well kept lawns with uniformly trimmed Irish yews among formal beds, some box-edged, filled with roses or bedding plants. Next, past croquet and tennis lawns among several huge trees and well-filled modern shrub borders, and then moving steadily upwards through the main part of the garden. There are several distinct sections here with herbaceous plants, a hosta collection, a small stream garden, trees and shrubs in variety from about 100 years old to recent plantings, including many magnolias and the rhododendrons that flourish in the more open conditions. The top of this semi-formality is well above the house and adjoining parish church and gives views of the buildings, the extensive wooded park and the distant car park. From this point at about 400ft (122m) above sea level a straight path leads steadily down to the third, more heavily wooded, completely informal section in which large-leaved rhododendrons have been more recently planted and are growing well above the bracken. This will no doubt fill to become a Cornish woodland garden of the future. In all one can admire the skill and art of those who do the gardening. **F.S.**

3 miles SE of Bodmin; turn south off A38 Bodmin to Liskeard road (signposted)

SX 0864

Daily: Apr to Oct 1100–1800; Nov to Mar daylight

Peak months: Apr to June

🅿 wc
🏠 *enter from B3268*
🍴 *Apr to Oct: daily; Nov and Dec: limited*
🐕 💐 🏺
🚆 *Apr to Oct*
🌿

Leonardslee Gardens WEST SUSSEX

The Loder Family, Lower Beeding, Horsham.
tel. Lower Beeding (040 376) 212

Leonardslee is aptly described in its attractive guide book as one of the largest and most spectacular woodland gardens in England. And this is no exaggeration for there are over 80 acres (32ha) of gardens comprising one of the best collections of mature and unusual trees, shrubs, rhododendrons, azaleas and camellias in the British Isles. The sturdy Georgian-style house built in 1855 is superbly sited 300ft (91m) above a fine panoramic view of the wooded valleys and lakes with the South Downs on the horizon. Sir Edmund Loder was the first of this famous family to begin planting and developing the gardens in the 1890s and it was he who raised many famous rhododendron cultivars, outstanding being the glorious Loderi crosses. These alone are worth seeing here in May and early June. The gardens have continued to flourish and develop under succeeding generations of the Loder family who still live here today. Plenty of time is needed to explore the gardens. Near the house are the massed shrubberies around the drives with spectacular specimen conifers, the rock garden ablaze with Kurume azaleas and dwarf rhododendrons in May and then the long descending paths through groves of more rhododendrons, camellias, magnolias and many others, to the lakes (old hammer ponds) and dells in the valley. Wild flowers and birdlife also abound in this marvellous place. **T.W.**

4 miles SE of Horsham at junction of A281 and A279

TQ 2127

Late Apr to mid-June: Wed, Thur, Sat, Sun and Bank Holiday Mon 1000–1800; Oct: Sat and Sun 1000–1700. Reduced rates for parties by prior arrangement

No peak season

🅿 wc
🍴 *limited*
🏠 🍴 🏺 🌿 💐 🎁

Levens Hall CUMBRIA

O. R. Bagot, Esq., Kendal.
tel. Sedgwick (0448) 60321

No topiary garden in the country has a finer display than at Levens where the garden and the topiary were laid out for Colonel James Grahme in 1692 by M. Beaumont, a pupil of Le Nôtre. Most of the original topiary work still exists in box and yew, massive and in all manner of unusual shapes, set in truly Stuart-style box-edged parterres. The beech hedge, 20ft (6m) high and the lime avenue, one of the earliest, at the end of the garden were planted by Beaumont. A circle of beech encloses a carpet of grass and herbaceous borders line grass walks to one of the early ha-has, while the brightest of flowers are underplanted in the topiary garden and there are more flowers in beds in the old orchard. Across the road from the garden is the old park taking in the gorge of the River Kent where the 1890 design is intact, although the park was on estate plans in 1170. There are deer here and an oak avenue, probably planted by the Countess of Suffolk and Berkshire in 1740, is in its prime and stone seats by the path give on to lovely vistas of the winding Kent. The house near the stable block was built for M. Beaumont. **K.L.**

5 miles S of Kendal by Levens Bridge on A6

SD 4985

Easter Sun to end Sept: daily 1100–1700. Parties at other times by appointment: reduced rates

Peak months: July to Aug

🅿 wc 🍴 🏠
🍴 *limited opening*
🏺 💐
🎁 *limited opening*
🚆 *limited opening*

3 miles N of Ipswich
take Claydon road at
A45 roundabout and
turn right immediately

TM 1350

Mid-May to mid-July:
daily 1400–1900

Peak month: June

⊖🚍⛅✿
🏛 by appointment
only

Lime Kiln Rosarium SUFFOLK

Humphrey Brooke, Esq., Claydon, Ipswich.
tel. Ipswich (0473) 830334

This is a romantic garden devoted to the preservation of old and rare roses and possessing at present a collection of over 500 varieties. The garden was started by Countess Sophie Benckendorff who, in the 1920s, designed an intimate formal garden with stone and brick paths around a mulberry and Irish yews. This contains mainly Victorian hybrid-perpetual roses and a few later varieties underplanted with hardy geraniums, Welsh poppies and hemerocallis. From 1956 the present owner extended the planting using the vegetable garden, the verges of the drive and a large lawn where there are collections of rugosa and wild roses. All the shrubs are allowed to reach a natural size; the only pruning consists of removing dead wood. As a result many have grown enormously large in spite of the chalky subsoil. This has influenced the character of the garden, which resembles in places that of the 'Sleeping Beauty'! The wildness will not appeal to everyone. Others will be enraptured by billowing masses of soft-coloured flowers tumbling over walls, trees, pillars and paths. None could fail to enjoy the intense rose fragrance augmented here and there by honeysuckles and philadelphus. The garden is naturally at its best around mid-summer. **M.R.**

14 miles S of Stranraer
off B7065

NX 0940

Apr to end Sept:
daily 1000–1700

Peak months: Apr to
Sept

🅿🚻⊖🚍🐕

Logan Botanic Garden
DUMFRIES AND GALLOWAY

Dept. of Agriculture & Fisheries for Scotland, Port Logan, by Stranraer (Wigtownshire)

Of all the gardens on Scotland's western seaboard, I believe that Logan Botanic Garden must have the most climatically favourable position. It lies on a narrow peninsula of land reaching to the south on the western side of Luce Bay, and although greatly exposed to prevailing winds, it is nevertheless relatively free of all severe frost. The potential of the garden to grow a range of less hardy plants was recognised by the McDoualls, who owned the garden at the beginning of the century, and possibly to an even greater extent by Mr Olaf Hambro, who succeeded the McDoualls at Logan. Eventually the property was gifted to the Secretary of State for Scotland for use by the Royal Botanic Garden, Edinburgh, as an annexe for more tender plants. Logan has the appearance of being a far more exotic garden than in fact it really is. The idea is suggested by cordyline, trachycarpus and dicksonia and the tall blue spikes of *Echium pinniana* in which the garden is abundant. The more familiar sight of primula and rhododendron in the woodland remind one of the other well know attractions of the garden, which can claim to be the first to have produced the now widely accepted style of garden known as peat walls. Throughout its 14 acres (6ha) the garden is a pleasure to explore, both for its established plants and the range of more exotic subjects. For colour it is essentially a spring garden, but for the plantsman, and one is tempted to say the cool glasshouse enthusiast, Logan will provide a new adventure. **E.R.**

3½ miles NE of
Garforth on B1217
Towton Road

SE 4435

Daily 1030–dusk

Peak seasons: spring
and late summer

🅿🚻🚍🐕
🍴⛅🎪🏛

Lotherton Hall WEST YORKSHIRE

Leeds City Council, Aberford.

The skilful use of sun-orientated walls and shelter belts of trees has made this 10-acre (4-ha) garden in the Plain of York a congenial home of tender trees, shrubs and climbers rare in the North. It is the creation of the late Mrs L. G. D. Gasgoine in the early part of this century, very probably advised by her great friend Miss Ellen Willmott of 'Genus Rosa' fame. Both house and garden were given to Leeds Corporation in 1968 by her son, Sir Alvary. A formal rose garden in box-edged parterres is on the garden front where a border under a sheltering wall is a study in blue. At right angles to the rose garden an avenue of Victorian pyramidal yews leads the eye to a vista stop of a white period summerhouse. Through the stolidly buttressed yew hedge is the walled sun-trap garden where flower, surprisingly, a range of slightly tender shrubs. Roses and heliotrope in box-edged borders scent the garden in high summer. Through a wrought iron gate a William and Mary sunken garden is reached with spiral box, classical urns and a lily pool. Beds around are full of herbs and walls give shelter to plants which are rare for these parts. The ha-ha, now filled in, is a mecca for primula, astilbe and meconopsis and the giant hogweed. A rockery glen of 1912 with its mature accompanying acers is an 'up-and-down' walking experience and near to is one of the earliest of brick-on-edge tennis courts. There are working shire horses and a large aviary. **K.L.**

Luton Hoo BEDFORDSHIRE

The Wernher Family, Luton.
tel. Luton (0582) 22955

Entering the park at the Luton town end of the estate, one's first glimpse of the landscape which Lancelot ('Capability') Brown created in the 1760s is the two lakes in the valley of the River Lea. When the house and its adjoining gardens are reached, tree-studded vistas open up which reflect Brown's genius for landscaping and the further tree planting which was carried out in the 19th century. Below the paved terrace on the south side of the house are two terrace gardens, the first with lawns on either side of the broad pathway and bordered on all sides by shrubs and climbers, perennials and annuals, the second an imposing rose garden of Italianate design. Its focal point is a circular pool and fountain from which radiate outwards box-edged rose beds. Standard roses and topiary specimens of different shapes and sizes provide further interest for the eye. Two domed pavilions and formal yew hedges enclose the garden. In a sylvan dell in the park is the rock garden, which is not a rock garden in the accepted sense but an extremely appealing garden of a different kind, with rock outcrops, a grotto and cascade, and a serpentine pool with water-lilies spanned by a stone bridge. Plantings of trees, shrubs, conifers and herbaceous plants create delightful effects with their diverse forms and colourings. **R.P.**

SE *outskirts of Luton, entrances off A6129 Wheathampstead road*

TL 1119

End Mar to mid-Oct: Mon, Wed, Thur, Sat and Good Fri 1100–1800; Sun 1400–1800. Reduced rates for parties by prior arrangement

No peak season

Lyme Park CHESHIRE

The National Trust, Disley, Stockport.
tel. Disley (066 32) 2023

Originally a hunting park, the Palladian mansion terraces still look over more than a 1,000 acres (405ha) of parkland and moorland on the edge of the Peak District. It was in the late 19th century that Lord Newton laid out the surrounding sunken gardens, steps, terraces, the graceful glass-roofed orangery and the Italian garden and fountain still to be seen from above in all its formal parterred glory, planted up twice a year to give a blaze of floral colouring. Other flower beds and two long herbaceous borders continue the floral interest across the lawns to a hedged rose garden and even the borders which are hedged by hollies and yews are full of roses and other climbing plants lacing the hedging. There is a pond, a setting for a statue of Neptune fishing, and a water feature bridged by a stone construction of 1756. In the distance is an eyecatcher, a lanthorn tower, and by the streamside a ravine is now a garden glade side-planted for a long season of flowering with primulas, hostas, rhododendrons, azaleas, hydrangeas, astilbes and a mixture of philadelphus for fragrance. Looking over the Italian, or Dutch garden as it is sometimes called, on the west front is the Vicary Gibbs' garden, to commemorate the gift of this once celebrated gardener from Aldenham, of choice trees and shrubs, the Algerian oak, *Aesculus* hybrids, *Cornus kousa*, *Malus* 'Gibbs' Golden Gage', and *M.* 'Aldenhamensis'. **K.L.**

6½ *miles* SW *of Stockport;* S *of A6 with entrance in western outskirts of Disley*

SJ 9683

Daily 0800–sunset

No peak season

by appointment only

limited opening

limited opening

Magnolia House SUFFOLK

Mark Rumary, Esq., and Derek Melville, Esq., Yoxford.
tel. Yoxford (072 877) 321

This immensely appealing garden of around half-an-acre (0.2ha), totally enclosed by mellow brick walls clothed in notable climbing and wall plants, is both beautiful to the eye and of absorbing interest. This, however, is hardly surprising for its owner, Mark Rumary, is a garden designer of distinction. Trees, shrubs, hardy perennial and bulbous plants have been inter-related to provide interest throughout the year, with the peak period being late May to early July. It is, in fact, a series of four completely integrated but separate gardens. The main garden adjoining the 18th-century house is comprised essentially of beguiling plantings framing a shapely lawn; beyond a yew hedge, painted scarlet in summer by the flowers of the perennial climber *Tropaeolum speciosum*, is a 'white' garden and to one side a garden in which soft flower and foliage colours are combined with a raised pool of classical design. To the east of the house is another small garden separated from the road by a screen of pleached hornbeams. This beauty and serenity has been created in just over 20 years. Above all, this is a garden of ideas with its component parts being of a size to which almost any garden owner could relate. In particular, it provides lessons on how plants can be used with effect, even beautiful but dubiously hardy shrubs like the white-flowered, fragrant *Carpenteria calfornica*, where the right micro-climate exists. **R.P.**

On A1120 in centre of Yoxford village

TM 3968

Open a few times each year, ring for details. Sun 1400–1800

Peak months: May to Aug

4 miles N of
Barnstaple off B3230
Barnstaple—
Ilfracombe road

SS 5437

Daily: dawn–dusk

Peak months: Apr to
Aug

limited opening:
parties any day by
appointment

Marwood Hill DEVON

Dr J. A. Smart, Barnstaple.
tel. Barnstaple (0271) 42528

Only in 1962 did the owner burst forth from the confines of the walled garden, where he had gardened from 1949, to plant trees and shrubs on the sloping pastures to the south. Now 12 acres (5ha) of this and the opposite slope of mown grass are planted with numerous species and cultivars of most kinds of garden plants, of many of which the owner can say 'from seed I collected in . . .'. An important interest is the camellia and a large greenhouse was built in 1969 to produce perfect blooms of many of the best. Neither they nor rhododendrons dominate the scene. A comprehensive collection of camellias is tucked away behind the church. In the same year the stream, which flows from east to west some 50ft (15m) below, was dammed, to be followed 8 years later by a lower dam to give three broad ponds and a stretch of bog with a wide range of water-loving plants. Also in 1977 another greenhouse was erected for tender Australian plants. Earlier a rock garden was made in a hillside quarry. The walls of the first garden are very well clothed with climbing and scrambling plants; there is a well kept rose garden and many new plants are added to the whole each year. A recent feature is a Leyland's cypress/larch shelter belt to the west which is being steadily thinned to accommodate many potentially large and mostly uncommon trees that will grow rapidly upwards among the nurse crop of the belt. A well kept plantsman's garden, full of interest. **F.S.**

5 miles S of Derby off
A453 West
Bridgford—Ashby-de-
la-Zouch

SK 3825

Daily exc Sat:
1400–1730

Peak seasons: June to
July and autumn

by appointment
only

limited opening

limited opening
limited opening

Melbourne Hall Gardens DERBYSHIRE

The Marquess of Lothian, Melbourne, nr Derby.
tel. Melbourne (033 16) 2502

Probably the only existing formal garden of the early 18th century left in England is at Melbourne Hall, where London and Wise from 1701 onwards created this Le Nôtre French-style lay-out for Thomas Coke. There are some 16 acres (6.5ha) from the house terrace to the far side of the Great Basin framed by tall, mature taxodiums and on which is situated one of the most elegant of British garden ornaments, the open, wrought iron 'Birdcage', or arbour, of 1706 by Robert Bakewell. By the side of the main lawns, bisected by a path edged with tonsured yews and leading the eye to the lake and the Birdcage, is the 200yd (183m) yew tunnel, older by many years than the garden lay-out. To the south between hedges there is a vista stopped by Van Nost's great Urn of the Four Seasons, a gift from Queen Anne to Coke. From this focal point and from fountain basins radiate a series of allées between woodland discovering many more Van Nost lead statuettes of cherubs, Mercury, Perseus, and Andromeda in yew niches. There is a Victorian grotto enclosing a mineral water spring with a verse inscribed by Caroline Lamb, wife of the 2nd Lord Melbourne, Queen Victoria's first Prime Minister. There is a 17th-century dovecot with an ogee roof now a muniment room. **K.L.**

8 miles NW of Kelso
off A6089

NT 6439

Easter weekend and
then May to Sept:
daily exc Sat
1230–1700. Reduced
rates for parties by
prior arrangement

Peak months: July to
Aug

Mellerstain House BORDERS

Lord Binning, Gordon, (Berwickshire).
tel. Gordon (057 381) 225

The formal landscape garden is a rarity in Scotland and therefore likely to make a greater impression than it would south of the border. Kinross House is a good example of this form of art, Mellerstain, I believe, is superb. Surprisingly enough, the landscape is a fairly recent creation having been laid out as late as 1909 by Sir Reginald Blomfield. It relies almost entirely upon architectural features starting with a balustrade-topped terrace to the immediate south of the house, with ornate stairways leading to an area formerly of intricate parterres, now planted with roses, then to a broad grass walk with a lake in a woodland setting. The Cheviot Hills make a focal point in the far distance. In early summer colour is brought to the woodland by azaleas and rhododendrons. A very appropriate addition to the property has been made by Lord Binning's mother, the Countess of Haddington, whose love of roses has manifested itself in a splendid collection of shrub roses to the west of the house. Mellerstain is a remarkable monument to that great Scottish architect, Robert Adam, with the setting for the masterpiece wonderfully achieved by Blomfield. It is, and will, remain one of the treasures of Scotland. **E.R.**

Montacute House SOMERSET

The National Trust, Montacute, nr Yeovil.
tel. Martock (0935) 823289

The very formal gardens were first planned when Montacute House was built in the late 16th century. They were later changed in 1845 by William Phelips and remain largely unaltered to this day. Entering the gardens through a yew hedge, clipped in such a way that it looks almost like a large moss-covered bank, the cedar lawn comes into view with two magnificent sweet chestnuts, *Castanea sativa*, standing in one corner. In the borders surrounding the east court, herbaceous perennials and roses give plenty of colour during the summer months. Tucked under the raised walk which separates the east court from the north garden, and edged with clipped yews and American thorns (*Crataegus lavallei*) is a border of shrub roses which includes *Rosa gallica officinalis*, *R. versicolor* and *R. alba* 'Maxima' with *Hosta fortunei* planted as ground-cover. Passing the orangery that stands at the west end of the raised walk, the very imposing west drive sweeps away from the house edged with yews, beeches, limes and cedars. Turning into the south drive where variegated hollies and golden yews grace the right hand side, there stands one of the largest Monterey cypresses, *Cupressus macrocarpa*, in the country, its height is well over 100ft (30m). On the left California redwoods grow. **A.S.**

4 miles w of Yeovil on A3088

ST 5016

Daily 1230–1800

No peak season

P **WC**
🚽 *by appointment only*
🎁 *Apr to Oct*
🏛 *limited opening*

Moseley Old Hall STAFFORDSHIRE

The National Trust, Fordhouses, Wolverhampton.
tel. Wolverhampton (0902) 782808

This is the house to which Charles II fled, and was hidden, two days after the Royalist's defeat at Worcester. When the National Trust was given the property in 1962 by Mrs W. Wiggin, the garden had disappeared and the half-timbered house hidden in a skin of blue-grey bricks. A complete replanting was necessary, so Graham Thomas, with the advice of Miles Hadfield, and money raised by the National Trust's Wolverhampton Centre, set about the re-creation of a garden of the mid-17th century. Do not expect a gaudy mis-representation of a knot garden of the kind that became fashionable under the Victorians. Remember that garden plants were still cultivated for practical purposes, for food, medicine, or with which to scent the house, remember also that the vast riches of China and Japan were still untapped. The Moseley knot garden is a copy of one designed in 1640, and portrayed in a manuscript in the library of Magdalen College, Oxford. A box hedge surrounds beds edged with dwarf box, and filled with gravel of differing colours. On the wooden arbour are trained *Clematis viticella*, and the deliciously scented virgin's bower, *Clematis flammula* from Southern Europe. A nut walk and roundel leads to the King's Gate. A small herb garden and an orchard planted with fruit trees current in the 17th century completes this small but interesting garden. **E.F.**

4 miles N of Wolverhampton, w of A460 Wolverhampton—Cannock road

SJ 9405

March and Nov: Wed and Sun. Apr to Oct: Wed, Thur, Sat, Sun and Bank Holiday Mon, plus Tue after Easter, Spring and end-Aug bank holidays. 1400–1800 (sunset if earlier). Parties at other times by appointment

Peak season: Summer

P **WC** ♿
🚽 *by appointment only*
🐕 🎁 🏛

Mottisfont Abbey HAMPSHIRE

The National Trust, nr Romsey.
tel. Lockerley (0794) 40757

The Augustinian Priors chose this beautiful sequestered place beside the River Test (still a fine Trout river) for the Abbey, and the 'font' or spring from which its name derives still wells up clear water in a shaded dell near the old house. On the Dissolution the buildings were embodied into a large gabled country house by William Sandys, Chamberlain to Henry VIII, and later enlarged in the 19th century and surrounded by magnificent trees, lawns and parkland, with walled kitchen gardens away to the west. The National Trust acquired Mottisfont in 1957 and in 1972 created in the walled kitchen garden the superb rose gardens for which this place is now internationally famous. The emphasis is on old shrub roses and climbers, many richly scented and many now rare in cultivation diligently collected by the great expert Graham Stuart Thomas, who also designed the garden. A visit in June and July is quite magical. Association of spring and summer herbaceous plants extend the season and provide contrast. A further rose garden is being developed in a second walled garden to house shrub roses of mainly German and Continental origins. In complete contrast, the extensive parkland and shady walks around the old house enable one to admire the magnificent trees. A pleasant paved walk and lime avenue, a paved octagon with enclosing yew hedges can also be found. **T.W.**

4½ miles NW of Romsey off A3057 Romsey—Andover road

SU 3226

Apr to end Sept: Tue to Sat (exc Good Fri) 1430–1800. Parties at other times by appointment

Peak months: June and July

P **WC**
♿ *limited*
🚽 🐕 🎁
🏛 *limited opening*

6 miles w of
Aylesbury between
A41 and A418 in
Nether (or Lower)
Winchendon village, E
of the church

SP 7412

May to Aug: Thur
and Bank Holiday
Sat, Sun and Mon
plus additional
weekends in June and
July 1430–1730.
Parties at other times
by appointment

Peak months: Apr to
June and Oct

Nether Winchendon House BUCKINGHAMSHIRE

Mrs Spencer Bernard, nr Aylesbury.
tel. Haddenham (0844) 290101

In the 18th century the manorial Tudor house came into the hands of the
Bernard family who have lived here ever since. In the early 19th century Sir
Scrope Bernard restored and embellished the house in the 'Strawberry Hill'
Gothic style. The house stands on a grassy platform with a flagged stone
terrace on its eastern side which looks down to the River Thames. Here since
1954 the present members of the family have developed an ornamental
arboretum of many different trees to replace elaborate formal gardens too
expensive to maintain. The trees are flourishing in the fertile river terrace soils,
and cut-leaf beech, cercidiphyllum, liquidambar, the unusual hickory
(Pterocarya), and many flowering malus, double cherries and whitebeams are
noteworthy – all planted since 1956. Spring bulbs abound and there are
attractive riverside willows. On the sweeping lawns nearer the terrace is a
massive silver-variegated sycamore planted in 1810, a large ash and many
other trees. The other gardens to the south and west are on the older pattern of
formal enclosures, although no record survives of any Tudor garden. One
garden is a plain rectangle of grass flanked by a yew hedge and walls with
attractive borders of roses and herbaceous plants and massed climbers. The old
kitchen garden accommodates a tennis court and small rock garden. The
entrance drive is flanked by a young avenue of dawn redwoods (Metasequoia)
replacing an old lime avenue. T.W.

9 miles SE of Thirsk
off A19 Thirsk—York
road, SE of Coxwold
village

SE 5576

Mid-May to end Aug:
Wed 1400–1800.
Other days for parties
of 20 and over by
appointment

No peak season

Newburgh Priory NORTH YORKSHIRE

Capt. V. M. Wombwell, Coxwold
tel. Coxwold (034 76) 435

Gardening has gone on here since 1145 when an Augustine Priory was built on
the site of which old stew ponds still tell their historic story. The outstanding
feature of the entrance drive are vast topiary yews cut into the shape of an
Earl's coronet created before 1803 when the last Earl Fauconberg died.
Topiary continues on the house front interspersed with flower beds. By the
side of the house leading the eye over the lake, man-made in 1780, is an avenue
of topiary peacocks, birds and dogs. Straight ahead from the house front is a
cherry avenue and to the right is a tree-lined avenue to the 'Wild Water
Garden' a grand conception of Captain V. M. Wombwell created in 1938.
Different trees of the avenue are marked by plaques to show they were planted
by royalty. The water garden on a sloping hillside is filled with
rhododendrons, azaleas, bamboos, astilbe, acers, flowering trees and shrubs.
On level ground at the foot of the slope are many variously shaped stone
troughs and containers of rare and unusual alpines. In a roofless building by the
house are lawns surrounded by narrow borders containing figs. A walled
kitchen garden still holds vegetable and fruit and walls filled with both fruit
and climbers. In the house are two oil paintings of the garden as it was in the
early 1700s and a vault holding Cromwell's headless body. K.L.

4 miles SE of Ripon
off B6265 Ripon—
Boroughbridge road

SE 3667

Apr to end Sept:
daily exc Mon but inc
Bank Holiday Mon

No peak season

1-mile walk

limited opening

Newby Hall NORTH YORKSHIRE

R. E. J. Compton, Esq., Ripon.

Gardening has gone on here since Sir Edward Blackett built Newby in 1705,
extended by Robert Adam in the mid-1700s. Early drawings show a square
and compass lay-out. Remaining from those days is the 18th-century east to
west walk edged by 17th-century Venetian statuary against yew and purple
plum and the elegant balustrading on the south front. It was the late Major
Edward Compton who took over a Victorian garden in 1921 including the
stepped and water-coursed rock garden attributed to Ellen Willmott, and the
long (1,050ft, 320m), wide sloping border from the house down to the River
Ure. In 1929 he converted croquet and tennis lawns into a species rose, a July
and an autumn gardens. In what was a period sunken rose garden he created
Sylvia's garden planted with his late wife's favourite flowers. Near what was
once an iris walk is the long, winding pergola walk. A tropical garden near the
river shelters behind its high walls many magnolias, Azara microphylla,
Xanthoceras sorbifolium, Embothrium lanceolatum and Carpentaria californica.
There is a 150-year-old tulip tree, Liriodendron tulipifera, and in sun-spangled
woodland stand hydrangea, camellia, rhododendrons, many acers and a
wealth of spring flowers. The large kitchen garden is now a children's
playground and unobtrusively round the rockery edge runs a miniature train.
K.L.

Newstead Abbey NOTTINGHAMSHIRE

Nottingham City Council, Linby.
tel. Mansfield (0623) 792822

Founded as a priory between 1163 and 1173, Newstead Abbey gardens and grounds have evolved over the centuries. The poet Byron lived here and there is a statue and verses to his favourite dog. The millpool of the priory was enlarged to make the upper lake. Water from this lake runs into the garden lake by an ornamental cascade behind which the visitor can view the Abbey and pleasure ground through the 'window' of water. From the lake, by two streams, the way is to a Japanese garden of the early 20th century with stepping stones, humpbacked bridges and appropriate plantings. The old walled kitchen garden is now the rose garden with a fountain and many old-fashioned, shrub and climbing varieties. The rock garden nearby is an early elaborate example with a heather garden of recent planting. Old yews here form a tunnel. Through the rose garden is the iris garden, formerly the fruit garden, where pears, quite old, are festooned over and around the paths. Sheltered by massive yews is what was once a tropical garden and nearby is a stew pond. There is Eagle Pond in Devil's Wood surrounded by walnuts. Adjacent to the Abbey is the so-called Spanish garden centred by an Iberian wellhead but really a knot garden where the compartments, box edged, are filled with flowers in season. The monks' garden is a dense planting of trees and many paths. There are trees planted by Dr Livingstone and Stanley. **K.L.**

4 miles s of Mansfield on A60 Mansfield—Nottingham road

SK 5454

Daily exc 25 Dec: 1000–dusk

Peak months: Apr to June

🅿 wc ⊖ 🏛 ☂
❤ 🚻 ✿ 🎁
🎪 limited opening

Northbourne Court KENT

The Lord Northbourne, Northbourne, Deal.
tel. Sandwich (0304) 612643

A series of intimate, enclosed gardens protected by high brick walls are the especial feature of Northbourne and everywhere a profusion of plants carefully selected for colour, fragrance and individuality, reflecting the personality and sensitive artistry of the late Lord Northbourne, who largely developed the gardens. Northbourne Court has Saxon origins but the main structure of the garden is Jacobean with the tiers of terracing inside several acres of high brick walls, acting as raised walks or prospects, that once faced across to the long vanished house in the time of James I. The present house dates from the 18th and 19th centuries. Its great historic barn, farm buildings and massed old evergreen oaks, provide atmosphere and valuable protection to the gardens from the cold north-east winds that can blow across this rather exposed part of East Kent. The well-drained soils and the maritime climate – the sea is only a few miles away – and the warm walls offer homes for many interesting plants with emphasis on late spring, summer and early autumn effects. The smaller courts around the house are richly clothed with plants, on the walls especially, while the brick or paved 'floors' are a mosaic of massed pinks, junipers, grey-foliaged plants, and many more. Great copper urns and old pots are spilling over in summer with fuchsias and blends of foliage and colour. **T.W.**

4 miles E of Deal, between A256 and A258 (signposted in Northbourne village)

TR 3453

May to Aug: several Sun 1400–1830 and Wed 1400–1800 under National Gardens Scheme

Peak months: June and July

🅿 wc
🚻 by appointment only
❤ limited opening
🏛 🚻 ✿ 🎁

Nymans WEST SUSSEX

The National Trust, Handcross.
tel. Handcross (0444) 400 321

Nymans is a large garden with associated woodland and parkland, noted for its many mature rare trees and shrubs and its association with the Messel family who have been largely responsible for its creation and development. Mr Ludwig Messel purchased a then-enlarged Regency house with fine lawns and cedar trees in 1890 and immediately began developing the gardens and grounds. He turned the old walled flower orchard into a delightful flower garden transected by the famous summer border inspired by Robinson and Jekyll, and planted out such rare trees as Nothofagus (southern beeches), magnolias and richly naturalized with bulbs. He made some of the first heather gardens in the country, a sunken garden with Japanese lanterns, and the great stone wisteria-clad pergola, a favourite feature of so many Italian gardens. After 80 years, a renovation programme is planned for this feature. His son, Colonel Messel succeeded in 1916 and he became a tremendous gardener and plant enthusiast. He laid out more of the gardens planting freely and developing the area called Tasmania on the west side of the main road. He rebuilt the house in a Jacobean style but it was sadly destroyed by fire in 1947. His daughter, Anne, Countess of Rosse, still lives here and supervises the garden for the National Trust to whom it was bequeathed in 1954. Allow plenty of time to explore the many contrasting features in this fine garden. **T.W.**

4 miles s of Crawley, just E of A23 Brighton road on B2114

TQ 2729

Apr to end Oct: Tue, Wed, Thur and Sat 1400–1900 (sunset if earlier); Sun and Bank Holiday Mon 1100–1900 (sunset if earlier). Parties of 15 or over at other times by appointment

No peak season

🅿 wc 🚻 ❤
✿ 🎁 🎁

½ *mile* s *of Pangbourne, turn east off A340 and left at T junction*

SU 6376

Open frequently from Feb to Sept by appointment and on several Sun under National Gardens Scheme

Peak months: Mar, Apr, June, July

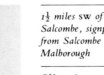*gardening societies only* *occasional*

Old Rectory Cottage BERKSHIRE

A. W. A. Baker, Esq., Tidmarsh, Reading.
tel. Pangbourne (073 57) 3241

This is a 2-acre (0.8ha) plantsman's paradise, remarkable for its rare and unusual plants, and the fact that it has been created in some 20 years from a cottage garden jungle. The Bakers were attracted by the capabilities of the site when they arrived in the late 1950s. Two quite different kinds of garden have evolved after 25 years, each merging imperceptibly with the other. Round the house, an informal cottage-garden style is characterised by grass paths, island beds and an abundance of plants carefully chosen for shape, texture, and colour contrasts. Concealed boundaries of the garden are a backcloth of gold, purple, grey and variegated trees and shrubs. Every wall is covered with a climber or wall shrub. The rock garden is a delight in May and June. Very different in character is the wild garden, cool, shaded paths wander among willows, poplars and old apple trees to the lake and the delightful river. Spring bulbs, primulas, hellebores, ferns and hostas, festoons of roses over the trees, lilies of many species and varieties, and bold foliage and waterside plants are all to be discovered here. Sawdust, horse manure and old hay mulches have been liberally used on the chalky clay soils throughout this garden to give wonderful fertility and growth. **T.W.**

1½ *miles* sw *of Salcombe, signposted from Salcombe and Malborough*

SX 7336

Daily

Peak season: spring to early summer

 ½-*mile walk* *limited opening*

Overbecks Garden DEVON

The National Trust, Sharpitor, Salcombe.
tel. Salcombe (054 884) 2893

A first glance at the level rectangular lawn running to the west of this 70-year-old house might make one think that this is just another quite ordinary garden. Brief thought of the approach road and study of the interesting plants in the borders, a look up to the sheer cliff at the end of the lawn and another glance south to the sea and estuary gives a very different impression. In the 6 acres (2.4ha) of well kept broken hillside there are many secluded corners in which to sit or stand and admire the views. Close at hand there are unexpected plants and groups of plants. There are recent plantings among 80-year-old trees and shrubs and several other areas of lawn or pathway, a rocky hollow with alpines and other suitable plants, narrow lawns with herbaceous plants and a wall from which to look down on to the propagating area (not open to the public). Other features include straight walks and walls shaded by magnificent magnolias and winding paths through large shrubs among which some clearing and replanting is going on. The Chusan palms are everywhere, grown from seed from the original specimens and in every corner there are half-hardy and tender plants to interest the curious and test the knowledge of the plantsman. Below it all there is the sea and water with yachts in summer and wind and waves before and after. A small conservatory houses well grown oranges and lemons and behind it the main part of the house fills and empties with passing youth hostellers. **F.S.**

7 *miles* sw *of Swaffham; turn* N *off A134 at Oxborough*

TF 7401

Early Apr and May to end Oct: Mon to Wed, Sat and Sun 1400–1800. Reduced rates for parties of 15 or over by prior arrangement

Peak season: summer

limited

Oxburgh Hall NORFOLK

The National Trust, Oxborough, nr King's Lynn.
tel. Gooderstone (036 621) 258

The glory of these gardens is the large intricate parterre which decorates a sunken lawn to the east of the fortified house, and which is probably unique in British gardens. It was created about 1845 by the Beddingfield family, descendants of the original builders of the house, who copied one they had seen in a garden near Paris. The original design has since been traced back to a book on garden design written by Anton Joseph Dazallier d'Argeville in 1709. The pattern is carried out in box-edged beds and panels of grass, set out on gravel with clipped yew sentinels; the beds are filled with blue ageratum, yellow tagetes, grey santolinas, ruta and stachys. Forming a background to the parterre is a yew hedge and behind this a classic herbaceous border planted against the Gothic-style brick wall of the kitchen garden which supports climbing roses, honeysuckles and clematis. To the south of it is a shrub border containing a standard pink *Wisteria floribunda*. The walled garden contains a young orchard of plums, quinces and mulberries. Near the chapel which stands in the grounds, are traces of a Victorian 'wilderness' which it is hoped to restore. **M.R.**

Oxford College Gardens OXFORDSHIRE

University of Oxford

Only a limited selection of College gardens is mentioned here of the many that exist. The selection concentrates on those that are usually open more regularly during the vacations. In most Colleges the gardens are in the form of quadrangles of great diversity of size, character and planting, but surrounded invariably by wonderful architecture. Founded in the 13th century, the gardens of *Balliol* have a quiet and austere stateliness with many unusual climbers, attractive borders and fine trees. More than five centuries old, the main gardens of *New College* have the romantic background of the old city walls against which a great mixed border is a splendid sight from May to the autumn. The famous mound or 'mount', a popular feature of Tudor gardens, was built about 1530. Lofty mature trees are also a feature of this garden. The unique tiny quad. of *St Edmunds Hall* is worth a visit alone for its atmosphere of a remote past wholly undisturbed. The old cloisters of *Magdalen* lead into the great second quad. with its mixed borders while away to the north-east side but with groves of trees are the famous Magdalen walks. Other remarkable gardens include those of *St John's* and *Trinity*, *Worcester* with its extensive lake, terraces and superb standard of maintenance, and *Christchurch Meadow*, an ancient river water pasture, where in May thousands of fritillaries are in flower. **T.W.**

In town centre

SU 5205

Most gardens are open daily in the afternoon but times vary

Oxford University Botanic Gardens

OXFORDSHIRE

University of Oxford, Rose Lane, Oxford.
tel. Oxford (0865) 242737

These, in fact, comprise three separate botanical gardens located in different places. The first is the main garden described here. The second is the small one-acre (0.4-ha) Genetic Garden founded in 1945 and designed to illustrate the process of plant evolution. Located at the edge of the University Parks, it is usually open in University hours. Finally there is the 50-acre (20-ha) Nuneham Arboretum founded in 1830 and open on weekdays April to September and situated at Nuneham Courtenay, south of Oxford. The main botanic gardens are the oldest in Britain and the second oldest in Europe, being founded in 1621 as Physic Gardens with the main purpose of cultivating plants for use by herbalists and apothecaries. In 1840 they became known as the Botanic Gardens and Professor Daubeny, an assistant curator, proposed many new and wider fields of study involving co-operation with botanists and zoologists. There are many fine trees and groups of plants and different areas to be discovered here. Collections of shrubs, of herbaceous, rock and water plants in beautifully constructed habitats, a fine and comprehensive range of 300 species and varieties of wall plants, many rather rare or half-hardy but enjoying the protection of the warm walls; a valuable demonstration of historical roses illustrating the origin of garden roses; and the glasshouses rebuilt in 1970 and housing a wide range of tropical, economic and ornamental plants. **T.W.**

In town centre, off High Street (either opposite Magdalen College Tower or from Rose Lane)

SU 5205

Mar to Oct: Mon to Sat 0830–1700, Sun 1000–1200 and 1400–1800; closed Good Fri. Oct to Mar: Mon to Sat 0900–1630, Sun 1000–1200 and 1400–1630; closed Christmas Day

No peak season

Packwood House WARWICKSHIRE

The National Trust, Lapworth, Solihull.
tel. Lapworth (056 43) 2024

Traditionally the clipped yews were said to have been planted during the Commonwealth, and to represent Christ preaching to the multitude. In fact modern research reveals that the greater part of them were planted as small topiary specimens in the middle of the last century. The attractions of this garden are, however, by no means limited to the austere beauty of these clipped trees. The south, or Carolean, garden has a gazebo at each of its four corners, from which it was possible to look over the surrounding countryside. The raised terrace walk was originally built to provide views of the elaborate parterres below. It is now planted with flowers whose colours blend with those in the lower garden. The colour scheme changes annually but is always striking. On the south face of the terrace wall are thirty round-headed niches in pairs built to house a colony of bee-skeps. In the area to the west, originally known as the fountain court, is a cold plunge called the Roman Bath, but few Romans would have been tempted by this dark water. Anyone interested in historic parterres or in Jekyll-style planting will delight in this unusual place. **E.F.**

11 miles SE of central Birmingham off A34; turn eastwards onto B4439 at Hockley Heath

SP 1772

Apr: Wed to Sun exc Good Fri but inc Bank Holiday Mon 1400–1700. May to Sept: Wed to Sun, plus Bank Holiday Mon 1400–1800. Oct: Sat and Sun 1400–1700

No peak season

by appointment only

Centre of Wisbech on
northern bank of
River Nene on B1441

TF 4510

Apr to mid-Oct:
Mon, Tue, Wed, Sat
and Sun 1400–1800

No peak season

P ⬛ ⬤
🗄 by appointment
only
⬤ ✿ 🏛

Peckover House CAMBRIDGESHIRE

The National Trust, North Brink, Wisbech.
tel. Wisbech (0945) 583463

Peckover is a handsome Georgian house but the garden is essentially early Victorian, laid out at a time when many strange new plants were arriving from foreign lands, and designed to show off these acquisitions. It affords a rare opportunity to see a garden of this period. In recent years, whilst care has been taken to respect the original style – for instance a newly planted border reinterprets carpet bedding using hardy instead of tender plants – more flowers have been added, particularly roses, honeysuckles and clematis. The sensitively maintained garden covers 2½ acres (1ha), most of it surrounded and subdivided by high walls, creating that sense of mystery which old town gardens often possess. The section immediately behind the house is most strongly Victorian, with trim lawns, gravel paths and shady walks through shrubberies of laurel, spotted aucuba and variegated holly, underplanted with ferns, hostas and asarum. There are two summerhouses, one rustic with columns of pine logs, the other white-painted with green lattice decoration which faces a circular lily pool and topiary peacocks with herbaceous borders beyond. A greenhouse contains ancient orange trees which fruit regularly, and colourful conservatory plants including plumbago and begonias. Near by is a shady fern house. **M.R.**

N of junction of A5
and A55

SH 6172

Apr to late May and
Oct: 1400–1700. Late
May to Sept and bank
holiday weekends
1100–1700. Reduced
rates for parties of 20
and over by prior
arrangement

No peak season

P ⬛ ⬤ 🗄 🐕
⬤ ✿ 🎁 🏛

Penrhyn Castle GWYNEDD

The National Trust, Bangor.
tel. Bangor (0248) 53084/53356

The castle, built in 1827 by the architect Thomas Hopper, dominates the surrounding country and from it there are magnificent views north to Anglesey, south to Snowdonia. This exposed position takes the full force of the wind and the park has recently been devastated. The wellingtonia planted by Queen Victoria in 1859 has, however, survived. From the Ice Tower a path leads to the walled garden. The top terrace is a Victorian parterre with the three lily ponds and a loggia. The box-edged beds are filled with fuchsias and the fountains edged with a purple hebe. There are interesting shrubs on the walls including an old plant of Leptospermum scoparium, the tea-tree from New Zealand. The middle area of sloping lawn is dominated by an old specimen of Pinus pinaster, the maritime pine, and contains shrubs that provide colour throughout the year, witch hazel, camellias, magnolias, honeysuckle, and hydrangeas. The vermilion flowers of Embothrium coccineum, the Chilean fire bush, are conspicuous in early summer, to be followed in August by the exquisite white flowers of the eucryphias. Below is a wild garden, through which oozes what was once a stream. Here beyond an overgrown bamboo screen grow enormous plants of Gunnera manicata from Brazil, there are also plantings of Japanese maples, 'Black Boy' palms, and eucalyptus, both the latter from Australia. **E.F.**

5 miles W of
Tonbridge, off A26
Tonbridge—
Tunbridge Wells road
on B2176

TQ 5244

Apr to end Sept:
daily exc Mon but inc
bank holidays
1230–1800

Peak months: June
and July

P ⬛ ⬤ 🗄 ⬤
🗄 ✿ 🎁 🏛 ⚓

Penshurst Place KENT

The Viscount De L'Isle, VC, KG, Penshurst, Tonbridge.
tel. Penshurst (0892) 870307

Undoubtedly one of the finest and best preserved heritage houses in the country, standing in parkland and surrounded by its old walled gardens whose outline has changed little since the Elizabethan period. The excellent guide to Penshurst tells the story of the great house, its zenith at the time of Sir Philip Sydney and visits by Royalty, its long period of neglect and the great revival during the last century. Penshurst lies in the River Medway valley close to the charming village and church. Within the boundary walls are a series of gardens, some still being developed by the present Lord De L'Isle. The greatest open space is the Italian garden, a large sunken parterre laid out with geometric patterns of box and a dwarf red variety of polyantha rose round a central oval pool. Axial walks lead away past the great south front of the house where boldly planted attractive borders are colourful in summer with old roses, grey, yellow and pink shrubs and perennials. Two wide borders leading from the entrance gate are backed with fine old apple trees, carefully retained, since much of this area was once an orchard. The rose garden is a simple, effective design of mainly pink and red roses underplanted with grey-blue herbs. A magnolia garden, nut garden, grey garden are also here while beyond the great lime avenue is an interesting farm exhibition area and an adventure centre for children. **T.W.**

Pitmedden Garden GRAMPIAN

National Trust for Scotland, Pitmedden, Ellon, (Aberdeenshire).
tel. Udny (065 13) 2445

Although the great garden of Pitmedden may have been a glorious and inspiring sight in its original conception by Sir Alexander Seton, a tragic fire of 1880 destroyed the house and with it any hope of knowing the designs which were used. In 1956 The National Trust for Scotland sought the help of the late Dr James Richardson to re-establish the garden. There are four parterre designs, three of which were adopted from contemporary patterns known to have existed at the Palace of Holyrood, Edinburgh, the fourth Richardson devised in the form of the Seton Coat-of-Arms. All are outlined in boxwood and filled each year with some 40,000 annual flowers, a historical inaccuracy necessary in the 20th century to attract visitors to the garden, and one, I believe, which preserves the original purpose to 'amaze and delight' those who saw it. The central walk of the 3 acre (1ha) garden is flanked by yews shaped in a contemporary style used by Andre le Nôtre, still to be seen at Vaux le Vicomte on the outskirts of Paris. Seventeenth century reproduction garden seats are being acquired to fill the yew butteresses, and suitable plants for the period are gradually being found. With allowances for the necessity to use modern methods of maintenance and means of attracting visitors, Pitmedden is, nevertheless, as authentic a reproduction of a period garden as one can hope for with minimal labour and other financial restrictions. To the idealist it may be imperfect, but even they must agree that Scotland would be the poorer without it. **E.R.**

14 miles N of Aberdeen on A920 Oldmeldrum—Ellon road, 1 mile W of Pitmedden village

NJ 8927

Daily: 0930–dusk. Reduced rates for parties

No peak season

Plas Newydd ISLE OF ANGLESEY

The National Trust, Llanfairpwll.
tel. Llanfairpwll (0248) 714795

In a sense the most important feature of this garden is the magnificent view of Snowdonia across the glittering waters of the Menai Strait. This is not to decry the fine shrub garden that has been developed south of the house within the shelter of trees planted to Repton's suggestion. The climate is mild, the atmosphere damp, the soil fertile and ideally suited to lime-haters such as rhododendrons, camellias, eucryphias and embothriums. Many of these shrubs are planted in island beds within the flow of well-maintained grass, tending towards J. C. Loudon's 19th-century gardenesque style, emphasising the plants themselves. Outstandingly successful are the great hedges of *Viburnum tomentosum* 'Lanarth'. To the north of the house there is an Italianate terrace garden created in the 1920s. The top terrace contains specimens of *Itea ilicifolia* and *Carpenteria californica*, the walls clothed with the evergreen *Clematis armandii*, backed by a hedge of clipped bay. On the lower terraces are twelve Mediterranean cypress. On the middle terrace grow roses, *Rhododendron yakushimanum*, heaths and Kurume azaleas. Further to the north, within a wood following the Strait, is a rhododendron garden just cleared and reopened to the public. **E.F.**

2½ miles SW of Menai Bridge on A4080

SH 5269

Apr, Sept and Oct: daily exc Sat 1400–1700. May to Aug and all bank holidays 1200–1700. Reduced rates for parties of 20 and over by prior arrangement

Peak season: Spring

Polesden Lacey SURREY

The National Trust, nr Dorking.
tel. Bookham (31) 58203/52048

The present elegant house was built in the 1820s by Joseph Bonsor who also enlarged the estate and planted more than 20,000 trees. He had purchased the estate and an older house from the playwright, Richard Sheridan, whose 25 years of ownership saw the making of one of the finest features of Polesden, the long grass promenade named after him. Early in this century Captain and Mrs Greville bought Polesden and developed most of the garden as it exists today. The whole estate was left to the National Trust in 1942. The Trust has produced an excellent plan and guide to the gardens detailing all the main trees, shrubs and roses and other garden features. After the long beech and lime avenues comes the marvellous surprise of the house set below the brow of the hill, with its thyme-studded lawns, and colourful flower beds. There are lovely views from here and the pinetum and Sheridan's walk to the left. To the right lie the enclosed gardens all linked to the house by interconnecting walks and vistas. There the dominant feature is the rose garden with its many pergolas covered in mostly Edwardian rambling roses, a splendid central Venetian well-head and fine mixed borders. Here there is also a rather original lavender garden, an iris garden, and outside the walls an informal winter garden and a curious thatched bridge. A rock and shrub bank exhibits high mature ground cover at its best, with a more informal area of grass and shrubs below. **T.W.**

3 miles NW of Dorking, turn S off A246 Leatherhead—Guildford road at Great Bookham

TQ 1553

Daily 1100–sunset. Reduced rates for parties on Tue to Thur by prior arrangement

Peak months: May to Aug

limited opening

limited opening
limited opening

1 mile S of Welshpool on A483; pedestrian access from High Street, Welshpool

SJ 2105

Early Apr, May, June and Sept: Wed to Sun 1300–1800 exc Good Fri. July and Aug: Tue to Sun 1300–1800. Bank Holiday Mon 1130–1800

Reduced rates for parties of 20 and over by prior arrangement

No peak season

Powis Castle POWYS

The National Trust, Welshpool.
tel. Welshpool (0938) 4336

It is difficult to overpraise Powis, for it has everything, a marvellous site, a park whose natural contours out-landscape Brown, formal terraces, flowing woods, lime and lime-free soil, a head gardener of exceptional ability, the whole dominated by its rose-red castle. Designs for the terraces were probably commissioned by the first Marquess between 1680 and his exile in 1688. They are a unique example of the formal Italianate style in Britain, and command views as extensive and superb as any villa in Tuscany. The planting is carefully documented in the excellent guide to the gardens by Graham Stuart Thomas and John Sales, and the list of plants excites envy. The key to the romantic appearance of the terraces lies principally, however, in the huge clipped yews, which date from the original planting, and in lead figures, probably by Van Nost, that adorn the balustrade above the orangery. The area below the castle hill to the north was converted to a pleasure garden some 70 years ago. The woods surrounding the main lawn below the terraces have been developed horticulturally during the present century. The acid soil is favourable to conifers and rhododendrons, which mingle happily with the original oaks. From the main vista magnificent views can be obtained of the Castle and terraces in one direction and of the Long Mountain and the Clee Hills in the other. So short an entry cannot cope with the richness of the planting which is remarkable at all seasons of the year, both for its variety and its artistry. E.F.

7 miles W of Abingdon and ½ mile S of A420 Oxford—Swindon road on B4508

SU 3696

Apr to May: Wed, Thur and Sun. June to late Oct: daily exc Mon and Fri. Bank Holiday weekends: Sat to Mon 1400–1800. Reduced rates for parties by prior arrangement

Peak months: June, July and Oct

Pusey OXFORDSHIRE

Pusey Garden Trust, nr Faringdon.

When Mr and Mrs Michael Hornby bought Pusey in 1935 they found the house neglected, the lake silted up and the parkland and trees engulfed in Victorian shrubberies. Their first decision was to ask Geoffrey Jellicoe in 1937 to create a spacious paved terrace from which to view the lake and distant vistas beyond. From 1947 they began creating the ornamental garden. Borders were carefully planned and planted, the water garden developed across the lake and the many walks furnished with suitable plants. Visitors can follow a circular tour of the gardens. After the entrance gate, comes a fine double border with reds shading to blues and yellows and silver and white as the distant lake comes into view. A great mixed border sweeps in a curve to the right, against the walls of the kitchen garden, also richly stocked with roses, clematis and many other plants. The paved terrace in front of the house is studded with pads of carpeting rock plants and bright with urns of flowers. To the left is an area of shrub roses and ground-cover plants, then the orange bed and thence across the lake by the Chinese bridge to a series of luxuriant water gardens, and through glades to pleasure gardens and shrubberies until one completes the circuit at Lady Emily's garden – walled and bright with flowers from spring to November. There are also many fine trees at Pusey from the huge old planes, cedars and beeches to many new and vigorous magnolias, sorbus and maples. T.W.

4 miles E of Haslemere and 1¼ miles S of Chiddingfold on A283 Milford—Petworth road

SU 9634

Late Apr to early June: Sat and Sun 1400–1900

Peak months: May and June

by appointment only

Ramster SURREY

Mr and Mrs Paul Gunn, Chiddingfold.
tel. Haslemere (0428) 4422

An extensive woodland garden with many good specimens of unusual trees and shrubs and spectacular displays of rhododendrons and azaleas in late May and June. Sir Harry Wechter Bt. laid out the woodland gardens in the early 20th century in conjunction with the then famous Gauntlett nurseries whose land adjoined Ramster. He also enlarged an Elizabethan farm house into the present Gothic-style house that is actually rather detached from the gardens and not open to the public. In 1920 the estate was bought by Sir Henry and Lady Norman and the latter, sister of the first Lord Aberconway of Bodnant, was responsible for completing the layout of the garden and introducing rhododendrons, azaleas and many other plants. The present owner is Lady Norman's daughter. An arrowed, recommended route guides one through the very informal arboretum. Winding paths and glades offer plenty of unexpected encounters with many fine groups of plants beneath a canopy of oaks, some fine larches and other trees. A dark, silent pool not far from the house is massed with bamboos, great mushrooms of Japanese cut-leaf maples and many waterside foliage plants with here and there Japanese stone lanterns. There are also splendid magnolias of many species, carpets of bluebells, and particularly striking towering banks of the pink rhododendron 'Cynthia' lining the drive. Allow plenty of time to explore this fascinating wild garden. T.W.

Regent's Park GREATER LONDON

Dept. of the Environment, The Store Yard, Inner Circle, Regent's Park, NW1.
tel. (01) 486 7905

Some 470 acres (190ha) of loveliness might well be a fitting description of this much-appreciated park – a park known not only for Queen Mary's Rose Garden but also for the bedding which is carried out in the Broad Walk. The park is still much the same as it was when it was designed for the Prince Regent in the early 19th century, with the well-known inner and outer circles being central to the layout. Queen Mary's Rose Garden is considered one of the finest of its type in this country and probably in the whole of Europe, including more than 60,000 roses both modern and old-fashioned. Also within the boundary of the rose garden is the begonia garden, which is also a great summer attraction. The flower walk – also part of the original concept – is a series of beds planted with a wide range of bedding plants. Again, trees are one of this park's great assets. A small and little-known garden where peace and quiet rules is situated near the entrance to St John's Lodge. Three circular beds form the design with each bed smaller than the last, as approached from the gate. A large lake is used for boating – except round Heron Island – but it is not fished, although fish are present. Heron Island is so named because a few years ago a family of herons decided to nest there and rear their young, as they have been doing ever since. This park is also noted for its water-fowl.

Within the Outer Circle, off Marylebone Road, Park Road, Prince Albert Road, Albany Street

TQ 2783

Daily

Peak seasons: spring, summer

Rievaulx Terrace NORTH YORKSHIRE

The National Trust, Rievaulx, Helmsley.
tel. Bilsdale (043 96) 340

Rievaulx Terrace of 1754 by Thomas Duncombe, son of the creator of Duncombe Terrace which, evidence shows, was to have been linked to Duncombe, is one of the outstanding achievements of 18th-century picturesque and romantic landscapes. Its serpentining half mile (0.8km) of grass lawn innovatively breaks away from any formal line-up and from this winding walk, high above Ryedale, are seen from the almost precipitous escarpment 13 differing bird's-eye views of the 1131-founded Rievaulx Abbey. Originally the wavy line of trees on the far side was interplanted with flowering shrubs and a gateway here was the entrance to the terrace from the estate road from Duncombe. At the terrace beginning is a Palladian Ionic temple, used as a banqueting house, with furniture by Kent, exquisite frescoes by Borgnis c.1760, and elaborately carved woodwork. At the far end is a domed Tuscan temple, circular and on a raised podium, of 1758, its interior enriched by colourful Italian plasterwork. From its raised platform the view is into the valley of the Rye, the abbey, a medieval pack horse bridge and over moors, ridge and vale to the distant Cleveland Hills. Visitors so overcome by the sheer majesty of this imaginative conception have been known to walk the lawns in bare feet! **K.L.**

2½ miles w of Helmsley on B1257

SE 5886

Apr to end Oct: daily exc Good Fri 1030–1800

No peak season

Ripley Castle NORTH YORKSHIRE

Sir Thomas C. W. Ingilby, Bart. Ripley, nr Harrogate.
tel. Harrogate (0423) 770152

This 14th-century castle lived in by the same family since 1250 looks over a mid-18th-century Brownian landscape, though Dorothy Stroud, his biographer, does not record it. But there is no doubt when one looks from the contemporary battlemented terrace to two serpentining lakes islanded and stemming from a crystal cascade which divides a tree-studded park of beech and oak under which deer and cattle browse, this is definitely Brown. The lake disappears in a steep cascade under a pretty Victorian ironwork bridge. From the north-facing terrace a few steps and a path take one to the walled flower garden. The wall is terminated by two balustraded, stone-built summerhouses, contemporary with the 1820 orangery in the centre. Thick-stemmed wisteria and other climbers clothe the rest of the wall under which is a herbaceous border and on the two spacious lawns are roses in ornamental beds. The central path here makes for a short avenue of fastigiate yews and a wrought iron gate to the reserve garden where trained fruit decorates the walls and a circular brick-pillared rose pergola, flanked by box-edged parterres, is terminated by a trimmed hornbeam hedge. A narrow sun-trap garden for early fruit and vegetables is reached through a wooden door. The orangery leads to a long woodland walk to a temple vista stop and under a stepped stone platform for a bird's eye view of garden and village. **K.L.**

4 miles N of Harrogate just off A61 Harrogate—Ripon road

SE 2860

Good Fri to end Sept: daily 1100–1800. Reduced rates for parties of 25 or over

Peak months: July to Aug

limited opening

Rosemoor Garden Trust DEVON

Lady Anne Palmer, Great Torrington.
tel. Torrington (080 52) 2256/3919

1 mile SE of Great Torrington on B3220 Exeter road

SS 5117

Apr to end Oct: daily dawn–dusk. Reduced rates for parties

No peak season

P wc ⊖ ⊞ 🛉
🦽*by arrangement only*
⛩ ☂ ✿ ❀

A steepish drive runs up through trees from a road beside the River Torridge to the personal gardens which started out in 1959 from the small surroundings of this pleasant country house. It now extends to 7 acres (3ha) and 'one more' field is soon to be planted. Many rare plants surround and clothe the house and there is always something new to be seen during each visit. Smooth lawns and shrub borders extend eastwards to a pond with water-loving plants in and around it. Peat banks support dwarf rhododendrons and other suitable plants. Further on at the end of the garden, and exit drive, there is a collection of smaller and truly ornamental trees and it is this type of planting that is to be extended into the next paddock. A hard tennis court has been broken, covered with soil and shredded bark and planted with shrub and trailing roses among many other varied plants. Other larger roses fill spaces between and clamber over pyrus, prunus and other trees to give generous colour for much of the summer. In the conifer plantation, now being steadily thinned, on the steep hillside above the main garden many species and cultivars of *Rhododendron* and related genera have been planted. Many of the rare plants in the garden are propagated in the mist on benches under the tunnels and in frames. All is carefully tended under the watchful eye of the owner and gives the impression that every plant is separately cared for. **F.S.**

Rousham Park OXFORDSHIRE

C. Cottrell-Dormer, Esq., nr Steeple Aston.
tel. Steeple Aston (0869) 47110

10 miles S of Banbury; turn E off A423 Banbury—Oxford road at junction with B4030 and take 1st turning to left

SP 4725

Daily: 1000–1800

No peak season

P wc ⊖ ⊞
🦽*limited opening*

Rousham is an almost perfect example of the first English landscape park of the early 18th century. It was largely the work of William Kent who also remodelled the 17th-century house. In the gardens he softened an earlier formal design by Bridgeman and fully exploited the charming setting of the River Cherwell and its valley. From the house he created vistas, the main one to the north looking towards a fine statue of a lion and horse, and in the far distance a triple arched 'ruin' or eye-catcher. Kent's main gardens lie in pleasant woodland glades on the north slope of the Cherwell, where by means of serpentine paths, its classic features are cleverly sited, the Cold Bath with its elaborate waterways, the seven-arched arcades or portico (Praeneste) and the ponds and gentle cascades in Venus Vale, a green, quiet place where great carp swim lazily in the pools. A Temple of the Mill in rustic Gothic is also here and everywhere fine trees. In complete contrast is the series of charming walled gardens. The main former kitchen garden with dipping pond and old espalier apples now combined with a mixture of luxuriant climbers on pergolas with herbs and flowers beneath. A charming pigeon house (its revolving ladder still operates) stands in a miniature parterre or knot garden of box hedges and roses. There are mulberries, magnolias and restful grass and seats here, a perfect place for meditation. **T.W.**

Royal Botanic Garden, Edinburgh
LOTHIAN

Dept. of Agriculture & Fisheries for Scotland, Inverleith Row, Edinburgh.
tel. Edinburgh (031) 552 7171

At Inverleith, with access from Inverleith Row or Arboretum Row

NT 2576

Daily exc 25 Dec and 1 Jan: Mon to Sat 0900–dusk, Sunday 1100–dusk

No peak season

wc ⊖ ⊞
🦽*limited opening*
✿ 🏠

The Royal Botanic Garden, Edinburgh, is one of three plant-taxonomic research institutions run by the British Government. Plants are grown in Edinburgh and at three outstations, the Younger Botanic Garden, Benmore (near Dunoon), Logan Botanic Garden (near Stranraer) and Dawyck Arboretum (near Peebles). Over 12,500 species are cultivated from all parts of the world, but with an emphasis on plants from the Himalaya and China. Nearly half the living plants are of known wild origin, and the living collection is used for botanical research. The whole garden is landscaped and plants are grown in a semi-naturalistic setting. The extensive rock garden with about 4,000 different species of plants is world famous. The exhibition plant houses which were opened in 1967 are also fully landscaped and contain a large collection of tender plants including palms, orchids, ferns and tropical economic plants. Two newer houses opened in 1978 display research collections of several plant families including the *Ericaceae* (heath family). The garden is known for its extensive collection of rhododendrons (about 400 species) most of which flower between March and June. Other Garden features include a wild garden, woodland garden, arboretum, peat walls, annual and herbaceous borders, a demonstration garden, heath garden and pond.

Royal Botanic Gardens, Kew
GREATER LONDON

Kew Road, Richmond, Surrey.
tel. 01 940 1171

A landscaped garden of over 300 acres (121ha) evolved from 18th-century Royal pleasure gardens overlaid by formal 19th-century features with modern additions and a reproduced 17th-century garden. Historic buildings include Kew Palace and Queen Charlotte's Cottage. Pagoda, Orangery, Temples, Ruined Arch, Botanical Museums and Marianne North Art Gallery. Extensive botanical collections (c.50,000 different types of plants) from around the world are housed in greenhouses, arboretum and herbetum. Collections under glass range from the giant Amazon water-lily to minute arctic-alpines with comprehensive display collections of aroids, bromeliads, cycads, carnivorous plants, ferns, orchids, palms, succulents, and regional plantings such as for plants from Australasia, the Canary Islands and Southern Africa. The extensive herbaceous collections are displayed in the Natural Order Beds, Grass Garden, Duke's and Queen's Gardens and the large arboretum includes a great variety of trees with many historic or rare specimens, collections of magnolias, oaks, pines, etc., lake and ponds, and special features such as berberis and rhododendron dells, azalea, bamboo, heath and rose gardens. The Queen's Cottage grounds form a natural bluebell wood and are kept as a nature reserve planted with native trees and shrubs. Large areas of the arboretum are planted with bulbs.

On A307 between Richmond and Kew Bridge

TQ 1876

Daily except Christmas Day and New Year's Day, 1000, closing times vary from 1600 to 2000 according to season

No peak season

only guide dogs
limited

Saling Hall ESSEX

Mr and Mrs Hugh Johnson, Great Saling, Braintree.

The present owners began to develop this garden about 10 years ago, but the previous occupant, Lady Carlyle, had laid excellent foundations, notably around the house. The land extends to 12 acres (5ha) and the opportunity has been taken to create areas of distinctive character, both in style and atmosphere. Each section skilfully leads to the next via a suitable area of transition. The old Dutch-gabled house is approached past natural ponds, fine chestnuts and a group of Japanese cherries. Formality then takes over, with rows of Lombardy poplars and pleached limes flanking the forecourt. The house overlooks, on the south side, a symmetrically planned walled garden. Around the sides and flanking the middle path are borders of shrubs, roses, plants and bulbs, producing mostly blue, pink and pale yellow flowers. Rows of slim conifers stand like sentinels, with *Chamaecyparis lawsoniana* 'Pottenii' against the walls and shorter *Juniperus hibernica* along the path. A paved walk leads through a semi-woodland area with good ground cover to a shady water and bog garden. An alternative route leads into a park-like arboretum containing many interesting young trees. Against a steep shrub-covered bank has been built a curving pool, the design of which shows oriental influence. **M. R.**

6 miles NW of Braintree off A120 Great Dunmow—Braintree road; house beside church at N end of village

TL 7027

Early May to July and Sept to mid Oct: Wed to Fri 1400–1700. Parties at other times by prior arrangement

Peak months: May, June and Oct

Sandringham House and Gardens
NORFOLK

H.M. The Queen, Sandringham.
tel. King's Lynn (0553) 2675

The spacious grounds of Sandringham bear the imprint of successive royal owners since it was first occupied by Edward, Prince of Wales, in 1862. The house is surrounded by enormous lawns and magnificent trees. From the public entrance a path runs through a woodland glade with shrubberies in which colour is provided from the camellias, cultivars of *Erica carnea* and massed daffodils of spring to the autumn berries of sorbus and cotoneasters. For the months between there are rhododendrons and azaleas, philadelphus and lavenders, hydrangeas and lilies. (Most of the plants are labelled.) This exemplary modern planting was carried out under the direction of T. H. Finlay of the Savill Gardens. Completely different in style is the formal garden adjoining the house, designed by Geoffrey Jellicoe for King George VI. Enclosed by pleached limes, box hedges create a number of enclosures, some containing small lawns, others hardy plants and roses. At the end is a statue of Father Time, purchased by Queen Mary. Near the south-west corner of the house are two lakes fed by water from natural springs which flows through rock outcrops planted with moisture-loving subjects. A further rock garden is planted with dwarf conifers and heathers, and nearby stands Queen Alexandra's summerhouse. **M. R.**

8 miles NE of King's Lynn off A149 King's Lynn—Hunstanton road

TF 6928

Apr to Sept: Mon to Thur 1030–1700; Sun 1130–1700. Closed late July and early Aug

No peak season

1½ miles from Egham
in Wick Lane,
Englefield Green,
approx 1 mile w of
A30

SU 9870

Savill Garden: Mar
to late Dec: daily
1000–1800; Valley
Gardens: Daily,
dawn–dusk

Peak months: Apr to
Oct

🅿 wc ⊖ ¹-mile walk
🚌
🐕 in Valley Gardens
🍴 in Savill Gardens
🚗 in Valley Gardens
🍷 in Savill Gardens
🛒 in Savill Gardens
🎁 in Savill Gardens

Savill Gardens and Valley Gardens BERKSHIRE

Crown Estate Commissioners, The Great Park, Windsor.
tel. Windsor (95) 60222

These large scale Royal gardens are set in the magnificence of Windsor Great Park, its 4,500 acres (1,821ha) of planned and planted woodlands and vistas including the ancient royal hunting forests. The Savill Garden was laid out first, from the mid-1930s, by Eric Savill the then Deputy Surveyor, who combined a keen eye for landscape and a great horticultural knowledge with a drive and persuasive persistence that impressed the Royal Family. He created 35 acres (14ha) of vistas, glades and ponds, clothing all with a rich adornment of acid soil-loving rhododendrons, azaleas and countless other trees and shrubs. He went for bold group plantings now at their most mature and effective stage. The well sited restaurant must have one of the finest woodland garden views in the country. The gardens are still developing with a Jubilee Garden for autumn colour, new herbaceous borders, a dry garden of plants in gravel, walls and raised beds, and an attractive and tempting plant centre near the car park.

The Valley Gardens lying to the south of the Savill Gardens were also laid out by Eric Savill who from 1947 created 400 acres (162ha) of superb woodland gardens exploiting a series of valleys lying along the north bank of Virginia Water, the attractive, very large 18th-century artificial lake. Bold planting was again practised in groups of four to nine trees or shrubs, with spectacular massing as in the famous Punch Bowl of evergreen azaleas, at its best in late May. There are 50 acres (20ha) of rhododendrons, azaleas, camellias, maples, hydrangeas to mention only a few, and autumn colour is also outstanding. Eric Savill was knighted in 1955 for his achievements which are now being continued and extended by the present Keeper of the Gardens, John Bond. He has created 10 acres (4ha) of unique heather and shrub garden in old dry gravel pits, and is now establishing the National Collections of Rhododendrons, Pieris, Dwarf and Slow-growing Conifers and other genera. **T.W.**

6 miles w of
Tunbridge Wells on
A21 Hastings road
just s of Lamberhurst

TQ 6835

Apr to Oct: Wed to
Sun, exc Good Friday
but inc Bank Holiday
Mon 1400–1800 (or
sunset if earlier).
Reduced rates for
parties by prior
arrangement

No peak season

🅿 wc 🚌 🍷 🛒 🎁

Scotney Castle KENT

The National Trust, Lamberhurst, Tunbridge Wells.
tel. Lamberhurst (0892) 890651

A perfect example of the picturesque period of landscape gardening, created in the late 18th and early 19th century using the ancient ruined castle in its lily-studded moat as the romantic feature among rambling wooded walks and rocky paths. The De Scotene family once possessed the castle, but it was the Hussey family who in the 18th and 19th centuries created the Scotney we see today, building a large 'Gothic' house on a commanding terrace well above the lake, and turning the old castle into a picturesque ruin. There are really no formal or flower gardens at Scotney, the essential features being the framework of magnificent trees, beeches, oaks and limes and some cedars and other evergreens of great size and character, and informal walks down the quite steep-sided valley in whose floor lies the old castle and its lake. The rich, acidic clay soils are fine for rhododendrons, azaleas, kalmias, magnolias and other May and June flowering shrubs. Autumn effects are also spectacular here. An old, secluded quarry from which stone was taken to build the house, was made into a large rock garden, with steep, mysterious paths crossing the rocky outcrops. The old castle with its walls and courtyards have been attractively planted, using herbs and fragrant plants. The moat is colourful with water-lilies, and its margins attractive with natural waterside associations. **T.W.**

Seaton Delaval Hall TYNE AND WEAR

Lord Hastings, Whitley Bay.
tel. Seaton Delaval (0632) 371493/373040

One of Vanbrugh's masterpieces is Admiral George Delaval's mansion Seaton Delaval, built in the early 1700s. This great theatrical pile was gutted by fire but still rises above its garden and parkland to dominate the scene. From the front the view is down to the distant port of Blyth and the North Sea, from the south it is over rolling parkland to ruined Tynemouth Priory. The garden on the west side of the house, designed by James Russell in 1950, was purposely made reminiscent of the original. It is a sunken one reached from a balustraded platform by two flights of wide steps, from where is seen, as it was meant to be, the patterns of the box parterres. At the far end behind a recessed seat is a David and Goliath statue by Baccio Bandinelli. During 1959–62 a shrubbery was cleared from the east and west sides of the main block and lawns laid. At the end of the enclosed lawn is a box-edged rose garden. Rhododendrons and azaleas and other flowering shrubs were planted here in 1964 and another classical statue of Samson and a Philistine by Gian Bologna was moved here. Bays are formed into buttresses on the wall side of the rose garden where shrub roses, peonies and a large buddleia are principal features. Clipped hollies are on this level as well as an unusual hypericum hedge to the small enclosed garden and greenhouse. **K.L**

4 miles N of Whitley
Bay on A190 off
A193 Whitley Bay—
Blyth road

NY 3376

May to Sept: Wed,
Sun, Bank Holiday
Mon 1400–1800

Peak months: June
and July

Sewerby Hall Park HUMBERSIDE

East Yorkshire Borough Council, Bridlington.
tel. Bridlington (0262) 73769

At Sewerby is a garden on the very cliff top overlooking the North Sea. Here a hall or manor has stood since Norman times and Anglo-Saxon and Roman remains have been found in the park. There are 50 acres (20ha) of garden and woodland where tender trees and shrubs defy the North Sea gales. Much of the present layout is basically the work of Mr Yarbrugh from 1841 onwards. In front of the 1715 house is a balustraded lawn on which is the three-coloured laburnum, *Laburnocytisus adamii*, a fine stand of copper beech and *Acer negundo*. Turning left from the house front the formal garden is dominated by six massive monkey puzzle trees and steps leading to an open temple and planted around, giving a sub-tropical effect, are yuccas, fatsias, the palm, *Chamaerops humilis*, foxtail lilies and lovely weeping birch (*Betula pendula* 'Youngii'). Under the woodland border to this lawn appears a succession of flowers. A path through the trees comes to a principal feature of Sewerby, the old English garden where topiary-worked yew hedges and box-edged geometrically shaped beds give the formal parterre effect even when bright with cottage garden flowers during the summer. There is a Georgian conservatory full of flowers and colourful foliage and through a wrought iron gate is a walled rose garden planted in ornamental box-edged beds. A walled walk on the outer wall protects many tender hebes, pittosporums, cistus and olearias. **K.L**

2 miles from centre of
Bridlington off B1255
Bridlington—
Flamborough road

TA 2068

Daily: 0900 to dusk

Peak months: May
and late Aug to early
Sept

limited opening

Sezincote GLOUCESTERSHIRE

Mr and Mrs D. Peake, Moreton-in-Marsh.

This is Xanadu come to England. The house, an amazing Hindu-Mogul fantasy in the manner of Akbar, was completed in 1805 by Samuel Pepys Cockerell for his brother Charles, who had served in the East India Company. The finest view of it can be had from the bridge over the lowest pond, where its amber walls, copper dome and the pinnacles of the pavilions, temples and stables stand out among the trees. Reverse the position and from the front of the house or from the curving orangery, surely the most enticing greenhouse corridor in England, look at the park. The great Lebanon cedars to the left were planted by Humphry Repton, their under-canopy, misty pink cherries, by Lady Kleinwort and Graham Thomas; the lake is Repton's, while the view across the Evenlode valley is English countryside at its most magical. Three parts of the garden in particular retain an exotic atmosphere. The south garden, between the house and the orangery, is laid out in Mogul fashion with canals and paths crossing at right angles, representing the rivers of life. Here restricted space prevents a full realisation of the Indian original. Moving to the temple pool, there is a temple, designed by Thomas Daniell, to Surya, Hindu god of the sun. The Indian influence culminates at Daniell's Bridge decorated with Brahmin bulls, and below which, coiled round a tree trunk, is a metal three-headed serpent. The planting of the stream expands and contracts, until it reaches the island pool, spanned by a bridge. Here under the repose of the cedars reflected in the deep clear water, with, in spring, the turf bright with anemones and bluebells, the garden ends and culminates. **E.F.**

4 miles N of Stow-on-
the-Wold, off A44
Moreton-in-Marsh—
Broadway road

SP 1731

Jan to end Nov:
Thur, Fri and Bank
Holiday Mon
1400–1800

No peak season

limited opening:
parties by appointment
only

10 miles N of Lewes
on A275 Lewes—East
Grinstead road

TQ 4125

Apr to mid-Nov: Tue
to Sat (exc Tue after
Bank Holiday Mon
and Good Fri)
1100–1800; Sun and
Bank Holiday Mon
1400–1800 (sunset if
earlier). Reduced rates
for parties by prior
arrangement

Peak seasons: spring
and autumn

🅿 ♿ ⊖🚻 ⚕
🍴 *limited opening*
🏛 💐 🎁

Sheffield Park Garden EAST SUSSEX

The National Trust, Uckfield.
tel. Danehill (0825) 790655

A great landscaped arboretum originating in the 18th century and richly planted over the succeeding centuries with magnificent groups of contrasting trees, conifers and massed shrubs around a series of extensive lakes. The 'Gothic' house dating from the 1770s and its terraces should really afford the finest views of the landscaped gardens where 'Capability' Brown was asked to assist with the layout, but the house, now under separate ownership, is divided from the gardens by screen planting. Humphry Repton also improved the designs in the late 18th century and added two more lakes to the original lake. A Mr Arthur Soames bought Sheffield Park from the Earl of Sheffield in 1909 and he transformed the gardens and parklands with an immense and imaginative programme of planting, using a great variety of North American trees. The tupelo trees are the finest planting in Great Britain and are brilliant in red and flame colours in mid-October. This is a fine time to see this garden, the tinted maples, swamp cypress, the tupelos contrasting with dark pines and blue cedars and reflected in the mirrors of the lakes on a still fine day. Rhododendrons and azaleas are also colourful in May and June. Under the skilled and effective management of the National Trust new areas are still being opened up in the 80 acres (32ha) or more of woodland and parkland. **T.W.**

2 miles S of
Sheringham off A148
Cromer—Holt road

TG 1441

May and June: daily.

Peak months: mid-
May to mid-June

⊖🚻 🍴 🏛 💐

Sheringham Hall NORFOLK

Thomas Upcher, Esq., Upper Sheringham.

Sheringham Hall was amongst that last works of Humphry Repton, the Red Book showing his proposals being produced in 1812. He regarded it as his masterpiece. It is fitting that his crowning achievement should have been created in the county in which he grew up and in which he chose to be buried. Besides the park, Repton and his eldest son designed the neo-classic house for Abbot Upcher, ancestor of the present owner. Repton decided to place the house in the shelter of a wooded hill facing south and to forego views of the sea. Instead, it looks out on to rising, undulating land with the hilltops crowned by woods – a prospect of great beauty. The kitchen garden with a small formal rose garden was set at some distance from the house. In recent years a temple to Repton's design has been built overlooking the park. In the mid-19th century the woods were thickly planted with rhododendrons raised from seed collected by Wilson. During the 1950s the land between the house and walled garden was developed with a small lake, lawns, flowering trees and informal borders of shrubs, whilst the woods behind the house were planted with well-chosen camellias, azaleas and rhododendrons. **M.R.**

5½ miles E of Stafford
on A573 Stafford—
Rugeley road
(entrance at Milford)

SJ 9822

Mid-March to late
Oct: Tue to Fri and
Bank Holiday Mon
(closed Good Fri)
1030–1730; Sat and
Sun 1400–1730

No peak season

🅿 ♿
⊖*1-mile walk*
🍴 🐕
limited opening
💐
🏚 *limited opening*
🏛

Shugborough STAFFORDSHIRE

The National Trust, nr Stafford.
tel. Little Hayward (0889) 881388

Shugborough is the result of Admiral Lord Anson's voyage round the world from which he returned in 1744, bringing with him a prize ship, that made the family fortune. He also brought *Lathyrus nervosus*, a blue, scented pea, eaten by his sailors in Patagonia, and always known as Anson's Blue Pea. What makes Shugborough unique is its array of garden monuments, of which a painting by Nicholas Dahl (when all were complete and as yet unravished) can be seen in the house. They are based on Revett's drawings and include the Tower of the Winds, a Triumphal Arch and the Lanthorn of Demosthenes. A Chinese pagoda was swept away in a disastrous flood in 1795. To the south of the house by the River Sow is the wild garden. The dark purple rhododendrons and pale yellow azaleas create a pleasing contrast, without the usual incursions of cerise and scarlet. Walk as far as the Chinese House, erected in 1747 by the Admiral from a sketch made by one of his officers in 'Centurion'. The present cast-iron bridge, erected in 1813, is painted in the colour of Chinese lacquer. The clipped yews round the house are remnants of a Victorian layout, re-vitalised in 1966 by Graham Thomas, who designed a rose garden with arched entrances, pillars, and standards reminiscent of Bagatelle, near Paris, in which grow favourite roses of that period. **E.F.**

Sissinghurst Castle Garden KENT

The National Trust, Sissinghurst, nr Cranbrook.
tel. Cranbrook (0580) 712850

These world-famous gardens attract over 100,000 visitors each year creating problems for those who keep up the remarkable standards notwithstanding. To enjoy a reasonably peaceful visit to Sissinghurst, choose a week day or a weekend early or late in the season or go early, or late in the afternoon. Once an important seat in the 16th and 17th centuries with a hunting park and royal visitors, a long decline in its fortunes ended with only fragments of the original great buildings remaining by the early 20th century, notably the fine gate house and red brick tower. Harold Nicolson and Vita Sackville-West bought the ruins in 1930 and during the next 20 years or so created the fascinating garden we can enjoy today. The story is dramatically told in Nigel Nicolson's guide to the gardens. The magic of Sissinghurst is that in a relatively small enclosure of 6 acres (2.4ha) a series of garden rooms has been made, each one furnished quite differently with rich collections of plants, and linked by vistas, walks and hedged paths so that the garden seems much larger than it really is. The old walls have been beautifully planted, and there are themes throughout the seasons, a red border, white garden, spring walk and an old orchard massed with bulbs of many kinds. A unique experience is the bird's eye view of the garden from the tower. **T.W.**

6½ miles NW of Tenterden and 1 mile E of Sissinghurst village on A262

TQ 8237

Apr to mid-Oct: Tue to Fri 1300–1830 (exc Good Fri 1000–1830); Sat and Sun 1000–1830. Reduced rates for parties by prior arrangement

No peak season

Sizergh Castle CUMBRIA

The National Trust, Sedgwick, nr Kendal.
tel. Sedgwick (0448) 60285

Probably the largest collection of hardy ferns in the country is at Sizergh, a lovely old mansion built round a Pele Tower of c.1350. The present garden lay-out of lawns, lake and limestone rock garden was designed and executed by the noted nursery of nearby Ambleside, T. R. Hayes and Son, in 1926. An approach garden of ancient yews, island beds of shrub roses, lilac and colourful underplanting of lilies and many different geraniums leads to old gate piers. Here a steep walk climbs to a high terrace and sheltering wall. The wall and bed beneath hold osmanthus, olearias, *Solanum crispum*, ceratostigma and caryopteris. From the house front a lawn leads to a small lake and a tree-filled island. On the far side the sloping lawns are flowery meads, in spring a cloud of pheasant's eye narcissus and later alive with wild orchis and other flora of the limestone soils. The ¾ acre (0.3ha) sunken rock garden, which contains over 100 differing species and varieties of ferns, is surrounded by surprisingly large 'dwarf' conifers. Japanese maples give their spring and autumn colour to the evergreens and a great variety of alpines, bog plants and marginals are planted in and among the ferns which include many varieties of the royal fern, unusual polypodias, blechnums, dryopteris and many more. **K.L.**

3½ miles S of Kendal on A6 Kendal—Morecambe road

SD 4088

Apr to end Sept: Wed, Thur, Sun, Bank Holiday Mon and other Mons in Aug. Oct: Wed and Thur 1400–1745. Reduced rates for parties of 15 or over by prior arrangement

No peak season

limited opening

Sledmere House HUMBERSIDE

Sir Tatton Sykes, Bart. Sledmere, Driffield.
tel. Driffield (0377) 86208

An exemplary Brownian landscape is the setting for this Georgian house of 1751–83 with its magnificent Joseph Rose Graeco-Roman style interiors and its library modelled on the baths of Diocletian. Brown's plan for the whole estate of 2,000 acres (809ha) hangs there. Under Sir Christopher Sykes the old village was removed, a model village and the famous race-horse stud stables built, all part of the surrounding house scene. The entrance is by way of the cupola-topped stable block onto lawns flanked by colourful herbaceous borders and climbing plants on the mellow brick walls and dotted with chestnuts well over 200 years old and stately cedars through which glimpses of the village church are seen. In 1911 an Italian garden was created in a recess adjoining the house with water, stone urns and statuary. Walls on the three sides are filled with climbers. From the south front of the house the view is of a typical Brown landscape: lawns marching up to the house foundations and sloping away to rise again by a later added pool and fountain to rolling landscape dotted with fine beech, elm and oak into the far distance where Brown's signature, a belt of trees, closes the view. Left from the house through woodland paths is a kitchen garden containing old glass and by its side a peculiar shaped rose garden and a walk of flowering trees, shrubs and wall climbers. **K.L.**

7 miles NW of Great Driffield off B1251 and B1252

TA 9465

Easter weekend (Good Fri to Tue), Suns in Apr, then daily (exc Mon, Fri) May to late Sept and all Bank Holiday Mon: 1330–1730

Peak months: June, July, Aug and Sept

215

Snowshill Manor GLOUCESTERSHIRE

The National Trust, nr Broadway.
tel. Broadway (0386) 852410

By 1919 Snowshill had become a semi-derelict farm when it was bought and restored by the architect Charles Wade. By 1923 Mr Wade, using Mr H. Baillie Scott as designer, had laid out the garden, incorporating the old farm buildings including the dovecot, and using the spring that rises under the house to feed a series of pools and troughs. 'One of his maxims was that the plan of the garden is more important than the flowers', writes Graham Thomas. Wade favoured gardens that do not disclose all their delights at a single glance, so his garden is organised in a series of terraces and outdoor rooms. He also had a predeliction for mauve and blue flowers which he considered to contrast ideally with surroundings of Cotswold stone. Visitors will notice that the doors, windows and gates of the house and farm buildings are painted in a deep turquoise blue that has become known as Wade Blue. It is no mean achievement to have made a garden of great variety in a small space which is in complete empathy with the house it surrounds. This garden is in the Hidcote and Sissinghurst tradition, full of charm, and only lesser in renown as it is smaller in scale. **E.F.**

Spetchley Park HEREFORD and WORCESTER

R. J. Berkeley, Esq., Spetchley, nr Worcester.
tel. Spetchley (090 565) 213/224

In the time of Rose Berkeley, sister of the great gardener Ellen Willmott, Spetchley Park was one of the wonders of England, and although it is no longer possible to maintain it to the highest standards, it remains a place to be admired and loved. The entrance is now through the melon yard, where a foretaste of the quality of the planting is obtained, for on the walls are *Bignonia capreolata*, *Campsis* 'Madame Galen', *Fremontodendron californicum*, and *Trachelospermum jasminoides*. Here also are to be found specimens of the olive, the double pomegranate and of lemon-scented verbena. Magnificent borders full of rare shrubs surround the old kitchen gardens. The alcove of Bath stone faces the fountain gardens, inspired by Ellen Willmott, in which the thirty six beds within yew hedges and flanked by stone paths, were filled by botanically arranged families of plants. The rose lawn, with the conservatory to the north, a fine cut-leaved beech, *Fagus sylvatica heterophylla* beside it and frame of tall pines and cedars is the focus of the garden; and from here the pattern of the lake, moat, woods and garden becomes clear. A walk past the cork lawn, dominated by the Luccombe oak, an evergreen cross between the turkey oak and the cork oak, leads to the new lawn with its collection of sorbus, and other trees for autumn colour. Return through the copse with its magnolias, azaleas, low-growing trilliums and huge cardiocrinums. To the discerning this garden is a constant delight. **E.F.**

Spinners HAMPSHIRE

Mr and Mrs P. G. G. Chappell, Boldre, Lymington.
tel. Lymington (0590) 73347

This is a remarkable plantsman's garden *par excellence*, created and developed by Mr and Mrs Peter Chappell over the past 25 years, around a small retreat of a house that they found hidden away in a neglected oak wood when they arrived here in 1960. On this wooded slope high above Lymington River, with its acidic gravelly soils and patches of deep clay and humus, they made the gardens removing scrub and thinning the tree canopy with great care and foresight so as to retain the spirit and atmosphere of the adjacent New Forest. Paths wander up and down between fascinating groups and masses of many distinctive plants. In spring the forest floor is rich with cyclamen, trilliums, erythroniums, hellebores, the unusual bloodroot (*Sanguinaria*) to mention only a few, while above and around are magnolias, followed by species and hybrids of rhododendrons selected for cream and apricot, scarlet and blue flowers and for foliage and texture. Lower down the paths open out, and the trees give way to open clearings. Deeper soils favour massed beds of geraniums, hostas, irises, meconopsis, primulas and many ferns and unusual grasses all carefully and beautifully combined. On the grassy slopes are fine specimen trees. Mulching and leafmould dressings are a key to the healthy appearance of all these plants. Most tempting of all to enthusiasts is the nursery here, a plant-hunter's paradise, including many rare and unusual plants probably unobtainable elsewhere. **T.W.**

Springfields Gardens LINCOLNSHIRE

Springfields Horticultural Society Limited, Camelgate, Spalding.
tel. Spalding (0775) 4843

A show garden for British bulbs and corms was opened here in Spalding in 1966 after over two years of work. The 25 acres (10ha) of lake, woodland,,sunken garden, paved walks, lawns and glasshouses in spring display over 1,000,000 bulbs and corms of more than 3,000 varieties. Some 300 tulip varieties are to be seen in two large greenhouses. Narcissi from the country's experimental horticultural stations and the Daffodil Society are grown in trial beds along with tulips from the Agricultural Development Advisory Service. This congress of beauty can be seen from early April to late May. In 1976 Springfield's opening season was extended to September with the highlight, the blooming of over 12,000 roses, both old and new, selected by the British Association of Rose Breeders. There are water-lilies in the lake, bedding-out and dahlias on the terraces, an eclectic collection of summer-flowering plants, trees and shrubs, all providing interest and brilliant colour in late summer. There is a maze of *Cupressocyparis leylandii* planted in 1977 to commemorate the Queen's Silver Jubilee. The gardens were designed by Carl Van Empelen, known for his Sterling Forest Gardens in New York and work on the Continent. In February every year the largest forced flower show in Britain is held in the gardens. **K.L.**

1 mile E of Spalding on A151 Spalding—Holbeach road

TF 2624

Apr to mid-May and mid-June to end Sept: daily 1000–1800. Reduced rates for parties of 30 and over by prior arrangement

No peak season

Stourhead WILTSHIRE

The National Trust, Stourton, Warminster.
tel. Bourton (0747) 840348

The breathtaking landscape gardens of Stourhead were designed in 1741 by Henry Hoare the Second when he created a series of lakes in a sloping woodland setting with vantage points to view the monuments and temples across the sparkling waters of the lake. Looking from the Temple of Flora the view is of the Pantheon standing serenely on a grass mound, more often than not reflected in the still water. Walking northwards along the path that encircles the lake one passes rhododendrons, magnolias, acers and magnificent specimens of sequoiadendron, metasequoia (the dawn redwood) and London plane. Many varieties of pine and abies are planted on the hillside above the path as it turns westwards, winding its way to the damp and rather eerie Grotto from which a marvellous view of the Stone Bridge, the Bristol Cross, brought from Bristol in the 18th century, and Church is seen. The Temple of Apollo towers above an enormous tulip tree, *Liriodendron tulipifera*, planted at the water's edge and when the leaves turn a brilliant yellow in the autumn, the bright red foliage of adjacent acers provides a striking contrast of colour. In the same area, a very good specimen of *Davidia involucrata*, the handkerchief tree, can be seen at its best in early summer. **A.S.**

10 miles S of Frome, just W of B3092 Frome—Gillingham road

ST 7735

Daily: 0800–1900 (or sunset if earlier)

No peak season

Oct to Feb

Mar to mid-Dec
limited opening: parties by appointment only

Stourton House WILTSHIRE

Col. and Mrs A. S. Bullivant, Stourton, nr Warminster.

This lovely 4-acre (1.5-ha) garden is filled with very interesting plants, including flowers that are grown specially for drying such as achillea, delphiniums and *Physalis franchettii*, the Chinese lantern. Elegant tree peonies, so beautiful in June, and herbaceous perennials grow in fan-shaped beds enclosed by high hedges in the small sheltered formal garden. In spring hundreds of unusual narcissi with split coronas bloom in an area next to the tiny water garden and rock garden. Not far from the front of the house, dwarf conifers and heathers fill the newly made peat beds, together with dog-tooth violets and the splendid deep purple-flowered *Fritillaria persica*. The high leafy canopy provided by mature trees in the woodland garden helps to protect the many rarities growing below, spectacular magnolias, rhododendrons, camellias and the marvellous pink-tinged green and white leaved *Pieris japonica* 'Variegata', mingle with primulas, meconopsis and the fern-leafed *Corydalis cheilanthifolia*, a mass of dainty yellow flowers in April. Nearby, in the shade of an enormous holly tree, many different kinds of hydrangea grow, giving good colour in late summer and featuring the most attractive white and green foliage of the variegated hydrangea. **A.S.**

11 miles S of Frome on B3092 next to Stourhead National Trust property

ST 7734

Apr to Nov: Sun and Thur 1100–1800

No peak season

by appointment only

3 miles NW of
Buckingham off A422
Buckingham—
Brackley road

SP 6737

Easter weekend, then
mid-July to early
Sept: Fri to Sun plus
Aug Bank Holiday
Mon 1300–1800

No peak season

Stowe School BUCKINGHAMSHIRE

Allied Schools Limited, Buckingham.
tel. Buckingham (0280) 813650

The visitor must not expect to find a garden here in the horticultural sense of
the word, but rather a vast landscape park in whose development 200 years
ago or so, some of the most notable architects and landscape gardeners of the
18th century were employed. The sense of arrival at a country seat of more
than dramatic properties is immediate as one takes the long straight avenue
past the Boycott pavilions to the main entrance at the north front of the house.
Walking round and standing on the great portico of the mansion one
immediately realises the scale of this great place. The house was enlarged for
Viscount Cobham by Sir John Vanbrugh the architect of Blenheim Palace
fame, and its huge façade once looked out across a formal Versailles-type
garden to a distant skyline Corinthian Arch. The Arch is still here, but the
formal gardens were gradually softened and broadened by William Kent and
later 'Capability' Brown to form a classical paradise garden of temples,
monuments, wooded groves and distant clumps and belts of trees, of
serpentine lakes, classical bridges and great rolling vistas. Some of the avenues
of the formal period were left. The school is involved in a lengthy programme
of restoration and tree planting, a commendable long-term effort in order to
ensure a landscape for tomorrow's generation. **T.W.**

3 miles SW of Ripon
off B6265 Ripon—
Pateley Bridge road

SE 2767

Daily exc 25 and 26
Dec, 1 Jan and Good
Fri. Early Mar and
mid-Oct to Feb:
0930–1600 (Sun Nov
to Feb 1400–1600).
Mid-Mar to May and
Sept to mid-Oct:
0930–1830. June to
Aug: 0930–2100

Studley Royal Country Park
NORTH YORKSHIRE

The National Trust, nr Ripon.
tel. Sawley (076 586) 333

If the South Sea Bubble had not burst this unique landscape would probably
have never existed. For Chancellor John Aislabie retired here in disgrace and
from around 1730 until his death in 1742 transformed the wild, rugged, steep-
sided narrow valley of the River Skell into a shimmering formal garden set in
magnificent greenery. The Skell was formed into a large lake running by
grotto cascades into canals to form the Moon Pool and its two adjoining
crescent-shaped pools. The water then runs over a formal rusticated cascade
between two Venetian fishing houses into a large lake and a steep, hillside
waterfall on its far side. Buildings both Gothic and classical adorn the grounds,
a beautifully proportioned banqueting house by Colin Campbell of c.1727,
the Temple of Piety, lead statues by the waterside and, over stepping stones by
the last cascade, an uphill path leads to a steep, stygian, rocky tunnel grotto.
This leads to a high viewing walk starting from an octagonal Gothic folly to
Tent Hill, to Surprise View, where, through a door in a small building, in the
distance by the Skell, stands Fountains Abbey. William, John's son, added a
Chinese temple, no longer there, and the obelisk terminating a long avenue of
trees aligned on the towers of Ripon Cathedral. The house was burned down
in 1946 but the handsome stable block by Campbell of 1728 remains. **K.L.**

6 miles NE of
Cheltenham off A46
Cheltenham—
Broadway road

SP 0327

Mar to Oct: daily
1100–1730. Parties in
winter months by
appointment. Reduced
rates available

No peak season

Sudeley Castle GLOUCESTERSHIRE

The Lady Ashcombe, Winchcombe.
tel. Winchcombe (0242) 602308

This is a large and popular place, so try to choose a time when crowds will not
spoil the Tennysonian atmosphere of the garden. Maude might easily have
wandered among the lavender and rosemary of the Queen's Garden, laid out
in imitation of a medieval original by Emma Dent in the mid-19th century.
Victorian too are the domed, clipped yews by the park balustrade, and the
bastion-like yew hedges with openings and tunnel walks that flank this
charming knot garden. The pleasure grounds are well planted with cedars and
limes, and many younger specimens of planes and sweet chestnuts. The canal is
now devoted to a collection of waterfowl. Another romantic incident is
provided by the ruin of the magnificent tithe barn; in front there is a
rectangular lily pool and at either side it is buttressed by hedges of yew and
groups of the white Japanese cherry 'Shirotae'. Strong climbers such as
wisteria, and *Clematis montana*, clothe it appropriately. The castle is in itself
highly romantic, so the whole, park, wide views, and garden combine
together to create a place in which Scott and Tennyson would have delighted.
E.F.

Sutton Park NORTH YORKSHIRE

Mrs N. M. D. Sheffield, Sutton-on-the-Forest, York.

Sutton Park is a 1962 creation by Percy Cane of a terraced garden using the original terracing and planted up in a most colourful and tasteful way by the owners since that time. The garden surrounds a medium-size Georgian house framed by lawns and a paved terrace with views over pastoral landscape said to be by Brown. The south garden side of the house has this spacious York-stone paved terrace punctuated with grass and beds. Wide stone steps lead to the first terraced rose garden with beds set in trim turf behind which are statues surrounded by the scented autumn-flowering *Clematis flammula*. The last terrace is marked by a lily tank and terminates in a high beech hedge shaped into a semi-circular niche for a white marble seat. There are delicate ironwork gazebos on one of the terraces and at the side of the house is a paved and pebbled area broken by beds of lavender and hydrangea in orange tubs, a present from Blenheim Palace. Glades on the east side of the terraced gardens lead to a woodland walk between forest trees, exotic and Japanese cherries to a temple, all created by the present owners. Columnar conifers most skillfully placed by the terrace walls add height to the picture and planting has been carefully designed to give differing colour patterns, as on the paved terrace where mauve, grey and pink predominate. **K.L.**

8 miles N of York on B1363 York—Helmsley road

SE 5867

Apr to end Sept: Sun, plus Tue and Thur (May to end Sept), Good Fri, Easter Sun and Mon, all bank holidays 1400–1800. Wed by appointment all year and other times by arrangement. Reduced rates for parties —

Peak months: Apr to July

Tapeley Park DEVON

Miss Rosamond Christie, Instow, Devon.
tel. Instow (0271) 860528

The half-mile (0.8-km) drive runs east from the main road at about sea level to the impressive brick-faced house standing 200ft (61m) above the sea. A former bowling green and flower beds to the west of the house have been cleared to make way for public putting greens. There is much of interest in this Domesday site and the 10-acre (4-ha) garden has evolved from a typical Victorian/Edwardian layout to meet the limitations of present-day finances. The main front of the house faces south above steeply falling terraced ground that was once landscaped as an 'Italian' garden. The walls supporting the terraces, and those of the house, are clothed with a variety of shrubs and climbers. Borders below the walls are filled with roses, shrubs and herbaceous plants. Statues, Irish yews and palms produce an exotic air and a tunnel of evergreen oak runs down beside the steps. They are of brick from top to bottom. One of the summerhouses has the family name of 'toot', perhaps derived from the west-country expression for look-out. East of the house a lawn extends to a mixed border backed by a wall, well clothed with a sloping shrubbery above. Stone steps (said to be of rejected tombstones) lead up from this lawn through massive pines, that also impress themselves on the landscape, to the walled kitchen garden in which concrete-framed greenhouses of 50 years ago remind one of the changing fashions and efficiency of construction since then. **F.S.**

1½ miles S of Instow on A39 Barnstaple—Bideford road

SS 4829

Good Fri to Oct: daily (exc Mon) but inc Bank Holiday Mon 1000–1800. Nov to Apr: daily 1000–dusk. Reduced rates for parties by prior arrangement

No peak season

by appointment only

Tatton Park CHESHIRE

The National Trust, Knutsford.
tel. Knutsford (0565) 3155

The gardens of 60 acres (24ha) and its 1,000 acres (405ha) of parkland show the changes of over 200 years. The garden at Tatton is divided into two, east and west, by the long walk terminating in a Grecian temple of 1820. Repton drew up a 'Red Book' for landscaping the parkland for the Egertons and the Italianate terraces, fountain and formal pool were laid down by Paxton in 1847, the vista over them being to deer grazing in parkland, tree studded and marked by a long mere or lake. Tatton has the best representation of a Japanese garden, dated 1910, in this country with its Shinto temple brought from Japan, tea-house, miniature pagoda and Fuji Yama, all created by Japanese workmen. This is by the Golden Brook and lake which mirrors exotic trees and a host of azaleas and rhododendrons, many planted since 1940, a last count giving over 600 different species and varieties. A Victorian fernery houses Antipodean tree ferns; there is an orangery of 1818 by Wyatt still housing oranges, a maze of box, an African hut and a glade of *Metasequoia glyptostroboides*, a leach pool with fountain and clipped topiary work. A paved rose garden with fountain is yew hedge enclosed and nearby the tower garden is the home of flowers and rare shrubs. The long L-shaped border is divided into sections by buttressed yew. Roses and clematis clamber through clipped holly, there is both an arboretum and a pinetum, a magnolia collection, a tiered fountain and arbour. **K.L.**

4 miles S of Altrincham, between A560 and A50, off A5034

SJ 7581

Easter to mid-May and Sept to early Oct: daily exc Mon 1200–1630 (Sun and Bank Holiday Mon 1100–1700). Mid-May to Aug: daily exc Mon 1100–1730 (Sun and Bank Holiday Mon 1100–1800). Early Oct to Easter: daily exc Mon 1300–1600 (Sun and bank holidays 1200–1600). Closed 25 Dec. Parties at other times by appointment

by appointment
limited opening

5 miles E of Colchester just beyond Elmstead Market on A133 Clacton road (signposted)

TM 0625

Feb to mid-Nov: Mon to Sat; mid-Nov to end Jan: Mon to Fri 0900–1700

Peak months: Apr to Oct

P ⓦ ⊖
🚻 *by appointment only*
🏮 ♈ ❦

The Beth Chatto Gardens ESSEX

Mrs Beth Chatto, Elmstead Market, Colchester.
tel. Wivenhoe (020 622) 2007

This is amongst the few influential gardens to have been created since the last war and it is full of lessons for the modern gardener on cultivation and maintenance, and above all on plant selection and grouping. The style is naturalistic and achieves its effects by the artistry with which the plants have been combined with each other and used in conjunction with water, grass and paving. On a 4-acre (1.6ha) site differing habitats have been created so that a wide range of plants can be cultivated. For plants adapted to grow in boggy conditions there are the banks of five large spring-fed ponds, whilst for those which must survive the long hot summers of countries drier than our own, there is a sharply draining gravel slope. Between these extremes are lightly shaded moist areas for woodland plants like hellebores and hostas. The emphasis throughout is on foliage and in particular that provided by perennial plants, many of them uncommon, and on species rather than cultivars. At the same time there is no shortage of flowers and in this, bulbs play a major part, from the crocus and snowdrops of late winter through to sternbergias and nerines, which are still in flower in November. **M. R.**

3 miles N of Trowbridge, just S of B3107 at southern end of Holt

ST 8662

Apr to end Oct: Mon to Fri 1400–1800. Other times by written application

No peak season

P
🚻 *by appointment only*
❦

The Courts WILTSHIRE

The National Trust, Holt, nr Trowbridge.
tel. Trowbridge (0225) 782340

Once an old wool mill, but now forming one wing of the house, 'The Courts' was made larger by 17th-century additions, when the building was converted for use as a court. By incorporating the old ponds and ditches once used for washing the wool, Lady Goff designed a series of very intriguing gardens sheltered by clipped yew hedges and joined by mossy stone paths. In 1950 many unusual trees were planted by Miss Goff in a meadow beyond the boundary of yews, including the elegant fern-leaved beech, *Fagus sylvatica heterophylla*. Many interesting features fill this 7-acre (3-ha) garden, a cool fern garden where rodgersia grows with many varieties of ferns round a tiny pool. The long rectangular lily pond is filled with pink water-lilies, blooming from May onwards, and bordered by a long bed of phlox on one side and roses on the other, the whole area being enclosed by mixed shrub and perennial borders. From the old wool washing pond where gunnera is planted, the path winds between little channels of water, before entering a formal garden filled with roses and old-fashioned plants such as honesty, cowslips, bluebells and bergenias naturalizing even between the slabs of stone on the paths and steps. **A. S.**

½ mile W of A10 from Royston to Cambridge at the level crossing on the road from Shepreth to Meldreth

TL 3947

Daily Peak months: April to Sept

⊖ 🚻 🐾

The Crossing House CAMBRIDGE

Mr and Mrs D. Fuller, Meldreth Road, Shepreth

Although only a quarter of an acre (0.1ha) in extent, and sandwiched between a main railway and a road, this garden is outstanding in three respects. Firstly it contains an amazing number of choice plants, many rare, others old favourites, but all selected by the eye of a connoisseur; secondly it shows how a strong, simple plan can transform an unpropitious site; and lastly it is that most exceptional thing, a successfully scaled down garden – a real 'tour de force'. This small masterpiece has been created over fourteen years by Margaret Fuller aided by her husband, who controlled the level crossing until automatic gates were installed. The design, which is full of original touches, incorporates a tiny lawn, pools with a cascade, banks for alpines and two hexagonal greenhouses. The spread of perennials and alpines and the size and shape of trees and shrubs are skilfully controlled to keep them in scale and prevent overcrowding. If a plant does get too big it is given away and some new discovery takes its place. Bare patches are not allowed and there are annuals and half-hardy plants in pots ready to fill any gaps. Every inch is used and the garden has even spread to the far side of the tracks! **M. R.**

The Fox-Rosehill Garden CORNWALL

Carrick District Council, Melvill Road, Falmouth.

One of several gardens in the district made by the Fox family during the last century, this one has been taken over by the local council and is preserved as a rare and unusual public garden. Some 2 acres (0.8ha) in area it is near but not in sight of the sea; it retains a number of massive trees and large shrubs including vast griselinias, tree rhododendrons, an embothrium, pines and other forest trees from early plantings. Lawns and some coarser grass planted with a range of bulbs provide space for walking and sitting and set off the plants, while broad smooth walks give access to all parts. Many tender shrubs found only in the mildest gardens widen the interest and much recent planting will provide a continuing display of camellias, magnolias and rhododendrons for many years to come. Such rarities as cestrum, prostanthera, musa (banana), tibouchina and many acacias are to be found against walls and in secluded corners. There are large specimens of the palms, trachycarpus and cordyline, that are so common in this part of Cornwall; the latter by its alternative name giving its name to one of the longer thoroughfares in the town – Dracaena Avenue. All is well kept, many plants are well labelled, there is hardly a popular geranium or forget-me-not in sight but *Geranium maderiense* and *Myosotidium hortensia* more than make up for them in the eye of the plantsman. A modern touch is a group of variegated and coloured phormiums from New Zealand. **F.S.**

On B3290, main road through centre of Falmouth

SW 8032

Daily

Peak season: spring

The Garden House DEVON

Fortescue Garden Trust, Buckland Monachorum, nr Yelverton.
tel. Yelverton (0822) 584769

A modern garden, created since 1945, in 2 acres (0.8ha) within the walls of part of a medieval monastery and now spread to some 7 acres (3ha) of mixed planting with closely trimmed lawns and flourishing trees. A small part of an ancient turret gives a bird's eye view of the enclosed garden. Known in the South-west for the very best forms of many of the numerous species and cultivars which, from the beginning, the first owner, Lionel Fortescue, collected from far and wide. The garden is not being allowed to ossify under the recently created Trust but is being cherished by the present gardener and opened to provide vistas to carefully selected trees and distant views, while former thoughtful groupings are being maintained and improved. Lines of Leyland's cypress, planted in the early days after the war, rather dominate some parts of the garden but provide essential shelter from cold winds from the moors above. The developing nursery is producing plants for sale from the rarer and better of the plants to be seen in flower or form by discerning visitors. The stony soil is naturally acid but the old walls have raised the pH in the enclosed part. So there are borders of carefully blended rhododendrons near the entrance with other unusual shrubs extending down to where the less acid soil allows the cultivation of a wide range of herbaceous and alpine plants on the banks and flat ground among the ruins. A garden in which to browse and buy something new to take home. **F.S.**

1 mile w of A386 Plymouth—Tavistock road, between Buckland Monachorum and Crapstone

SX 4968

Apr to end Sept: Mon, Wed and Fri 1430–1900, exc bank holidays

Peak months: May and July

The Gardens of the Rose HERTFORDSHIRE

The Royal National Rose Society, Chiswell Green Lane, St Albans.
tel. St Albans (0727) 50461

This 12-acre (5-ha) garden contains one of the finest – some would say the finest – collection of roses in the world, with around 30,000 bushes representing every category of rose, modern, species and old-fashioned. Situated at Chiswell Green, some two miles from the centre of St Albans, it has been the home of the Royal National Rose Society since 1960. The display gardens surround a substantial house which is the Society's headquarters, with the main axis of the garden being the broad, rose-flanked pathway leading from the house to a circular pool bisected by an extensive curved pergola, a feature of great beauty when the climbing roses with which it is adorned are in bloom. But this is but one of many major features and, in addition to the main displays, there is also a series of small, intimate gardens where roses are grown in association with other plants in conditions approximating to those obtaining in countless home gardens. These include a garden of miniature roses. Of great importance, too, is the trial ground, where new roses are subjected to three years of rigorous judging, with those which are deemed worthy of it receiving the Society's coveted awards. **R.P.**

2 miles sw of St Albans, w of A405 off B4630

TL 1204

Early June to Sept: Mon to Sat 0900–1800, Sun 1400–1800

Peak months: late June to early July

5 miles SW of
Reading, between A4
and A33 in Burghfield
village

SU 6668

Feb to Oct: last Wed
of month exc Aug
1100–1600, also by
appointment

Peak months: June
and July

The Old Rectory BERKSHIRE

Mr and Mrs R. Merton, Burghfield, nr Reading.
tel. Burghfield Common (073 529) 2206

A most ingeniously designed and planted garden of about 6 acres (2.5ha), full of surprises and many different features, and still comparatively young since, apart from the 18th-century house and the mature trees, the remainder has been created over the past 30 years. A border beneath the house windows is planted in themes of blue, yellow and white with irises, sages, lavenders, and eryngiums. The paved south terrace is gay with beautifully planted pots and containers, a special feature of the garden. On the warm walls are sun-loving climbers. On the east side is a sheltered south-west facing border with two notable specimens – a fine 20-year-old *Magnolia grandiflora* 'Exmouth' and the August-flowering golden rain tree, *Koelreuteria*. Lilies, roses and geraniums thrive everywhere. Next to the lean-to conservatory is a small intimate paved 'French garden' with pots of hibiscus, citrus, oleanders, and scented pelargoniums. The main vista from the south terrace is the double herbaceous border backed by mature yew hedges. Beyond this is a wild or spring garden which leads to a large natural pool where massed azaleas and rhododendrons give colour and backing. A cool, shaded church walk passes beneath mature oaks and yews. There are other notable features in this very English country garden where old-fashioned plants and colour themes are the special characters beloved by the owners. **T.W.**

5 miles NE of
Tewkesbury off B4079

SO 9436

May to Sept: Thur,
also several Sun under
National Gardens
Scheme and other
charities, 1400–1900

Peak months: June to
Sept

Sun only

The Priory HEREFORD AND WORCESTER

Mr and The Hon. Mrs Peter Healing, Kemerton, nr Tewkesbury.

Mr Healing is a lover and grower of plants, interested in the unusual but not in thrall to novelty; he has had the vision to combine rare treasures with the less rare in colour groupings deriving from William Robinson and from Gertrude Jekyll. The soil is limy, ph7.5, so it is encouraging to find *Meconopsis regia* at home and cardiocrinum, grown from seed, about to flower. *Hebe hulkeana* is happy under a wall, and the fern, 'Mrs Goffey's Very Fine Variety', is a feathery wonder. The new garden, used for vegetables until 1974, has been designed to be at its best in June and July, and here the tones are soft, silver, pink and lavender. *Polemonium* 'Pink Beauty', is a key plant in May. The central path is of round stepping stones, dug up by the Healings while making the garden, over which the plants spill, behind them rise old-fashioned and species roses, and then the dark wall of a yew hedge, a fine example of controlled profusion. Knowledge, the eye for a good plant, and the capacity to plan (the original layout was done on paper during Mr Healing's war-time service with the RAF, and he has found little need for change) have combined to produce a garden of unusual distinction, the whole animated and infused by the owner's evident love of the place and of its plants. **E.F.**

W of A360 in centre
of Devizes

SU 0061

Mon to Fri
0800–1300, 1400–1630;
Sat 0900–1230

No peak season

The Wansdyke Nursery and
The Pygmy Pinetum WILTSHIRE

Mr and Mrs D. van Klaveren, Hillworth Road, Devizes.
tel. Devizes (0380) 3008

A visit to the Pygmy Pinetum is a rare treat for all collectors and admirers of dwarf and slow-growing conifers. Started in 1959 by Mr H. J. Welch, it houses the largest collection of this type of conifer in the British Isles, with over 1,200 varieties, all well labelled, growing in the rock gardens, raised beds and borders. The Pinetum was taken over in 1979 by Mr and Mrs van Klaveren, who plan to enlarge this already very comprehensive collection. How attractive these conifers look in the rock gardens where they blend well with the mellow stone used – the beautiful blue-grey foliage of *Picea pungens* 'Globe' and the flat-growing *P. pungens* 'Koster's Prostrate' mix with unusual dwarf yews, many with variegated or golden leaves – and planted among them are flowering cherries which give added overhead colour in spring. Three tiny pools on different levels are overhung by salix, *Acer palmatum* 'Dissectum Atropurpureum' and the very lovely pendulous *Cedrus libani* 'Sargentii' under which *Anemone blanda* and other small bulbs are planted. Strolling round the Pinetum one marvels at the great variety, shape and colour of the conifers from *Juniperus communis* 'Compressa', a miniature column suitable for growing in a sink or trough, to *Picea glauca* 'Alberta Globe', shaped like a ball with bright green foliage, and the larger, conical *Sequoiadendron giganteum* 'Pygmaeum'. **A.S.**

Threave Garden DUMFRIES AND GALLOWAY

National Trust for Scotland, Threave House, Castle Douglas,
(Kirkudbrightshire).
tel. Castle Douglas (0556) 2575

When Major Alan Gordon presented the Threave Estate to the Trust in 1948,
the thought of establishing a school of gardening there almost certainly had
been discussed, but no-one at that stage could ever really have imagined the
large, varied and extremely interesting garden which 25 years and many
students would produce. The School began in 1960 with the first six residential
students. They, and those who succeeded them, have had the task of
developing and extending the garden, and to them also has fallen a large
measure of the maintenance of the 80 or so acres (32ha) of grounds. Essentially
a teaching establishment, Threave has gradually acquired a wide collection of
plants, as well as several types of garden embracing rock, water, woodland,
rose and peat gardens, all built around the old walled garden, retained largely
in the Scottish tradition of vegetable plots, or breaks dissected by paths and
backed by flower beds. The walls support fruit and several large, modern
glasshouses include some designed for display and instruction. In addition to
all of this, Threave has become an attraction to thousands of visitors each year.
It is doubtful if even the imaginative Alan Gordon could have seen his home
converted so successfully to a hostel for young people, or foreseen the
immense pleasure his fields of wheat and barley would eventually provide for
those who enjoy horticultural delights. It is, nevertheless, through his
generosity and to his credit that Threave owes its continued existence. **E.R.**

*1 mile W of Castle
Douglas off A75
Gatehouse of Fleet
road*

NX 7561

*Daily: 0900–1700.
Reduced rates for
parties*

No peak season

🚻♻
💧*limited opening*
♿🎁

Tintinhull House SOMERSET

The National Trust, nr Yeovil.

After moving to Tintinhull at the beginning of this century, Dr S. J. M. Price
laid out the very beautiful small formal gardens to the west of the house,
starting with the walled Eagle Court. In 1933 Captain and Mrs F. E. Reiss
came to live at Tintinhull and they were responsible for planning the lovely
gardens to the north of the house and for introducing many of the unusual
plants. The running of the gardens is now in the capable hands of Penelope
Hobhouse. A path from the west front of the house leads through the Eagle
Court with bergenias and hellebores blooming in spring in the left border
under splendid flowering cherries, while tulips and bearded iris mingle with
perennials on the right. Charming dog-tooth violets, anemones and hardy
cyclamen contrast well with cone-shaped clipped box along the stone path.
Before walking through the tranquil Fountain Garden, look back at the
superb view of the west front of the house. Kniphofias (the red hot pokers),
peonies and sweet peas trained up tripods blend well with the vegetables and a
good collection of herbs in the kitchen garden, where the summer air is filled
with the scent of the roses and honeysuckle climbing the pillars by the central
path. A tranquil scene is viewed from the loggia in the Pool Garden where
water-lilies bloom in early summer. **A.S.**

*5 miles NW of Yeovil
and ½ mile S of A303
on eastern outskirts of
Tintinhull village*

ST 5019

*Apr to end Sept:
Wed, Thur, Sat and
Bank Holiday Mon
1400–1800*

No peak season

🅿🚻♻
🚗*by appointment
only*
♿🏪

Trelissick Garden CORNWALL

The National Trust, Feock, nr Truro.
tel. Devoran (0872) 862090

With some 350 acres (142ha) of tree-dotted park and deciduous woodland this
20-acre (8-ha) garden has variety of form and magnificent views from many
vantage points in lovely surroundings. The stately house with its small
orangery stands 150ft (46m) above King Harry Ferry which crosses the River
Fal nearby. It can only be seen from a distance as, with its terrace and
immediate surroundings, it is not open to the public. There are several distinct
and distinctive gardens within the whole. Firstly, in the angle of two walls, a
collection of tender plants and, opposite, a fig garden with 10 cultivars of that
luscious fruit, backed by a collection of ivies on other walls and brightened by
many named fuchsias. The outer walls of the large kitchen garden, not open,
provide many more lengths of backing for tender and half-hardy plants. A
shaded dell has tree ferns and many other suitable plants. Crossing the public
road by an old bridge one comes into a miniature parkland with many
interesting trees, including conifers, and shrubs in lightly mown grass and a
pleasant meander of closely cut grass paths. Back in the main garden more
grass and gravel paths lead through camellias and rhododendrons to open
lawns with old and young trees and a wide range of shrubs, including
summer-flowering kinds of which hydrangeas are particularly plentiful.
Everywhere are glimpses of the waters of the Fal and the surrounding park and
wood which can be walked through. **F.S.**

*4 miles S of Truro on
B3289 above King
Harry Ferry*

SW 8449

*Apr to end Oct: Mon
to Sat 1100–1800, Sun
1300–1800 (sunset if
earlier)*

*Peak months: Apr to
Aug*

🅿🚻🚗💧♿🎁🌢

Off B3266, just s of
St Tudy on
Wadebridge road

SX 0675

Daily: Apr to end
Sept 1400–1800

Peak months: Apr to
June

P⊙
⌂by appointment
only

Tremeer Gardens CORNWALL

Dr G. C. Haslam and Mrs C. Hopwood, St Tudy, Bodmin.
tel. Bodmin (0208) 850313

The drive is lined on the north by flowering cherries and then by the vegetable-garden wall. It ends at the east-facing front door of the 80-year-old house. To the north is a bank of heather and small-leaved rhododendrons. Above and beyond, narrow grass paths lead round beds and borders filled with others of the same genus. They feature all over this 7-acre (3-ha) garden for it once belonged to two dedicated rhododendron enthusiasts. Most are labelled and are probably between 10 and 30 years old. Returning to the start the obvious route takes one onto a terrace with borders under the south wall of the house and an extension to the west. The walls are mostly clothed with shrubs and climbers with low-growing plants at their feet. A few steps down there is another border of small rhododendrons and some other shrubs facing two level lawns. Across to the south one may plunge into more rhododendrons, opposite the foot of the steps or at either end, to find more narrow paths wandering so that almost every plant can be seen. They include some camellias and other shrubs and small trees. At the lowest level a stream has been partially dammed to produce a narrow irregular pond or broad slow-moving stream with water plants and duck. Situated 350ft (107m) above the sea and not many miles from the north Cornwall coast the rainfall is high and the growth of lichen strong. Colour is provided well into the summer by other genera but also by many late-flowering hybrids mostly, say the labels, crosses involving the late-flowering R. 'Polar Bear'. **F.S.**

3 miles s of Stoke-on-
Trent off A34
Stafford—Stoke road

SJ 8641

Daily exc 25 Dec and
1 Jan: 0830–dusk

Peak months: July
and Aug

Pwc⊙**🚻**
🅃👜🚪👑

Trentham Gardens STAFFORDSHIRE

J. L. Broome, Esq., Stone Road, Trentham, Stoke-on-Trent.
tel. Stoke-on-Trent (0782) 657341

The great terrace, designed by Nesfield and Sir Charles Barry, is a knockout. In the dour potteries landscape it is impossible to conceive of anything more lavish. In 1847 67 men were employed in the garden, now the consumption of gardeners and bedding plants has been much reduced but the effect remains sumptious and in excellent taste, probably better than when the garden was at its height in the 1840s under the 2nd Duke of Sutherland. The drama of the contrast between the elaborate Italian garden and the smooth immensity of Brown's lake beyond is breathtaking. The central walk thrusts straight down and from the steps in front of the now demolished house to the copy of Cellini's statue of Perseus with the head of Medusa, now re-instated in its old position after a stay at Sutton Place. The attraction is so strong that the eye is held firmly to the central vista, the statue, the lake, and the eyecatcher on the hill beyond; but this is not all this garden has to give. The rose garden, the clematis walk, the rock garden and the peat garden are all of horticultural interest, as is the garden for flower arrangers, but these can be found elsewhere, the point of Trentham is prodigious display on a scale unequalled since the days of Absolute Monarchs, and of which Le Nôtre, master of a million flower pots, would not have felt ashamed. **E.F.**

sw corner of island

SV 8914

Daily: 1000–1600

Peak months: May to
Aug

wc⊙**🅃**👜
🍷💟🎁

Tresco Abbey CORNWALL

R. A. Dorrien Smith, Esq., Tresco, Isles of Scilly.

Unique is an over-used word in descriptive writing but there is no garden quite like this sub-tropical outpost. Fourteen acres (6ha) of south-sloping gardens are protected by 50 acres (20ha) of sheltering trees. This shelter is essential for the plants that are grown on this low-lying island in the Atlantic. Augustus Smith from Hertfordshire started to make this garden nearly 150 years ago and several succeeding generations of his family have continued to collect and receive from collectors and to plant and maintain these truly magnificent gardens. Within the shelter of Monterey cypress and pine, plants from the Southern Hemisphere and the Mediterranean are grown as in a vast greenhouse. Large palms in greater variety look happier than on the mainland, acacias abound within the shelter plantations and pelargoniums act as ground cover. Cinerarias and other South African annuals seed themselves and the vivid red of the startling beschorneria contrasts with the flourishing arum lilies. Plants known as house plants elsewhere not only grow in the gardens but thrive among native plants outside it. Colour is everywhere so that the non-gardener must be impressed; the wide variety and rarity of trees, shrubs, climbers, bulbs, succulents, herbaceous and annual plants make a visit a necessity for anyone with any interest in plants or gardens, while the approach by sea or air is a spectacle in itself. **F.S.**

Trewithen CORNWALL

Mr and Mrs A. M. J. Galsworthy, Grampound Road, Probus, nr Truro.
tel. St Austell (0726) 882418

Standing just above the 250-ft (76-m) contour this 28-acre (11ha), almost level, garden would often be swept by Cornish gales if it were not for the many mature native and exotic trees in and around it. They provide the framework in which George Johnstone, author of *The Asiatic Magnolias*, created the present garden in the 56 years before 1960. Many of his laurel windbreaks are no longer necessary and have been removed but there has been wise planting of new mixed shelter belts around the outside to maintain the serenity of this beautiful garden. The ha-ha beyond the east lawn and walk gives good views of massive trees in the well-farmed park. Among the numerous kinds of trees and shrubs the broad lawn, running some 200yd (183m) south from the 250-year-old house, is the hallmark of the place. Cross and recross this lawn to savour the views in both directions and the noble, 100-ft (30-m) tall trees. Many side paths reveal a wider range of woody and other plants, both mature and young. The newer plantings, often in gaps left by gale-felled old giants, include many modern camellias and rhododendrons which add to the numerous rarities and old favourites. Other plantings are in an area leading to the old cock pit and in a grass field within the new shelter belt. The formal walled garden, with its pool, roses and climbers, is worthy of attention on the way in, or out; note the wisteria dominating the pergola and the old yew at the far end. **F.S.**

6 miles E of Truro on A390 Truro—St Austell road

SW 9147

Mar to end Sept: Mon to Sat 1400–1630

Peak months: Mar to May

🅿 ♿ ⛲ 🚻
🐕 ☕ 🌱 🐾
♿*limited opening*

Tyninghame LOTHIAN

The Rt Hon The Earl of Haddington, KT, MC, Dunbar, (East Lothian).
tel. Dunbar (0620) 860330

Tyninghame is one of the few family estates in Scotland which has not diminished. Its tradition of gardening began in the early 17th century and when the house was enlarged in 1828, the garden on the south side was redesigned and replanted. On the west side of the house, beyond a formal rose garden, Lady Haddington made what may be considered as one of the most outstanding shrub rose gardens to be found in the country, with a reproduction of an 18th-century folly with an Italian statue of Summer as a centre-piece. The surrounding beds are packed with an excellent selection of roses, supported by colour combinations of clematis and herbaceous plants such as cimicifuga and bulbous plants like agapanthus. In contrast, a 4-acre (1.6-ha) walled garden has been greatly simplified by the removal of herbaceous borders, leaving only what were considered to be outstanding features. The 'apple walk' is such a one, first planted in 1891 as a pergola of closely planted trees and covering a distance of over 400ft (122m). Classical statues stand on well maintained grass against a yew hedge, replacing the borders formerly used to decorate this area of the garden. A woodland garden is rich with azalea, rhododendron, philadelphus and even embothrium. Beneath the light shade of large oaks grow sorbus and acer and the enormous spread of a large parrotia. Throughout drifts of primroses and wild hyacinths are yet another delight in this garden of so many different horticultural treasures. **E.R.**

8 miles W of Dunbar off A198 North Berwick road

NT 6279

June to end Sept: Mon to Fri 1030–1630

No peak season

🅿 🚻
⛲*1-mile walk*
🪑 🐾
♿*only parties, by appointment*

University of Leicester Botanic Garden
LEICESTERSHIRE

Council of the University of Leicester, Beaumont Hall, Stoughton Drive South, Oadby, Leicester.
tel. Leicester (0533) 717725

The University of Leicester has in the years since 1947 achieved successfully the very difficult feat of creating a botanic garden from a number of separate private gardens – four in this case, with the houses of the original properties being converted into student residences. All the houses were built early this century and their presence adds much to the interest of the 16-acre (6.5-ha) garden, especially as the character of the plantings around them have, to a considerable extent, been preserved, and mature trees, many fine specimens of their kind, abound. Special features include an arboretum, a collection of hollies and others of roses and skimmias. The rose beds depict the evolution of this most popular flower from ancient times to the present, while the skimmias are the National Collection of this valuable genus of evergreen shrubs. Other features include limestone, sandstone, water and herb gardens, and a conservation garden, which will house National Collections of garden cultivars of *Viola* and *Hesperis*. Heathers, woodland and herbaceous perennial plants are all well displayed. There are no less than nine glasshouses housing diverse collections of plants, from alpines to succulents and mixed ornamentals. This admirable garden deserves to be better known. **R.P.**

3 miles SE of city centre off A6 London road, opposite Leicester racecourse

SK 6200

Mon to Fri: 1000–1700

Peak months: May to Oct

♿ ⛲ ☕ 🌱 🐾

9 miles NW of Chester
off A540 Chester—
West Kirby road
(signposted)

SJ 3076

Daily exc 25 Dec:
0900–dusk

Peak months: May,
early June and July to
Oct

University of Liverpool Botanic Gardens (Ness) CHESHIRE

Mr J. K. Hulme (Director), Ness, Neston, South Wirral.
tel. (051) 336 2135

Now the botanical gardens of the University of Liverpool, this 50 acres (20ha) of land on the Wirral started as the private garden of A. K. Bulley, who first sent George Forrest, Kingdon Ward and R. E. Cooper plant hunting. Many of the plants introduced by the collectors were first grown at Ness and the original *Pieris formosa forrestii* and many of Forrest's Asiatic primulas are still grown there. Ness is also historical in that the well-known seeds firm, Bees, who introduced the first coloured, penny seed packets was started here by Bulley. Today Ness has the finest heather garden in the country, a rose garden set out to demonstrate the evolution of the family, a woodland garden sheltering rhododendrons and many of the tender South American trees and shrubs. A large rhododendron and azalea collection dazzles the eye while collections of sorbus and magnolias add interest. A long double herbaceous border contrasts with the smaller scale, but delightful, terrace garden with delicate climbers on its walls. Two small, compartmented gardens are paved and parterred to make colourful resting places. The Ledsham Herb Garden laid out in 1974 displays all the culinary herbs in separate beds and nearby is a rose pergola and laburnum arch. A lower area called the 'Pingle' is a stream- and pool-fed garden and there is a bulb meadow too. A water garden houses endangered native plants and there are greenhouses for a tropical touch. **K.L.**

Canongate, in centre
of St Andrews

NO 5016

Daily: summer
1000–1900, winter
1000–1600

No peak season

limited opening

University of St Andrews Botanic Gardens FIFE

University of St Andrews, St Andrews.
tel. St Andrews (0334) 76161

Since its foundation in 1889, the University of St Andrews Botanic Garden has seen many changes and it was not until 1960, when $18\frac{1}{2}$ acres (7.5ha) were set aside, that relative calm now prevails. The subsequent development of the Garden has attracted visitors from all over the world. On offer to the discerning public are tree and shrub borders around the perimeter of the Garden culminating in the central area of peat, rock and water features which contain a large number of species from all over the temperate world. There are plant order beds for the botany students to study the differences between families, and herbaceous and bulb borders for use in botanical teaching. In the early months of the year bulbs and spring-flowering shrubs provide considerable interest and this is followed by the early alpine plants drawn from mountain ranges from the four corners of the world. Peat-loving plants produce a floral display from early February commencing with rhododendrons and continuing with primulas, meconopsis, lilies, etc., and culminating with brilliant blue carpets of autumn gentians intermixed with startling autumn colours set against dark evergreens. It is in essence a garden for all seasons for there are always plants in flower, from deepest winter to high summer. **E.R.**

In SE outskirts of
York; university
signposted off A64 to
avoid city centre

SE 6350

Daily

Peak months: May to
July and late Sept to
Oct

University of York Gardens
NORTH YORKSHIRE

Heslington, York.

A water garden on a grandiose scale has been constructed at York University; it has been created since 1950 yet is engagingly married to the Elizabethan Heslington Hall. The Hall's own garden is of massive topiary yews and a charming gazebo reached by steps, the old and new being cleverly linked by a canal pool and a small fish pool, part of a 19th-century landscape attempt, which now form the headwaters of a large lake around which many of the university buildings are grouped. The suggestion for this waterscape came from the late Frank Clark and was carried out by a committee. It is a most imaginative lay-out with Rialto-type bridges, covered walks above the water, stepping stones, fountains, a harbour side with slipways and bollards with buildings which in some cases hang over the lake, and in others rising from it in Venetian fashion. Trees and flowers, lily tanks and loggia promenades link the colleges and the waterscape, while wild fowl on the water and boating make for life and movement on the scene. A Henry Moore group of figures finds, surprisingly, an appropriate place on the edge of the topiary garden. It is interesting to note that the construction of the 14-acre (5.6-ha) lake and the waterways generally was the cheapest way to rid the site of boggy ground and surplus water. **K.L.**

Upton House WARWICKSHIRE

The National Trust, Edge Hill.
tel. Edge Hill (029 587) 266

Upton House stands less than a mile (1.6km) to the south of the battlefield of Edgehill, and the ground behind it slopes into a deep coombe. In 1927 Lord Bearsted's architect, Morley Horder, developed wide terraces behind the house and planted them with lavender, catmint and the old Scots rose 'Williams Double Yellow'. A good time to visit is June when this rose is in flower. The garden was originally laid out to provide food for the household, fruit and vegetables on the warm south slope, and fishponds in the valley below. On the slope between further, descending terraces, shrubs and low-growing perennials are planted that flourish in conditions of shallow soil and sharp drainage, valerian, tree lupins, lavender, sages, laburnums, brooms, irises, lithospermums and aubrieta, well worth studying by those faced with similar conditions. Good borders of sun-loving perennials are set beneath the terrace walls. A neat vegetable garden, laid out in the style of a French potager, is the last trace of the once extensive vegetable and fruit growing. In a coombe below, round the corner, were three ponds, now reduced to one, the sites of the other two occupied respectively by a bog garden and a planting of flowering cherries. **E.F.**

7 miles NW of Banbury on A422 Banbury—Stratford road

SP 3546

Apr to Sept: Mon to Thur 1400–1800, also Bank Holiday Mon and several summer weekends (see National Trust handbook). Reduced rates for parties by prior arrangement

Peak months: June to Sept

Vann SURREY

Mr and Mrs Martin B. Caroe, Hambledon, nr Godalming.
tel. Wormley (042 879) 3413

Vann is a particularly good example of a now all-too-rare Gertrude Jekyll garden still perpetuated in her style. The name derives from a 'fenne' or bog as the site is quite low lying on moist clay soils in this secluded and wooded unspoilt part of Surrey. The old brick and timbered part-16th and part-17th century house was considerably enlarged in 1907 to 8 by W. D. Caroe, the present owner's grandfather. Gertrude Jekyll advised on the layout of at least some of the 4½ acres (1.8ha) of gardens, which with woodlands, orchards and vegetable garden combine an attractive blend of formal and informal styles. Through a clipped yew arch, one enters a hedged rectangular garden divided up by paths and lawns and attractively planted with a cottage garden blend of old roses, hardy fuchsias, tree peonies, lavenders and grey-leaved plants. The wisteria-clad pergola bounds the north side of the formal lawn with borders making an effective mixture of semi-shade-loving plants. Away from the house lies a beautifully planted 'natural' pond overhung with willows and this is partially fed by a charming stream that passes between yew hedges, its damp course massed with cowslips, mossy saxifrages and roses. A bridge wreathed in wisteria is a feature. Below the pond lies a valley woodland garden known to have been laid out by Gertrude Jekyll. A stream and small connecting pools are all richly planted with many herbaceous and native plants. **T.W.**

4 miles S of Godalming; turn E into Vann Lane off A283 at Chiddingfold post office: house 2 miles down on left

SU 9838

Open few times each year under National Gardens Scheme. Other times by appointment

Peak months: Apr to June

Wakehurst Place Garden WEST SUSSEX

The National Trust, Ardingly, nr Haywards Heath.
tel. Ardingly (0444) 892701

A very large and scenically magnificent garden covering a naturally dramatic site of woodlands, rocky valleys, streams and lakes where a vast collection of rare and unusual trees, conifers, shrubs and many other plants is grown. There is a spectacular display of rhododendrons and azaleas in May and early June. Gerald Loder, later to become Lord Wakehurst, purchased the Elizabethan house and 500-acre (202-ha) estate in 1903 and spent the next 30 years developing the gardens and landscaping and planting the estate on an ambitious scale. His successor, Sir Henry Price, continued the programme, and on his death in 1963 bequeathed Wakehurst to the National Trust, who then leased it to the Royal Botanic Gardens at Kew for scientific botanical and conservation research. Such is the scale, the diversity and the infinite variety of plants here that visitors are recommended to obtain a copy of the excellent guide to the gardens and the trail booklet. Notable features to summarise briefly here are the beautifully planted Sir Henry Price Memorial Gardens and the walled garden areas, the heather garden, the streamside walk called 'The Slips' and the rock garden where magnolias, acers and dogwoods flourish, and then for the adventurous the fascinating circulating ramble through Westwood Valley to the lake, along the rock walk and back by Bethlehem wood, marvellous with bulbs in the spring. **T.W.**

1½ miles NW of Ardingly on B2028

TQ 3432

Daily (exc 25 Dec and 1 Jan): Jan, Nov and Dec 1000–1600; Feb and Oct 1000–1700; March 1000–1800; Apr to Sept 1000–1900. Reduced rates for parties by prior arrangement

Peak seasons: spring and autumn

12 miles w of Morpeth on B6342 Colwell—Rothbury road, just s of Cambo

NZ 0384

Daily: Apr to Sept 1000–1900; Oct 1000–1800; Nov to Mar 1000–1600. Reduced rates for parties of 20 or over

Peak months: June to Aug

P **wc** ○
◻ *by appointment only*
ⵜ
◖ *limited opening*
ⵉ
▥ *limited opening*
▦ *limited opening*
⚘

Wallington NORTHUMBERLAND

The National Trust, Cambo, Morpeth.
tel. Scots Gap (067 074) 283

A garden's progress through the years can be seen at Wallington both on the ground and in plans to be seen in the house. Both parkland and gardens, like the house, are largely the work of Sir Walter Calverley Blackett from 1728 to 77. Both west wood and east wood were planted by him, west wood with its middle pond and boat house pond, ice house and wishing well and east wood with the China pond called after a Chinese building which adorned it and garden pond with its Portico House by Garrett of 1740 still standing. Brown helped with the tree planting in the park and designed a grotto and a teahouse. A long pathway through native woodland leads to the Neptune Gate into the walled garden first made by the Blacketts in 1760 but altered by the Trevelyan family. In 1938 Lady Trevelyan created the viewing platform above a fountain pool from where a flower-edged stream winds into a shrubbery at the far end. From the terrace is an even better view across the garden and the rolling countryside. There are lead statues on the parapet wall of 18th century origin and at the rear of the terrace a large conservatory, overlooked by the Owl House of 1765, housing a giant fuchsia and heliotropes. The walled garden contains a rose pergola, yew hedges, ornamental trees, honeysuckles, many climbing old roses and ornamental shrubs. **K.L.**

4½ miles s of Edenbridge: turn off B2026 Edenbridge—Hartfield road at Cowden Pound and left at 1st crossroads

TQ 4641

Open few times each year under National Gardens Scheme and at other times by appointment for parties

Peak months: May to July

wc ◻ ◖ ▦ ⵝ

Waystrode Manor KENT

Mr and Mrs Peter Wright, Cowden, nr Edenbridge.

Mentioned in Domesday, this venerable, timbered house with its Tudor carvings makes a perfect setting for the lovely gardens around it. Since 1963 the present owners have enlarged and developed some 6 acres (2.5ha) of gardens making full use of sheltering copses, ancient trees and other trees planted by a previous owner in the 1930s. A series of four spring-fed ponds are also welcome features. A shaded, woodland drive leads down to the old house, where a pleasing composition of wisteria-clad barns, old dovecot and soft-coloured planting sets the scene for the manor gardens. The style is mostly extensive and informal, with massed islands and groups of shrubs and specimen trees in undulating, well mown lawns. A delightful more formal and intimate paved garden to the south-east of the house is richly planted with mixed old roses, shrubs and perennials, urns and statuary and leads to a small white garden with glimpses of the Weald through a wrought iron gate. In a nearby former orchard, roses festoon apple trees with clematis for late-summer colour. A charming pond with natural planting near a restored oast house contrasts with the cleverly designed and sited swimming pool. A pink *Robinia hillieri* is a lovely fern-leaved tree here. Changes in level have been accommodated by richly planted stone walls. An informal arboretum is being made to the north and the latest venture is a woodland garden along the drive. Waystrode Manor is a garden for all seasons, and beautifully maintained. **T.W.**

9 miles sw of Gloucester on A48 Gloucester—Lydney road

SO 7214

Apr and Oct: Sat, Sun and Easter Mon 1100–1700. May to Sept: Wed to Sun and Bank Holiday Mon 1100–1800

No peak season

P ○
◻ *by appointment only*
▦ ⵉ

Westbury Court Garden GLOUCESTERSHIRE

The National Trust, Westbury-on-Severn.
tel. Westbury-on-Severn (045 276) 461

Kips view of 1707 shows the garden at the height of its development after the construction of the T canal, probably by Maynard Colchester II in about 1715, and when the Elizabethan manor house was still standing. The digging of the long canal was begun by Maynard Colchester in 1699, he completed the garden house in 1703. No garden of this type, with its emphasis on formal water, clipped evergreens and horticulture, a style which was typical of the Netherlands, has survived to an equal extent even in Holland itself. When the National Trust, with the help of generous benefactions, took over the gardens in 1967 the place was in ruins, the canals silted up, the hedges dying and no flowers at all. Over 1,000 cu ft (28m³) of silt have been removed from the canals, the hedges re-planted, and the walls covered with varieties of fruit current in the late 17th century. In the small walled garden next to the gazebo nearly a hundred species of plants grown in England before 1700 have been planted. It is also a rose garden with some forty kinds of old roses, including the true, very rare, old musk rose, the apothecary's rose, and 'Rosa Mundi'. Anyone interested in experiencing the intimate charm of formal gardens before their wholesale devastation by Lancelot ('Capability') Brown should not fail to visit Westbury. **E.F.**

West Dean Gardens WEST SUSSEX

The Edward James Foundation, West Dean, Chichester.
tel. Singleton (024 363) 301

Although the gardens have existed at West Dean since the early 17th century, the present extensive park and informal, romantic grounds date largely from the 19th century to match the large semi-Gothic style, flint and stone house built in 1804 to a design by James Wyatt. When the American Edward James purchased the house in 1891 he made further alterations and extensions. The present gardens of some 30 acres (12ha) are essentially informal and largely retain their 19th-century character with some later additions in the early 20th century. Outstanding features are the trees, many planted by visiting Royalty and European aristocracy 70 to 80 years ago. The two Lebanon cedars flanking the approach drive are much older, probably more than 200 years. Other interesting features include the 300-ft (91-m) colonnaded pergola, designed by the architect Harold Peto in 1911, leading to an extraordinary gazebo, an Edwardian feature with its floor of knapped flints and horses' molars. Two magnificent fern-leaved beeches stand on either side of the pergola. Pausing for tea, perhaps in the elegant cast iron conservatory, one can explore a spring garden, and wild garden and then return via the front lawn with views across the Sussex downland, to the walled garden where much new restoration work is in progress. **T.W.**

5 miles N of Chichester on A286 Chichester—Midhurst road

SU 8713

Apr to end Sept: daily 1100–1800. Reduced rates for parties by prior arrangement

Peak months: May and July

Westonbirt Arboretum GLOUCESTERSHIRE

Forestry Commission, Tetbury.
tel. Westonbirt (066 688) 220

The idea of an arboretum can be daunting, but this is not true of Westonbirt, for Robert Holford, who began the plantings in 1829, had a genius for grouping and was as much concerned to satisfy the eye as to form a scientifically arranged collection. This was the time when David Douglas was exploring North America and it is inevitable that Holford's arboretum should concentrate on the flood of new conifers that he introduced. Their arrangement, however, into glades and avenues and the subsequent underplanting with flowering trees and shrubs avoids boredom while allowing us to view from sufficient distance the grandeur of Douglas fir, noble pine, coast redwood and sequoia. The Forestry Commission, who now own and run the arboretum, are carrying on the planting tradition and developing new collections notable among which is the Hillier Glade of ornamental cherries. Visitors should not confine their visits to the original arboretum but cross the valley into Silk Wood, where in the shelter of old oak woods and hazel coppice are collections of native and American species, and where a major delight is in walking among magnificent trees on a spring carpet of primroses, wood anemones and bluebells. Come without fail both in spring and autumn, where the colours of leaves are at their best, and choose, if you can, a sunny day. **E.F.**

3½ miles SW of Tetbury on A433

ST 8690

Daily: 1000–dusk

No peak season

by appointment only

Weston Park SHROPSHIRE

The Earl of Bradford, Weston-under-Lizard, nr Shifnal.
tel. Weston-under-Lizard (095 276) 207/385

The Park is a distinctive and successful creation of the great Lancelot ('Capability') Brown, who was engaged in 1762, together with James Paine, to layout the park and its architectural features. Surprisingly there is no large lake, normally a hallmark of Brown's landscapes, instead we have Church Pool, bordering the main drive, Temple Pool, behind Paine's Temple of Diana, and Park Pool, the largest, south-west of the house. The original plantings in Temple Wood are by Brown, but under the last Earl, an accepted expert on forestry, much replanting was done. The 'doyen' of the trees is however an oriental plane, which is supposed to have been planted when the house was built in 1671. It is now within the garden, but is thought originally to have been in the park. In 1865 the 3rd Earl had the formal terrace gardens on the south front constructed, and there formal bedding continues to be practised. At the same time he built the orangery, now used as a tea room for visitors. Flower lovers may consider that this aspect is neglected, but others interested in garden architecture, in trees, or noble landscape will find their visit worthwhile. **E.F.**

6 miles E of Telford on A5 Telford—Cannock road

SJ 8010

Apr, May and Sept: Sat, Sun and bank holidays. June to Aug: Tue, Wed, Thur, Sat, Sun and bank holidays 1100–1900. Reduced rates for parties by prior arrangement

Peak months: May to early June.

3 miles w of High
Wycombe, s of A40
Oxford road at
western end of West
Wycombe

SU 8395

Easter and Spring
bank holiday Sun and
Mon, Mon to Fri in
June, daily exc Sat in
July and Aug:
1415–1800

No peak season

P WC ⊖ 🎁 ⍩
🏠 limited opening

West Wycombe Park BUCKINGHAMSHIRE

The National Trust, West Wycombe.
tel. High Wycombe (0494) 24411

This beautiful landscaped park is now considered to be 'one of the most perfect expressions in England of the Natural School of Gardening'. The Dashwood family acquired the manor of West Wycombe in 1698. The 2nd Baronet, Sir Francis Dashwood, enlarged the house to its present day appearance and created the park. He began work on the park in 1735, and continued it until 1785. A pupil of 'Capability' Brown's was involved with damning a stream to make the great lake. Humphry Repton 'tidied up the park' in about 1794 removing odd buildings and thinning trees. The 10th Baronet gave the house and grounds to the National Trust in 1943. The present Sir Francis Dashwood runs the estate of 4,000 acres (1619ha) and the house. A plan available to visitors shows the main features to see, the fine views from the house, the lake, its islands, cascades, and temples. New planting and renovation is in progress to restore the park to its 18th-century grandeur. Nearby are the famous Hell Fire Club caves, another of the 2nd Baronet's diversions, and the church he rebuilt on the hill. Close by is the dominating mausoleum with its niches to take the urns in which were to be preserved the hearts of the members of the club. The beautifully preserved village is also owned by the National Trust.
T.W.

2 miles SE of
Godalming on B2130
road to Hascombe

SU 9142

Daily during daylight

Peak months: May
and Oct to Nov

P WC ⊖
🏠 by appointment
only
🍽 limited opening
🐕 ⍩
🏠 limited opening

Winkworth Arboretum SURREY

The National Trust, nr Hascombe, Godalming.

The Arboretum dates from 1938 when Dr Wilfred Fox MD, FRCP, an enthusiastic horticulturist, bought 5 acres (2ha) of neglected woodland. Working mainly alone and also helped by friends he cleared and planted the main area of the Arboretum which eventually extended to about 100 acres (40ha). He gave Winkworth to the National Trust in 1952. The original character of the site, a dramatic wooded hillside overlooking two lakes 'a valley quite unspoilt, of pastoral and wooded character' is today one of the great qualities of the Arboretum, the other being the quality and diversity of the plantings, now maturing in the 40 years or more since it all began. Dr Fox's plan was to create really bold groups of species, going for seasonal effects and contrasts. The Trust today offers two trail walks. A spring walk and an autumn walk highlighting the two seasons when a visit is particularly recommended. In spring there are early magnolias, cherries and malus (ornamental crabs) and in late spring massed azaleas and rhododendrons, while bluebells, wood anemones and wild flowers are everywhere. In autumn, preferably early to mid-October, there are brilliant effects from Japanese maples and cherries, the plum-coloured Indian gum (*Liquidambar*), and along the lakeside the orange and scarlet-leaved tupelo trees (*Nyssa sylvatica*) seen against the steely blue of Atlas cedars. There are many more beautiful trees to find here. **T.W.**

5 miles E of Woking
off A3 Guildford—
London road

TQ 0657

Daily exc Christmas
Day: Mon to Sat
1000–1900 (sunset if
earlier), Sun
1400–1900 (sunset if
earlier). Reduced rates
for parties by prior
arrangement

No peak season

P WC ⊖ 🎁 🍽
⍩ 🏠 ⍩ 🎁

Wisley Garden SURREY

The Royal Horticultural Society, Woking.

The outstanding garden of the Royal Horticultural Society ranking among the finest in Europe for its well labelled, comprehensive collections of hardy plants and many new special demonstration areas aimed at the gardening public. The garden began in the 1870s when Mr G. F. Wilson purchased 60 acres (24ha) of wild, damp oak and birch woods and began to develop the area. In the oak wood near the western boundary he created his famous wild garden and he constructed the ponds and mass planted these with waterside plants. In 1904 the Society moved here from their overcrowded site in Chiswick. The wild garden was largely retained with many of Wilson's specimen trees and shrubs and these still form the bulk of the mature planting in this area today. In 1911 the rock garden was constructed. The alpine house was built in 1926 and the great collections of rhododendrons and azaleas were planted on Battleston Hill from 1937 onwards. The pinetum was created in the early 1900s and considerably extended from 1946 onwards, including the planting in 1948 of the first seedlings of the newly introduced dawn redwood, *Metasequoia glyptostroboides*. Many other additions and improvements have been made between 1946 and the present day, particularly in glasshouses, demonstration gardens, visitor facilities and extensive new trial grounds. **T.W.**

Woodside DEVON

Mervyn T. Feesey, Esq., Higher Raleigh Road, Barnstaple.
tel. Barnstaple (0271) 43095

This quite steeply sloping garden of barely 2 acres (0.8ha) facing south above
the town and River Yeo is crammed with a considerable collection of a great
variety of plants, almost all carefully labelled. The owner, an architect and
author of the recent Wisley handbook on grasses and bamboos, particularly
enjoys plants whose leaves or general outlines have grace or a symmetrical
quality. His other interest is in collecting unusual forms of plants, those with
unusual leaf shapes, variegations and other aberrations. These he culls from the
botanic gardens of the world and from any chance contact and one can find
trays of tiny pots, each with seed and label, standing on a terrace in the sun or
beside a path in the shade according to need. There are many tall trees and
shrubs around the sides of the garden with narrow paths on which to visit
them. Raised beds in the centre are covered with gravel to reduce weed
growth and filled with numerous small plants. From time to time a large plant,
that has exceeded its position or has become old or unshapely, is removed to
make way for newcomers. Great attention is needed by visitors in order to get
the best from this garden, to spot the variations and not miss the rarities. An
apparent weed may have double flowers or unusual leaves and a tiny plant
from Moscow may be growing happily beside another from Rome. There is
much to be found in this concentrated plot. **F.S.**

*Off A39 Lynton road
on outskirts of
Barnstaple*

SS 5634

*Open few times each
year under National
Gardens Scheme and
other times by
appointment*

No peak season

🅿 ⓦⓒ ♿ 🐕 ⟟
🍴 *occasional*

Wrest Park BEDFORDSHIRE

Dept. of the Environment, Silsoe.
tel. Cambridge (0223) 358911 ext. 2285

Both the 19th-century mansion and gardens are French Renaissance in style –
elegant, and almost uncannily well suited to the flatness of the Bedfordshire
terrain. To stand by the rose garden and look over the parterre is to have the
eye drawn with magnetic compulsion to the great garden below the terrace. A
magnificent marble fountain, lead statues from Holland dating back to the
17th century and others brought to the gardens after the Great Exhibition of
1852 provide a link with the formal Long Water canal which provides the axis
for the whole design. Beyond the canal is the domed pavilion, the work of
Thomas Archer in 1709–1711 and a focal point of commanding presence. This
scene of grandeur, with acres of mown grass and magnificent trees framing the
formal features, was created by the 1st Duke of Kent in the early 18th century.
Lancelot ('Capability') Brown was engaged between 1758 and 1760 to carry
out alterations, these consisting of rides and vistas through the woods and the
creation of a river. On the west side of the gardens is the 18th century Bowling
Green House, in the Palladian style; an orangery dating from 1836, a bathhouse and cascade. With their long vistas and matchless symmetry, these
gardens are a tribute to the artistry of man and nature. **R.P.**

*10 miles N of Luton
on A6 Luton—
Bedford road*

TL 0835

*Apr to end Sept: Sat,
Sun and Bank
Holiday Mon
0930–1830*

No peak season

🅿 ⓦⓒ 🍴 🐕
🍴 ⛲ 🍴 🏛

Wroxton Abbey OXFORDSHIRE

Dr J. R. Seagrave (Director), Wroxton, Banbury.
tel. Banbury (0295) 73551

Fairleigh Dickinson University of New Jersey, USA acquired Wroxton
Abbey with 56 acres (23ha) of grounds in 1963 after a long period of neglect.
The outstanding features of the gardens are the 18th century designs, a unique
example of the early picturesque style of gardening. Traces of earlier more
formal gardens can still be found but it was the leading exponent of the natural
landscape and picturesque style, Sanderson Miller, who laid out the grounds.
His designs make use of flowing lawns, specimen trees and woodlands, of
natural-looking waters and eye-catching buildings. Colourful flower borders
were not a feature of this style of landscape gardening. These came later in the
19th century and a rose garden and terrace walk of this period can be found
between the Doric Temple and the double flight of steps that lead to the flower
garden and what was called Her Ladyship's Pool. Much restoration work of
the long neglected grounds is now in progress and visitors should see the Great
Pond and Cascade, Serpentine River, Drayton Arch, Chinese Bridge and
Mount, Doric Temple and a stone built ice house, all disposed in a broad valley
setting richly clothed with fine trees and ornamental woods. Cedars are
outstanding and many Victorian conifers such as monkey puzzle and
cypresses. **T.W.**

*2½ miles NW of
Banbury just S of
A422 Stratford—
Banbury road*

SP 3141

*Apr to Sept: Mon to
Fri 1200–dusk. Other
times by appointment*

No peak season

🅿 ♿ 🍴 🐕 🍴
🏛 *by appointment
only*

County Guide to the Gardens

AVON
Dyrham Park

BEDFORDSHIRE
Luton Hoo
Wrest Park

BERKSHIRE
Old Rectory Cottage
Savill and Valley Gardens
The Old Rectory

BUCKINGHAMSHIRE
Ascott
Cliveden
Nethern Winchedon
Stowe
West Wycombe Park

CAMBRIDGESHIRE
Anglesey Abbey
Cambridge University Botanic Garden
Cambridge University Colleges
Peckover House
The Crossing House

CHESHIRE
Arley Hall
Chester Zoo Gardens
Dunham Massey
Lyme Park
Tatton Park
University of Liverpool Botanic Gardens (Ness)

CORNWALL
Antony House
Chyverton
Cotehele
Glendurgan House
Lanhydrock
The Fox-Rosehill Garden
Trelissick Garden
Tremeer Gardens
Tresco Abbey
Trewithen

CUMBRIA
Holker Hall
Levens Hall
Sizergh Castle

DERBYSHIRE
Chatsworth
Hardwick Hall
Melbourne Hall Gardens

DEVON
Bicton Park
Bickham House
Dartington Hall
Killerton House
Knightshayes Court
Marwood Hill
Overbecks Garden
Rosemoor Garden Trust
Tapeley Park
The Garden House
Woodside

DORSET
Abbotsbury Sub-Tropical Gardens
Compton Acres
Cranborne Manor Gardens
Forde Abbey
Highbury

ESSEX
Hyde Hall
Saling Hall
The Beth Chatto Gardens

GLOUCESTERSHIRE
Barnsley House
Batsford Park Arboretum
Hidcote Manor Garden
Sezincote
Snowshill Manor
Sudeley Castle
Westonbirt Arboretum
Westbury Court Gardens

GREATER LONDON
Regent's Park
Royal Botanic Gardens, Kew
Hampton Court Palace Gardens
Isabella and Waterhouse Plantations

HAMPSHIRE
Exbury Gardens
Hinton Ampner
Jenkyn Place
Mottisfont Abbey
Spinners

HEREFORD AND WORCESTER
Abbey Dore Court
Berrington Hall
Burford House Gardens
Hergest Croft Gardens
Spetchley Park
The Priory

HERTFORDSHIRE
Ashridge
Benington Lordship
Capel Manor Institute
Hatfield House
The Gardens of the Rose

HUMBERSIDE
Burnby Hall Gardens
Sewerby Hall Park
Sledmere House

KENT
Bedgebury National Pinetum
Eyhorne Manor
Great Comp
Northbourne Court Garden
Penshurst Place
Scotney Castle
Sissinghurst Castle Garden
Waystrode Manor

LEICESTERSHIRE
University of Leicester Botanic Gardens

LINCOLNSHIRE
Gunby Hall
Harrington Hall
Springfields Gardens

NORFOLK
Blickling Hall
Bressingham Hall
Oxburgh Hall
Sandringham House and Gardens
Sheringham Hall

NORTHAMPTONSHIRE
Boughton House and the Dower House
Coton Manor
Deene Park

NORTHUMBERLAND
Cragside
Wallington

NOTTINGHAMSHIRE
Flintham Hall
Newstead Abbey

OXFORDSHIRE
Blenheim Park
Brook Cottage
Oxford University Botanic Garden
Oxford University Colleges
Pusey
Rousham Park
Wroxton Abbey

SHROPSHIRE
Benthall Hall
Hodnet Hall Gardens
Weston Park

SOMERSET
Barrington Court
Brympton d'Evercy
Clapton Court Gardens
Hadspen House
Montacute House
Tintinhull House

STAFFORDSHIRE
Alton Towers
Clive Memorial Gardens
Moseley Old Hall
Shugborough
Trentham Gardens

SUFFOLK
Beares
Great Thurlow Hall
Haughley Park
Helmingham Hall

Lime Kiln Rosarium
Magnolia House

SURREY
Claremont Landscape Garden
Polesden Lacey
Ramster
Vann
Winkworth Arboretum
Wisley Garden

SUSSEX
Borde Hill Garden
Cobbler's Garden
Denmans
Great Dixter
Heaselands
Horsted Place
Leonardslee
Nymans
Sheffield Park Garden
Wakehurst Place Garden
West Dean Gardens

TYNE AND WEAR
Seaton Delaval Hall

WARWICKSHIRE
Charlecote Park
Packwood House
Upton House

WILTSHIRE
Bowood House
Stourhead
Stourton House
The Courts
The Wansdyke Nursery and Pygmy Pinetum

YORKSHIRE
Beningbrough Hall
Broughton Hall
Castle Howard
Duncombe Park
Harewood House
Harlow Car Gardens
Lotherton Hall
Newburgh Priory
Newby Hall
Rievaulx Terrace
Ripley Castle
Studley Royal Country Park
Sutton Park
University of York Gardens

WALES
Clwyd
Erddig
Gwynedd
Bodnant Garden
Penrhyn Castle
Isle of Anglesey
Plas Newydd
Powys
Powis Castle
South Glamorgan
Dyffryn Botanic Garden

SCOTLAND
Borders
Abbotsford
Kailzie Gardens
Mellerstain House
Dumfries and Galloway
Logan Botanic Garden
Threave Garden
Fife
Falkland Palace
Kellie Castle
University of St Andrew's Botanic Gardens
Grampian
Crathes Castle Gardens
Cruickshank Botanic Garden
Pitmedden Garden
Highland
Inverewe Garden
Lothian
Royal Botanic Garden, Edinburgh
Tyninghame
Strathclyde
Achamore House Garden
Brodick Castle Gardens
Crarae Woodland Garden
Culzean Castle
Glasgow Botanic Garden
Tayside
Branklyn Garden
Cluny House
Edzell
House of Pitmuies

An A to Z of Gardening and Botanical Terms

Acaulescent
A botanical term meaning stemless or practically stemless. The specific epithets *acaulis* and *acaule* are derived from the same root and are often applied to plants with flowers which are either stemless or carried on extremely short stems.

Achene
A botanical term for a seed vessel or fruit that is dry, contains only one seed and does not split open along a clearly defined line or lines. The fruits of a buttercup are of this type.

Acid
Chemically an acid is a substance, an aqueous solution of which will turn the blue litmus dye pink in contrast to a base or alkali which turns pink litmus dye blue. As far as the gardener is concerned he can think of acid substances most helpfully as those which are sharp and sour and have the property of combining with alkalis to form salts which are in the main neutral in reaction, i. e. neither acid nor alkaline.

The term is important to gardeners because soils are either acid, neutral or alkaline and this may have an important bearing on their fertility, the kinds of plants which they will grow and even the suscept- ibility which these plants may show to certain diseases. For example, most members of the heather family, *Ericaceae*, which includes heathers, rhodo- dendrons, pieris and andromeda, will only thrive in soils which are to some extent acid. By contrast, most members of the brassica family, *Cruciferae*, which includes cabbages, brussels sprouts, kale and wallflowers, succeed best in soils which are neutral or slightly alkaline; if planted in markedly acid soils, they are often heavily infected with club root disease.

Acidity and alkalinity can be measured by various means, but are usually expressed in terms of a scale which is known as the pH of the substance tested. If the substance is described as being pH 7.0 it is neutral, that is to say, neither acid nor alkaline. If it is described as having a pH above 7.0, for example pH 7.5, it is alkaline, whereas if the figure is below 7.0, for example pH 6.5, the substance is acid. In general the most satisfactory reaction for a garden soil, in which many different plants are to be grown, is between pH 6.5 and pH 7.0. Soils with readings below 6.0 become difficult for many plants except those that thrive in acid conditions. Similarly, above pH 8.0 trouble may be experienced with many plants and there may be signs of severe mineral deficiency (a form of starvation), owing to the lock- ing-up of certain essential foods in the soil.

In the British Isles, the degree of acidity of most soils is controlled by the amount of lime they contain. A soil containing free lime will always be to some degree alkaline and therefore unsuitable for the really acid-loving plants. It is, however, possible for lime to be present in the soil without being free. This so-called active lime (i. e. lime that has combined with humus and the finest soil particles or colloids) is a vital constituent of all fertile soils. The less active lime there is, the more acid the soil will usually be; harmful acidity can, in consequence, always be remedied by giving dressings of lime (see Lime). Acidity may be caused by an excess of organic matter in the soil and also by poor aeration (see Aeration). In consequence, besides treatment with lime, cultivation, which improves both aeration and drainage, must be considered as a possible method of counteracting acidity.

Acute
A botanical term often applied to leaves, indicating termination in a sharp point. The term differs from acuminate in that in this instance the sides of the point are either straight or curved slightly outwards.

Adpressed, see Appressed.

Adventitious
A botanical term for a growth or organ produced by a plant at a place which would not normally have a growth or organ of that type. For example, if a willow stem is cut off and inserted in the soil in autumn or winter, it will almost certainly produce roots from the base; these are known as adventitious roots because they would not have been produced had the branch been left to grow on the tree. In the same way, if a tree is cut down, buds and, later, shoots may be produced near the top of the stump, despite the fact that there were no buds there previously. These are known as adventitious buds.

Aeration
Applied to gardening this means the presence of air spaces between the soil particles, an important factor in all fertile soils. Many cultural operations are concerned with the improvement or maintenance of satisfactory aeration. For example, a lawn which has been subject to heavy wear will become so consoli- dated that little or no air can penetrate the soil. To remedy this the gardener perforates it with a spiked roller, or even with the prongs of an ordinary garden fork, so letting in air and restoring the fertility of the soil.

Coarse sand is a usual ingredient of most loam- based seed and potting composts and some soilless ones because it prevents the more adhesive consti- tuents of the mixture from binding too closely together and so excluding air. Digging, forking and hoeing, though necessary for other reasons, are also valuable because they increase aeration. In a soil which contains insufficient air, harmful bacteria and other micro-organisms thrive and acid conditions are rapidly produced.

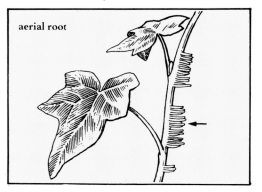

aerial root

Aerial root
Any root which appears above ground level is known by this name. Aerial roots are most important to certain orchids which in nature live on trees where there is little or no soil. These orchids obtain most of their nourishment from the moisture in the air which they absorb by means of these aerial roots, as well as by their leaves. Some climbing plants, such as ivy, cling by means of aerial roots.

Alkaline
The opposite of acid; a substance the aqueous solution of which turns pink litmus paper blue. See Acid.

Alternate
A term applied to leaves which are placed singly on the stem at different heights in contrast to leaves which are in pairs opposite one another or in whorls, several together.

alternate

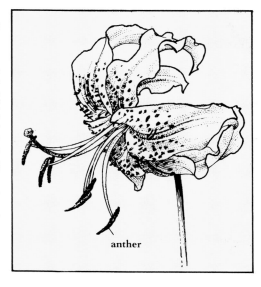

anther

Anther
That part of the flower which produces pollen, the male sex cells of the plant. The anther itself forms part of the stamen, the remainder of which usually consists of the filament, a thread-like stem which bears the anther. In some flowers anthers are of considerable size and add greatly to the decorative properties of the bloom, e. g. the central cluster of golden anthers in a single rose, the large yellow anthers in a white lily or the nearly black anthers in some tulips.

Plant breeders often remove the immature anthers from flowers which have been selected as seed parents. This is done in order to prevent fertilization with their own pollen and the process of removal is known as emasculation.

Ants
These are enemies to the gardener for two reasons; they loosen the soil and so disturb the roots of plants, and particularly of seedlings, and they trans- port aphids from one plant to another. They do not themselves attack plants directly. Ants can be destroyed by dusting the soil around their nests with HCH or derris or by watering the nests with tri- chlorphon. Several proprietary ant-killing prepara- tions are also offered and these should be used according to manufacturers' instructions.

Apical
At the summit or tip of a branch or any other organ.

Aphid
The collective name for the many louse-like plant pests which are known in gardens by such popular names as greenfly, black fly or dolphin fly, American blight and blue fly. Aphis is the scientific name of one genus. Though aphids differ considerably in appearance and in the plants which they attack, all the numerous species have this in common, that they obtain their food by sucking the sap of plants. As a result of their attack plants are weakened and shoots or leaves frequently become curled or other- wise distorted. More serious still, aphids frequently act as carriers of virus diseases, picking up the virus from infected plants and inoculating previously healthy ones with it.

Most aphids prefer the young shoots and leaves and will be found clustered around the tips of the

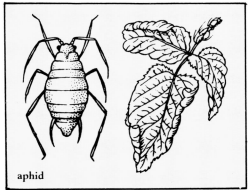

aphid

former and on the lower surfaces of the latter; but some species are confined to the roots.

Among the substances most effective in killing aphids are derris, diazinon, dimethoate, formothion, HCH, malathion, menazon, nicotine, pirimicarb, pyrethrum and resmethrin. In general, insecticides should be used immediately aphids are seen and be applied directly to the insects in the form of a wetting spray. Derris may also be applied as a dust but this as a rule is less effective. In any case it is desirable to repeat the application two or three times at intervals of about a week in order to catch the new generations before they start to breed. However, these methods can be modified when using systemic insecticides which are actually absorbed by the plant and enter its sap. As systemic insecticides are more persistent and do not need to come directly into contact with the insects that are to be killed, they may be applied in advance of an expected attack and applications need not be repeated so frequently. Systemic insecticides in the above list are dimethoate, formothion and menazon, see Systemic.

Appressed
A botanical term meaning closely pressed together and often applied to leaves which are closely pressed to the stem. Adpressed has the same meaning.

Arachnoid
A botanical term meaning like a cobweb. The specific epithet *arachnoideus* is derived from the same root. Thus *Sempervivum arachnoideum* is a houseleek in which the rosettes of leaves are densely covered with fine white filaments like cobwebs.

Arboretum
A garden or park devoted exclusively or mainly to the cultivation of trees and shrubs, though in practice the term is usually confined to collections of botanical interest.

Aril
A complete or sometimes incomplete covering to the seed of some plants. It is often of a fleshy nature and may assist the dispersal of the seed by animals.

Articulate
Jointed; a term used botanically to describe any part of a plant which has nodes or joints at which separation from the parent plant may be expected to occur naturally.

Ascending
A term applied to stems which are neither prostrate nor erect but curve upwards, or are produced obliquely.

Asexual
Literally sexless. In gardening chiefly used for methods of propagation not involving seed e. g. division, cuttings, layers, runners, grafts and buds.

Awn
Any thread-like attachment to a fruit or seed, though the term is most commonly applied to the beard of some grasses and cereals.

Axil
The angle between a leaf stalk or leaf and the stem on which it grows. At this point there is usually a bud, either a growth bud or a flower bud, and this may be referred to as the axillary bud. It is growth buds of this character that are used in the particular form of grafting known as budding.

Bacteria
These are very simple forms of life, each individual consisting of no more than one cell. Ordinary fertile soil teems with bacteria of many different kinds and they are so minute and so prolific that they may number millions in a few grams of soil. Some bacteria may be harmful to plants, but many are indirectly beneficial because they assist in the decay of organic matter in the soil, in the release of chemical plant foods and, in some cases, in the actual fixing of nitrogen (itself one of the most important plant foods) from the atmosphere.

Bearded
With long hairs, as in the case of the dense growth of hairs which occurs on the lower petals or falls of some irises. A beard of this character can often add considerably to the beauty of a flower. The long awns of barley and certain ornamental grasses are also known as the beard and this is reflected in the common name, e.g. bearded wheat.

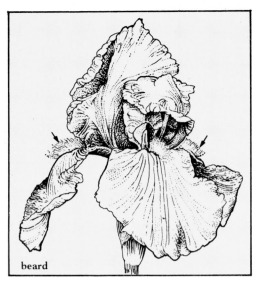

beard

Bedding plant
Any plant used for temporary display in the garden, a feature which is known as bedding out. Bedding plants may be annuals, biennials or perennials, and can be hardy or half-hardy. A typical example is the geranium (correctly called pelargonium), a half-hardy perennial which is grown in great numbers for planting out in late May or early June and provides a bright display in the garden during the summer months. Bedding plants are usually planted at two main seasons, in early autumn when plants such as wallflowers, forget-me-nots, double daisies, tulips and hyacinths are put in for a spring display, and in late spring, when plants such as geraniums, marguerites, heliotropes, French and African marigolds, stocks and asters are put in for a summer display.

Bees
The common honey bee is usually a friend to the gardener for by carrying pollen from flower to flower it helps to ensure fertility in fruit trees and seed production in a great many other plants. Occasionally this activity may be a nuisance, for example if the gardener is attempting to make particular crosses between one plant and another and needs to be certain that they have not already been pollinated by means outside his control. Under such circumstances he will be well advised to protect, with muslin, Cellophane or paper bags, those flowers which have been selected to produce seed and to do this early before there is any chance that they are ready to receive pollen.

The humble bee is also a great distributor of pollen and because of its long proboscis it is capable of pollinating some flowers which are beyond the powers of the honey bee. Because of its size it can make a mess of delicate flowers and is occasionally a nuisance, particularly to exhibitors.

Another kind of bee is a real pest in the garden because of its habit of cutting pieces out of the leaves of roses, lilacs, privet and rhododendrons. It uses the pieces to build its nest. The pieces are usually bitten out of the edge of the leaf, which has a deeply

scalloped appearance as a result. The damage is sometimes attributed to slugs but the holes are cleaner and more regular in outline than those made by slugs. Unfortunately there is no very satisfactory remedy though some leaf-cutting bees may be caught with butterfly nets.

The term bee is also applied to the petaloid centre of a delphinium floret.

Bicolour
This botanical term means two coloured and is usually applied to flowers in which one colour is sharply contrasted with another.

Bipinnate
Twice pinnate; a botanical term applied to leaves which are composed of several separate segments which are themselves divided into separate segments.

Birds
From the gardener's standpoint birds may be roughly classified in three groups, one composed of kinds such as the owls, wagtails, flycatchers, tits, swallows, woodpeckers, swifts, cuckoos, robins and hedge sparrows, which are entirely, or almost entirely, beneficial; a second composed of such birds as the thrush, blackbird, starling, magpie, rook, jay and chaffinch, which do some harm but probably, on balance, more good and so are to be reckoned as friends rather than foes; and a third, of which the wood pigeon, stock dove, bullfinch and house sparrow are notorious members, which do more harm than good.

Jays can do considerable damage to peas and fruit but they also eat great numbers of insects, slugs, mice and other garden pests. They can be kept away from the pea pods if pea rows are covered with netting. Small fruit bushes can be protected in the same way. Some birds pick up seeds but few are capable of scratching and so have no means of getting at seeds which have been properly covered; in any case vulnerable seeds can be efficiently protected with dark thread drawn tightly between sticks to form a network over the seed bed. Sparrows often do damage to brightly coloured flowers, especially to crocus and polyanthus. Again the most effective remedy is to cover the plants with tightly drawn and dark-coloured thread. Bullfinches attack the buds of fruit trees and bushes. Protection with netting is often the only effective remedy though bird scarers fixed among the trees may have some effect. The damage is usually done in late winter as the buds start to swell.

Tits are also sometimes accused of destroying buds but on closer examination it will almost always be found that these buds are already attacked by insects and that it is the latter, not the buds themselves, that the tits have been after. Even if such buds had not been damaged by the tits, it is very unlikely that they would have developed into healthy shoots or flowers. Spraying with proprietary bird repellents may do good but usually it is necessary to repeat the application of these after heavy rain.

Black fly, see Aphid.

bird protection

Blind

A plant is said to be blind when loss of the growing point causes cessation of growth. This condition is frequent in the case of seedlings of cabbage and other members of the brassica family, particularly if these have been attacked by maggots of the cabbage root fly. At first sight the plants can appear quite healthy, but a closer examination will show that they have no central growing shoots and that, in fact, growth is at a standstill. Such plants are quite useless and should be discarded, as no treatment will make them regain their growing points.

Bract

A modified leaf found at the base of a flower stalk, or on the stem of a flower cluster, or forming part of the flower head itself, as in the involucral bracts found in members of the daisy family, *Compositae*. Bracts are sometimes highly coloured and as decorative as the flowers with which they are associated or even more so. Examples of this kind are to be found in *Salvia horminum*, which has showy purple bracts, the poinsettia, *Euphorbia pulcherrima*, which has scarlet bracts.

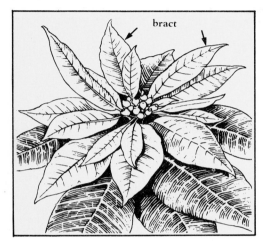

bract

Broadcast

The practice of scattering seeds more or less evenly all over the surface of soil instead of confining them to straight lines or drills. In the garden broadcasting is used for grass seed to form a lawn and occasionally for seed of annuals which are to form irregular groups. Broadcasting seed is done with a quick flick of the wrist and care should be taken to pick up a similar quantity of seed each time.

Broadcast seed may be covered either by scattering fine soil over it or by raking the surface.

Bud

An embryo shoot, flower or cluster of flowers. Buds vary greatly in shape and character and a study of them is often of great practical assistance to the gardener, enabling him to judge the progress of growth and to decide how and when a shoot should be pruned or whether any pruning is necessary. In particular, the fruit grower must learn to distinguish between growth buds and fruit buds. In general, growth buds of fruit trees are comparatively small and lie close against the shoots, whereas fruit buds are larger and more prominent and often stick out from the shoot or form extensive clusters known as spurs. A growth bud contains within itself the embryo of a shoot but it may in time change its character and develop into a fruit bud which, despite its name, contains not a fruit but a flower bud or buds capable of producing fruits.

Bug

A member of the order *Hemiptera*, which consists of insects with biting and sucking mouthparts, and contains, apart from species of direct interest to the gardener, such well-known characters as the bedbug, water-boatmen or pond-skaters. The frog hopper or cuckoo spit insect is a well-known garden pest. The majority of the 1,500 British species are sap suckers, which makes the order one of very great importance in horticulture. It includes, for example, the capsid bud and also many species of aphid, popularly known as greenfly, white fly, black fly and plant lice. Mealy bug on vines and greenhouse plants generally is also included and so are the various scale insects which attach themselves like limpets to the bark, stems or leaves of plants, sucking their juices. Lastly there is the rhododendron bug, a small black creature which attacks rhododendron leaves, giving them a rusty appearance beneath and a mottled look above.

Bulbil

The very small bulbs which form on some plants and which, if detached and planted in suitable soil and situation, will, in time, grow into full sized bulbs. The tiger lily, *Lilium tigrinum*, is a familiar example of a plant that forms bulbils on the flowering stems, in the axils of the leaves.

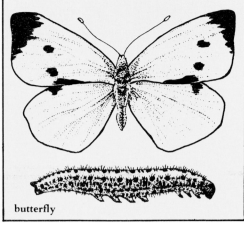

butterfly

Butterflies

Most butterflies are harmless as far as the gardener is concerned, and some help to carry pollen from flower to flower and so effect pollination. There are, however, some exceptions, notably the cabbage white butterflies, both large and small. The bright green caterpillars of these creamy white butterflies attack not only cabbages but all kinds of brassicas and many other plants. They are capable of defoliating plants completely. Spray or dust directly an attack is observed with a good insecticide such as derris, carbaryl or trichlorphon. On a small scale hand picking will be useful.

Calcareous

Containing chalk or lime. This term is applied in the garden principally to soils containing chalk or lime, which are sometimes referred to as calcareous soils. A calcareous rock is one composed mainly or entirely of chalk or limestone.

Calcicolous, Calciphilous

Both words have a similar import, the first meaning living on chalk, the latter chalk loving. They are applied in gardens to those plants that like lime or chalk in the soil and may be contrasted with calcifuge.

Calcifuge

Disliking lime or chalk in any form. The term is frequently used to describe plants which are limehaters, such as most rhododendrons and heathers.

Callus

The growth which forms naturally over any wound made in a plant, e. g. if the limb of a tree is cut off, after a few weeks a thickening of the tissues underlying the bark will occur round the wound and this callus will gradually extend until the whole wound is covered and new bark is formed over it. In a similar manner a cutting forms a callus at the base and this callus in time covers and seals it. In this case roots may appear both from the callus and from the tissues immediately above it.

Calyx

The outer whorl of a flower, formed of sepals, in contrast to the inner whorl formed of petals. These sepals are sometimes united in the form of a cup or tube and are sometimes separate. Frequently the calyx is green and not particularly conspicuous or decorative, but in some instances the calyx segments are highly developed and more brightly coloured than the petals. This is notably the case with the many varieties of clematis, in which the showy part of the flower is formed of the calyx, and the petals are either completely absent or inconspicuous. Many of the highly developed garden forms of hydrangea also depend on large, coloured calyces (plural of calyx) for their decorative value. In some flowers, e. g. magnolias and lilies, there is little or no differentiation between sepals and petals all of which play an equally conspicuous part in forming the flower. They may then be collectively known as tepals,

Cambium

Botanically this name may be given to any plant tissue other than that at the growing points (shoot and root tips and buds) which retains the power of growth. However, when the term is used in horticulture, it is almost invariably confined to the very narrow layer of active tissue which exists between the bark and wood of dicotyledons. It is of vital importance to the grafter because it is at this point alone that active cell growth can take place to unite stock and scion. When the bark is peeled from a young stem that is in active growth, part of the cambium adheres to the wood and part to the bark. It is this fact which makes it possible to bud plants by placing a piece of bark carrying a bud in close contact with the 'wood' (it is actually the thin layer of cambium cells covering the wood) of a stock from which a small portion of bark has been peeled. When a cutting is inserted in the rooting medium it forms a callus from the exposed ring of active cambium at the base and it is from the cambium and this callus that new roots are formed.

Canker

A general name given to various diseases which cause the bark or skin of plants to split and decay, the diseased area often being surrounded by enlarged tissue growth. When this happens on trees, growth above the canker wound may at first merely be checked, but later, if the wound spreads so that it completely encircles the branch, all that area above the canker is killed. There are proprietary remedies on the market which will often cure canker wounds and, if not, will usually prevent their spread. These should be used in accordance with manufacturers' directions. It is always wise to cut away the cankered bark and wood until clean healthy tissue is reached. This should be done with a sharp pruning knife and afterwards the clean wound should be painted with an approved wound dressing.

Capillary attraction

The force which causes liquid to rise through any very fine tube or the tiny spaces between closely packed particles. It is capillary attraction which draws moisture through a sheet of blotting paper or oil up the wick of an oil lamp, and it is the same force which enables moisture to rise in the soil from the water reserves below. At one time it was supposed that hoeing was effective in preventing loss of moisture by evaporation from the surface because, by loosening the surface soil, the fine spaces through which water may rise by capillary attraction were broken up. Experiment has not supported this belief, for it has been shown that the loss of moisture by evaporation from unhoed soil is no greater than that from soil which has been hoed frequently. Apparently in this case the dried cap of soil which forms on unhoed soil is as effective in preventing loss of moisture as the layer of broken soil.

Capsid bugs

A group of insects some of which are plant pests though some are useful as they prey on other insects, notably red spider mites. The harmful capsids are small greenish or reddish insects. They obtain their food by sucking sap from the leaves, stems, fruits and flowers of plants. As a result the plants are weakened and there is usually considerable distortion and sometimes the formation of corky-looking scabs. This last sympton is common on apple fruits. Flower buds attacked frequently fail to develop and may be one sided, a deformity often noted in chrysanthemums. Relatively few capsid bugs can cause a great amount of damage because they are fairly active insects which pass readily from one part of a plant to another or from one plant to another. Capsid bugs can be killed by spraying with HCH or a systemic insecticide. In greenhouses, diazinon can be used as a spray or aerosol.

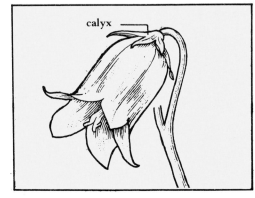

calyx

Capsule

A dry fruit which splits to discharge its seeds and which has more than one carpel. Examples are the seed pods of the poppy, iris and cabbage.

Caterpillar

The larval stage of a butterfly or moth, the complete cycle being (1) egg, (2) caterpillar or larva, (3) pupa, chrysalis or cocoon, and (4) adult insect or imago (butterfly or moth). There are, therefore, as many different kinds of caterpillars as there are butterflies and moths, but by no means are all garden pests. Nevertheless a considerable number of caterpillars, and particularly the caterpillars of moths, do feed on garden plants, and some inflict a great deal of loss on the gardener.

For the purpose of treatment caterpillars may be conveniently split into three groups – (1) those that feed on the outside aerial parts of the plant, mainly leaves, but occasionally shoots as well; (2) those that feed within the tissues of the plant either by tunnelling holes into the fruits as do the caterpillars of the codling moth, or by tunnelling into the shoots or branches, as do the caterpillars of the leopard moth and currant clear wing moth; and (3) those caterpillars that feed on the underground parts of the plant. Caterpillars of this third group are frequently referred to as cutworms. They spend their lives in the soil and gnaw the roots or those parts of the stem which are at or beneath the soil level.

Caterpillars which move by looping their bodies are known as loopers.

Leaf- and stem-eating caterpillars are usually dealt with by means of insecticides such as HCH, derris, trichlorphon or carbaryl. The object is to cover the leaves and stems with a fine film of poison either just before an attack is likely to start or as soon as one in observed. Then the caterpillars are poisoned directly they begin to feed.

Stem- and fruit-boring caterpillars are not so easy to deal with, in fact in the case of stem-borers it is usually necessary to extract them one by one from their tunnels with the aid of a length of flexible wire. Fruit-borers may be killed with the aid of stomach poisons provided these are applied to the fruits before the caterpillars have entered them.

Cutworms or soil caterpillars may be dealt with by dusting the soil with a fumigant such as finely powdered naphthalene or paradichlorbenzene and hoeing this in, or by dusting or watering the soil with carbaryl or trichlorphon

Catkin

A particular kind of flower spike,usually unisexual and pendulous, in which flowers are stalkless and have small, scale-like bracts. The hazel, birch and willow are familiar examples of catkin-bearing trees.

Cauline

A botanical term meaning pertaining to or attached to a stem.

Cell

The unit of plant tissue, microscopic in size and consisting, as a rule, of a nucleus embedded in protoplasm and cell sap, and bounded by a thin wall. Cells at the tips of shoots and roots and in the cambium layer have the power of multiplication by division, by which means the plant grows.

Chalk

Chalk, which is one of the common geological formations in the British Isles, is carbonate of lime, otherwise known as calcium carbonate, and is chemically identical with limestone, though it is much softer. Chalk is converted into quicklime by burning it in kilns, and quicklime in turn is converted into hydrated lime by slaking it with water or by exposing it to a damp atmosphere. Chalk itself is valuable in the garden for correcting acidity, but it should be ground finely as, if applied in lumps, it is extremely slow in action, in fact the lumps may remain practically unchanged for many years. Some gardeners prefer using finely ground chalk to hydrated lime because it is less likely to scorch tender leaves and roots, it is more pleasant to handle and its effect is steadier and lasts longer. It is also said to be better for light, sandy soils because of its tendency to hold moisture and therefore to correct the natural dryness of these soils. It can be employed in potting composts in place of ground limestone and is in fact one of the recognized ingredients of the John Innes seed and potting composts. For this purpose it is usually applied at the rate of ¾oz (21g) chalk to each bushel of compost. In the open garden, it is used at rates varying from 6oz to 2lb to the sq yd (200g to 1kg per sq metre) according to requirements. It can be applied at any time of the year but should not be used at the same time as dung or sulphate of ammonia, with either of which it will combine to liberate ammonia gas with resultant loss of nitrogen.

Gardens on chalky soils present their own problems as the soil is likely to be alkaline and therefore unsuitable for the cultivation of acid-loving plants such as rhododendrons and heathers. Moreover, an excess of chalk may result in the locking up of certain other essential plant foods, notably iron, magnesium and potassium. It is because of this lack of available iron and magnesium on chalk soils that plants growing in such places often have yellow foliage – a condition known as chlorosis and due to lack of chlorophyll or green colouring matter. Iron and magnesium are both essential ingredients of chlorophyll. It is not possible to overcome these deficiencies simply by adding iron and magnesium as ordinary salts such as sulphate of iron or sulphate of magnesium, as these almost immediately become locked in the soil, but special chelated forms of these chemicals are available which remain available to plants for a considerable time. They are also referred to as sequestrols.

It may be possible to lower the alkalinity of such soils by giving heavy dressings of acid substances such as dung, peat and oak leafmould. Chalky soils tend to be very wasteful of humus and consequently high rates of manuring with bulky manures such as dung and compost are likely to be required to maintain full fertility.

Plants which thrive in chalky soils include aubrieta, most members of the dianthus family, *Caryophyllaceae*, including the pink and border carnation, gypsophila, irises, centranthus, helianthemums, scabious, wallflowers, clematis and also all members of the cabbage family, *Cruciferae*. Some saxifrages grown on chalky soil secrete a solution from special glands on the edges of the leaves which evaporates leaving the chalk on the surface of the plant.

Chlorophyll

The green colouring matter of plants which is particularly developed in the leaves. Chlorophyll is a highly complex substance, which has the unique property of being able to utilize the energy of sunlight for the purpose of synthesizing the complex chemicals upon which plants live from simple chemicals supplied from the soil and air. This process is known as photosynthesis. Oxygen is formed during photosynthesis. Plants with white or yellow leaves lack chlorophyll, and are unable to carry out photosynthesis. Lack of chlorophyll may be brought about by many causes including the action of viruses or inherited genes and the lack of certain chemicals in the soil such as iron and magnesium. See Chlorosis.

Chlorosis

Loss of chlorophyll or green colouring matter in a leaf or leaves as a result of which they become yellow or white. As it is the chlorophyll which enables the plant to manufacture its food from raw materials obtained from air and soil, it follows that without chlorophyll the plant will become starved and may in severe cases be killed. Chlorosis may be a symptom of disease, notably of certain virus diseases, but in such cases it is more usually referred to as mosaic, the term chlorosis being reserved for yellowing caused by purely physiological conditions. Two of the commonest causes are lack of iron and lack of magnesium. Lack of iron is itself usually due to excessive alkalinity and cannot be countered directly by applying iron salts to the soil, as this iron is rapidly rendered unavailable. See Chalk.

Ciliate

Fringed with hairs; a botanical term applied mostly to leaves which have margins of the character, as in *Rhododendron ciliatum*.

Cladode

A stem which has taken on the function of a leaf. A well-known example is the apparent leaf of the common Butcher's Broom, *Ruscus aculeatus*, which is not really a leaf at all but a flattened stem. It can be observed that the small white flowers are borne in the centres of these 'leaves' which proclaims their true character as stems.

Clasping

Botanists apply this term to leaves which partly or wholly surround the stem from which they grow.

Classification

Classification of plants is a matter for botanists, but it is of interest to gardeners because they frequently use the names which have been applied by botanists working to their classification rules. Popular names are used in some cases, as for example for roses, wallflowers, forget-me-nots, marigolds, lilac, but for many plants no popular names exist or there are so many different species bearing the same popular name that confusion occurs. A good example of this is the barberry, of which there are now close on 200 species in cultivation, any of which can be referred to as a barberry. In order to make it quite clear which species is being referred to, it is almost essential to make use of botanical nomenclature.

This nomenclature is based upon scientific examination of the plants in an effort to trace their relationship one to another – a kind of family tree. The system of nomenclature is governed by international rules which are respected in every country throughout the world. Because of this the gardener as well as the botanist has an international language at his disposal, by which he may communicate with gardeners in other lands and, if he desires, purchase plants from abroad with reasonable certainty that he will make his requirements quite plain.

The primary classification of plants is into those which flower and which are botanically called phanerogams, and those which do not flower and are called cryptogams. Ferns and fungi are familiar examples of non-flowering plants.

Flowering plants are obviously of greater importance to the gardener, and these are again subdivided into two great groups according to the method of carrying their seeds. In one group, known as gymnosperms, the ovule or female cell, which, when fertilized, will develop into a seed, is exposed, whereas in the other class, known as angiosperms, the ovule is protected in an ovary. Pines, firs, cedars and other cone-bearing trees are familiar examples of gymnosperms, while apples, roses, tomatoes and peas are angiosperms.

The angiosperms are themselves subdivided into two classes according to the number of seed leaves or cotyledons which they produce when the seed germinates. One class is known as monocotyledon because its members only have one seed leaf – the onion and the lily are examples known to everyone. The other class is known as dicotyledon because normally its members produce two seed leaves – tomatoes and marigold are of this type.

Within these major divisions of the vegetable kingdom the individuals are grouped according to their families, genera, species and varieties or cultivars. From the gardener's point of view, it is the last three which are of most importance, but it is desirable to have some understanding of the whole system in order to be able to understand the relationship between plants.

The species is the unit and all plants within the species will resemble each other closely, only differing in minor qualities such as colour, size of flower, earliness and so on. Species which resemble one another fairly closely and may be considered to have some common ancestry, are grouped together in genera, and genus and species between them provide the botanist with his mechanism for nomenclature, known as the binominal system. By this, each plant receives two names, the first designating the genus to which it belongs and the second the species. Thus *Ranunculus* is the generic name of the various species of buttercup, of which there are many. The common creeping buttercup is known as *Ranunculus repens*; the meadow buttercup, which is more erect in habit and does not creep about to the same extent, is *Ranunculus acris*; and the marsh buttercup, *Ranunculus lingua*. Exactly the same principle applies to garden plants – the barberries all belong to the genus *Berberis*, but each separate species has its own name so that the common barberry found in this country is *Berberis vulgaris*, while the beautiful deciduous barberry found in China by the collector Wilson, is known as *Berberis wilsonae*; the holly-leaved barberry which fills our gardens with orange blooms in April is *Berberis darwinii*; and so on. Example of Classification

Family : *Ranunculaceae*
Genus : *Delphinium*
Species : *elatum*
Variety : 'Bridesmaid'

Any small variation within the species may be indicated by varietal names; thus, *Berberis thunbergii atropurpurea* is a form of Thunberg's barberry which has purple-coloured leaves. Sometimes varietal names are given as fancy or vernacular names. This is common with species or hybrids which are very variable and have been highly developed in gardens, as with roses and chrysanthemums. With these, such names as Etoile de Hollande, Crimson Glory, Shot Silk, The Favourite, Loveliness and so on, are really varietal names in English form, and this is permitted by the international rules of nomenclature. Such names are referred to as horticultural names as distinct from true botanical names. In botanical nomenclature varieties which have arisen in cultivation are known as cultivars to distinguish them from varieties that have occurred in nature. It should be noted that names of genera and species can only be given after a plant has been properly examined and identified by a trained botanist and a full description published in a magazine or other publication accepted by botanists for this purpose. Horticultural names of garden-raised varieties could, however, be given by gardeners who have no botanical qualifications, but rules are laid down, and among the most important of these is that no two plants of the same genus can bear the same varietal name, and all fancy names should be as simple as possible, and not include titles such as Mr, Mrs, Captain and so on, which might cause confusion. Horticultural names are only valid if published with a recognizable description in a recognized horticultural or botanical periodical or in a dated horticultural catalogue.

Genera are themselves grouped in families, according to their supposed relationship in the evolutionary scheme. Thus the buttercup already referred to belongs to the family *Ranunculaceae*, a family which also includes the obviously allied marsh marigold or caltha, together with other plants not, to the layman, so obviously related, as for example columbine (aquilegia), aconitum, delphinium and love-in-a-mist (nigella).

Claw
The stalk-like base of a petal in plants such as dianthus.

Clone
All plants produced vegetatively from one original parent.

Collar
That part of a plant where the stem or stems join the roots. With some plants it is important to keep the collar at soil level.

Composite
A member of the daisy family in which many small individual flowers or florets are united in one head. See Compound flower.

Compost
This word is used by gardeners in two quite distinct ways. A compost heap is a heap composed of garden refuse of one kind and another, such as grass clippings, soft hedge trimmings, vegetable leaves and so on, possibly with the addition of dung and straw which will rot down and provide suitable material for digging into the soil. Compost is also the term employed by the gardener for all kinds of soil mixtures used for rearing seedlings or growing pot plants.
Soil composts for the cultivation of seedlings and pot plants were at one time of many diverse kinds as it was believed that quite different mixtures were required for plants of differing character of growth. Extensive research work carried out by the John Innes Horticultural Institution has shown that it is possible to accommodate practically all the plants commonly grown in gardens and greenhouses in a few standard mixtures. These mixtures are known as John Innes seed compost and John Innes potting composts. The potting composts are numbered 1, 2 or 3, the number indicating the fertilizer content – the higher the number the more fertilizer the compost contains.
Soilless composts Since these John Innes composts were devised and proved successful many other seed and potting composts have been made up, some of which dispense with soil altogether as being the most difficult ingredient to standardize and the one most likely to introduce diseases, pests or weed seeds. Some of these are based on peat, sand and fertilizers, some on peat and vermiculite and some on peat and fertilizers only. Highly satisfactory results are obtained with all types but rather different techniques must be adopted in potting and aftercare, mainly little or no firming of the compost and less frequent watering. All the same, care must be taken not to allow peat composts to becomes really dry as it is then very difficult to get them moist again.

Compound
This term is used by botanists to describe leaves, flowers or fruits which are composed of two or more similiar parts. Thus a rose has a compound leaf composed of several leaflets joined to a common stalk.

Compound flower
A flower which consists of a number of separate florets, or small flowers, united in one head as in the daisy family, *Compositae*, and also in the teasel or scabious family, *Dipsaceae*.

Cone
The clustered flowers or fruits of conifers. The flowers are unisexual and the female clusters develop into the typical scaly, and usually hard, cones which open to discharge the seeds they contain.

Container-grown plants
Many plants, including small specimens of shrubs and trees, are grown by nurserymen for sale in containers from which they can be transplanted to the garden with a minimum of root disturbance. In consequence, provided the plants are subsequently watered in dry weather until they are properly established, they can be planted at any time of the year when soil conditions are suitable. The containers may be tins, pots of various kinds or quite thin polythene bags. Before being sold plants should be sufficiently established within the container to permit this to be removed without the soil falling off the roots. All containers, except those made of compressed peat, sawdust or treated paper, must be removed before planting and care should be taken to do this without damaging the roots or disturbing the soil. The plants should then be planted in the ordinary way and well watered in if the soil is dry. Trees and shrubs may require staking until they become established.

Convolute
A botanical term which means rolled up longitudinally.

Cordate
Heart shaped; a botanical term applied, as a rule, to leaves which have a pair of rounded lobes at the base.

Corm
A storage organ differing from a true bulb in being composed mainly of thickened stem and therefore in being solid throughout and not made up of separate layers or scales. Such scales as it possesses are thin and papery and serve only for protection. Familiar examples of corms are gladiolus and crocus, which may be compared with the sectioned bulb of onion and daffodil or the scaled bulb of lily. The tiny corms that form round the parent corms are known as cormels or cormlets.

Corolla
The inner leafy whorl of a flower composed of the petals. It may be contrasted with the outer whorl or calyx which is composed of sepals. In most flowers it is the corolla which provides the display, the calyx being less showy and of a more protective character. However, there are occasions when the calyx is more showy than the corolla, as for example in clematis, and there are other flowers in which corolla and calyx contribute equally to the showiness of the bloom, as in the lily.

Corona
Botanically any appendage which separates the corolla of a flower from its anthers, but in gardens the term is almost exclusively reserved for the cup, crown or trumpet of a narcissus (daffodil).

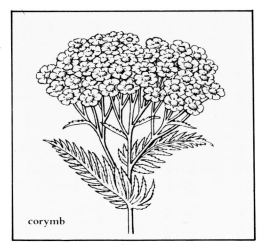

corymb

Corymb
A botanical term for a flat-topped or nearly flat-topped flower cluster, in which the stalks of the various flowers which compose it do not start from a common point as in an umbel. The youngest flowers are in the centre. A familiar example of a flower cluster of this type is to be found in the yarrow – *Achillea millefolium*.

Cotyledon
A seed leaf, of which there is only one in monocotyledons and two in dicotyledons. The seed leaves are usually the first to appear, though in some plants, e. g. pea, they remain below ground. As a rule they differ considerably in character from the leaves which appear later. Usually they are much simpler in structure and are generally completely undivided and regular in outline. Cotyledons are important to the gardener because their state of development is an indication of the best time at which seedlings should be pricked out. Also the gardener should learn to distinguish the cotyledons of cultivated plants from those of weeds, so that he may destroy the latter at an early stage before they have had time to rob the garden plant seedlings of food. It used to be considered that seedlings should not be pricked off until they had formed at least their first true leaves beyond the cotyledons, but more recent research has suggested that many seedlings pricked out in the cotyledon stage give the most satisfactory results.

Crenate
A botanical term applied to leaves the margins of which have shallow, more or less rounded teeth.

Cross-fertilization
A flower is said to be fertilized when pollen reaches the ovules and unites with them to start the formation of seeds. It is said to be self-fertilized or self-pollinated when the pollen comes from the same plant as that producing the ovules and cross-fertilized (cross-pollinated) when the pollen comes from another plant. It should be noted that cross-fertilization does not mean merely the transference of pollen from one flower to another, but from the flower of one plant to that of another plant.

Cross-fertilization is useful to the gardener because it often enables him to combine the characteristics of two different varieties. As a rule, cross-fertilization is only successful with plants that are closely related. Varieties of the same species can usually be cross-fertilized without difficulty though, as already remarked, this is not always so with fruit trees. Plants belonging to different species, but of the same genus, can sometimes be cross-fertilized, but it is seldom that plants belonging to different genera can be successfully cross-fertilized. Gardeners sometimes hear tales of dahlias being crossed with chrysanthemums, tulips with daffodils and so on. These can be dismissed as sheer nonsense.

Crossing, see Cross-fertilization and Hybrid.

Crown
The upper part of the rootstock from which the shoots grow. The term is usually confined to plants with a fairly fleshy or woody crown as in peony, lupin, delphinium and rhubarb. The term is also occasionally used loosely to cover the whole of a root, particularly of a root lifted for forcing, for example, rhubarb and seakale.

Crucifer
Any plant belonging to the family *Cruciferae*. The name has reference to the four petals arranged in the form of a cross which is characteristic of the flowers of all plants in this family, e. g. wallflower, arabis and cabbage.

Cultivar
A botanical term for a variety that has either arisen or is maintained in cultivation as distinct from a variety that occurs naturally in the wild.

Cup, see Corona.

Cyathium
An inflorescence which is typically seen in the euphorbias. It consists of a cup-shaped involucre of bracts surrounding a single, long-stalked female flower and several male flowers, each consisting of only one stamen.

Cyme
A head of flowers in which the oldest flower ends the growth of the stem and younger ones come from one or more side shoots behind it, each in turn ending its growth. Where there are many branches

the head is often in the shape of an inverted cone, with the oldest flower in the centre; where the stems are solitary the whole head may tend to curl up as in the borage family. In the pink family two branches usually occur at each forking. Compare with a raceme, a type of flower head in which the youngest flower ends the growth.

Dead heading
The removal of faded flower heads. It is an important operation in the cultivation of some very free-flowering rhododendrons as, if the flower heads are allowed to remain and carry seed, few flower buds are likely to be formed for the following year.

Deciduous
A name given to plants which lose their leaves in winter. It is particularly applied to trees and shrubs and may be contrasted with the term evergreen, which is applied to a plant which retains its leaves throughout the winter. Deciduous trees and shrubs are of many different kinds and may have little in common, but there is one important cultural point which applies to most of them, namely that they are best transplanted during the period when they are leafless or practically leafless, roughly from about the end of October to the end of March. For town planting deciduous plants have the advantage over evergreens, that they start afresh each year with a clean lot of leaves. The old leaves of evergreens are apt to get so coated with grime and soot that they are more of a liability than an asset to the plant.

Decompound
A botanical term meaning more than once compound.

Dehiscent
A botanical term used to describe a seed pod or anther which splits open to discharge its contents.

dehiscent

Dentate
A botanical term used to describe leaves which have rather coarsely toothed edges.

Dicotyledon
A plant with two cotyledons or seed leaves in contrast to those which have only one cotyledon or seed leaf and are known as monocotyledons. The distinction is very important from the botanical viewpoint and provides one of the fundamental methods of grouping plants for classification.

Digging
There are many different methods of digging the soil, but all have two main objects – the destruction of weeds and the breaking up of the soil so that air may penetrate and the natural processes of decay, by which plant foods are liberated, may be speeded up. Sometimes digging also provides an opportunity for mixing manures or fertilizers with the soil.

There are three principal systems of digging, which may be described as plain digging or single spit digging; double digging or digging to a depth of two spits, and trenching or digging to a depth of three spits. A spit is the depth of the blade of a spade, roughly 10in (25cm).

Digitate
Hand like; a botanical term used to describe leaves which are composed of several separate leaflets all joined at one point as in the horse chestnut.

Dimorphic
Existing in two forms.

Dioecious
A botanical term applied to plants in which the flowers on any one plant are either entirely male, i.e. with stamens and no pistils, or entirely female, i.e. with pistils and no stamens. An example is *Skimmia japonica*, and if the female plants of this are to produce berries, a male plant must be placed near to them. The same thing applies to some varieties of holly and also to the sea buckthorn, hippophae. See Monoecious.

Disbudding
The process of removing surplus buds or shoots. Disbudding is an important item in the cultivation of many flowers particularly when required for show. Roses are restricted to one flower to each stem, other flower buds being removed at an early stage. Carnations are frequently restricted in the same way to one flower to each stem, and the practice is common with chrysanthemums when large flowers are required. As a rule, it is the central or terminal bud that is retained and the side or axillary buds that are removed, but occasionally this rule is reversed. It may, for example, be reversed where roses with very full flowers are concerned, particularly early in the season or when the weather is unusually wet, the reason being that the central or terminal buds are liable to be too full of petals and to ball or fail to open properly as a result. The smaller side buds will give slightly smaller flowers which will open with less difficulty when conditions are adverse.

By removing shoots or buds the gardener concentrates the whole strength of that particular stem on the remaining bud and forces it to develop to its fullest extent. As a rule disbudding is carried out as early as possible, which in practice means just as soon as the buds that are to be removed can be conveniently handled. If the work is delayed, the development of the bud that is to be retained will be checked and occasionally the gardener makes use of this fact as by delaying disbudding he can produce a slightly later and, if necessary, a slightly smaller flower.

Disbudding is usually done by pinching or rubbing out the unwanted buds between the first finger and thumb, but occasionally the point of a penknife is used.

Disk or disc florets
The small, often tubular florets or flowers which form the compact centre of the compound flowers of daisies and other members of the *Compositae* or daisy family. Usually these florets are surrounded by ray florets which make the whole head or flower more showy.

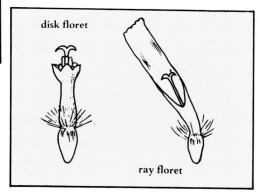

disk floret

ray floret

Distichous
Arranged in two opposite rows, one on each side of the stem.

Dormant
A condition of temporary cessation of activity. Few plants are completely dormant in the sense that no changes are going on within them, but some plants and particularly those with storage organs such as bulbs, corms or tubers, may have a prolonged period of apparent dormancy. This is usually, though not invariably, in winter. Familiar examples of plants which are dormant in summer are nerine, the bulbs of which are almost completely at rest from about midsummer until August, and the greenhouse cyclamen which has a period of semi-dormancy at the same time of year. Deciduous trees and shrubs, that is those which lose their leaves in autumn, are described as being dormant from the time their leaves drop until the buds begin to swell in late winter or early spring.

Buds are said to be dormant when they are inactive. Buds of this type are to be found on most trees

and shrubs at any time of the year.

Many seeds have a period of dormancy after they ripen and during this time will not germinate however favourable the conditions. There are, however, other seeds which have no such period and can be germinated as soon as they are ripe.

Dot plant
A plant of taller growth used in a groundwork of lower plants to stand out as an individual specimen. In formal bedding schemes dot plants are often used to break up the monotonous line that would result from using nothing but plants of the same height. Any plant can be used as a dot plant if it is naturally taller than the plants with which it is to be associated or if it can be trained to make it stand up above them. Sometimes the same kind of plant can be used both as groundwork and dot plants, e. g. ivy-leaved pelargoniums may be allowed to sprawl on the ground except for an occasional specimen which is trained up a stick.

Double flowers, see Flore Pleno.

Drawn
If plants are grown in the dark or crowded together they will become excessively tall, thin and weak, a condition described as drawn. Seedlings and young plants grown in greenhouses or frames are particularly susceptible and it is for this reason that they are often placed on shelves near the glass or raised on inverted pots placed on the staging so that they get as much light as possible. It is also partly to avoid this danger that it is recommended that seeds be sown thinly and seedlings pricked out early.

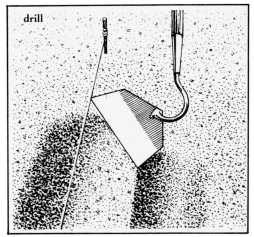

drill

Drill
A narrow furrow or groove made in soil for the purpose of receiving seeds which are to be sown in straight lines, as opposed to broadcast sowing. The act of preparing such drills is described as drawing drills or drilling. There are various ways in which this may be done. Frequently a draw hoe is used for the purpose, in which case it is held with one corner to the soil and pulled along in a series of smart but controlled jerks. Some gardeners prefer to use a dutch hoe held almost vertically, again with one corner only presented to the soil. The hoe is then drawn smartly towards the body. For making small drills in frames or small beds a pointed stick is often used, and another useful method is to press a rake handle into the soil. There are also mechanical implements which will not only prepare the furrow, but also drop the seeds into it at regular intervals.

The important thing in all drilling is that the drills shall be of the same depth throughout and that this shall be the correct depth at which the seeds should be sown. Beginners usually have a tendency to make drills which are too deep and vary in depth. The work is made much easier if the seed bed itself has been well prepared, and is even in texture and free from large stones. A garden line should be stretched tightly to mark the line of the drill and the tool which is to be used should be kept close to this line throughout. It will be found that if the tool, whether it be hoe, stick or mechanical implement, is operated firmly and rather rapidly it will be less liable to be deflected by small inequalities or obstacles.

For most seeds, drills should be no more that ½in (13mm) deep. For just a few large seeds such as those of peas and beans, drills of 1 to 2in (2.5 to 5cm) deep are required.

When seeds have been sown in drills, they are covered by drawing back the displaced soil into the drill and this is best done either with a rake drawn diagonally across the drill.

Edging

This term may be used in several ways; to describe the act of trimming the edges of lawns or the selection or use of plants to edge beds and borders.

Lawn edging may be done with a special tool (see Edging Iron) or with a sharp spade, and the grass that grows over the edges may be trimmed with long-handled shears or a variety of mechanical devices made specially for this purpose. When actually cutting the soil to straighten a lawn edge, a line should first be stretched to ensure that the cut really is straight, alternatively a long straight-edged plank can be used held in place with the feet.

A great many small plants are used for edging and one dwarf form of evergreen box, *Buxus sempervirens* 'Suffruticosa', is known as edging box because of its popularity for this purpose. It can be kept to a height and width of a few inches by repeated clipping and is often used for edging formal beds.

Elliptic

A botanical term used in describing a shape which is widest at the middle point and narrows towards each end.

Ensiform

Sword shaped; a botanical term usually applied to leaves.

Entire

A botanical term applied to a leaf with an unbroken margin, without any teeth, notches or divisions.

Epiphyte

A plant which grows upon another plant without actually being a parasite upon it. Many orchids are epiphytic, growing in the branches of trees but obtaining their nourishment from the air and from decaying matter collected in crevices of the bark.

Ericaceous

Belonging to the heather family, *Ericaceae*, which includes, in addition to the heathers themselves, *Erica* and *Calluna*, such allied genera as *Daboecia*, *Rhododendron* (including azaleas), *Kalmia*, *Arbutus*, *Vaccinium*, *Gaultheria* and *Pernettya*. Many members of this family dislike lime and prefer acid soils.

Evergreen

Any plant which retains its leaves throughout the year, in contrast to a deciduous plant which loses its leaves and then, after a period of dormancy, produces new ones. However, even evergreens do shed their leaves and produce new ones, though the process is more or less continuous and there is no time at which the plant is bare. Some plants behave in an intermediate manner, shedding all or most of their leaves in very cold weather but retaining them throughout a mild winter. The common privet is an example and such plants may be termed semi-evergreen.

Evergreen trees and shrubs play an important part in the furnishing of the garden, particularly since they will provide foliage at all times of the year. Too great a reliance on evergreens can, however, give a heavy appearance to the garden and they should be interspersed with deciduous types.

Evergreen trees and shrubs are of many different kinds and no general treatment can be prescribed to suit all, but one feature which most of them have in common is that, unlike deciduous trees and shrubs, they have no marked period of dormancy and cannot be transplanted while dormant. Experience proves that, in general, evergreens, with the exception of evergreen conifers, transplant most satisfactorily either in early autumn (September, October) or in spring (April, May). Evergreen conifers can be transplanted successfully between November and March.

Everlasting

A popular, though slightly misleading name for certain flowers, which, because of their dry and chaffy petals, can be kept for a long period. Familiar examples are statice and helichrysum. Everlasting flowers of this character should be cut just before they reach their maximum development. They should be dried by tying the stems in small bundles and hanging them head downwards in a cool airy shed or similar place where they are not directly exposed to sunshine. Frequently the dry stems have not sufficient strength to carry the rather heavy flowers and must be replaced by wires.

F₁ Hybrid

Literally a first-filial, i. e. a first generation hybrid. Hybrids of this type can be valuable because of their vigour and uniformity. They are made from parents carefully selected for their desirable qualities and their proved suitability for producing reliable progeny in the first generation. As a rule pollen from the selected male parent must be conveyed by hand to the selected female parent, a slow and costly proceeding which partly accounts for the higher price of F₁ hybrid seed compared with open-pollinated seed of similar plants. But sometimes it is possible to make use of male-sterility or other inbred peculiarities to enable F₁ hybrid seed to be produced without hand pollination. The F₁ hybrid must be remade every time it is required. If a plant of the F₁ is fertilized with its own pollen an F₂ hybrid will be produced, i. e. a second generation hybrid, and if a plant of this generation is self-fertilized an F₃ hybrid will result, i. e. a third generation hybrid. Usually these second and third generation hybrids differ markedly from the F₁ but occasionally stable hybrids can be produced, at least at the F₂ stage, and as these can be produced much more cheaply by open pollination in the field, they have a commercial value.

Falls

The sepals of certain types of iris which hang downwards in contrast to the petals which stand up and form that part of the flower known as the standards.

Family

A group of related genera. See Classification.

Farinose

Covered with a white, bluish or yellow dust-like meal.

Fascicle

A small cluster or bundle of flowers, leaves or roots.

Fastigiate

A botanical term meaning erect in habit. It is applied chiefly to trees and shrubs which in normal forms have spreading branches but in particular varieties have branches which are upright. Two familiar examples are the Lombardy poplar, which is a fastigiate form of the black poplar, and the Irish yew, which is a fastigiate form of the common yew.

Female flower

A flower which bears pistils but no stamens, in contrast to a male flower which bears stamens and no pistils, and a hermaphrodite flower which has both pistils and stamens.

Fern

Non-flowering plants belonging to the group named *Filices*. The leaves of ferns are known as fronds and are often very beautiful. Ferns do not produce seeds but spores.

Fertile

That which is able to produce abundantly. The term is used by gardeners both to describe varieties of plants which are able to produce good crops, in contrast to other varieties of the same kind of plant which do not produce so abundantly, and also to describe soils which are rich, in contrast to those which are poor. The term self-fertile, frequently applied to certain varieties of fruit, means that these varieties are capable of producing abundant crops when fertilized with their own pollen, in contrast to self-sterile varieties which will not produce crops unless fertilized with pollen from another tree or bush of the same kind of plant, but of a different variety.

Fertilization

The union of two cells of opposite sex to produce a new individual. In flowering plants fertilization is effected by the growth of a pollen grain down the pistil of a flower until the male cell in it fuses with the ovule. As a result a seed is formed and this on germination produces a new plant. Fertilization is not only important as a means of producing new plants but also from the gardener's standpoint it is important as a means of producing fruits as many plants will not develop their fruits unless fertilized. The problem is further complicated by the fact that, though some plants are self-fertile i. e. they will produce seeds and fruits from a union between their own pollen and ovules, others are self-sterile i. e. they will only produce seeds and fruits when cross-fertilized with pollen from another variety of the same kind of plant.

Plant breeders carry out their controlled fertilization of particular flowers by emasculating the intended seed parents some time in advance and covering these prepared flowers with greaseproof paper or muslin bags to protect them from chance fertilization. The chosen pollen can then be brought to these flowers on a camel-hair brush when the stigmas are sticky and in a suitably receptive condition.

Fertilizer

Any substance used in fairly concentrated form as a plant food in contrast to bulky manures such as dung, compost, sewage sludge and seaweed. Popular fertilizers are sulphate of ammonia, nitrate of soda, dried blood, hoof and horn meal, bonemeal, basic slag, superphosphate of lime, sulphate of potash and muriate of potash. See Organic and Inorganic.

Fibrous

This term is used by gardeners in two ways: to distinguish plants with masses of fine roots from those with much coarser or more fleshy roots, e.g. fibrous-rooted begonias from tuberous-rooted begonias; and to describe loam containing a lot of plant roots, particularly roots of grass, which give it a fibrous texture. Such loam is the best to use for potting and seed composts.

Filament

The slender stalk which bears an anther.

Flora

All the plants that grow in a particular country or locality or a book describing such plants.

Flore pleno

A botanical term used to describe flowers which are double, that is to say, which have more than the characteristic number of petals, e. g. the familiar double-flowered form of *Gypsophila paniculata* is botanically known as *Gypsophila paniculata* 'Flore pleno'.

A double-flowered form of hollyhock

Floret

One of the individual flowers which make up the head of a composite flower, as in the daisy. The florets which form the cushion-like centre of a composite flower are known as disk florets, while the outside florets which carry ornamental petals are known as ray florets.

Flower

A flower is a short reproductive shoot, the stem or axis of which may be thickened or flattened (receptacle).

In a perfect flower the leaf or leaves at the end of this stem have been modified to form the carpel(s) or female organ(s). These are surrounded by stamens which are leaves altered to bear the male organs. These in turn are frequently surrounded by attractively coloured leaves or petals, protected by green leaves or sepals. See overleaf.

In semi-double or double flowers the stamens and/or the carpels develop in a more leaf-like form as petaloids or extra petals and often halfway stages can be found with one half a stamen and the other apetal.

An opened pea pod can be seen as a leaf with seeds borne on the margins, supplied by veins from a midrib.

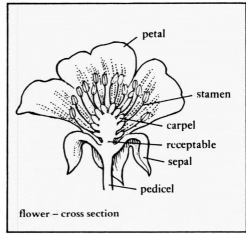

flower – cross section

(labels: petal, stamen, carpel, receptable, sepal, pedicel)

Bulbs for forcing should be brought indoors when the shoots are well formed

Fly

A general term used by gardeners not only for a number of genuine flies which are pests in the garden, but also for some insects which are not flies at all. Among the latter may be mentioned the black fly and the greenfly, both of which are aphids; the white fly which is closely related to the scale insects and superficially is more like a tiny moth than a fly, and the frog fly which resembles an aphid rather than a fly.

Forcing

The practice of hurrying plants into growth, flower or fruit by the application of heat or some other means.

Forcing bulbs, It is most important that before bulbs are introduced to heat, they should be given a period during which they can develop an adequate root system. With narcissi, tulips and hyacinths, this is ensured by plunging the pots or other receptacles containing the bulbs, in a cool place out of doors, for a period of at least eight weeks before they are introduced to a greenhouse. Sand, sifted ashes or peat are materials commonly used for plunging and the pots or boxes are completely covered to a depth of 2 or 3in (5 or 8cm). Other bulbs are not plunged but are placed in an unheated frame or sheltered place out of doors for a similar period before being forced.

Plants and bulbs that have been forced are usually so much weakened by the process that they are either of very little use afterwards or else must be allowed several years of normal culture before being forced again.

Forcing shrubs Many shrubs, including roses, are potted and brought into the greenhouse for forcing. Only strong, well-grown plants should be used for this purpose and it is an advantage if they are really well established in the pots before they are forced. The plants in their pots are grown in the open for most of the year, usually with the pots plunged to their rims in a bed of sand or ashes to reduce evaporation. They are brought into a cool greenhouse in the autumn or early winter and are only subjected to a really warm atmosphere for the last few weeks before flowers are required. Indian azaleas, *Deutzia gracilis*, lilacs, *Prunus triloba*, hydrangeas and *Cytisus fragrans* are popular subjects for forcing in this way. Provided great heat is not used and the plants are well looked after during the summer, being properly and regularly fed, watered and pruned, they will not suffer in constitution and can be gently forced several years in succession. After hard forcing, however, a prolonged period of recuperation may be required.

Formal garden

A term used to describe any garden or part of a garden designed on a more or less geometrical pattern, in contrast to an informal garden in which the lines are more flowing and irregular and the balance less obvious. It was rarely used in connection with gardens until the publication of *The Formal Garden in England* by Reginald Blomfield in 1892. No hard and fast rules can be given for formal gardens and every kind of intermediate type exists between the completely formal garden, as exemplified by the old English knot gardens in which beds contained elaborate patterns in clipped box or other plants and were arranged with absolute symmetry, to the completely informal wild or woodland gardens, which became so popular towards the close of the 19th century and in which it is sometimes difficult to have any organized plan.

Frost

A great many plants are damaged to a greater or lesser degree by temperatures below freezing point. In consequence, frost is one of the big problems with which the gardener has to contend. See Protection.

Fruit

Literally the seed-bearing organ of a plant. A dry pea pod is as much a fruit in this sense as is a peach. In gardens, however, the term is usually confined to edible fruits.

Fungicide

Any substance which will kill fungi. As many plant diseases are caused by fungi, fungicides are of great importance to the gardener. The ideal substance is one which, while very poisonous to fungi, is completely harmless to garden plants. This may never be fully attained but several chemicals or combinations of chemicals come sufficiently close to it to have a wide application in the garden. Popular fungicides are benomyl, Bordeaux mixture, calomel, chloraniformethan, dinocap, maneb, quintozene, sulphur, thiophanatemethyl, thiram, triforine and zineb.

Fungus

One of the important divisions of the vegetable kingdom. Fungi are of many different kinds and differ greatly in appearance, habit and method of growth. All are alike, however, in lacking green colouring matter and therefore in being unable to manufacture their food from simple chemicals, using for the process energy derived from the sun. In consequence they must obtain food supplies ready made and this many of them do by attaching themselves to living plants which possess the green colouring matter necessary for photosynthesis. They are, in fact, parasites and like most parasites they can live only by weakening or, in some cases, actually killing their hosts. It is for this reason that many fungi are correctly regarded by the gardener as enemies, for they are the cause of many plant diseases.

Not all fungi are similarly harmful. Many are not parasites but saprophytes, living on plant tissue or other organic matter which is already dead. Frequently these saprophytic fungi perform a very useful function in promoting the decay of dead material and hastening the liberation of the chemical plant foods which it contains and also the production of the humus which is so valuable in the maintenance of soil texture. There are even some fungi which are valuable as human food. The most familiar is the mushroom which has become an important commercial crop.

Gene

The physical unit of inheritance. The development of every characteristic feature in a plant or animal is controlled by a gene or genes. It will be realized, therefore, that even a fairly simple organism will have a great many genes, yet each is so small that the complete set characteristic of that organism is reproduced in every living cell. Individual genes are collected together into rod-like bodies known as chromosomes which themselves form a part of the nucleus of each living cell.

Germination

The first stage in the growth of a seed. In order to ensure germination, the seed must not only be living, but also must be provided with certain physical conditions, including a reasonable quantity of moisture, a sufficiently high temperature and some air. The precise degree of temperature required for germination varies from one species to another and almost invariably plants from tropical

Protecting the crowns of herbaceous plants that are likely to suffer from frost damage. Dry bracken is held in place with split canes or wire netting. See also Protection, page 247

regions require a higher temperature than those from temperate regions. These temperatures may vary from as little as 7°C (45°F) for plants from cold regions to as much as 27°C (81°F) for tropical plants.

Many seeds lose their power of germination fairly quickly, and with all seeds the power of germination tends to be lowered with the passage of time. Stories concerning the germination of seeds after many thousands of years can be dismissed as false, but it is quite possible for some seeds to germinate after periods of 10, 20, 50, or possibly even 100 years. It has been estimated that delphinium seeds lose at least 50 per cent. of their germinating power within the first 6 or 8 months.

The majority of seeds appear to germinate most readily and satisfactorily when the soil in which they have been sown is exposed to a fair amount of light, but some seeds will only germinate in the dark. Air is essential to germination, and it is often through lack of air that seeds buried too deeply fail to germinate or germinate badly.

Many seeds go through a period of dormancy after ripening during which they cannot germinate no matter what the conditions. Others will germinate the moment they are ripe or even before they are ripe.

The provision of a good tilth for seed beds or of a suitable compost for seed pans and boxes is very important because they provide the physical conditions of moisture and air which are essential to germination. If the tilth is faulty or the compost too fine, the soil will pack down so closely over the seeds that air will be excluded and germination prevented or retarded. If the soil is too loose it will dry out so quickly that there may not be sufficient moisture to complete germination.

Glabrous
This term means no more than not hairy though it is wrongly used in the more positive sense of smooth.

Glaucous
Bluish grey, covered with a bloom. A term often used in the description of leaves or stems.

Globose
Spherical or nearly so; a term used to describe flower or seed heads of that shape.

Greenfly, see Aphid

Hardening-off
The process of gradually accustoming plants to a cooler atmosphere than that in which they have previously been grown. If the change from one temperature to another is made too rapidly, plants will suffer a severe check to growth which may retard them by many weeks or even kill them outright. Hardening-off is particularly important when plants are raised in a warm greenhouse for the purpose of being transplanted out of doors later on. The plants should first be moved to the coolest part of the house and then, after a week or so, taken to a frame. The lights of the frame must be kept closed at first but after a few days may be opened an increasing amount on all fine days until eventually they can be removed altogether. If a cold wind is blowing it may be possible to raise the frame lights on the leeward side and so continue to harden-off the plants within, without exposing them to chilling draughts. At all times the appearance of the plants must be the gardener's guide as to how quickly he can proceed. If they continue to grow and they remain a normal colour, all is well, but if growth suddenly stops and leaves begin to turn blue or develop brown streaks or blotches, it is highly probable that the change to a lower temperature is being made too rapidly.

Hardy
A rather ambiguous term which means no more tr an that the plant to which it is applied will survive frost. Without some qualification it says nothing about the degree of frost the plant will stand and this varies greatly not only from one species to another but also between individuals within a species and according to the locality from which they have been obtained. Other factors, such as soil and air moisture, feeding, the degree of ripening the plant has received and its stage of growth, affect its hardiness. In general, young growth is more susceptible to cold than old growth, young plants more susceptible than old ones and all plants more susceptible when the soil is wet, the air humid or growth is soft because of an excess of nitrogen in the soil.

Plants may become temporarily tender if grown for some time in a greenhouse, but will recover their hardiness if they are gradually accustomed to cooler temperatures. So plants reared in the greenhouse in late winter or early spring must be gradually hardened-off before they are planted out in the late spring or early summer.

Half-hardy The term half-hardy is used for plants which will stand little or no frost and can be grown out of doors during the summer months but require protection in winter. A half-hardy annual is one which is too tender to be sown out of doors until quite late in the spring, but can be raised in a greenhouse or frame from a late winter or early spring sowing and can then be planted out in late spring or early summer.

Hastate
In the form of an arrow-head or halberd. A botanical term usually applied to leaves which are of this shape.

Head
Botanically this term is used to describe a dense cluster or a short dense spike of flowers. Gardeners often use it in a much looser sense to cover such unrelated objects as a head of lettuce, a head of cauliflower, a head of cabbage, a head of celery – meaning one well developed specimen of the vegetable named.

Heart shaped
A term synonymous with cordate and used, as a rule, to describe leaves which have pairs of basal lobes giving them roughly the form of the heart on a playing card.

Heel
When a cutting of a plant is prepared by pulling a side shoot away from the main shoot from which it grows, the small strip of bark and wood which will be dragged away from the main shoot and remain attached to the bottom of the cutting is referred to as a heel. In consequence this type of cutting is sometimes called a heel cutting. As a rule it is the practice to trim off the thin end of the heel leaving only a small piece, like a little knot, at the base of the cutting. Some cuttings seem to strike more readily or with greater certainty if taken with a heel, whereas others do better if prepared entirely from young growth with no older wood attached at the base. Unfortunately there is not sufficient information available to say which plants respond best to either method.

Heeling-in
The process of planting temporarily until permanent planting can be undertaken. If the plants arrive from the nursery or elsewhere during bad weather or when for any other reason it is inconvenient to plant them in their final positions a trench may be dug out in any convenient place and the plants laid close together with their roots in this. The soil is then returned and made firm over the roots with the foot. Plants heeled-in in this manner will usually remain in good condition for several weeks if necessary.

Herbicide
Any chemical that will kill plants. All weedkillers are herbicides and since weeds are simply plants in the wrong place, a subtle distinction which no chemical can make, herbicide is the more scientific term. However, gardeners usually refer to such chemicals as weedkillers and they are more fully described under that heading.

Hermaphrodite
Of both sexes. In botany applied to flowers which have both anthers (male organs) and pistils (female organs).

Hip (or Hep)
The fruit of a rose.

Hirsute
Hairy; a botanical term used to describe the coarse or rough hairs which are to be found on the leaves or stems of some plants.

Hormones
A name given to certain organic chemicals, some of which are formed naturally in the tissues of plants and some produced artificially, which exercise a controlling influence on some aspects of growth or development though they are not themselves plant foods.

Hormones artificially enable the gardener to

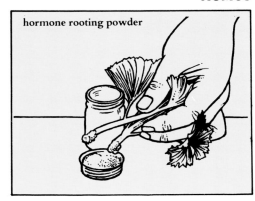
hormone rooting powder

promote changes in the development of plants at times of year, or under conditions, when they would not normally occur. Root-forming hormones such as alpha-naphthalene-acetic acid can be exceedingly useful in hastening the formation of roots by cuttings or layers. They are prepared commercially both in liquid form for dilution with water and as powders in which the base of a cutting can be dipped or which can be sprinkled on the wounded portion of a layer.

Hose-in-hose
A term used for a type of abnormality which sometimes affects flowers, particularly those of primroses, cowslips and mimulus. In these abnormal forms the bloom appears to be duplex, one perfect flower being carried inside another. Sometimes these hose-in-hose varieties have considerable beauty and have been selected and cultivated as garden plants.

Humidity
The amount of moisture in the atmosphere. This is expressed as a percentage of complete saturation but it should be borne in mind that the total amount of water that can be held in the air will vary according to the temperature of the air. The hotter it is the more water it can contain. Thus 100 per cent. humidity at a low temperature would represent a far lower water content than 100 per cent. humidity at a high temperature. One of the reasons for recommending fairly high temperatures for certain greenhouse plants, such as cucumbers and some tropical orchids, is that this allows the high degree of humidity to be maintained which these plants require.

Humus
This name is given to the residue left when organic matter of any kind decays. It is a somewhat loose term as it is applied both to organic matter which is only partially decayed and may still contain considerable traces of its original structure, such as leaves, plant stems and animal refuse, and also to the end product of decay which will be a fine, dark brown or black sticky substance bearing no trace of its original source. In a strictly scientific sense the word humus should be confined to the latter product.

Organic matter at all stages of decay is of value in the soil because it improves its texture, giving it a spongy character which enables it to hold moisture without becoming waterlogged and also because it provides the most suitable medium for bacterial activity. It is upon the bacteria which multiply in humus that the soil depends for the breakdown into suitable plant foods of many of the complex chemicals which are contained in it. Soil which is deficient in humus will soon become infertile no matter how well it is supplied with chemicals, unless special measures are taken to ensure that these are available as plant foods and also to maintain the fertility of the medium by artificial means, as is done in those special methods of cultivation which come under the general term hydroponics or soilless culture.

The humus content of soil can be increased by applications of animal manure, leafmould, decayed vegetable refuse, peat, spent hops, seaweed, shoddy, straw, chaff, fish waste and offal. Smaller, but still useful, quantities of humus are also supplied by such organic fertilizers as hoof and horn meal and bonemeal and those also have a stimulating effect on bacterial activity.

All organic matter is gradually destroyed in the soil by the natural processes of decay and all measures of cultivation tend to hasten this natural rate of destruction. The more thorough and more frequent the cultivation, the more rapidly will the loss proceed and it is for this reason that soils which are intensively cultivated must be more heavily manured with humus-producing substances than those which are little disturbed. In a natural soil which is not cultivated, as for example, a meadow, a sufficient supply of humus is maintained by the decay of vegetation and the decaying bodies of worms and other creatures.

Hybrid

To the geneticist any plant which is not true-breeding for all the genetical factors under consideration is regarded as a hybrid. In the garden the term is seldom used in this way, but is confined to the progeny of crosses between plants of different species or, at the very least, to crosses between plants of markedly different varieties of the same species. For the purpose of botanical nomenclature, the term is confined to the progeny of crosses between distinct species or genera.

Hybrid plants produced from the union of different parents will, as a rule, show some characteristics of both parents, though they may possibly resemble one parent far more than the other. Progeny of any primary hybrid, i. e. the progeny from a cross between two species, though differing in small degree one from another, will generally show a considerable amount of similarity. If each of the parent plants is completely homozygous, i. e. it is itself true-breeding, the progeny will also be extremely uniform and this is the basis of the F_1 hybrid technique (see F_1 Hybrid). Sometimes hybrid plants are themselves sterile, but when they are not their own progeny will usually show a much greater degree of variation than the original hybrid. This is due to the innumerable recombinations of genes which can occur in the second and succeeding generations. These facts are made use of by breeders, who often employ the primary or F_1 hybrid when they wish to produce a plant of known character, while they may exploit succeeding generations when in search of fresh possibilities.

Hybrid plants are often more vigorous than either of their parents.

Imbricate

Overlapping; a botanical term used to describe leaves and bud scales which overlap one another like the tiles on a roof.

imbricate

Incurved, Incurving

Flowers with petals all or many of which curl inwards to form a ball-like bloom. It is used chiefly for chrysanthemums; incurved implying an almost perfectly ball-shaped flower, incurving a less globular flower in which some of the petals may not curl inwards. The opposite of recurved, reflexed.

Inflorescence

The flowering part of a plant which may be composed of one or more flowers arranged in many different ways. See Panicle, Raceme, Head.

Inorganic

The opposite of organic; in the strict interpretation any chemical compound not containing carbon. Inorganic chemicals, such as sulphate of ammonia, nitrate of soda, muriate of potash, sulphate of potash, sulphate of magnesium, play an important part in the feeding of garden plants and these or similar substances are frequently used to maintain fertility of the soil. Inorganic chemicals do not enrich the soil in humus and as a rule do little or nothing to improve its texture – in fact they may harm the texture of the soil. In consequence they have sometimes been condemned, but, if properly used, they do no harm and a great deal of good. Inorganic forms of nitrogen are, in general, cheaper

than organic forms and several of them, such as sulphate of ammonia and nitrate of soda, are quicker in action than any organic source such as hoof and horn meal or dried blood. Provided humus in sufficient quantities is applied in other forms (see Humus), correct feeding of the soil with inorganic foods can do nothing but good.

Insect

Strictly speaking this term applies only to a particular section of the animal kingdom, all members of which have six legs, and bodies composed of three distinct sections – a head, thorax and abdomen, as in butterflies, moths, bees, wasps, beetles and flies. Insects usually have a life cycle consisting of four distinct stages: first the egg, then the larva (popularly known as a grub, maggot or caterpillar), then the pupa or chrysalis and finally the perfect insect or imago which can be a bug, beetle or fly. The term insect is often loosely used in the garden for a great many small creatures which are not true insects at all e. g. spiders, centipedes, woodlice and even some worms.

Insecticide

Any substance which will destroy insects. Some insecticides are stomach poisons, some are contact poisons and some combine both properties. Stomach poisons must be eaten by the insect or other small creatures before they are effective in destroying them, whereas contact poisons have only to be brought into contact with the body of the insect to have their effect. Both types are of importance to the gardener, the stomach poison because it enables him either to prepare poisoned baits which are placed here and there for the insects to devour, or to use the plants themselves as baits, coating them with a thin film of the stomach poison so that the insect is poisoned by the first few bites it takes. Contact poisons provide an important means of destroying those insects which do not actually devour leaves or stems, but suck the juices from them by puncturing them with a proboscis or similar organ. Greenflies and other aphids are of this type and cannot be destroyed with stomach poisons unless this can be introduced to the sap of the plant (see Systemic).

Internode

That portion of the stem of any plant situated between two joints or nodes.

Involucre

The whorl of bracts which is to be found close beneath some flowers or flower clusters. An involucre is a prominent feature of all flowers of the daisy type.

involucre

Irrigation

The artificial application of water to land usually for the purpose of stimulating the growth of plants and so increasing the weight or quality of plants produced. In a really dry country irrigation can be an indispensable preliminary to any cultivation. In the British Isles the comparatively heavy rainfall somewhat obscures the value of irrigation. Nevertheless it has been proved time and again that droughts do occur sufficiently frequently and intensely to make irrigation a paying proposition, at any rate so far as the more valuable vegetable crops are concerned – lettuces, spring onions, early carrots, french beans and ridge cucumbers.

The most primitive form of irrigation consists in cutting channels across the ground and flooding these with water. This gives fairly good results but greater efficiency can be obtained by applying water overhead in the form of a fairly fine spray. A great

deal of ingenious apparatus has been developed to spray water efficiently in this way. A simple and well-known type is the revolving lawn sprinkler in which two or three fine jets, mounted horizontally on a rotating axis, drive themselves round by the reflex force of the water passing through the jets. Impulse sprinklers are rotated by the jet of water striking and deflecting a spring-loaded hammer which knocks the spray nozzle around. Both these types water a circle, whereas oscillating sprinklers cover a rectangle and can be moved so that every portion of ground receives an approximately equal amount of water. Such sprinklers may be either quite small and suitable for home use, or they may be extensive line installations portable but intended primarily for commercial uses.

A further development has been the introduction of apparatus which is capable of adding carefully graded quantities of fertilizer to the water so that the crops are fed at the same time as they are watered.

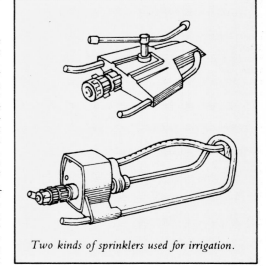

Two kinds of sprinklers used for irrigation.

John Innes Composts, see Compost.

Joint

Where applied to plants this term is synonymous with node and indicates the point of junction between a leaf or leaf stalk and a stem. A plant is said to be short jointed when the joints occur very frequently along the stems, the spaces between them being small, and long jointed when the joints are comparatively few in number and widely spaced. Plants tend to become abnormally long jointed when deprived of light or grown in too much heat.

Juvenile

Some conifers produce two quite distinct types of growth – one in the seedling state and while the plant is still young and another which gradually replaces it as the shrub or tree becomes mature. This distinctive type of early growth is frequently referred to as juvenile growth, in contrast to the later type which is referred to as adult. Some other non-coniferous trees and shrubs exhibit a similar difference between leaves on young and old plants, many species of eucalyptus being notable examples.

Keel

The boat-shaped part of a leguminous flower such as a pea or lupin. The rest of the flower is composed of an erect petal, the standard, and two lateral petals, the wings.

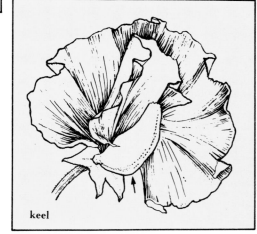

keel

Knot garden
A type of garden very popular in Britain in the 16th and 17th centuries, and now regaining popularity, in which patterns, often of a very elaborate nature, are made with plants, usually clipped evergreen plants such as the edging box, *Buxus sempervirens suffruticosa*. Such gardens were usually close to the home or adjacent to a raised terrace or walk so that they could be viewed from above and enjoyed as a more or less flat pattern on the ground.

Labellum
The lip of a flower. A term frequently used in the description of the flowers of orchids.

Lanceolate
A botanical term meaning lance shaped and usually applied to leaves which are considerably longer than they are wide and taper at both ends.

Landscape gardening
Strictly the art of laying out ornamental grounds so that they blend with the surrounding landscape. The 18th century was the great period of landscape gardening in Britain and its principal exponents were William Kent, Lancelot (Capability) Brown and Humphry Repton. However, the concept has never been abandoned and many of the finest gardens of the 19th and 20th centuries have been designed as miniature landscapes in themselves or to form a part of the existing landscape.

The term has also been loosely applied to all forms of garden design and construction.

Lateral
A side shoot or branch in contrast to a leading or terminal shoot found at the end of a branch. The term is frequently used in connection with the training and pruning of fruit trees.

Latex
The milky sap found in some plants e. g. poppies, dandelions and spurges (euphorbia).

Ligulate
Strap or tongue-shaped.

Lime
To the chemist, lime is the popular name for calcium oxide which the gardener knows as quicklime. In the garden the term lime is loosely employed for several different forms of calcium, but most commonly for calcium hydroxide, otherwise known as hydrated or slaked lime. Ground chalk and ground limestone may also come under this general term and are often used to 'lime' the soil.

Calcium is a plant food and very occasionally it may become so deficient in the soil that lime in some form or other must be added to increase the calcium content. More frequently, however, lime is not required because calcium is deficient, but because it is an alkali which neutralizes acids in the soil, see Acid.

Lime in one of its forms is always used to correct excessive acidity. The more lime is applied the more will the soil be changed in the direction of alkalinity. No hard and fast rules can be given as to the amount of lime required to produce any given change as this will depend on the nature of the soil. Thus more lime is required to produce a given change on a soil that is heavily supplied with humus than on one that is markedly lacking in humus; in other words an acid sand can be corrected with a dressing of lime much smaller than that needed for an acid peat. Ground chalk and ground limestone will produce the same effect as hydrated lime but about twice the quantity will need to be applied. Chalk and limestone are slower in their action on the soil than hydrated lime or quicklime, although the rate increases the more finely the chalk or limestone is ground; in fact, if it were possible to grind them as finely as the powder which is naturally formed when quicklime is slaked, there would be little difference in their speed of action. Quicklime is quite as effective as hydrated lime at the same rates of application and also has marked insecticidal properties because of the heat generated as it slakes in the soil. It is, however, a very unpleasant material to handle as it tends to burn the skin and burst any bags in which it is stored.

Lime tends to encourage some fungi which cause disease and discourage others, e. g. the fungus which causes club root disease of cabbage and other brassicas cannot thrive in a distinctly alkaline soil and is therefore checked by heavy applications of lime, whereas the fungus which causes common scab disease of potatoes thrives in an alkaline soil and is encouraged by heavy applications of lime.

In addition to these important functions, lime also has a marked physical effect on the texture of clay soils. This is due to the fact that lime will make the minute particles of such a soil cling together to form larger granules which make a soil more open in texture and less liable to bind or become waterlogged. This process is referred to as flocculation. Regular liming of clay soils is usually adopted as part of the cultural treatment to improve them, but it must be carried out in connection with acid-alkaline reaction tests.

Lime can be applied at any time of the year but it is usually most economical to use it in the autumn or early winter on heavy soils, and in late winter or early spring on light soils. It is generally applied as a topdressing and then left to be washed down by rain, or it can be worked into the uppermost soil with rake or fork. Lime in any form should not be applied at the same time as animal manure, particularly fresh animal manure, as it reacts with this to liberate ammonia gas which escapes into the air and represents a heavy loss of nitrogen, one of the most important plant foods contained in dung. Usual policy is to apply lime to land that was manured a year previously but if this cannot be done the manure should be well dug in first and then the lime applied as a topdressing a few weeks later.

Lime-hating plants
Some plants, notably rhododendrons and heathers, dislike free lime in the soil and grow best in soils that are moderately or even highly acid. See Calcifuge. Such plants are to be contrasted with others that either tolerate free lime, and are therefore known as lime-tolerant plants, or prefer soils that are chalky or limy in which case they are called calcicolous or calciphilous.

Linear
Long and narrow; a botanical term used in the description of leaves which are of this shape.

Lip
In some flowers all the petals or sepals are not of equal size, but one or more may be larger and so form a distinctive lobe or lip. The Latin word for lip is *labellum* and the family of plants known as *Labiatae*, of which mint and salvia are familiar examples, mostly have markedly lipped flowers.

Loam
A mixture of clay, sand and humus but the term is by no means a precise one and many different types of soil may be referred to as loam. The ideal loam sought after by experienced gardeners as a basis for potting composts, will contain enough sand to keep the soil open and enough clay to prevent it drying out rapidly. Good loam always contains a considerable quantity of fibre provided by the dead and decaying roots of grasses and other small plants. This fibre helps to maintain the open texture of the loam and when loam is being prepared for potting composts great care should be taken not to remove all the fibre from it by sieving it too finely. Loam which differs considerably from this ideal, may be described by qualifying adjectives such as light loam, meaning one containing a high proportion of sand; heavy loam, containing a high proportion of clay, and fibrous loam, containing an unusual amount of fibre. The term chalky loam is sometimes employed, but this type of soil is more correctly referred to as marl.

Loam is usually cut from the top spit of meadows. The turves should be stacked grass-side downwards in a heap and allowed to remain for at least twelve months, so that the grass may decay. Stacked loam will remain in good condition for a number of years, particularly if the stack is built with a ridged top to throw off rain.

Male
Flowering plants all make use of the functions of sex and have male and female organs, though the way in which these are disposed differs considerably from one kind of plant to another. The majority of flowers are monoecious, i. e. there are both male and female organs in the same flower. The male organs are known as stamens and consist of anthers attached to filaments. There are also type of plants in which the flowers are dioecious, i. e. some carry only male organs (stamens) and others carry only female organs (pistils). There is still further differentation in certain plants in which all the flowers on one plant will be of one sex only. Examples are holly (ilex), sea buckthorn (hippophae) and *Skimmia japonica*. In these plants which produce nothing but male flowers are male plants and those with only female flowers are female plants.

Mealy bug
One of the most troublesome greenhouse pests. The insects are small and whitish, and they protect themselves with a white or greyish, waxy substance which at first sight looks like a little tuft of cotton-wool. The mealy bugs move about slowly on the stems and leaves of many greenhouse plants, and live by sucking sap from the plant. Growth may be greatly weakened as a result. Fumigation is effective, while on a small scale mealy bug may be controlled by sponging the leaves and stems with derris insecticide. Spraying with derris, pyrethrum, diazinon, or with petroleum oil emulsion are other possible methods of keeping this pest in check.

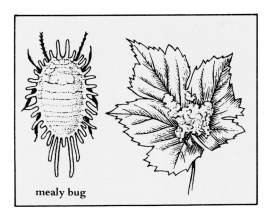
mealy bug

Mice
Great damage can be done to seeds and seedlings and to bulbs, corms and tubers of all kinds by mice. Crocus are particularly favoured and so are pea and bean seeds and those of marrows, cucumbers and melons. Mice may be killed with one of the many advertised mouse poisons. Under glass, trapping is often the most effective remedy with either break-back traps or cage traps baited with fat, nuts, chocolate, cheese or, probably best of all, cooked dried peas. Pea and bean seeds and small bulbs can be protected by rolling them in red lead prior to sowing. The seeds should first be moistened with either water or a very small quantity of paraffin.

Midrib
The central vein of a leaf.

Mildew
A general name given to a number of diseases caused by various fungi which can be classified in two main groups; the powdery mildews, so called because they produce a powdery white or grey surface mould on leaves and stems, and the downy mildews which are deeper seated and may often produce a downy outgrowth particularly on the under surfaces of the leaves.

One kind of powdery mildew is to be found on peas, particularly those maturing rather late in the season. Another powdery mildew is common on chrysanthemums, and again is most noticeable in the autumn. Roses may be attacked by powdery or by downy mildew but the former is much more common. Plants commonly attacked by downy mildews are anemone, stocks, lettuce, onion, cabbage and spinach.

All these mildews thrive in damp, cool conditions. Under glass, ventilation and a rather dry atmosphere are means of keeping them at bay.

Dinocap is a good specific against powdery mildew including the powdery rose mildew. For downy mildews zineb and copper fungicides such as Bordeaux mixture should be used. Several systemic fungicides, including benomyl and thiophanate-methyl, also give good control.

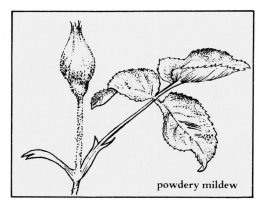
powdery mildew

Moles

Moles can be destroyed by trapping, by poisoning and by gassing. Special steel traps are made for the first purpose, and these are set across the underground runs. A piece of turf or some soil should be removed to allow the trap to be placed in position, and should then be replaced round the trap in order to exclude light, to which moles are very sensitive. Gloves should always be worn when setting traps as moles have a keen sense of smell and will easily be scared by human scent. Traps are most likely to prove effective if set across main runs and particularly those leading towards water, as these are likely to be used frequently.

Poisoning may be effected by using worms as bait and placing strychnine on these. Calcium carbide, which is not poisonous, is sometimes recommended for gassing, and though the acetylene gas which it produces may drive moles away, it will not kill them. Special smoke generators, or fusees, are manufactured for killing or driving out moles. They are ignited and placed in the main runs.

A simple and effective method of keeping moles out of specific areas of land, e. g. preventing their access to a lawn, is to surround the area with naphthalene moth balls dropped into small holes about 3in (8cm) deep and 3 to 4in (8 to 10cm) apart.

Monocotyledon

A plant which normally produces only one cotyledon or seed leaf. This may be contrasted with a dicotyledon which normally produces two seed leaves. The distinction is an important one to the systematic botânist as it serves to distinguish one great group of flowering plants from another. The lily family *Liliaceae*, the amaryllis family, *Amaryllidaceae*, the iris family, *Iridaceae*, and the grasses are familiar examples of the great group of monocotyledons, whereas the cabbage family, *Cruciferae*, the buttercup family, *Ranunculaceae*, and the daisy family, *Compositae*, are examples of dicotyledons.

Monoecious

The name given to a plant which has flowers of two sexes, some with stamens or male organs only, and some with pistils or female organs only, but flowers of the two kinds are borne on the same plant. A familiar example is the common hazel, the male flowers of which form the familiar and showy catkins, while the female flowers are small, red, and held closely to the stems.

Moss

The name for one of the great divisions of the vegetable kingdom. Mosses are of many different genera and species and in some conditions of soil and climate they provide the major vegetation of the land. For example, there are areas in Britain and even greater ones in Sweden almost completely covered by a dense growth of sphagnum moss and as the older plants die and decay, deposits of peat are formed which are known, because of their origin, as sphagnum peat. This moss peat is of particular value to the gardener as it is extremely absorbent of moisture and is of a fibrous or granulate nature, relatively free of dust, so that it does not tend to clog composts in which it is used.

Besides being of use to the gardener in the way just described, moss can also be a great nuisance and it may become a serious weed on lawns, entirely destroying the grass. Mosses are usually an indication of certain conditions of the soil. They are most likely to be found abundantly where the soil is naturally rather poor and damp, with high acidity and bad aeration.

In consequence, when mosses behave as weeds in the garden, the first line of attack should be to rectify the conditions which may have encouraged them. Drainage may be improved, soil fed with fertilizer or suitable animal manures, and it may sometimes be possible to admit more light by cutting dense trees or lopping branches.

If none of these measures is possible, or having been tried, all fail to effect a sufficient improvement, the moss must be attacked directly. This may be done with various chemicals, particularly mercurial compounds such as calomel. Proprietary anti-moss dressings, which include these chemicals, are available and should be used as topdressings according to the manufacturers' instructions.

Permanganate of potash is a useful and safe chemical for killing moss, though not so effective as the mercurial compounds. It should be used at the rate of 1oz to a gallon (28g to 4.5l) of water – a gallon (4.5l) being sufficient to treat one square yard (sq metre) of moss.

Sulphate of iron is probably a more efficient moss-destroyer and also a cheaper one and this should be used at the rate of ¼ to ½oz per sq yd (8 to 17g per sq metre), preferably mixed with several times its own bulk of sand to act as a carrier and ensure even distribution.

Hormone weedkillers do not destroy moss and may even indirectly encourage it by killing weeds which were previously in competition with the moss, and so leaving the moss a free hand.

Moth

Insects which are closely allied to butterflies, but may be immediately distinguished from them by the fact that the antennae of British butterflies are always clubbed at the end whereas those of moths are not clubbed though they may be feathery. Moths fly at night and many species are garden pests, not because the moths themselves do any damage to plants but because they lay eggs which then hatch out into caterpillars that feed on plants.

Familiar examples of moths which are troublesome in the garden are the cabbage moth, the caterpillars of which are green or reddish grey and feed on all kinds of brassica; the clearwing moth, the caterpillars of which attack currant bushes, boring their way into the pith of the stem and so causing the stem to wilt; the goat moth, the caterpillars of which are large and able to bore into quite large branches of trees, causing similar damage to that of the clearwing moth; the leopard moth, which attacks trees and shrubs in the same way as the goat moth; the pea moth, the whitish caterpillars of which are all too familiar in pea pods, and the so-called winter moths, including the March moth, the caterpillars of which feed on the young leaves of apple and other fruit trees in the spring. There are many others which may prove troublesome.

It is nearly always the caterpillars and eggs rather than the moths themselves that are most vulnerable. The caterpillars can usually be poisoned by spraying affected plants with insecticides such as HCH, carbaryl, derris or trichlorphon. The eggs may sometimes be killed by spraying with tar oil wash, DNC wash or similar preparations, but unfortunately these can only be used on hard-wooded plants while they are dormant in winter. They cannot be applied to plants in leaf or to soft-stemmed plants because of their caustic action on these.

Mulch

Any fairly heavy topdressing applied to the soil. Mulches usually have a threefold purpose, partly to feed the soil and plants growing in it, partly to slow down surface evaporation and so conserve moisture in the soil and partly to check growth of annual weeds. Mulches generally consist of some fairly bulky organic material such as strawy manure, chopped straw, grass clippings or peat. They may be applied at any time of the year, though spring and early summer are probably the most favoured times. As a weed suppressor the mulch can be particularly useful in shrub borders in which fairly heavy dressings can be spread and renewed from time to time throughout the year, with the result that weeds are persistently smothered and little further cultivation is required.

It has been suggested that a good mulch of grass clippings of 1in (2.5cm) or more in thickness applied to rose beds in early spring and maintained by occasional additions throughout the summer, will not only encourage more vigorous growth of roses, but also will check the spread of black spot disease. This it does by preventing spores of the fungus which causes the disease from being splashed or blown from the soil on to the stems or leaves of the roses.

The more loose and littery the material of which a mulch is composed, the better will be its capacity for preventing evaporation of moisture from the soil. Such mulches will also act as heat insulators, maintaining the soil at a more even temperature than would otherwise be the case. A drawback to mulches is that they are sometimes rather unsightly but this is not true of peat mulches which can have a very pleasant appearance.

Naturalize

The practice of growing certain plants under as nearly natural conditions as possible. For example, daffodils are said to be naturalized when they are planted in grass and left to look after themselves. The term is also used to describe plants from foreign countries which have established themselves so well in the country into which they have been introduced that they behave like native plants and are able to maintain themselves without the aid of the gardener. When plants have been naturalized in this manner for a very long time it is often difficult to decide whether they are, in fact, foreign plants which are naturalized or are genuine natives. A case in point is the stinking hellebore, *Helleborus foetidus*, which is found growing, apparently wild, in many parts of Britain, but usually on or near the sites of Roman encampments. This lends colour to the belief that this is not really an indigenous British plant but one brought over by the Romans nearly 2,000 years ago.

Nectar, Nectary

Nectar is the sweet liquid secreted by some flowers apparently with the function of attracting insects and so securing pollination, as the insects carry pollen from the anthers to the stigmas of the flowers. It is from the nectar of flowers that honey bees produce honey and from the pollen that they prepare the substance known to bee keepers as bee bread. This nectar is produced from glandular tissue which may be concentrated in one place which is then known as a nectary e. g. the spur of a violet.

Node

The joint of a stem at which point a leaf is borne or has been borne. Cuttings which are severed just below a joint are frequently described as nodal cuttings, whereas those which are severed midway between joints are described as internodal cuttings. A growth bud or buds will be found at each node. The cambium layer at this point is usually more capable of producing adventitious roots or buds than the cambium in other parts of the stem. See Joint.

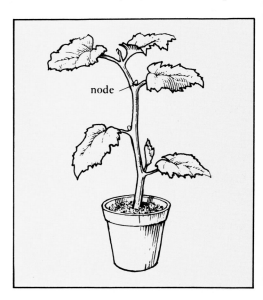

node

Oblanceolate

Lanceolate but with the broadest part near the apex.

Obovate

A term used to describe leaves that are oval in outline.

Obtuse

Blunt or rounded; a botanical term used in the description of leaves which are of this character.

Offset

A young plant produced vegetatively alongside another plant and easily detached from it. The term is most commonly applied to bulbs and corms which usually produce offsets freely as a natural means of increase. The term, however, is also applied to fibrous-rooted plants, particularly to plants which form a number of separate crowns of shoots rather loosely connected together. Propagation by removal of offsets is really a form of propagation by division. Offsets, being vegetative in origin, almost invariably resemble the parent.

Opposite

A botanical term describing a particular mode of producing leaves, in which the leaves appear in pairs on opposite sides of the stem. This may be contrasted with alternate, in which the leaves are produced singly and are usually arranged in a roughly spiral formation on the stem.

Orbicular

Circular, or nearly so, in outline; a term usually applied to leaves.

Organic

Any chemical compound of carbon. As a great many organic chemicals are derived from living organisms, the term is often loosely used to describe substances obtained from such organisms, in contrast to those obtained from non-living sources. For example, the terms organic gardening and organic manuring are frequently used to describe those systems of gardening and manuring which rely exclusively on bulky animal manures and vegetable composts and make no use of concentrated fertilizers. This, however, is really a misuse of the word, as there are many organic chemicals which are synthetically produced in the laboratory.

Plants are not designed by nature to make direct use of organic substances, their food being simple inorganic chemicals which they then synthesize, with the aid of sunlight, into the more complex organic substances, such as sugars, starches and proteins. The importance of organic substances in the soil lies in the effect which they have on soil texture and the micro-organisms which live in soil. Most organic substances undergo a process of decay in the soil and this decay is brought about largely by the activities of fungi. bacteria and other micro-organisms. In the absence of sufficient organic matter, these micro-organisms are reduced in numbers and, unless suitable inorganic foods are applied in carefully controlled quantities (as is done when using hydroponic and other soilless methods of cultivation), the soil quickly becomes un-balanced in food and the growth of plants is retarded or prevented. The presence of an abundant population of micro-organisms, particularly fungi, in the soil, improves its texture, helping drainage in wet weather and at the same time enabling the soil to absorb sufficient moisture to withstand reasonable periods of drought. It will be seen, therefore, that any wise system of gardening will take into account the value of both organic and of inorganic substances and will not rely on one to the exclusion of the other.

Ovary
The seeds of a flowering plant develop from ovules that have been fertilized with pollen. That part of the plant which contains the ovules is known as the ovary.

Ovate
In outline like an egg; a botanical term used in the description of leaves which are of this shape.

Ovule
A female sex cell, after fertilization it becomes the seed.

Palmate
Divided in the form of a hand; a botanical term used to describe leaves which are deeply divided into several lobes. The term digitate has a somewhat similar meaning but is usually reserved for leaves that are composed of several separate leaflets united to a common stalk at the base.

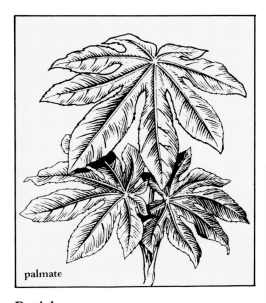
palmate

Panicle
A particular kind of flower cluster consisting of several separate branches each of which carries numerous stalked flowers with the youngest at the top.

Pappus
The tuft of hairs or bristles found in the flowers of some members of the daisy family (*Compositae*) and which later enable the seeds to become airborne.

Parterre
A level area of any shape or size usually containing a design or pattern. Frequently the design was defined by formal edgings of clipped box or other shrubs. It was a form of gardening highly developed by French designers of the 17th century, and is now occasionally making a return on formal sites.

Parterres were intended to be seen as a pattern, for which reason they were often placed near a building or beside a raised terrace or partly surrounded by a raised walk from any of which vantage points they could be viewed from above. They varied greatly in their complexity from plain parterres of quite simple design and usually set in grass to parterres of embroidery in which the patterns might be exceedingly elaborate and carried out with the aid of coloured earth, gravel, sand and other materials.

Parterres were usually further ornamented with clipped evergreen shrubs and sometimes with vases, urns, statues, balustrades and other architectural objects.

Peat
Dead vegetation in an arrested state of decay. Peat is most likely to be formed from deposits of vegetation which has grown on heathland or in some boggy areas. Peat varies greatly in both its origin and its character, and while some peat is of great value to the gardener as a source of humus, other samples are of much less value being either too acid or of poor texture. Good grade peat has to a considerable extent replaced leafmould as a source of humus in potting composts, partly because it is relatively free of spores of fungi and of other organisms which may cause disease, and also of weed seeds, but even more because it decays more slowly than leafmould and therefore retains its nature in the soil for a longer period. The best peat for this purpose is that derived from deposits of sphagnum moss, but any fibrous peat which is not too dusty in texture, and not too acid, may be used.

For outdoor use to improve soils lacking in humus, a wider range of peats can be used without harmful effects. However, it is wise to avoid those which are of a very dusty nature, as these will tend to clog up the soil rather than improve its texture. If peats of a very acid nature are used, it is often desirable to give a dressing of lime at the same time to counteract this acidity. For outdoor use, peat can be employed in the same way as leafmould at rates from 6 to 12lb per sq yd (3 to 6½kg per sq metre). Finely-broken peat is also a useful topdressing for shrub borders, lawns and vegetable crops, to protect the surface soil from the heat of the sun and encourage moist, cool conditions in which roots thrive.

Some plants, notably members of the heather family, *Ericaceae*, delight in peaty soils. When these are grown in places in which the soil is not naturally of this type, it may pay to import considerable quantities of peat, both for forking into the soil prior to planting and for use subsequently as topdressings. As these plants also like acid conditions, it will not, as a rule, matter if the peat is somewhat acid.

It is customary to dry peat thoroughly before it is made up in bales or bags for sale, as dry peat weighs considerably less than wet peat. In this condition, however, it is rather difficult to make it absorb moisture, so before dry peat is used, whether in potting composts or for digging into the soil, it should be thoroughly moistened. This may be done by spreading it out and soaking it or, if it is purchased in plastic bags, by opening these at one end, pouring in water and leaving it to soak in.

panicle

parterre

Pedicel
The stalk of a single flower.

Peduncle
Usually applied to the main stalk of a cluster of flowers, but can be used for the stalk of a single flower. See Pedicel.

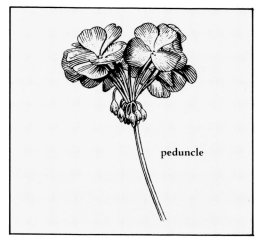
peduncle

Peltate
A botanical term used to describe leaves in which the stalk is attached within the leaf margin, as in the common nasturtium, *Tropaeolum majus*.

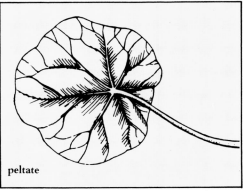
peltate

Perfoliate
Penetrating the leaf; a botanical term applied to stems which are apparently completely encircled by the leaf, e. g. juvenile form of *Eucalyptus gunnii*.

Perianth
The name given to the outer parts of a flower which enclose the reproductive organs. Usually the perianth will comprise both sepals and petals but sometimes one or other may be missing or there may be no clear differentiation between them. In narcissi the term perianth segments is used for those parts which form the more or less flat part of the flower against which the trumpet or cup, known as the corona, is displayed.

Pest
A very loose term used in the garden to describe any member of the animal kingdom which may damage plants. Thus there are many insects which are garden pests and also many other small creatures which do not belong to the insect family as, for example, mites, woodlice, millepedes, slugs and snails. The term may also be used to cover mice, rats and even some destructive kinds of birds.

Petal
One of the separate leaves of the corolla of a flower, usually coloured.

Petaloid
Resembling a petal; a botanical term used to describe parts of a flower which though not true petals nevertheless resemble petals in many respects. For example, some peonies have small petal-like parts forming a boss in the centre of the flower. These are really modified stamens, not true petals, and such blooms are described as having a petaloid centre.

petaloid

Petiole
The botanical term for a leaf stalk.

pH, See acid.

Photosynthesis
The process whereby green plants make use of the energy of sunlight to convert simple chemicals into complex carbohydrates and proteins. Oxygen is formed as a waste product. Photosynthesis depends upon the green colouring matter or chlorophyll found in the leaves and often also in the younger stems.

Pilose
A botanical term used to describe leaves or stems which have long, soft hairs.

Pinching
A term used to describe the removal of the tips of growing shoots, see Stopping.

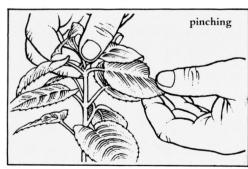
pinching

Pinnate
Like a feather; a term for leaves composed of several leaflets attached on either side of a common stalk as in the rose.

Pinnatifid
A botanical term, for leaves notched or cut in a pinnate manner, but not actually composed of separate leaflets. Pinnatisect has the same meaning.

Pip
The word is used in two ways, to describe the seeds of apples, pears and allied fruits and for the individual flowers of auriculas and some other primulas, especially those for show purposes.

piping

Piping
A particular kind of cutting which is sometimes used for propagating pinks and other members of the dianthus family. Pipings are obtained by pulling a young shoot out at one of the joints. The shoot is simply grasped between finger and thumb, just above a joint, while the stem below the joint is held firmly. A steady pull will then bring the shoot cleanly away, and it is ready for insertion without any further preparation. Pipings are usually made from young non-flowering shoots and are taken in early summer. They are treated in exactly the same way as cuttings.

Pleach
The practice of training the branches of trees in one plane to produce a narrow screen or hedge. Lime is commonly used because its flexible branches can easily be tied down to training wires or canes or can be intertwined (the word has the same origin as plait), but almost any tree can be pleached. Hornbeam and yew were at one time much used. Conveniently placed stems are trained as they grow and others are cut out.

Plenus(a), Pleniflorus(a)
With double flowers, see Flore pleno.

Plumose
Plumed or feathery; a botanical term used in the description of flower or seed parts which are of this form.

Pollen
The male sex cells of flowering plants are carried in dust-like particles known as pollen. To effect fertilization these must be transferred to the stigmas of the flowers where they germinate to form pollen tubes which grow down the style taking the male cell to the egg cells in the ovules.

Pollination
The act of transferring pollen from the anthers to the pistil of either the same flower or another flower with the object of causing fertilization. Pollination may be encouraged by jarring plants while in bloom, by dusting their flowers lightly with a camel-hair brush or rabbit's tail tied to a stick, or sometimes syringing them with water.

Pompon
A flower that is small and globular. It is used particularly for dahlias and chrysanthemums with flowers of this type but can be applied to other plants as well.

Potting soil
The mixture of soil used for potting: generally termed a compost.

Pricking out
The operation of transferring seedlings from the pots, pans, boxes, or beds in which they have been raised to other containers or beds in which they can be given more room. This is a task requiring great care, as in most cases seedlings will still be very small and tender when they are transplanted and it is easy to damage their roots severely or crush their leaves and tender shoots by undue pressure with the fingers. At one time it was recommended that pricking out should always be delayed until the seedlings had at least their first true leaves, as distinct from the seed leaves or cotyledons which are the first to appear. Investigation has shown, however, that less check is inflicted on growth and better plants result if the seedlings are pricked out while in the seed-leaf stage, and before they have any true leaves.

The seedlings should be removed from the containers or beds with as little injury to the roots as possible. For this purpose a sharpened wooden label is often very serviceable as it can be used like a small trowel to lever the plants up. If the seedlings tend to be at all crowded in the seed beds, great care should be taken to separate them. Holes for them are made with a wooden dibber, the thickness of which will vary according to the size of the seedlings being handled, but will average about ⅝in (15mm). This dibber should have a rounded end. With one hand the hole is made in the prepared soil with the dibber, and with the other the seedling is carefully placed in position. The seedling should be held by its seed leaves. Make sure that the hole made is big enough to accommodate the roots without any unnatural doubling up or cramping, then press the soil round the roots with the rounded end of the dibber.

For a few days after pricking out it is wise to keep the seedlings in a slightly warmer and damper atmosphere than they have been accustomed to and with less ventilation and more shade from strong sunshine. As soon as they have become established in their new quarters, and begun to grow again freely, the original conditions should be restored.

For pricking out very small seedlings which it would not be possible to grasp at all easily, use may be made of a small, forked stick to lift the seedling and hold it in position while the hole is being prepared and the roots are being firmed in it.

lifting seedling

inserting with dibber

water gently

Protection
In the garden protection is usually required for one of four reasons: to guard plants against injury caused by low temperatures; to protect them from injury caused by high winds; to shield them from excessive

sunshine, and to shelter them from excessive rain-fall. Naturally methods used for these four quite different objects will vary greatly and much ingen-uity is sometimes displayed in providing protection of one kind or another.

The most obvious method of protection is that provided by glass in the form of a greenhouse, frame or cloche. Glass will give adequate protection against both wind and damp, and though by itself it will not be sufficient to keep out severe cold, particularly if prolonged for more than a few hours, it will give some measure of protection. It can also be used as a shield against strong sunshine if it is coated with limewash, one of the many advertised shading compounds, or something of that kind. A drawback to glass is its comparative costliness, its weight and its fragility.

Many substitutes for glass have been tried including various plastics. None of them appears to be quite as good as glass from the point of view of encouraging plant growth, but most of them give useful protection against winds and damp. Screens and shelters of various types can be easily made from some of them to stand round or over plants without disturbing them in any way.

Newly planted trees and shrubs, particularly ever-greens, sometimes suffer severely during the first few months from the effects of wind. This is due more to the drying effect of the wind than to its chilling effect, and provided the plants can be shel-tered in some way from the main blast, they usually pull through quite satisfactorily. For this kind of windbreak wattle hurdles are excellent. Hessian sacks may also be used, nailed to strong wooden uprights. Yet another alternative is to use evergreen branches thrust into the soil like peasticks. All protection of this kind, applied for the purpose of keeping off wind, should be in the form of an open-topped screen, no attempt being made to cover the plant above as this would only cause it to make premature growth which would be more than ever susceptible to injury.

Slightly tender shrubs planted against walls can usually be protected from winter cold by placing one or two wattle hurdles in front of them. If the weather should be very severe, the space between the hurdles and shrubs can be stuffed with clean (i.e. disease free) dry straw or bracken. Once again no attempt should be made to close in the top.

Some herbaceous plants require a measure of protection from severe cold in winter. Two familiar examples are gunnera and eremurus. Both can be cut down to ground level in the autumn, and a simple method of protecting the crowns is to place a piece of wire netting over each, bent in the form of a low tent, and then to cover this with a good thick layer of straw or bracken with a further piece of netting pegged on top to prevent the whole from being blown away. The purpose of the lower piece of netting is to stop the covering material from pressing too closely on the crowns and possibly causing them to rot. Another method sometimes used, particularly with eremurus, is to cover the crown with a cone of sand or ashes which can be left in position until the shoots push through it in the spring.

Some perfectly hardy plants are very susceptible to excessive wet in winter, notable amongst these being many alpine plants from high altitudes, particularly those with rather woolly or hairy foliage. On their native mountains they are protected by a deep layer of frozen snow in winter and this keeps them perfectly dry. In our climate they are frequently wet and this tends to make them rot. The remedy is to support a pane of glass a few inches above each plant, but with the sides completely open, so that there is a free circulation of air. The piece of glass can be supported on sticks with notches cut in them, or on bent wires. Ordi-nary cloches are not suitable as they keep the plants too warm and encourage premature growth.

Many plants suffer from the effects of strong sunshine in summer. This is particularly true in the greenhouse where the heat on a sunny day can become very intense, but it can also happen out of doors, especially with evergreen shrubs from coun-tries in which the climate is very wet and the sky frequently covered with clouds. This is the case with many of the Asiatic rhododendrons, which in Britain often suffer more damage from hot sunshine than from frost. The remedy in this case is to plant in the protection of trees or in a similar shady place. Under glass it is often very difficult to keep the temperature sufficiently low in summer, though shade can be provided by the means already described. Few small greenhouses have adequate provision for ventilation. There should be ventila-tors both in the sides and in the roof, so that a free circulation of air can be obtained when required.

protection

Pruning
The act of cutting back a plant in any way, particu-larly applied to the cutting back of fruit and orna-mental trees and bushes for the purpose of control-ling their shape and regulating the crops of flowers and fruits which they produce. Pruning is one of the most difficult arts which the gardener has to master, and one upon which opinions vary greatly.

There are four main purposes of pruning: (1) to form the specimen according to the requirements of the gardener; (2) to remove superfluous parts so that the energies of the plant can be concentrated upon what really matters; (3) to remove worn out, damaged or diseased parts, and (4) to control the quantity and quality of flowers and/or fruits produced. Different methods of pruning will be required for each different object.

Pseudobulb
A bulb-like growth that is not a true bulb. The term is particularly used for the thickened stems of some species of orchid. These serve as storage organs for food and moisture while the orchid is at rest.

Pubescent
Downy; a botanical term used to describe leaves or stems which are covered with soft but short hairs.

Punctate
Derived from a Latin word meaning a point and generally used to describe a surface marked with dots or depressions.

Pupa
That stage in the life history of an insect in which it is encased in a hard covering or shell, e. g. chrys-alis of a moth. It occurs immediately after the larval or grub stage and is followed by the adult flying stage.

Raceme
A botanical term used to describe elongated, unbranched flower clusters in which each flower is attached by a stalk to a main stem and in which the lower flowers open first. A hyacinth flower is of this type.

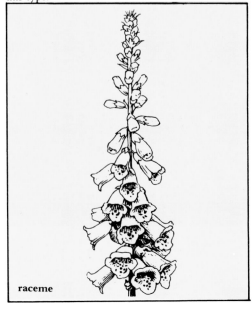

raceme

Radical
Belonging to the root of a plant.

Ray florets
The outer florets of certain members of the daisy family in which the central disk of disk florets is surrounded by other showier florets each with a strap-shaped corolla. See Disk, page 238.

Recurved, Reflexed
Curved or bent downwards. A botanical term used in the description of leaves and petals which are formed in this way. It is also used by gardeners to describe a particular type of flower in which the petals curl outwards. Thus a reflexed chrysan-themum has mainly outward curling petals in contrast to an incurving chrysanthemum, or incurve, which has inward curling petals.

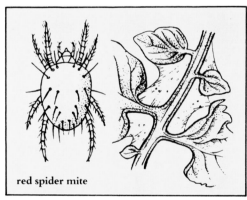

red spider mite

Red spider mites
The name of these familiar pests is rather misleading as they are neither spiders nor are they red. They belong to the family of mites and are brownish or at most reddish brown in colour. They are so small that they can only just be seen with the naked eye. A hand lens will reveal them as having roundish bodies and eight legs. They cluster on the undersides of leaves, chiefly in the angles of the veins, and they live by sucking sap. As a result the leaves develop a mottled appearance, usually greyish or bronzy in colour.

Red spider mites thrive in a hot dry atmosphere and are discouraged by moisture and low temperat-ures. Under glass attacks can often be prevented by giving ample ventilation and maintaining a damp atmosphere by frequent syringing with clear water. Fumigation with azobenzene or the use of azoben-zene aerosols will usually give complete control if an attack does occur. Chlorbenside, derris, dimethoate, diazinon, dicofol and malathion are other chemicals that can be used to control red spider mites.

Reflexed, see Recurved.

Reniform
Kidney-shaped; a botanical term used to describe leaves, etc. which are of this form.

Resting
Most plants have a period at which they make little or no growth, and are then said to be dormant or resting. In some plants, notably bulbs, this resting season is extremely marked and may continue for several months, whereas in other plants, particularly greenhouse evergreens, there is very little real

resting. The plants are in growth most of the time, though possibly more slowly at one period than another.

It is most important that plants should have their normal period of rest at the right time of the year. For example, with many greenhouse-grown bulbs it is necessary to reduce the water supply as the resting season approaches to encourage top growth to die down, and then to withhold water altogether while the bulbs are at rest. Most plants require less water and less warmth during the resting period, though their requirements will differ according to their nature and the climatic conditions of their native habitat. Plants from tropical places, with a high or continuous rainfall, are likely to have a less marked resting period, whereas plants from cold areas, or from those in which there are long seasonal periods of drought, are likely to have a more clearly marked resting period.

Reticulate
A term meaning netted and often applied to leaves with a netted pattern of veins or markings. However, petals may also be so marked and some bulbs are covered with a netted membrane e. g. *Iris reticulata*.

Revolute
A botanical term describing leaves in which the margins are rolled backwards, such as rosemary and heaths.

Rhizome
An underground stem usually growing more or less horizontally and producing shoots at a distance from the parent plant. Common examples are the bearded or German iris and couch grass.

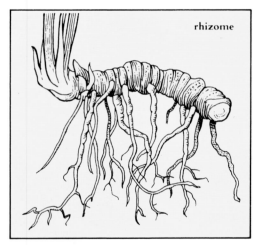

rhizome

Rootstock
A term sometimes used by gardeners for the stock as distinct from the scion in a grafted or budded plant. Thus an apple may be described as grafted upon Paradise rootstock. The word also has a botanical meaning and is used to describe rhizomes, particularly rather short or more or less erect rhizomes such as those found in many ferns.

Rough leaves
A term sometimes used for the first leaves that appear on a seedling after the seed leaves or cotyledons. Its point is that, whereas the seed leaves are always simple (i. e. with a smooth outline), the true leaves that follow are often indented, saw edged or otherwise diversified.

Rugose
Wrinkled; a botanical term used mainly to describe leaves which have a wrinkled surface as in *Rosa rugosa*.

Runner
A popular name for a stolon, i. e. a rooting stem produced at soil level. Some plants have the habit of producing runners freely and using them as a normal method of increase. A familiar example is the creeping buttercup, one plant of which is soon capable of throwing out sufficient runners to cover quite an extensive area of ground. Violets increase themselves in the same way, and so do most strawberries, though the alpine varieties do not produce runners.

The attitude of the gardener towards runners will depend upon the plant in question and the purpose for which he needs it. The buttercup runners are an unmitigated nuisance to him, and must be destroyed by every practicable means. The violet and strawberry runners provide a ready method of increasing stock, but if not needed for this purpose they should be removed at an early stage, as they tend to weaken the main plant and to overcrowd the bed.

Runners usually produce a succession of small plantlets along their length, each of which is capable of rooting and forming a new plant. When runners are used for propagation, it is generally advised that the number selected per plant should be strictly limited, usually to 5 or 6 per plant, and that only the first plantlet formed on each runner should be retained, the rest of the runner being removed. By this means really sturdy young plants are produced.

Runners are quite capable of rooting and making plants when left entirely to their own devices, but to make certain of it the gardener usually pegs the plantlets firmly to the soil, or holds them in position with a stone, making sure that they are well watered should the weather become dry. Sometimes the runners are pegged down into pots so that, when rooted, they can be transferred elsewhere with a minimum of root disturbance.

It is generally advisable to sever rooted runners from their parents a few days before it is intended to transplant them elsewhere. This minimizes the shock which otherwise might be inflicted by depriving a plant of the food supplies which it gets from its parent and also, at the same time, damaging some of its own roots. Great care should be taken to select runners only from good, healthy plants.

Rust
A general term applied to a variety of diseases caused by different fungi which are alike mainly in the fact that they produce rusty coloured outgrowths on the leaves or stems of the plants attacked. These outgrowths may be in the form of rust coloured spots as with antirrhinum rust, carnation rust and chrysanthemum rust or larger rust coloured pustules as with hollyhock rust and mint rust. Rose rust has the appearance of rather bright orange spots or patches on the undersurface of the leaves. The so-called rust of rhododendrons is not caused by a fungus but by the attacks of rhododendron bug.

Almost all the rust diseases are difficult to eliminate but frequent sprayings with thiram or zineb are likely to give a considerable measure of control. Treatment of this type should be supplemented by careful removal of all affected leaves or shoots which should be burned immediately. Rust-resistant varieties of antirrhinum have been produced and may be grown where the disease has proved particularly troublesome. Mint rust does not, as a rule, yield to any treatment and affected plants should be removed and burned.

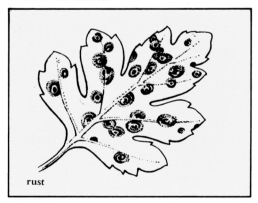

rust

Sagittate
Arrow shaped; a botanical term used to describe pointed leaves which have two lobes projecting backwards giving them roughly the shape of an arrow-head.

Samara
A nut or indehiscent fruit with a wing at the upper end. A typical example can be seen in the fruit of the sycamore.

Sand
This is chiefly of value for the cultivation of plants in greenhouses and frames, though occasionally it is used out of doors to lighten heavy soils. Sand usually has no manurial value, though in a few instances it may contain lime, usually in the form of crushed shells. It is, however, almost always used for its purely mechanical effect on the soil. It helps to keep the finer particles of soil apart and so improve drainage and aeration. For these purposes rather coarse and angular sand is to be preferred to sand that is fine and composed of smooth particles. The

sand recommended for the John Innes seed and potting composts will grade from very tiny fragments up to pieces that only just pass through an ⅛in mesh sieve. Such a sand may form up to a quarter of the bulk of a seed or potting compost. This proportion will vary according to the nature of the soil itself and the kind of plant which is to be grown in it.

Pure sand is also sometimes used as a rooting medium for cuttings. It has the merit of encouraging very rapid formation of roots, but it suffers from the drawbacks of containing no nutriment whatsoever, so that cuttings, if allowed to remain in it for any length of time after they have formed roots, will become starved, and also that it dries out rapidly so that frequent watering is essential in warm weather.

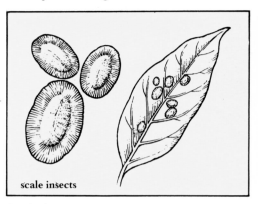

scale insects

Scale insects
A great many related insects pass under this general name. Their characteristic is that they are protected, at any rate during some part of their life cycle, by a scale. They attach themselves limpet-fashion to the branches, stems or leaves of the plants to be attacked and they then suck sap from them. The scales which cover them vary considerably in size, colour and shape. Often leaves or stems which are attacked by scale insects become coated with a sticky substance, and sooty mould grows on this so that the shoots have a blackened appearance.

In the open, fruit trees, aucubas, rhododendrons, yews and beeches are particularly liable to be attacked, while under glass, orchids, ferns, palms, camellias and all kinds of foliage plants are favourite victims of the scale insects. Fruit trees can be cleared by spraying in winter with a tar oil winter wash when dormant or with DNC at bud burst. Under glass plants may be sprayed with petroleum emulsion insecticide, or treated with diazinon or malathion aerosols. In small attacks the scales can be removed one by one with the point of a knife, and the stems or leaves washed subsequently with soapy water.

Scale leaves
Rudimentary leaves such as those which envelop the growth buds of many plants or form the dry, membranous covering of some bulbs. Bulbs are themselves composed of fleshy scale leaves which in some species of lily can be detached and grown on in damp sand into complete bulbs.

In some plants green stems perform most of the normal functions of leaves and such leaves as remain are of a rudimentary nature and this is also true of some parasitic plants.

Scape
A flower stem growing direct from the ground and bearing no leaves. The flower stems of hippeastrum, daffodil and dandelion are of this type.

Scion
Any shoot or bud separated from its parent plant and joined to another plant with the object of forming a union with it, as in grafting or budding. The scion is that part of the grafted or budded plant that provides the aerial shoots or branches, in contrast to the stock which is that part of the partnership which provides the roots.

Seaweed
This is valuable as a manure for the land and great quantities are gathered in many parts of the coast. The most suitable seaweeds for this purpose are the bladder wrack or fucus, which is also the commonest of all seaweeds on most of the coast of the British Isles, and the long, broad, ribbon-like seaweed known as laminaria. Such seaweeds can either be dug in wet, as gathered, at the rate of 10 to 20lb per sq yd (5½ to 11kg per sq metre) or they may be spread out thinly in the sun to dry, and then

be dug in at 2 to 3lb per sq yd (1 to 1½kg per sq metre). Wet seaweed. if stacked, rots very quickly, and, though it is still suitable for use as a manure, the smell is most unpleasant. Dried seaweed, on the contrary, if built into cone-shaped or beehive-shaped stacks, can be stored for long periods without rotting and without an unpleasant smell.

Seaweeds vary considerably in their analysis, but an average wet sample may be expected to contain about 0.5 per cent nitrogen, 0.1 per cent phosphoric acid and 1 per cent potash. It will be observed that the ratio of potash to nitrogen and phosphoric acid is unusually high for a bulky manure – certainly much higher than in any animal droppings.

Numerous proprietary fertilizers and liquid feeds are prepared from seaweed and these should be used according to manufacturers' instructions.

All forms of seaweed tend to improve the texture of the soil, sometimes to a degree which appears disproportionate to the quantity applied. These effects appear to be due to the humic and alginic acids which seaweed contains. These act as soil conditioners causing fine particles to aggregate into larger granules which provide more air space and better drainage.

Seed

Seeds provide the normal method of reproduction for most flowering plants. A seed results from the fertilization of an ovule (in the ovary) by the pollen, and contains an embryo which grows to form a new plant when the seed germinates. This new plant will have some of the characteristics of the pollen parent as well as some from the seed parent. Only in a very inbred race of plants will it appear identical with both parents. (As many flowering plants can be self-pollinated this does aid uniformity.) As the seed ripens the ovary wall becomes the fruit wall.

The seed often contains a store of concentrated food, e. g. starch or oil, either within the embryo or surrounding it, which is used during its early growth. The seed is prevented from drying out by a thick coat or covering – the testa. In large seeds, such as sweet pea, this seed coat is often chipped by the gardener before sowing, in order to speed up the intake of water. Seeds do not usually carry any virus disease which may be present in the parent plant and are thus an important means of raising virus-free stock. But this is not always true of fungal diseases which may be seed borne.

The fruit wall may fuse with that of the seed, e.g. sunflower, or at least be shed with it and not split to let the seeds out while still on the plant, e. g. hazel nut.

Seed Leaf

The first leaf or leaves produced in a seed. Seed leaves are also known as cotyledons.

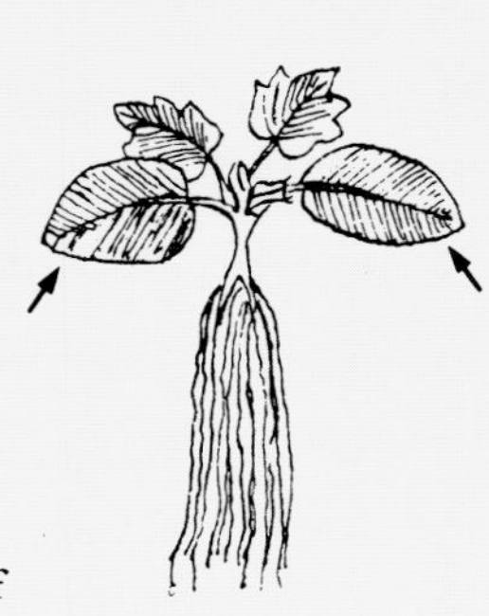

seed leaf

Segment

A subdivision into which any part of a plant may be divided.

Self-fertile

Any plant which is capable of producing seeds when fertilized with its own pollen. In garden practice the term is most used in connection with fruit growing, and is of importance because so many varieties of fruit are not self-fertile, i. e. they will only produce seeds (and therefore only produce a crop of fruit) when fertilized with pollen from another variety of the same kind of fruit. This can be a drawback, particularly in small gardens in which it is not desired to grow several different varieties of the same kind of fruit.

Self-pollination

The pollination of a plant with its own pollen or with the pollen of an identical plant.

Self-sterile, see Sterile.

Semi-double

A rather loosely defined term which may be applied to any flower which has more than the normal number of petals but has not had all or most of its stamens and pistils changed into petals as with a fully double flower.

Sepal

One of the separate leaves forming the calyx of a flower.

Sequestrol

A name for certain organic chemical complexes used for curing mineral deficiencies in soils. Iron and magnesium are the two chemicals usually offered as sequestrols in which form they remain available for some time as plant foods even in soils (mainly those that are markedly alkaline) in which, if applied as inorganic salts, e. g. sulphate of iron or sulphate of magnesium, they would rapidly undergo chemical changes which would render them insoluble and therefore unavailable. Sequestrated chemicals (also known as chelated chemicals) are available for dry or liquid application and should be used according to manufacturers' instructions.

Serrate

Saw edged; a term applied to leaves which have toothed margins of this type.

Sessile

Not stalked; a botanical term used in the description of leaves and flowers which have no stalks.

Sex

Flowering plants exhibit the characteristics of sex, i. e. they bear both male and female organs, the purpose of the female being to produce seeds, and of the male to fertilize the female egg cells or ovules. The essential male organs are known as stamens and consist of anthers and filaments, while the essential female organs are known as pistils and consist of stigmas, styles and the ovaries in which the seeds are developed. A great many plants produce flowers containing both male and female organs; these are known as hermaphrodite. But in some kinds of plants certain blooms have male organs only while others have female organs only. Such plants are known as monoecious. In other instances male and female flowers are borne on separate plants and plants of this character are termed dioecious. Those producing male flowers only are referred to as male plants, those with female flowers only as female plants.

Single

A term used by gardeners in contrast to double, and meaning a flower with the normal number of petals.

Sinuate

A botanical term describing a leaf whose margins are more or less deeply waved.

Slip

A term synonymous with cutting, though it is generally used for that type termed a heel cutting. It is also applied to small pieces or single shoots which can be detached with some roots – these are really small divisions and are sometimes referred to as Irishman's cuttings.

Slugs

Many different species of slug may be found in the garden and not all are equally damaging. Slugs live on decaying vegetable matter as well as on living plants, and some species, particularly the very large slugs, appear to be more scavengers than pests. It is the small grey and black slugs that are most damaging. These eat leaves and stems and are quite capable of destroying small plants completely. The small black slug is particularly fond of fleshy roots, such as those of the potato, into which it will bore. Slugs feed at night and hide by day. In consequence they are often not noticed and the damage they cause is erroneously put down to other pests. They are most likely to be active in mild, damp weather. Slugs can be destroyed by hand picking after dark with the aid of an electric torch and by trapping in small heaps of vegetable refuse placed on the soil and turned over each morning so that any slugs that have hidden beneath can be collected and destroyed. The most effective method, however, is to poison them with a suitable poison bait such as bran and metaldehyde or to water soil and plants with a liquid slug killer based on metaldehyde.

Snails

The damage done by snails is very similar to that caused by slugs. Snails are most likely to be troublesome in greenhouses and near buildings. They are particularly fond of sheltering by day on walls or stones, particularly if they can find protection, as, for example, under ivy on a wall. Possible hiding places should be examined and snails collected. Snails can be killed with the same poison baits as slugs.

Soil

Soils may be broadly classified in several different ways, e.g. as light, medium or heavy, according to the proportion of sand or clay that they contain; as alkaline, neutral or acid according to their pH; as coarse or fine according to their texture; light or dark according to their colour, and mineral or organic according to the amount of humus contained. All these points are of importance to the gardener, and have some bearing both on the manner in which he will treat the soil in order to improve it for the cultivation of plants, and also on the kinds of plant which can be grown successfully in it.

For general garden purposes, the ideal soil will probably be a medium loam, fairly well supplied with humus, well drained, and with a pH of about 6.5. Soils which contain appreciable quantities of lime or chalk are almost always alkaline in reaction, and are consequently unsuitable for the cultivation of lime-hating plants such as heathers and rhododendrons. Soils with a very high percentage of humus are often acid in reaction and the same is true of many sandy heathland soils. When the pH reading is below 5.5 many cultural difficulties are experienced and numerous plants fail to thrive, but the acid-loving plants such as rhododendrons and some heathers delight in such conditions.

The colour of soil may be influenced by the amount of humus which it contains, and by other factors, including the use of soot. Dark soils absorb more sun warmth than light soils, and consequently tend to encourage the early growth of plants. Bad drainage has a retarding effect on growth, and by contrast well-drained soils are frequently early. Contrary to popular belief, plants cannot live on humus and humus-rich soils are not always highly fertile though they can usually be rendered fertile by suitable treatment, which will include thorough cultivation and, usually, heavy liming. The chief value of humus in the soil is the mechanical effect which it has on it, enabling it to absorb moisture readily and yet maintain a fairly open texture which allows air to penetrate and surplus water to drain away. Soils that are deficient in humus tend to dry out very rapidly in summer and, if they also contain clay, may set very hard after heavy rain or if they have been walked on. Humus-producing substances such as animal manure, decayed vegetable refuse and peat will tend to correct these faults.

Plants, in addition to requiring water in the soil and carbon dioxide and oxygen in the atmosphere, need as food a variety of chemical salts, all of which will be present in greater or lesser quantity in any fertile soil. It may well be, however, that the soil is deficient in one or more of these chemicals and that its fertility can, therefore, be increased by adding suitable chemicals to it. This is the justification and the basis for all feeding with chemical fertilzers.

In addition to containing minerals and decaying organic material, all natural soil contains a vast population of microscopic organisms including fungi and bacteria. Some of these are harmful to plant life, some neutral and some beneficial. In a fertile and healthy soil the beneficial micro-organisms will be in excess of the harmful ones, but the balance can be upset either by infection of healthy soil with disease-causing organisms, or by bad physical conditions, particularly lack of aeration and waterlogging. Under such conditions the healthy organisms tend to be destroyed and the harmful ones to be encouraged. Beneficial micro-organisms are useful for numerous reasons, including the physical effect which they exert in making the soil more granular in texture and, therefore, better drained and aerated, and for their chemical effect in breaking down organic matter into simple inorganic chemicals in which form they are available as plant food. Some harmful micro-organisms attack plants directly, living in their tissues and bringing about decay; some break down the chemicals the plants can absorb, releasing nitrogen and ammonia to the air; while others produce acids in the soil which are themselves harmful because they lower the pH of the soil and make it unsuitable for all but those plants which like extremely acid conditions. Soils in the open can usually be kept in healthy condition by regular and intelligent cultivation, including digging, forking, and the application of bulky organic and concentrated inorganic manures.

It may sometimes happen that the soil becomes so heavily infected with some disease-causing micro-organisms that remedial measures must be taken. Then it may well be necessary to sterilize the soil to get rid of these harmful organisms. It is not possible to sterilize in a completely selective manner, killing only the harmful organisms and sparing all those that are useful, but if the sterilization is carried out in one or other of the approved manners it will be found that, while the disease-causing organisms are destroyed, sufficient of the useful kind will remain to build up a thriving micro-population within a few weeks. This process will be encouraged if the soil contains an adequate amount of humus and of nitrogen.

Many cultural operations, including digging, forking and ploughing, are intended to improve the aeration of the soil and so encourage the multiplication of beneficial organisms, all of which require air for their existance. In contrast many harmful micro-organisms thrive in the absence of air, and it is for this reason that waterlogged or badly cultivated soils tend to become unhealthy.

Cultural operations such as digging and forking also tend to hasten liberation of plant foods locked up in the soil in chemical forms unsuitable for the use of plants. Cultivation of this kind is usually followed by an increase of fertility, but reserves of food in even the most fertile soil are not inexhaustible and if the cultivation is continued year after year without any other treatment, there will come a time when the fertility of the soil will begin to decline. After that, the more it is cultivated the more quickly will it lose fertility. This inevitable process can only be prevented by feeding soils which are under cultivation, and for this purpose both manures of bulky organic character and concentrated fertilizer are useful.

Although plants require twelve or more different chemicals from the soil, and seem to derive some beneficial effect from several more, only five or six of them are likely to be readily exhausted. The three most often in short supply are nitrogen, phosphorus and potash, and after this iron, magnesium and calcium. Boron, manganese and molybdenum may occasionally be deficient for the needs of certain crops and zinc and copper are two other chemicals that may very occasionally have to be added.

Nitrogen, phosphorus, potash, magnesium and other useful chemicals are contained in bulky animal manures and in decaying vegetable refuse. They can also be applied in the form of chemical salts such as sulphate of ammonia, superphosphate and sulphate of potash. Calcium is contained in many substances including wood ashes and organic matter. When lacking in the soil, it is usually applied in the form of lime, ground chalk or ground limestone.

A soil that is in natural condition and not cultivated tends to retain its chemical and physical balance as a result of the decay of vegetation and the death and decay of small creatures, including insects, in the soil, and also by droppings of animals. When cultivated, the balance of these natural processes is completely altered and fertility is impaired unless manuring is practised, as already outlined.

Bad drainage, in addition to resulting in bad aeration and the consequent increase in the population of undesirable micro-organisms, also tends to chill soils and make them late. It is often possible to hasten the growth of plants considerably by improving the drainage of a heavy wet soil.

Soilless composts
Seed, cutting and potting composts based on peat, sand, vermiculite, etc. but excluding soil. See Compost.

Spadix
A particular type of flower spike in which the stem is thick or fleshy and the insignificant flowers are more or less embedded in it. As a rule it is surrounded by a spathe as in the arum lily (zantedeschia) and anthurium.

Spathe
A special type of inflorescence, found in aroids and palms and well exemplified by the arum lily, in which one leaf or bract is folded around a central spadix consisting of a column-like spike of flowers.

Spatulate
Shaped like a spatula; a leaf which is oblong, rounded at the apex and tapering gradually at the opposite end.

Specimen plant
Any plant which is grown so that it can be viewed from all sides as distinct from being grouped with other plants.

Sphagnum
A genus of mosses which are usually found in damp or boggy places. They make very dense growth which, because of its power to absorb moisture like a sponge, makes an excellent packing material for plants or for the stems of cut flowers. It is also extensively used in orchid potting compost, for which purpose it is chopped up finely. A wad of sphagnum moss is sometimes placed in the bottom of earthenware pots and pans in which seeds are to be germinated or cuttings struck, the idea being that it produces good drainage and yet holds sufficient moisture to keep the compost moist. Sphagnum moss is almost invariably used by florists as a basis for wreaths.

Decomposing sphagnum forms a particular kind of peat, usually known as sphagnum peat or moss peat. It is a suitable kind of peat for use in the garden, especially in seed and potting composts. Good sphagnum peat should be fibrous or granular in texture and should not contain a great deal of fine dust which would clog up the compost and impede drainage.

Spike
A flower cluster very closely resembling a raceme but differing from it in having individual flowers which are stalkless or nearly so. The term is often loosely used by gardeners for any elongated flower cluster. For example, the flowers of delphiniums are often described as spikes though in fact many of them are racemes.

Sport
Strictly speaking any variation from the normal in the character of a plant may be termed a sport, but in garden practice the term is usually reserved for variations which occur apart from seed. For example, it will sometimes happen that some of the flowers on a chrysanthemum plant will be of a different colour from the other flowers on the same plant and this variation is termed a sport. The genetical term for such a variation is a mutation.

Sports occur spontaneously in many plants and some kinds of plants are particularly liable to produce sports. They are common, for example, in chrysanthemums and also in some varieties of polyantha pompon roses, particularly those with orange flowers which frequently sport to red. It must be clearly understood that sporting is by no means confined to a change in colour, but may affect any characteristic of the plant. In roses, bush varieties sometimes sport as vigorous climbing forms, and many of our best climbing roses have been obtained in this way.

Sporting is due to a change in the character of one or more genes carried in the chromosomes. If such a change occurs in the apical cell of a bud or growing shoot, the growth produced by that bud or shoot will be of a new type, though the remainder of the plant will remain unchanged. Such sports can only be perpetuated from material obtained from the sporting shoot or shoots. In the case of chrysanthemums, for example, if one shoot of a plant produces blooms of a different colour and it is desired to perpetuate this colour, cuttings must be obtained from this particular shoot and not from other shoots or from the base of the plant. This may necessitate using material which would normally be considered unsuitable for the purpose of making cuttings, but once plants of the new variety have been established, normal cutting material can be obtained.

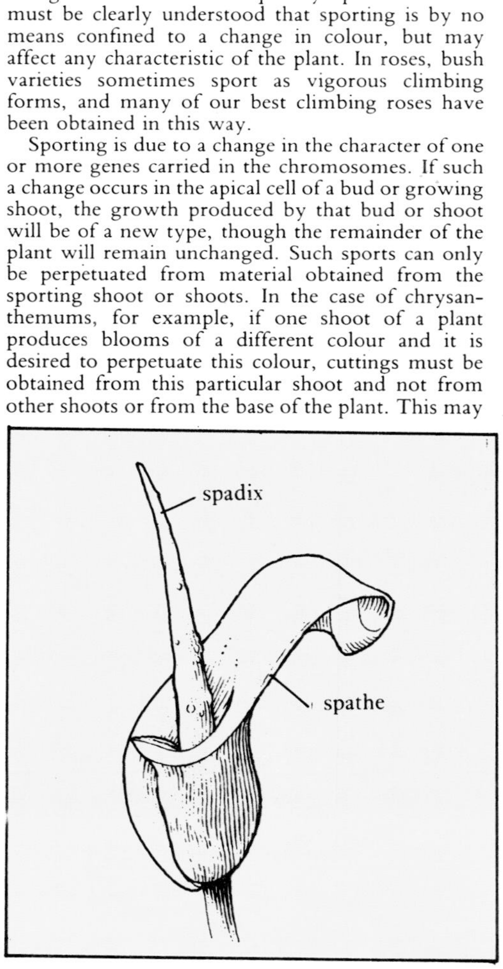

Spraying
Many chemicals used to destroy insects or fungi are most conveniently applied to plants in the form of a liquid spray. Many different types of apparatus have been produced for the purpose of applying such sprays, and these range from simple hand syringes, consisting of a plunger working inside a tube fitted with a fine nozzle, to complicated mechanically driven apparatus, capable of spraying liquid in a fine mist at considerable pressure over a large area.

Normal spraying in the open garden is usually done with some form of syringe or hand-operated pump, though in larger gardens small, mechanically-driven spray plants are employed, some operating from petrol and some from electric motors. The essential with all good spraying apparatus is that the liquid must be broken up into a fairly fine spray. Too coarse a spray may cause damage to the plants, as some insecticides and fungicides will scorch tender leaves, flowers and fruits, if applied too heavily. A second point of importance is that the spray must be produced with some force, so that it penetrates between the branches or leaves of the plant and covers all with equal efficacy. Weak spraying will result in partial coverage of the outer leaves, and pests and diseases will continue to thrive undisturbed in more out-of-the-way places. For the same reason it is often important to wet the undersides of the leaves of the plants as well as the upper surfaces. To enable this to be done conveniently it is an advantage to have the spray nozzle cranked at an angle to the lance or barrel of the spraying apparatus.

Wherever possible spraying should be done in dry, still weather. Most of the insecticides and fungicides in common use adhere firmly to the plants when dry, but if rain falls while they are being put on or within an hour or so of their application, they may be washed off or diluted to such an extent as to be ineffective. This difficulty does not occur with systemic chemicals which are actually absorbed by the plant. Spraying in windy weather is always a trying and wasteful operation. Unfortunately both these instructions are counsels of perfection which must often be ignored, as frequently the time margin for spraying is small, and it must be carried through almost irrespective of the weather.

It is seldom wise to spray with insecticides while plants are in bloom, as at this time they are usually visited by many beneficial insects including honey bees, and the sprays which kill harmful insects are often fatal to useful insects as well. A further warning is that many of the sprays used against insects are also poisonous to warm-blooded animals including human beings, and kill some fish. All must be handled with care, and must be kept out of reach of children and unauthorized persons. Protective clothing is necessary when applying some dangerous chemicals and rubber gloves should always be worn when mixing them. All utensils and spraying apparatus should be thoroughly washed after use, and the containers carefully disposed of. Always read manufacturers' instructions before using sprays.

Stamen
The stamen is the male organ of the flower and it usually consists of two parts – a thin stalk or filament, and a head or anther. It is the latter which produces pollen with which egg cells in the ovary of the flower are fertilized. When hybridization is carried out ripe pollen is transferred from the male to the female parent, and where possible it is wise to remove all stamens from the flower which is to carry seed, so that there is no chance of accidental self-pollination. This removal of stamens should be done quite early in the development of the flower before the anthers have become ripe and started to shed their pollen. It may be necessary to remove the petals of the expanding flower to get at the stamens so that they can be cut off with a small pair of pointed scissors.

Sometimes stamens become changed into petals and it is in this way that many semi-double and double flowers are produced. In the former instance only some of the stamens may be converted into petals, but in fully double flowers all or most will have been changed. Sometimes the stamen changes into a complete and fully-developed petal, in other instances the petal is small and of a different character from the normal petal. It is in this latter manner that the petaloid flowers seen in some forms of peony and also in certain camellias are produced.

Standard

A term with both a botanical and a horticultural application. Botanically a standard is the upper petal of a flower of the pea family, but gardeners also apply the term to the broad upright petals found in some irises including the so-called bearded irises. In pea flowers the standards are in contrast to the keel and wings; in irises the standards are in contrast to the falls.

Horticulturally the term standard is applied to any tree or shrub grown on a bare stem several feet in height. Most trees automatically assume a standard habit as they age, because the lower branches fall off leaving a bare trunk of varying height.

Stellate

Star like; a botanical term used to describe any organ with parts that radiate in the form of a star and often applied to hairs.

Sterile

A name given to any plant or flower which is incapable of producing seed or taking part in the production of seed. Thus the showy, bracted flowers of hydrangeas are sterile, producing neither ovules nor pollen. Some very double flowers are sterile because all the sex organs have been converted into additional petals.

Sterile is also sometimes used to describe soils of very low fertility and also to describe plant-growing media of various kinds, e. g. peat, sand and vermiculite, which are unlikely to contain any organisms harmful to plants.

Stigma

The end of the pistil, or female organ, of a flower on which pollen is retained. Usually the stigma becomes sticky when the flower is ready for pollination.

Stipule

A leafy outgrowth at the base of the leaf stalk, sometimes with a small accessory bud in its axil.

Stock

A name given to that part of a grafted or budded plant which produces the roots, or to plants grown specifically for the purpose of providing roots for budding and grafting. Thus rose stocks are often seedlings of the common dog rose, *Rosa canina*, or rooted cuttings of *Rosa rugosa* or *Rosa polyantha*. Stocks for apple trees are nowadays generally of some form of Paradise apple, though at one time seedling crab apples were freely employed. Pears are frequently worked on stocks of quince or seedling pear. The wild gean (*Prunus avium*) is the common stock for cherries, while various plums, usually raised from layers or suckers, are used for stocks upon which to grow garden varieties of plums. Choice rhododendrons are often grafted on stocks of seedling *Rhododendron ponticum*. So the story might be continued for many other plants which are commonly increased by grafting or budding.

It is important to realize that though the tissues of stock and scion (that part of the graft or budded plant which produces the branches) normally remain entirely distinct, the stock can nevertheless influence the growth and behaviour of the scion in many ways. This is very clearly illustrated in the various Paradise stocks used for apples. Some of these tend to dwarf the varieties grown upon them, and to encourage very early maturity and heavy cropping. Others, by contrast, tend to produce much larger trees which reach maturity later in life, though they may continue to live longer than the dwarfed trees.

The influence of the stock on top growth is also clearly seen in roses. Varieties worked on *Rosa rugosa* tend to make a great deal of growth in the first few years, and to flower very freely, but the flowers are seldom of the same high quality, nor are the bushes, as a rule, as long lived as those on *Rosa canina*.

It may be asked why stocks should be employed at all. The answer is twofold, first, that there are some plants which it is difficult to propagate vegetatively by any means other than grafting or budding, and secondly, that the influence of the stock is often of real value to the gardener.

Stolon

Any shoot which runs along the surface of the soil, forming roots as it goes. See Runner.

Stomata

The pores found on leaves, mainly on the under surface, which can open and close to control the amount of evaporation from the leaf.

Stool

Any plant that is used solely or mainly for propagation. Thus the old roots of chrysanthemums after the blooms have been gathered are referred to as chrysanthemum stools, their main purpose then being to provide cuttings from which a stock of young plants can be produced for flowering the following year.

stool

Stopping

The removal of the growing tip of a plant usually with the object of making it produce side branches, though sometimes the intention is quite literally to stop further growth of that shoot.

Stopping is applied to a great many plants, particularly those of a herbaceous character, but is of primary importance in the cultivation of chrysanthemums and perpetual flowering carnations.

Stratification

A term used by gardeners for the practice of exposing seeds to frost to hasten or improve germination. Some seeds germinate much better after a period of stratification than without it. This is true of hard-coated seeds of some hardy plants including numerous trees and shrubs. Seeds to be stratified are frequently placed in shallow pans or boxes and covered with sand, after which they are placed out of doors in a fairly exposed position and left there throughout the winter without any protection. The following spring the seeds are sown in the ordinary way, either out of doors or in boxes or pans of soil. When seeds are stratified in this way, it is often wise to protect the boxes or pans from the attacks of mice and this may be done by placing fine mesh wire netting over them.

Strobile

A cone-like structure found in cycads and some other plants.

Style

The stem of the pistil or female organ of a flower which joins the stigma to the ovary.

Sub-globose

Somewhat globe shaped.

Sub-shrub, see Suffruticose

Subtropical

A term which has no precise definition but is used in gardens to describe those plants which come from regions near to the tropics of Cancer and Capricorn, and which in gardens require intermediate greenhouse rather than hot house treatment. Many subtropical plants can be placed out of doors for the summer months, but all are injured by more than a degree or so of frost.

Succulent

A term applied to all plants with thick, fleshy leaves or with thickened or fleshy stems which take the place of leaves. The cacti comprise one group of succulent plants characterized by certain botanical features which bring them within the family *Cactaceae*. Many succulent plants are found wild in regions which are subject to long periods of drought, and the succulent habit is of benefit to the plants by enabling them to withstand such periods without undue loss of moisture. It is not true, however, that succulents require to be kept comparatively dry all the year round, for they must have periods of fairly abundant moisture in which they

can replenish their stores of sap. Very often in partly desert regions there is heavy rainfall for a time. In cultivation it is usually desirable to water succulents fairly freely while they make their growth and to give them some moisture even during the dormant season.

Sucker

Any growth which comes direct from the roots of a plant or from the stock of a grafted or budded plant may be called a sucker. Suckers on grafted and budded plants have a special importance as they will resemble the character of the rootstock and not of the scion which has been grafted or budded upon it. If such suckers are allowed to remain, the plant will have two distinct types of top growth, and as stocks are frequently more vigorous than the plants worked upon them, the suckers will in time tend to smother the scion growth and kill it altogether. Many bushes of *Rosa rugosa* to be seen in neglected gardens have arisen in this way, the garden rose having originally been budded on *rugosa* stock and the latter having been allowed to produce suckers indiscriminately until eventually the garden rose was destroyed, and only the suckers remained. Suckers from grafted or budded plants should, therefore, always be removed at the earliest possible opportunity. Care should be taken to cut them off cleanly, close to the roots from which they grow or to the stem of the rootstock if they grow from this on plants which have been grafted or budded above ground level. If any stumps are left, fresh suckers are likely to be produced from them. Frequently suckering is caused in the first instance by bruising the roots through careless soil cultivation. A callus forms over each wound and from this callus adventitious buds and eventually sucker growths are produced.

Suckers produced by plants which are growing on their own roots, as distinct from grafted or budded plants, are not harmful in the same way since they are of the same character as the rest of the plant and may serve to extend it. Such suckers are sometimes of value as a means of propagating the plant. The suckers can be detached with a few roots and planted on their own to form new specimens. This kind of propagation is commonly used for raspberries and also such ornamental shrubs as *Rhus typhina* and bamboos.

Suffruticose

A term used to describe perennial plants (sometimes known as sub-shrubs) in which the upper part is soft and herbaceous, but the lower part is woody. The wallflower is a familiar example.

Summer pruning

Any pruning done during the months of June, July or August. The purpose of summer pruning is usually to check the vigour of trees and shrubs and to encourage the formation of flower buds.

Synonym (Syn)

An alternative name. In botany many plants have at different times been known by different names and it is part of the systematic botanist's task to discover which is the correct name. Others may be listed as synonyms.

Systemic

A term applied to certain chemicals which enter the sap of the plants to which they are applied instead of remaining on the outside. Some insecticides such as menazon and dimethoate are of this character and have several advantages over corresponding non-systemic insecticides. For one thing only those insects are destroyed which actually feed on the sap or tissues of the plant or are hit by the chemical when it is being applied. Useful insects are not at great risk. Another advantage of the systemic insecticide is that it is more readily spread all through the plants as it goes wherever the sap goes. However, there is considerable difference in the freedom of movement of different systemic chemicals and also, sometimes, of the same chemicals in different plants. External applications, by contrast, may miss many parts of the plant they are meant to protect. A third merit is that such insecticides cannot be washed off by rain, though as a rule they do disintegrate within the plant, some more rapidly than others.

A drawback of some systemic insecticides is that they are poisonous to warm-blooded animals (including human beings), as well as to insects. As they are within the plant it is impossible to get rid of them by wiping or washing and even cooking may not remove them.

There is also a range of systemic fungicides,

including benomyl, chloraniformethan and thiophanate-methyl. These are especially useful against the fungal diseases black spot and powdery mildew.

Some weedkillers are systemic, notable examples being paraquat and diquat, both of which not only enter into the sap of the plant but also undergo chemical changes within the plant which bring about its death. Again they have the advantage of being unaffected by rain and of passing through the plant even when only applied to part of it.

Temperature
In the case of every seed or plant there is a minimum and maximum temperature below and above which it suffers injury; a minimum temperature below which growth ceases though the plant is not injured, and an optimum temperature at which growth is most rapid. Obviously it is an essential part of the gardener's art to know approximately what these temperatures are with respect to every plant which he proposes to cultivate. There are not many seeds which germinate at temperatures below 7°C (45°F), and the majority of seeds of greenhouse or half-hardy plants require temperatures between 13 and 21°C (55 and 70°F). to ensure germination. Most plants from temperate regions grow freely in temperatures between 10 and 21°C (50 and 70°F). Plants from tropical regions usually require temperatures between 18 and 27°C (64 and 81°F). for rapid growth. These are general figures to which many exceptions would have to be recorded.

Plants can become accustomed to temperatures considerably different from those to which they would normally be exposed, and, having become so accustomed, may be damaged by temperatures which they could normally have endured. It is for this reason that comparatively hardy plants which have been grown for a period in the greenhouse become more tender than they would normally be, and must be accustomed at gentle stages to ordinary outdoor conditions. By contrast, some plants which, when first introduced to this country appear to be too tender to be grown out of doors during the winter, gradually become acclimatized (probably by a process of selection of the hardier seedlings produced) and eventually can be left out of doors with safety, except during the most severe winters.

Exceptionally high temperatures can do quite as much damage as low ones, and one important item in the management of greenhouse plants in the summer is to prevent the temperature from reaching excessive heights during very bright sunshine.

Tender
A rather vague term used in several different ways when applied to plants. Perhaps the best definition of a tender plant would be one that is injured by frost, but in many instances plants are said to be tender when they will not stand out of doors without protection in an ordinary winter. Such plants may be able to withstand a few degrees of frost, but will succumb when the temperature reaches those lower levels which are commonly experienced at some time during the winter in that place. Degree of susceptibility to frost may differ quite a lot according to the stage of growth and the conditions under which the plant has been grown. Thus young growth is usually more tender than old growth as a result of which spring frosts are usually more damaging than autumn or winter frosts. Also it is usually considered that shoots or leaves which are very full of moisture are more likely to be injured than those that are less turgid.

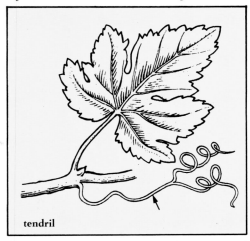

tendril

Tendril
Thin, usually spiral, organs produced by some

plants as an aid to climbing. Tendrils may be modified leaves or leaflets or modified leaf stalks or shoots. They are all very sensitive to contact, with the result that they twine round any suitable support. Familiar examples of plants which produce tendrils are peas, passion flowers and grape vines.

Tepal
The individual segment of any flower in which there is no clear distinction between sepals and petals. The term is most commonly used in describing the flowers of magnolias and of the amaryllis family.

Tomentose
Covered with a close mat of hairs; a botanical term used in the description of leaves and stems which have a covering of this type. The covering itself is referred to as a tomentum.

Topdressing
A term used by gardeners to describe the application of some substance to the surface of the soil, in distinction to working something into the soil. Topdressings may consist of bulky substances such as dung or compost, though with these the process is more frequently referred to as mulching. More usually topdressings consist of artificial fertilizer, lime or some other fairly concentrated substance. Topdressings provide a convenient method of feeding plants while in growth. When soluble chemical fertilizers such as sulphate of ammonia, nitrate of soda, superphosphate of lime and sulphate of potash are applied, it is important not to exceed quantities recommended by experts, as otherwise there may be too great a concentration of the chemical in the surface soil with consequent injury to roots. It is also frequently important to keep topdressings to the soil only and not spread them over stems and leaves. Superphosphate of lime and sulphate of ammonia can both be very damaging to foliage and so can fresh soot. It is sometimes recommended that topdressings of fertilizers should be mixed with the surface soil by hoeing. This seems a matter to be dictated by tidiness rather than by utility.

Transpiration
The giving off of water vapour through the stomata of the leaves.

Tread, Treading
Seed beds are often trodden before being sown and when large plants, shrubs and trees are planted the soil is generally trodden firmly around the roots. The main purpose of treading seed beds is to provide a reasonably firm soil which will not subsequently subside unevenly. Moreover, moisture can rise from below by capillary attraction in such a soil and it will not dry out so rapidly as one that is left loose. Treading when planting has two objects, to get soil into close contact with the roots and to hold the plant securely in the ground until such time as it has made sufficient new roots to provide its own secure anchorage.

Where treading is to be carried out it is essential that the soil be in suitable condition, neither so wet that it sticks to the boots nor so dry that it is impossible to consolidate it by treading.

Trifoliate
Three leaved.

Tripinnatifid
A botanical term to describe a three-segmented pinnatifid leaf.

True-breeding
A plant is said to be true-breeding when its flowers, having been pollinated with their own pollen, produce seed which will give seedlings with all the essential characters of the parent. Thus with a variety of sweet pea, it can only be regarded as true-breeding if the seed saved from it after self-pollination will produce plants bearing flowers of the same character and colour as those of the parent. It is important to observe that the term is relative and not absolute. No plant reproduces itself true in every minute detail. It is a question of what is important from the gardener's standpoint. The geneticist describes a true-breeding plant as homozygous, and one that is not true-breeding as heterozygous or hybrid.

Trumpet
A term used to describe flowers that have the flaring shape of a trumpet. It is also used to describe the enlarged cup or corona of that class of narcissi known as trumpet daffodils.

Tuber
A thickened underground stem or root used for the storage of food, often in the form of starch. Familiar examples are the potato, a stem tuber, and the dahlia, a root tuber. The tuberous begonia may be contrasted with the crocus and its corm which resembles the tuber in some particulars, but is covered by a membranous coat. The difference between root and stem tubers can be determined by whether or not they produce eyes or buds. The stem tuber always has eyes, whereas the root tuber has not.

Tunicate
Enclosed in a thin, loose, outer membrane, usually applied to bulbs or corms.

Umbel
A botanical term used to describe flower clusters in which the flower stalks or branches all arise from a common point at the top of the main flower stem. The flower head of a carrot is of this form.

umbel

Undulate
With wavy margins; a botanical term applied to leaves, etc. which are of this character.

Unisexual
Of one sex only. The term is used by botanists for flowers which produce stamens but no pistils, or pistils but no stamens. This is the opposite of hermaphrodite. The begonia provides a familiar example of a plant with unisexual flowers.

Variegated
Of two or more colours. As a rule the term is applied only to foliage and stems, but it may occasionally be used in connection with flowers that are blotched or marked with more than one colour. The commonest type of foliage variegation is due to lack of chlorophyll or green colouring matter in some parts. As a result patches of yellow or white appear and these may either be regularly disposed in bands or along the veins, or they may be irregularly disposed in spots or blotches all over the surface of the leaf. Variegation, especially of the spotted or blotchy type, is often a symptom of virus infection, and diseases known as mosaic show this symptom

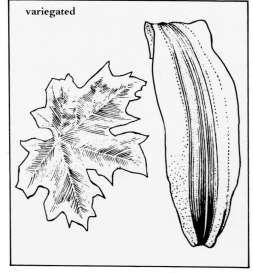

variegated

in a marked manner. Variegation can also be an inherited characteristic unconnected with any pathological condition. The handsome leaves of many kinds of maranta and the silver-variegated leaves of *Pilea cadierei* are of this kind. Variegations also arise as sports or mutations from normal unvariegated forms and usually in such cases the variegation occurs as a chimaera, i. e. tissues of two or more kinds occur, one often overlying the other like a glove but not covering the whole leaf or stem. As a result where both layers occur the normal colour is seen but where there is only one layer a different colour may appear.

Variegated plants are often of great decorative merit. As a rule those that occur as chimaeras or as a result of virus infection can only be propagated true to type by vegetative means, i. e. by cuttings, grafts, or layers, but plants that are naturally variegated can usually be increased by seed. Variegated plants are often a little weaker in growth than their normal green counterparts, this being due to the lack of chlorophyll which is essential to the process of photosynthesis by which the plant manufactures its foodstuffs, with the aid of energy obtained from sunlight. Often variegated forms tend to revert to normal forms. Branches or stems bearing normal green leaves must be cut out as soon as observed or, because of their greater vigour, they may soon crowd out the variegated parts of the plant.

Variety
A division used in the classification of plants, see classification.

Venation
The arrangement or pattern of the veins in a leaf.

Vernalization
This name is given to various techniques by which seeds or plants can be made to pass through, at a greater rate than normal or at an unusual season of the year, those physical and chemical changes which would normally occur in winter. By this means seeds or plants may be brought into a condition in which they will start into growth rapidly directly they are subjected to sufficient light and warmth and given sufficient moisture.

Watering
The correct application of water to plants, and particularly to plants grown under glass, is one of the most important parts of the gardener's art and one of the most difficult to master. Too much water may result in the soil becoming waterlogged, as a result of which air will be driven out of it and the roots of the plants will be suffocated. Moreover, over-watering results in chilled soil and retarded growth. On the other hand if insufficient water is applied growth may come to a standstill, for all the nourishment which plants take from the soil must be in solution.

The commonest fault is that of watering too frequently but in insufficient quantity. As a result the surface inch or so of soil is kept moist most of the time, but beneath this the soil becomes dry. As most of the plant's roots are well below the surface, it follows that growth under such conditions is poor. When watering pot plants it is necessary to give sufficient at each application to moisten the soil right to the bottom of the pot.

The method of applying water must always be considered with care. Most watering cans are fitted with roses, and often with roses of two different kinds, one fine the other coarse. Fine roses should only be used for sprinkling cuttings or other plants that need no more than an overhead damping. This method of watering gives a deceptive appearance of moisture on top. Small pools soon start to collect on the surface yet the soil beneath may be quite dry. Much inadequate watering is due to the frequent use of fine roses. Coarser roses are better, but for all watering of well-established plants the water should be applied direct from the spout of the watering can, held close to the soil to avoid disturbing the surface with a powerful jet of water. When watering out of doors no rose should be used except for very small plants. The best kind of watering in the open is with an irrigation plant of some kind which can be left to run for several hours and will give a rain-like spray. By this means the soil will be adequately moistened without being unduly beaten down. See Irrigation.

At one time it was supposed that the temperature of the water used for greenhouse plants was important, and that this must be at least equal to the air temperature of the house in which the plants are growing. Experiments have not confirmed this view and it does not seem that cold water gives plants any severe or prolonged check. Nevertheless, common sense would suggest that it it undesirable to use extremely cold water for plants that are growing in a warm atmosphere.

It is possible to feed plants as they are watered, in fact, water itself must be regarded as an important food element. Further plant foods can be added to it either in the form of chemicals, or by steeping bags of manure, soot, etc. in the water.

Weed
Any plant growing where it is not required. No hard and fast division can be made between weeds and cultivated plants. Thus grass is a weed in a bed or border or on a path but is a highly desirable plant in a lawn. Snow-in-summer, *Cerastium tomentosum*, can be attractive and useful if kept within bounds, but can become a troublesome weed if allowed to spread too freely.

Weeds can be killed mechanically by hoeing, hand weeding and digging, or they may be killed with various chemicals. When the true definition of a weed is grasped it will be realized how impossible it is to find any chemical which will kill all weeds and spare all cultivated plants.

Weeds may be classified as annual and perennial, and, in general, the former are easier to destroy. If they can be prevented from ripening and distributing their seed all trouble will be at an end, provided that the soil is not already full of seeds from earlier crops which have not been controlled. Perennial weeds, by contrast, can continue to live and spread for years without ever producing a seed. Most are weakened and killed in time if they are repeatedly cut off at or just below soil level but some, such as ground elder, couch grass, bindweed and horsetail, show resistance even to this treatment. Some annuals will continue to develop and ripen their seeds even after they have been pulled up or cut down. Groundsel is particularly troublesome in this way and so should always be removed bodily if it is in flower at the time that it is attacked.

Weedkiller
Various chemicals can be used to kill weeds, but it may be observed that as a weed is simply a plant in the wrong place, all weedkillers are liable to damage some plants that are not regarded as weeds. For garden use weedkillers may be classified in three main groups: contact, selective and residual.

Contact weedkillers kill plants to which they are directly applied and some may remain for a time in the soil, killing or damaging the roots of plants. Sodium chlorate is of this latter kind and so it is usually unsafe to plant or sow anything for some weeks or even months after its application. By contrast, paraquat and diquat, which are also contact weedkillers, are inactivated by the soil and so have no effect on roots and do not damage plants put in or seeds sown after their application.

Selective weedkillers kill some types of plants but not others. Some kill many broad-leaved herbaceous weeds such as plantains, daisies and buttercups, but are relatively harmless to grass, so they can be applied to lawns to kill the weeds in them. Lawn sand made with sulphate of ammonia and sulphate of iron is also selective on lawns since it lies on and scorches the comparatively broad leaves of weeds but slips off narrower, more vertical leaves of grass.

Residual weedkillers remain as a residue or film in the soil, checking the germination of seeds or killing seedlings and small plants as they attempt to emerge. Simazine and dichlobenil are two of the most valuable weedkillers of this type for garden use.

Some weedkillers, not naturally selective, can be made so by the manner of their application. Paraquat, diquat and glyphosate can be applied direct to the leaves of weeds amongst growing plants, particularly shrubs, roses and fruit trees, provided they are kept off the leaves and soft stems of the garden plants or trees. They will not harm the roots of these plants since they are inactivated by the soil. Simazine and dichlobenil in moderate doses can be applied to soil beneath shrubs, roses and fruit trees since their roots are too far down to be harmed by them.

All apparatus used for the application of weedkillers should be thoroughly washed after use. If possible such apparatus should not be used for any other purpose.

Because of the danger of drift when fine sprays are applied it is usually safer to apply liquid weedkillers from a can or other container fitted with a sprinkle bar which can be held close to the ground or to the weeds to be destroyed, but this method does tend to use up rather more weedkiller than when it is sprayed through a fine nozzle.

Weeping
A term applied to the naturally pendulous habit of some trees and shrubs and also to the practice of training certain plants, including roses, in such a manner that they appear to have a pendulous habit. One of the most familiar examples of a natural weeping habit is to be found in the weeping willow, *Salix babylonica*. There are weeping forms of a great many other trees including the common birch, beech, ash, hornbeam and elm. Many conifers also have weeping forms, including *Chamaecyparis lawsoniana*, the common larch, yew and *Picea ormorika*. *Picea breweriana* is of naturally weeping habit.

White Fly
Tiny white winged insects which sometimes infest plants in such numbers that, if disturbed, the flies appear in a dense white cloud. Many greenhouse plants are attacked and there are allied white flies which attack plants out of doors.

In addition to the flies themselves damage is done by the scales which precede the adult stage and are attached like minute limpets to the lower surface of the leaves. Sap is sucked from the leaves and they are fouled with a sticky grey excrement which blocks up the breathing pores (stomata) in the leaves and prevents them from functioning properly. Though plants are seldom killed by white fly they are often severely weakened.

Under glass the most effective method of destroying white flies is by spraying or dusting with BHC, diazinon, malathion or carbaryl. An alternative is to fumigate with tetrachlorethane, an older method which has been largely superseded.

A small wasp-like insect, known as *Encarsia formosa*, preys upon the scales and, if introduced to a greenhouse in which there is a heavy infestation, will soon reduce it very considerably. Scales that have been attacked by this parasite have a distinctive dark appearance and contain the eggs of the parasite. If a leaf bearing scales of this kind is hung up in a greenhouse containing white fly, the parasite will be produced from the eggs and will multiply rapidly. This useful parasite is killed by fumigation with tetrachlorethane and also by cool temperatures so it cannot be over-wintered in an unheated greenhouse.

Out of doors fumigation is useless as a means of controlling white fly, but a fair measure of control can be obtained by occasionally spraying with HCH, carbaryl, diazinon or malathion.

Whorl
A botanical term used to describe the arrangement of several leaves or flowers in the form of a circle at one joint or node on a stem. The flowers of *Primula japonica* are borne in whorls.

Wind
Moving air can have a considerable influence upon the behaviour of plants, particularly if it is moving at such a velocity as to constitute a strong wind or gale. The influence may be one of two ways, either direct disturbance of the plant, which, in severe form, may result in roots of the plants being dragged bodily out of the soil, or an increase in the rate at which water is lost from the leaves by surface evaporation. The former needs little comment as the results are obvious, but damage of the latter kind may often be puzzling and be attributed to causes other than wind. Familiar symptoms are browning of leaf margins or a mottled browning of the whole leaf, and such markings may easily be mistaken for those caused by disease. Sharp draughts in greenhouses or frames will cause precisely the same symptoms, particularly on the tender young leaves of such plants as tomatoes or grape vines. Almost precisely similar damage can be caused under glass by sun scorch, and it is sometimes difficult to decide whether a particular outbreak of scorching is, in fact, due to strong sunshine or to draughts.

Out of doors, wind damage causing leaf scorching may be confused with damage caused by frost, and it is not possible to give any general rules by which one kind of damage may be distinguished from the other. The atmospheric conditions which have been prevailing during the few days before the damaged is observed will usually give the clue. Some plants which are highly resistant to wind damage are extremely sensitive to frost damage and vice versa. A good example of the former can be found in *Senecio rotundifolius*, which in some very exposed gardens in Cornwall is used as an outer windbreak against Atlantic gales in positions in which few other evergreens would survive, yet is killed by temperatures a few degrees below freezing point. See Protection.

Index

Page numbers in italics indicate line illustrations